Mastering™ 3ds max® 4

Cat Woods

Alexander Bicalho

Chris Murray

SYBEX®

San Francisco • Paris • Düsseldorf • Soest • London

Associate Publishers: Cheryl Applewood, Dan Brodnitz
Contracts and Licensing Manager: Kristine O'Callaghan
Acquisitions and Developmental Editor: Mariann Barsolo
Editors: James A. Compton, Suzanne Goraj
Production Editor: Dennis Fitzgerald
Technical Editor: Scott Onstott
Book Designer: Maureen Forys, Happenstance Type-o-Rama
Graphic Illustrator: Tony Jonick, Rappid Rabbit
Electronic Publishing Specialist: Maureen Forys, Happenstance Type-o-Rama
Proofreaders: Nelson Kim, Laurie O'Connell, Yariv Rabinovitch, Nancy Riddiough
Indexer: Ted Laux
CD Coordinator: Christine Harris
CD Technician: Kevin Ly
Cover Designer: DesignSite
Cover Illustrator: Jack D. Meyers

For those who want to understand
—Cat Woods

To my family and friends
—Alexander Bicalho

Acknowledgments

Thanks to Spirit for giving me this opportunity and helping me through it. For inspiration, I thank Barbara Kingsolver (*Animal Dreams*) and Ursula Le Guin (*the telling*) as well as my solsiblings circle.

I thank the people who supported me to this point in my life: Becky Taber, Leslie Walper, Nancy Naugle, and Paul Bindels. Also my teachers: Alex Lindsay, Ben de Leeuw, Ken Robertson, Jeff Abouaf, Bob Hone, Jon Zax, Celia Pearce, Bert Monroy, Barbara Mehlman, Marc Abraham, and Michele Matossian. Thanks to Theresa Lumiere in Sausalito for repairing my back spasm and to Beta Nineties Computer in San Francisco for building my computer. Special thanks to Jerek Carnelian for "moving the wheel."

Thanks to all the people who worked on this book: my co-author, Alexander Bicalho, as well as all the people who contributed projects so that I could give sufficient attention to the writing. My deepest thanks to Scott Onstott, who not only provided several complex projects but was also an excellent technical editor on the book, and to Jason Wiener, who provided projects encompassing tutorials in many chapters and traveled great distances in order to help me out. My sincere thanks to other contributors to the book (John Matsubara, Tom Meade, Mark Zarich, Kay Pruvich, and Blue Bactol) as well as to those who contributed their art (S Fitts, Elizabeth Murray, and Stasia McGehee). Thanks to Chris Murray for initiating the project and to my other editors (Jim Compton, Dennis Fitzgerald, and Suzanne Goraj), who were patient through various ordeals, especially Mariann Barsolo, who makes it a priority to build a good working relationship with an author. Thanks to Maureen Forys for her book design and layout work. Thanks also to Darlene Zandanel, Cheryl Applewood, Carl Montgomery, Erica Yee, Juanita Tugwell, Tony Jonick, and Donna Crossman.

—*Cat Woods*

I would like to thank my family and friends for all their support. I would also like to thank Borislav Petrov, Larry Minton, Ravi Karra, and Simon Feltman for their help. They were my MAXScript teachers. I also would like to thank all the Sybex crew for their patience and support. I cannot forget Scott and Cat who did amazing work on this book, and Chris Murray and Alex Monteiro for all their work on the previous book.

—*Alexander Bicalho*

Contents at a Glance

Contents

Introduction

The goal of this book is to teach you 3ds max while giving you a solid grasp of the context of computer graphics (CG) and its role in the creative process. My hope is to inspire you to make art—to express yourself in the medium without being encumbered by worries or confusion about the technical side of it. In order to get to that point, you have to be familiar enough with the technical issues that they are barely a conscious consideration, much like you might drive a car without thinking much about which gear is engaged. Developing that kind of facility takes a willingness to be in over your head for a while—and a lot of practice.

This is not an exhaustive book on 3ds max. (I defy anyone to write a truly exhaustive book on a program of this depth. Besides being a set of at least a dozen encyclopedias, it would be obsolete within an hour when the next plug-in was written.) This book is designed to raise the base level of understanding of developing max users, providing a solid foundation in the essential concepts of 3D computer graphics and exploring some of the more complex subjects in detail to stretch you into unfamiliar territory. Because of this breadth of scope, not every topic can be covered in depth. We have not shrunk from the challenge, however. We have included chapters on character animation and MAXScript, for example, when there are whole books written about character animation and Alexander has already written a whole book on MAXScript. There are whole books written about virtually every topic in CG. We have aimed to acquaint you with the various facets of the big picture of CG and to direct you to resources for exploring particular facets in greater depth. We hope that we have effected a good compromise between breadth and depth.

This book is best suited for people who have played around with 3ds max, and perhaps learned parts of the program in detail, but are missing some of the basics and want to take themselves to the next level in their progress toward true mastery. The book can also be used by beginners, as it reviews the basic tools and concepts of max before moving on to more advanced material. The book moves quickly, however; beginners should give themselves extra time to play around with the tools and get the feel of the program as they work through the book. Keep in mind that there is no single, straight path to learning computer graphics. The topics interlock and depend on each other, so the process of learning CG is inherently circular. It is not possible to confine the discussion of any one topic to a particular phase of the workflow. Since printed books unfold information in a linear progression, consider your completion of the course of the book the first cycle in a spiraling process of achieving mastery.

Advanced users may want to skip through to the new features (see the table of new features inside the back cover). Advanced users may also gain something from reading through the book as a whole: it can help you organize the vast range of subjects involved in 3D computer graphics into a manageable structure; and it can remind you of the whole cycle of the work flow, facilitating your progress to the next level of mastery.

To avoid wasting your time with endless repetitions of the same steps, the book assumes that you are learning as it progresses. In early tutorials, every step is recorded in minute detail. After a few instances of this, the steps may be summarized in a more general instruction, assuming that you know the procedure by now. We realize that you may be jumping around in the book, however. If you find a step summarized that you do not understand, try skimming back to a place where this was covered in more detail. For example, if you don't understand a reference in a later chapter to "Go to the Vertex sub-object level," go back to Chapter 3 or 4, where this is explained more precisely.

For most of the tutorials, incremental .max files are available on the CD. Whenever you are told in the text to "save your file as filename.max," you can find on the CD an example of that file. If you get stuck on something or are interested in only part of a tutorial, you can also start with that file and continue with the rest of the exercise. Always copy the CD files to your hard drive before trying to use them. Also copy any map files to your 3dsmax4\Maps directory.

The "Hands-on max" sections at the end of many chapters are more complex tutorials, building on the preceding exercises. The pace of these tutorials is faster than the rest of the exercises. If you find one too advanced, try reviewing the preceding chapters and try it again later.

While you are learning, give yourself time to just play with the program, explore it, let things blow up on you and learn from the experience. There is no linear way to learn max, since everything affects everything else and since there are at least half a dozen ways to do most things. Have fun with it. If it stops being fun, take a break from it.

Be sure to also take care of your body as you work. Nothing you create in CG is worth being debilitated by severe eyestrain, tendinitis, or carpal tunnel syndrome. Get an ergonomic setup that works for you. Drink lots of water. Take breaks to stretch, change the focus of your eyes, and yes, even have a life. (Do as I say, not as I do.)

The different parts of the book, summarized later in this Introduction, will serve to usher you into the realm of computer graphics and animation. Once there, we trust you will continue your explorations in order to offer back to the world something of meaning and value.

—*Cat Woods*

Who Should Read This Book

Mastering 3ds max 4 has something to offer artists of all backgrounds:

- Those curious about the development and uses of computer graphics

- Traditional or digital 2D artists looking to develop skills in 3D computer graphics

- Those interested in deepening their understanding of the issues involved in CG

- Students interested in developing technical skills as part of an overall artistic process

- Web designers who want to know how to add 3D content to their sites and 3D animators who want to know how to display their work on the Web

- 3D artists familiar with another 3D program who wish to learn max

- Max artists who wish to update their knowledge for max 4

What's in the Book

Here's a quick preview of what's covered in each part of the book. Cat Woods introduces her Parts I–V, and Alexander Bicalho introduces his Part VI.

Part I: Introduction and Theory

The three introductory chapters (Part I of this book) are what I wish someone had told me when I was first learning max. Chapters 1 and 2 provide a grounding in essential computer graphics, 3D, rendering, and max concepts. These concepts will serve you throughout the book and give you an overview of the context and history of computer graphics. Chapter 1 also discusses in some depth what is involved in taking on the many learning curves involved in making animated digital art. This may grow in meaning for you as you immerse yourself in the task of learning max. Chapter 3 is a kind of reference guide to the whole max interface.

I'm convinced that reading these three chapters would have saved me thousands of dollars in classes and many hours of futzing around and pulling my hair out in frustration. There's nothing wrong with futzing, of course; in fact, there's no way of avoiding it when exploring the program. However, Part I offers you a way to improve the quality of your experimentation and use your time more efficiently by giving you the groundwork of understanding you need.

Part II: Modeling

To use a 3D program, you need to build 3D models. In Part II, you learn general principles for building and optimizing these models intelligently. You will model in mesh, patch, and NURBS surfaces. You will learn modeling techniques appropriate to the different outputs and build complex models using these techniques.

Part III: Applying Texture Maps and Materials

Part III teaches you how to "paint" your models with materials. In Chapter 7, you will learn how materials are built and will apply maps to various material channels. You will learn how to assign mapping coordinates and will do this in great detail for a character designed for a game environment. Chapter 8 moves on to more advanced materials topics and tutorials.

Part IV: Animation

Part IV teaches you how to animate in max. You will explore the different animation tools and methods available and create animations using these. The three chapters build on concepts introduced in Part I in progressive depth, from simple animation through various types of complex character animation. You will not only follow the steps of tutorials, but at the same time learn about the considerations going on behind the steps. This way you will know how to approach a completely different type of project and can better translate your animation skills between different software packages.

Part V: Refining the Rendering

Part V focuses on topics that affect the final appearance of the rendering by adjusting pixel colors. While lighting, special effects, and camera work are not similar jobs in the real world, their CG counterparts are very much related. Part V is about the packaging of rendered images for the best presentation. In Chapter 12, you will learn the characteristics of CG lights and apply different lighting setups to dramatically change the appearance of your scene. Chapter 13 covers the many options for rendering, including alternate renderers and network rendering. Chapter 13 also covers the "post-process" effects available in the Environment window. In Chapter 14 you will learn how to cut and cross-fade between cameras and pre-rendered images, how to apply special effects within the Video Post window, and how to composite images within max and in discreet combustion.

Part VI: Using MAXScript

MAXScript has become a very important part of 3ds max. Using MAXScript, you can create scripts and macros that automate repetitive tasks, help you animate your scenes, and build your own geometry and plug-ins.

Chapter 15 introduces the basics of the MAXScript language and gives you a foundation for understanding how it works. Chapter 16 uses tutorials and exercises to demonstrate how to manipulate scenes and work with objects, modifiers, materials, and more. Chapter 17 teaches how to create a user interface (UI) for your scripts and how to create Macro Scripts and add them to menus and quads. Chapter 18 shows how MAXScript can help you animate objects and access animation parameters. You will also learn how to create and manipulate bitmaps, and how to control rendering, including Render Elements and network rendering. Chapter 19 explores advanced scripting, with scene management tools, max UI management, max file I/O, and callbacks. Chapter 20 introduces tools and plug-in scripts and their seamless integration to the UI. You will learn how to create plug-in scripts that extend familiar objects and plug-ins that create objects and modifiers.

Conventions Used in This Book

Throughout this book, the following symbols will help you find specific information when you need it and accelerate your ability to learn 3ds max.

This is a Tip. Tips are helpful hints that demonstrate efficient, effective procedures to accomplish your task.

This is a Warning. Warnings alert you to bugs, hazards, and other potential problems or areas where you need to proceed with caution.

In tutorial exercises, this symbol flags the places where you need to use a project file from the accompanying CD-ROM in order to complete the exercise. For the best performance, always copy the necessary CD files to your hard drive. With map files, it is particularly important to copy the maps to your 3dsmax4\Maps directory.

This symbol identifies key 3ds max or CG concepts that are critical to understanding a topic. A table of key concepts is provided inside the front cover.

Key
Concept

This symbol identifies features that are new in 3ds max 4. If you're familiar with previous versions and want to skim a topic for the latest changes, look for this marker. A table of new features is provided inside the back cover.

This Is a Sidebar

Sidebars develop specific ideas and expand upon information that is related to the chapter's primary topics.

Typography and Capitalization   This book uses **boldface type** to mark any text you should enter as you are doing the exercises, and `this typeface` for filenames and directory paths, URLs, and MAXScript code.

To make our text as clear as possible, this book capitalizes all menu options and interface selections even when they are not capitalized on screen. We also capitalize the names of all the objects you'll create in working through the exercises; in some cases, however, object names may be lowercased in the corresponding files on the CD-ROM.

Finally, note that we follow discreet's new style of lowercasing the trademarked names of most of its software: 3ds max 4, combustion, character studio, and mental ray, for example.

Interface Illustrations   When taking shots of the 3ds max interface, we focused on how to best illustrate the point of the text. We sometimes changed the interface colors from the defaults in order to improve the contrast for print or add emphasis.

Missing Maps   If you get a warning naming missing map files when you open a `.max` file or try to render, it means that max doesn't know where to find the bitmap images used in the file.

You have three options for fixing map paths:

- Copy the maps or the whole map directory to your `3dsmax4\Maps` directory (recommended).

- Go to Customize ➜ Configure Paths and add the path to the directory where the map files are located.

- Go to Utilities ➜ More ➜ MapPath Editor. Click Edit Bitmaps, select the missing maps, type in the file path, and click Set Path.

Contributing Authors

Many people created art or projects for this book. Here's a look at each of them and what they did.

Scott Onstott Scott Onstott received a Bachelor of Arts degree in Architecture from the University of California at Berkeley in 1992. He worked in several prominent interior architecture firms in San Francisco until 1997, when he started private consulting. Scott has taught hundreds of students at UC Berkeley Extension, San Francisco State University, and the Academy of Art College in San Francisco. Scott is an author and technical editor of books on AutoCAD, 3ds max, 3ds Viz, Lightscape, Photoshop, Illustrator, Dreamweaver, and Fireworks.

Scott contributed the museum gallery project, the NURBS cartoon project, the dinner table project, materials exercises, the tablecloth project, and the Cornell box projects. He also worked as a technical editor on the book.

Jason Wiener Jason Wiener has worked as a professional illustrator, a high school English teacher, and a Web designer. He currently makes his living as a 3D artist for a number of game companies and publications and lives in San Francisco. More of his work can be found at http://www.madwomb.com.

Jason contributed the ongoing "Intrepid Explorer Jim" project and the tendrilhead project, as well as numerous plates in the Color Gallery.

Mark Zarich Mark Zarich has been doing 3D graphics and animation since 1991, when he worked with the Amiga platform. He studied 3D Arts at the Multimedia Studies Program at San Francisco State University. He has worked on a number of projects, using a variety of 3D software, and is now working at Pulse Entertainment, where he focuses on real-time 3D for the Web. Mark can be contacted via his Web site at www.zarich.net.

Mark contributed the Pulse Producer and Creator project.

Blue Bactol Blue Bactol is a 3D artist and technical consultant based in San Francisco. Her experience ranges from architectural visualization to interactive design for games, virtual environment design, character modeling, and animation. After narrowly escaping a career in the San Francisco Ballet, Blue began fiddling with computers as a graphic designer for screen-printing. She graduated with a certificate in 3D Arts from San Francisco State University, where she can still be found lurking about. Blue has lectured for both the University of California at Berkeley and San Francisco State University and is an instructor of 3ds max, 3ds viz, and render farm set-up. She can be reached at `blue@blueha.com`.

Blue contributed the drafting table project, the RLA compositing project, and information on network rendering. She also modeled and textured the "Punch" character shown in the Color Gallery and used on the title pages for this book.

Tom Meade   Tom Meade studied film at Boston University, and moved to San Francisco to participate in the growing new-media industry after earning his BA in film production in 1996. He worked on several interactive CD-ROM games as a 2D production artist before swallowing the 3D pill. Over the past year he has done 3D illustrations and visual effects work for *Wired* magazine and dvGarage. Tom is currently a 3D product specialist at Pulse Entertainment.

Tom contributed the Bath camera-mapping project.

John Matsubara   John Matsubara graduated from UC Berkeley in 1995 with a double major in biology and art. After spending a few years in the biotech industry, he realized he needed to do something to satisfy the right side of his brain, which had been neglected since school. He began taking classes three years ago in 3D graphics at the Multimedia Studies Program at San Francisco State University and has been in love with the genre ever since.

John contributed the guitar modeling project.

Other Contributors

Kay Pruvich   Kay Pruvich is a fine artist and 3D animator in the San Francisco Bay Area. She holds a BFA degree in Painting from the University of Washington and has a background in Theater Arts. She has also studied CG and art at the College of Marin, West Valley College, and San Francisco State University Multimedia Studies Program. She is proficient in 3ds max, Maya, Photoshop, and After Effects. Most recently, Kay contributed to an animation in 3ds max as part of "Breaking the Code: Sequencing the Arabidopsis Genome" for the National Science Foundation International Conference celebrating the completion of the Arabidopsis Genome. This project can be viewed at `http://www.nsf.gov/od/lpa/news/press/00/pr0094_2.htm`. Kay may be reached at `cerces9@aol.com`.

Kay contributed the vase still life and a contour drawing.

S Fitts   S Fitts is an illustrator, photographer, and Web-designer working in Rhode Island and Houston, Texas. He is currently studying Illustration and Photography at the Rhode Island School of Design. He can be reached at `sfitts@pdq.net`.

S contributed a cartoon.

Elizabeth Murray   Elizabeth Murray has a background in technical theater and film. She worked professionally in New York City for eight years before moving to San Francisco. She returned to school in 1999 to study computer graphics, specifically modeling environments and texture mapping. She continues to study and is a teaching assistant. She is currently an intern with Alex Lindsay at dvGarage.

Elizabeth contributed plates in the Color Gallery.

Stasia McGehee   Stasia began using 3D Studio in 1992, when she moved to California to work at Twin Dolphin Games as a character animator. Since then, she has been using 3ds max to model avatars for Internet applications. More of her work can be seen at `www.stasia3d.com`. Stasia has a B.F.A in Painting from Memphis College of Art and a Master's in English from the University of Wisconsin, Madison. Currently she is a technical writer for Pulse Entertainment.

Stasia contributed plates in the Color Gallery.

Special Acknowledgment

Marc Abraham   We would like to extend special thanks to Marc Abraham. Several of the methods described in this book for modeling and texturing characters were based on his design and instruction. He spent over a year in the Open Lab of San Francisco State University's Multimedia Studies Program training students in modeling and animation in 3ds max—purely for the love of it—and was one of the best teachers many of us had. He currently works on 3D multimedia products for Macromedia. Examples of his work can be found at `http://www.geocities.com/dfa0445/`. We wish him the greatest success.

—*Cat Woods, Blue Bactol, Jason Wiener,
Kay Pruvich, and Elizabeth Murray*

Help Us Help You

As you work through this book and begin exploring 3ds max on your own, you may think of additional topics you would like us to cover in future editions, as well as other ways we might improve the book or its CD-ROM. Feel free to send any suggestions to us via `www.sybex.com`. (For advice about how to accomplish a particular task, however, please check the User Reference under the 3dsmax Help menu, discreet's support site at `www.discreet.com/support/`, or it's web forum at `http://support.discreet .com/~max` before contacting us. You'll usually find an answer much faster that way.)

You may also contact Cat at `cat801@hotmail.com`. Be sure to include "`3ds max`" in the subject line. Please allow up to several weeks for a response.

Alexander can be reached through his Web site at `http://www.origamy.com.br`.

We wish you much luck and enjoyment in your pursuit of this art.

Part I
Introduction and Theory

In This Part

n Part I, you will get a grounding in the concepts and history you need to understand to work effectively in max. Chapter 1 gives you an overview of computer graphics, the history of its development, and how it is used. Chapter 1 also discusses the learning process itself and the particular challenges of juggling and balancing everything you need to learn to create good 3D animations. In Chapter 2, you will learn essential concepts of CG, 3D, animation, and max. These concepts will serve you throughout the book. It is said that people need to encounter a piece of information 8 times before they really learn it. Being introduced to the important ideas early will help you assimilate the information better when you encounter them again in later chapters. You may want to re-read Chapter 2 after you have learned more of the specifics in later chapters. Chapter 3 is a kind of reference guide to the max interface, covering all of the main toolbar buttons and command panels as well as many other sections of the interface.

Image Creation with Computer Graphics

3ds max

Chapter 1

C omputer graphics tools give us a means of creating images that touch an audience. In that sense, your computer with 3ds max installed is not so different from a box of crayons. Remembering this from time to time as you plow through the intricacies of the program can help to demystify the work. Computer graphics (CG) and 3D applications give us a sophisticated, highly controlled way of making images; this process is rooted in the long history of image creation and should be understood in that overall artistic context.

In the course of this book, you will examine the principles and issues of creating CG images as we follow a project through the whole artistic process. As you do that, you will learn the concepts you need in order to understand what is going on with 3D and how you can use it to achieve an artistic goal, in enough detail to know how to pursue your own areas of special interest.

If you are learning a 3D application for the first time, the material in this chapter will give you a sense of the field you are entering. Even if you are coming to max from another 3D application, this material may still be of value. It will give you a synopsis of the development and uses of 3D computer graphics and a reminder of the central challenges of creating art in this form. Topics include:

- The balance of technology and art
- Film, digital video, and real-time 3D output
- 3D interfaces
- Scientific visualization
- Personal expression and the artistic process
- Message, vision, and storyboarding
- Finding a career in 3D
- Quick history of seeing, rendering, and digitizing images

Learning Technology

The distinction between making images with a 3D application and making images with a 2D application—or a box of crayons—is that in 3D graphics, the original file holds a description of three-dimensional information from which the images were calculated, as if a camera took photos of the scene. This is made possible by complex mathematical simulations of three-dimensional reality, all hidden by a user-friendly interface.

Every aspect of 3D computer graphics requires substantial explanation, and each topic can be examined to a theoretical and mathematical depth far beyond the scope of this book. Volumes have been written on each nuance of 3D simulation. The topics are also all interlinked: you can't understand what you're doing when modeling or animating without knowing something about rendering, for example. To understand the nature of 3D and the ways you can use it, you need to be acquainted with each of the topics to a certain extent. We will introduce these topics in this chapter and return to them in progressively more depth throughout the course of the book. As you'll see, learning computer graphics and 3D imaging ultimately involves looking at the world anew and examining your preconceptions about what you see.

For exhaustive depth on a particular subject of interest within CG, consider attending courses or seminars at the SIGGRAPH convention, held every summer in the US (www.siggraph.org).

It's important to keep in mind—in order to avoid overwhelming frustration—that no one on the planet knows everything about 3D. It isn't possible. The technology has developed in myriad explosions of information. Undertaking to learn all of it would be a Sisyphean task. Learn enough of the big picture of 3D to understand the principles involved and have a sense of context about it; then choose an area you wish to master.

Cartoon by S Fitts

For any particular detail of information, there will be people who will act as if you should know that already. To continue learning the technology, you can't let that kind of condescension intimidate you or stop you from asking questions. An antidote to the competitive condescension among technically savvy people is the more cooperative approach to building knowledge. Connecting and communicating with other CG artists will facilitate your progress tremendously. Max itself has a community of 100,000 users, many of whom are willing to share their knowledge and help solve problems.

The 3ds max Web board is an incredible knowledge base for max users. Go to `http://www2.discreet.com/support/max/index.html`.

Achieving mastery within computer graphics requires a long-term commitment, one that may take many years. If you remain in the field, you will continue to refine your knowledge and skills for the rest of your life. You will definitely encounter situations where you don't understand what's wrong and feel completely stuck. Getting past these places requires patience with yourself and with the process of learning. Take breaks when you've reached your limit with a problem, and then come back when you're fresh. The only thing that can entirely stop your progress is giving up.

Learning Art

In learning to use max, you will want to do more than just understand its technology; you will also want to be able to use the software to make art. To do this, you need grounding in a variety of artistic disciplines as well. If you want to create your own 3D animations, it will help to give yourself some background in creative writing, traditional drawing and painting, sculpture, cinematography, and animation. You will want to understand the basic principles of storytelling and visual metaphor; of line, perspective, and shading; of modeling in three dimensions; and of lighting, camera work, editing, and special effects. That's a lot of learning curves to broach at once. As anyone in these fields knows, any one of them takes years, if not decades, to master.

The same exhortations about the patience and persistence needed for learning technology apply to learning art, too. You can't know all of it, but you can steadily improve your overall understanding. You can also work in teams with other people where you can focus on one area of expertise. If you end up working in the film industry, you will definitely specialize. It still helps your work to know something of the big picture and how the different facets of the work affect each other.

Putting Technology and Art Together

One of the biggest challenges in developing your skill as a 3D artist is balancing your development of technical skills with development of artistic vision. You need to develop both—free visionary creativity and linear analytical thought—in order to master CG. If one of these kinds of mental activity is dominant in you, make a point of strengthening your nondominant side by giving yourself challenges for that side. Because the technology changes so fast, it is easy to overemphasize technical education at the expense of art. If you think you might be falling into that trap, set aside time for feeding your inner artist—for example, you could enroll in a class on figure drawing or literature.

How 3D Computer Graphics Are Used

Unless you've been living on a desert island, isolated from all modern technology and media, you have seen plenty of 3D imagery. 3D applications are used in the creation of video games; films; architectural design and presentation; advertising; courtroom reenactments and forensics; scientific visualization and illustration; choreography; industrial design; training in the medical, aviation, and sports fields; news illustration; and information design. Just within film, 3D imagery is used to scope out expensive action shots; to make animatics, animated storyboards that sketch out a scene; to add obvious special effects, like the dinosaurs in *Jurassic Park*, as well as less noticeable special effects, like the puppies in *101 Dalmatians*; to make photorealistic animation; and to make cartoon animation that looks hand drawn. CG is used to turn medical data into images that aid doctors in diagnosis. It is used to build online virtual worlds and "avatars," virtual bodies that you use to navigate these worlds. It is used to model real-life situations in order to predict potential problems or to plan possible innovations.

When you encounter 3D computer graphics, it is through a two-dimensional image that has been *rendered* from the 3D scene file. Rendering means portraying the three-dimensional world in a flat 2D image; in CG, this means to calculate from the scene information what appears on the screen. Since the final product of 3D art is some kind of rendered image, our discussion of max will return to the concept of rendering repeatedly.

Delivering to Film, Digital Video, or Real-Time 3D

One essential distinction between different types of 3D imaging is whether the image is prerendered, as with a film, an AVI digital video file, or an architectural still, or is rendered "on-the-fly"—in real time, as in games. Real-time 3D gives you the option of adding interactivity, so the user can choose different animations, move objects, make choices by clicking on objects, or input information that affects the display on the screen. Prerendered images allow you to use very high-quality processor-intensive images, composite different images together to create special effects, output to film or video, and tell a story exactly as you envision it. Table 1.1 gives some examples of how and why real-time or prerendered 3D is used.

Table 1.1 Real-time 3D vs. Prerendered 3D

	REAL-TIME 3D	PRERENDERED IMAGES
Where Used	Video games	Film, TV, digital video, print
	VRML or Web 3D in browser	
	Viewport in max	Scanline renderer in max
Advantages	Allows user interaction and input	High-resolution images (looks good)
	Easily made nonlinear	Gives you complete control over user experience of story
	Processing time hidden from user	
	Rendered immediately	Lower processing time
	Broad applicability	
Disadvantages	Uses less precise shortcuts to ensure real-time response	Must still be highly compressed for Internet delivery
	Depends on user's processing power	Fewer opportunities for nonlinear interactivity—each prerendered segment is linear
	Can't do sophisticated compositing	

The production pipeline for the different uses of 3D also varies greatly. In film, a prerendered high-resolution image may be composited among hundreds of other images in a single shot. This post-production work is a major part of the pipeline for much film work. Prerendered low-resolution images to be used in digital video for the

Web are highly compressed before being embedded in a Web page. For real-time games and Web 3D, the animated and textured geometry itself is exported to the game engine or embedded in a Web page.

Offering New Interfaces

A growing use for interactive real-time 3D is in creating interfaces to information. The metaphor of moving through three-dimensional space to find information draws on our familiar experience of the real world: we travel places to get somewhere; we look in their desk drawer to find something; we don't know what's on a piece of paper, but we know where we left it. 3D interfaces can therefore be more intuitive than the standard directory tree structure for organizing and accessing information. Virtual spaces are emerging as a popular new kind of information architecture.

A standard HTML browser, like Navigator, Internet Explorer, or Opera, gives users some interactive options: typing a URL, using a bookmark, and clicking the back and forward buttons. We experience the browser and often the Web site itself as two-dimensional. The site may link to pages through clickable text or image buttons, but there is no three-dimensional scene for you to navigate. A 3D interface will still be viewed through the 2D display on the screen, but it contains three-dimensional infor-mation that allows you to navigate through the space. These interfaces present a user with landscapes, buildings, and corridors to explore, with events defined by the user's interaction with objects and characters encountered in the space, much like a computer game. In this case, the object is not to win a game, but to provide the user with the con-tent of the Web site.

Virtual worlds are one example of a 3D interface. In such worlds, you can have a private meeting in your virtual home or attend a convention in a large hall. All your interactions occur through the simulation of a three-dimensional environment. Figure 1.1 shows a view within Active Worlds, a Web site containing many virtual worlds. As 3D interfaces continue to develop, standard Web browsers and the Web as a whole may include more 3D information. Perhaps in a few years you won't be click-ing forward and back buttons but navigating the "space" of the Internet as an avatar or in a 3D vehicle.

To check out some possibilities of virtual worlds and avatars, visit Active Worlds at `http://www` `.activeworlds.com`*. After installing their software, you can explore whole 3D worlds of interaction.*

Figure 1.1 *Active Worlds is an example of the 3D interface of a virtual world.*

Other 3D interfaces are the 3D equivalents of Flash for the Web, such as Pulse, included on the CD for this book, and Cult 3D. These applications allow you to make an interface of three-dimensional characters and objects that anyone can view and that you can design to respond to user input or launch applets.

 Appendix A of this book is a tutorial on exporting animated content from max to interactive real-time 3D for the Web.

Aiding Design and Experimentation

Visualization in many scientific fields (e.g., biochemistry, physics, and astronomy) has been greatly aided by computer graphics. Once translated into visual images, even very complex data can be easily interpreted. In addition to illustrating data, CG can also be used to design experiments and analyze probabilities in advance to narrow the range of variables to be tested. Computer-aided design is used extensively in the automotive, aeronautic, electronic, and textile industries. CG can be used to aid the imagination in all types of design, from choreography to architecture. Because simulation is generally so much cheaper than staging a performance of an entire dance troupe, for example, and so easily edited, CG allows more experimentation in the design phase. Instead of being forced to commit to a certain path fairly early on, a designer can take all manner of permutations of an idea to their logical completion before making a decision (or presenting options to decision-makers). The software handles the computations, freeing the designer to focus on comparing the results of different routes rather than on figuring out the results.

The caveat to this is that a 3D simulation of an experiment is only as good as the premises on which it is based. It is easy to be convinced by a visual simulation, because vision involves its own mental processes separate from our analytical minds. When using 3D to simulate a test that would be expensive in the real world, bear in mind that the assumptions of the simulation need to be carefully analyzed before you commit to a course of action.

Using 3D for Personal Artistic Expression

It's been said of animators that they are shy actors, finding expression through the performance of their characters in front of an audience. While max has many professional uses, it is increasingly also used as a richly expressive medium by individuals working towards personal artistic goals. In the same way that Macromedia Flash swept the Internet and offered many artists the opportunity to make animated 2D art, 3D programs are becoming increasingly accessible to a wide range of people interested in taking advantage of the artistic possibilities.

In making your own animations and video, you are undertaking all the jobs of an animation team yourself. You are in the director's chair; you are the screenwriter; you are the actors, the lighting crew, and the camera crew. If you have an idea for a substantial project, consider making connections with other 3D artists and forming teams to get the work done. Whether you do all the work yourself or build a team to help you, your project will go through the following general stages.

Finding Your Message

Presumably you want to do something with max, not just find out what the software does. This may sound obvious, but you need to know what it is you want to do when you start a project. Creating art involves putting something of yourself into it, conveying something of meaning to an audience. This book cannot show how to offer a meaningful message, but you will learn how to use max within the framework and considerations of the artistic process. What you have to say or offer through that obviously can only come from you.

Before you even think of a story, ask yourself what you want to do, who your audience is, and how you want to affect your audience. Advertisers often understand this principle better than artists, because their message is so simple and easily verified by sales: "Buy this product." An artist's message can be deeper than this and less easily formulated. But know it. Know who you are and whom you are addressing. If you are working as part of a group, know the mission statement of the group and the purpose of the project. It sets the tone for all your work. You, as the art director of your piece, need to know its direction.

As an example of a project purpose, consider this book: our purpose is to inspire the creation of meaningful 3D art while teaching people the concepts and techniques of 3D computer graphics in 3ds max. For the ongoing "Intrepid Explorer Jim" project you will work on throughout the book, our purpose is less profound: to entertain and amuse while teaching the essentials of modeling, texturing, and animation in max.

Formulating Your Vision

To enact your message through moving imagery, you need a story. The traditional five-act structure has provided for effective storytelling since ancient times:

1. The first act introduces the characters and sets up the conflict.

2. The second act elaborates on the conflict and extends it. Acts one and two together form the "rising action" of a story.

3. In the third act, a turning point is reached. This point of no return is the culmination of the conflict, the crucial point that determines the inevitable transition from the initial situation to the final one.

4. The fourth act presents the consequences of the turning point, with a natural slowing of the pace for reflection and emotional response. Act four generally constitutes the "falling action" of a story.

5. The fifth act is the climax, the destiny that was determined by the turning point. In a tragic story, this will include hard-hitting emotional consequences. In a comic story, the climax involves the resolution of all threads of conflict and exposure of all deception. The fifth act should generally contain a bit of both, though. A comic resolution with no emotional impact can leave an audience empty and bored. A tragic emotional ending with no resolution can leave an audience empty and depressed. To leave an audience with the sense that they have been given something, include a note of empathy in the resolutions and a note of hope in the harsh destinies.

The acts do not need to be clearly marked or divided. The overall parabolic flow of the story usually means that the first act will relate to the fifth somehow, as the second will relate to the fourth.

Keep this dramatic structure in mind when formulating your story. It may not always be applicable to a short farcical animation, but it's a good blueprint for drama that will move an audience.

Storyboarding

When you have a story in mind, the next step is *storyboarding*. The storyboard process was originally developed and perfected by Disney studios for hand-drawn celluloid ("cel") animation. It is now used for virtually every kind of movie or TV project, anything that involves images changing over time. Everything you do in your animation is based on the storyboard, so storyboarding is an important step. It saves you from modeling and animating objects that won't be seen. It gives you a guide to which you can refer when questions come up during production. Most importantly, it forces you to formulate your idea visually. You want to think out the angles and zoom of the camera, the movement within the scene, the flow of the action line over time—anything that affects the composition or continuity of the shot.

The Art of the Storyboard *by John Hart (Focal Press, 1999) is an excellent guide for storyboarding, including many tips and tricks for drawing useful storyboards.*

For the ongoing project, let's say we have a vignette of Intrepid Explorer Jim entering a cave with a torch, looking around and falling through a hole. A simple storyboard for this might look like Figure 1.2, a four-panel storyboard, book-ended with black. Panel 1 fades up from black to flickering light as Explorer Jim cautiously approaches the camera, holding a torch. Panel 2 cuts to close shot of Explorer Jim's face as he turns his head nervously from left to right. Panel 3 shows Explorer Jim's eyes go large with surprise as he drops from under his hat before the cut back to full shot. Panel 4 shows a large hole in the ground with the empty hat fluttering down above and the dropped torch lying nearby. The shot fades to black as the torch sputters and dies.

Note that while Jason Wiener, who drew this storyboard, is an accomplished artist, a storyboard doesn't have to be this detailed. You can plan out the main forms of your shot in the simplest of line drawings. If you are unhappy with your own drawing ability and can find an artist to help you, so much the better.

Storyboard by Jason Wiener

Figure 1.2 *A storyboard for the "Intrepid Explorer Jim" animation you'll create in later chapters*

Creating Your Vision in 3D

The bulk of this book will cover the steps for taking your idea as sketched out by your storyboard and bringing it to fruition in max. The process involves:

- Modeling—creating the geometric objects that make up your scene

- Texturing—applying images to the surfaces of your objects

- Animating—adding motion to your objects or changing them over time

- Lighting—adding shadow, color tone, and mood to your scene

- Rendering—creating the series of 2D images of your action by shooting through a virtual movie camera

This process can be taken further in post-production by editing and compositing rendered images with other images; you'll get a taste of this kind of work in Chapter 14, "Post-Production and Compositing."

Finding a Career in 3D

Working in 3D can be highly competitive, with some jobs much more so than others. If you are just starting out, consider spending several years building your art and software skills before going for that animator's job at Pixar. There are also many other fields within 3D, where you might be able to put your previous background to work.

In film work, especially, there are many highly specialized job descriptions. Skilled programmers can work on something as detailed as one shading algorithm or physics simulation; for example, the rushing water in *Antz* was created with detailed models of water movement written in a proprietary programming language. On the other end, an entry-level CG job in film is wire removal, where wires and unwanted features are removed frame by frame from a shot through a process called *rotoscoping*, involving the use of complex animated mattes. You can specialize just in modeling, just in texturing, just in character animation, just in lighting, or just in compositing. If you can draw well, you could be a storyboard artist. If you can create detailed realistic digital paintings, you could work as a matte painter. As you will see when Chapter 8, "Advanced Materials," discusses camera mapping, many impressive shots involve the use of a few detailed 2D images used as mattes. Film work also offers a variety of jobs in writing, producing, and directing. Your greatest asset in moving up the ladder of film is the training of your eye to notice and understand what makes moving images convincing.

The book CG101: A Computer Graphics Industry Reference, *by Terrance Masson and Steve Weiss (New Riders, 1999), in addition to presenting a comprehensive background in CG history and technology, contains a section on specific CG job titles and descriptions available in the film industry.*

Work in the video game industry is also very competitive. Because game companies are smaller, however, fewer people are so narrowly specialized as in film. Chances are you'll have to be skilled in a variety of 3D areas to land a job with a game company. For example, a character animator at a top special-effects company might only need to know how to animate well, because an interface of sliders, programmed in a proprietary language, has been provided to add or adjust every type of movement needed. At a game company, it is more important to know the ins and outs of a computer application in order to animate characters. In film, there are often separate animators for effects and for characters, whereas in games, an animator needs to be familiar with all the types of animation needed. The nature of the skills involved in gaming is different, too; film work is high-resolution and generally as detailed and accurate as possible, while games require more "cheats" and doing a lot with limited resolution. Max is very widely used in the game industry because of its array of tools for game development. Max is also increasingly used in film work because of its range of tools for creating cinematic effects.

Beyond the highly sought-after jobs in film and games, there are the many options mentioned earlier, where 3D can be incorporated into fields involving some kind of visualization or design. For example, law firms often require 3D graphics in their legal and forensic work. Any experience or understanding you have in a field can help you in creating high-quality CG projects in that field. While some industries can easily support staff CG artists, many projects are offered on a contract basis.

Many 3D artists work as independent contractors. You can sign up at `http://www.3dsite.com` *to receive a newsletter of available jobs and contract work for 3D artists.*

Web work in 3D is growing. Web development companies increasingly use max for creating digital video or to export to Flash, Pulse, or another Web application. The trend toward 3D interfaces is not likely to stop. If you develop the skills to put 3D art on the Web, you not only have the ability to reach a huge audience with your work, you also have a marketable skill for which the demand is increasing. If you have a background in Java or JavaScript programming, with advanced skills in HTML coding, you could also put this to use programming interactive behaviors for Web 3D content.

If you are good at understanding engineers and translating their language to artists, another career opportunity in 3D lies in explaining the technology to others. Schools need max teachers, and people will also pay for private lessons. 3D software companies need technical support people to coach users through difficulties with the software, and they need technical writers and editors to document applications. If you are good at managing creative people, understand the artistic big picture, and also understand the business side of the big picture, project managers are needed for many sorts of CG projects.

Creating a Great Demo Reel

The primary calling card of a 3D artist is the demo reel. It is still the standard of the industry.

A demo reel should include only your very best work. If you are not confident of something, don't include it. The first 15 seconds should be a fast-paced overview of all your work. (If you last past 15 seconds, you've impressed someone.) Do not include clichés (no bouncing chrome spheres, tunnel fly-throughs, or exploding space ships) or controversial material unless you are absolutely sure it is appropriate to the company to which you are applying. Do include a checklist of the work involved in the project and exactly which work you did.

If you excel in a certain area, focus on that in your demo reel. For example, if you want to be a texture artist, focus your demo reel on your textures. Don't distract attention from your specialty by including mediocre character animation if that is not your strong suit.

The medium for your demo reel should be VHS video. CDs are often thrown away. If you want to send a CD, make sure you have explicit permission first.

Processing Images: Some Background and History

Now that you know why you might want to use max, let's back up and look at the history of image creation. As mentioned at the beginning of the chapter, knowing the context of CG images will help you use them effectively.

Seeing

Most of us depend upon our sense of sight so much that we take the act of seeing for granted and fail to notice the complexity and mystery of the process. Visual perception involves not just the eyes, but also the visual cortex of the brain, with relays into even deeper parts of the brain. We don't have the equivalent of data recorders for color and brightness values; we have a whole visual *mind* that interprets as it sees.

There are three types of cones in the retina, sensitive to long, medium, or short wavelengths of light. As the cones receive light from the environment, this information is processed simultaneously by the visual cortex. Our visual system organizes visual input involuntarily, to assemble our visual environment in a meaningful way without the participation of our conscious minds. From a survival standpoint, this is crucial; we need to be able to interpret the visual pattern of "predator" instantaneously, without having to engage the analytic processes of the mind.

Visual information is processed by different mental "channels." We recognize objects through the form channel. Because the ability to distinguish forms in the environment is essential to survival, this level of information is given a high priority by our visual system. Color information is processed in a lower-priority channel, and we will often associate it with nearby form information. Our eyes determine a color by estimating its *reflectance*, its tendency to reflect light, from the differences between nearby colors. (Reflectance is different from brightness, the actual energy reflected. Black can be quite bright if a strong light is shining on it, but it will have the same reflectance and still be perceived as "black" even if it is brighter than a nearby "white.") This is why our perception of color is affected by neighboring colors; reflectance is estimated differently by the visual system depending on the differences present in a given scene. A third visual channel processes movement and stereoscopic depth. We are able to perceive even slight movement—another survival mechanism for recognizing predators. Stereoscopic depth is assembled from the slight difference in vantage point between the right eye and the left. The difference is negligible farther away and becomes more significant for closer objects. The visual system automatically puts these differences together in the mind as an interpretation of depth.

As Figure 1.3 illustrates, all of this visual processing is performed preconsciously, before the image ever reaches the conscious mind for further interpretation. This is why visual images can be so powerful and why "a picture is worth a thousand words." Images engage a visual mind that is quicker and able to process a lot more information simultaneously than the conscious mind can analyze.

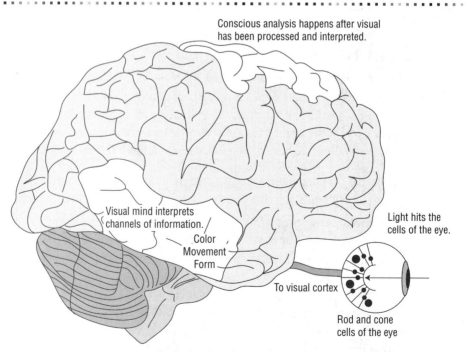

Figure 1.3 *Visual processing occurs preconsciously, before analysis.*

A great book for learning about both the science of visual perception and the applications of computer graphics in scientific visualization discussed earlier is Visualization, the Second Computer Revolution, *by Richard Mark Friedhoff and William Benzon (WH Freeman, 1991).*

Rendering

While there are individual differences in visual systems—for example, one person may have poor perception of stereoscopic depth while another may be much better than average at form recognition—the properties of seeing just described are relatively universal. As soon as we start discussing the topic of rendering an image in two dimensions, however, we move into the realm of cultural conventions and traditions. These conventions begin to shape our perceptions while the process of interpreting the visual is still preconscious. Because of this, a book about image creation is obviously going to be limited by the cultural heritage of its authors—in this case, the Western tradition rooted in the European "Renaissance." We will discuss some of these cultural conventions and how they affect modern image-creation. Keep in mind that you may have a visual perspective from a different culture or a different way of seeing things that has something to offer outside the conventions discussed in this book. The most exciting developments in art have brought in something from outside the conventions.

Our overall perception of a three-dimensional scene includes auditory and sensory cues as well as all the cues of binocular vision and the instantaneous mental interpretations of the brain. When we attempt to reduce all this to a single two-dimensional image, we make many choices about what data to emphasize and what to leave out. Contour drawing, like that shown in Figure 1.4, for example, emphasizes form with lines that follow all the objects perceived by the mental form channel. Photography emphasizes hue and brightness information by translating light energy reaching a single lens into chemical reactions that create an image. A young child's drawing will typically emphasize simple symbols that the child has learned for representing significant people and features of the child's life. Each rendering choice succeeds in communicating the representation to the extent that the viewer understands the rendering convention. While something as pictorial as a photograph is more universal than a sketch of obscure symbols, there are certain cultures that do not recognize a photograph as representing something three-dimensional. As "obvious" as the photographic image may seem to us, we are still accessing our library of cultural cues in order to interpret it.

"Poppy" contour line drawing by Kay Pruvich

Figure 1.4 *Contour line drawings emphasize form information.*

Artistic conventions of representation are called *schemata*. Because the visual mind is so quick that it bypasses conscious analysis, these schemata become conventions not only in rendering but in how a culture thinks and perceives. A visual vocabulary is built within a cultural tradition, with its own givens, iconography, and metaphor.

During the Renaissance period, artists in the Western tradition became enamored of perspective and realistic shading in drawing. They used grids to teach themselves how to record and map brightness values the way a camera lens does today. They closed one eye to avoid the discrepancy between the vantage points of the two eyes for near objects. They developed schemata to cue viewers to 3D perspective in flat images:

- The way forms overlap is a cue to depth because foreground objects block the line of sight to objects behind them.

- Gradations of shading, the placement of light highlights, and the placement of dark shadows all cue the viewer to depth by implying the fall of light rays across a three-dimensional arrangement of objects.

- Detail perspective cues the viewer to depth because objects in the foreground can be seen more clearly, and with finer detail, than objects in the background.

- Linear perspective involves two cues: the horizon line itself, below which objects appear to shrink and move upward with distance and above which objects appear to shrink and move downward with distance, and converging lines towards vanishing points.

- Aerial perspective gives another depth cue, because the shorter wavelength of blue light can penetrate the atmosphere more easily than longer wavelengths, causing features in the distance to have a more bluish tint.

Figure 1.5 shows a painting by Raphael vividly illustrating the discoveries about perspective being explored during the Renaissance.

These pictorial schemata are more universal than symbolic ones, but as we discussed earlier, they still involve a mental interpretation based on conventions. For example, the converging lines of linear perspective assume the 90° angles of level square buildings, generally arranged along straight streets. We can be fooled by this expectation. In miniature sets for stop-motion animation, linear perspective is exaggerated by slanting the walls inward toward the back, making the set appear deeper than it is. Someone whose life had been spent in round huts and whose visual experience did not include a lot of 90° angles would not come to an image using linear perspective with the same expectations and might interpret it differently.

In the modern world, photography and these conventions of rendering are widespread enough that the schemata are effective visual communication tools for a large audience. The principle of surrealism—to use the conventions of realistic rendering on an imaginary environment—applies broadly to computer graphics, and especially to the way 3D applications work. Thoroughly understanding the principles of realistic drawing and painting is a huge advantage in using max effectively and artistically.

Figure 1.5 The School of Athens *by Raphael shows the Renaissance fascination with perspective.*

Digitizing Images

In order to be manipulated on a computer, an image needs to *digitized*, or represented in the form of digits. The computers we use store all information as combinations of 1s and 0s, each digit (1 or 0) of which is called a bit. The number of bits used to store a piece of information determines how many choices (*values*) are available for that item. For example, if you have eight bits to describe a value of gray between black and white, your number of choices would be 2^8 or 256 shades of gray. That's two choices (1 or 0) raised to the power of eight to account for every possible combination of those two choices among the eight digits ($2 \times 2 \times 2 \times 2 \times 2 \times 2 \times 2 \times 2$). A grayscale image requires eight bits to describe each value of gray in the image.

To render images on the CRT (cathode ray tube) screen of a computer, an image must be described as an array of single-color blocks called picture elements or pixels.

The 2D array of pixels is called a bitmap. How many bits the computer needs to store the image in a file format depends on several things: how many pixels are in the image, the color *depth* or the number of choices of colors for each pixel, and whether the image is being stored pixel by pixel or through a mathematical description of the image.

The Way Computer Graphics Works *by Olin Lathrop (Wiley, 1997) goes into great depth about the technical backend of how pixel values are calculated for a CRT. This may be of particular interest if you are looking to buy a monitor or video card for your computer.*

Like Hermann Hesse's Glass Bead Game, digitizing allows information and ideas to be easily conveyed and translated between different disciplines and formats. Since imagery itself is another kind of universal language, digital images are a particularly versatile coin of the realm. Any kind of information can be converted to numerical data, any kind of numerical data can be represented in visual images, and images can be used to manipulate other images.

This was the revolution brought about by Photoshop. When John and Tom Knoll first created Photoshop in 1988, it was designed for translation between image file formats. It soon became apparent that once images could be expressed as arrays of pixels described by three numbers determining pixel color, images could then be easily manipulated through mathematical algorithms and other software tools. The 2D image-manipulation techniques first made possible by Adobe Photoshop have become standard in CG. You use them in 3D when making texture maps, making alpha channels for materials, and altering rendered images in post-production. If you are going to work in computer graphics, you need to master, in addition to max, at least one pixel-based image-editing program such as Photoshop.

Some useful guides for learning important image-manipulation techniques are Photoshop Channel Chops *by David Biedny, Bert Monroy, and Nathan Moody (New Riders, 1997);* Mastering Photoshop 6 *by Steve Romaniello (Sybex, 2001); and* Photorealistic Techniques in Photoshop and Illustrator *by Bert Monroy (New Riders, 2000). Another source of excellent teaching on Photoshop is the 500-page online course by Barbara Mehlman at* http://www.sfsuonline.org.

Adding Motion to Images

Another visual language well developed in modern culture is that of moving images. The individual images that form a moving picture are still. The appearance of motion depends on a property of the eye that continues to perceive light after the light is gone. This property is called *persistence of vision*. When images are presented to the eye quickly enough and with enough continuity between them, the eye interprets a series of images depicting a form in different places as the movement of that form. The rate at which this continuity becomes apparent is called *flicker fusion*. A film camera photographs action at increments of time to be played back at the same speed. Each photograph is called one *frame* of the film. In animation, we simulate the movement of forms by creating an image for each frame, as if the form had been photographed in motion, and then playing the frames back in sequence. To figure out how much change is needed between frames in order to create the illusion of a specific motion, early animators studied film frame by frame. Figure 1.6 shows an early sequence of frames by Eadweard Muybridge of a galloping horse. Looking at film or video frame by frame is still a good way to figure out how to animate that kind of motion. In addition, in the many years that animation has been studied, general principles and techniques of good animation have been formulated. We will discuss some of these principles in the animation chapters later in the book.

Figure 1.6 The Horse in Motion *by Eadweard Muybridge, an early example of a sequence of frames forming moving images*

Motion pictures brought about the vocabulary of visual metaphor called *cinematography*. This field is another example of a cultural tradition of seeing and interpreting images. For example, when a character is filmed from underneath, the image is understood by the visual mind to connote power attributed to that person. Like other examples of visual interpretation, these metaphors may vary in how broadly they are understood. Most of us in the modern world have seen enough moving images in this tradition that our visual minds understand the metaphors even if we have never studied cinematography or analyzed the meaning of the camera work in a movie. If you want to make moving images yourself, it is well worthwhile to learn these visual conventions so that you can communicate effectively within the form and choose when to depart from tradition.

Digital Cinematography by Ben de Leeuw (Morgan Kaufmann, 1996) covers the meaning of the visual conventions of film, with tips on how to use these in the context of 3D animation.

Key
Concept

Simulating Three Dimensions

The premise of 3D computer graphics is that by using the understandings of visual images developed in the world of art and photography, imaginary objects described in three dimensions by a computer file can produce images as if the viewer were looking at them. The most elementary 3D file stores only the coordinates of points (called *vertices*) and the *polygons* that comprise them. A polygon is a multi-sided shape that defines a surface. (Since it takes a minimum of three points to determine a planar surface, "polygons" are generally three-sided in this use of the word. These three-sided surfaces are also called *faces*.) The surface is one-sided, with a *normal* pointing outward at right angles to the surface. A normal is a unit vector, a mathematical term that simply gives a direction in space—in the case of a surface normal, the direction that the surface is facing. Polygons can be formed into meshes that simulate three-dimensional objects. Figure 1.7 shows the normals of the polygons (in this case, triangles) of a spherical mesh.

The simplest rendering of a 3D file is called *wireframe*, which omits surfaces and draws only the points and the line segments between them. Through calculations based on the conventions of realistic shading and perspective rendering, the surfaces can be drawn to various degrees of realistic detail. (Chapters 2 and 7 discuss various shading algorithms.) With the exception of ray tracing, discussed in Chapters 7 and 8, these calculations consider only the surface properties of objects. There is no substance described in a 3D file, only the surfaces that can be seen from the vantage point being rendered.

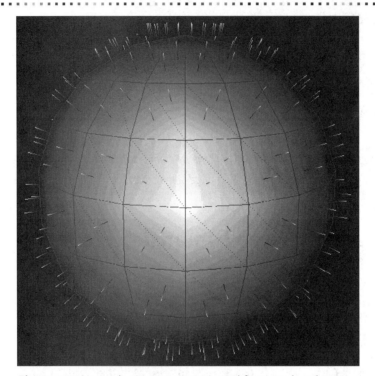

Figure 1.7 *Normals are vectors projected from each polygon determining which direction its surface faces.*

The very powerful aspect of a 3D CG file is that once a scene is described, it can be "photographed" from any vantage point. Consider how difficult it can be to draw a scene with the perspective exactly correct. How many artists could also look at a scene, draw it, and then give you another accurate drawing when you told them you wanted to look at the scene from a vantage point 15 inches below and 7 inches to the left of the first drawing? Possibly an old-school Disney animator. How many could look at a scene and draw it accurately if you told them you wanted to look at the scene from a point just behind the ear of a character in the far left corner? You'd be hard-pressed to find one; and yet, this is easy in max once you have modeled your scene.

Remembering the Context

CG simplifies the complexity of real life in order to create a simulation that can be calculated. There is no physical camera with an actual lens taking pictures of a real scene. In the computer, there is no actual light bouncing off an actual object to reflect to the camera. You are creating the illusion with mathematical approximations. As this book delves further into max, you will learn more about the simplifications being made and the considerations involved in using them. Keep in mind, when learning max, that the familiar concepts of our real world are useful metaphors for 3D simulation. Don't confuse the interface metaphor to mean that the approximation will behave exactly as the object would in real life. For example, a CG light has very different capabilities and limitations than a real light, as you will learn in Chapter 12. You have to maintain some awareness of what you're really working with in order to use the simulation effectively. Knowing the basis of the simulation allows you to decide where a shortcut trick will make no difference, where the difference will be negligible, and where it won't work for your purposes.

There is a tradeoff between making the accuracy of a simulation and the computational burden of generating it. As a result, 3D artists and animators working under deadline have to keep in mind the cost of each decision in terms of its impact on render time.

On a broader level, we can return to the concept of schemata: conventions in representation and perception. 3D imagery has its own schemata that can be misleading. For example, space ships can't really fly the way they do in movies and on TV, but people don't find scientifically plausible simulations convincing. They already "know" how space ships fly: just like jet planes do in the Earth's atmosphere. This is also an example where knowing your purpose and your audience makes a difference. If you are educating students about the probable appearance of real space flight, you will want to research the realistic details to make your simulation accurate. If you are entertaining an audience accustomed to space ships with jet-plane behavior, you will want to follow that convention, at least until such time as your audience has more experience with actual space flight.

Further Innovations in 3D

The 3D computer graphics field continues to explode with new developments. 3D scanners are available that will scan a physical object into a matching surface and texture map in a 3D file. 3D "printers" are used in the manufacture of precision metal parts; the object is designed very precisely in a 3D file and then output to a device that makes a wax mold of the object, into which the metal can be poured. Holograms not only store three dimensions of information, but can be viewed in three dimensions of reality rather than only through a 2D rendering. (These are rare exceptions to the assertion that will be repeated throughout this book: that the final output of a 3D file is always a 2D array of pixels.) In animation, character motion is often recorded from actors' movements using motion capture techniques. This motion information can then be loaded onto a 3D character. Photogrammetry techniques, in which several photographs are taken of an object from different vantage points, can be used to create accurate 3D models and textures of real-world objects.

Check out RealVIZ products for their capability of generating 3D models from images and other advanced image recognition features: `http://www.realviz.com`.

Each innovation in the technology tends to bring up some concern about what will happen to the job market. For example, traditional animators were often concerned about computer animation, just as computer animators became concerned about the later innovation of motion capture animation. Generally, the artistic skill required— for instance, the traditional animator's eye for motion between frames or the character animator's skill at getting a precise nuance of motion from a 3D character—can never be replaced by the technology. The jobs change, but they are not eliminated. Excellent animation skills are much more valuable for getting a job animating on a computer than just knowing an animation software package, so traditional animators find themselves using the tool of the computer to exercise the same artistic skill. Character animators find themselves using the tool of motion capture files to satisfy the same goal of their trained eye.

As technological developments automate more and more jobs that were formerly done by hand, job market values follow a general trend. While there are many economic and social forces at work, what has the most enduring value over time is what can't be automated and what humans do better than computers. This means anything involving original thinking and creativity, anything involving a higher order of comprehension, anything where a qualitative or holistic assessment is required, and anything that involves understanding meanings, emotions, or qualities of the human soul. As more tools are developed that perform the tasks that can be done by rote, we may find ourselves increasingly able to focus on those irreplaceable tasks of finding inspiration, conceiving design, and communicating meaning. What is ultimately of value is the ability to convey meaning.

Summary

The purpose of this chapter was to orient you to the task of learning 3D computer graphics and "mastering 3ds max." You were introduced to the myriad uses of 3D in today's world, in industry and by individual artists, as well as some of the many possible career paths in 3D. You got a quick course in the science of visual perception, art history, and digital image processing in order to develop a sense of context of your work in max. In the next chapter, you will delve further into the essential concepts of CG and how they are implemented in 3ds max.

Getting Oriented to max

3ds max

Chapter 2

This chapter will help you understand concepts that are essential for using max. Some of these concepts are specific to max; some apply equally to other 3D programs as well. While you can skip ahead and start learning the interface and tools, understanding how max is designed and how 3D works can make what you're doing in max much more comprehensible. You can set up your projects and your workflow more efficiently if you know what you're dealing with. We will come back to these concepts throughout the book in order to deepen your comprehension as you learn how they apply.

On the other hand, some people learn best by trying a lot of things out, having things break, and then figuring out what they did wrong. If you learn best that way, you may want to skip this chapter for now and start working on the projects in the later chapters of the book. If you do that and get confused about something, remember to come back to this chapter. You may even want to review it from time to time as you learn the program. The concepts make more sense the more ways you are exposed to them. Topics include:

- Coordinate systems and orientation

- Max objects and sub-objects

- Modifiers and space warps

- The transform matrix

- CG keyframe animation

- Information definition and organization

- Object relationships

- CG shading and texture-mapping

Understanding Your Orientation

In order to describe a 3D scene, you need a reference point. In an empty computer file, with none of the kinds of reference points one has in real life, max needs to define a reference point called the *origin*. Three perpendicular reference planes through the origin define the World coordinate system. The World coordinate system is the Cartesian coordinate system that defines the space of the World object of max. The three reference planes are collectively called the *Home Grid*.

There are different coordinate systems you can use in max to move and orient objects. As you'll see, each system can be useful in certain situations. You will understand the different systems better if you understand how the traditional Cartesian coordinate system of three dimensions is applied in max. In Figure 2.1, you can see the Cartesian coordinate system. Notice that the positive X axis points to the right, the positive Y axis points up, and the positive Z axis points toward you. The origin is located at (0,0,0). This orientation is useful to remember when using the Screen coordinate system, discussed in Chapter 3, and when dealing with imports from or exports to other programs.

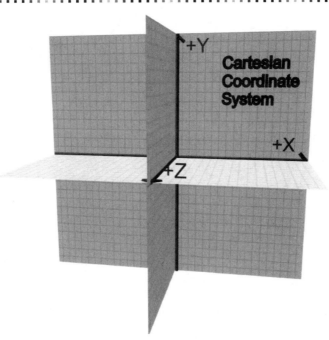

Figure 2.1 *The traditional Cartesian coordinate system*

The designers of max took the "desktop metaphor" of the graphical user interface quite literally. The World coordinate system of max assumes that the XY plane is lying flat on a desktop in front of you rather than mounted vertically on the screen. The result can be seen in Figure 2.2. The origin is still at (0,0,0) and the positive X axis still points toward the right, but the positive Y axis points *away* from you and the positive Z axis points up.

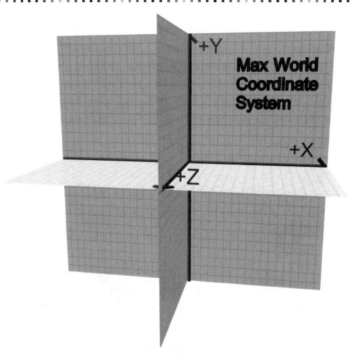

Figure 2.2 *The max World coordinate system*

The World coordinate system applies to the space of the World as a whole. When you assign coordinates in the World system, they are considered *absolute* coordinates. The other coordinate systems are *relative* to something else, either the screen or an object other than the World. You will learn about these coordinate systems in more detail in Chapter 3. The important thing for now is to know which way is up: in max, Z is up.

Max will allow you to create a piece of geometry and name it "World." Don't do this. It is only confusing and can cause errors for plug-ins and exports.

Viewing a 3D Scene File

Once you have a reference point and have oriented yourself, you need a way to look at your 3D scene. When you first open max, you see an interface that looks like Figure 2.3. You will learn about the interface and how to use it in great detail in Chapter 3, but for now notice the four windows that take up the bulk of the screen. These are *viewports* that present you with views of your scene information. The viewports use a separate viewport renderer that renders in real time so that you can see updates as you work.

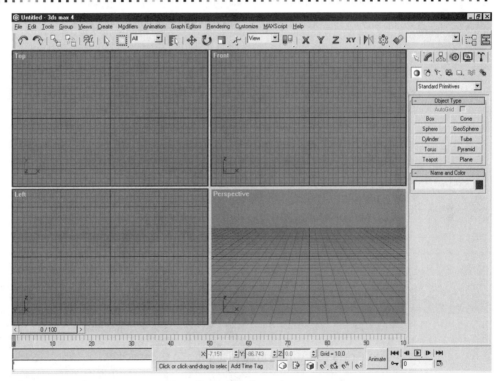

Figure 2.3 *The starting max interface with four viewports*

The two types of views that appear by default are *orthogonal* and *perspective* views. Orthogonal views show you exactly where each point lies in the coordinates of the viewing plane, because they do not show objects appearing to get smaller in the distance. The three orthogonal views that come up by default are

Top	Looking down on the XY plane
Front	Looking forward at the XZ plane
Left	Looking from your left side at the YZ plane (with the positive Y pointing toward the left)

Some 3D applications call "Left" the view from "stage left" or the scene's left rather than your left. Keep this in mind if you switch programs or are accustomed to another program.

The perspective view in the lower right draws your scene from a single vantage point, as if through a camera lens, with the rules of linear perspective applied. The perspective is not drawn all the way to the horizon line. In order to maintain real-time response, the appearance of the perspective grid is estimated.

Figure 2.4 shows two views of the same scene, the left an orthogonal view from the front and the right a perspective view from the front. The orthogonal view shows objects at their actual relative sizes, regardless of distance, at the exact coordinates where they lie on the World XZ plane. The perspective view shows the objects closer to the way they would look in real life, with perspective projection. The distant object appears smaller, and the lines of the floor grid are converging in the distance.

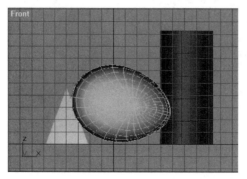
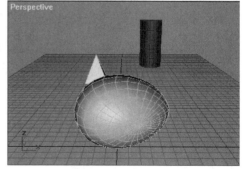

Figure 2.4 *The same scene viewed through orthographic and perspective projection*

The World Is Made of Objects

Once you have a window into a 3D scene, you can see, as in real life, a world of objects. In CG, the terms world and object have more specialized meanings. Max was written in C++, an object-oriented programming language. Object-oriented programming encapsulates information, functions, and properties into modules of programming code called objects. In max, everything is tracked by objects. The word object gets used in different senses when talking about max:

- the technical sense of actual programming code objects, upon which all max objects are based (sometimes called *nodes*)

- discrete items that are represented by some kind of icon in a viewport, whether a piece of geometry or one of the nonrendering objects, such as helpers, space warps, and emitters

- a piece of geometry

It should generally be apparent from the context which sense of the word is being used. What the different senses have in common is that the term *object* defines a certain boundary of organization. You can have many objects in a scene. You have already been introduced to one object in max, the World object. Since the World object is not shown in the scene, it is sometimes called an "imaginary" object. There is one World object per max file that max uses to reference all other objects of the file. The World is the top of the hierarchy of your scene. You can see the hierarchy of your scene in the Track View window.

 If you click the Track View button on the toolbar, you will open a Track View window. (You will use the Track view in Chapters 9 through 11 on animation.) The pane on the left shows the hierarchy of the scene, as seen in Figure 2.5. At the top of the list is a globe icon named World. If you click the minus sign next to it, everything else closes up under it; you are *collapsing* the view hierarchy.

Figure 2.5 *The hierarchy of an empty scene*

This hierarchy illustrates another feature of object-oriented programming: Different kinds of information are passed from object to object according to hierarchies. Information attributed to the World object is passed to everything in the scene file.

Geometry Objects

The most obvious type of object is a type that will render in your scene: geometry. Geometry objects have surfaces, generally one-sided, as explained in Chapter 1. They are not solid; they are like eggshells. Since CG models are just descriptions stored in the computer, multiple objects can occupy the same space. They have no substance. Unless dynamics properties are added to simulate collisions, objects will pass right through one another like ghosts rather than solid objects. (You will learn more about dynamics in Chapter 10.)

There are three types of surfaces in max: mesh, patch, and NURBS. You will learn the nature of these surfaces in much more detail in the modeling chapters (Chapters 4–6). Mesh objects are the most common, since all 3D programs have mesh objects. Mesh objects can be primitives, editable meshes, editable polys, compound objects, or modified versions of these.

Primitives

A *primitive* in computer graphics is one of the basic modeling objects from which other objects are built. Max includes in its programming instructions for building and drawing these primitives.

Point

A *point* is exactly that: a point location at one set of coordinates in space. As soon as a point is connected to another point by a line segment, it is called a *vertex*.

Segment

A *segment* is the line connecting two vertices. If a segment is bounding a polygon, it is also called an *edge*. A segment is sometimes called a *vector primitive*. This is because the instructions defining a segment can be reduced to a point and the distance and direction from that point to the end point. A *vector* is a mathematical concept that includes both a distance and a direction. The vectors used most commonly in 3D are unit vectors that specify only a direction, such as the surface normal discussed in Chapter 1. The usage of the word "vector" to mean a line segment is most commonly seen in reference to vector-based drawing programs such as Illustrator, Freehand, and Flash. These programs, like max, store information about lines as mathematical instructions rather than as pixels, allowing for much smaller file sizes.

Mesh Primitives

Mesh primitives are basic modeling forms for which max has building instructions. These generally have a set of creation parameters that you can adjust to get the size and shape you want. The most frequently used mesh primitives are the sphere and the box. You will use some of the others in later chapters. As long as max has a set of instructions for building an object, almost any kind of mesh can be a primitive. The teapot, for example, is a complex object made of several pieces or *elements*, yet it is a primitive in max. Figure 2.6 shows a teapot with its four elements separated. Max has a set of instructions for building a teapot when you drag out its dimensions in the viewport or enter its creation parameters directly.

Figure 2.6 *Teapot primitive with its four elements separated*

The ubiquitous CG teapot comes from historic developments in 3D computer graphics. In 1975, Martin Newell first modeled a teapot at the University of Utah, in order to test shading algorithms. This "Utah teapot" is part of the culture of computer graphics, almost a mascot at this point.

Editable Mesh

All mesh objects are made of polygons with vertices and edges. In mesh primitives, the vertices and polygons are generated by the instructions max has about that primitive. The same form can also be "baked" into a mesh of explicitly defined vertices and polygons by converting or collapsing the original object to an *editable mesh*. Two file formats that define all objects as explicit meshes this way (by naming vertices and polygons) are the Drawing Exchange Format (DXF) file, a kind of Rosetta Stone in translating models between software packages, and the Virtual Reality Modeling Language (VRML) file.

Mesh models are defined by vertices and polygonal surfaces. The terms *polygon* and *face* are often used interchangeably in CG literature, depending on who is defining them. A face is always a three-sided planar surface. In some contexts in max, a "polygon" can have more than three sides. In previous max versions, all meshes were modeled with faces, even though some of the edges between the faces of a polygon were hidden. Now max 4 has introduced true polygonal modeling, without hidden edges. You will model in both types of mesh in Chapter 4. Since renderers understand only three-sided "polygons," however, max has to translate polygons of greater than three sides into triangles for rendering. Therefore, when max is counting polygons for rendering, the term "polygon" is synonymous with "face" or "triangle."

Compound Objects

Compound objects in max are exactly what they sound like: objects made out of other objects. The computations involved can be very complicated, and, consequently, compound objects are often unstable. Because of this, when you begin modeling with compound objects in Chapter 4, you will be instructed to take extra precautions for backing up your files. You will learn about all the compound objects in Chapter 4, but it's useful here to describe the two most common, Booleans and lofts.

Booleans

Booleans are so called because they are calculated using a kind of mathematics called symbolic logic, invented by George Boole. This is the math of logical true/false operations, such as *OR*, the union of two sets; *AND*, the intersection of two sets; and *NOT*, the subtraction of one set from the other. Applying this to geometry gives the first approximation of solid objects in CG. Only surfaces are rendered, but with Booleans, max calculates the surface based on the corresponding solid geometry being added, subtracted or intersected. An example of CG Boolean operations can be seen in Figure 2.7.

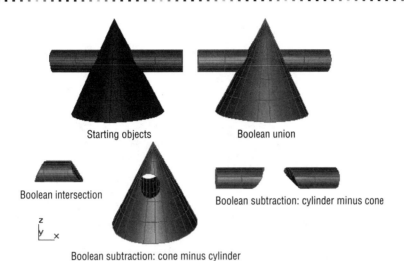

Starting objects   Boolean union

Boolean intersection

Boolean subtraction: cylinder minus cone

Boolean subtraction: cone minus cylinder

Figure 2.7 *Boolean operations applied to a cone and cylinder*

Lofts

Lofting is a term that originated in ship-building to describe the process of forming the shape of a ship's hull. You can think of a ship's frame as a skeleton, with a "spine" running lengthwise and "ribs" forming cross-sections. In max, any 2D shape can serve as a cross-section to be lofted along any path to create a 3D shape. You can also modify the resultant form with loft deformations. Lofting provides a lot of modeling options, for objects that can be described that way, and it is used to create basic forms that can be further modified. Lofts can be output as mesh or patch surfaces. Figure 2.8 gives you an idea of how loft objects work. You will model more detailed objects using lofting in Chapters 4 and 5.

Splines

The term *spline* also originated in ship-building, where a piece of steamed wood would be shaped into a curve by distorting it with clamps and pairs of pegs ("ducks"). Mathematicians borrowed the word to describe curves in terms of mathematical functions. In computer graphics, a spline is a curve defined by mathematical functions rather than a series of straight line segments. A French automotive engineer named Pierre Bézier came up with the way to describe curves using points and the tangents of the curve

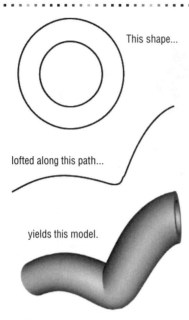

This shape...

lofted along this path...

yields this model.

Figure 2.8 *A shape lofted along a path yields a basic 3D form that can be further modified.*

going into and out of those points. In max, the word *spline* is generally used to mean the Bezier splines used for shapes and patch surfaces. Bezier splines are also fundamental to most vector drawing programs as well as to the Pen tool in Photoshop, and many forms of typography. You will return to the subject of Bezier splines in progressively more depth when using them to build models in Chapters 4 and 5. Bezier tangents are used in a variety of places in the interface as well.

Patches and NURBS

There are two types of spline-based surfaces in max: patches and NURBS. *Patches* are based on Bezier splines, while *NURBS* are based on a different kind of spline you will learn about in Chapter 6. Spline-based surfaces are defined by a different set of instructions than meshes; they have different types of vertices that allow curves between vertices, unlike polygonal meshes, which always have straight edges between vertices. Since renderers still understand only triangles, these surfaces are converted to faces for rendering in the viewport and the production render. One of the useful features of spline-based surfaces is that you can set different conversion properties for the viewport than for the final render, allowing you to maintain real-time response in the viewport while maintaining modeling detail in the final render. For NURBS, the subdivision into polygons can actually be calculated on the fly, based on how close the object is to the camera and various parameters that you assign. This is the real benefit of NURBS; the cost is that the surface calculations put a great demand on your processor at render time.

Mesh primitives can be converted to NURBS, and any mesh object can be converted to a patch object. NURBS and patches can also be converted to meshes. Using the methods and tools of one object type to get part of the way and then converting to another type (usually mesh) is common modeling practice. The tricky part is knowing how to optimize your model for the best result when converting. In Chapter 5, you will model Intrepid Explorer Jim in patches using the Surface Tools method, convert the patch model, and then optimize the mesh.

Editing Levels

Many objects in max have *sub-objects*. Another important concept to be aware of when working in max is the editing level, or *sub-object level*, of the object you are currently working on. This level determines which sub-objects of the object are available for selecting and editing. Editable mesh objects have vertex, edge, face, polygon, and element sub-object levels. When you are working at one sub-object level of an object, you can't select sub-objects on another level, nor can you select another object in your scene until you return to the object level.

Different kinds of objects have different sub-objects. A compound object has sub-objects of the two objects (called *operands*) that formed it. If you stay aware of your editing level, you will avoid a lot of confusion common to beginners, and you will have a better idea of how to go about doing what you want to do.

Modifiers

Modifiers do exactly what the name says: they modify objects. Modifiers are encapsulated sets of instructions to apply to your object. Max records your application of modifiers in an ordered list called the *modifier stack*. The bottom of the stack is the original primitive or editable mesh object, and each modifier is applied in the order named in the stack, from the bottom to the top. The stack works like a list of instructions for a factory assembly line: take this object, have the Modifier 1 department alter the object according to these specifications, then have the Modifier 2 department alter the object according to these specifications, and so on. A sub-object selection at one level is *passed up the stack* to the next modifier.

Modifiers have sub-objects called *gizmos* that determine their range of application. They may also have a center or plane of application sub-object. These sub-objects can often be moved, scaled or rotated to change the application of a modifier.

The modifier stack can be edited by moving modifiers, by copying and pasting them from other modifier stacks, or by deleting them or turning them off or on. The stack can also be *collapsed*, effectively converting everything that's been done to it into a mesh with no history. You would preserve the modifier stack when there is a possibility of wanting to change a modifier's parameters or if you want to animate modifier parameters. You would collapse a modifier stack when you want to save yourself the memory allocated in the modifier stack.

The Edit Mesh Modifier

One important modifier, *Edit Mesh*, gives you almost all the same tools for editing meshes as collapsing to an editable mesh does. The difference is that Edit Mesh, being a modifier, will allow you to go back and change your base object or modifiers that you applied before it in the stack. Edit Mesh is a huge modifier, containing about 80 percent of the programming that made up the predecessor of max, 3D Studio DOS, so you should use it only when you have to.

If you have made edits, navigating down the stack under an Edit Mesh modifier brings up the warning shown in Figure 2.9. You can still edit beneath it, but you have to be careful of changing the sub-object selections that you pass up the stack to Edit Mesh. If you change the number of segments the base object has, for example, you will be sending more vertices up the stack. If you had made edits to a certain selection of vertices in Edit Mesh, those edits will become garbled when applied to the new geometry. The vertices will have new numbers and your edits will be applied according to the vertex numbers of your original object.

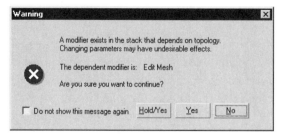

Figure 2.9 *Warning message when navigating under an Edit Mesh modifier*

Space Warps

Space Warps are like modifiers that work in World space. They have a specific range of effect in space. When an object is bound to a space warp, the effect applies only when the object is within range of the space warp. Many modeling modifiers are also available as space warps. This is useful when animating; it allows you to apply temporary changes to a model as it moves through space or to simulate the presence of physical forces in your scene. Some space warps apply dynamics properties to geometry to simulate the physics of collision and bouncing. In this case, a geometry object defines the range of effect of the space warp, and the colliding objects are bound to the space warp.

Particle Systems

Particle systems are objects that simulate complex arrangements and movements of clusters of particles by defining the creation and movement of the particles according to procedures that describe the whole system. This way, you don't have to create every single piece of geometry and animate them all individually. Particle systems are an example of *procedural* animation, animation defined by procedural instructions carried out by the computer rather than being hand-animated piece by piece. In max, the animation is built in to the particle system object; all you have to do is adjust the parameters of the system to fine-tune it for your purposes. Particle systems are used to model streams of water, smoke, swarms of insects, and even crowd scenes. Particle systems can also be used for modeling stationary mesh objects.

Other Max Objects

Other objects available in max include *helper objects*, nonrendering objects that help you measure or manipulate your scene; cameras, to control the composition of your scene the way you would with a real camera; and lights, to control the color and contrast of your rendering. There are *systems objects* that, like particle systems, have a number of objects and animation instructions or constraints built into them. *Dynamics objects* are special mesh objects that have dynamics properties built in for physics simulations, comparable to a mesh object bound to a particular space warp.

Key
Concept

Understanding Transforms

Each object in a max file has its own orientation. The World object is oriented around the origin of the World coordinate system at the XYZ coordinates of (0,0,0). Any other object is oriented around its pivot point, the origin of the local coordinate system defining its *object space*. The pivot point is defined by max relative to the World origin. Each object has a *transform matrix* that tells max where it is located and oriented in World space. A matrix is just an array of numbers. The transform matrix is an array of the position, rotation, and scale values for that object relative to the World. This information is computed separately from other object information, as you will learn in "Object Data Flow" later in this chapter. The matrix algebra behind it can be complicated for a nonmathematician, but to a computer, it is simple arithmetic. You don't have to understand the math, but it's important to grasp how max is storing this information when you start to animate, especially when you want to animate a whole character. We will come back to this topic repeatedly.

Rotation is defined and controlled differently in different applications. Since most animation data is recorded with rotation values, it is much more difficult to translate animation between programs than models.

Understanding CG Animation

Transform data changing over time is one form of animation involving movement. Any parameter or value that changes over time can be a form of animation.

As you learned in Chapter 1, animation involves creating the illusion of motion through a succession of images, called *frames*, played fast enough to fool the human eye. In the history of animation, there are two main styles of animation: straight-ahead and pose-to-pose.

Straight-Ahead Animation

Straight-ahead animation means creating each frame of the animation in order, with incremental changes between the images. This is the technique used to create stop-motion animation. In stop-motion, physical models are shot frame by frame for each increment of motion. The model is moved slightly, a picture is taken; then the model is moved again, and another picture is taken. This is a time-consuming, labor-intensive process, but it can be used to create masterpieces like Tim Burton's *Nightmare Before Christmas* or Nick Park's Wallace and Gromit animations. The technique also results in a certain style of motion. In the earlier days of stop-motion, the style was a little jerky, because the increments of movement were made larger to save film. More modern stop-motion is broken down into smaller increments for smoother motion, but it can still evoke that style at times. Movement in stop-motion can also seem less scripted, if done well, because the animator has to think at each frame how a movement naturally progresses.

Pose-to-Pose Animation

In *pose-to-pose animation*, significant poses are *keyframed* and the transition frames filled in afterwards. This technique was first developed for cel animation.

In cel animation, each frame is painted on pieces of celluloid called *cels* that are combined and shot onto film. Disney Studios developed cel animation into a stream-lined production pipeline by dividing the painting of cels into two main tasks: drawing the significant poses and drawing all the transition frames between these poses. The best, most experienced artists were reserved for drawing the *key* frames of the significant poses, called, naturally enough, *keyframes*. The apprentice artists then took on the arduous task of drawing all the in-between frames, called *tweens*.

For example, if Mickey were to hit a tennis ball, the keyframe artists would decide which were the most important poses to tell the story of Mickey hitting a tennis ball. Those poses might be broken down as shown in Table 2.1.

Table 2.1 Breakdown of Action into Keyframes of Poses

KEYFRAME NUMBER	POSE
Keyframe 1	At rest
Keyframe 2	Racket down, ball in hand
Keyframe 3	Weight back, racket coming up, ball in air
Keyframe 4	Full backswing, ball falling
Keyframe 5	Middle of serve, contact with ball
Keyframe 6	Last half of serve, ball out of frame, racquet heading downward, weight forward
Keyframe 7	Follow-through

After drawing these key poses, the keyframers would give them to tweeners to paint all the frames of the motion that take place between these keyframes. Because of the sheer number of frames to be tweened, tweening could be a very tedious job, although obviously indispensable.

Keyframe Animation in max

Computer animation generally uses the *keyframe* method. The software allows you to be the keyframer and the computer to be your team of tweeners. When you use max to animate, you are saved all the tedious work of drawing key poses by hand and getting someone else to figure out how to draw the in-between frames. You instead have the responsibility of creating the right keyframes and instructing max how to draw the frames in between to get the timing you want. Chapters 9 through 11, on animation, examine this task in much greater detail.

Max stores the keyframes of your animation in *tracks* for a particular object. You had a preview of tracks when you looked at the Track View window earlier in this chapter. Every object in max has many animatable tracks. For example, every object has a position track that records the values of the position transform over the course of an animation. If the object's position does not change at all over the course of an animation, it will have no *keys* in that track. As soon as the object's position is animated to change over time, at least two position keys will be stored in that track. A key stores the value of a particular animated track. A frame that contains any keys is considered a keyframe in CG animation.

Key Concept

Parametric vs. Explicit Definitions

Keyframes are only one of the ways that animation data is stored. A max file stores a huge range of information in a variety of different forms. Widely disparate types of data can still fit a general scheme of the ways that information can be stored. Let's consider some examples and see the pattern that emerges.

CG objects can be defined in different ways. One very laborious way to define a mesh object is to write a VRML file that names every point and polygon of your object and import that into max. This would explicitly define the vertices and surfaces of your object. Even if you named a thousand coordinates exactly three units from the origin, max would understand it as a thousand points connected by however many polygonal surfaces, not as a sphere with a radius of 3. It would be a lot of work to then redefine every coordinate in order to change each point at a radius of 4 units from the origin.

In contrast, a *parametric object* is calculated by max based on parameters you enter. These parameters can be altered later, even after you apply other modifiers to your object. You tell max to create a sphere and then set its radius at 4. If you later change your mind, you can come back and change it to 5 or 22. This parametric property of information is an important concept to understand, because it applies to so many things. If you collapse your parametric sphere to an editable mesh, the parametric properties are gone. The sphere, while it looks the same, is converted to a different object type that is more explicit. You can continue to change the object, but you can't go back and change the initial radius or number of segments.

Modifiers applied to an object usually have parameters of their own. These parameters can also be altered later, even after you apply other modifiers to your object. Some modifiers serve to give you parametric control of your geometry again, although not with exactly the same creation parameters as the initial object. For example, max has a modifier called XForm that you could apply to your mesh sphere and then scale to change its radius. The scale value that changed the size of the sphere would then be available as a parameter of your XForm modifier, even though you lost the radius parameter itself.

This distinction between explicit data and data stored parametrically, as an algorithm or procedure, comes up again and again in CG. When assigning texture maps, as you will do in Chapter 7, you can use a procedural map, which defines the map according to certain parameters you can change, or you can use a bitmap, in which every pixel has been defined explicitly before you apply it. Patch and NURBS surfaces are parametric; the renderer translates them into polygons at render time. You can specify the translation into polygons differently for the final render than for the viewport.

Objects can be more procedural or more explicit by degrees. An editable mesh is more explicit than a sphere, for example, with every vertex defined in space; yet the edges and polygons are still defined by instructions in the computer, similar to a line drawing in a vector-based drawing program. (The final rendered image of the object, equivalent to an image in a pixel-based drawing program, would be the most explicit.) A patch surface is more parametric than an editable mesh, but more explicit than the tessellations of a NURBS surface, where the polygonal subdivision is calculated on-the-fly at render time.

Procedural animation is animation using expressions and scripts that provide instructions rather than explicit keyframes. A *particle system* is a kind of procedural animation, where the instructions are hidden by the interface. An *expression controller*, as described in Chapter 10, is more procedural because all the animation is in the expression, while particle systems have parameters that can be keyframed. Animation expressed as samples at a set number of frames, like motion capture data, is the most explicit type of animation.

max Hierarchies of Information

In addition to the form of the stored information, understanding the organization of that information is also crucial to understanding how a max file works. In object-oriented programming, parts of the program are modular and values are passed from one object to another. The order in which values are passed is very important. Getting the results you want out of max is a lot easier when you understand how it stores information. It's like knowing how the program thinks. If you wanted to get good results out of an employee you were managing, you would want to know how that person approached things so you could give instructions they could clearly understand. With max, if you don't give instructions that it can understand, no alternative management practice will get you the results you want.

You have already seen an example of a hierarchy in max—the overall hierarchy of the scene visible in Track view. Another example is the modifier stack, which applies changes in the exact order specified. Another crucial ordering of information is max's object data flow, of which the modifier stack is one part.

Object Data Flow

Critical to using max effectively is understanding the order in which max evaluates information. Unlike humans, who massively parallel-process information, computers must evaluate data linearly, one step at a time. The order of evaluation is called the *object data flow*. As you have seen, similar changes can be applied in different ways; for example, you could alter an object by modifying its creation parameters, by applying a modifier, by scaling it, or by binding it to a space warp. Applying changes in one level of the data flow will have different repercussions than applying them at another level.

What you do to an object in the interface gives max a set of instructions it will use when rendering: Start with this object, add these modifiers in this order, apply this transform, apply the effects of these space warps, and consider these object properties. Where in the data flow you need to apply changes depends on the specific needs of a project. For example, if you are exporting models separately from animation data, only the first two levels will export, so you don't want to put modeling changes in the transforms.

You can see graphic suggestions of the object data flow in the Track view and modifier stack of an object that has modifiers and space warps applied. Neither of these is exactly a graphic representation of the object data flow. The modifier stack does not list transforms or object properties at all, and some animatable object properties show up at the bottom rather than the top of the tracks for an object. Yet the images below, of the hierarchy of the Track view (left) and the modifier stack (right) for the same object, give you some insight into max's object data flow directly from the interface.

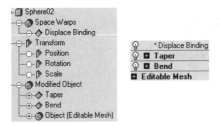

Object data in max flows in this order:

1. Master object evaluated.

2. Modifier stack applied.

3. Transform matrix applied.

4. Space warp bindings applied.

5. Object properties evaluated.

Step 1: Master Object Evaluated

First in the data flow order is calculating the master object. Max evaluates the object type, its pivot point, and the creation parameters of a parametric object or the vertex positions and polygon definitions of an editable mesh object.

The pivot point, as mentioned earlier, defines the position and orientation of the local coordinate system relative to the World. Max also evaluates where the pivot point is located relative to the object as a whole.

Step 2: Modifier Stack Applied

Max's second step in evaluating the information contained in a scene file is to apply the modifiers in the order specified in the stack. The order can make a big difference. Since sub-object selections are also passed up the stack, selections also can make a big difference.

In Figure 2.10, the same object has been modified with Skew and Stretch. The difference between the Skew modifier being applied before the Stretch modifier and vice versa is apparent. When the object is skewed first, the stretch is applied in a different direction than the skew. When the object is stretched first, the skew is applied to the whole stretched object, so the stretch itself is skewed.

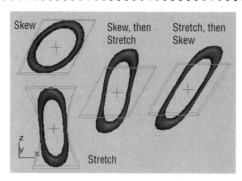

Figure 2.10 *Results of applying Skew and Stretch modifiers in different order*

In Figure 2.11, the same object has had a Stretch modifier applied with the same settings. In the object on the left, however, the sub-object selection of vertices to be passed up the stack to the Stretch modifier extends farther down the object.

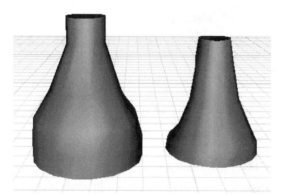

Figure 2.11 *The result of applying Stretch to different sub-object selections*

The modifier stack contains the history of an object, albeit a history that can be edited. You can erase the history and all its editable options by collapsing the stack. The creation parameters and modifier stack no longer exist, leaving you with the mesh object you have created thus far.

Step 3: Transform Matrix Applied

The third step in the object data flow is applying the transforms. Transforms do not carry a history like modifiers, because transform information is stored in a matrix or table rather than an ordered list. What is preserved in the object data flow is the transform matrix relative to the master object in World space. If the transforms of an object are animated (i.e., the object is animated to move, rotate, or scale), the changes in the transform are calculated for each frame and stored in the respective keys for the transform tracks.

The order of the transform matrix in the object data flow can cause many problems down the line if you don't understand it. Since the transforms are calculated after *all* the modifiers, it doesn't matter whether you use them before applying one of your modifiers.

Figure 2.12 shows two cones scaled nonuniformly on X and Y and with a Bend modifier applied. The starting cones were identical, and both times the scaling was performed *before* the Bend. However, for the cone on the right, max applied the scaling *after* the Bend, because the scaling was in the transform. You can see how the Bend gizmo itself was scaled. The cone on the right was scaled within the object space by using an XForm modifier before the Bend modifier was applied. This put the transform in the modifier stack in the desired order.

Figure 2.12 *A Bend applied to identical scaled cones. The first was scaled directly; the second was scaled with an XForm modifier.*

The XForm modifier was designed to allow you to apply your transforms to the XForm gizmo so that the changes are made in the modifier stack rather than in the transform matrix. If you have already applied transforms to the object as a whole, you can move them all into the modifier stack using a utility called *Reset XForm*. Reset

XForm takes the rotation and scale values out of the transform matrix and applies them to an XForm modifier added to the object. If you wanted to move this transform information into the base object, you could then collapse the XForm modifier into the mesh.

Another way to use the Move, Rotate, and Scale tools at an earlier level of the object data flow than the transform matrix is to apply them on a sub-object level. If you move all the vertices of a mesh at a sub-object level, so that the geometry is taking up the same space as another object five feet behind it, this is recorded as a change in the vertex positions of the master object instead of as a change in the object's transform. You would rarely make such an extreme adjustment of vertex positions when modeling; you would be more likely to scale vertices together or apart or move them slightly. The point is that no matter how extremely you change the sub-object positions, the overall object still has the same position.

In the Track view, you can see the values of an object's transforms under the transform tracks for that object. Figure 2.13 shows a view of the tracks for three spheres that look identical. The first is a sphere with a radius of 20 and no transforms or modifiers applied. You can see that Sphere01 shows 100% scale in the Transform track and a Radius value of 20. The second has a radius of 40 and an XForm Modifier applied, with the gizmo scaled 50%. You can see that its Radius track shows a value of 40 and the Scale value of its *modifier gizmo* is 50%. The third sphere has a radius of 40 and was scaled directly 50%. You can see that it has no modifiers applied, its Radius value is 40, and the Scale value of its *transform* is 50%. Get comfortable with looking at tracks, because they are a source of a lot of information that is useful for deciphering problems.

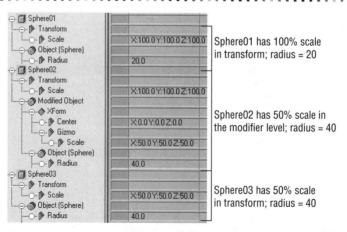

Figure 2.13 *Radius, Transform, and Modifier tracks for three spheres that appear to be identical*

Step 4: Space Warp Bindings Applied

The fourth step in the data object flow is applying space warp bindings. Many geometry deformations available as modifiers are also available as space warps. The difference is that space warps are best used for animated effects rather than for modeling. The same reasoning applies as with using transforms for modeling, because, regardless of your order of application, space warps won't be calculated until after all the modifiers and transforms. Since the effect of space warps is determined by an object's location in space, they have to be calculated after the transforms. Space warp bindings will also always appear in the modifier stack above all the modifiers, regardless of when they are applied. This gives you a graphical indication of their place in the object data flow.

World space modifiers, noted in the interface with an asterisk, are calculated with space warps in the object data flow, after transforms.

Step 5: Object Properties Evaluated

Object properties are evaluated last in the data flow. Most of these either cannot be animated or have to do with viewport display rather than final rendering, so they don't require a lot of special consideration. The name of an object, its base color, the material assigned to it, its visibility, and its motion blur properties are all object properties. These are considered uniquely for each object, regardless of the connections it may have to other objects.

The object data flow shows us how max passes information from the master object, through the application of modifiers, transforms, space warps, and object properties, to the renderer. Figure 2.14 shows a graphical representation of this flow. Understanding how information passes through the application prepares you better for using it.

Understanding Object Relationships

Another way information is organized in a max file involves the different ways that objects can be related to each other. Some of these relationships are hierarchical; others are lateral. Understanding the different ways objects can be connected to each other is crucial to using max effectively. Objects can be attached, instanced, referenced, grouped, or linked. Each connection has entirely different rules designed for specific purposes.

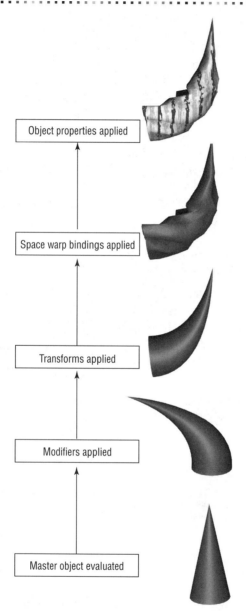

Figure 2.14 *Graphical representation of object data flow*

Attaching

Attach is an option available in various edit modes, such as editable mesh or editable spline. When you attach one object to another, they become a single object with the original two objects becoming sub-objects of the whole object. Attaching is used when modeling to build complex objects out of pieces. You will use Attach a lot when modeling with Surface Tools in Chapter 5.

Instancing: Passing Master Object and Modifier Information

In object-oriented programming, objects can be *instanced*, a form of duplication in which any change made to an instance of the object affects all of the instances. In max, geometry and other types of objects can be cloned as instances, so that changes that you make to either the original object or the clone refer to all of them. Any changes to the master object, and any modifiers applied, will be passed between instanced objects. The transform matrix is not passed between instances, nor is anything above the transform matrix in the data flow, like a binding to a space warp or an object property.

Instances pass master object and modifier information between all instances until you make an instance unique. At that point, changes made to the object will no longer affect the original object or its instances. Use instances when you are creating a lot of objects that will be identical and want to tweak them all simultaneously.

Modifiers themselves can also be instanced. A modifier can be copied and pasted from one object into the stack of another object as an instance, so that changes to the parameters of the modifier that you make to one object are applied to all instances of that modifier, even if the modifier is applied to completely different objects. Materials and maps can also be instanced, as you will see in Chapters 7 and 8.

A *reference* is another kind of clone that passes master object and modifier information in one direction, from the original object to the reference, but not from the reference to the master object. References are often used to see changes in the final version of an object while applying edits at a lower level. For example, when you build a spline cage with Surface Tools in Chapter 5, you will apply a surface to a reference of the spline cage. This way you can see the final surface while editing the spline cage without having to turn the surface on and off.

A *copy* is a clone that inherits everything from the original object at the time of cloning but does not pass any master object or modifier information thereafter. A copy is a unique object. An instance or reference that has been made unique is equivalent to a copy. No more information is passed.

There is no way to change an existing unique object into an instance or reference of another object. The only way to make instances or references is to clone another object.

Grouping

Grouping allows you to select and move a set of objects together easily. When a modifier is applied to a selection of multiple objects, whether or not they are grouped, the modifier affects the objects based on their position within the group, as shown in Figure 2.15. An instance of the modifier is applied to each object with the extent of its gizmo adjusted to account for the whole group.

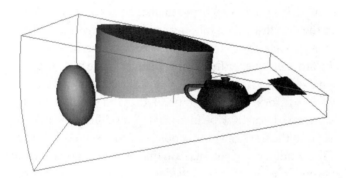

Figure 2.15 *A Bend modifier applied to a selection of multiple objects affects objects based on their position in the group.*

Groups can be nested within groups. Groups can be opened and closed, if you want to change an object within a group and then regroup them; they can be ungrouped to the next level down; and they can be "exploded" to separate every object.

Think of groups as a way of organizing your scene while building it. Don't try to use groups for setting up animatable characters. You will group objects in Chapter 4 when you model an exhibit table that groups a display case model with a nested group of objects that form the table model.

Linking: Passing Delta Transform Information

Linking objects means creating a hierarchy in which one object, the child, is linked to another, the parent. Hierarchies are used for animating, especially for animating complex characters. Objects are linked in hierarchical chains from the end child object to the root parent object.

As mentioned earlier in this chapter, each object has a transform matrix containing its position, rotation, and scale data relative to the world. Once a linkage is established, the object's transform is defined relative to the parent object rather than to the world. Any change in the parent's transform, called the *delta transform*, is passed down the chain to all the children below it in the hierarchy. This way, when you rotate a character's upper arm at the shoulder, the lower arm and hand don't get left behind.

In the discussion of hierarchical animation in Chapter 11, you will see how to define which transform data gets passed along the chain and how to specify limits to apply when animating.

Shading in Computer Graphics

Since you will be looking at renders of your file—in the viewport and in the production renderer, it's important to understand the basics of what you will be seeing. As you learned in Chapter 1, the three dimensions of the objects in your max file are simulated in the rendered image by shading surfaces using the schemata of Western art. Let's look at some different types of basic shading.

In Figure 2.16, you can see four perspective views of the same sphere. The viewport on the upper left is set to Wireframe. This shows you only the edges between polygons. The viewport on the upper right is set to Facets shading. This is the oldest type of CG shading.

In both of these display modes, you can see every facet of the sphere. The viewport on the lower left is set to Smooth. It is the same sphere with the same number of segments, but here it appears smooth, because the viewport renderer is calculating the shading to simulate a smooth surface. The sphere's surface is still made of flat facets, but the color values of the pixels of one facet are now blended in gradations across the polygon to make it appear rounded and smooth. This method of interpolating the color value of the pixels between the vertices of a polygon was invented by Henri Gouraud and is now called *Gouraud shading*. To display an object with the edges between polygons smooth-shaded this way, you need to turn on *smoothing*. Smoothing can be turned on for a primitive in its creation parameters. In a mesh, edges are smoothed if a) the polygons are in the same smoothing group (a property you can assign), and b) the angle between the edges is greater than the smoothing angle you assign.

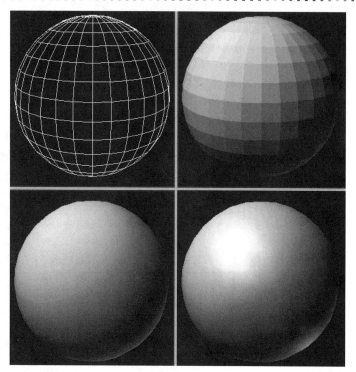

Figure 2.16 *A sphere displayed with four types of shading: Wireframe (upper left), Facets (upper right), Smooth (bottom left), and Smooth & Highlights (bottom right)*

The viewport on the lower right is set to Smooth & Highlights shading. This shading method, called *Phong shading* because it was invented by Bui Tuong-Phong, adds in specular highlights by interpolating the surface normals between vertices. Recall from Chapter 1 that the surface normal determines which way the surface of a polygon is facing. By interpolating the normal across the surface, CG software like max can calculate the value of each pixel independently, with a surface direction that more closely approximates a rounded surface. This innovation allows artists to add specular highlights and reflections.

Texture Mapping

The next advance in shading was the ability to apply bitmaps to a surface. These bitmaps are also called *texture maps*. Texture maps can include reflection maps, which affect the specular reflection; opacity maps, which affect the transparency; and bump maps, which affect the depth shading; as well as the regular "wrapping paper" sort of map called a diffuse map.

Texture maps are applied according to a *texture space*, which has a coordinate system separate from that of the object. Since the coordinates X, Y, and Z are already used to describe the object space, the coordinates U, V, and W are used to describe the object's texture space. These coordinates are called *mapping coordinates*, *UVW mapping*, or just *UVs*. U and V describe the surface, while W is the axis perpendicular to the surface used to describe rotations of the UVs. In max, geometry objects can have multiple bitmaps applied, as well as multiple sets of mapping coordinates, because you might want to use one set of coordinates for one map and another set of coordinates for another.

You can also control which pixels of a texture map are projected onto which polygons of the geometry. You will learn about texture mapping in much greater detail in Chapters 7 and 8.

Extensibility

One of the most powerful aspects of a program like max is that it is fully extensible. Programmers can use discreet's software developers' kit, or SDK, to write plug-ins that can add almost any kind of functionality to the program. Many plug-ins are available free of charge; others can be pricey. Plug-ins often appear as separate utilities, but they can also appear anywhere in the interface: as new parametric primitives, as modifiers, as materials, and so on.

Even if you don't have the level of programming skills involved in using the SDK, you can still write scripts in MAXScript, as you will learn in Part VI of this book.

Summary

In this chapter you became more familiar with the structure and logic of max. You learned how the max World is defined and oriented. You were introduced to the various types of objects used in max. You learned several key concepts: how transform data is stored, what it means to define objects parametrically, how max processes data, how information can be passed between objects, and how surfaces are shaded. You were introduced to CG animation in keyframes. You got a peek at the tracks where max stores its animation data for a scene. With this grounding in the core concepts of max, you are ready to get on with the business of using the program. In the next chapter you will become familiar with the max interface.

Meeting the
max Interface

3ds max

Chapter 3

The max interface gives you access to thousands of features and commands. Many of these can be accessed in multiple ways. The interface is also so customizable that one user might not recognize the customized interface of another user. Like most of today's object-oriented applications, max has menus and tools that are context-sensitive, so you might not come across some aspect of the interface until you tackle some very specialized feature. Plug-ins also add new options to the interface.

In this chapter, you will get to know the essential areas of the max interface, starting from when you open max for the first time. Knowing how these areas work will help you know how to go about a specific task and the basic tools available to aid you. You can also come back to this chapter at any time as a reference guide to the user interface if you get stuck.

Topics include:

- The main areas of the interface

- The Command panels

- Creating, modifying, and manipulating objects

- The main toolbar

- Menu commands

- Viewport navigation and shading

- Customizing the interface

An Overview of the Interface

When you open up max for the first time, the interface looks as shown in Figure 3.1. As you learned in Chapter 2, the four viewports are your windows into the max scene. Above them is the main toolbar, probably the most recognizable part of the max interface, with buttons for all the main tools. You can customize this toolbar and create your own toolbars. If you roll your cursor over a blank area of the toolbar, you should see a hand icon. By dragging on the toolbar when you see this icon, you can scroll to see the rest of the toolbar.

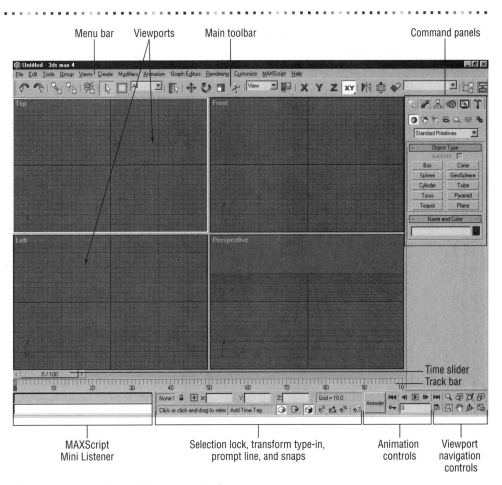

Figure 3.1 *Overview of the max interface*

Whenever a part of the interface doesn't fit on the screen, hold your cursor over a blank part of the interface, wait a second until you get the pan hand icon, and then drag that part of the interface to scroll farther. You might want to set the resolution of your screen higher (using the Windows Display control panel) to see more of the interface. This will also make everything smaller on the screen, making text less readable. A common working resolution for 3D is 1024 × 768.

Above the toolbar is the Menu bar, which offers many commands you will examine in this chapter and in the course of this book. Many of these commands are also available elsewhere in the interface. On the right side of the screen is the Command panel area, with tabs for six panels. The Command panels are highly context sensitive, offering a vast number of possible rollouts depending upon the object selected.

The bottom area of the interface contains the MAXScript Mini-Listener for recording commands in MAXScript; status information and prompts to give you feedback about the current action; tools to help you navigate viewports and manipulate objects; and a time slider, track bar, and animation controls to help you navigate within the time span of your animation. A blank max file has a default of 100 frames at 30 frames per second (fps) or a little over three seconds. MAXScript will be covered in Chapters 15 through 20 (Part VI).

Showing the Tab Panels   Choosing Customize ➜ Show UI ➜ Show Tab Panel will bring up the Tab panel shown here. This includes 10 tabbed toolbars with icon buttons for most of the commands in the Create and Modify panels and the Rendering menu. Right-click on a blank area of the Tab panel and, in the context menu that appears, uncheck this option to put it away.

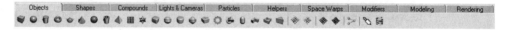

When you are first familiarizing yourself with max tools and workflow, you will probably depend mostly on the toolbar and menu items. As you become more proficient, you can increase your efficiency with more use of the context-sensitive quad menus and keyboard shortcuts. While all of these tools are customizable, we will stick to the default menus and keyboard shortcuts in this book. You will also access commands in different ways to become acquainted with the range of your user interface (UI) options.

Command Panels

The Command panel area holds most of your commands for modeling and animating. Many of these commands are accessible from other areas of the interface. The six panels, whose tab icons are shown below, are Create, Modify, Hierarchy, Motion, Display, and Utilities. (Note: We refer to the tabbed panels within the Command panel as *panels* to be consistent with the 3ds max documentation. Similar elements in other parts of the interface are described in the max documentation and this book as *tabs*.)

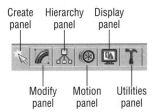

Create panel   Hierarchy panel   Display panel

Modify panel   Motion panel   Utilities panel

Rollouts   A *rollout* is a section within a command panel partitioned off by a title bar. If a panel section title has a + symbol, this bar can be clicked to roll out the subsection. To roll up the section, click the title bar (which will now have a – symbol) again. Right-clicking a blank area of a Command panel allows you to navigate through the rollouts. Below is an example of the right-click menu for the Create panel when a primitive is selected. Rollouts with check marks are open. By choosing one of the rollout names, you can navigate directly to that rollout. You can also close the rollout you are in, close all the rollouts, open all the rollouts, or reset the rollouts to their defaults.

You can move rollouts around by dragging the label of one above or below another.

Spinners   *Spinners* are numerical entry fields with up and down arrows to the right. You can type values directly into the fields and press Enter, or you can click the arrows to increase or decrease the value by a set increment. (You can set this increment in Customize → Preferences → General. In the Spinners section, the Snap value sets the increment. Use Snap must also be checked.) By dragging up or down on the spinner, you can spin through to the desired value. Pressing the Ctrl key while you do this will spin faster; pressing the Alt key will spin slower. Right-clicking while you're dragging sets the spinner back to the last value. To return to the default value, right-click on one of the spinner arrows. Table 3.1 gives you an easy reference for controlling spinners.

Table 3.1 Spinner Controls

TO CHANGE SPINNER THIS WAY	DO THIS
Increase/decrease by increment	Click up/down arrow
Spin value up/down	Drag up/down on spinner
Spin faster	Press Ctrl while dragging
Spin slower	Press Alt while dragging
Return to last value	Right-click while dragging
Return to default value (or sometimes to zero or lowest allowed value)	Right-click one of the arrows
Add/subtract from existing value	Type R before value (e.g., type **R-3** to subtract 3 from existing value)

You can show and hide the Command panel area by pressing 3. You can move it or make it into a floater by right-clicking in a blank area at the very top and choosing Dock → Left or Float.

The Create Panel

You'll use the Create panel to create most of your objects in max. This is where you access the commands to create all kinds of geometry (mesh, patch, or NURBS objects), compound objects, splines, particle systems, dynamics objects, space warps, lights and cameras, helper objects, and various systems. The Create panel contains six tabs, and each of these has a drop-down menu such as the one for Geometry shown below. Even if a drop-down has only one standard option as a default (as with the Lights, Cameras, and Systems tabs), plug-ins are often available that add options to these drop-downs. Spend some time navigating through the Create panel to check out all the tabs and drop-down options. It will help you remember what's available and where to find it when you need it. Table 3.2 lists the tabs within the Create panel and describes the options available in each.

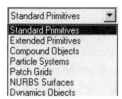

Table 3.2 Tabs of the Create Panel

Tab Icon	Tab Name	Use
	Geometry	Creates mesh primitives, patches, NURBS surfaces, compound objects, particle systems, and dynamics objects.
	Shapes	Creates splines and NURBS curves.
	Lights	Creates different types of lights.
	Cameras	Creates different types of cameras.
	Helper Objects	Creates nonrendering dummy objects for animating, measuring devices, gizmos for effects, manipulators, camera reference points for camera matching, and VRML helper objects.
	Space Warps	Creates forces and space warp deformations or modifications to affect animated objects and simulate physics.
	Systems	Creates bones and various other systems. The biped system of the character studio plug-in is accessed here.

Creating Objects

When you create objects in the Create panel, you begin by clicking the button for the type of object you're creating. You can then size the object either by dragging its dimensions out in the viewport or by entering its dimensions numerically. Here's a quick look at each method.

Creating Objects by Dragging

To try the dragging technique, go to the Create ➜ Geometry panel and click the Box button. Once the button is activated, it turns yellow. Drag a square out in the perspective viewport. A rectangle is drawn on the floor grid. Release the mouse button and move your cursor upward in the viewport. Click again to set the height of the box. You now have a box. Notice that the Box command is still active. If you click in the viewport again, you will continue to create boxes. Delete the box by pressing the Delete key on your keyboard. Right-click in the viewport to deactivate the Create Box command.

Creating Objects Numerically

While you're still in the Geometry tab of the Create panel, click the Sphere button. On the Create panel, open the Keyboard Entry rollout. In the Radius field, type a value of **35**. Click the Create button. You have now created a sphere. If you drag the Radius spinner now, you can adjust the radius interactively. Once you click anything else, however, you can modify your creation parameters only in the Modify panel, not in the Create panel. Deactivate the Create Sphere command by right-clicking in an empty area of the viewport. Keep this file open, because you will use it while exploring the interface in upcoming sections of this chapter.

The Modify Panel

The Modify panel is where you will do a great deal of editing. After you first create an object, you can modify its creation parameters only in the Modify panel. You also apply and edit modifiers here.

Select the sphere you created in the previous section, by clicking on it in the viewport. At the top of the Modify panel you'll see the object's name and color. These, as you may remember from Chapter 2, are both object properties. You can edit the object name here by simply typing in a new name. You can edit the object color by clicking the color swatch and choosing a new color from the Object Color palette.

The Modifier List

Underneath the object name and color swatch is a drop-down called the Modifier List, which includes all the modifiers currently available. In max 4, it is organized in sets according to modifier type to aid you in finding the modifier you need. Modifiers marked with an asterisk are World space modifiers. These are calculated with space warps in the object data flow, because they are calculated based on World space rather than object space. Table 3.3 lists the major modifier types and what they are used for. We will cover specific applications of various modifiers throughout this book.

Table 3.3 Major Modifier Types

MODIFIER TYPE	MODIFIERS IN SET	DESCRIPTION	COMMON USAGE
Selection	Mesh Select Patch Select Poly Select Vol. Select	Allow you to make sub-object selections of geometry to pass up the stack to the next modifier.	MeshSelect is used most often to send a selection of vertices or faces to a deforming or editing modifier. It is also used to clear a sub-object selection.
Editing	Edit Patch Delete Patch Delete Mesh Edit Mesh Face Extrude Normal Smooth Tessellate STL Check Cap Holes VertexPaint Optimize MultiRes	Allow you to edit geometry.	Many of the mesh-editing modifiers are included in Edit Mesh. It is best to use the smallest modifier you need for what you are doing. For example, if you just want to flip the normals of a surface, use the Normal modifier rather than Edit Mesh.
Animation	Skin Morpher Flex Melt Linked XForm PatchDeform PathDeform SurfDeform *PatchDeform *PathDeform *SurfDeform	Allow you to apply animatable deformations to your geometry.	Flex is commonly used to add secondary animation to a moving object; for example, long ears flopping in response to motion.

Table 3.3 Major Modifier Types *(continued)*

MODIFIER TYPE	MODIFIERS IN SET	DESCRIPTION	COMMON USAGE
UV Coordinate	UVW Map Unwrap UVW UVW Xform *Camera Map Camera Map *MapScaler *Surface Mapper	Allow you to change the mapping coordinates of your object.	UVW Map is used to assign mapping coordinates. Unwrap UVW is used to assign which vertex in the geometry should be mapped to which pixel in the texture map.
Cache Tools	Point Cache *Point Cache	Allow you to save out and cache vertex animation data (new in max 4).	Point Caches are used to improve playback of animation by recording and caching animated vertex positions.
Subdivision Surfaces	HSDS Modifier MeshSmooth	Allow you to subdivide geometry.	MeshSmooth is commonly used to increase the smoothing of a model for higher-polygon models.
Free Form Deformations	FFD 2x2x2 FFD 3x3x3 FFD 4x4x4 FFD (box) FFD (cyl)	Allow you to deform geometry with a lattice.	An FFD modifier is applied and then the points of the lattice are moved around to pull the geometry in that direction. The position of these points can also be animated.
Parametric	Bend Taper Twist Noise Stretch Squeeze Push Relax Ripple Wave Skew Slice Spherify Affect Region Lattice Mirror Displace XForm Preserve	Allow you to deform geometry according to the parameters of the modifier and the placement and scale of its gizmo.	The Noise modifier is applied to model many sorts of irregularities in surfaces. The noise can be animated to simulate natural movement.

New

Table 3.3 Major Modifier Types *(continued)*

MODIFIER TYPE	MODIFIERS IN SET	DESCRIPTION	COMMON USAGE
Surface	Material MaterialByElement Disp Approx *Displace Mesh	Allow you to change the surface properties of geometry.	The Material modifier, also included in EditMesh, can be applied to change the material of a selection of faces.
Conversion	Turn to Poly Turn to Patch Turn to Mesh	Allow you to convert between types of geometry without collapsing the stack.	A Turn to Mesh modifier might be applied to a patch object to see how it will convert to mesh. These modifiers can take up a lot of processing power, so use them only when necessary.

Modifier Sets

Below the Modifier List is a set of modifier buttons, the Selection modifier set. Click the Configure Modifier Sets button slightly farther down the panel and look at the options below Show Buttons in the menu. All the sets of modifiers you saw in the Modifier List are available as sets of buttons. When you choose one of these, a different set of modifier buttons becomes available in the Modify panel. If you uncheck Show Buttons, no modifier buttons will display. If you choose Configure Modifier Sets from the menu, you can make your own set of modifier buttons. When the Show All Sets In List box is checked, the Modifier List is organized into the sets described in Table 3.3; when it is unchecked, the Modifier List is organized as it was in previous versions of max, with object and World space modifiers separated and sorted alphabetically.

Making Your Own Set of Modifiers

You can create your own sets of the modifier buttons you use often for certain tasks. Click the Configure Modifier Sets button and choose Configure Modifier Sets. Type in the name for your new modifier set at the top. Set the number of buttons you want. Select a button and, in the list of modifiers on the left, double-click the modifier you want for that button. Once you've assigned all the buttons, type in a name for the new set and click Save. Click OK. Your new set will appear at the top of the list of sets.

The Stack View

New

Between the buttons of the current Modifier set and the Configure Modifier Sets button is an area called the Stack View, redesigned for max 4. This is the same modifier stack that max has always used, but its display and features have been altered. To see how it works, first make sure your sphere is still selected by clicking on it in the viewport. You should see an object name displayed in the Stack View. Right-click the name in the Stack View and choose Convert To: Editable Mesh. The Stack View should now display "+ Editable Mesh." Click the plus sign to see the sub-object levels displayed beneath Editable Mesh. Click the word Vertex. The vertices of your object should be displayed in the viewport and the Vertex sub-object button in the Selection rollout should now be active, as shown in Figure 3.2.

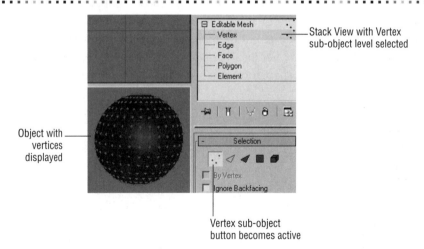

Figure 3.2 *The Stack View with the Vertex sub-object selected activates the Vertex sub-object button.*

Expanding the Command Panel

Max 4 has the option to expand your Command panel area so that you can see much more of it at once when you need to. To expand the Command panel:

1. While still at the Vertex sub-object level, right-click in a blank area of the panel and choose Open All.

2. Put your cursor at the left edge of the panel until it turns into a horizontal double-headed arrow.

3. Drag the edge of the Command panel to the left until you have four panel rows.

4. Drag the edge back to return to the normal interface. Click Editable Mesh again to return to the Object level.

Using the Transform Gizmo to Alter the Modifier Effect

When you use the Modify panel to apply modifiers, you can alter their parameters in the panel and access their gizmo sub-objects to alter the application of the modifier. Let's look at this:

1. Click the Configure Modifier Sets button again and choose Parametric Modifiers.

2. Click the Stretch button to apply a Stretch modifier to your object.

3. In the Parameters rollout farther down the panel, drag up on the Stretch and Amplify spinners to stretch your object.

4. In the Stack View, click the plus sign next to Stretch. Click the word Gizmo to go to the Gizmo sub-object of the Modifier. The gizmo of the modifier, which appears as a framework around the object in the viewport, should turn yellow.

5. The Move tool in the main toolbar should be automatically activated. If not, click the Move tool button. A *transform gizmo* appears as an XYZ axis in the center of the object. Roll your mouse over the red X axis of the transform gizmo until it becomes highlighted in yellow. Then drag that axis to the left to move the Stretch gizmo. Your object should start stretching toward the new placement of the gizmo. Figure 3.3 shows an example.

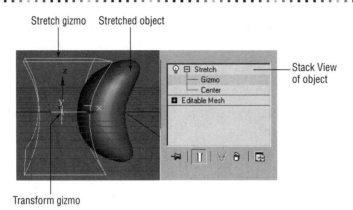

Stretch gizmo   Stretched object

Stack View
of object

Transform gizmo

Figure 3.3 *The effect of the Stretch modifier altered by moving its gizmo*

Click the word Stretch in the Stack View to get back to the Object level.

The *transform gizmo* represents the location of the pivot point when you are transforming (moving, rotating, or scaling) an object. It is a tripod showing the three axes of the local object space: X (in red), Y (in green), and Z (in blue). Use the transform gizmo to constrain the motion of a transform along an axis while you drag the mouse: roll over the axis name until it highlights in yellow and then drag to constrain to that axis; drag the corners between axes to constrain to that plane.

Dragging Modifiers from the Stack View to the Viewport

In max 4, you can now copy or instance modifiers to other objects just by dragging from the Stack View to another object in the viewport:

1. In the Create panel, click the Sphere button and drag out another sphere in the viewport. Right-click in the viewport to deactivate the Sphere command.

2. Click on your original stretched sphere and go to the Modify panel. Drag the word Stretch from the Stack View to the new sphere. When you see the + cursor, release the mouse button. The new sphere now has a Stretch modifier applied to it, copying all the settings of the original modifier.

The Stack View Menu

Right-click the word Stretch to bring up the new Stack View menu. This menu allows you to turn modifiers on and off in the viewport and renderer independently. *Off* turns the selected modifier off in both the viewport and the renderer; it has the same effect as clicking the light bulb icon in front of the modifier name. *On* turns the modifier on in both the viewport and the renderer and does the same thing as toggling the light bulb icon back on. You must use the context menu to turn modifiers on or off independently.

You can also use this menu to rename modifiers and copy and paste them from here to the stack of other objects.

Quad Menus

The context-sensitive quad menus are new in max 4 and give you access to many of the editing commands available in the Modifier panel with a simple right-click:

1. Reset max (File ➜ Reset).

2. In the Create panel, click Box.

3. Drag out a box in the viewport.

4. In the Modify panel, right-click Box in the Stack View and choose Convert To: Editable Mesh.

5. Now right-click the box in the viewport to bring up the quad menu.

Quad menus are highly context-sensitive, so you will encounter many different versions of the menus through the course of this book. All of them, however, follow the general layout shown in Figure 3.4. The two menus on the right are the same for any object, including access to the transform tools (like the Move tool you used earlier), the Object Properties dialog, and various display settings. The lower-right menu also includes access to the new Manipulate mode, which we will discuss in the main toolbar section of this chapter.

The two menus on the left are context-sensitive to the editing level of your object, the type of object, and the active tool or command in the program. The last command used continues to be active until you choose a new command. The last command used in any quadrant is available by clicking the inner yellow square of that quadrant.

The steps above brought up the quad menu for an editable mesh object, as seen in Figure 3.4. The editable mesh commands will be covered in Chapter 4. Manipulators and parameter wiring are covered later in this chapter, in the "Manipulate Mode" and "Parameter Wiring" sections. Track view is covered in more depth in Chapters 9 through 11.

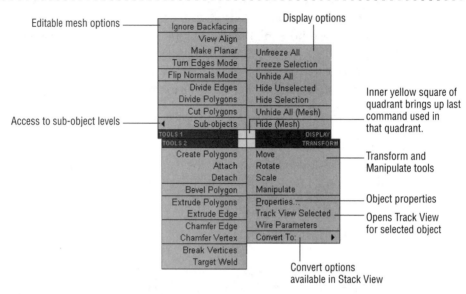

Figure 3.4 *The quad menu for an editable mesh object*

The Hierarchy Panel

The Hierarchy panel is used mainly to set and adjust constraints on linked hierarchies (introduced in Chapter 2 and covered in detail in Chapter 11).

Hierarchies are usually set up to animate complex characters with jointed limbs. The two main methods for animating these hierarchies are *forward kinematics*, in which the delta transform is simply passed down the hierarchy, and *inverse kinematics*, in which you move the endpoint of a chain to a desired position (such as a foot to the floor) and the computer calculates the movements of the rest of the chain. The Hierarchy panel contains three tabs, accessed through the three buttons at the top of the panel, that give you tools for adjusting your hierarchy and for setting constraints on forward kinematics (FK) and inverse kinematics solutions (IK). You will learn about forward and inverse kinematics in more detail in Chapter 11.

Pivot

In the Pivot section, you can move and reorient the pivot point of an object. Because transforms are passed through the hierarchy, this is where you can adjust an object's position without affecting its children, and you can adjust the pivot point of an object independently of the rest of the object.

While the Pivot section is very useful when adjusting hierarchies, you can use it for moving the pivots of unlinked objects as well. Here's an example:

1. With your box still selected, click the Pivot button on the Hierarchy panel. Then click the Affect Pivot Only button.

2. Under Alignment, click the Center To Object button. This moves the pivot from the base to the center of the box. If you left the pivot here, the box would pivot around its center when rotated.

Always remember to click the Affect Pivot Only button again to turn it off when you are finished adjusting the pivot point. Otherwise, when you go to rotate the object, you will rotate the pivot point instead.

3. Click the Reset Pivot button to return the pivot to where it started.

The Don't Affect Children button allows you to move a parent object without passing the transforms to the children. This is essentially the same as unlinking the object, moving it, and relinking it, so it can be quite handy when you need to adjust a hierarchy.

Link Info

In the Link Info section, you can set constraints for the movement of hierarchies in regular FK. The Locks rollout is for preventing movement, rotation, or scaling along a specific axis. The Inherit rollout is for specifying exactly which transforms will be passed to the object's children. For example, you could specify that only the rotation around the object's Y axis will be inherited by its child objects.

IK

The IK tab is for setting constraints for some of the IK solutions available in max. Chapter 11 covers a variety of IK options, including the new IK solvers, with applications to character animation.

The Motion Panel

The Motion panel gives you access to many of the animation tools and controls that are also available in the Track View. You can adjust keys and the tangents going in and out of them, and you can assign or change animation controllers. You use these controls to adjust the motion of an animated object. The new IK solvers are edited in the Motion panel, and the character studio plug-in for biped character animation is also set up and modified through this panel. Chapters 9 through 11 cover animation and the use of this panel.

The Display Panel

The Display panel gives you options for controlling the display of objects in the viewport. The Display Properties rollout lists certain Object Properties, which are also available by right-clicking and choosing Properties from the Quad menu. Table 3.4 lists the key features available in the Display panel. These features are also available in a floater in Tools → Display Floater.

Table 3.4 Key Display Features

DISPLAY PROPERTY	WHAT IT DOES
Hide	Removes the object from viewport display, although it will still exist in your scene.
Unhide	Returns object to viewport display. Pressing **5** will bring up the Unhide By Name dialog.
Freeze	Makes object impossible to select in the viewport (it will appear gray).
See-Through	Makes an object semi-transparent so that you can see through it while you are working. Toggle this on and off by pressing Alt+X.
Vertex Ticks	Displays vertices in viewport.
Edges Only	Hides the edge between the faces of a poly. The default is on; uncheck this to display the hidden edges.

The Utilities Panel

The Utilities panel gives you access to utility programs. Many of these are plug-ins that ship with max, and many more are available free of charge. Still others can be bought from software developers. Table 3.5 explains the key utilities available within max.

Table 3.5 Key Utilities in max

UTILITY	DESCRIPTION
Asset Browser	An improvement on an already-great tool called the Asset Manager, this utility allows you to see all image and .max files in a directory. Now allows you to browse the Internet as well.
Bitmap Path Editor	Allows you to change the path of bitmaps used in your scene.
Color Clipboard	Allows you to sample any color in a rendering or in the Material Editor and copy it to a clipboard to use elsewhere. You can save and load these clipboards. You will use the color clipboard in Chapter 12.
Follow/Bank	Allows you to add bank to a trajectory without using the path controller.
MAX File Finder	Allows you to search for .max files containing information that you specify; for example, one that uses a certain bitmap or contains a certain Keyword field.
Polygon Counter	Allows you to find the exact number of faces in a mesh. You will use the polygon counter in the Optimization tutorial in Chapter 5.
Rescale World Units	Allows you to rescale selected objects or the entire scene without affecting the scale value.
Reset XForm	Mentioned in the last chapter, allows you to put rotation and scale data into an XForm modifier. You will use Reset XForm in Chapter 11 after setting up a hierarchy.
UVW Remove	Allows you to remove mapping coordinates and material assignments.

Pressing Q toggles on the display of a polygon count for selected objects. It displays in the viewport rather than in a dialog box like the Polygon Counter utility.

The Main Toolbar

The main toolbar holds the essential tools for manipulating objects in max. Before we discuss those tools, however, you should take a quick step to make the toolbar fit better on most screens. This is a good idea because the rendering buttons at the end of the toolbar are used quite often, and constantly scrolling to reach them can slow you down.

Shrinking the Main Toolbar

Let's fix those wasteful large toolbar buttons:

1. Open up max.

2. From the menu bar choose Customize ➜ Preferences. On the General tab, in the UI Display section, uncheck Use Large Toolbar Buttons.

3. Click OK and close max. When you reopen max, you should have a toolbar of smaller buttons that looks as shown.

The Quick Reference Card included in the box with 3ds max gives you labeled graphics of all toolbars in the interface. Use it while you're learning the interface.

Learning the Toolbar Contents

Some of the tool buttons contain a variety of tools arranged in a flyout, some launch dialogs, and most can be accessed in other ways. Table 3.6 describes the tool buttons, flyouts, and dialogs available on the main toolbar. The tools are described in more detail in the sections following.

You can show or hide the main toolbar by pressing Alt+6.

Flyouts   A small triangle in the lower-right corner of a tool button indicates that a *flyout* of other button options is available. Essentially, the buttons on a flyout represent a grouping of related but mutually exclusive options or tools. Click and hold your mouse on a flyout button to display the flyout. To select a button from the flyout, drag your mouse over your choice and release. Your choice will remain the visible button until you change it. For example, Figure 3.5 shows the Scale tool and the three choices within its flyout (Scale, Non-uniform Scale, and Squash). Here, Scale is the "default" scaling tool that currently appears on the toolbar; choosing Squash from the flyout would both launch the Squash tool and leave the Squash button visible on the toolbar.

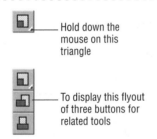

Hold down the
mouse on this
triangle

To display this flyout
of three buttons for
related tools

Figure 3.5 *Example of a tool button flyout: the Scale tools*

Modal and modeless dialog boxes   Dialog boxes come in two types: a *modeless* box can remain open while continuing work on the scene; a *modal* box must be completed or canceled before continuing with any further functions. Track View, Schematic View, the Material Editor, and Video Post are modeless, so you can keep them open as you work. The Mirror and Array tools are modal, so you need to finish them or cancel to work on your scene. The Select By Name dialog comes in two versions: the default available on the toolbar is modal, but a modeless floater that does the same thing is also available.

Table 3.6 Tools on the Main Toolbar

Icon	Name	Description
	Undo	Undoes the last action.
	Redo	Redoes the last action undone.
	Link	When active, dragging from child object to parent object sets up a hierarchical linkage. You will use the linking tools in Chapters 10 and 11.
	Unlink	Unlinks selected objects of a hierarchy.
	Bind To Space Warp	When active, dragging from geometry to a space warp object binds it to the space warp. You will use this tool in Chapters 9 and 10.
	Select	When active, allows you to select objects without moving them. Also good for deactivating command buttons.
	Selection Region flyout	Allows you to select objects by drawing a marquee around them in the viewport. Flyout options are Rectangular, Circular, and Fence.
	Selection Filters drop-down	Makes categories of objects selectable or nonselectable in the viewport.
	Select By Name	Brings up a dialog box with many options for selecting exact objects or collections of objects.
	Move	Moves objects in viewport.
	Rotate	Rotates objects in viewport.
	Scale flyout	Scales objects in viewport. Flyout options are Uniform, Non-uniform, and Squash.

Table 3.6 Tools on the Main Toolbar *(continued)*

ICON	NAME	DESCRIPTION
	Manipulate	Makes manipulators (built-in or custom helper-objects) visible and usable in the viewport.
	Reference Coordinate System drop-down	Allows you to choose the coordinate system you want a transform tool to reference.
	Transform Coordinate Center flyout	Allows you to choose the center you want a transform tool to reference. Flyout options are Pivot Point, Selection Center, and Coordinate System Center.
	Restrict to Axis	Constrains transform to a single axis.
	Restrict to Plane flyout	Constrains transform to a plane. Flyout options are XY, YZ, and ZX.
	Mirror	Brings up the Mirror dialog box to mirror and/or move an object along specified axes.
	Array flyout	Brings up the Array, Snapshot, or Spacing dialog box to make arrangements of clones.
	Align flyout	Aligns objects in the scene. Flyout options are Align, Normal Align, Place Highlight, Align Camera, and Align to View.
	Named Selection Sets	Creates a new selection set or selects an already named selection set.

Table 3.6 Tools on the Main Toolbar *(continued)*

Icon	Name	Description
	Track View	Brings up the Track View for viewing data in your scene or adjusting animation.
	Schematic View	Brings up the Schematic View for setting up hierarchies and viewing linkages and references.
	Material Editor	Brings up the Material Editor for building and applying materials or maps in your scene.
	Render Scene	Brings up the Render Scene window to choose from many options for rendering.
	Quick Render flyout	Renders the active viewport using the current render settings. Flyout options are Production, Draft, and Active Shade.
	Render Type drop-down	Allows you to choose whether to render the entire view, a certain region, or just selected objects.
	Render Last	Renders the viewport that was last rendered with the last render settings used.
	ActiveShade Floater	Opens an interactive ActiveShade render as a floater window. ActiveShade views will update only when the lighting or materials change.

Selection Tools

Being able to select exactly which objects or sub-objects you want is critical for anything you want to do with max. When there are many objects in a scene, it can be tricky to select exactly which object(s) you want without selecting the others. Fortunately, max has a wide array of selection tools to make selection easy. The transform tools are all technically selection tools as well. The formal name of the Move tool, for example, is Select and Move. We will deal with these separately and refer to them by their simple names. The general rules of selection in max apply to the transform tools as well.

Adding and Subtracting Selections

In max, you hold down the Ctrl key to add to selections, and you use the Alt key to subtract from selections. If you are accustomed to other programs that use Shift to add to selections, you will probably make a mistake in max. Shift in max is used with the transform tools to clone objects. Just remember Ctrl+Z to undo.

Region Selection

The Region Select options allow you to draw a marquee in the viewport to select objects. You will often use a marquee in one view to get a starting selection, and then subtract using a marquee in another view. With Fence selection, you can draw a marquee of any shape. These tools work in conjunction with the Window/Crossing Selection toggle, located in the area next to the Snaps at the bottom of the interface.

Crossing Selection　Everything within the marquee as well as everything it crosses will be selected.

Window Selection　Only what is entirely within the marquee will be selected.

Selection Filter

The selection filter makes certain object types selectable and others not selectable. The default is for all objects to be selectable. The Combos option (in the Selection Filter drop-down) brings up the Filter Combinations dialog box, where you can create any combination of general or specific object types to be available as a selection filter.

Named Selection Sets

A named selection set allows you to select a particular set of objects or sub-objects easily. To create a selection set, select the objects or sub-objects you want in it, type in the name in the Named Selection Sets field, and press Enter. The set will then be available in the drop-down list for selection. You can share sub-object selections between animation controllers, and you can copy and paste them between modifiers at the same sub-object level by using the Copy and Paste buttons in the Named Selection Sets section of the Selection rollout under the Stack View.

To edit or remove a named selection set, use Edit ➜ Edit Named Selections.

The Select By Name Tool

The Select By Name button brings up the Select Objects dialog, shown in Figure 3.6. This dialog allows you to select objects by name. In addition to the alphabetical option, the Sort section also allows you to sort by object type, color, or size, making it easy to select by these properties as well. The List Types section allows you to filter certain object types from the dialog by unchecking their checkboxes. You have access to named selection sets; with Select Subtree checked, you can select all the children of an object with the parent. With Select Dependents checked, you can select all the instances and references of an object with it. Display Subtree lets you see the hierarchical linkages between objects.

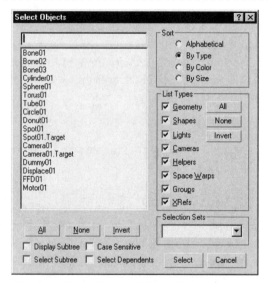

Figure 3.6 *The Select Objects dialog box*

Select By Name is much more useful if you give the objects in your scene names that will help you identify them. Leaving your scene with Box01 through Box55 will make it very difficult to know what you're doing.

You can use the Select By Name tool with other tools as well. For example, you can use it when binding an object to a space warp for selecting both the object and the space warp. Use Select By Name to select the object to be bound, click the Bind To Space Warp button, and then click the Select By Name button again to choose the space warp. This time the dialog will come up with a Bind button instead of a Select button, and it will show you only the space warps in your scene. The Align tools can also be used this way; the dialog box in this case will have a Pick button and show you the other objects in the scene as alignment targets. The Link tool can also be used this way, showing a Link button. The limitation of the modeless Selection Floater (Tools ➜ Selection Floater) is that it doesn't work this way with these tools. You would use the floater when you wanted to make a series of selections and perform edits on each selection in between selections.

Pressing the H key brings up the Select By Name dialog.

Transform Tools

Use the transform tools to move, rotate, or scale objects. As you have seen, they are accessible through the quad menu as well as the toolbar buttons, and the transform gizmo appears as a default, giving you options for constraining the transform. Constraints don't affect uniform scaling, dragging to create objects, or the transform type-ins. Table 3.7 shows the various ways of constraining a transform.

Whenever an object is selected and one of the transform tools is active, you can toggle between the display of the transform gizmo and a simple axis icon by pressing X. (To turn off the display of both the gizmo and the icon, uncheck Views ➜ Show Transform Gizmo.)

Table 3.7 Constraining Transform Tools to a Single Axis or Plane

TRANSFORM CONSTRAINT	ACTION USING TRANSFORM GIZMO	BUTTON ON TOOLBAR	KEYBOARD SHORTCUT
Constrain to X	Drag on the red X-axis	X	F5
Constrain to Y	Drag on the green Y-axis	Y	F6
Constrain to Z	Drag on the blue Z-axis	Z	F7
Constrain to plane	Drag on the corner between the two axes of the plane	XY, YZ, or ZX	F8 cycles through options

Key Concept

Coordinate Systems

The constraints you place upon transforms work according to the coordinate system being used by the viewports. In Chapter 2 you learned about the World coordinate system of max, where X points to the right, Y points away from you, and Z points up. If you choose World in the Reference Coordinate System drop-down, your transform gizmo will show you the axis directions in World space. Constraining to X will constrain to the World horizontal axis, regardless of which viewport is used.

The other coordinate system discussed in Chapter 2 was the one from traditional mathematics, where Z points toward you and Y points up. In max, this is called the Screen coordinate system, because it is relative to your computer screen rather than to the floor of the World. The default coordinate system in max, View, uses the World coordinate system for the perspective view and the Screen coordinate system for the orthogonal views. With the default View active in the Reference Coordinate System drop-down, the three orthogonal views (Front, Top, and Left) will always show X pointing to the right and Y pointing upward.

You can also constrain transforms using other coordinate systems. Table 3.8 describes each of the coordinate systems. The grid system is useful if you have created a grid helper object and activated it by right-clicking it and choosing Activate Grid. This makes the grid object the one displayed in the perspective view and makes the Grid coordinate system relative to the active grid rather than the Home Grid.

Table 3.8 Reference Coordinate Systems for Transform Constraints

COORDINATE SYSTEM	DESCRIPTION
World	Constrains relative to max world coordinates.
Screen	Constrains relative to screen (X horizontal, Y vertical, +Z toward) for each view. This means that constraining to Z in the perspective view will move the object at an awkward slant based on the angle of projection.
View (default)	Screen for orthogonal views, World for perspective view.
Local	Constrains relative to selected object's pivot point.
Pick	Constrains relative to object next picked.
Parent	Constrains relative to object's parent. (Parent of an unlinked object is the World.)
Grid	Constrains relative to an activated grid.

Transform Coordinate Centers

Rotation and scaling are also applied relative to a center. The Transform Coordinate Center flyout gives you three options for this center: Pivot Point, Selection Center, and Coordinate Center.

Pivot Point The pivot point of an object is the default transform center for rotation and scaling. (The pivot point of a selection of multiple objects is the selection center.) The pivot point for an individual object is not always the center of the object. Some objects, such as boxes, have a default pivot at their base instead of their center; spheres have a checkbox option to place the pivot at the base rather than the center; and pivot points can always be moved or reoriented.

 When the Animate button is on, Pivot Point is the only transform center available; the other options are grayed out. You can turn off this restriction on the Animate tab of the Preferences dialog box (Customize ➜ Preferences) by unchecking Local Center During Animate. Be careful of doing so. It is better to use a dummy object or move the pivot point than to change the transform center for animation.

 Selection Center Uses the center of the selection as the transform center for rotation and scaling. This is useful when an object's center is different from its pivot point.

 Coordinate Center Uses the origin of the coordinate system chosen in the Reference Coordinate System drop-down. For Local, this is the same as the pivot point; for World, Screen, and View, this is the World origin. For Pick, Parent, and Grid, this is the pivot point of the picked, parent, or grid object.

The Transform Type-In Dialog Box

Right-clicking on any of the transform tools brings up the Transform Type-In dialog box, seen in Figure 3.7. You can keep this dialog box open and click a different transform tool to switch to the type-in controls for that tool. The dialog box gives you two options: entering exact values relative to the World, in the Absolute section on the left; and entering an offset to the current values relative to the active coordinate system, in the Offset section on the right. After you enter an offset value, the Offset section resets to zero, ready to accept a new offset. The World section always tells you the exact values relative to the World. You can undo transform type-in changes with the Undo button while the dialog is open, but Ctrl+Z won't work until you close the dialog.

 The new transform type-in status fields at the bottom of the interface give you an alternate access to the same functionality. See "Transform Type-In Status Fields" later this chapter. You can also bring up the Transform Type-In dialog by pressing the F12 key.

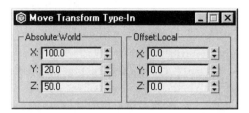

Figure 3.7 *The Transform Type-In dialog box for the Move tool*

Cloning Objects

You can easily clone an object using the transform tools by holding down the Shift key as you transform the object. This brings up the Clone Options dialog box, giving you a choice whether to make a copy, instance, or a reference. By spinning up the number of copies, you can create a series of copies separated by the same increment of transform values that you used to bring up the dialog. You are cloning and adding a transform at the same time. This is very similar to how the Mirror and Array tools work.

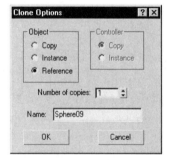

If you brought up the Clone Options dialog box by mistake, because your hands are trained to adding selections in other applications (using the Shift key), just click Cancel.

Manipulate Mode

Max 4 has new manipulators for controlling parameters of objects from the current viewport. Manipulators are built into the UVW Map modifier, the hotspot and falloff of a spotlight, the reaction parameters of a reactor animation controller, and the swivel angle of an HI IK solver. New manipulator helper objects are also available for wiring to any parameter you choose.

When you activate the Manipulate tool in conjunction with either a select or transform tool, you can see and use these manipulators in the viewport.

Parameter Wiring

Parameter wiring means hooking up a parameter from one object to a manipulator or a different parameter on another object. Let's set up a simple example of a manipulate mode using a new manipulator slider and the new parameter wiring feature:

1. Reset max (choose File ➜ Reset).

2. In the Create panel, click Teapot and drag out a teapot in the perspective viewport.

3. In the Helpers tab, choose Manipulators from the drop-down list at the top of the panel.

4. Click Slider and then click in the perspective view. A slider should appear. Right-click in the viewport to deactivate the Create Slider command.

5. Now hook up one of your teapot parameters to the manipulator. Right-click on the teapot and choose Wire Parameters from the lower-right quadrant. A popup menu comes up. Choose Object (Teapot) ➜ Radius.

6. A dotted line appears. Move your cursor to the slider manipulator and click on the slider. A second popup menu appears. Choose Object (Slider) ➜ Value.

7. This brings up the Parameter Wiring dialog box. Click the directional arrow from the Slider value to the Teapot radius.

8. Click the Connect button and close the dialog box by using its close box. Your teapot has disappeared.

9. Click the Manipulate mode button on the toolbar. Drag the slider of the manipulator. The Teapot radius is wired to your slider. You can use this to create viewport sliders for animation, for example. You might rig up a slider to perform a specific rotation or to deformation of an object. You can also wire parameters to a parameter of another object.

10. Click the Manipulate mode button again to turn it off. Now if you drag the slider, it doesn't change the teapot.

The Complex Transform Tools

With the complex transform tools, you can have transforms calculated by the computer to create a desired result. These tools include the Mirror tool, the Array tools, and the Align tools. Examples of using these tools are found in Chapters 4 and 5.

Mirror

Clicking the Mirror tool icon brings up the Mirror dialog box. You can choose to mirror an object about a specified axis or plane. By changing the Offset value from 0.0, you can see the new placement of your object interactively.

You can choose to move the original object or a clone, and you can choose whether clones are copies, instances, or references.

The Array Tools

The Array tools work similarly to holding Shift while transforming. As with Mirror, you can choose whether to clone and whether the clones are copies, instances, or references.

Array   Arranges clones of an object according to specified combinations of transforms. You can choose which transforms to use for the array (move, rotate, and/or scale). You can choose whether to specify the increment of the transform applied or the total amount (which will be divided by the number of clones you choose). You can choose which axes you want the transform relative to; for example, you might choose one axis of rotation or three axes of position. You can add a second and third positional dimension to the array (2D or 3D options), making extra clones offset in position along the axis you specify.

Make sure you choose your transform coordinate center before using the array tool for rotational arrays. If you choose a rotation array in order to get a circle of objects but have the pivot point transform center chosen, all the objects will be rotated around in the same space. Use the reference coordinate system transform center and either rotate around the origin or use the Pick coordinate system to pick a center.

Snapshot   Creates clones of an object at specified times in an animation. Another way to make arrangements of objects is to animate an object moving through the positions you want it. You can also take a single mesh snapshot of an animated morph, for example. You can specify the snapshot as a single clone (of the frame you are on) or a number of clones over a range of frames. You can make this an ordinary clone (copying all animation, parameters, and history) or you can create a mesh snapshot.

Spacing   Makes clones of an object along a specified spline path or between two points. You can choose the number of clones and specify an offset. You also have a variety of options for how the clones are spaced and how the path is followed.

The Align Tools

The Align tools enable you to move an object in order to achieve a desired result.

Align   Aligns an object to the chosen axes of another object. To use it, select an object, click the Align tool, and then pick a second object to align with the first. In the dialog you can choose the axes of alignment.

Normal Align   Aligns an object to the normal of another object. To use this tool, select an object, click the Normal Align tool, and then drag along the surface of the selected object. You should see a blue arrow showing you the normals of the faces. When you find the normal of the face you want to align to another object, release the mouse. Then drag along the surface of the object you wish it to align to. You should see a green arrow showing you the normals of the target object. When you find the normal you want your object to align to, release the mouse. A dialog box comes up, allowing you to add position and rotation offsets, which you can see interactively in the viewport.

Place Highlight   Moves a light to place a highlight on an object. To use it, select a light and then click the Place Highlight tool. Drag along the surface of the object on which you will place the highlight. The light moves and allows you to see the highlight placement interactively. Release the mouse when you have found the highlight you want.

Align Camera   Moves a camera to point at a normal of an object. To use it, select a camera, click the Align Camera tool, and drag along the surface of the object until you get the camera position you want.

Align to View   Aligns a selected object to the current view. To use it, select an object and click the Align to View tool. You can choose the axis of alignment.

Undo/Redo

By default, max lets you undo up to 20 previous actions. You can change this in the General tab of the Preferences dialog (Customize ➜ Preferences) under Scene Undo to up to 500. In practice, however, the number of levels of undo you can get also depends on the amount of RAM your computer has. The Undo/Redo buttons refer to changes only to objects in the scene. Viewport changes can also be undone but are stored in a separate buffer with a separate undo/redo.

Keyboard shortcuts for object changes are Ctrl+Z for Undo and Ctrl+A for Redo. For viewport changes, Shift+Z is Undo and Shift+A is Redo.

Right-clicking the Undo or Redo button gives you a list of recent changes in the undo buffer. You can select where in the history you want to undo or redo to. For example, clicking Undo after selecting the commands in the history shown here would undo back to the Bevel command. You could also click the Undo button repeatedly or press Ctrl+Z repeatedly to do the same thing.

Some commands cannot be undone, at least not dependably. These include creating compound objects, editing in Track View, applying modifiers, and assigning maps. If you are uncertain whether to go through with one of these actions, you should do an Edit ➜ Hold first. This saves an actual file of everything in your scene; you can retrieve it later with Edit ➜ Fetch.

The Schematic View

The Schematic View is a large dialog box where you can see your hierarchies in Hierarchy mode and your references in References mode. (An instance is a two-way reference.) The same Link and Unlink tools found on the main toolbar are also found here, allowing you to set up your hierarchies within the Schematic View. The advantage of setting them up here is that you can arrange them in a structure that resembles the character you are linking, giving you a visual reference to the chain you want to animate.

In Reference mode, references appear as yellow triangles coming out of the sides of an object name. If you click on a modifier or an object in Reference mode, all references of it will turn yellow along with it.

Other Toolbar Options

Other tools on the main toolbar were described in Table 3.6 and are covered in more depth elsewhere in the book. You will examine the Materials Editor in Chapters 7 and 8, the Bind To Space Warp tool in Chapters 9 and 10, the Track View in Chapters 9 through 11, the linking tools in Chapter 11, and the rendering tools in Chapter 13.

Menu Commands

You've already used several of the Menu commands. Many Menu items are available more conveniently elsewhere in the interface. Table 3.9 describes commands from the Menu bar that are not already described in another interface section.

Table 3.9 Menu Commands to Remember

MENU COMMAND	DESCRIPTION OF USE
File➜ View Image File	Plays back a rendered animation file or views any image file.
File ➜ XRef Objects and XRef Scene	References an object or scene in another .max file. (Examples in Chapter 4.)
File ➜ Summary Info	Provides info on number of objects of each type, number of vertices and faces, and a list of plug-ins loaded or not loaded. Allows you to edit the Comments field. Displays the time it took to render the last frame, the last animation, and the last Video Post queue rendered.
File ➜ File Properties	Allows you to edit Title, Author, Comments, Keyword, and other filing information. On the Contents tabs, you can view a list of all the contents of your scene, including all materials, bitmaps, xrefs, and plug-ins used.
Edit ➜ Hold	Saves a copy of the current scene exactly as it is in case something can't be undone.
Edit ➜ Fetch	Retrieves the scene saved with Edit ➜ Hold.
Tools ➜ Display Floater	Brings up handy modeless dialog box with display commands (Hide, Unhide, Freeze, Unfreeze, Object Display Properties, and scene display filters).
Tools ➜ Selection Floater	Brings up a modeless version of the Select By Name dialog box.
Tools ➜ Isolate	Hides the rest of the scene while you edit an object.

Table 3.9 Menu Commands to Remember *(continued)*

MENU COMMAND	DESCRIPTION OF USE
Tools ➜ Light Lister	Allows you to view and edit the properties of all the lights in your scene. Covered in detail in Chapter 12.
Group commands	Explained in Chapter 2. Allows you to Select a set of objects and Group them. Can also Open and Close, Ungroup, or Explode. Attach and Detach add and subtract members from a group. (Example in Chapter 4.)
Views ➜ Save/Restore Active View	Saves the view of the active viewport to a buffer. Restores last saved active view.
Views ➜ Viewport Background	Allows you to use an image in the background of your viewport. Viewport backgrounds are often used as modeling templates. (Example in Chapter 8.)
Views ➜ Show Dependencies	When the Modify panel is active, will highlight in pink all the references or instances of a selected object.
Create menu	Gives you access to commands on the Create panel.
Modifiers menu	Allows you to apply modifiers without using the Modify panel.
Animation menu	Covered in detail in Chapter 9 and 10.
Graph Editors	Accesses the Schematic and Track View dialog boxes.
Rendering menu	Covered in depth in Chapters 13 and 14.
Customize menu	Covered in more detail at the end of this chapter.
MAXScript menu	Covered in depth in Chapters 15–20.
Help ➜ User Reference	Displays the official online documentation of max.
Help ➜ Tutorials	Displays max tutorials covering a wide variety of subjects.

Exploring Viewports

In addition to providing you with an interactive display of what is happening in your scene, the views displayed in the viewports are also crucial for manipulating objects in your scene. As we have seen, the Screen coordinate system, used as a default in orthogonal views, allows transforms to be constrained to the view plane. Views are also critical for getting the correct sub-object selection when editing: by selecting in one view and then subtracting from or adding to the selection in another view, you can get the precise selection you need.

All of the views are accessible by right-clicking the viewport label and choosing the view you want for that viewport.

Perspective View

A perspective view displays the scene with an angle of view, as a camera lens does, or a single eye. The angle of view, called the *field of view* or FOV, creates the effects of perspective projection that make objects in the distance appear smaller than those in the foreground and gridlines appear to converge toward the horizon. In max, a perspective view can be at any orientation. The default field of view is 45°, but you can change this in the Rendering Method tab of the Viewport Configuration dialog, covered in "Viewport Configuration" later this chapter.

To get back to the default Perspective view angle and orientation, hide everything in the scene and Zoom Extents All (Ctrl+Shift+Z).

Axonometric View

An *axonometric* view displays the scene with parallel projection, where the angle of view is 0. All grid cells are the same size whether near or far, and receding lines do not converge in the distance. In max, this is also called the User view. (Technically, both perspective and axonometric views are user views, because they are views determined by the user rather than facing a specified plane.) If you are looking at a perspective view and want to see it without the perspective distortion in the distance, you can press U to switch to an axonometric view of the same orientation.

An orthogonal view is a special type of axonometric view, using parallel projection but facing one of the Home Grid planes. The orthogonal views available in max are the default Top, Front, and Left, plus the Bottom, Back, and Right.

Special Views

In max, you can also show the view from a camera or light (spot or directional light). These views have special viewport controls that enable you to adjust the placement and parameters of the camera or light interactively. A Grid view allows you to view your scene relative to an activated grid. If there is no grid object activated in the scene, a Grid view is relative to the Home Grid, just as the regular views are. You can also display the

Track View, Schematic View, Asset Browser, or MAXScript Listener in a viewport. The new Active Shade view allows you to adjust lighting and materials interactively. See "Active Shade View" for more detail later in this section.

Viewport Controls

Max has four main sets of viewport navigation controls. Figure 3.8 shows the standard set (for all axonometric views), the perspective set, the camera set, and the light set. The standard and the perspective set are similar, and the camera and light set are similar.

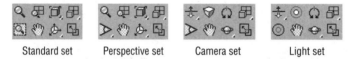

| Standard set | Perspective set | Camera set | Light set |

Figure 3.8 *Max viewport controls for axonometric, perspective, camera, and light views*

Tools in All Viewport Controls

All of the viewport controls have three buttons in common: Pan/Truck (hand), Zoom Extents All, and Min/Max.

Pan or Truck   The hand tool allows you to move your vantage point in the plane of the screen by dragging in the viewport. It is called Truck in the Camera and Light viewport controls, because you are actually moving the camera or light in order to do this.

If you have a three-button mouse, you can pan just by dragging in the viewport while holding down the middle mouse button. The mouse control needs to be set to Pan/Zoom in Customize → Preferences → Viewport. (In the Control Panel of your computer, "2" on the Buttons tab of the Mouse controls also has to be set to Middle Button.)

Zoom Extents All flyout   Zooms to fit in all viewports. The icon with the gray box fits the entire scene to the viewports; the icon with the white box zooms to fit selected objects to the viewports.

Whenever a viewport control has an icon with an object shaded gray, it is relative to the scene; when it is shaded white, it is relative to the object selection; when it is shaded yellow, it is relative to the sub-object selection.

Min/Max Toggle   Maximizes or minimizes the active viewport. It's a waste to use this tool button. Use the W keyboard shortcut instead.

Tools in Standard and Perspective Controls

These tools are found in both standard and perspective viewport controls:

Zoom   Zooms in or out of the view as you drag up or down in the viewport.

If you have a three-button mouse with a wheel, you can zoom by rolling the wheel in the viewport. The mouse control needs to be set to Pan/Zoom in Customize ➔ Preferences ➔ Viewport. In some computer configurations, the mouse also needs to be set up in the Windows Control Panel.

Zoom All   Zooms in or out of all views as you drag up or down in the viewport.

Zoom Extents flyout   Zooms the active view to fit either the whole scene or the selected objects.

Arc Rotate flyout   Rotates the view using an arcball. If you drag on one of the handles in the four directions of the arcball, you constrain the rotation to the horizontal or vertical axis of that screen. If you drag your mouse inside the arcball, the scene rotates without constraint. If you drag your cursor entirely outside the ball, you constrain the rotation to the Z axis of that screen. The flyout options are Relative To Screen, Relative To Selected Object, and Relative To Selected Sub-Object.

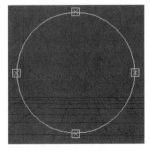

Region Zoom   Zooms into a region you specify by drawing a marquee in the viewport.

In the perspective view, Region Zoom is part of a flyout under Field of View.

Tool in Perspective and Camera Controls

A tool found in perspective and camera views is the Field of View control.

Field of View   Increases or decreases the angle of view of the perspective projection. In a camera view, you are actually altering the camera's Lens Size parameter. As the FOV gets smaller, the perspective flattens, as with a zoom lens. As the FOV gets larger, the perspective starts to distort, as with a wide-angle lens. If you widen the field of view too far, everything in the scene distorts radially.

Tools in Camera and Light Controls

Special viewport controls in the camera and light views actually alter the placement or properties of the camera or light object. Consequently they are undone with Ctrl+Z rather than Shift+Z.

Dolly flyout   Moves the camera/light forward and back. Options are moving Camera/Light, moving Target, and moving Both.

Roll   Rotates the camera/light around the forward axis, similar to constraining to Z with arc rotate in a perspective view.

Orbit/Pan rollout   Rotates the camera/light around its target (Orbit) or rotates the target around the camera/light (Pan). Note that Camera/Light Truck is similar to Pan in the Standard controls, while Camera/Light Pan is similar to Arc Rotate. These terms come from real-life camera and lighting work. The good thing is that Pan in the Standard controls and Truck in the Camera/Light controls both use the hand icon.

Assigning a keyboard shortcut to Rotate View will bring up the most recently used tool in this flyout when a camera or light viewport is active.

Tool in Camera Controls Only

A tool that is found only in the camera viewport controls is the Perspective control.

Perspective   Moves the camera forward and back with a compensatory change in FOV to keep the same area in view. Thus, only the perspective is adjusted.

Tools in Light Controls Only

Tools that are found only in light viewport controls are the Hotspot and Falloff controls.

Hotspot   Interactively adjusts the hotspot of the light in the central area of the cone.

Falloff   Interactively adjusts the falloff of the light around the cone.

Viewport Rendering Levels

The viewport uses its own real-time renderer so that you can see the results of changes interactively as you make them. In order to maintain real-time response, viewports are rendered with simpler shading methods. The default shading in max is Wireframe (no shading) for the orthogonal views and Smooth + Highlight in the perspective view. You can choose the rendering level by right-clicking the viewport label and choosing the level or by opening the Viewport Configuration dialog box.

Bounding Box   Displays only the bounding boxes of objects.

Wireframe   Displays only the edges of polygons, with no surfaces.

Z-buffered Wires   Hides the back of the wireframe and any objects behind other objects, because it is calculating the Z-buffer or Z-depth: the relative distance of objects from the camera or plane of view.

Lit Wireframe   Displays the wireframe mesh but adds lighting.

Facets   Displays objects with faceted shading, regardless of whether smoothing is turned on.

Facets + Highlight   Displays objects with faceted shading and highlights.

Smooth   Displays objects with Gouraud shading, smoothing between vertices, but with no specular highlight.

Smooth + Highlight   Displays smooth shading between vertices and adds specular highlights.

ActiveShade View

The new max 4 ActiveShade view, available as a floater or viewport, provides a somewhat interactive render that is quicker than a full production render yet displays materials with multiple textures including bump, reflection, and other maps. It updates materials and lighting changes interactively. You can access the ActiveShade floater in the Rendering menu or by clicking the ActiveShade button on the toolbar. You can make a viewport an ActiveShade view by right-clicking the viewport label and choosing Views ➔ ActiveShade. You can have only one ActiveShade floater or viewport at a time, and it cannot be maximized.

To update the ActiveShade view after a change (to something other than materials or lighting), right-click in the viewport and choose Initialize from the lower-right quad menu. Selecting an object before choosing Active Shade makes only that object Active Shade, speeding up the render considerably. To turn off Active Shade in a viewport, right-click in the viewport and choose Close in the upper-left of the quad menu.

Resizable Viewports

You can change the relative size of the viewport windows just by dragging the center point between the viewports. For example, dragging this point down and to the right expands the top view (in the upper-left) while shrinking the other three. To get back to the default viewport size, right-click the center point and choose Reset Layout.

Viewport Configuration

You can access the Viewport Configuration dialog box by right-clicking a viewport control, by right-clicking a viewport label and choosing Configure, or by choosing Customize ➔ Viewport Configuration. This window gives you access to many of the same viewport options you've encountered elsewhere in the interface, including rendering level and the FOV of a perspective view. You can turn selection brackets off or display selected objects with edged faces. (Edged faces are useful when modeling, so you can see the faces of your model.) You can disable a view to speed up redraw time when you are working on a complex object within one view. The Layouts tab gives you a choice of configurations for your viewports. To change the layout, click one of the configurations at the top; the configuration will display in the central area of the tab, allowing you to click each area and choose a view for that viewport from a popup menu.

Viewport Shortcuts

You will need to become facile with making viewport changes easily, so it is worthwhile to learn some of the keyboard shortcuts for common viewport changes. Table 3.10 lists useful keyboard shortcuts for navigating viewport controls.

Table 3.10 Keyboard Shortcuts for Viewports

Viewport Change	Keyboard Shortcut
Undo viewport change	Shift+Z
Maximize/minimize view toggle	W
Zoom Extents All	Shift+Ctrl+Z
Zoom Extents Selected	E
Zoom region	Ctrl+W
Redraw all viewports	1
Wireframe/Smooth & Highlight toggle	F3
Show Edged Faces toggle	F4
Shade Selected Faces toggle	F2
See-through display toggle	Alt+X
Texture correction toggle	Ctrl+T
Disable viewport	D
Top view	T
Front view	F
Left view	L
Perspective view	P
Bottom view	B
Back view	K
Right view	R
Axonometric User view	U
Camera view	C
Spotlight view	Shift+4 ($)
Grid view	G

Status Bar, Locks, and Snaps

At the bottom of the interface are a variety of tools that also help you see and control what you're doing in the viewport. Figure 3.9 shows these controls. You learned about

Window/Crossing Selection earlier, in the "Selection Tools" section. The Plug-in Keyboard Shortcut toggle overrides the main keyboard shortcuts when activated, replacing them with other keyboard shortcuts used for special purposes.

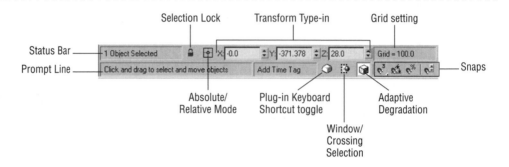

Figure 3.9 *Status, Lock, and Snaps controls*

The Status Bar and the Prompt Line

The status bar tells you how many objects you have selected, and the prompt line below it gives you a context-sensitive prompt for what max expects next. If a tool isn't working as you expected, this is a good place to check. If the prompt line says "Click and drag to begin creation process," for instance, you have left one of the Create command buttons active and need to right-click in the viewport to deactivate it.

Transform Type-In Status Fields

In max 4, the XYZ display fields are now convenient transform type-in fields. They work similarly to the Transform Type-In window described earlier. When nothing is selected or one of the transform tools is not activated, these fields display the coordinates of the mouse cursor. When you are dragging an object, the fields display the relative transform being applied. When you have multiple objects selected, only the values you type in are applied to the objects.

> **Absolute/Relative Mode**   Absolute/Relative mode is a toggle that applies when you are transforming an object. Absolute applies transforms in World space; Relative applies the transforms relative to where the object was when you started.

Selection Lock

Selection Lock locks your selection so that you can click in the viewport and perform operations without changing the selection. This is another thing to check if something isn't working as you expected: Did you leave a selection of an object or sub-object locked?

The keyboard shortcut toggle for Selection Lock is the Spacebar.

Snaps

Snaps enable you to move objects in fixed increments or to align objects precisely with each other. When they are off, you can choose locations between gridlines (or whatever you are snapping to in the snap settings). Table 3.11 summarizes the snap tools.

Table 3.11 The Snap Tools

Icon	Tool	Function
$\begin{array}{c}2\\2.5\\3\end{array}$	Snaps flyout	Snaps to gridlines or other features, according to the Grid and Snap settings. 3D snaps in all three directions. 2D snaps in the active plane. 2.5D acts like projection to objects behind so you can look through a grid object.
	Angle Snap	Snaps to a certain angle increment when rotating.
	Percent Snap	Snaps to a certain percentage increment when scaling.
	Spinner Snap	Changes a spinner parameter by a given increment to single clicks on a spinner. (Spinner snap increment set in Customize ➜ Preferences, and Use Snap must be checked.)

You can change the Grip and Snap settings by right-clicking any of the snap buttons or by choosing Customize ➜ Grid and Snap Settings. In the dialog box that appears, on the Snaps tab, set whether you want to snap to the grid or to some other piece of geometry. In Options, you can set the snap strength and choose axis constraints.

Pressing S toggles Snap on and off. Pressing A toggles Angle Snap on and off.

Adaptive Degradation

Adaptive degradation is used to give you better real-time response in a complicated scene. It is on by default. Adaptive degradation redraws to the viewport rendering level when possible and to lower levels when redraw speed is being affected. The rendering level is set in the Rendering Level tab of the Viewport Configuration dialog box, and the lowest acceptable level is set on the Adaptive Degradation tab. When adaptive degradation override is on, the display will redraw to the viewport rendering level, regardless of how it affects redraw speed.

Animation Controls

The animation controls allow you to navigate in time in your scene, access animation keys, and animate your objects. Figure 3.10 shows the time slider, track bar, and animation controls. These controls are covered in detail in Chapters 9 through 11. The time slider allows you to scrub through the time of your animation and go to a specific frame. The Go To Frame field allows you to type in a frame number and press Enter to go to that frame. The playback controls work like VCR controls with play/stop, fast forward, and reverse, as well as first frame and last frame buttons. The track bar shows all the keyframes for a selected object as red boxes along the time line. The time configuration dialog allows you to set and rescale the active segment of an animation. Key mode, when on, snaps the time slider to keys in the animation.

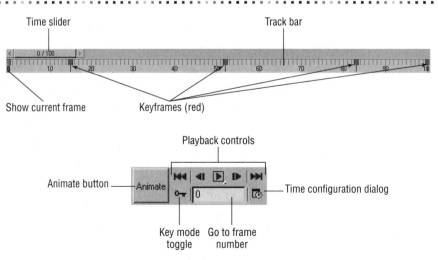

Figure 3.10 *The time slider, track bar, and animation controls*

The Animate Button

The Animate button allows you to set animation keys interactively. When this toggle is off, the changes you make apply to the entire animation. When it is on, the changes you make apply to that frame only (unless you are at frame 0). As soon as you have two frames with different values in a certain parameter, you have an animated change. You can animate very easily by going to a different frame (using the time slider or the Go To Frame field), turning Animate on, and making a change. Frame 0 is a default keyframe in max (except in character studio Biped animation). When the Animate button is on and you change a parameter at a frame other than zero, your change is animated over time from frame 0 to that frame. At frame 0 the parameter has its original value, and by the new keyframe, your change is fully implemented. It's always a good idea to turn the Animate button off as soon as possible after you've made a change. Otherwise, you may be animating a lot of things that you don't intend to animate.

The keyboard shortcut for toggling the Animate button is N.

Customizing the max Interface

You've already encountered a lot of options for customizing the max interface. You can access the Customize User Interface dialog box with Customize → Customize User Interface or by right-clicking a toolbar and choosing Customize. In this window, you can make your own toolbars with buttons for commands you use often for certain types of work, set your own keyboard shortcuts, add your own quad menu items or Menu bar items, and change the colors of the interface.

Assigning Keyboard Shortcuts

To assign your own keyboard shortcut, go to the Keyboard tab of the Customize User Interface window. Select the command you want a shortcut for. If there is already a shortcut for it, it will display in the list. Type in your shortcut in the Hotkey field. If the key is already assigned to another command, that assignment will be displayed. You can still reassign it if you choose. Then click Assign. Click the Save button to save out your shortcuts as a .kbd file. You can load a different .kbd file from here or from Customize → Load Custom UI Scheme.

Customizing Toolbars

To add an item to the main toolbar, just drag it from the Toolbars tab to the main toolbar. Any buttons from the Tab panels are available for your customized toolbars, as well as any commands in the interface. To create your own toolbar, click New, name your toolbar, and drag buttons into it. Click Save to save your settings.

To remove a button from a toolbar, just Alt+drag it off the toolbar and click Yes to delete.

Customizing Menus and Interface Colors

To add Menu or quad menu items, drag from the list of commands on the left of the Menus or Quads tab to the menu on the right to which you want to add it. To remove an item, highlight it and press the Delete key. The Colors tab of this window was part of the Preferences dialog in previous versions of max. You select the area of the interface on the left, select a new color on the right, and click Apply Colors Now to change the interface colors.

Saving Your Custom Scheme

You can save your interface layout settings in files in the 3dsmax4\ui directory. You can then take these files with you and copy them to the same directory on another computer in order to load them there. Be careful not to overwrite the defaults. Table 3.12 lists the different custom settings files you can save. Customize → Save Custom UI Scheme saves all your current settings in these files. Customize → Load Custom UI Scheme allows you to load settings from these custom settings files.

Table 3.12 Custom Scheme Files

Custom setting	File Type
Keyboard shortcuts	.kbd
Interface layout, tab panel, and toolbars	.cui
Interface colors	.clr
Menu bar and quad menu items	.mnu
Quad menu behavior, layout, and colors	.qop

Preferences

Customize ➜ Preferences brings up a dialog with many tabs that apply to different areas of max. You have already used it several times, and you will be coming back to it as necessary throughout the book. Take some time to look through the tabs and acquaint yourself with the vast array of choices in the dialog.

File Locations

Customize ➜ Configure Paths allows you to tell max where to find files. This is where you add new paths for bitmaps and plug-ins, especially if your file was brought in from another computer with in a different directory structure. You need to copy any special bitmaps and plug-ins as well as the .max file and tell max the new file location. To do that, go to the Bitmaps or Plug-ins tab, click the Add button, choose the directory you want to add (you can check Add Subpaths to add all the directories below it), and click Use Path. To change the default location for saving .max files, go to the General tab and highlight Scenes. Click Modify, find the new directory, and click Use Path. Click OK to leave the dialog.

Summary

In this chapter, you were introduced to all the main areas of the max interface. You learned about the major types of commands available in the command panels as well as every tool on the main toolbar. You discovered several options for accessing commands from different parts of the interface. You learned the key Menu bar commands, how to navigate and manipulate objects in viewports, and the basic animation tools in max. You learned a variety of ways to customize your interface.

In the next chapter, you will be introduced to the general principles of modeling and will learn the variety of ways to go about polygonal modeling in max.

Part II
Modeling

In This Part

In Part II, you will learn different options for building models in max. You will learn principles of modeling that apply to any 3D application as well as procedures and methods unique to max. You will model in the three different data types of mesh, patch, and NURBS surfaces. You will work on simple examples of single techniques as well as larger complex modeling projects that build on these techniques. You will model a "high-res" human character and then optimize it for a low-res environment.

Mesh Modeling

3ds max

Chapter 4

I n this chapter, you will learn the principles of modeling in general and the specifics of mesh modeling in max. You will use a variety of different modeling methods. You will edit mesh primitives and create meshes from splines using modifiers, create different compound objects, model editable mesh and editable poly objects, build an architectural model, and assemble a large project from smaller ones using external references. Topics include:

- The art of modeling

- Planning models

- Modeling with primitives, modifiers, and compound objects

- Bezier splines

- Modeling meshes from Bezier splines

- Merging geometry from different files

- Editable mesh modeling

- Editable poly modeling

- MeshSmooth and NURMS

- Modeling with externally referenced objects

The Art of Modeling

After two chapters chock full of CG theory and max technology, it is time to get back to art. (You can see why it is a challenge to keep a balance between the two in CG: there's just so *much* technology to contend with.) Modeling is an inherently artistic process. In several places in the longer tutorial projects, the instructions amount to "move things around until they look right." This skill may be intuitive, artistic, and not easily reduced to sets of instructions, but it benefits from training and practice.

When you model in max, you use the same principles as with real-life sculpture. The difference between a good model and a bad model (aside from any mistakes caused by misunderstanding the tool) is that the person who constructed the bad model did not pay attention to the form. If you are modeling real life, look at real life. You want to forget what you "know" about the thing you're modeling – put aside your preconceptions and *look* at the object. When modeling a hand, don't think of what a hand is *supposed to* look like. Look at actual hands. Ask your friends if you can sketch their hands. If you build a face based on what your analytical mind has stored about faces, you will get a symbolic representation rather than realistic proportions and believable expression. Symbolic representations can work for cartoonish models, but even then, the best cartoonish models demonstrate a sense of reality that has been exaggerated rather than a lack of awareness of form.

"Seeing is forgetting the name of the thing one sees." —Paul Valery

To better their acquaintance with form, CG artists benefit greatly from ordinary 2D drawing practice. To help yourself model figures, do figure drawing. Take figure drawing classes, or draw in the park. As much as possible, draw from life rather than from a photo. Especially with modeling, it is vital to look at things from multiple angles; you need an awareness of the three dimensions in order to learn from the process.

Choosing a Modeling Method

As you learned in Chapter 2, a surface in max can be a polygonal mesh, a patch surface, or a NURBS surface. For geometric forms, machines, or architectural models, polygons are definitely the way to go. Polygons are the cheapest model in terms of processing efficiency and, because they are linear descriptions in the first place, handle straight lines very well.

For modeling organic forms with smoothly curved surfaces, patches and NURBS have some advantages over polygons, because they are based on mathematical descriptions of curves. You will use patch modeling in Chapter 5 and NURBS modeling in Chapter 6. A third option for organic modeling is using subdivision surfaces on meshes. The subdivision surface technique, applied through the MeshSmooth, HSDS (for "hierarchical subdivision surface"), or Tessellate modifiers, subdivides polygons for smoother curvature. This way you can quickly build a model with few polygons ("low-poly") and then subdivide the surface to make a higher-resolution "high-poly" model.

Max offers extra versatility by allowing you to convert between the different data types. NURBS and patch models can be converted to polygonal models and then further edited with mesh tools. Meshes can also be converted to patches or NURBS and then edited with the corresponding tools and methods, although this is not generally recommended. You are free to experiment with whatever works for you.

Developing a modeling style is personal. What works fabulously well for one person will be a hair-pulling bundle of frustration to another. You may find using loft deformations to be completely intuitive, for example, while your co-worker finds them unreliable and prefers to move each vertex with Transform Type-In commands. There are multiple ways to achieve almost any modeling goal. You may also decide to go part of the way with one method and then convert the object type and continue modeling.

For an amazingly in-depth look at modeling techniques, check out form Z: Modeling for Digital Visual Effects and Animation *by David Rindner (Charles River Media, 1999). While it covers modeling in form Z specifically, most of the techniques and information apply to modeling in any 3D application.*

Mesh Basics

The oldest type of CG model is the mesh surface. As mentioned in Chapters 1 and 2, a mesh is made of vertices and polygons. In max, up until this release, the polygon sub-object of a model was always made up of triangular faces—the polygons that count at render time. With max 4, you now have the additional option of a true polygonal object. Both editable poly and editable mesh surfaces are polygonal meshes. The editable poly type just doesn't have hidden edges within a square polygon.

Planning Models

When you sit down in front of your computer to start modeling, what do you have? Perhaps you have a vision of what you want to create, or perhaps a project manager handed you a set of instructions. Whatever the case, it helps to plan how you are going to go about modeling, thinking the process through before starting. You need to consider animation needs: decide how you're eventually going to animate your model and consider how this affects your modeling. When you are animating, the object data flow discussed in Chapter 2 will become much more relevant. You also need to consider your final output: will this be a low-poly or high-poly model? Will it be prerendered or rendered in real-time?

In the beginning, when you are learning how to model, you will make many false starts, starting over each time from scratch. There's nothing wrong with this process; don't get impatient with it. Just be aware of the difference between following a guided tutorial, where everything has been planned out for you, and designing and modeling a project of your own. Once you've tried enough exercises to feel that you understand the tools and want to start your own complex project, spend considerable time in the designing and planning phase. Trial and error is always involved, but it makes a huge difference to have an idea of what you want to do and how you're going to do it. If your method doesn't work, take a break for a bit and then—literally—go back to the drawing board. Go back to the design and planning phase and think through your Plan B before sitting in front of the computer again.

Saving and Managing Files

Over the course of this book, you will work on some complex continuing projects. In this chapter you will start using and saving .max and map files. Versions of project files are available on the CD that comes with this book. In order to work most efficiently, you should make a project folder on your hard drive for saving your .max files for each chapter. (You'll use some of the project files from the CD as you work through the exercises. These are marked with the symbol at the left; when you see that, make sure the file is copied to your hard disk. Other files duplicate work you will be doing in the exercises and are provided simply as a convenience. You'll get the most benefit out of these projects by creating them yourself and using the CD files only for reference. Keep your own project files separately on your hard drive.)

To change max's default directory for saving files, go to the General tab of the Configure Paths window (Customize ➔ Configure Paths) and select Scenes in the list. Click Modify and browse to your project directory. Click the Use Path option and then OK.

Obviously, when working on big projects, you will want to save your work often. A good rule of thumb is to save your work immediately after you have completed a task. Then, if max or your computer crashes, you won't have to redo too much work.

You can count on computers crashing from time to time. Sometimes a crash will corrupt your working .max file. Corrupt files may be only partially broken or completely unusable. A complicated CG file often contains millions of bits of information. Sometimes files can lose a few bits of information without affecting you; at other times critical bits will be lost, destroying your file. The chance of significant corruption grows as your files grow in complexity and size. Even if you save your work regularly, you can still lose everything just when you have almost finished your project.

Saving your file is not enough. To be safer, when you reach a milestone, save your work under a different filename. This way, if your file becomes corrupted, you can use the last saved version of your file because it exists as a separate uncorrupted file. The clearest and simplest way to do this is to use a numerical naming scheme and *increment the filename when you save*. After a while you will start to accumulate many incremental .max files. You can later delete the oldest files, but keep at least three of the newest files as a contingency in case of data corruption.

You can easily increment files in max by naming the first file filename01.max *and then clicking the + button in the Save File dialog box each time you want to save a new version. This automatically saves the file as* filename02.max, *and so on.*

Modeling with Primitives

The mesh primitives in max can be used for modeling in a variety of ways: you can create a cartoonish character by linking up an arrangement of simple primitives; you can apply modifiers to primitives to deform them; you can use primitives as the initial operands of compound objects; and you can use the Editable Mesh or Editable Poly tools to edit primitives into complex models.

The simplicity of a model does not determine the sophistication of the animation. A model made out of primitives can be completely convincing as a character if the quality of the animation is good enough. For example, "Fluffy," the animated short about a dog made entirely out of primitives, demonstrated that a believable character can be conveyed through expressive animation in a well-considered script even without sophisticated modeling. You can find Fluffy on video at http://www.odyssey3d.com/comanfes.html.

Reviewing the Creation of Primitives

You will use mesh primitives as starting points for much of your modeling. In Chapter 2, you created box and sphere primitives, both by dragging in the viewport and by numeric entry. Let's go over the process again and pay attention to some of the details.

1. Right-click in any empty area of the perspective viewport to activate it. You can tell which viewport is active by the yellow border around it.

2. Press W to maximize the perspective viewport. Click the two-dimensional Snap button at the bottom of the screen. This allows you to snap the corners of the box to the grid points. In the Create panel, click Geometry ➜ Box. Drag a Box from one grid point to another. This sets the Length and Width parameters of the Box. Release the mouse button and then move the mouse up or down without clicking to see the height of the box change interactively. When you are happy with a size, click to set the Height parameter. Press Delete to delete the box.

   You have a chance to change the parameters of an object on the Create panel immediately after creating it. If you deselect the box by clicking elsewhere in the viewport, the parameters for the box disappear.

3. Now let's create a torus using the keyboard entry method. Click the Torus button. Open the keyboard entry rollout. In the X, Y, and Z fields enter 10, 0, 10 as the location for the torus's pivot point. Set the minor radius up to 20 and the major radius to 10. Click Create. A torus appears 10 units above and 10 units to the right of the origin.

   The X, Y, and Z values of the Keyboard Entry rollout specify where the pivot point of the object will be placed when you click Create.

4. Change the name of the torus by clicking in the text box where it says Torus01, typing in a new name, and pressing Enter.

Remember to name your objects clearly as you model. Don't wait until you are trying to figure out whether you want to select Box81 or Box47 to start giving objects meaningful names. Get in the habit of naming objects as you create them. It will save you time in the long run.

5. Change the object color of the torus by clicking on the color swatch to open the color picker. By default, objects are assigned a random color to help you distinguish different objects.

Changing object color is different from applying materials, covered in Chapters 7 and 8. Object color is useful while modeling to help you better differentiate objects.

Other primitives are created in the same fashion. Experiment with creating primitives until you feel comfortable with both the dragging and keyboard entry creation methods. Some of the primitives have an extra parameter that must be set while you are creating them. For example, making the cone primitive requires an extra click to set the Radius 2 parameter. Zoom out or rotate the view if you need to make more room on the screen for your primitives.

The "Viewport Controls" section of Chapter 3 covers view navigation in detail. You may want to review the use of these controls.

Modeling with Modifiers

As you learned in Chapters 2 and 3, max uses the modifier stack (also called simply the "stack") to apply changes to an object in a specified order. *Modifiers* are algorithms that can be applied to affect your objects. The stack contains the accumulated history of an object, starting with the base object, and continuing up through all the modifiers in the stack. The stack represents a pipeline of computation as base objects are loaded into memory first, and then modifiers are loaded in order from bottom to top. Therefore, the sequence of modifiers in the stack is significant.

Some modifiers apply only to one type of surface (mesh, patch, or NURBS), and some turn an object into a certain type (the Conversion modifiers, for instance, or Edit Mesh). In general, though, you go about modeling with modifiers the same way with any type of surface. Again, you can also apply modifiers to one type of geometry and then convert to another type, as you will do in the Landscape tutorial later in this chapter. Table 4.1 describes the key modeling modifiers that apply to meshes or that generate meshes.

Table 4.1 Key Mesh Modeling Modifiers Available in Max

MODIFIER	PURPOSE
Deformation Modifiers	
Bend	Bends the selection up to 360° around a chosen axis.
Displace	Deforms a mesh according to the grayscale values of a bitmap. You'll use Displace in the Landscape project later in this chapter.
FFD	Deforms a mesh with a lattice. You'll use an FFD in the Shark project later in this chapter.
Ripple	Deforms a mesh according to chosen ripple parameters.
Skew	Offsets the geometry along chosen axes and according to the extents of the modifier gizmo.
Stretch	Stretches an object along an axis while maintaining its volume by scaling down along the opposite axes.
Taper	Scales an object differently at one end than another, according to amount and curve values set.
Twist	Twists geometry around a chosen axis.
Wave	Deforms the mesh according to chosen waveform parameters. You'll use Wave in the Seascape project later in this chapter.
Lattice	Converts the edges of the mesh into struts of a lattice. You'll use Lattice in the Display Case project later in this chapter.
Noise	Applies random variations to a surface, according to animatable parameters. You'll use Noise in the Seascape project later in this chapter.
Push	Moves vertices outward or inward along the average normals.
Relax	Smooths surfaces by moving vertices relative to an average center point.
Spherify	Distorts a model toward a spherical shape by a chosen percentage.
Squeeze	Squeezes vertices of a model radially toward its pivot point while squeezing or stretching axially.
XForm	Deforms a mesh using transform tools in the modifier stacks.
Spline Modeling Modifiers	
Edit Spline	Accesses and edits sub-object levels of splines without collapsing to an editable spline.
Extrude	Builds geometry projected perpendicularly outward from a selected spline or polygon. You'll use Extrude in the Table Top project later in this chapter.

Table 4.1 Key Mesh Modeling Modifiers Available in Max *(continued)*

MODIFIER	PURPOSE
Spline Modeling Modifiers	
Fillet/Chamfer	Rounds out adjacent corners of a spline symmetrically. (Adds vertices with curved tangents between Corner vertices.)
Lathe	Builds geometry based on the rotation of a spline around a selected axis. (The axis of rotation can be moved.) You'll use Lathe in the Dome project later in this chapter.
Spline Select	Makes sub-object spline selections to pass up the stack to the next modifier.
Trim/Extend	Removes pieces of intersecting splines to adjacent points of intersection or extends a segment of a spline to the next point of intersection.
Mesh Modeling Modifiers	
Bevel	Extrudes splines or polygons with Outline parameters.
Cap Holes	Builds polygons across holes in meshes.
DeleteMesh	Deletes selected vertices or polygons. (Improves viewport response time while working on other sub-object levels; you can then delete this modifier or turn it off in the renderer.)
Edit Mesh	Moves, welds, or adds vertices; transforms, extrudes, bevels, chamfers, cuts, or slices polygons; transforms, extrudes, cuts, slices, or turns edges; assigns material IDs, smoothing groups, or vertex colors; flips normals. Can't animate sub-object positions, as in Editable Mesh, without XForm modifier.
Face Extrude	Extrudes faces or polygons.
Mesh Select	Makes mesh sub-object selections to pass up the stack to the next modifier. Changes the sub-object selection.
Normal	Flips normals of a surface (part of Edit Mesh).
Smooth	Smooths adjacent polygons or creates a hard edge on a smooth surface by assigning smoothing groups (part of Edit Mesh).
Volume Select	Makes mesh sub-object selections to pass up the stack according to a volume rather than direct selection. Position of volume gizmo is animatable.
Subdivision Modifiers	
MeshSmooth	Subdivides polygons to add detail and smoothness to a model. New features allow you to add creases or hard edges where needed. You'll use MeshSmooth in the Shark project later in this chapter.

Table 4.1 Key Mesh Modeling Modifiers Available in Max *(continued)*

MODIFIER	PURPOSE
Subdivision Modifiers	
HSDS	Subdivides polygons adaptively to add detail to specific areas of a model.
Tessellate	Subdivides selected faces of a model. Also subdivides at polygon sub-object level.
Polygon Reduction Modifiers	
Optimize	Reduces the number of polygons in a model. Works best on geometric or architectural models. Figures and faces need be optimized with more mesh resolution in some places and less in other, as detailed in Chapter 5.
MultiRes	Reduces the number of vertices in a model (or part of a model) to a specified percentage or number. Merges vertices within a specified threshold.

Experimenting with Modifiers

In Chapter 2, you applied modifiers and altered the application of a modifier by transforming its gizmo. Before you start making models, let's try out another modifier to practice using modifiers and adjusting their application.

1. In the Create panel, click Sphere and drag out a sphere in the perspective viewport.

2. In the Modify panel, click the Configure Modifier Sets button and choose Parametric Modifiers. Make sure Show Buttons is checked.

3. Click the Twist button. In the viewport, an orange box appears around the sphere, showing us the gizmo of the Twist modifier. In the modifier stack, the word Twist appears above the word Sphere.

4. In the Parameters rollout, spin up the Angle value to about 800. Spin the Bias up and down to see how that affects the twist. Change the Twist Axis to X to make the twist horizontal rather than vertical.

5. Under Limits, check Limit Effect. The twist goes away. Spin up the Upper Limit to about 35, and spin down the Lower Limit to about –35.

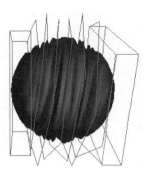

6. In the modifier stack, click the plus sign in front of the word Twist and click Gizmo to select the gizmo. Right-click the modifier gizmo's transform gizmo in the perspective viewport and choose Rotate. Press A to turn on Angle snap. Roll over the letter Y on the transform gizmo until it turns yellow. Drag down on the letter Y to rotate the gizmo around its Y-axis until the status line reads 30°. Press A again to turn off Angle snap.

The term gizmo *refers to the bounding box that modifiers use to affect the objects they are applied to. The gizmo appears in orange when not selected and in yellow when selected. The gizmo indicates the position, scale and orientation of the modifier; it lets you know how that modifier is working. As you saw in Chapter 3, transforming a modifier's gizmo alters the modifier's effect.*

7. Right-click the transform gizmo and choose Scale. Drag the transform gizmo up to stretch out the twist a little. Then right-click the transform gizmo and choose Move. Drag the XZ corner of the transform gizmo up and to the right slightly. Click the word Twist in the stack to get back to the object level. All the changes that you've made to the object since Step 5 were caused by transforming the modifier gizmo. These changes are also animatable.

Modeling a Display Case with the Lattice Modifier

Let's use another modifier, Lattice, to model a display case from a simple box. You will use this display case later in the chapter, as part of a larger project, so create the box to the specifications given.

Except as noted, the tutorials in this chapter assume that units are set to US Standard, Feet with Fractional Inches, $^1/_8$ inch. The home grid is set to 1" with 12 divisions per major division. Steps 1 and 2 below describe how to choose these settings. If you come back to these tutorials after changing settings, using File → Reset, shutting down, or changing computers, go through these steps again.

1. After resetting max (File → Reset), bring up the Units Setup window (Customize → Units Setup). Choose US Standard. Choose Feet w/Fractional Inches from the drop-down, $^1/_8$ in the drop-down next to that, and Inches as the default unit. If you work with the metric system, you can select that in the Units dialog instead. The units for this project will be given in US Standard.

2. Right-click the Snap button to open the Grid and Snap Setting window. Click the Home Grid tab. Change the Grid Spacing to 1" and set Major Lines every 12th. Finally uncheck Inhibit Grid Subdivision Below Grid Spacing and close the dialog box. The settings given here set up the grid for working in feet and inches and ensure that your grid lines are always drawn in foot increments, no matter how close you zoom in.

3. Press Shift+Ctrl+Z to Zoom Extents.

4. Create a box (choose Create → Geometry → Box) at the origin with these parameters:

   - Length = 3'0"
   - Width = 3'0"
   - Height = 2'0"

5. Name this object DisplayCase01. Change its object color to black. Right-click the viewport label and check Edged Faces. Increase the number of segments in the Parameters rollout. Notice that the visible form of the box remains the same.

   As a default, the box has the minimum number of segments defining its mesh (Length Segments, Width Segments, and Height Segments all equal 1). The only thing that adding more segments changed is the topology of the box. The term *topology* describes the mesh structure of objects, independent of form. Form is, however, affected by topology, as you shall see.

6. With the box still selected, click Lattice on the Modify panel.

The Lattice modifier converts the topology of an object to a geometrical lattice of struts and joints. *Joints* are the points of intersection in an object's topology. *Struts* are segments that connect the joints. The Lattice modifier expresses topology directly with adjustable parameters.

7. In the Modifier stack, click the word Box. Set the Length, Width, and Height Segments back to $1 \times 1 \times 1$. The lattice now has the minimum number of struts and joints.

8. Click the Lattice modifier in the stack. In the Geometry section of the Parameters rollout, choose Struts Only from Edges. In the Struts section, set Radius = 0.5″ and Sides = 6, and check End Caps and Smooth. Save your work as `DisplayCase01.max`.

Display Case project by Scott Onstott

Modeling a Landscape with the Displace Modifier

In this exercise, you are going to use the Displace modifier to model a landscape. In a later tutorial, you will add a road to this landscape.

The tutorials in this chapter assume that units are set to US Standard, Feet with Fractional Inches, 1/8 inch. The home grid is set to 1" with 12 divisions per major division. Steps 1 and 2 of the Display Case tutorial describe how to choose these settings. If you come back to these tutorials after changing settings, using File → Reset, shutting down, or changing computers, go through those steps again.

The Displace modifier pushes vertices of a surface up or down based on the grayscale values of a chosen bitmap. Values lighter than 128 gray raise the corresponding geometry, while values darker than 128 gray lower it. Figure 4.1 shows the grayscale bitmap you will use to deform a flat surface into a landscape (`landscape.bmp` in the Chapter 4 CD files). The whitest pixels represent the peaks, the darkest pixels represent the valleys and low-lying areas, and the many shades of gray represent the intermediate sloping areas in the landscape.

Figure 4.1 *The landscape grayscale image*

You could start with a mesh plane to make the landscape. To get a more smoothly continuous surface, you will start out with a patch and later convert the displaced patch to mesh. You could also start with a NURBS surface and get a similar result. Figure 4.2 shows the different results from applying the same Displace modifier to a patch with 25 segments in each direction and a mesh plane with 50 segments in each direction. Notice the smoother, more detailed contours of the patch surface.

1. On the Create panel, go to Geometry ➜ Patch Grids and click Quad Patch. Using the Keyboard Entry rollout, create a patch at the origin with these parameters:

   - Length = 24′0″

   - Width = 24′0″

2. The QuadPatch needs to capture the fine detail in the topography, so increase the number of segments now. In the Parameters rollout, set Length Segs = 25 and Width Segs = 25. (If you clicked off the patch after creating it, switch to the Modify panel to enter these parameters.)

3. With the patch still selected, click Displace from the Parametric Modifier buttons on the Modify panel.

Patch grid, 25 X 25 segments

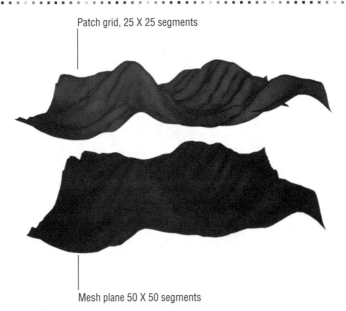

Mesh plane 50 X 50 segments

Figure 4.2 *The same Displace applied to a patch and a mesh plane*

4. Click the button marked None under Bitmap in the Image section of the Modify panel. In the file browser window, select `landscape.bmp` from your project folder and click Open.

5. Set Strength to 10′0″ and watch your patch object get displaced. The amount you select for the strength parameter is very subjective—10′0″ looks about right. Change the name of the object to Landscape. Your landscape should look like the Patch Grid model in Figure 4.2.

6. Save your work as `Landscape01.max`.

Landscape Bitmaps

The grayscale bitmap in Figure 4.1 was created using image editing software; specifically, Corel Bryce 4. Bryce is an excellent program for creating 3D landscapes. Bryce makes its 3D landscapes using an internal displacement technique. You can also use the advanced pixel-manipulation features in Bryce to create grayscale 2D bitmaps that can be exported. Alternatively, you could also use filters in Adobe Photoshop to manipulate the pixels of a bitmap. Although detailed image manipulation instructions for pixel-based drawing programs is beyond the scope of this book, you need good image manipulation skills to use max effectively. Chapter 1 includes recommendations for useful Photoshop books, and there are tutorials available on the Internet.

Modeling Meshes from Bezier Splines

Another way to use modifiers to model meshes is to start with Bezier splines and apply the Extrude or Lathe modifiers. These modifiers create mesh geometry based on a starting spline: Extrude projects the spline forward at a right angle and creates the connecting geometry; Lathe rotates the spline around an axis and creates the connecting geometry. Before you try using these modifiers, let's take a closer look at splines.

Using Bezier Splines

As introduced in Chapter 2, Bezier splines are curved or straight lines described mathematically by the tangents into and out of a vertex. To generate the mesh geometry you want, you need to know how to manipulate splines. Bezier splines are also the basis of patch surfaces, and facility with Bezier splines is particularly vital to working with Surface Tools to create patch models. You need to be able to edit them when creating Loft or ShapeMerge compound objects and when making animation paths. Bezier handles are also part of the loft deformation, function curve, and map output curve interfaces. You may want to review this section when dealing with Bezier splines or handles in another area of max.

Although there are other types of splines, including NURBS, the word "spline" is generally used to mean Bezier splines.

1. Choose File ➜ New. Leave the New All box checked and click OK. Press Shift+Ctrl+Z to Zoom Extents.

2. In the Create panel, click Shapes ➜ Circle. In the front viewport, drag from the origin outward to create a circle.

3. Right-click the circle and choose Convert To: Convert to Editable Spline.

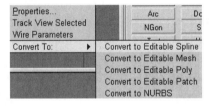

4. In the Modify panel, click the plus sign in front of Editable Spline in the modifier stack.

   Notice that there are three sub-object levels for splines: Vertex, Segment, and Spline. An Editable Spline object can contain more than one spline; the Spline sub-object level allows you to select and manipulate the splines the object comprises. *Segments* are defined as the curve between two vertices.

5. Click Vertex in the stack.

Note that there are only four vertices in this circle. Because splines can describe curvature with tangents into and out of a vertex, an entire circle can be mathematically described by just these vertices. However, don't be deceived. The curvature is still being approximated by straight-line segments by the renderer.

6. In the Interpolation rollout, spin the Steps value down to 2. Now your circle looks less round. Spin the Steps down to 0. Now you have a square. Set the Steps back to 6 and check Adaptive.

The Steps parameter allows you to choose how many straight-line segments are being used to approximate a curve. When Optimize is checked, the Steps parameter is used for curved spline segments and no steps are used for straight segments. When Adaptive is checked, more steps are used for sharp curves, fewer for gentle curves, and none for straight segments. When neither Optimize nor Adaptive is checked, the Steps parameter is applied to all segments, whether straight or curved. This is especially significant when you are generating a mesh from splines, because the steps will become vertices in your extruded or lathed mesh. Figure 4.3 illustrates how Step settings of a spline affect a generated mesh.

Editing a Bezier Spline

The vertices of a spline have four options for interpolating the tangents of the curve between them: Smooth, Corner, Bezier, and Bezier Corner. Let's look at what these do to a spline.

1. Still at the Vertex level of your circle, click one of the vertices of the circle in the front viewport. Yellow tangents with green handles appear. These are Bezier handles controlling the tangents into the vertex.

2. Right-click the vertex and look at the upper-left quad menu. Notice that Bezier is checked.

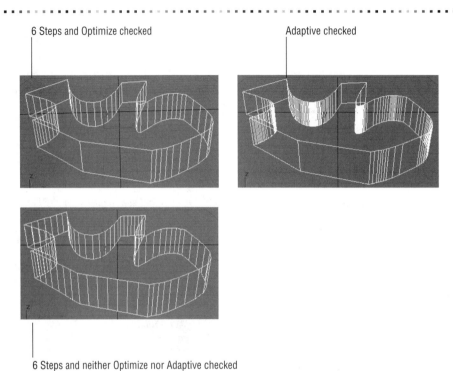

6 Steps and Optimize checked

Adaptive checked

6 Steps and neither Optimize nor Adaptive checked

Figure 4.3 *Extrusion of same spline with different Steps settings*

Table 4.2 describes each spline vertex type in max.

Table 4.2 Vertex Types of Bezier Splines

VERTEX TYPE	DESCRIPTION	USE
Corner	No curvature in or out of the vertex. No handles.	Good for sharp corners and straight lines.
Smooth	Curvature in and out of the vertex is calculated automatically. Handles are not available.	Good for creating very smooth curves where you don't need to control the exact curvature.
Bezier	Bezier handles on either side of the vertex are dependent, moving together.	Good for creating smooth transitions between curves.
Bezier Corner	Bezier handles for controlling the curvature on either side of the vertex are independent.	Good for abrupt changes in curvature and changing from straight lines to curves.

3. Drag the green Bezier handle in the front viewport. Notice that the curvature changes on both sides of the vertex simultaneously.

4. Right-click the vertex and choose Bezier Corner. Now drag the Bezier handle of the upper curve. This time only the curve on that side of the vertex changes, allowing for sharp change of curvature at the vertex.

5. Right-click the vertex again and this time choose Smooth. The handles disappear, and a very smooth curve reappears, but you can no longer change the curvature.

6. Right-click the vertex again and this time choose Corner. The segments on either side of the vertex are now straight as they reach the vertex. Figure 4.4 shows examples of the four vertex types for the same spline.

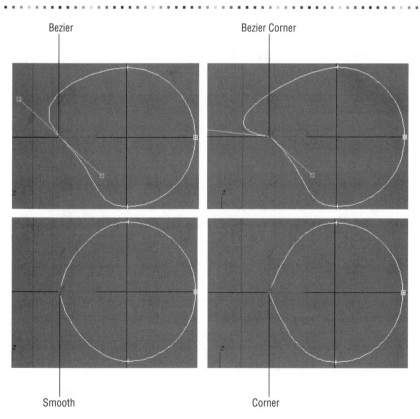

Figure 4.4 *Different vertex types with examples of possible curvature*

Lathing a Dome

Now let's use a spline to make an Islamic dome. You will use this dome in a larger architectural project later in the chapter, so build it to the specifications given. The dome's complex curvature doesn't look like any available primitive. Since it is radially symmetric, you can draw the cross-section of the dome and create the surface by spinning the cross-section 360 degrees by using the Lathe modifier.

Creating the Spline Cross-Section

First you will use spline creation and editing tools to create the cross-section you will later lathe.

1. Choose File ➜ New. Leave New All checked and click OK. Press Shift+Ctrl+Z to Zoom Extents.

2. Click within the front viewport to activate it and press W to maximize it.

3. Click the Line button (Create ➜ Shapes ➜ Splines ➜ Line). In the Creation Method rollout, choose Initial Type = Corner and Drag Type = Smooth.

Initial Type *means the type of vertex you get when you click once;* Drag Type *means the type of vertex you get when you drag the direction of a tangent out, then let go to drag to the vertex position, and click. Note that you can't create Bezier Corner vertices by dragging. You can always change your vertex types and move them once you have created a spline.*

4. Press S to turn on snap. Watch the status line as you roll over intersections of the grid. As an intersection is highlighted in cyan, indicating that clicking will snap to that point on the grid, the status line tells you its exact position. Roll over grid points until you find –9′0″ X, 0′0″ Y, and 16′0″ Z. Click once. Be careful not to make any extra clicks. The first vertex is a corner vertex.

5. Roll your mouse to –9′0″ X, 0′0″ Y, and 22′0″ Z. This time, *hold down the mouse button* as you drag a tangent. Drag to about –7′0″ X, 0′0″ Y, and 24′7-4/8″ Z before releasing the mouse. Release the mouse and roll over the grid until you find 0′0″ X, 0′0″ Y, and 28′0″ Z. Click once. Then right-click to finish your line. Right-click in the viewport to deactivate the Line tool. Press S to turn off snap.

6. In the Modify panel, change the name from Line01 to Dome. Your line should look like the one in Figure 4.5. If it doesn't, you can edit your vertices using the spline editing techniques described earlier, start over, or open up Dome01.max from the CD files for this chapter.

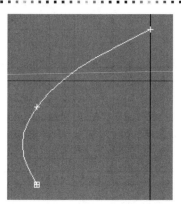

Figure 4.6 *The Curve to create using the Line command*

7. In the modifier stack, click the Spline sub-object button in the Selection roll-out. This does the same thing as if you had chosen Spline in the modifier stack. If you click the plus sign in front of the word Line in the stack, you will see that the Spline level is already highlighted to indicate that you are now in the Spline sub-object mode.

8. Click the line in the viewport. The line is now highlighted in red, indicating that the entire spline has been selected. Right-click in a blank area of the panel and choose Geometry to display the Geometry rollout. Notice that many of the controls are grayed out, indicating that they are not available in this sub-object level. Scroll down in this rollout until you find the Outline button.

9. Using the Outline spinner, drag up and down to see the effect of the Outline tool. Release the mouse button to finish the command. Press Ctrl+Z to undo after you have experimented.

A quick way of canceling a command in process is to click the right mouse button. When dragging a spinner, right-click while you are dragging with the left mouse button to cancel. This allows you to experiment with parameters without fear of "messing things up."

In the Outline field, type –1′ and press Enter. You now have the basic cross-section of your dome.

10. Let's adjust the vertices of your cross-section to make the exact shape you want. Right-click the object in the viewport and choose Sub-objects ➜ Vertex from the upper-left quad. This is yet another way to navigate between sub-object and object levels.

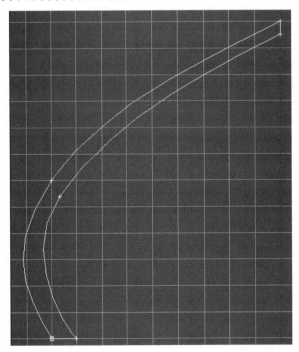

Spline ✓	Unbind
Segment	Line
Vertex	Curve
Top-level ◀	Sub-objects

11. Right-click the spline again and choose Move. Click the vertex that is very slightly to the right of the center of your Dome. In the status line Transform Type-In, type 0 for the X value and press Enter. Click the vertex that is a little lower and to the right of that one and enter **0** for X. For the same vertex, type **R 4.5** in the Z value and press Enter. The vertex moves up 4.5 inches. Move the other vertices so that your cross-section looks like Figure 4.6. Save your file as Dome02.max.

12. Click the word Line in the stack to get back to the object level.

Figure 4.6 *A completed cross-section of the dome*

Applying the Lathe Modifier

Now that you have the cross-section shape of the dome, you can apply the Lathe modifier to make a 3D object.

1. Click the Configure Modifier Sets button and choose Patch/Spline Editing. With the dome spline selected, click Lathe.

2. Press W to minimize the front viewport. Right-click in the perspective viewport to activate it. By default, the axis of rotation of a Lathe is around the Z axis through the center of the object. You can transform the Axis sub-object of the Lathe modifier to change this, but there are also three convenient preset buttons in the Align section of the Parameters rollout. Click Max to get your desired dome shape. This rotates the cross-section around Z through the maximum X value of the spline. This completes your dome. Save it as `Dome03.max`.

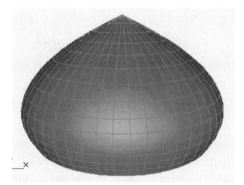

Extruding a Table Top

The other modifier that creates mesh geometry from starting splines is Extrude. Since polygons themselves can be extruded, and Extrude is part of the Edit Mesh modifier and Editable Mesh tools, it is included in the Mesh Editing modifier set. In this exercise you'll use the Extrude modifier to create a table top, which can be conceived as a flat plane extruded to a certain thickness.

1. Choose File → New. Leave New All checked and click OK. Press Shift+Ctrl+Z to Zoom Extents.

2. Right-click in the top view to activate it. Press S to turn on Grid Points snap. Activate the Rectangle button (Create ➜ Geometry ➜ Shapes ➜ Splines ➜ Rectangle). In the Keyboard Entry rollout, enter these values and then click Create:

   - $Z = 2'8''$

   - Length = $4'0''$

   - Width = $6'0''$

   - Corner Radius = $0'6''$

3. In the Modify panel, choose the Mesh Editing modifier set and click Extrude. In the Parameters rollout, type **2″** in the Amount field and press Enter. Change the name from Rectangle01 to Tabletop01.

4. In the perspective view, navigate the view until you are looking down at the table top from an angle.

You navigate the view using the Zoom, Pan, and Arc Rotate tools. Get comfortable using these tools to change your point-of-view. Practice navigating until you feel confident in your ability to see things from all sides. If you have a three-button mouse, click and hold the middle wheel down to Pan and roll the wheel to Zoom. (See Chapter 3 for how to set up a three-button mouse for max.)

5. Apply an Edit Mesh modifier. Go to the Polygon sub-object level. Press the F2 key to shade selected faces in the viewport. Click the top polygon of Tabletop01. Right-click in the Modify panel and navigate to the Edit Geometry rollout. Type **1″** in the Extrude text box and press Enter. Type **–1″** in the Bevel field and press Enter. The table top now has a beveled edge.

6. If you look closely, you can see faceted polygons in the corners of Tabletop01. These appear simply because they make up the structure of the mesh. To make this object look better, you need to do something more. In the perspective viewport, select all the polygons of the mesh. Press F2 to turn off shading of selected faces. In the Surface Properties rollout, enter **40** in the field next to the AutoSmooth button and click AutoSmooth. The table corners now appear smoother. The Auto smooth value sets the maximum angle between polygons when they should be smoothed in a viewport or render with at least the Smooth rendering level. This does not change the topology of the mesh.

The above steps could have been done with Extrude, MeshSelect, FaceExtrude, Bevel, and Smooth modifiers. Because you were using so many features included within the Edit Mesh modifier, however, you used it instead. You also could have collapsed to an editable mesh and used the same tools there.

7. Return to the object level. Save your work as `Table01.max`. You will build the legs for the table in the next section on loft objects.

Modeling with Compound Objects

Chapter 2 introduced the concept of compound objects. These objects allow you to model complex forms from simple starting objects, called *operands*. Table 4.3 describes the different types of compound objects in max.

Table 4.3 Compound Objects in Max

COMPOUND OBJECT	DESCRIPTION
Loft	Projects a cross-section along a spline path, creating connecting geometry.
Boolean	Subtracts, intersects, or adds the volume of one geometry to another.
Conform	Deforms one object to the contours of another object.
Connect	Creates geometry connecting a hole in one geometry to a hole in another.
ShapeMerge	Adds polygons to a mesh defined by a closed spline projected onto the mesh.
Terrain	Creates geometry connecting topographical contour lines imported from a CAD program.
Mesher	Creates mesh snapshots of animated procedural objects on a per-frame basis (like using the Snapshot tool to make a mesh snapshot of an object at each frame).
Morpher	Obsolete. Replaced by Morpher modifier. The Morph compound object is included in max in order to support files from versions of max prior to MAX R3, when Morpher was introduced. Morphing will be explained in more detail in Chapter 9.

New

Modeling Table Legs as Loft Objects

As you learned in Chapter 2, the term *loft* was taken from traditional wooden boat-builders to describe the process of creating the complex geometry of a ship's hull. Lofting has been around in computer graphics for a long time; in 3D Studio R1 (for DOS) lofts were the main modeling technique available.

To learn this technique, you are going to make legs for your table. As shown in Figure 4.7, each table leg consists of three parts: the cylinder, the cap and the leg itself.

Figure 4.7 *The finished Table model*

Modeling the Cylinder and Cap with Primitives

The cylinder and cap can be modeled out of primitives. The legs you will loft from splines.

1. Open the Table01.max file you created in the Table Top tutorial or from the CD files.

2. Right-click the top view to activate it. Create a cylinder (Create ➜ Geometry ➜ Cylinder) with Radius = 2″ and Height = 9″. Set the Height and Cap Segments to 1 and the Sides to 18.

3.   In the top viewport, move the cylinder near one of the corners of the table, but not on the extreme edge.

4. You need to align Cylinder01 with Tabletop01. Make sure Cylinder01 is selected and click the Align tool. Now click Tabletop01. In the Align dialog box, check Z axis and select Maximum for the Current Object and Minimum for the Target Object.

5. With your cylinder still selected, choose Edit ➜ Clone. In the Clone Options dialog box, change the name to Cap01 and select Copy.

6. With Cap01, go to the Modify panel and set the Radius to 2.5″ and the Height = -1″. Save your file as Table02.max.

Creating the Splines for the Loft

Now that you have completed a cylinder and cap, let's move to a leg. As you saw in Figure 4.7, the legs have a complex form that can be described by a series of cross-sections along a curved path.

1. Start from where you left off in the last section or open Table02.max from the CD files for this chapter. You are going to draw the basic profile of the leg with a line. Right-click in the front viewport to activate it and press W to maximize it. Press S to turn on Grip Point snap. (You may want to right-click the Snap button and check that only Grid Points is checked.)

2. Click the Line button (Create ➜ Shapes ➜ Splines ➜ Line). Set both Initial and Drag Types to Corner. Draw a line in the front viewport as shown in Figure 4.8.

. . . .

Figure 4.8 *Draw this line in the front viewport.*

3. You need to make the line curvilinear. Go to the Vertex sub-object level. Select the two middle vertices. In the Modify panel, click the Fillet button. Spin up the Fillet field until you get a line shaped like that in Figure 4.9. Return to the object level and name the line LoftPath01.

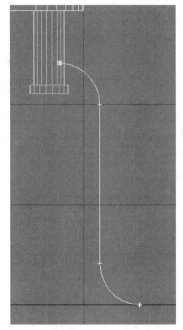

Figure 4.9 *The filleted line to be used as the Loft path*

4. Press W to minimize the front view and right-click in the top view to activate it. Draw a small circle near the base of the line you just completed (Create ➔ Shapes ➔ Splines ➔ Circle). Set its Radius to 1″. The exact position of the circle doesn't matter since it is being used as the cross-section to be lofted. Name this object LoftShape01.

Lofting the Table Legs

Lofts are composed of at least two parts: a *path* and one or more *shapes*. It may be easier to understand lofts if you imagine the wooden hull of an old boat. The boatbuilders made the hull by creating cross-section *shapes* acting as ribs, giving the hull a form. The surface planking was laid up on top of the ribs, following a *path* from bow to stern. You are going to loft a table leg with a single cross-section shape (the circle) that follows a curved path (the line). Later you will articulate the form of the leg by deforming the loft object.

1. Choose Edit ➜ Hold.

Compound objects are generally not undoable, even when they appear to undo. Always do an Edit ➜ Hold before creating a compound object.

2. Select LoftPath01. Click the Loft button (Create ➜ Geometry ➜ Compound Objects ➜ Loft).

3. Notice that in the Creation Method rollout, there are buttons called Get Path and Get Shape. Click Get Shape.

When creating a loft, you have the options Get Shape or Get Path. The object that is selected when you begin the loft stays put and becomes the one that you don't "Get." The other spline that you "Get" will be moved to a position based on the first vertex of the initial spline. In most cases, it is better to start a loft with the path and click Get Shape, because you generally want the path of a loft in a particular orientation.

4. Max is now waiting for you to select your cross-section shape. Click Loft-Shape01. A new object called Loft01 appears.

5. Right-click a blank area of the Modify panel and navigate to the Skin Parameters rollout. Set Shape Steps to 3 and Path Steps to 5. The loft is a smoothly curving circular form.

Deforming the Loft to Articulate the Shape

To give the leg a more complex shape, you need to scale the cross-section asymmetrically at different places along the path. To do this you use a Scale loft deformation.

1. Right-click a blank area of the Modify panel and navigate to the Deformations rollout. Click the Scale button. This brings up the Scale Deformations dialog box, shown in Figure 4.10.

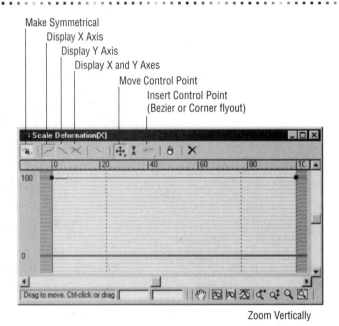

Figure labels:
Make Symmetrical
Display X Axis
Display Y Axis
Display X and Y Axes
Move Control Point
Insert Control Point
(Bezier or Corner flyout)
Zoom Vertically

Figure 4.10 *The Scale Deformations dialog box*

2. Scale deformations are used to scale the loft shapes along the X and Y axes of the path. Often it is convenient to lock the X and Y axes together, to deform the loft symmetrically along the path. You are going to deform the loft asymmetrically, however, so click the Make Symmetrical button to deactivate it.

3. Click the Display Y Axis button. You are going to scale this axis first.

4. Zoom Vertically out until you can see 300 percent in the vertical axis of the Scale Deformation dialog box. You need more room here to adjust the scale

curves. This graph represents the amount the loft is being scaled (the vertical axis) along the path (the horizontal axis). The dashed vertical lines represent the two middle vertices along LoftPath01. No scale has been applied yet, so the graph is flat.

5. Click the Move Control Point button. Drag the second control point (on the right) up to 200 percent in the vertical axis (scale). Observe how this deforms Loft01.

6. Click the Display X Axis button. You will set the scale in this axis separately.

7. Drag the left control point up to 300 percent and the right control point down to 40 percent. Now Loft01 is scaled asymmetrically, but it still doesn't look like a very good table leg.

8. You need more points on this graph curve to refine the scale deformation. Click the Insert Corner Point button. Click two points on the scale graph curve close to the vertical dashed lines. This creates two new corner points.

9. Click the Move Control Point tool again. Drag the two new corner points down the vertical dashed lines to 100 percent.

10. Click the Display XY Axes button to show both axes at once. Figure 4.11 shows the completed scale deformation curves. When your curves match these, close the Scale Deformation dialog box.

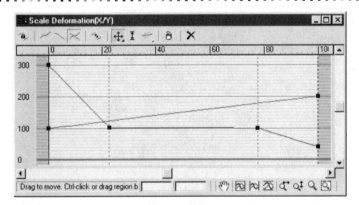

Figure 4.11 *Scale deformation curves*

Positioning the Pieces of the Leg

Now you have to assemble a leg from the pieces you've created.

1. Right-click the perspective viewport to activate it. Align Loft01 to Cylinder01 by matching their centers in both the X and Y positions.

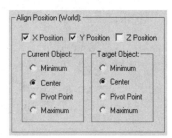

2. Press S to turn off snap. In the front viewport, use the Move tool to drag Loft01 along X just enough to position the top of the leg emerging from Cylinder01. Position it along Y so that it is just above Cap01. The position of Loft01 doesn't have to be perfect, just as long as it intersects slightly with Cylinder01.

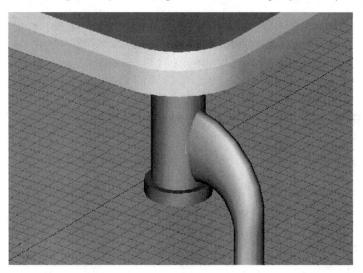

3. Select the loft in the perspective viewport. In the Hierarchy panel, click Affect Pivot Only. Align the pivot of Loft01 to the center of Cylinder01 in both X and Y positions.

4. Turn off Affect Pivot Only. Now Loft01's pivot is centered on the Cylinder01/Cap01 assembly. Right-click the loft in the perspective viewport and choose Rotate. Rotate the loft –45 degrees around the Z axis. You can either drag interactively or type the value in the Transform Type-In text box.

You could have also performed the same rotation using the Pick coordinate system, picking the cylinder, and choosing the Reference coordinate system transform center for your rotation.

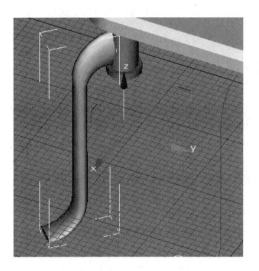

Now you have finished the table leg's three parts: Cylinder01, Cap01, and Loft01. Next you need to group all three objects together. *Groups* are organizational objects that can contain any number of objects or other groups. Groups themselves have no parameters; and when selected, they do not show up on the Modify panel. Groups do have a pivot point so that you can transform collections of objects together as a single group.

5. Press H to Select by Name. While holding down the Ctrl key, select Cylinder01, Cap01, and Loft01. Then click Select.

6. Choose Group ➜ Group. In the Group dialog box, type **TableLeg01** for the Group name. TableLeg01 now has a bounding box surrounding all three objects.

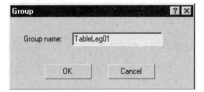

7. With TableLeg01 still selected, click Affect Pivot Only on the Hierarchy panel. Right-click the pivot point and choose Move. In the status line Transform Type-In, move the group's pivot to the origin by entering 0,0,0 for X, Y, and Z. Turn off Affect Pivot Only.

8. Click the Mirror tool. In the Mirror dialog box, select X as the mirror axis and Instance as the clone selection. Another leg is created, an instance of the first.

If you need to review the concepts of instances and other clones, see Chapter 2.

9. Select both table legs. Click the Mirror tool again. Select Y as the mirror axis this time and Instance as the clone selection.

10. Choose Tools ➜ Display Floater and click Hide by Name. Select LoftPath01 and LoftShape01, and click Hide.

11. Select all five remaining objects. Click Group ➜ Group and type **Table01** for the group name.

Group objects together when they logically belong together and the parts are stationary relative to each other; and nest groups to better organize your scene. This makes it easier to manage these models in future projects. Also be sure to give meaningful names to all the parts of your models; this will make a big difference when you want to modify something you made over a year ago in a new project.

Aligning the Table to Rest on the Grid

You have one last problem: the table legs are sticking down below the grid. You need to move the table up so that the legs rest on the grid.

1. Create a rectangle anywhere in the perspective viewport (Create ➜ Shapes ➜ Rectangle). Select Table01 and align the Minimum of Table01 to the rectangle you just created in the Z position.

To make an object (whose pivot point isn't already on the grid) rest on the grid, align the object in the Z position to a 2D object that is itself on the grid.

2. Delete the rectangle; it was only needed as a reference for the alignment in the last step.

Merging In the Display Case

Your table will have a display case on its top surface for displaying exhibits in the gallery you will build later in the chapter. Let's put the display case on the table now.

1. Choose File ➜ Merge. Browse to the DisplayCase01.max file you created earlier or from the CD files for this chapter. Click Open.

2. In the Merge dialog box, select the DisplayCase01 object and click OK.

3. A copy of your display case appears underneath your table. Align the Minimum of DisplayCase01 in the Z position with the Maximum of TableTop01. Now the display case is in the proper position on top of Table01.

4. Select [Table01] and Display Case01. Create a group named Exhibit01 containing these objects.

5. Save your file as Table03.max.

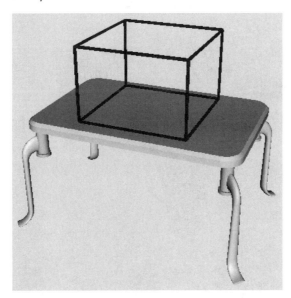

Exhibit table project by Scott Onstott

Modeling Pendentives with Booleans

As you learned in Chapter 2, the Boolean compound object in max is calculated using symbolic logic, a branch of mathematics created by George Boole. Boolean operations in max allow you to use two starting objects, called *operands*, to model a new object that is the intersection, subtraction, or addition of the two objects. Booleans require a lot of processing, so there is rarely any reason to use them for adding geometry. You use Booleans when your model requires cutting one object out of another object or calculating the intersection of the two.

Multiple Booleans are very tricky, not to say buggy, in max. One thing that seems to help is to keep your starting object the same through successive Booleans. That is, the first object selected (Operand A) is Operand A for each Boolean operation (it will look different but have the same object name).

You are going to use a Boolean to model pendentives. *Pendentives* are architectural structures that allow a round dome to sit atop a square base. They were first used by the Byzantine emperor Justinian when building the Hagia Sophia church in Constantinople in the fifth century CE. Figure 4.12 shows the pendentives that you are going to build. You will be using these in your larger architectural project later in the chapter, so model them to the specifications given.

Figure 4.12 *Pendentives*

Setting Up the Operands

The idea for modeling the pendentives is to create a box and cut away from it with a sphere. In order to do that, you need to create a box and a sphere of the correct size and proportions to be operands for the Boolean subtraction.

1. Choose File ➜ New. Leave New All checked and click OK. Press Shift+Ctrl+Z to Zoom Extents.

2. You want to make a box measuring 20′×20′×10′ to begin the volume of the gallery. Click Create ➜ Geometry ➜ Box and open the Keyboard Entry rollout. Set Length to 20′, Width to 20′, and Height to 10′. Click the Create button. A box is created at the origin. Change its name from Box01 to Pendentives. Feel free to change the object's color to suit you. Zoom in and center the object in the perspective viewport.

3. Using the Keyboard Entry rollout, create a sphere with a Radius of 13′. Change the Hemisphere parameter to 0.5. The Hemisphere parameter makes a partial sphere. Using a value of 0.5 means you have exactly half a sphere. Change the Segments parameter of the sphere to 100. You are going to need 100 segments in the sphere to meet the needs of the model. Right-click the perspective viewport label and choose Edged Faces. Figure 4.13 shows the two operands so far.

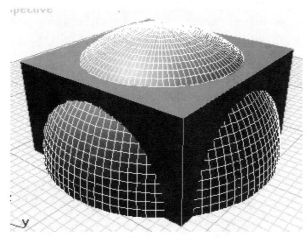

Figure 4.13 *The box and sphere operands for the Boolean operation*

Subtracting the Sphere from the Box

Now you're ready to cut the sphere shape out of the pendentive.

1. You want the box named Pendentives to be Operand A of your new Boolean. Deselect the sphere by right-clicking an empty area of the viewport. Select the box, and choose Edit ➜ Hold.

2. In the Create panel, choose Compound Object from the drop-down in the Geometry tab. Then click Boolean. This defines your selected object as Operand A of the Boolean.

3. Now you need to define Operand B of your Boolean. Click the Pick Operand B button. Notice that the prompt line at the bottom of the interface reads Pick Operand. This tells you that the program's mode expects you to pick an object as an operand. You can't do anything else until you pick an object to complete this mode. Click the Sphere to define it as Operand B. As you saw in Figure 4.13, the resultant Boolean (A minus B by default) looks like four architectural pendentives. Save your work as `Gallery01.max` in your project folder.

Adding a Road to the Landscape using a Conform Object

The Conform compound object works with two meshes, called the Wrapper and the Wrap-To objects. Using these two input meshes, Conform makes a new compound object. You will add a road to the landscape you created earlier, using a Conform compound object to get the road to conform to its topography.

Modeling a Road

You need to make a road that will eventually conform to the topography of the landscape. To accomplish this, you need to draw the plan of the road first.

1. Open the `Landscape01.max` file you created earlier in the chapter or from the CD files for this chapter.

2. Click in the perspective viewport to make it active. Press T to change it to a top view, press Shift+Ctrl+Z to zoom Extents All, and press W to maximize the viewport.

3. You need to be able to see the landscape yet also see the spline you are drawing for the road. Select the landscape and press Alt+X to put it in see-through mode. Click Create ➜ Shapes ➜ Splines ➜ Line. In the Creation Method rollout, set Drag Type to Corner.

4. You need to place the road between the two mountain ranges, running just about vertically down the middle of the landscape. Start your line in the middle of the valley, on the top edge of the landscape. Continue clicking points of your line every few feet (the grid is set to 1′ intervals), going down the valley until you reach the bottom edge of the landscape, as shown in Figure 4.14. Right-click a blank area of the viewport to deactivate the Create Line command.

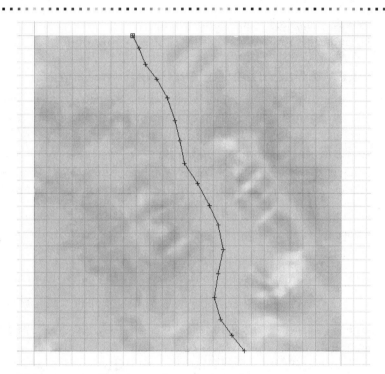

Figure 4.14 *A line drawn through the valley*

5. Press the H key and select the line. In the Modify panel, go to the Vertex sub-object level. From the menu bar, choose Edit ➜ Select All. All the vertices of the line are selected. Position the mouse directly over one of the vertices and right-click. Choose Smooth from the upper-left quad.

6. Go to the Spline sub-object level. Select the single Spline that defines Line01. In the Modify panel, type **6″** in the Outline field and press Enter.

7. Switch back to the Vertex sub-object level. Zoom in on the upper part of the spline. Move the top two vertices of Line01 close to the edge on the Landscape. However, be sure to keep the vertices inside the landscape. Do the same for the bottom vertices. Move the road vertices to maintain the same road width. Go back to the object level.

8. Apply the Extrude modifier to the line. Set the Amount to 1″. Change the name of Line01 to Road.

9. Press W to minimize the viewport. In the front viewport, move the road above the landscape. You don't have to be exact. Save your work as `Landscape02.max`.

Preparing the Operands for the Conform Object

To make the Conform object, you want your operands to be a simple as possible, so you will collapse the displaced patch landscape to an editable mesh. You also need to be able to distinguish the road from the landscape in the completed compound object. To do that you will assign each component object its own material ID number so that the corresponding faces of the compound object will be assigned that ID number. You can then use a special max material to assign different colors to the different material IDs.

1. Select the landscape and press Alt+X to return to opaque shading. Press P to change the shaded viewport back to perspective. Arc-rotate the perspective view to see your scene.

2. Right-click on the landscape and choose Convert to: Convert to Editable Mesh.

3. Select the Landscape object. Apply the Material modifier. Set the Material ID to 2.

4. Again right-click on the landscape and convert it to an editable mesh. This collapses the landscape into a mesh with a material ID of 2. The material ID of the road is 1 by default. Right-click on the road and convert it to an editable mesh.

Conforming the Road to the Landscape

Now that both road and landscape objects have been prepared, you are ready to make the Conform compound object. The object that is selected when you click Conform becomes the Wrapper object. In this model, road will be the Wrapper. The landscape will be the Wrap-To object.

1. Choose Edit ➜ Hold.

2. Select the Road object. Click Create ➜ Geometry ➜ Compound Objects ➜ Conform.

3. Right-click in the perspective viewport to make it active. Press T to switch it to a top view. This is necessary because you will project the road onto the landscape using this active viewport.

4. Click the Pick Wrap-To Object button and select the landscape in the top viewport. After a moment, the new Conform object appears. Press P to switch back to the perspective viewport.

If you select the landscape in the wrong viewport, Edit ➔ Fetch and go back to step 2. Don't try to undo.

5. Notice that the Road object is gone; it has been subsumed into the compound object. Rename the compound object "Road and Landscape".

Using a Material to Distinguish the Components

At this point, you can't pick out the Road object from the Landscape; they are both the same color. You need to make a special material that has two parts. Then you will be able to distinguish both parts of the compound object.

This use of materials is a quick run-through just so you can pick out the road from the landscape. Chapters 7 and 8 will explain materials in depth.

To distinguish the road from the landscape by material:

1. Press M to open the Material Editor.

2. Click the button marked Standard on the right hand side of the Material Editor. The Material/Map Browser appears. Select Multi/Sub-Object and click OK.

3. A small dialog box appears called Replace Material. Select Discard Old Material and click OK.

4. In the Multi/Sub-Object Basic Parameters rollout in the Material Editor, click the Set Number button. Set Number of Materials to 2 and click OK.

5. The Material Editor now shows a Multi/Sub-Object material with two sub-materials. When you apply this Multi/Sub-Object material to the compound object, the first sub-material (with Material ID 1) will be applied to the polygons of the road and the second material (with Material ID 2) will be applied to the polygons of the landscape. Click the color swatch next to the first material. Select a dark gray color from the Color Selector.

6. Click the color swatch next to the second material. Select a dark green color from the Color Selector. Click the Close button on the Color Selector. Rename the material from "1 – Default" to "Landscape and Road" in the text box in the middle of the Material Editor.

7. With the compound object selected, apply the new material by clicking the Assign Material to Selection button in the Material Editor. Close the Material Editor.

8. In the Conform parameters, change the Standoff distance to 5.

9. Right-click the Conform object and collapse to an editable mesh. Save your work as Landscape03.max.

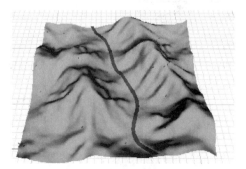

Landscape project by Scott Onstott

Using the Terrain Object

The Terrain compound object generates a mesh from contour line drawings exported from AutoCAD. Civil engineers and landscape architects map the slope of terrains with topological contour drawings. Each curve in these drawings represents a single elevation relative to some common reference point. The closer these lines are together, the greater the change in elevation and, therefore, the steeper the slope of the terrain. Contour drawings are typically drawn in Computer Aided Design (CAD) programs like Autodesk AutoCAD, Bentley Microstation, or Graphisoft ArchiCAD. The AutoCAD DWG file format has become a standard for transferring CAD data between systems. To prepare contour lines for export to max, in the source program move each line to the actual height it represents in the Z axis. Then save or export to the DWG format.

You will import CAD contour data that has already been prepared this way:

1. Choose File ➜ New. Leave New All checked and click OK. Press Shift+Ctrl+Z to Zoom Extents.

2. You start by importing the CAD contour data. From the menu bar, select File ➜ Import. The Select File to Import dialog box appears. Open the Files of Type pop-up list and choose AutoCAD (*.DWG).

3. Browse to select the file `Site Contours.dwg` included in the CD files for this chapter. Click Open. Check the Merge Objects With Current Scene radio button and click OK.

4. Leave all the default settings alone in the Import AutoCAD DWG File dialog box. Click OK.

5. The contour lines appear in the viewport. Click the object to select it.

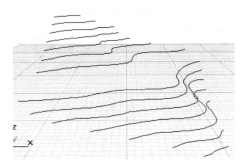

6. Choose Edit ➜ Hold. Click Create ➜ Geometry ➜ Compound Objects ➜ Terrain. In the Modify panel, change the Form to Graded Solid.

7. Change the viewport display to Edged Faces. Now you can see the topology of the Terrain. Notice that there are too many faces.

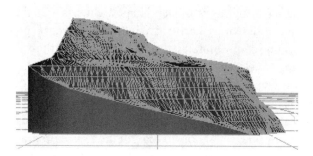

8. Open the Simplification rollout. Check Use 1/4 of Points in the Horizontal section. Now the Terrain has more efficient topology and still describes the same form. Turn off Edged Faces in the viewport display.

9. Open the Color by Elevation rollout. Click the Create Defaults button. This sets different colors at varying elevations to further highlight the sloping Terrain. In the Color Zone section, change the Base Elev to 7′0″. Change the Base color to a medium warm gray. Check the Solid to Top of Zone radio button. (This is optional; it affects the way the colors will blend between elevations.) Click the Add Zone button. In this way you can create your own colors at selected elevations.

Counting Polygons

In any polygonal mesh, there is a balance between having too many faces and not enough. When there are too many faces, unnecessary geometry has to be held in RAM, stored on disk, and calculated during the rendering process. This can overwhelm the capacity of your computer, bringing its performance to a crawl. Rendering unnecessary faces means wasting valuable time. On the other hand, not having enough faces in a mesh makes objects appear blocky or jagged. The optimum number of faces depends on the object's form, your modeling methods, and the intended use for the geometry. Real-time games and Web 3D use low-poly models. If you intend to render a close-up of an object, plan to include more faces in its topology. If you are using a model only in the background of a scene, you can probably get away with using fewer polygonal faces. If you are planning to animate objects, fewer faces can probably be modeled because motion is forgiving—objects tend to blur a bit when moving. Knowing the right number of faces to use comes with experience.

10. Save your work as Terrain.max.

Terrain project by Scott Onstott

Editable Mesh Modeling

You've already done some editable mesh modeling. The tools in editable mesh mode are also virtually identical to the ones in the Edit Mesh modifier. Many of these tools, as you have seen, are also available as smaller modifiers. The thing to remember about working in editable mesh (editable poly or editable spline) is that you don't maintain a history the way you do when you are modeling in the modifier stack. When working in editable mesh, you can only go back as far as your undo buffer will hold. If you close the program or run out of undos, it is difficult, if not impossible to get back to a point further back in the process. That said, it is a powerful modeling method and definitely the "cheapest" in terms of computer overhead. Once you learn all the tools available, you can work around most difficulties.

Modeling a Guitar Using Editable Mesh

The method of modeling in editable mesh (or editable poly) is to start with a simple primitive, collapse it to an editable mesh, and then move vertices and extrude and scale polygons to get the basic form you want. After that, you subdivide the surface to create the level of detail appropriate to your output. You have used some of the editable mesh tools (Extrude, Bevel, changing material ID, smoothing) already and will use them throughout the book. In this tutorial, you will get a sense of the overall method.

1. Choose File ➜ Reset.

For this tutorial, you are putting the Units back to the default of max units. You will be changing it back afterward.

2. In the front viewport, drag out a cylinder (Create ➜ Geometry ➜ Cylinder). Give the cylinder the following dimensions:

   • Radius: 150

   • Height: 100

   • Height Segments: 2

   • Cap Segments: 2

   • Sides: 30

   Right-click in a viewport to deactivate the Cylinder button.

3. In the Modify panel, right-click Cylinder in the stack and choose Convert To: Convert to Editable Mesh. Change the name of the object to Guitar.

4. Go to the Vertex sub-object level. With the Circular option chosen from the Selection Region flyout, use the Select tool in the front viewport to select the inner ring of vertices of the cylinder cap that is facing forward.

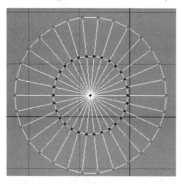

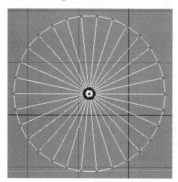 5. With the Non-Uniform Scale tool, scale these vertices down the front viewport in the YX plane so that the circle is small but not quite a point.

6. In the front viewport, select the vertices on the perimeter of the cylinder that are just above the vertices in the midsection of the circle. Draw a region around one of the vertices highlighted in Figure 4.15; then hold the Ctrl key and draw a region around the other. You should have six vertices selected if you look at the bottom of the Selection rollout.

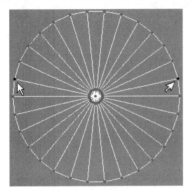

Figure 4.15 *Select these vertices*

7. In the Soft Selection rollout, check Use Soft Selection and set the falloff to 125. Soft selection allows partial selection of vertices, with gradations of selection, to allow transforms to be applied across an area of vertices with a falloff.

8. Nonuniformly scale the vertices toward the center of the cylinder until a guitar-like form is achieved. Uncheck the Use Soft Selection option.

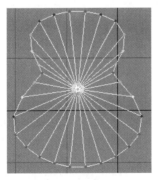

9. In the front viewport, select the inner circle of vertices on the cylinder cap. In the left viewport, hold the Alt key and draw a region around the vertices on the back of the guitar. This subtracts those vertices from the selection, leaving you with just the front vertices selected. Non-uniformly scale these up to be the size of a hole for the guitar. Move the vertices so that the circle lies more in the top half of the guitar.

10. Activate the top viewport and press K to change it to a back viewport. Select the inner circle of vertices on the back of the guitar. In the left view, Alt+select (subtract) any vertices from the front of the guitar that got selected as well. At the bottom of the Edit Geometry rollout, click Collapse to collapse these vertices to a single vertex.

11. Go to the Polygon sub-object level. Select the polys inside the inner circle on the front of the guitar (Alt+select any on the back). In the Edit Geometry rollout, click Extrude, type in a value of **–5**, and press Enter. Press the Delete key to create the hole of the guitar.

12. Select the two polygons at the very top of the guitar. Constraining to X, non-uniformly scale them up in the front viewport until they reach the appropriate size for the bridge of the guitar.

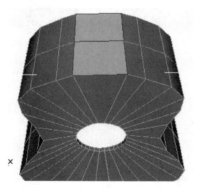

13. Holding the Alt key, de-select the top polygon toward the back of the guitar. With the front polygon selected, perform an Extrude with a value of 40. Constraining to Y, non-uniformly scale the polygon in the Y direction in the perspective viewport until it reaches half its size or less. This will determine the thickness of the bridge. In the top viewport, move the polygon down, constrained to Y, so that the front edge is flush with the front face of the guitar.

14. With the top polygon of the bridge still selected, extrude a value of 250 to form the bridge.

15. To form the end of the bridge, extrude the same polygon with value of 10. Constraining to X, non-uniformly scale outwards slightly in the top viewport. Extrude with a value of 75. Extrude with a value of 10 and non-uniformly scale slightly inward in X in the top viewport. This completes the bridge.

16. Go to the Vertex sub-object level. Select the vertices of the end of the bridge except for the vertices that are shared with the neck of the bridge.

17. In the left viewport, rotate the vertices backward around Z so they are bent back about 20 degrees. Move the vertices back in the X direction so that the neck is not crimped.

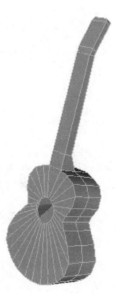

18. The basic form of the guitar is now complete. Press M to open the Materials Editor. Check 2-sided in the Basic Parameters rollout. Click the Diffuse color swatch and choose a color for your guitar. Click the Assign Material to Selection button. The 2-sided material allows us to see the inside polygons through the hole of the guitar. Save your work as Guitar.max.

Guitar project by John Matsubara

Editable Poly Modeling

As covered previously, the new editable poly object is very similar to editable mesh except that it allows true polygons rather than polygons with hidden edges of the triangular faces. Editable poly has subdivision surface with the MeshSmooth modifier built in, and since editable poly objects have no problems with hidden edges, the tessellation is better. Editable poly includes the tools familiar from editable mesh modeling, plus the new Borders sub-object level that allows you to cap holes easily and the Weld Edges command.

Modeling a Shark as an Editable Poly

In this tutorial, you will model a shark starting from a box primitive, converting it to editable poly, and using the editable poly mesh editing tools. As with editable mesh, all the modeling work is done within sub-object levels of the box. After creating the form of the shark, you will subdivide its surface using the MeshSmooth modifier. Finally, you will apply free form deformations to the polygonal mesh to create a second shark in a different physical position from the first.

1. After resetting max (File ➜ Reset), bring up the Units Setup dialog box (Customize ➜ Units Setup). Choose US Standard. Choose Feet w/Fractional Inches from the drop-down, 1/8 in the drop-down next to that, and Inches as the default unit. If you work with the metric system, you can select it in Units Setup instead. The units for this project will be given in US Standard.

2. Right-click the Snap button to open the Grid and Snap Setting dialog box. Click the Home Grid tab. Change the Grid Spacing to 1″ and set Major Lines every 12th. Finally uncheck Inhibit Grid Subdivision Below Grid Spacing and close the window. The settings given here set up the grid for working in feet and inches and ensure that your grid lines are always drawn in foot increments, no matter how close you zoom in.

3. Click Create ➜ Geometry ➜ Box. Using the Keyboard Entry rollout, create a box with these parameters:

    *   Length = 3′0″

    *   Width = 1′0″

    *   Height = 1′0″

4. In the Modify panel, change the topology of the box by adjusting these parameters:

   • Length Segs = 3

   • Width Segs = 3

   • Height Segs = 3

   Change the name of the box to Shark.

5. Turn Edged Faces on in the viewport display. Right-click the word Box in the stack and choose Convert to: Convert to Editable Poly.

6. Click the plus sign in front of Editable Poly in the stack. Notice that the Editable Poly object has five sub-object levels: Vertex, Edge, Border, Polygon and Element. Select Polygon. You are going to do most of your modeling in this sub-object level.

Shaping the Nose and Dorsal Fins

1. Select the middle polygon on the front of the box and move it in the Y direction to make the nose of the shark.

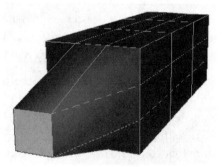

 Don't worry about being too accurate when modeling the shark. Organic forms don't tend to have numerical precision—instead, they are rich in proportion. Simply move polygons around until they "look right."

2. Select the middle polygon on the top surface of the shark. You are going to form this into the dorsal fin. In the Modify panel, put your mouse over one of the spinner arrows for Extrusion and drag the mouse up. You are interactively extruding the selected polygon. Release the mouse after making a nice dorsal fin. Be careful not to do this more than once. If you do click the mouse button several times, just undo and try again.

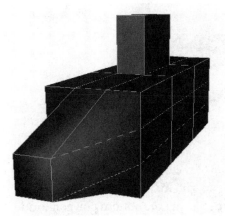

3. Drag the Outline spinner down to make the top of the dorsal fin smaller. Move the polygon back in the positive Y direction to give the fin a swept appearance.

Forming the Tail

1. Arc-rotate around to the back of the shark body. Select the middle polygon on the back side. Zoom out a bit so you have room to move. Move this polygon a little less than 3′ in the positive Y direction to form the tail of the shark.

2. Select both the top of the tail and the bottom. You have to arc-rotate after selecting the top polygon to be able to see the bottom of the tail. Hold down the Ctrl key while selecting the bottom polygon to add it to the selection.

3. Right-click in the left viewport to make it active and press R to change it to a right view. In the Modify panel, click the Slice Plane button. Press A to turn on Angle snap. With the Rotate tool, position your mouse over the Z axis (blue) of the transform gizmo in the right viewport and rotate the Slice plane 90 degrees.

Slice creates new polygons within an editable poly. Select polygons to cut, position or rotate the slice plane, and then click Slice to create new topology wherever the slice plane intersects selected polygons. (Don't confuse this with the Slice modifier, which operates on the object level.)

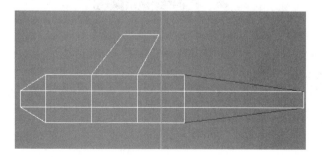

4. Move the Slice Plane in the X direction about three-fourths of the way across the tail. Click Slice. New topology has been created by Slice where the Slice Plane intersects the selected polygons. Click the Slice Plane button to turn it off.

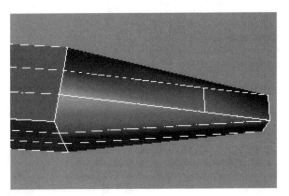

5. Deselect all four polygons by clicking in any blank area of the viewport. Select the two new polygons at the end of the tail. Arc-rotate after selecting the top polygon and hold the Ctrl key while selecting the bottom polygon. Extrude these two selected polygons a little over 1′ to create the tail fins.

6. Type −1″ in the text box next to the Outline tool and press Enter to make the fins a little smaller. Move the selected polygons back a bit in the positive Y direction, to give the fins a streamlined look.

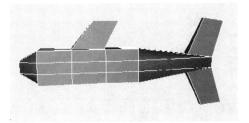

Extruding the Front Fins

1. Go to the Edge sub-object level. Arc-rotate underneath the shark and select the two edges on the sides of the upper section of the shark's body.

2. Type **1″** in the Chamfer field and press Enter. New topology is created.

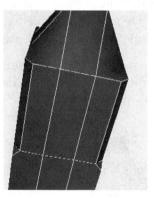

3. Go to the Polygon sub-object level and select the two new polygons that were created in the last step. Extrude these polygons about 9″.

4. Move the selected polygons back in the positive Y direction to give the front fins a more streamlined look. Go to the object level.

5. You now have the basic form of your shark model. Save your work as Shark01.max.

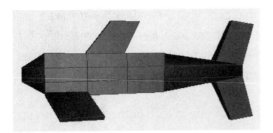

Using the MeshSmooth Modifier

Applying Subdivision Surfaces to a low-poly mesh is a powerful modeling technique. The amount of modeling effort required to create a low-poly model is low compared to the high-poly complexity of the resulting mesh. Your model of the shark is a "low-poly" model because it is composed of very few polygons. It was relatively easy to build such a low-poly model. The shark looks blocky because it is defined by so few polygons. By applying Subdivision Surfaces to the object, you can greatly increase the complexity of the shark's form. This greater complexity will make the shark look more streamlined and organic:

1. Choose the Subdivision Surfaces buttons from the modifier sets. Apply a MeshSmooth modifier in the to the shark model. Note that the default is the NURMS setting.

NURMS is a play on the word NURBS, covered in Chapter 6. The term emphasizes the ability to set relative weights from vertices of the low poly mesh, similar to weights of NURBS control points.

2. In the Subdivision Amount rollout, change the number of iterations to 2. Be careful not to increase this number beyond 3 or 4 because you will probably crash the computer. Each iteration applies a greater level of complexity to the polygonal mesh.

3. Max 4 has new features for fine-tuning the subdivision of NURMS. At the bottom of the Local Control rollout, check Display Control Mesh. This shows you a lattice of your original low-poly model around the subdivided model. Go to the Vertex level of the MeshSmooth modifier. Select the two vertices on the back end of the dorsal fin and spin up the Weight value to draw the mesh closer to these vertices. While MAX 3 had the NURMS option of assigning vertex weights from the control mesh, max 4 now allows you to edit these weights within MeshSmooth, without having to go back down the stack to the base object.

You could also apply subdivision surface by clicking the MeshSmooth button in the Subdivide rollout of the editable poly object. NURMS is the default setting of the MeshSmooth modifier, but it needs to be checked when using the version built into editable poly. Under Surface properties, check NURMS Subdivision. In this exercise, the modifier version is used in order to access the control mesh lattice.

4. Select the vertices on the back tip of each of the fins and turn up the Weight.

5. Go to the Edge sub-object level *of the MeshSmooth modifier* (not the editable poly). Select the two edges that form the crease between the two fins of the tail. Use Window Selection and draw a square region around the edges in the right viewport; then hold Alt and click the two side edges in the front viewport to subtract them.

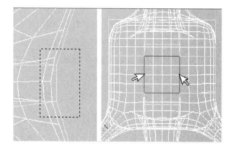

 6. Spin up the Crease value to draw the mesh closer to these edges. Crease allows you to create an actual crease or a more precise adherence to the base form of a model where needed. This gives you much more detailed control over the form of your model. Select edges for greater Crease value where you want more creasing in your model.

7. Deselect all the edges and return to the Object level. Save your work as Shark02.max.

A recent technology on the Internet uses Subdivision Surfaces to represent complex 3D models on client computers. The low-poly model is the only thing transmitted across the Internet, and each user's computer subdivides the mesh as necessary to create the intended complex 3D model. This technology efficiently uses limited bandwidth to display complex 3D geometry. Go to `http://www.kaon.com` *or* `http://www.viewpoint.com` *to check out this technology.*

Free Form Deformations

Let's make a second shark in a slightly different conformation than the first. Using a Free Form Deformation (FFD) modifier on a clone of the shark allows you to bend and deform it differently. FFD modifiers have a lattice that "pulls" the mesh toward them as you move the points of the lattice. Of the available FFD modifiers, FFD 2x2x2, FFD 3x3x3, and FFD 4x4x4 are special cases of the FFD (box) modifier with the specified number of lattice points. More control points allow you finer control over the free-form deformations. The FFD (box) modifier allows you to select the number of control points you would like in each dimension. FFD (cyl) uses a cylindrical lattice of control points. To deform a copy of the shark:

1. Hold the Shift key while moving the shark model to the side. In the clone options dialog, choose Copy and rename the clone Shark_alt.

2. Apply a FFD (box) modifier from the Free Form Deformations set to Shark_alt. Click the Set Number of Points button. In the Set FFD Dimensions dialog, set Length to 3, Width to 2, and Height to 2, making a 3x2x2 lattice of control points.

3. Expand the FFD (box) modifier by clicking the plus symbol in the stack. Click on the Control Points sub-object level.

4. Select the four control points on the Shark's left rear side. Move these control points a bit in the positive X direction. Observe how the polygonal mesh is deformed as a whole. The effect is concentrated closest to the selected control points.

5. Transform other control points as you wish, to deform the second shark into a different swimming position than the first. Exit sub-object mode. Save your work as `Shark03.max`.

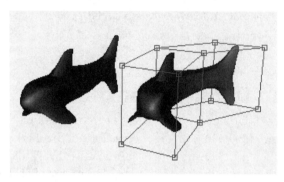

Sharks project by Scott Onstott

Hands-on max: The Museum Project

Now you are going to bring together some of the smaller projects made while learning modeling methods as parts of a larger project. You are going to model a gallery building that uses the dome and the pendentives you've already built. This building will be a museum exhibiting some of your projects. Inside the museum you will display three exhibits within exhibit tables. In one of the display cases will be your landscape and road project; another will become an aquarium for a couple of your sharks; the third will contain your terrain object with a miniature gallery building sitting on it.

In order to complete this project, you need to make a water surface for your shark aquarium and you need to model the gallery building itself.

Animating a Sea Surface with Noise and Wave Modifiers

First let's make an animated water surface for your sharks. As with the landscape project, use a patch surface in order to get smoother contours than you would get with a polygonal plane:

1. Choose File ➔ New. Leave New All checked and click OK. Press Shift+Ctrl+Z to Zoom Extents.

2. Using the Keyboard Entry rollout, create a patch grid for the sea surface (Create ➜ Geometry ➜ Patch Grids ➜ QuadPatch). Create the patch at the origin with these parameters:

   - Length = 24'0"

   - Width = 24'0"

3. You will need more topology to form convincing waves on the surface of the seascape. In the Modify panel, change these parameters:

   - Length Segs = 10

   - Width Segs = 10

   - Name = Seascape

4. Apply a Wave modifier from the Parametric Modifiers set. Set these parameters:

   - Amplitude 1 = 0'6"

   - Amplitude 2 = 0'6"

   - Wavelength = 6'

5. To make it more interesting, let's apply another Wave modifier, with these parameters:

   - Amplitude 1 = 6"

   - Amplitude 2 = 6"

   - Wavelength = 9'

6. The second Wave modifier didn't seem to do much—yet. Go to the Gizmo sub-object level of the top Wave modifier in the stack.

7. Using the Rotate tool, rotate the gizmo about –15 degrees around the Z axis. If you prefer, you can type **–15** in the Transform Type-In. Now the second Wave modifier affects the Seascape object at an angle, resulting in a more complex surface. Exit the Gizmo sub-object level of the second Wave modifier by clicking the word Gizmo in the stack.

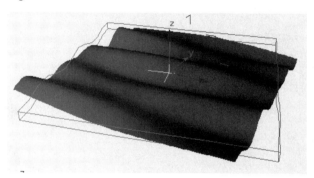

8. To introduce some random variation to the Seascape surface, you will make some noise. Apply the Noise modifier to Seascape from the Parametric Modifiers set.

The concept of noise—random variations in the background of a signal—can be applied in several contexts within max. On an old TV set with bad reception, the "snow" you see is an example of 2D visual noise. Noise can be used when designing materials to create a mottled or bumpy surface. Adapting this concept to geometry, noise can alter the topology of an object in random (but controllable) ways.

9. Set the parameters of the Noise modifier to these values:

   - Seed = 2
   - Scale = 4.0
   - Strength in the Z axis = 1′

   Now the Seascape surface appears less regular. Save your work as Seascape01.max.

Animating the Seascape

Now that you have modeled the Seascape surface, it would be nice to see it move. You will animate the parameters of the Wave and Noise modifiers to create the motion.

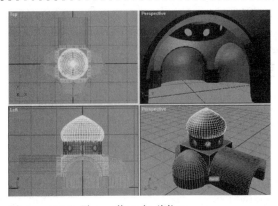

1. In the animation controls at the bottom right of the interface, click Go To End. This moves us to frame 100.

2. Click the Animate button next to the time controls. Notice that this button turns red and the active viewport is highlighted in red also. The red color means *be careful*—any changes you make now will be animated.

3. Click the bottom Wave modifier in the stack of Seascape. Change the Phase parameter to 1.0. Notice that there is a red outline around the spinner to indicate that this parameter is now animated.

4. Click the second Wave modifier in the stack. Change this modifier's Phase parameter to 1.0 also. Now this Wave will be animated also, keeping in phase with the other Wave modifier.

5. Click the Noise modifier in the stack. Check Animate Noise and set Phase to 50.

6. Click the Animate button to turn it off. The red color disappears.

7. Click the Play Animation button in the time controls and watch the Seascape move. Save your work as Seascape02.max.

Seascape project by Scott Onstott

Making the Gallery Building

To house all your exhibits, you're going to build a gallery building for your museum. The building will look like Figure 4.16 when you are finished.

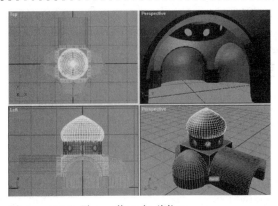

Figure 4.16 *The gallery building*

Modeling the Drum with Booleans

The drum is an architectural element that sits atop the pendentives, supporting the dome. The drum is penetrated by eight circular openings around its perimeter, as shown in Figure 4.17.

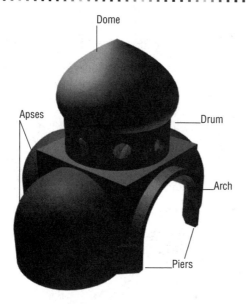

Figure 4.17 *Parts of gallery except the vault*

1. Open Gallery01.max from the Pendentives tutorial or from the CD files for this chapter.

2. In the Create panel, click Tube (Create ➜ Geometry ➜ Standard Primitives ➜ Tube). Since the drum needs to rest on top of the pendentives, and the pendentives are 10′ tall, you will create the drum at (0,0,10). Open the Keyboard Entry rollout and type these values:

   - Z=10′

   - Inner Radius = 8′0″

- Outer Radius = 9'0"

- Height = 6'0"

Click Create to make the tube.

3. Change the name of the tube from Tube01 to Drum. Change the object color if you wish.

4. To make the circular windows in the drum, you will again cut holes with Boolean operations. The holes are cylindrically shaped, so you will use a cylinder. Click Cylinder on the Create panel (Create ➜ Geometry ➜ Standard Primitives ➜ Cylinder). Using the Keyboard Entry rollout, make a cylinder at the origin with the following parameters:

- Radius = 1'6"

- Height = 2'0"

If you can't see the cylinder, navigate the view so that other objects do not obscure it.

5. If you imagine using this cylinder to make the openings in the drum, you will notice that you need to rotate it into position to cut the hole, and that you need to make seven other equally spaced cylinders. With the cylinder still selected, right-click it and choose Rotate. In the status line Transform Type-In, type 90 into the X field and press Enter.

6. Right-click in the top viewport to activate it. In this view, you are looking directly down on the object, as in a floor plan. You need to move the cylinder down along the Y axis until it looks like it is sticking completely through the drum. Make sure that snap is off, so that it doesn't interfere when you move the cylinder. Click the Move tool and position your mouse over the green Y axis of the transform gizmo in the top view. You will see it highlight in yellow when you are on top of it. Drag the mouse down in the top view until the cylinder crosses the drum. If you watch the Transform Type-In status, the Y field should be approximately –7'4".

7. Choose Arc Rotate Selected from the Arc Rotate flyout (the middle one with the white circle in the icon). With the cylinder still selected, use Arc Rotate Selected to rotate the view around the cylinder in the top view. The top view now changes to an axonometric user view.

8. You need to make eight cylinders like this one arrayed around the origin. To do this, you will move the cylinder's pivot point to the origin prior to using the Array tool. With the cylinder selected, click the Affect Pivot Only button on the Hierarchy panel.

9. Click the Move tool. Right-click the Move tool to bring up the Transform Type-In floater. Right-click the Y spinner of the Absolute:World section to set it to zero, thereby moving the pivot point to the origin. Click the Affect Pivot Only button again to turn it off.

10. You are now ready to make a radial array of cylinders for your Boolean. Click the Array tool. There are two major groups of controls in the Array window: Incremental and Totals. You want to array your cylinder a total of 360 degrees around the Z axis. Click the arrow on the right side of the word Rotate to enable the Totals group. Now type **360** in the text box next to the Z axis. Finally, type **8** next to the 1D count. Click OK, and the completed array appears.

At this point the array consists of eight separate cylinder objects. It would be tedious to Boolean out holes in the drum this way, and multiple Booleans can be unstable. Instead you will make the cylinders all one object.

11. Select one of the cylinders. Right-click it and choose Convert to: Convert To Editable Mesh.

12. In the Modify panel, open the Edit Geometry rollout and click Attach List. This opens a window listing all the objects in the scene. Select all the cylinder objects and then click the Attach button. Now all eight cylinders make up one object.

13. Click the Move tool. Type **13'** in the Z field of the status line Transform Type-In and press Enter to move the new cylinder mesh object up into position.

14. Select the Drum object. This will be Operand A in the Boolean. Now click Create → Geometry → Compound Objects → Boolean. Click Select Operand B. Click the cylinder mesh object, being careful not to accidentally select Pendentives. Save your work as `Gallery02.max`.

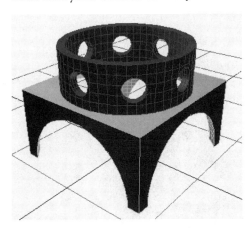

Modeling the Arches

Let's create the four semi-circular flanking arches framing the openings of the pendentive. You saw one of the arches in Figure 4.17. These can be made with tube primitives. You will create and position one arch and then array the other three around the origin.

1. Create a Tube object at the origin with the following parameters:

   - Radius1 = 8′0″

   - Radius2 = 9′0″

   - Height = 2′0″

2. In the Modify panel, adjust the following parameters:

   - Name = Arch01

   - Height Segments = Cap Segments = 1

   - Sides = 50

   - Slice On checked

   - Slice From = 90.0

   - Slice To = -90.0

Whenever you clone an object, max will automatically increment the object name. This means that if you clone an object called Kitchen, the first copy will be named Kitchen01, the next Kitchen02, etc. To stay organized, name the first object Name01. Then, if you decide to clone it, the naming system will stay consistent.

3. Rotate Arch01 90 degrees around the X axis.

4. Click the Align tool, and choose Pendentives as the target object. In the Align dialog box, check Y and choose Maximum for Current Object and Minimum for the Target Object. Arch01 is now properly aligned with the Pendentive.

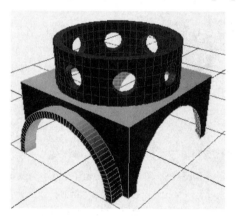

5. Now let's array the rest of the arches. Go to the Hierarchy tab and click the Affect Pivot Only button. Move the pivot to the origin point by making all the axes read zero in Absolute Mode of the Transform Type-In. Turn off Affect Pivot Only.

6. Click the Array tool and array four objects a total of 360 degrees rotated around the Z axis. Save your work as `Gallery03.max`.

Merging In the Dome

Your structure is now ready for the dome you built earlier in the chapter.

1. Choose File ➜ Merge. Choose the `Dome03.max` file that you created earlier or from the CD files for this chapter.

2. Select Dome from the Merge dialog box and click OK. The dome comes in right in place since you modeled it in the correct position.

When you plan to use a model in another file, position your model correctly relative to the origin point. This will make your model easier to merge or externally reference in another scene.

Modeling the Piers

Now let's model the piers beneath your existing structure. You saw two of the piers in Figure 4.17. You will draw the 2D plan of the piers and then extrude them to create a 3D volume.

1. First you need to move your existing structure up before constructing anything below the grid. Press H to Select by Name. In the Select Objects window, click the All button in the lower-left corner and then click Select.

Unless you have a good reason to do otherwise, plan to use the grid as a baseline that your objects rest on. For architectural subjects, the grid represents the ground plane.

2. Click Relative mode. In the Z field of the status line Transform Type-In, type **5′** to move all the objects up by that amount. Click the button again to return to Absolute mode.

3. Arc-rotate so you can see underneath and Zoom in on one of the corners of the structure. Right-click the viewport label and uncheck Show Grid to see everything more clearly.

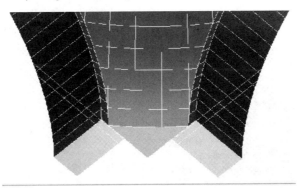

4. Choose Create ➜ Shapes ➜ Splines ➜ Line. Change both Initial and Drag Types to Corner in order to draw straight line segments.

5. You want to snap the Line to the vertices of the existing structure. Right-click the Snap button to open the Grid and Snap Settings window. Click the Clear All button, click Vertex, and close the window.

6. Turn 3D snap on. Remember to click and hold the Snap button to see the fly-out menu where you can select 3D snap.

 Notice that turning snap on is separate from choosing snap settings. You have to click the Snap button to toggle it on or off. Right-click the Snap button to select snap settings.

7. Draw a line around the area where the arch and pendentive meet. Draw your line in a counter-clockwise (CCW) direction. It doesn't matter which vertex you start with, as long as you proceed to draw the other vertices moving CCW. When you get to the end of the line, click the same vertex you started with. A very small dialog box will appear, asking you whether you want to close the spline—choose Yes.

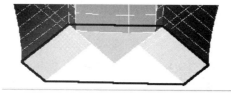

8. In the Modify panel, choose the Mesh Editing modifier set and click Extrude. Set the Amount to –5′ to extrude the line downwards. Change the name of this object to Pier01.

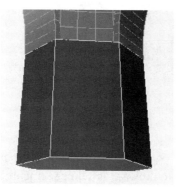

9. Navigate the view until you can see the entire structure. You need to array the other piers. On the Hierarchy panel, click Affect Pivot Only. Move the pivot of Pier01 to the origin. Turn off Affect Pivot Only.

10. Click the Array tool to open the Array window. Array four objects a total of 360 degrees around the Z axis. Save your work as `Gallery04.max`.

Modeling the Apses

Eventually, you will display modeling exhibits in your display cases on tables in the *apses*. Apses form half a spherical dome. You will need to make three apses in your Gallery. Refer to Figure 4.17 for a look at the finished apses.

1. Navigate so your view looks similar to Figure 4.18.

2. Go to the Splines section of the Create panel (Create ➔ Shapes ➔ Splines).

3. You are going to use the End-End-Middle Creation Method. This means you create the arc by clicking one-at-a-time on the end vertex, the other end vertex, and finally the middle vertex. Try making a few arcs on the ground for practice. Delete all the arcs when you understand how they are made.

4. The arc that is going to become the basis of your apse needs to snap to one of the existing arches. This is where AutoGrid comes in. AutoGrid allows you to create objects that automatically align with other objects. It works by making a temporary grid that exists while you are in the process of creating your new object. Let's try it. Check AutoGrid in the Create panel and then click the Arc button.

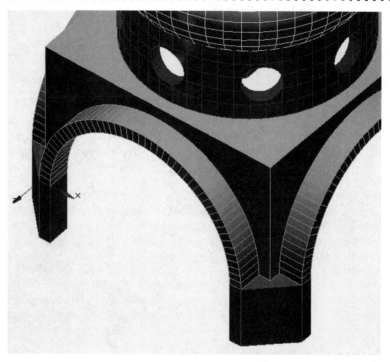

Figure 4.18 Navigate so that you have this view of the Gallery.

5. Make sure 3D Vertex snap is still on. For the first point of the arc, move your mouse over the corner of the base of one of the arches. You need to wiggle the mouse in small motions in this area until you see two things happen: first, the vertex snap icon should light up, indicating that you will make this arc on top of the arch; second, the AutoGrid gizmo needs to show the X and Y axis arrows aligning with the side of the arch. These axes together define the XY plane, and that is where the arc will be created. Figure 4.19 shows the placement of the vertices of the arc in steps 5 through 7.

6. Click and drag the mouse to the top of the arch. Release the button when you see the cyan crosshairs that indicate this point will snap to the top of the arch. If your viewport is set to Show Edges, this point is easier to see.

7. Move the mouse and click again when you can snap to a point on the outer edge of the arch. This completes the arc and sets its middle vertex. Change the arc's name to Apse01.

Figure 4.19 *The placement of the vertices of the arc using AutoGrid*

8. In the Modify panel, make sure the Radius of Apse01 is about 9′0″ and goes From 90.0 To 180.0. If Apse01 does not have these dimensions, delete it and repeat steps 5 through 8.

9. Change the Radius to 8′6″. This positions Apse01in the middle of the arch.

10. Apply an Edit Spline modifier from the Patch/Spline modifier set. Click the plus in front of Edit Spline in the stack. Click the Spline sub-object level. Click the object to select its only spline.

11. Scroll down the panel to the Outline group. Type –1′ in the Outline field and press Enter. Go back to the object level by clicking again on the word Spline in the stack.

Be sure to exit sub-object mode before applying any more modifiers. If you stay in sub-object mode when you apply a modifier, the modifier affects only your sub-object selection. You can tell when a modifier is being applied to a sub-object selection because it will have asterisks after its name in the stack.

12. Apply the Lathe modifier. Set these parameters:
    - Degrees = 180
    - Weld Core checked
    - Segments = 25

13. With Apse01 still selected, hold down the right mouse button on a blank area of the viewport and choose Hide Unselected.

14. Right-click in the front view to activate it. Shift+Ctrl+Z to Zoom Extents All.

When your model starts getting complicated, hide some of the objects you've already made to make it easier to see what you're working on. You can always unhide the hidden objects later on. Pressing the 5 key brings up the Unhide By Name dialog box.

15. Apply an Edit Mesh modifier to Apse01. Go to the Vertex sub-object level. Select a region that includes only the bottom row of vertices in the apse. Figure 4.20 shows the vertices to select.

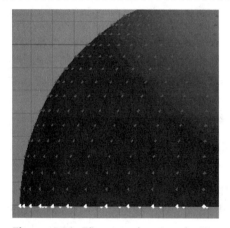

Figure 4.20 *The apse showing the Vertex sub-object selection*

16. Move this selection of vertices to a value of zero in the Z axis. To accomplish this, make sure the Transform Type-In is set to Absolute mode. Then change the value in the Z field to zero. Now Apse01 touches the ground.

17. Arc-rotate until you can see the upper part of the inside of the apse. Go to the Polygon sub-object level and select the two polygons on the inner surface by holding down the Ctrl key. Press F2 to shade selected faces. Figure 4.21 shows the selection.

18. Move this selection 2′ in the X direction. In Relative mode, type **2′** into the X Transform Type-In field and press Enter. Go back to the object level. Hold down the right mouse button on the viewport and choose Unhide All. Now the apse covers the arch from the exterior of the Gallery.

19. Move the pivot point of Apse01 to the origin. Array four Apses a total of 360 degrees around the Z axis. Save your work as `Gallery05.max`.

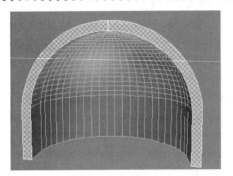

Figure 4.21 *The Apse showing the Polygon sub-object selection*

Modeling the Vault

All you need to complete the Gallery is the entry vault. This vault has the same form as the arches, only it is much longer. You could model it using several of the techniques presented in this chapter. However, it is easier to copy one of the arches and modify it to form the vault.

1. Select the exposed arch. Choose Edit ➜ Clone. The Clone Options window appears. Change the name to Vault01 and check Copy.

2. Now you have an exact copy of the arch in exactly the same position. Switch to the Modify tab and change the following parameters of Vault01:

   - Radius1 = 8'6"

   - Radius2 = 10'0"

   - Height = 20'0"

3. Change the color of Vault01 to something different than the Arches. You still need to make the vault reach the ground. Apply an Edit Mesh modifier to the Vault01 object. Go to the Polygon sub-object level and, holding the Ctrl key, select the two polygons on the bottom surface of Vault01. Move these polygons down to the ground plane by moving them –5' in the Z axis in Relative mode. Go back to the object level. Save your work as Gallery06.max.

See the finished gallery building in the Museum Gallery Project plate in the Color Gallery section.

Assembling the Museum with XRefs

Now that you've finished your gallery building, you are going to externally reference (*XRef* for short) some of your earlier project files as exhibits to complete your museum. When objects are externally referenced (XRef'd) into another file, the referenced geometry cannot be edited from the project file. Instead, if you want to change one of the models, you have to open its file and change it there. XRefs are useful when bringing together disparate components of a larger composition like this as well as when working in teams.

Team members may want to XRef each other's models while working on their own. For example, one team member might model the gallery building while another models the table. The team member working on the table might want to know the scale of the apse into which the table must fit. By externally referencing the gallery model into the table file temporarily, the team member can design the table to fit in the space allotted. When the table model is complete, she can detach the XRef from the model. Near the end of the modeling project, all the models can be XRef'd into an overall project model that contains everyone's work. The project model is then rendered or animated to produce the final output.

External references help you maintain your project data over time. For example, let's say you XRef'd the table model into several different projects. A few weeks later, the project manager tells you that the table has to be redesigned in all the projects to better fit the needs of the client. Because you used XRefs, you just need to modify the design of the table in its original file. All the tables used in your projects are automatically updated, because they reference the original table file.

Externally Referencing the Gallery Building

The first file you will externally reference is the gallery building itself. XRef the entire scene, rather than all the separate objects:

1. Choose File ➜ New. The New Scene dialog box appears. Select New All and click OK.

2. Choose File ➜ XRef Scene. The XRef Scenes dialog box appears. Click the Add button. Browse to the `Gallery06.max` file that you created earlier, or from the CD files for this chapter, and click Open. Close the XRef Scenes dialog box.

There are two types of XRefs: Scenes and Objects. Use XRef Scenes when you want to reference every-thing within a file. Choose XRef Objects when you want to reference only part of a scene. You can select the individual objects you wish to reference with XRef Objects.

3. Now the Gallery model is referenced in your new file. Press H to bring up the Select by Name dialog box. Notice that there are no objects in this scene. When you XRef a scene, you don't have access to the scene's objects; they simply appear in the new file.

4. Close the Select Object window. Save your work as Museum01.max.

Externally Referencing the Display Tables

The next step is to XRef three tables into your file, to put in the three apses. Since you know that you are going to have to move these tables to position them, XRef Objects is a better choice than Xref Scene.

1. File ➜ XRef Objects. Click the Add button in the XRef Objects window. Select the Table03.max file you created earlier, or from the CD files for this chapter, and click Open. A smaller XRef Merge dialog box (identical to the Select by Name dialog box) appears, showing a list of all the objects in the Table Scene. Select Exhibit01. Click OK.

2. Press H to bring up the Select by Name dialog box. Notice that there is now an object listed, in contrast to the XRef Scenes method. This object has curly braces around it to indicate its special XRef'd status. You cannot change the form of XRef'd objects.

3. Position the exhibit table within the gallery building by moving it in the nega-tive X direction into the apse on the left side.

4. Rotate Exhibit01 90 degrees about its Z axis. Position Exhibit01 so it matches Figure 4.26.

5. In the Hierarchy panel, click Affect Pivot Only. Move the pivot of Exhibit01 to the origin. Click the Affect Pivot Only button again to turn it off.

6. With the top viewport active, array three tables a total of 270 degrees around the Z axis. Save your work as Museum02.max.

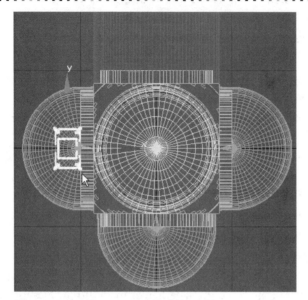

Figure 4.26 *Placement of table within apse*

Externally Referencing the Landscape Model

The landscape model contains only one object. This might suggest using XRef Scenes. However, you are going to need to transform the Landscape object to fit within one of the display cases on a table. It's easier to accomplish this if you use XRef Objects instead.

1. It is going to be easier to see the tables if you first hide the Gallery model. Click File ➜ XRef Scenes to bring up the XRef Scenes window. In the Display Options group, click the check box next to the word Box and close the window. Now the Gallery is displayed as a bounding box, and you can see through it easily.

2. Click File ➜ XRef Objects. The XRef Objects window appears. Click the Add button.

3. Select the Landscape03.max file you made earlier or from the CD files for this chapter. Click Open. Select the Road and Landscape object from the XRef Merge dialog box and click OK.

4. Now the Road and Landscape object appears in the top view. However, it is far too large. Click the Scale tool. In the status line Transform Type-In, type **10** in the X field and press Enter.

5. Align the Road and Landscape with Exhibit01. Center the objects in X, Y, and Z.

6. Zoom Extents Selected and arc-rotate to navigate your view close to Exhibit01. Scale Road and Landscape up a little bit so that it fits snugly inside the display case.

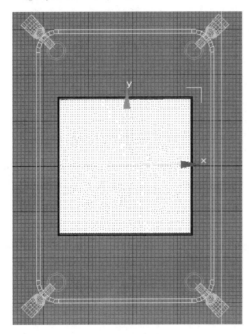

7. In the front viewport, move Road and Landscape down in the Y direction until it is near the bottom of the display case. Save your work as Museum03.max.

See the finished landscape exhibit in the Museum Gallery Project plate in the Color Gallery section.

Externally Referencing the Seascape and Sharks

Follow the same procedure in referencing and transforming the seascape as you did for the landscape.

1. Choose File ➔ XRef Objects. Click Add and select the Seascape02.max file you created earlier or from the CD files for this chapter. Click Open. Select the Seascape object from the XRef Merge dialog box. Click OK.

2. Notice in the top view that the Seascape is far too large. Click the Scale tool. In the Transform Type-In, type **12** in the X field and press Enter.

3. Align the seascape with Exhibit02. Center the objects in X, Y, and Z. In the front viewport, move seascape up until it is near the top of the display case.

4. The Shark model contains only one object, so you will use XRef Objects for this procedure. Choose File ➔ XRef Objects. Add the Shark02.max file you created earlier or from the CD files for this chapter. Click Open. Select the Shark and Shark_alt objects from the XRef Merge dialog box and click OK.

5. The sharks are also too large. Click the Scale tool. Scale the sharks down to a size that fits within a display case. Align the sharks with the Exhibit02. Center the objects in X, Y and Z. In the front and top viewports, move the sharks until they are within the display case.

6. Transform the sharks as you like underneath the seascape surface to make a pleasing composition. Save your work as Museum04.max.

See the finished seascape exhibit in the Museum Gallery Project plate in the Color Gallery section.

Externally Referencing the Terrain with a Miniature Gallery

You are going to XRef the terrain model and then place a small model of the gallery building itself on the terrain. Because there are many objects making up the Gallery model, and you want to reference the entire scene, it makes sense to use XRef Scenes rather than XRef Objects. However, you are going to need to transform the Gallery scene, both to make it smaller and to position it on the terrain model. To do this you will bind the entire scene to a dummy helper object.

1. Choose File ➔ XRef Objects. Add the Terrain.max file you created earlier or from the CD files for this chapter. Click Open. Select the Terrain object from the XRef Merge dialog box. Click OK.

2. In the top view, you can see that the terrain is too large. Click the Scale tool. In the Transform Type-In, type **12** in the X field and press Enter. Rotate the terrain –90 degrees around the Z axis. Align the terrain with Exhibit03. Center the objects in X, Y, and Z.

3. In the front viewport, move the terrain down until it is near the bottom of the display case.

4. Now you're ready to create the dummy to which you will bind your gallery scene. Drag out a small dummy object near the origin (Create ➔ Helpers ➔ Dummy). The exact size and position do not matter.

 Dummy *objects are non-rendering helper-objects used in many contexts to hold a position for something else. You are using a dummy for the XRef'd scene to be bound to. When you transform the dummy, the transforms will be passed to the XRef'd scene as well.*

5. Choose File ➔ XRef Scenes. Add the `Gallery06.max` file you created earlier or from the CD files for this chapter. Click Open.

6. Click Bind. Move the XRef Scenes window to the side of the screen by dragging its blue title bar. You are doing this in order to see the dummy object. Click the dummy object in one of your viewports. The word Dummy01 should appear directly above the Bind button. Now the dummy has become the parent of the XRef'd scene. Click Close.

7. With the dummy object selected, click the Scale tool. Type **2** in the X Transform Type-In field and press Enter. This makes this referenced gallery very small with respect to the "real" gallery building. Change the name of the dummy to Miniature Gallery.

8. Align the miniature gallery with Exhibit03. Center the objects in X, Y, and Z.

9. Navigate your view so you can see both the miniature gallery and the terrain. Rotate the miniature gallery around Z a bit and move it down until it intersects with the Terrain. Save your work as `Museum05.max`.

See the finished terrain exhibit in the Museum Gallery Project plate in the Color Gallery section.

10. Click Create ➜ Geometry ➜ Plane.

11. Create a large plane that is larger than the Gallery, centered on the origin. Name this object Ground Plane.

Placing Cameras in the Museum

Now that you have finished modeling and externally referencing everything in the Gallery project, you need to make some cameras. CG cameras behave in a way similar to real-world cameras. They use a camera lens analogy, to adjust the field-of-view (of perspective projection) just like in a real camera. Cameras with about a 50mm lens approximate the human eye fairly well. However, for architectural subjects, a slightly wide-angle lens is recommended. Let's make a camera and look through its lens.

1. Right-click in the front viewport to make it active.

2. Click Create ➜ Cameras ➜ Free.

Cameras come in two types: Target and Free. A target *camera uses separate camera and target objects that are linked. The camera will always point at its own target. The target camera allows complex animations where the camera can be keyframed separately from its target. A* free *camera has only the camera object without a target. In most situations, the choice of camera type is a matter of personal preference.*

3. Click a point on the screen somewhere inside the bounding box of the Gallery. Camera01 appears.

4. Right-click in the front viewport to make it active. Press **C** on the keyboard. This switches the selected viewport to camera view. Change the camera viewport to display Smooth + Highlights.

5. Now that your camera is inside the Gallery, let's display the Gallery model. Choose File ➜ XRef Scenes. Click the second Gallery file in the File list. Click the checkbox next to Box in the Display group to turn bounding box mode off. Click Close.

6. Right now the camera is pointing in the wrong direction. In the top viewport, rotate the camera around in the Z axis. Move the camera up or down in the left viewport until Camera01 has a view of one of the display tables.

7. With Camera01 still selected, go to the Modify panel and click the 24mm button in the Stock Lenses group. Now you can see more of the interior with Camera01.

8. In the camera viewport, use the camera viewport navigation controls (described in detail in Chapter 3) to further adjust your camera until you have a pleasing composition. Repeat steps 1 through 8 as needed to create additional cameras.

9. Save your work as Museum06.max.

See the finished museum gallery in the Museum Gallery Project plate in the Color Gallery section.

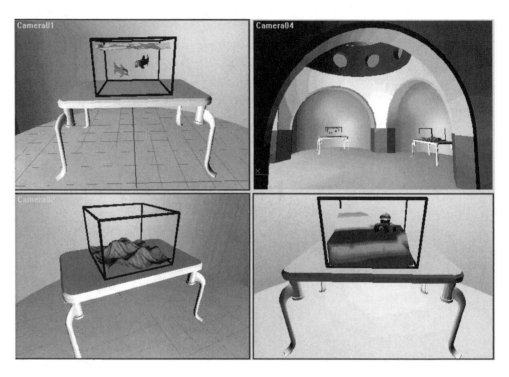

Museum Gallery project by Scott Onstott

Summary

In this chapter, you were introduced to the art of modeling and various methods of modeling polygonal meshes in max. You used modifiers to model from mesh primitives and splines. You used lofts, Booleans, and other max compound objects to construct complex models. You used the editable mesh and the new editable poly tools to model complex forms from simple primitives. You animated a surface by animating the parameters of modifiers. In the Hands-on max tutorial for this chapter, you will model a building with unusual architectural features and externally reference many of your smaller projects from this chapter into a larger project.

In the next chapter, you will learn about modeling in patches. You will learn max's Surface Tools and begin modeling Intrepid Explorer Jim for your ongoing animation project.

Patch Modeling

3ds max

Chapter 5

In this chapter, you will learn about Bezier patch surfaces and how to model them. You will look again at Bezier splines, the basis of patch surfaces, and the techniques for editing both splines and patches. You will learn different patch-modeling techniques: modeling directly in patches, converting from a loft object, and the popular Surface Tools method of modeling patches from splines. You will learn important pointers for successful modeling. Finally, you will model a detailed human head in Surface Tools, convert a patch model to polygons, and optimize a high-res model for a low-poly environment. Topics include:

- Spline-based organic modeling

- Bezier patches

- Bezier splines

- New patch and spline cage features

- Methods of patch modeling

- Spline cages and Surface Tools

- Modeling a human head using Surface Tools

- Optimizing a low-poly model

Spline-Based Organic Modeling

When modeling characters and other organic forms, you often need to create smoothly continuous surfaces that can be edited easily. You already learned one method of organic modeling in Chapter 4: subdivision of a polygonal surface using the MeshSmooth modifier with the NURMS option. The other two organic modeling methods are spline-based: Bezier patches and NURBS surfaces.

Since splines are a mathematical means of describing curves, they are especially well-suited to modeling smoothly continuous curved surfaces. You already took advantage of this characteristic of patches when you used patch grids in Chapter 4 to model a landscape with the Displace modifier and a sea surface with the Wave and Noise modifiers. Like Bezier splines, Bezier patches are defined by vertices and the tangents of the edges between the vertices. A patch grid was preferable to a polygonal plane for the landscape and sea surface models, because Bezier tangents describe actual curves while polygons approximate them with a series of small straight edges.

While Bezier patches involve the same mathematics as Bezier splines to describe curvature, patches describe an actual surface rather than just the lines between vertices. A patch can have either three sides (tri patches) or four sides (quad patches). Quad patches tend to be preferred when modeling smooth surfaces, except when a tri patch is necessary (to fill a hole in a model) or when it is helpful for modeling a particular detail. The vertices of patches can be coplanar (giving you Bezier handles that move together across the vertex) or corner (with independent handles).

Review of Spline Manipulation

Since patches are based on Bezier splines, it helps to develop a facility with Bezier splines before modeling in patches. You already used Bezier splines in Chapter 4 to build mesh objects with the Extrude and Lathe modifiers. Now let's review splines and the ways to manipulate them.

You may want to reread the "Editing a Bezier Spline" section in Chapter 4.

Splines are created in the Shapes tab of the Create panel. With the exception of the Create Line command, you have to collapse other shapes to an editable spline in order to access the sub-object levels of the spline. Splines have vertex, segment, and spline sub-object levels. The vertices of a spline are similar to the vertices of a mesh in the sense that they are single points in the coordinate space, but they differ in that spline vertices can define curvature between the vertices. A *segment* is the piece of a spline between two vertices. The spline sub-object is a connected set of segments. These segments have an order from the first vertex, marked with a special vertex icon, to the end of the spline. The vertices of a circle spline are shown in Figure 5.1. You can attach multiple splines with each as a sub-object "spline" of a spline object.

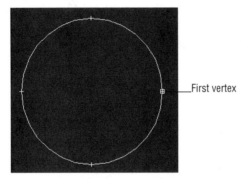

Figure 5.1 *Circle spline with first vertex marked*

Changing Vertex Types

Spline vertices come in four types: Corner, Smooth, Bezier, and Bezier Corner. Corner vertices are the most similar to mesh, because they have no curvature in or out of the vertex. Smooth vertices have smoothly continuous curvature in and out of the vertex, but you can't access the tangents to change the curvature. Bezier vertices have smoothly continuous curvature across a vertex, with handles of the tangents, called *Bezier handles*, staying locked to each other. Bezier Corner vertices have separate, independent Bezier handles defining curvature in and out of the vertex. Figure 5.2 shows the different vertex types. To switch between spline vertex types, right-click and choose the vertex type from the upper-left quad. To switch the type of multiple vertices, select them all, right-click one, and choose the new vertex type.

Adding Vertices

To add vertices to a spline, go to the Vertex sub-object level, click Refine, and click along the segment where you want to add a vertex. Refine will add a vertex at that point without changing the curvature of the segment.

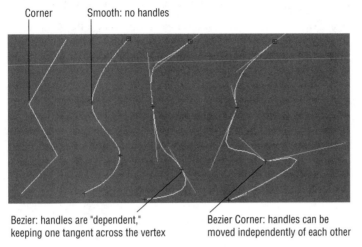

Corner   Smooth: no handles

Bezier: handles are "dependent,"   Bezier Corner: handles can be
keeping one tangent across the vertex   moved independently of each other

Figure 5.2 *Four types of vertices of Bezier splines*

Welding Vertices

Weld vertices when you want to connect vertices that are currently not connected. Of a selection of vertices, those within a specified weld threshold will be made into one vertex when you click Weld.

Max does not allow branching splines, so if you try to weld vertices of segments that are not connected in a linear fashion, you may get some unexpected results.

Fusing Vertices

Fuse vertices when you don't want them to be part of the same connected spline, but you do want them in exactly the same place. Note that this is different from welding, which makes the vertices part of the same connected spline.

Adding Segments

To create a new line segment in an existing spline, click the Create Line button and use it like the Line tool. Click it a second time or right-click in the viewport to turn it off.

Building and Editing Patch Surfaces

You have several options for modeling in patches in max. The traditional way is to start with a patch, subdivide it, add patches, and adjust their curvature. With patch and edge extrusion options, patch modeling in this way is easier than it used to be. Primitives, meshes, and loft objects can also be converted to patches and then edited in patch form. Max's Surface Tools provide an additional method of modeling in patches.

The old method of working with patches has been called "knitting a house." The advantage of learning this way of modeling is that it applies to most 3D applications, so you will be able to transfer your skills easily to a job that requires you to model in patches in a different program. The disadvantage is that it requires a great deal of patience and practice, but that's true of most things in 3D.

Creating Patches

Let's start by creating a patch and subdividing it.

1. Reset max (File ➜ Reset).

2. Click Quad Patch (Create ➜ Geometry ➜ Patch Grids ➜ Quad Patch).

3. Drag out a patch in the top viewport.

4. Right-click the patch and choose Convert To: Convert To Editable Patch.

You can also use the Edit Patch modifier, analogous to the Edit Mesh modifier for meshes. As with the other Edit modifiers, this modifier takes more memory than converting to an editable patch; use it when you want to retain access to the source object.

5. In the Modify panel, click the plus sign in front of Editable Patch in the stack. Click the word Patch in the stack to go to the Patch sub-object level. Select the patch object in the viewport. You can see that the whole object is selected; you have a single patch.

6. In the Geometry rollout, click the Subdivide button. Now select the patch object again. Only a quarter of the object is selected; there are now four patches.

You can subdivide patches at the Patch or Edge sub-object levels. Checking Propagate when subdividing propagates the subdivision through adjoining patches, all the way through the model. The only time you would not check Propagate is when you want to make a "hole" in your surface. If you have two patch edges adjacent to a single patch edge, the surfaces are discontinuous. You can then move the extra vertex of the side with two edges, shaping a hole in the surface of the object.

Shaping Patches

Adjusting patches to shape them is very similar to shaping Bezier splines:

1. Go to the Vertex sub-object level. Select the vertex in the center of the four patches.

2. In the front viewport, move the vertex upward to form a hill.

3. Move one of the Bezier handles on the vertex. Notice that the default is the Corner type with independent handles, like the Bezier Corner vertices of splines.

   There is a Bezier handle for each patch edge coming into a vertex.

4. Right-click the vertex and choose Coplanar from the shortcut menu.

5. Move one of the handles again. This time the handles are dependent, part of one tangent across the vertex.

 Like Bezier spline vertices, Coplanar patch vertices make it easier to create a smoothly continuous curve; Corner patch vertices make it easier to create a precise change in curvature, as do Bezier Corner spline vertices.

Soft Selection on Patches

 In max 4, you can also use soft selection on patch vertices, allowing for more organic sculpting of form:

1. Go to the Patch sub-object level and select all four patches in the viewport.

2. Click Subdivide twice, with Propagate checked.

3. Go to the Vertex sub-object level. Right-click the Modify panel and navigate to the Soft Selection rollout. Check Use Soft Selection. Select a single vertex in the viewport and spin up the Falloff. The surrounding vertices start turning yellow to indicate that a transform or modifier will be applied partially to these vertices.

 4. Click the Rotate tool and choose Use Selection Center from the transform center flyout. Rotate the vertices in the top viewport around Z. Soft selection gives you a very smooth swirling effect. Uncheck Use Soft Selection.

Ignore Backfacing Vertex Selection on Patches

Patches also now have an Ignore Backfacing check box so that you can select vertices only on the side of the model facing you. This makes it easier to adjust the vertices of a complex model.

Taking Advantage of Patch Surface Options

Patches are translated into polygons for rendering in the viewport and the renderer. You can adjust how many subdivisions are used to approximate the curvature of a patch. Part of the beauty of patch modeling is that you can set a different level of subdivision in the viewport, to keep a fast update while working, and a higher level in the renderer, to get very smooth curves:

1. Return to the object level. Navigate to the Surface section of the Geometry rollout of the Modify panel. Notice that there are separate settings for View Steps and Render Steps.

2. Right-click the label of the perspective viewport and choose Edged Faces from the shortcut menu. This shows us the effect of surface steps.

Edged Faces displays patch steps and polygons in viewports set to Smooth + Highlight.

3. Change View Steps to 15. Increasing the steps makes the patch surface much smoother, as can be seen in the before and after shots in Figure 5.3.

4. Change the View Steps to 5 and the Render Steps to 12.

5. Uncheck Show Interior Edges to show just the edges of the patches.

Adding New Patches

To continue to build in patches, you need to add patches at the edge level:

1. Go to the Edge sub-object level.

2. Select an outer edge of one of the patches on the perimeter of the surface on the right side.

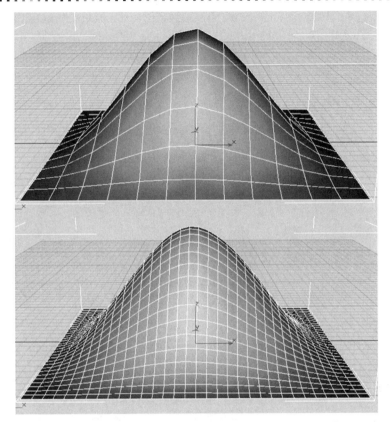

Figure 5.3 *Top, a patch surface with five steps; bottom, with 15 steps*

3. Click the Add Quad button in the Geometry rollout. Max adds a new four-sided patch to the selected edge.

Extruding Patches

Another way to add geometry to a patch surface is to extrude or bevel a patch, just as you extrude or bevel a polygon of a mesh:

1. Go to the Patch sub-object level. Select a patch on the surface and click Bevel.

2. In one of the viewports, drag upward on the patch to set the amount to extrude. Release the mouse and move inward to set the amount of the bevel. Click again to finish the bevel. Right-click in the viewport to turn off Bevel.

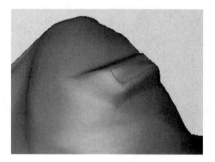

Extrude Edge on Patches

In max 4, extrusion is also enabled for the Edge sub-object level, giving you an alternative for adding a patch.

Shift-dragging an edge in the viewport extrudes a patch.

Attaching and Welding Patch Surfaces

As with mesh, spline, and NURBS objects, you can attach separate patches as sub-objects of one object. You can then "sew" the pieces together by welding vertices.

1. Return to the object level. Click the Mirror tool. In the Mirror dialog box, choose X for Mirror Axis, Copy for Clone Selection, and then spin up the Offset to create an object on the right side of the current object.

2. Select the first patch object. In the Geometry rollout, click Attach. Pick the mirrored patch object you just created. The new surface is now part of the same object as the first surface. Click the Attach button again to turn it off.

3. Go to the Vertex sub-object level. In the top viewport, region-select the four adjoining vertices. Turn the weld threshold spinner (next to the Weld button in the Geometry rollout) up to about 18 and click the Weld button. The four vertices should weld into two, connecting the surfaces of those vertices. If this doesn't work for you, undo and adjust the weld threshold until you find the value that will weld the adjacent vertices without welding the nonadjacent vertices. The surface is smoothly continuous across the welded seam.

Using Interior Vertices

The default Bezier handles control the curvature of the vertices on the corners of the patch. Additional control of the curvature is available through *interior vertices*. You can access these by choosing Manual Interior from the right-click shortcut menu on the Patch level, and then going to the Vertex sub-object level. Yellow squares appear that allow you to change the curvature of the interior of the patch.

Built-in Relax with Dial-in Smoothness

Patches now have the Relax modifier built into the editable patch data type. Let's see how it works:

1. Return to the object level. Navigate to the Surface Properties rollout. Check Relax.

Note that you can turn Relax off in the viewport independently.

2. Spin up the Relax value to 1.0. The patches get smoother.

3. Click up the Iterations one by one. The smoothing increases dramatically.

Be careful of increasing the Relax iterations. It is costly in terms of computer resources.

Converting a Loft Object to Patches

Another way of patch modeling is to get part of the way there through the techniques of mesh modeling you learned in Chapter 4, convert to patches, and continue to edit using the patch modeling methods above. All the mesh primitives can be converted to patches and, in an especially useful feature, loft objects can also be converted to patches. In this exercise, you will use a simple loft to get the beginnings of a whale model.

Shaping a Loft Using Scale Deformation

First, create a loft object to convert to patches:

1. Reset max.

2. Create a small circle in the left viewport (radius about 20).

3. Create a line across the top viewport, clicking once on the left and once on the right and then right-clicking to complete.

4. With the line selected, make a loft object (Create ➜ Geometry ➜ Compound Objects ➜ Loft).

5. Click Get Shape and then pick the circle.

6. Select your loft object and navigate to the Deformations rollout on the Modify panel. Click Scale.

7. In the Scale Deformation dialog box, click the Insert Corner Point button and click three places between the endpoints of the line in the dialog box.

8. Click the Move Control Point button to move the first point down. Notice that the loft is scaled proportionally as you do this.

9. Marquee-select the second and third points (of five total points) and right-click one of them. Choose Bezier Smooth from the shortcut menu.

10. Right-click the fourth point and choose Bezier Corner from the shortcut menu. Close the Scale Deformation dialog box.

11. Using the Move Control Point tool to move the points and the handles, create a graph that looks about like Figure 5.4.

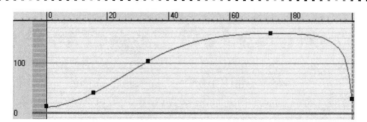

Figure 5.4 *Create a scale deformation like this one.*

Converting to Patches

When converting a mesh to patches, max assigns patches based on the number of faces of the mesh. To use patches efficiently, you want as few vertices as possible. Let's optimize the loft before converting it to patches.

1. With the loft still selected, navigate to the Skin Parameters rollout.

2. Change the Shape Steps and the Path Steps to 2. This reduces the complexity of the loft a great deal.

You can output a loft object directly to patches by checking Patch instead of Mesh under Output in the Surface Parameters rollout of the loft. The only problem with this is that it gives you no control over the number of patches you get. By adjusting the shape and path steps, outputting to mesh, and then applying an Edit Patch modifier, you get fairly precise control over the subdivision of the resulting patch object.

3. Apply an Edit Patch modifier to the loft. Since you are only using this as a starting point, it doesn't matter if the model is distorted at this point.

4. Go to the Vertex sub-object level. Move the vertices and their tangents to shape the object however you like.

5. Select the patches on the front undersides of the form, check Propagate, and click Subdivide. Do this again on patches that are where the fins should be extruded.

6. Holding the Ctrl key, select the patches where the fins should extend on either side.

Clicking Ignore Backfacing can help you avoid deselecting the patch on one side when you arc-rotate to the other side to select the other patch.

7. Click Bevel and extrude and bevel fins.

8. Drag the end patch of fin back in X in the front viewport.

9. To smooth things out when you are done, navigate to the Relax rollout, check Relax, and set the Relax Value to 1. Save your file as `loft_patch.max`.

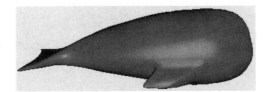

Using Surface Tools

Max Surface Tools allow you to model in patches by building a spline cage and applying a Surface modifier that creates a patch surface over the cage. The benefit of building a patch model this way is that it is relatively easy to make detailed edits to the spline cage that would be difficult to add to an established patch model. You can further model in patches or you can convert any patch surface to polygons and continue modeling from there.

Understanding a Spline Cage

To understand the principle behind Surface Tools, you need only consider the similarities between Bezier splines and Bezier patch surfaces. The vertices and tangents are very similar and are based on the same math. It makes sense, then, that you could draw an armature out of splines to define a patch surface. Unfortunately, max does not allow "branching" splines—splines that have more than two edges meeting at a single vertex—so a welded armature is impossible. How, then, can you build a "spline cage"?

How the Surface Modifier Works

Peter Watje, who designed Surface Tools, wrote the Surface modifier to operate on a single spline object with different spline sub-objects. If the spline vertices of a "cage" are coincident or within a specified threshold, Surface will create a patch surface with vertices corresponding to the meeting places of the splines. If a section of the spline cage has three sides, it will create a tri patch; if a section has four sides, it will create a quad patch; and if a section has more than four sides, it will leave a hole in the patch surface.

Consequently, in building a spline cage for the Surface modifier, you need to design your model with three or four spline vertices around a section that you want surfaced and five or more vertices around a section where you want a hole. Another consideration is that extra spline segments cause problems in the resultant surface, so you need to delete any duplicate spline segments. When moving vertices, it is important to remember that a "point" on the spline cage is not one welded vertex. It is often a number of coincident vertices that the Surface modifier will *interpret* as one vertex of the patch surface.

Manipulating a Spline Cage

When using Surface Tools to make a surface from a spline cage, it helps to know the techniques for making spline cages, adding to them, and manipulating them. All the techniques for manipulating splines discussed in Chapter 4 and in "Review of Spline Manipulation" earlier in this chapter apply to spline cages. Most often you will be using Refine to add vertices and manipulating the shape by changing vertex types and moving the Bezier handles.

How the CrossSection Modifier Works

The other modifier that makes up Surface Tools is the CrossSection modifier. CrossSection helps you build parts of your spline cage by taking splines and building a cage of splines around them, with the initial splines as cross-sections. You don't have to use the CrossSection modifier at all; the alternative is to create connecting lines manually between corresponding points of splines. CrossSection can save you some time, as you will see in the "Modeling a Human Head Using Surface Tools" tutorial later in this chapter.

CrossSection is easier to see than to describe in words, so let's look at it.

1. Reset max.

2. In the top viewport, create an ngon (Create ➜ Shapes ➜ NGon). An ngon is a shape of *n* number of sides. Set the sides to 8 and check Circular.

3. With the Move tool, Shift-drag the circle upward in the front viewport. Check Copy and 3 in the Clone dialog box and click OK. Scale down the second and last circle somewhat.

4. Select the bottom circle, right-click it, and choose Convert To: Convert To Editable Spline from the lower-right quad. In the Geometry rollout, click Attach. Pick the next shape above it and then the top shape, in that order. Click the Attach button again to turn it off.

It is very important, when applying the CrossSection modifier, to attach the splines in the logical order of cross-sections. Otherwise you will get chaos.

5. Apply a CrossSection modifier from the Patch/Spline Editing modifier set. Now you have a spline cage between the circle cross-sections.

CrossSection cannot be limited to a sub-object selection. A method for applying the CrossSection modifier to parts of a spline cage is explained in "Detaching Splines for the CrossSection Modifier" later in this chapter.

You just created a simple spline cage, so let's take a minute to see what it's made of:

1. Right-click the spline cage and collapse it to an editable spline again.

2. Go to the Spline sub-object level. Click different places on the "spline cage." Notice that the splines aren't really connected where they meet; they have vertices that are coincident at the meeting places.

It is important to remember that there is more than one coincident vertex at any branching point of a spline cage. These vertices need to be moved together and you do NOT want to weld them when prompted, because this may distort your splines. There is no way of making a completely welded spline cage, because splines can't branch.

Surfacing a Reference Spline Cage

Key
Concept

You want to be able to see the surface developing as you make changes to your spline cage. Especially when adjusting Bezier handles, where small changes can make the difference between a smooth surface and an unwanted crease, you need to see the surface respond interactively. To do this, you make a reference clone of the spline cage object and apply a Surface modifier to the reference. As you learned in Chapter 2, a reference has a one-way connection from the original object. Unlike a copy, any changes you make to the original will update in the reference. Unlike an instance, none of the changes you make to the reference (such as applying Surface) will apply to the original. This way you can edit the cage while watching the effect on the resulting surface as you work.

Some people like to model half the model as a spline cage, mirror it as a reference, and apply Surface to that, so the changes in the spline cage are seen in the other side of the model. This is not a good option if, like the author, you have even slight dyslexia so that the mirrored response of the reference surface is confusing. Some people like to keep the reference surface in the same place as the cage. In this case, you may want to view your reference surface in see-through mode by pressing Alt+X while it is selected. The exercises and tutorials in this chapter use the method of moving the reference surface to one side.

To make a reference surface:

1. Return to the object level. Shift-drag the spline cage to the right in the front viewport. In the Clone dialog box, choose Reference.

2. Select the new reference clone and apply a Surface modifier to it. Check Remove Interior Patches. If your surface is reversed, check Flip Normals, too. You have a continuous patch surface (based on your non-continuous splines)

except at the top and the bottom, where there are more than four vertices around the shape.

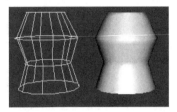

Creating Lines to Add Patches

To add a surface where there are too many vertices going around a shape, as in the spline cage you just built, use the Create Line tool within the editable spline tools:

1. Right-click the Snaps button, uncheck Grid Points, and check Vertex. Choose 3D Snap.

It's very important when working with Surface Tools to use vertex-only 3D Snap when creating new lines and to have snaps OFF when you are adjusting Bezier handles. Turn off snaps whenever you are done creating a line.

2. Zoom in to the model and create the lines shown in Figure 5.5. To create a line, watch for the cyan crosshair cursor that indicates a snap and click the first vertex, then, watching again for the cyan crosshair, click the second vertex. Right-click to end the line. This completes the top surface of this model. Now the Surface modifier will be able to make quad patches because each patch will have four vertices. Click the Create Line button again to turn it off. Turn off snaps.

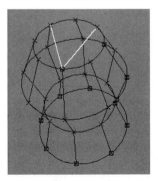

Figure 5.5 *Create these lines to add patches across the top of the model.*

Always right-click in the viewport or click the Create Line button again to turn off Create Line.

Detaching Splines for the CrossSection Modifier

Let's say that you have a spline cage and want to do the equivalent of extruding one of the areas defining a patch in the corresponding surface. If you just drag the vertices out, you won't get a crease in the model where you want it. If you clone the splines that border the area you want to "extrude," you also need all the splines defining the sides of the extrusion. You really want to use CrossSection, but CrossSection can't be limited to a sub-object selection, and CrossSection requires that the splines be attached in a logical order. If you applied CrossSection to your model, you would get a mess.

Let's look at an example using your spline cage:

1. Let's say you want to extrude just the area corresponding to the patch on the upper-left of the model. Click the Spline sub-object button and click around that area. Notice that you can't select that shape because the segments that form it are parts of other splines. To define the area you want to extrude, you need to select the segments that form it.

2. Go to the Segment sub-object level. Select the segments that surround this patch on the upper-left of the model. You will need to hold the Ctrl key and arc-rotate in order to get them, as shown in Figure 5.6.

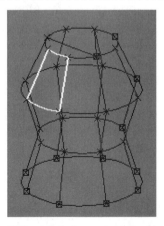

Figure 5.6 *Arc-rotate to select these segments.*

3. Toward the bottom of the Geometry rollout, check Copy and then click the Detach button. Click OK to detach a copy of the selected splines as a separate object (in the same place as the existing splines of your spline cage object). Return to the object level.

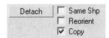

4. For CrossSection to work, the segments must be a single spline. Using Select By Name, select the Shape01 object that you just created. Go to the Vertex sub-object level and select all the vertices of the shape. With the weld threshold set to 1.0, click the Weld button. Go to the Spline sub-object level and select the shape; notice that you now have one spline.

5. Stay in the Spline sub-object level of the detached shape. Arc-rotate the front viewport so that the shape spline is perpendicular to the view. Choose the Screen coordinate system. Shift-drag the spline to the left along the screen X. Shift-drag the new spline to the left again along X.

6. Scale down the new spline sub-objects.

7. Return to the object level of Shape01. Apply a CrossSection modifier. You now have a second spline cage exactly in place to fit to the first one.

8. Before you attach the new spline cage to the first, you need to delete the extra spline that is a copy of the segments you originally attached. Collapse the Shape01 spline cage to an editable spline and go to the Spline sub-object level. Select the spline that is in the same place as the segments you detached and press Delete.

9. Now you are ready to attach the new area of the cage. Return to the object level and select the first spline cage. Click Attach and pick the Shape01 spline cage. Your model now includes the new spline cage extension. Right-click in the viewport to turn off Attach. Save your file as spline_cage.max.

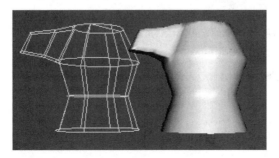

To model from here, you would adjust vertices and Bezier handles and continue to detach segments for using the CrossSection modifier, adding vertices and creating lines where needed. You will use this technique later in the chapter to model a human head.

Segment End Selection on Spline Cages

As you've learned, the points on a spline cage consist of more than one spline vertex. The best way to move the point, then, is to region-select the point in order to get all the coincident vertices. With the new Segment End option checked along with Area Selection, when you click on an end of a segment, you select the entire "knot" of vertices at that point in the spline cage. For the purposes of this chapter, you will still be told to region-select vertices—in order to get you accustomed to the idea of moving multiple vertices at the same point. As you grow more proficient with Surface Tools, you may want to take advantage of this new feature.

Soft Selection on Spline Cages

As with patches, splines also now have soft selection. If you check Use Soft Selection and spin up the Falloff, you can affect all the sub-objects in the surrounding area with a falloff.

Using Bind

An editable spline has a command called Bind that will bind a vertex to an edge. This allows the vertex to move with the edge whenever the edge moves.

Bind can also be used to get the Surface modifier to recognize what is essentially a five-sided patch. Beware of using this if you plan to convert to a mesh, and especially if you need to export the mesh to another program. When converted to meshes, five-sided patches create strange geometry that does not translate well to some formats, such as DXF.

Good Habits for Working with Surface Tools

Working with Surface Tools takes some getting used to. You'll pick up the habits that are most useful for Surface Tools one way or another; why not try these from the start rather than learning through painful experience?

Turn Weld Threshold to Zero   As mentioned earlier, you *don't* want to weld your vertices all the time. If you have any weld threshold set at the Vertex sub-object level, you will get an annoying prompt every time you move vertices together or create a line, asking you if you want to weld coincident endpoints. If you get this, click No. To avoid getting this message all the time, turn the weld threshold to zero until you actually want to weld. The only time you need to turn the weld threshold up is when you want to make whole splines from detached segments in order to use the CrossSection modifier.

When prompted whether to weld coincident endpoints, some people like to try Yes, see if it's what they want, and Undo if it's not. They do this because welding may result in a smoother surface. This is not recommended for beginning Surface Tools modelers. If you're not experienced in what to look for, you may accidentally weld vertices that completely screw up your model and may not notice it until you're much further along. You can always weld the coincident vertices of a specific point in the cage to see if this helps you. This gives you more control over how and where the welding happens.

Region-Select Vertices   While region selection is not entirely necessary with the new Segment End feature combined with Area Selection, it is a good habit to region-select vertices when you move them, in order to get all the coincident vertices. It also helps to remind you of what you're in fact dealing with: coincident vertices of several splines, rather than the welded point of an armature. You also need to region-select when fusing adjacent vertices.

Turn Off Axis Constraints   When you are moving vertices around, you don't want the snap settings to be using the axis constraints. Right-click the 3D Snap button and uncheck Use Axis Constraints on the Options tab.

Use Vertex 3D Snap when Needed and Then *Turn Snaps Off*   When creating a new line between two existing vertices or to move a vertex to be coincident with another vertex, you want 3D Snap ON and the snap settings to be set to Vertex. (Right-click the 3D Snap button, uncheck Gridpoints, and check Vertex.) To adjust Bezier handles, move points in the spline cage to a place other than an existing vertex, or draw a new spline with new vertices, make sure snaps are OFF. Pressing S toggles between snaps on and snaps off.

When your vertices still aren't coincident, even after using Vertex Snap, you need to fuse them.

Use Selection Center to Scale Vertices   You can scale Bezier vertices together the same way as you would with polygonal vertices in an editable mesh. The trick is that you have to choose Use Selection Center from the Use Center flyout in order to scale the vertices rather than the size of the Bezier handles.

Hide and Unhide Vertices   To prevent selection of the wrong vertices, select the vertices that you are not working with and click Hide in the Modify tab at the Vertex level. Click Unhide All when you want to work on a new section.

Turn On Vertex Ticks   If you want to be able to see your vertices even when they're not selected, turn on Vertex Ticks in the Display tab or Object Properties.

Save Versions Often   To avoid losing a lot of work, save a new version of your file fairly often. At the end of the day, you can keep the most recent versions and delete all those you no longer need.

Troubleshooting when Your Surface Disappears

Sometimes while working with Surface Tools, your surface, or part of it, will disappear. Don't panic (yet). Here are some possible reasons and solutions.

Redraw the Screen   It could be just a display problem. Press the number 1 to redraw the viewport, zoom in a little, or reopen the file.

Adjust the Threshold   If you just applied a Surface modifier and the surface or part of the surface isn't showing, try adjusting the Threshold in the Parameters rollout for the Surface modifier. Sometimes, for no apparent reason, the Surface modifier will be finicky about the threshold. Small increments can make a difference, as in the example shown in Figure 5.7.

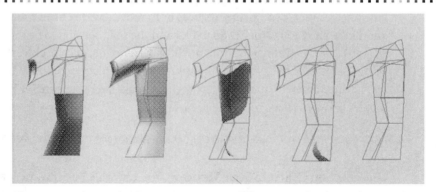

Figure 5.7 *Identical spline cages can get different results depending on the Surface threshold.*

Check Normals   As you've learned, the normal of a surface is the vector pointing outward from it that defines which side of a surface is facing and which is its back. By default, only the facing side is shaded. In the process of building your spline cage, the corresponding surface will interpret which side is the facing one differently as you go along. Try checking or unchecking Flip Normals (on the Surface modifier of the reference), and arc-rotate until you can see the other side of the surface. If you're still unsure, apply a material with the 2-Sided option checked in order to see both sides of the surface in the viewport.

Check the Number of Sides   You will only get a surface for a section of the spline cage bounded by three or four sides. Check to see whether the area that is missing a surface includes more than four points of the cage.

Fuse Vertices   Sometimes, even when using Vertex Snap, vertices aren't really coincident. The Fuse button within the editable spline commands makes selected vertices coincident without welding them together. If a section of your surface has three or four sides and still isn't showing a surface, region-select each of the points on the spline cage and click Fuse to make the vertices at that point coincident. Fuse moves the selected vertices to their average position.

Applying Surface Tools to a Complex Model

Working with Surface Tools on a complex project involves knowing the nature of what you are working with and applying these different techniques as appropriate.

In the "Modeling a Human Head Using Surface Tools" tutorial later in this chapter, the spline cage has already been planned for you according to the design of Jason Wiener and Marc Abraham. When designing your own model, you will have a lot more thinking to do. Map out your general strategy in your mind, before you even sit down at the computer. You want to put more vertices where you need more detailed definition. You want mostly quad patches in your result, so you want the corresponding areas of the spline cage to be defined by four points or "knots" in the spline cage.

Hands-on max: Modeling a Human Head Using Surface Tools

Now let's try a complex model: the human head. In particular, let's model the head of Intrepid Explorer Jim of our storyboard in Chapter 1.

The process for modeling the human form in Surface Tools is in part well-planned design and in part the intuitive, moment-to-moment feedback of your artistic eye. As mentioned before, you can learn the intuitive artistic skills as well as the technical ones. For example, artists often use the rough approximation that the body is seven or eight heads tall. This is why it is often best to begin modeling with the head. In this book, you will get the basic structure for Surface Tools modeling; making the model look expressively human is a matter for your own eye.

One good resource for modeling the human figure is An Atlas of Anatomy for Artists, *3rd ed., by Fritz Schider (Dover Publications, 1981).*

At the risk of belaboring the point, it really helps to be savvy with the tools you will be using, because it's impossible for a tutorial to describe every possible situation you might come across. If you haven't really grokked the concept of a spline cage and its reference surface, or if you're unsure of why you might want snaps on or off, for example, it's worth reviewing the preceding sections before continuing.

Creating the 2D Face Template with Splines

The production artist's slogan is "keep it simple." In this spirit, one of the best approaches to building a complex model of the human head is to start with a simple flat template of splines. To make a face template:

1. In the front viewport, create four rectangles to approximate half a head, nose, and mouth, and an eye (Create ➜ Geometry ➜ Shapes ➜ Rectangle).

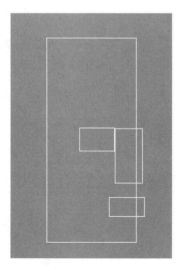

2. Right-click each rectangle and convert it to an editable spline.

3. For each rectangle, go to the Vertex sub-object level and click Refine. Refine the splines with new vertices that will prepare for lines to connect the inner geometry of the face. See Figure 5.8 for the vertices to add to each rectangle. Remember that you have to go back to the object level in order to switch to a different rectangle.

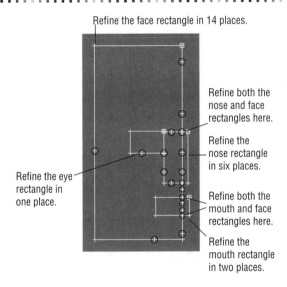

Refine the face rectangle in 14 places.

Refine both the nose and face rectangles here.

Refine the nose rectangle in six places.

Refine the eye rectangle in one place.

Refine both the mouth and face rectangles here.

Refine the mouth rectangle in two places.

Figure 5.8 *Refine rectangles of the face with these vertices.*

4. For each rectangle, go to the Vertex sub-object level, select all the vertices, right-click one of the vertices, and choose Corner. (Again, you have to go back to the object level between rectangles.)

5. In the nose and mouth rectangles, go to the Segment sub-object level and delete extra or redundant lines. See Figure 5.9 for the segments to delete.

6. Select the face rectangle. In the Geometry rollout, click Attach, and select the other three rectangles. Click Attach again to turn the button off. Rename the object face01.

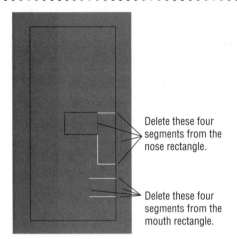

Delete these four segments from the nose rectangle.

Delete these four segments from the mouth rectangle.

Figure 5.9 *Delete these segments from the nose and mouth rectangles.*

7. Go to the Vertex sub-object level, region-select each of the seven places where there is more than one coincident vertex, and click Fuse for each set. Select the two vertices on the left side of the mouth and click Fuse.

8. Make sure your snap settings have only Vertex checked. (Right-click the Snap button and uncheck all except Vertex.) Turn on snaps. In the Geometry rollout of the Modify panel, click Create Line. Create nine lines connecting the eyes, the nose, the side of the chin, the corner of the mouth, and the top lip line, as shown in Figure 5.10.

PolyConnect should be unchecked when you use the Create Line command.

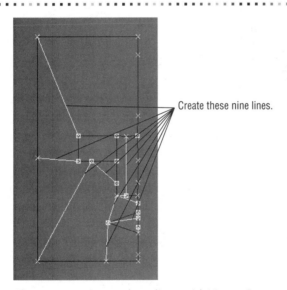

Create these nine lines.

Figure 5.10 *Create these lines with Vertex Snap on.*

9. Refine the new lines as shown in Figure 5.11. These vertices are added in order to add curvature of the face, the lower lip, and cross geometry of the nose.

10. With Vertex Snap on, create lines connecting these new vertices to the geometry of the face. These vertices add the lines that will be the face curves, contours between the eye and the chin and nose, the top of the lower lip, the cross contours of the nose, and contours of the cheek, as shown in Figure 5.12. When you are done, turn off snaps.

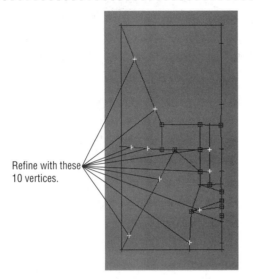

Refine with these 10 vertices.

Figure 5.11 *Refine the new lines with new vertices in these places.*

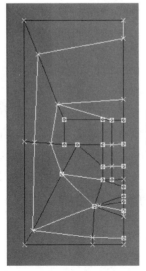

Create the 17 line segments shown in white.

Figure 5.12 *Create these lines with Vertex Snap on.*

11. Select all the vertices, right-click, and choose Corner.

12. Still working only in the two dimensions of the front viewport, region-select points of the developing spline cage and move them to look more like a face, as shown in Figure 5.13. How the face should look depends on the particular face you are modeling, of course. Save your work as Face01.max.

Figure 5.13 *Region-select vertices and move them to look more like the contours of a face.*

Adding the Third Dimension to the Template

Now that you have a 2D spline template that looks something like a face, you can start moving the vertices to their appropriate positions in the World Y-axis:

1. In the front view, region-select each of the four vertices between the endpoints of the outermost curve of the face (holding the Ctrl key to add to the selection). Switch to a left view and pull the vertices back. Region-select the vertices of the inner curves of the face and pull those back. Pull back the corners of the

eye and mouth. Pull forward the nose, lips, brow, and chin, depending on the features of the face you are modeling. Save your work as Face02.max.

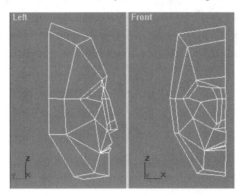

2. Now you need to be able to see the surface of the face you are building so you can adjust its curvature. Go to the object level and Shift-drag your face spline to the right. Choose Reference from the Clone dialog box.

3. Select the reference clone and apply a Surface modifier to it from the Patch/Spline Editing modifier set. Check Remove Interior Patches. You might also need to check Flip Normals if your surface is facing the wrong way. Adjust the threshold until you can see your surface (a value of .01 often works; if not, try .025 or .001). How many steps you use depends on whether you are making a high-poly or low-poly model. High-poly would use 5 to 10 steps; low-poly would use 0 to 2 steps. For now, use 5 steps so you can see the smooth contours of the face.

4. Go to the Vertex sub-object level. Select all the vertices of the face, right-click, and choose Bezier Corner. In the front view, move the vertices (region-selecting) and Bezier handles to shape and sculpt the face as you wish. This step and the next three steps are very much intuitive and according to your own artistic vision. Work on the three main curves of the face, shown in Figure 5.14, first. Then work on the five radiating contours. Then shape the eye, the nose, and the lips. Figure 5.15 provides a reference for how your model might look after shaping the contours in the front view.

If you have Area Selection checked and all your coincident vertices selected, you can click the Cycle button to cycle through the coincident vertices and shape the one you want. If Area Selection is unchecked, you will cycle through all the vertices of the spline (including the hidden vertices).

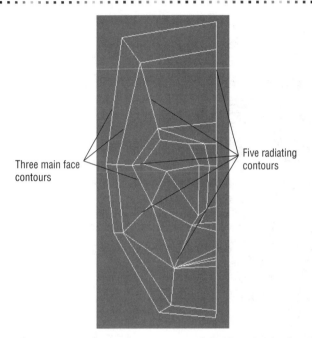

Three main face contours

Five radiating contours

Figure 5.14 *Shape the contours of the face in the front view.*

5. In the left view, move vertices (region-selecting) and Bezier handles to adjust the face contours to look correct in the left view. Figure 5.15 provides a reference for how your model might look after shaping the contours in the left view.

When moving vertices, especially when making subtle adjustments, it helps to switch to Corner type first, and then switch back to Bezier Corner to adjust the handles. Although moving a Bezier tangent of one vertex should not affect those of adjacent vertices, sometimes it will.

6. In the top view, move vertices (region-selecting) and Bezier handles to adjust the face contours to look correct in the top view. Figure 5.15 provides a reference for how your model might look after shaping the contours in the top view.

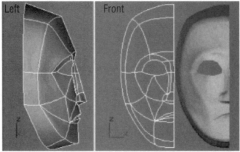

Model shaped in front view

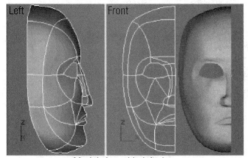

Model shaped in left view

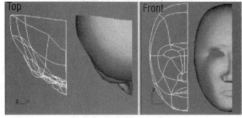

Model shaped in top view

Figure 5.15 *Contours of the face after being shaped in the front, then the left, then the top view*

You can also check Segment End and Area Select in the Selection rollout to move all the vertices at a certain place in the spline cage together. For the purposes of reminding you that there is more than one vertex at each point, these instructions will tell you to region-select each vertex.

7. Repeat steps 4 through 6, fine-tuning the form. Save your file as Face03.max.

When shaping your form, it helps a great deal to understand how spline tangents work. If you have a problematic crease, the problem is generally not with the line of the crease itself, but with the edges that are perpendicular to that crease. The flow of those edges needs to be continuous across the vertices. Adjust the Bezier handles of the vertices of those edges.

Adding a Nostril

Now that you have modeled the three-dimensional form of a face, you are ready to start adding the refinements of the facial features: nostrils, the interior of the mouth, and an eyelid. To add the nostrils:

1. Zoom in exceedingly close to the nose and add a single vertex to the line at the bottom of the nose. Notice that you now have a hole in the reference surface, because there are now five vertices around the bottom of the nose.

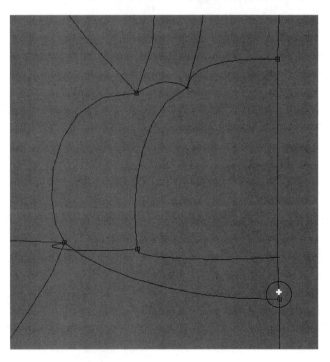

While working on the nostrils, you will need to use the front and bottom (press B) views as well as a view at an angle between these by arc-rotating the front view up.

2. Go to the Segment sub-object level. Holding the Ctrl key, select the five segments that make up the bottom of the nose. Use the Select tool rather than the Move tool, in order to not move the segments at all. Click Detach (without checking Copy). You will lose part of your surface for a while.

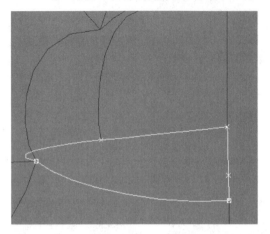

3. Return to the object level, select the new nose spline you just detached, and go to the Vertex sub-object level. Select all the vertices, set Weld Threshold to .003m, and click Weld to make one spline to use for the CrossSection modifier. Check the vertex selection in the Selection rollout before you click Weld. Select all the vertices again afterward, and check it again. The number of vertices should read "5 vertices selected" when you are done. Set Weld Threshold back to 0.

4. Return to the object level. Set the Transform Center to Use Selection Center. Holding the Shift key to make a clone, scale the nose spline down to the nostril size of your model (to about 40%). Check Copy in the Clone dialog box.

5. Select the original nose spline (the larger one). Click Attach and choose the nostril spline. Click Attach again to turn it off.

6. Apply a CrossSection modifier from the Patch/Spline Editing modifier set.

7. Select the face spline and click Attach. Select the nose spline. The surface of the nose should return to the reference clone, this time with a nostril hole. Click Attach again to turn it off.

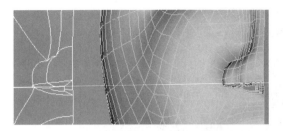

8. Go to the Vertex sub-object level. Turn on Vertex Snap. Add a spline across the center of the nostril. Turn off snaps.

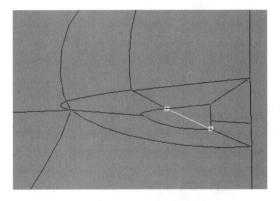

9. Add a vertex to the center of this new line.

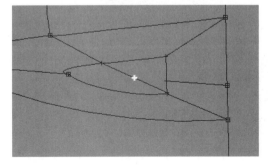

10. Turn on Vertex 3D Snap and create two lines to connect the inside of the nostril to the center vertex. Turn off snaps.

Click No if prompted to weld vertices.

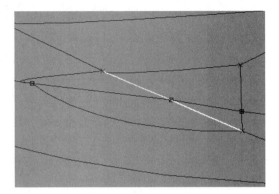

11. Select the vertex at the center of the nostril. From the side view, pull it up so that a nostril cavity appears in the reference clone. Adjust as needed to be sure it does not poke through the face.

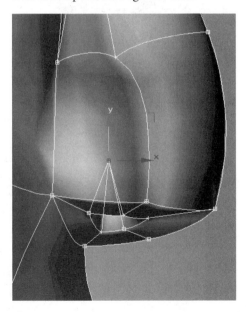

12. Adjust the small lines connecting the bottom of the nose to the nostril to make a rounded shape. Don't touch the lines along the center line of face. Save your work as Face04.max.

If you lose your surface at times other than when you have detached splines, remember to try the ideas in "Troubleshooting When Your Surface Disappears" earlier in this chapter.

Adding the Mouth

Continue to use the same methods to add a mouth to the face:

1. Add a vertex to the vertical line connecting the top and bottom of the mouth.

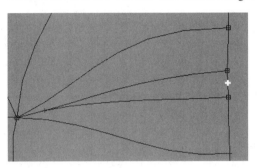

2. Turn on Vertex 3D Snap. Create a line from the new vertex to the side corner of the mouth. Turn off snaps.

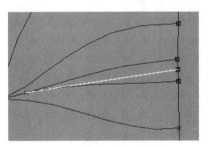

3. Select the vertex you added between the top and the bottom of the mouth. From the side view, pull it back so that a mouth cavity appears in the reference clone. Adjust Bezier curve handles to create a more curved mouth. Save your file as Face05.max.

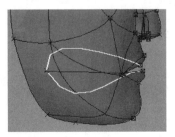

Adding an Eye

The process for building the eyelid is the same as that for the nostril, except there is no interior to build:

1. Return to the object level. Create a sphere to act as a placeholder for the eyeball. Remember that eyeballs are very big behind the skin and skull. The top should reach to the level of the eyebrow, the bottom halfway down the nose. Copy the sphere for the reference surface. Try to place the second sphere in the same place relative to the surface face as the original is to the spline face.

2. Select the face spline cage. Go to the Vertex sub-object level. Adjust the Bezier handles of the eye vertices so that the six vertices and the lines connecting them fit snugly around the eye sphere without the sphere passing through the skin.

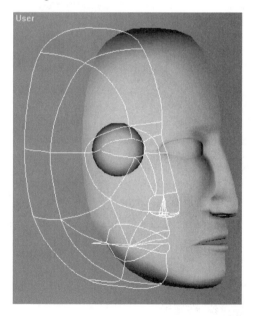

3. Go to the Segment sub-object level. Select the five segments around the eye and click Detach. You will lose part of your surface.

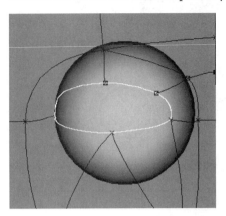

4. Return to the object level. Select the new eye spline. This is the outer edge of the eyelid. Go to the Vertex sub-object level, select all the vertices, turn up the weld threshold a little, and click Weld.

5. Return to the object level. With the Use Selection Center transform center active, hold the Shift key and non-uniform-scale in XY in the front viewport down to about 60% of the original. Choose Copy from the Clone dialog box. This is the inner edge of the eyelid.

6. Select the outer eye shape, click Attach, and select the inner eye shape.

7. Apply the CrossSection modifier to the combined eye shapes.

8. Select the face spline cage, click Attach, and pick the new eyelid spline. Click Attach again to turn it off.

9. Go to the Vertex sub-object level. Adjust the vertices and their Bezier handles to shape the eyelid around the eyeball.

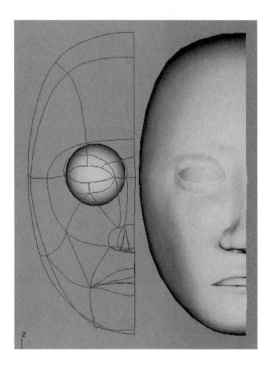

10. Go to the object level and select the reference surface and its eyeball. Click the Mirror tool. Choose X axis and Reference and spin up the Offset until the new reference is lined up along the centerline. Click OK.

11. Add a Relax modifier to the first reference surface to smooth it more.

12. Make adjustments to the eyes and nose vertices, watching the changes in the whole face. Don't worry about the crease down the center of the face. That will be eliminated later. Save your file as Face06.max.

Adding the Back of the Head

Now you are ready to build the back of the head:

1. In the left view, create a circle (Create ➜ Shapes ➜ Circle). The diameter should be about twice the width, from the side, of the head.

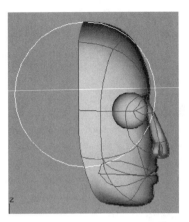

2. Right-click the circle and choose Convert To: Convert To Editable Spline. Choose Edit ➜ Clone and choose 1 and Copy.

3. Press A to turn on Angle Snap. Rotate the spline 90° so that it is going around the head like a headband. Shift-drag this spline down in the left viewport, and choose 2 and Copy.

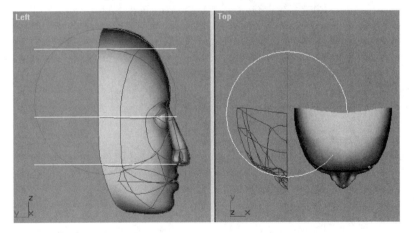

4. Scale the lower two splines so that they fit the head.

5. Select the original circle, click Attach, and pick the other three circles. Go to the Vertex sub-object level and adjust the vertices so that they better fit the form of the head you are modeling.

6. Select each of the three pairs of vertices of the back of the head that should be coincident and click Fuse after each. (Don't select them all and fuse all of them at once.)

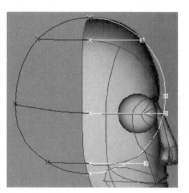

7. Go to the Segment sub-object level. Holding the Ctrl key, select the segments that extend beyond the back half of the head and delete them.

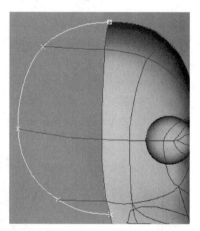

8. Return to the object level and select the face spline cage. Click Attach and pick the back of the head spline.

9. Go to the Vertex sub-object level. At each of the four places where the back of the head attaches to the face (the top of the head on the center line, and each of the three side connections), region-select the vertices and click Fuse.

10. Adjust the Bezier handles of the back of the head to make a smoother shape. Watch the changes in your reference clone. Save your file as Head01.max.

Preparing the Head for the Ear

In order to add an ear, you need to give your head model a place for it to attach:

1. Go to the Segment sub-object level. Select the four segments that form the back curve of the head and click Detach. You will lose the surface of the back of the head.

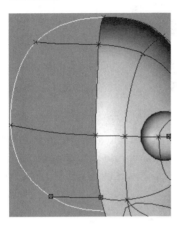

2. Return to the object level. Select the new spline. Go to the Hierarchy panel and turn on Affect Pivot Only. In the top viewport, move the pivot of the spline so that it is at the bottom of the spline as seen in the top viewport.

3. Press A to turn on Angle Snap. Holding the Shift key, rotate it 65° around Z in the top view, toward the middle of the head. Turn off snaps.

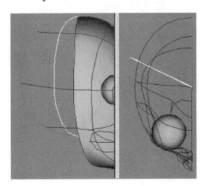

4. Select the new spline and go to the Vertex sub-object level. Adjust the Bezier handles to more closely fit the curve of the head.

5. Return to the object level and select the main body of the head. Add vertices where the new spline crosses the head.

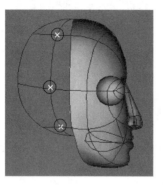

6. Return to the object level, click Attach, and attach the two head curves. At each of the four places where the new spline is to connect to the rest of the spline cage, region-select the vertices and click Fuse. This should restore the surface to the back of the head.

Adding the Neck

Now that you have the head topology complete, you are ready to add the neck:

1. In the top viewport, create a circle spline the size of the neck. In the left view, rotate it about 10° around Z. Right-click it and convert it to an editable spline.

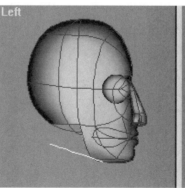
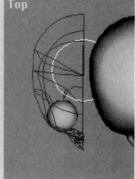

2. Go to the Vertex sub-object level. In the top view, add a vertex to the lower-left quadrant of the circle.

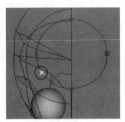

3. Go to the Segment sub-object level. Select and delete the two segments that form the right half of the circle and the segment on the lower part of the lower-left quadrant, leaving only the two segments in the upper-left.

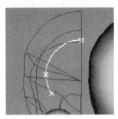

4. Return to the object level. Select the face spline cage, click Attach, and pick the neck spline. Click Attach again to turn it off.

5. Go to the Vertex sub-object level. Turn on Vertex 3D Snap. In the top view, create a line connecting the lower vertex of the new spline to the bottom of the chin.

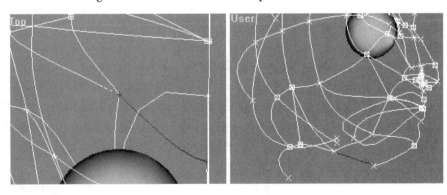

6. Arc-rotate to a user view where you can see the back of the head. Create a line from the back of the bottom of the head to the back of the neck. In the left viewport, create a line from the vertex on the side of the head to the vertex you just connected to the bottom of the chin. Turn off Create Line. Turn off snaps.

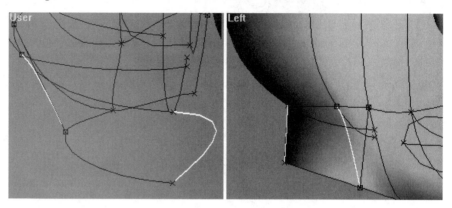

 Small changes (creating a new line, fusing vertices) in the spline cage can result in the surface being reversed. Try flipping normals on the reference surface if it seems to be inside out or invisible.

7. For the three connection points on the spline cage where the new splines intersect the rest of the head, region-select the vertices and click Fuse.

8. Adjust the Bezier handles of the new vertices to shape the neck. Save your file as Head02.max.

Adding an Ear

Now it will be easier to see what you are doing when you add an ear:

1. In the front view, create a rectangle about the size of an ear (Create → Shapes → Rectangle). Right-click it and convert it to an editable spline. While it is still selected, right-click it again and choose Hide Unselected from the upper quad.

2. Go to the Vertex sub-object level and adjust the Bezier handles to create the shape of the auricle of the ear.

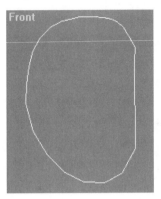

3. Return to the object level. Holding the Shift key, scale down the shape. Choose 1 and Copy in the Clone dialog box. Repeat this twice more so you have four concentric ear shapes.

4. Select the first outside shape, click Attach, and pick each interior shape in order toward the center. The order is significant for using CrossSection. Apply the CrossSection modifier. Collapse the spline to an editable spline.

5. Go to the Segment sub-object level. Select and delete the six segments shown in Figure 5.16.

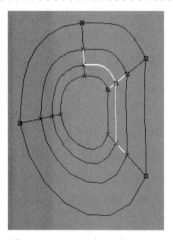

Figure 5.16 *Delete these segments.*

6. Go to the Vertex sub-object level. Region-select each pair of points on the spline cage circled in Figure 5.17. Press Fuse after each.

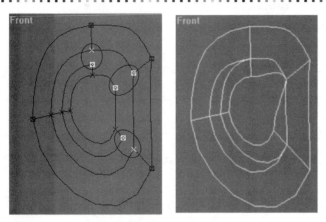

Figure 5.17 *Region-select and fuse each of the pairs of points circled on the left to create the arrangement shown on the right.*

7. Add a vertex to the area of the lobe where the little flap that covers the hole of the ear attaches to the rest of the ear on the surface of the head.

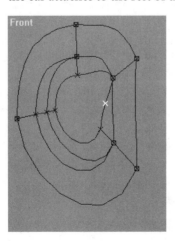

8. Turn on Vertex 3D Snap and create a line from the new vertex to the other side of the ear. Turn off snaps.

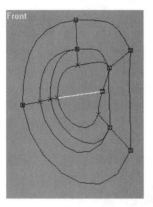

9. Return to the object level. Holding the Shift key, move the ear spline to the right. Choose 1 and Reference from the Clone dialog box. Select the new reference spline, apply the Surface modifier to it, and check Remove Interior Patches. You should be able to see the surface of the ear on the reference clone.

10. Select the original ear spline cage. Go to the Vertex sub-object level. In the front viewport, adjust the Bezier handles to shape the ear according to the model you are making. Go to the left viewport and adjust the Bezier handles from that view.

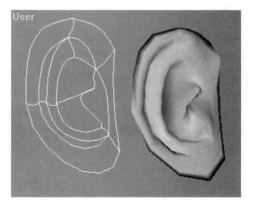

11. Return to the object level. Delete the reference clone of the ear. Press A to turn on Angle Snap. In the top viewport, rotate –80° around Z. In the front viewport, rotate 10° around Z. Press A to turn off snaps.

12. Press 5, select all your other objects, and click Unhide. Position the ear spline next to the face spline and rotate as necessary.

13. With the ear spline selected, go to the Segment sub-object level. In the left viewport, delete the line at the front of the ear.

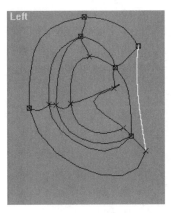

14. Return to the object level. Select the face spline, click Attach, and pick the ear spline. Click Attach to turn it off.

15. Go to the Vertex sub-object level. Arc-rotate and zoom in so that you can see the points where the ear needs to attach. Turn on Vertex 3D Snap and create two lines to connect the back corners of the ear to the head. Turn off snaps.

16. For each of the attachment points of the ear to the head, region-select the vertices and click Fuse. Save your file as Head03.max.

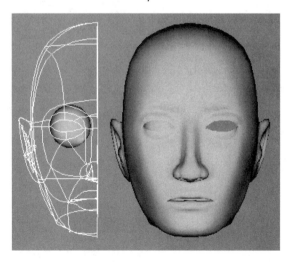

Adding Hair

One way of modeling hair is to include it as part of the geometry of the model and texture-map it with detail. Whether this works for you depends on the type of hair you are modeling and your final output. To add hair this way to the Intrepid Explorer Jim model:

1. Go to the Segment sub-object level. Select all the segments that cover the back of the head up to and including the hairline. Click Detach. You will lose the surface on the back of the reference head model.

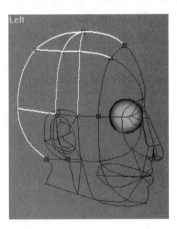

2. Return to the object level. Shift-drag the hairline spline a little bit further from the face and a little higher, to represent the top of the hair. Choose 1 and Copy from the Clone dialog box. Hide this new outer spline.

3. Select the original hairline spline and go to the Segment sub-object level. Select the 12 segments that are not part of the hairline (all the ones that will be inside the hair area when the two hair splines are attached) and delete them.

4. Unhide the outer hairline spline. Select the inner hair line, click Attach, and pick the outer hair spline. Click Attach to turn it off.

5. Go to the Vertex sub-object level. Turn on Vertex 3D Snap. Create seven lines to connect the top of the hair and the hairline. Turn off snaps.

6. Return to the object level, select the face spline, click Attach, and pick the hair spline. Click Attach to turn it off.

7. Go to the Vertex sub-object level and adjust the Bezier handles of the hair curves to shape the hair according to your model. Pay attention to the back of the head and the sideburns. Exit the sub-object level when done. Save your file as Head04.max.

Mirror and Merge the Other Side of Head

With half the head modeled, all you need to do is mirror it to make the other half and fuse the seams:

1. Delete the extra reference clone of your spline (face03). Move the remaining reference surface and its eyeball to the right to get it out of the way. Hide the reference surface and its eyeball.

2. With the front view active, mirror the face spline cage along X, choose Copy, and spin up the Offset to meet with the left side.

3. Select the new right half of the face. Go to the Segment sub-object level and select the 21 segments along the centerline of the face. Press Delete.

If you use Window selection rather than Crossing, you can just drag a marquee around the centerline of the model. Check in the Selection rollout to make sure you have 21 segments selected.

4. Return to the object level. Select the original left half of the face spline and attach the right half. Unhide the reference surface.

5. Go to the Vertex sub-object level. At each of the 22 points on the center line where the two halves of the face meet (including the inside of the mouth), region-select and click Fuse. You will have to arc-rotate to get the exact points on the spline cage without getting other points as well.

6. Return to the object level. Apply a Relax modifier to the head with a relax value of 0.5 and 1 iteration. Save your file as Head05.max.

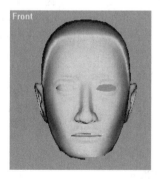

Intrepid Explorer Jim project by Jason Winter

The techniques you used for modeling the hat and the head are the same ones used for modeling the rest of the body. If you would like to look at the steps used to complete the Intrepid Explorer Jim model, files with the steps for the rest of the body are in the body_model_steps.max *file in the CD files for this chapter. The file contains a copy of the model at each step, and the models are named with the procedure of that step.* Hat_steps.max *shows the steps for modeling the hat,* cave_steps.max *the steps for modeling the cave, and* torch_steps.max *the steps for modeling the torch.*

If you want to duplicate the exact model used in later steps, you need to non-uniform-scale the head down before modeling the body. Jason found that he wanted a squatter head than he ended up with. It's best to apply a Reset XForm after doing this, to strip the scaling information out of the transforms.

As described in Chapter 2, Reset XForm is a vitally important utility. It is a good habit to use it when you've scaled or rotated an object while modeling. (Scaling or rotating on a sub-object level is fine; it's the transforms of the object that cause problems.) It won't make much difference while you are modeling, but when you animate, leftover transforms can completely screw up your animation. Sometimes it helps to also collapse the stack after resetting XForm.

Hands-on max: Optimizing a Low-Poly Model

Key Concept

If your model is for real-time games or Web 3D, you need to make it low-poly. The process of making a high-poly model lower poly is called *optimizing*. What you can get away with depends on the particular needs of your output, your model, and your animation. Optimizing is a process of making careful choices as to what geometry is absolutely necessary to preserve the distinguishing features of the character. Generally, try to get below a thousand polygons for most online applications, with half the polygons going to the body and half to the head.

In games, it is typical for arms and legs to have five sides with no subdivision between joints. Each joint, however, needs two subdivisions. A low-poly character will often have a well-textured mitten hand rather than five full fingers. Eyelids are often reduced to eight sides and the eyes are built in. The ears and nostrils can be flattened, with the geometry implied by a texture map. Although you could easily build a less-detailed model in the first place, many gaming companies do build high-res versions of characters for prerendered cinematics or to swap in for close-ups.

To make a patch model low-poly, you need to first convert from patches to polygons and then manually remove polygons to keep them where you need definition in the model and get rid of them where you don't need them.

The Optimize modifier is better for geometric structures than for organics. It gives you no control of where to keep polygons and where to eliminate them. It tends to make the organic models bland and lopsided. The new MultiRes modifier gives you more control, but it is still good to know the manual techniques for controlling precisely where polygons are removed. Whether these polygon reduction modifiers work for your model depends on the nature of the model and the limitations of your output.

Converting a Patch Surface to a Low-Poly Mesh

To convert the Intrepid Explorer Jim model to a lower-poly mesh:

1. Open `Intrepid_Explorer_Jim01.max` in the CD files for this chapter.

2. Notice that the body and head models are separate. This is in order to assign more patch steps to the head than to the body, because the facial features need more definition. Check that the Patch Steps of the Surface modifier of the head has been set to 2, while the Patch Steps of the body has been set to 1. (You will have to go to the Surface modifier in the stack for the head to see the Patch Steps.)

3. Collapse each object to an editable mesh. Save as `Intrepid_Explorer_Jim02.max`.

Manual Polygon Reduction

Using a low number of Patch Steps before converting is one form of optimizing. To optimize further, you need to manually weld selected vertices. Figure 5.18 shows how welding two neighboring vertices changes the polygon count of a surface from 12 to 10.

If you turn on the plug-in keyboard shortcuts button, the L key welds selected vertices.

Weld these two vertices.

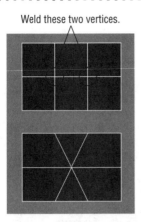

Figure 5.18 *Welding the two central vertices reduces this area by two polygons.*

The procedure for manual polygon reduction is to go through your model looking for places where you can get away with less resolution. You first perform a sequence of welds. For example, if you wanted to reduce the polygons on just the top section of the form shown in Figure 5.19, first weld the inner four vertices to one vertex. Then weld each pair of extra vertices on the side to a single vertex. Then target-weld each of the extra vertices to one of the corners, as shown in Figure 5.19.

Weld each pair of vertices along sides.

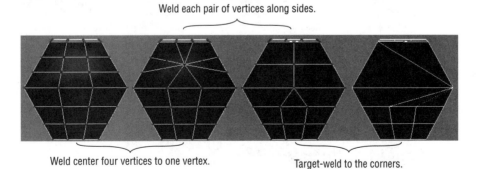

Weld center four vertices to one vertex.

Target-weld to the corners.

Figure 5.19 *Sequence of welds to optimize a specific section of a model*

Make sure you have Ignore Backfacing checked when selecting vertices so that you don't weld vertices from the front of a model to vertices on the back of a model. Also be careful in areas such as those between the fingers, where it is easy to select vertices from another part of the model with those from the part you want to weld.

Next, turn the edges as necessary (click Turn and click on the edge sub-object). The edges between the faces of polygons affect the shading across the polygon. Aim for quads (four-sided polygons) when possible, because they receive texture better. Figure 5.20 shows two arrangements of edges, one that makes for rounder shading, one that appears flatter.

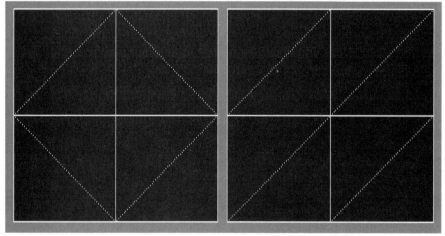

This arrangement of edges allows for rounder shading across polygons.

This arrangement of edges causes flatter shading across polygons.

Figure 5.20 *Turn edges to improve the smooth shading across the model.*

Use either the built-in polygon counter (press Q) or the Polygon Counter utility (Utilities ➜ More ➜ Polygon Counter) to keep track of your polygon count as you go along.

Replacing the Eye with Polygons

Using a texture map for an eye rather than a whole sphere reduces a lot of polygons. Let's optimize the eye of the Intrepid Explorer Jim model.

1. Go to the Vertex sub-object level of each object. Delete all the vertices on the right half of the model.

2. Hide the body object and zoom up very close to the eye. Since you are using a texture map for the eye, you need polygons. Go to the Polygon sub-object level. Click the Create button. You need to click the vertices in counter-clockwise order for the normal of the polygon to face you. Click on the eight vertices around the eye and then back on the first one to create the polygon shown in Figure 5.21.

Figure 5.21 *Create this polygon filling the eye.*

3. Go to the Edge sub-object level and click Divide. Click the edge that crosses the middle of the eye to create a new vertex there.

4. Click Turn and click the edges that don't go through the center vertex until they all go through the center vertex. Click Turn again to turn it off.

Intrepid Explorer Jim project by Jason Wiener

5. Go to the Vertex sub-object level. Select the center eye point and move it forward slightly.

6. Go to the Polygon sub-object level. Select all the polygons of the head. Navigate to the Surface Properties rollout and assign them all the same smoothing group. This will smooth out the edges on the eye. Save your file as `Intrepid_Explorer_Jim03.max`.

To continue optimizing, select vertices and weld where extra polygons are not needed. `Optimize_steps.max` *in the CD files for this chapter shows successive steps of manual polygon reduction for the Intrepid Explorer Jim model. An example of just using the Optimize modifier is also included for comparison.*

Summary

In this chapter, you learned more about Bezier splines and patches. You built models with different patch-modeling techniques and learned the advantages and disadvantages of each. You manipulated Bezier splines and patch surfaces. You learned how to use max Surface Tools to create patch models and created a complex organic model using this technique.

In the next chapter, you will learn about organic modeling using NURBS, the other spline-based system in max.

NURBS Modeling

3ds max

Chapter 6

This chapter will familiarize you with using NURBS to create smoothly curved models that are tessellated adaptively when rendered. You will learn the basics of using NURBS curves and surfaces, explore the advantages and disadvantages of NURBS, and build a model out of NURBS. Topics include:

- The nature of a NURBS model and its advantages

- Point and CV curves and surfaces

- Converting mesh primitives to NURBS

- Isoparms

- Tessellating NURBS for viewport and final render

- The NURBS creation toolbox and other NURBS tools

- Shaping and sculpting NURBS forms

- Modeling a vase with NURBS

- Modeling a cartoon character's head with NURBS

Non-Uniform Rational B-Splines (NURBS)

In Chapters 4 and 5, you learned about Bezier splines and used them to build mesh and patch models. Like Bezier patches, NURBS are also based on mathematically defined curves. A B-spline, short for basis-spline, is a mathematical concept including both Bezier splines and NURBS. A rational B-spline is one that is defined mathematically as the ratio of two polynomial functions. A non-uniform B-spline is one in which the influence of a curvature can be varied. A *non-uniform rational B-spline*, called NURBS for short, is used in CG to create models with control vertices that can be weighted to affect the curvature of the associated surface or curve. Fortunately for those of us who don't breathe the rarefied air of higher mathematics, we never have to understand any of the math involved to use NURBS.

Adaptive Tessellation

NURBS also have a feature that was their main "selling" point when they were introduced: adaptive tessellation. The tessellation of the NURBS surface into rendered polygons can not only be assigned a different level of detail for the viewport than the renderer, but also can be tessellated differently based on distance from the camera, so that you can tessellate more when rendering detailed curvature in a close-up and tessellate less when rendering a model in the background. The tessellation is calculated on the fly while you are rendering. Adaptive tessellation is now available in some forms of mesh models, so this advantage is less persuasive today.

Pulse Creator, included on the CD for this book, allows you to export a low-poly model from max and change it into a "wing object" whose tessellation is calculated adaptively based on the distance from the camera.

Using NURBS for Organic Modeling

As you learned in Chapters 4 and 5, polygons are the most efficient for modeling linear geometric forms, while spline-based modeling methods (in patches or NURBS) are good for modeling smoothly contoured surfaces. Industrial designers often use NURBS to model automobile designs, because NURBS allow very precise numerical control over complex curved surfaces. NURBS allow you to create objects with precise organic curves and topology that can be designed with animation in mind.

Mastering NURBS can be daunting; they are much more complex than other data types in max, the learning curve is steeper, and they are much slower to update in the viewport. Many max modelers switched from modeling in NURBS to Bezier spline cages with the Surface modifier applied, because the demand on the processor is less and because patch surfaces are more stable in max. Because of the popularity of NURBS modeling in programs like Rhino, Alias, and Maya, however, there will probably always be some demand for NURBS modeling in max. The curved surfaces of NURBS have a smoothness that is difficult to duplicate exactly with other modeling methods. It may also turn out to be the modeling method that is most intuitive and efficient for your needs.

NURBS Modeling Techniques

There are a variety of techniques for modeling NURBS objects. One method is to create a NURBS curve and generate a surface from the curves; another is to create a NURBS surface directly and sculpt it into organic forms by moving its CVs; still another method is to convert a mesh primitive into a NURBS object and adapt it from there. For example, a sphere can be converted to a NURBS object and then sculpted into a character's head. Once a NURBS surface is generated, it can be used to generate new NURBS curves, which can themselves be used to alter the surface or generate new surfaces.

NURBS curves are shaped by control vertices (CVs) that do not have to lie on the curve itself. Each CV has a weight, which determines the extent of its influence over the curve. By increasing the weight of a CV, you draw the corresponding curve or surface toward that CV. These are relative weights, so increasing all the CV weights identically will not change the curvature.

Working with NURBS Curves

There are two types of NURBS curves: point curves and CV curves. These are actually just alternate interfaces to the CV curve. In the case of point curves, the CVs are not accessible; points on the curve are accessible instead. You can convert between them at the Curve sub-object level so that you can move a point on a curve when necessary and get back to the CVs when you want to model that way. The underlying math is the same for both types of curves.

Shaping Point Curves

Let's start by creating and shaping a point curve:

1. In the top viewport, choose Create ➔ Shapes ➔ NURBS Curves and click Point Curve.

2. Click several points in the top view to create a NURBS point curve. Right-click to finish drawing. Notice that the curve flows through the points that you clicked.

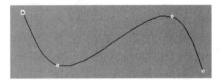

3. In the Modify panel, click the plus sign in front of NURBS Curve in the stack. Go to the Point sub-object level.

4. Select and move a few points. The curve always flows through these points. Moving the points affects the curve, but you don't have any handles for affecting the curve between them as you do with Bezier splines.

5. Click the Refine button and then click along the point curve to add points. Right-click in the viewport to turn off the Refine button.

6. Now move your new points around to change the curvature.

The only way you can control the curvature of a point curve is by adding points or moving them.

7. Go to the Curve sub-object level. Click the curve in the viewport to select it and then click Convert Curve. In the Convert Curve dialog box, make sure the CV Curve button is active, keep the defaults, and click OK.

8. The curve is now a CV curve. Go to the Curve CV sub-object level to see the CVs of the curve. The CVs are the little green boxes at the corners of the lattice around the curve.

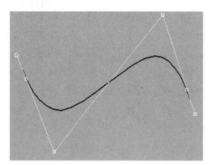

Shaping CV Curves

Now you have a CV curve made from a point curve, but let's back up and create one from scratch:

1. Go back to the object level of the curve and delete it.

2. Click Create ➜ Shapes ➜ NURBS Curve ➜ CV Curve.

3. Click once to create one endpoint, click another place to create a CV, click a third place to create another CV, click another place to create an endpoint, and then right-click to end the curve.

4. In the Modify panel, go to the Curve CV sub-object level. Your curve should look something like Figure 6.1. Notice that it is the lattice lines that run through the CVs you created, not the curve itself. The curve flows through the CVs only at the start and endpoints of the curve.

5. Select the first of the two CVs shaping the middle of the curve. In the CV section of the Modify panel, change the weight to 5. Notice how the CV pulls the curve toward itself more strongly; the curve gets closer to the lattice. This reveals how the lattice represents the outer bounds of curvature for the NURBS curve.

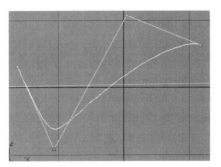

6. Select the second of the two middle CVs and move it. Notice that moving a CV changes the lattice lines and resultant curve.

7. In the Modify panel, click the Refine button. Click the curve between the two middle CVs to add a CV. Click the Refine button again to turn it off. Notice that the two CVs you started with have moved in order to keep the shape of the curve the same.

8. Move the new CV around to change the shape of the curve. Notice that if you move it closer to the last of the middle CVs, you get a sharper curve.

Two or three coincident CVs in a NURBS curve will give you sharper corners.

9. Return to the object level and delete the curve.

. . . .

NURBS curve   CV   Lattice line

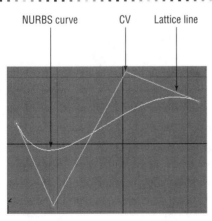

Figure 6.1 *NURBS curve with control vertex*

Working with NURBS Surfaces

As with NURBS curves, NURBS surfaces can be point surfaces or CV surfaces. You can convert between them at the Surface sub-object level in order to, for instance, add or move a point on a surface to model a certain detail and then convert back to a CV surface to model using the weights and positions of the CVs. Again, the two forms of surfaces are just alternate interfaces to the same mathematical object.

Shaping Point Surfaces

Let's look at a NURBS point surface:

1. Click Create ➜ Geometry ➜ NURBS Surfaces ➜ Point Surf.

2. Drag out a point surface in the perspective viewport.

3. In the Modify panel, go to the Point sub-object level. Move a point upward in the Z direction. Notice how the modified surface continues to flow through the transformed point.

4. Click Surf Row under Refine in the Modify panel. In the top viewport, click between the rows of points. This adds a new row of points for shaping the surface. You can use Surf Col to add columns of points across the surface as well.

5. Return to the object level and delete the surface.

Shaping CV Surfaces

Now let's take a look at a CV surface:

1. Click Create ➜ Geometry ➜ NURBS Surface ➜ CV Surf.

2. Drag out a CV surface in the perspective viewport.

3. In the Modify panel, go to the Surface CV sub-object level. Right-click the perspective viewport label and change the display to show Edged Faces. Move a CV upward in the Z direction. The surface bulges upward slightly. Notice that the CV surface does not flow through the CV itself.

4. Set Weight to about 4. Notice how the surface changes its shape—it gets closer to the lattice. As with the NURBS CV curve, the lattice represents the outer bounds of curvature for the NURBS CV surface.

5. Return to the object level and delete the surface.

Converting a Mesh Primitive to NURBS

One way to start modeling a NURBS object is to convert a mesh primitive to the NURBS data type. Primitives can be converted to editable meshes, editable polys, patches, and NURBS. When you convert a primitive to another data type, the object's form does not change, only the mathematical representation of that form. Let's see how this works:

1. Click Create ➜ Geometry ➜ Standard Primitives ➜ Sphere.

2. Using the Keyboard Entry rollout, create a sphere at the origin with a radius of 50.

3. In the Modify panel, right-click in the modifier stack and choose NURBS. The Sphere is converted to a NURBS surface. The modifier stack now shows the sub-object levels of the new data type. Once you convert data types, you can no longer access the creation parameters for the sphere.

4. Save your file as `Cartoon01.max`.

Understanding Isoparms

As you learned in Chapter 2, the U and V axes are used for describing the coordinate system of a surface for applying maps. This nomenclature is also used in NURBS for referring to the contour lines of a surface. These lines are called *isoparametric* lines: isoparms or iso lines for short. "Iso" means "same" in Latin. Isoparms have a constant U or V parameter in the NURBS math, similar to topographic contour lines that represent a constant elevation in a landscape. Remember that any NURBS surface is defined mathematically along its entire surface; iso lines simply aid the visualization of these surfaces.

Let's look at isoparms of the NURBS sphere you just made:

1. Right-click the viewport label of the perspective viewport and choose Wireframe.

2. Notice that the object's topology is represented in a new way. Figure 6.2 compares the topology of the sphere primitive with the topology of the same sphere converted to NURBS. As a mesh primitive, the sphere was composed of vertices and faces. After conversion to a NURBS surface, the topology is now represented by the isoparm contour lines.

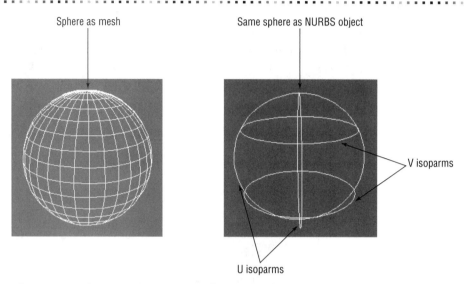

Sphere as mesh

Same sphere as NURBS object

V isoparms

U isoparms

Figure 6.2 *Sphere topology in mesh faces and NURBS isoparms*

Isoparms are also used in NURBS modeling as one of the ways to generate NURBS curves from NURBS surfaces (using the Create U Iso Curve or Create V Iso Curve tool) and to generate surfaces from curves (using the U Loft and UV Loft tools). This will be covered in more detail in "Using NURBS Tools" later in this chapter.

Approximating the NURBS Surface with Tessellation

All the data types in max besides NURBS are defined only at discrete points. These points, called vertices, are bridged by some sort of surface that connects these points. Meshes are defined by vertices and triangular faces connecting the vertices. Polys are defined identically to meshes, except that they can have quadrilateral (four-sided) surface polygons rather than only three-sided polygons. Patches are defined by spline vertices, the tangents going in and out of the vertices, and the patch surfaces connecting these vertices. NURBS, on the other hand, are defined at every point along their topology, making them the most mathematically accurate surfaces of all the data types. To be displayed in the viewport or renderer, NURBS have to be approximated by their tessellation into triangles.

As with patches, NURBS allow you to set different tessellation for use in the viewport than for rendering. In the Surface Approximation rollout of the Modify tab of a NURBS surface (object level), you can set the tessellation settings for the viewport and renderer. Table 6.1 describes the tessellation settings available in the Surface Approximation rollout for NURBS.

Unlike most radio buttons, these do not give you a single choice (between viewport settings or renderer settings). The Viewports and Renderer radio buttons work more like tabs: you check the Viewports radio button and choose your viewport settings, then check the Renderer radio button and choose your rendering settings.

Table 6.1 Tessellation Settings for NURBS

TESSELLATION SETTING	DESCRIPTION
Presets	Low, medium, or high tessellation.
Base Surface	Tessellation of surface before displacements or trims.
Surface Edge	Tessellation of edge of trimmed surface. By default locked to surface tessellation. With Lock off, can be tessellated independently.
Displaced Surface	Tessellation for surfaces with displacement maps applied. Available only for renderer.
Regular	Tessellation across the entire surface: U Steps is number of subdivisions across U axis of surface; V Steps is number of subdivisions across V axis of surface.
Parametric	Tessellation between rows and columns of CVs based on U and V values. Make sure you turn the U and V Steps down to 1 or 2 before switching to Parametric.
Spatial	Tessellation based on the size of the edges of the tessellation. Edge sets the maximum length of an edge when tessellated.
Curvature	Tessellation based on how sharply the surface is curved. Where the curvature changes sharply, the tessellation will be greater. Distance is how far the tessellated approximation can deviate from the NURBS definition. Angle is the maximum angle between tessellated faces.

Table 6.1 Tessellation Settings for NURBS *(continued)*

TESSELLATION SETTING	DESCRIPTION
Spatial and Curvature	Tessellation based on edge size and the sharpness of curvature. View Dependent, only available for the renderer, tessellates adaptively based on distance from the camera. When the camera is close up to an area, the area will be tessellated more; when the area is in the background, it will be tessellated less.
Merge	Determines how tessellation of surface sub-objects is changed to match adjoining sub-object surfaces. Zero means the tessellation is not changed.
Advanced Parameters	Controls algorithms for spatial and curvature tessellation settings.
Clear Surface Level	Clears all tessellation settings for surface sub-objects and locks them to the setting for the object level.

Let's look at the tessellation of the NURBS sphere:

1. Change the viewport display back to Smooth + Highlights. Turn on Edged Faces. Notice that the NURBS surface appears to be tessellated like a mesh.

2. In the Surface Approximation rollout, notice that the Viewports radio button is checked. You are setting the tessellation to be displayed in the viewport. This has no effect on the render. Click the High button in the Tessellation Presets group. Then click Low. The presets give you drastic differences in tessellation. Note that all three of these presets use the Spatial and Curvature tessellation method.

Dependent and Independent NURBS Sub-objects

As with splines in spline cages, NURBS curves and surfaces can be sub-objects of an overall NURBS model. NURBS curve and surface sub-objects can be independent or they can be dependent on another NURBS sub-object for their definition. The tools in the NURBS toolbox are mainly for creating new curves or surfaces dependent on other curves or surfaces. For instance, a Blend is defined by connecting two other sub-objects. If you change the sub-objects on which it depends, the blend sub-object changes to compensate. This change can also be animated, although it requires a lot of computer horsepower to calculate.

You can't access the CVs or points of dependent curves or surfaces, because they are dependent upon the parent curve or surface. You can make a dependent curve or surface independent with the Make Independent button; this will give you access to the CVs of points again, but ends the dependence on the parent sub-object.

As soon as you use Convert Curve or Convert Surface to switch between points and CVs, or to reparameterize, any dependency is broken.

With dependent sub-objects, you also have the option of replacing the sub-object on which they depend. For example, when you select a sub-object that is dependent on a parent surface, a Replace Base Surface button is available in the Modify panel. If you click this button, you can then click on a different surface to be the parent of the dependent sub-object.

Using NURBS Tools

All the NURBS tools can be accessed within the Modify panel of a NURBS object or sub-object. The tools that are available on the Create Points, Create Curves, and Create Surfaces rollouts are also available in the NURBS Creation toolbox. The toolbox, shown in Figure 6.3, can be brought up by clicking the NURBS Creation Toolbox button in the Modify panel of a NURBS object. Once turned on, it will be displayed whenever you are in the Modify panel of a NURBS object. Table 6.2 describes the commands in the NURBS toolbox and their functions.

If you use the rollouts on NURBS objects to create sub-objects, the creation parameters of these tools will appear at the very bottom rollout of the Modify panel. If you use the NURBS creation toolbox to create sub-objects, the creation parameters will appear in the first rollout of the Modify panel.

When using the NURBS sub-object creation tools, keep in mind that, except for the few tools that create independent NURBS sub-objects, the curves and surfaces you create are dependent on their parent sub-objects until you make them independent. You can make a curve or surface independent by clicking Make Independent in the Curve Common or Surface Common rollout.

Figure 6.3 *The NURBS creation toolbox*

Table 6.2 Commands in the NURBS Creation Toolbox

ICON	TOOL	DESCRIPTION
	Create Point	Creates an *independent* point.
	Create Offset Point	Creates a dependent point at a specified distance from an existing point.
	Create Curve Point	Creates a dependent point on a curve or at a specified distance from it.
	Create Curve-Curve Point	Creates a dependent point at the intersection of two curves.
	Create Surf Point	Creates a dependent point on a surface or at a specified offset from it.

Table 6.2 Commands in the NURBS Creation Toolbox *(continued)*

Icon	Tool	Description
	Create Surface-Curve Point	Creates a dependent point at the intersection of a surface and a curve.
	Create CV Curve	Creates an *independent* CV curve sub-object.
	Create Point Curve	Creates an *independent* point curve sub-object.
	Create Fit Curve	Creates a dependent point curve fitted to selected points on a point curve or point surface.
	Create Transform Curve	Creates a dependent curve that copies a selected curve but can be moved, rotated, or scaled independently of the parent curve.
	Create Blend Curve	Creates a smooth connecting curve dependent on the curves it is blending.
	Create Offset Curve	Creates a dependent curve offset from its parent curve.
	Create Mirror Curve	Creates a dependent curve that is the mirror image of its parent curve.
	Create Chamfer Curve	Creates a dependent curve that adds a straight bevel between two parent curves, trimming the curves to the bevel.
	Create Fillet Curve	Creates a dependent curve that adds a curved corner between two parent curves, trimming the curves to the corner.
	Create Surface-Surface Intersection Curve	Creates a dependent curve that is the intersection of its parents' surfaces.
	Create U Iso Curve	Creates a dependent curve that is the U isoparm at the point clicked on the parent's surface.
	Create V Iso Curve	Creates a dependent curve that is the V isoparm at the point clicked on the parent's surface.
	Create Normal Projected Curve	Creates a dependent curve that is the projection of a parent curve onto a parent surface along the parent surface's normals.
	Create Vector Projected Curve	Creates a dependent curve that is the projection of a parent curve onto a surface along the vector pointing into the viewport.

Table 6.2 Commands in the NURBS Creation Toolbox *(continued)*

Icon	Tool	Description
	Create CV Curve On Surface	Allows you to draw a dependent CV curve dependent upon a parent surface on which you draw it.
	Create Point Curve On Surface	Allows you to draw a dependent point curve dependent upon a parent surface on which you draw it.
	Create Surface Offset Curve	Creates a dependent curve at a specified offset from a parent curve on surface. The offset is along the surface normal.
	Create Surface Edge Curve	Creates a dependent curve on the boundary of the parent surface. Can also be the boundary of a trimmed surface.
	Create CV Surface	Creates an *independent* CV surface sub-object.
	Create Point Surface	Creates an *independent* point surface sub-object.
	Create Transform Surface	Creates a dependent surface that copies a selected surface but can be moved, rotated, or scaled independently of the parent surface.
	Create Blend Surface	Creates a dependent surface smoothly connecting and blending the curvatures of two parent surfaces.
	Create Offset Surface	Creates a dependent surface offset from the parent surface along the parent surface's normals.
	Create Mirror Surface	Creates a dependent surface that is the mirror image of the parent surface along a specified axis.
	Create Extrude Surface	Creates a dependent extruded surface of a parent curve along the axis of its gizmo.
	Create Lathe Surface	Creates a dependent lathed surface of a parent curve along the axis of its gizmo.
	Create Ruled Surface	Creates a dependent surface between two parent curves that bound it. Is similar to a U Loft between only two curves.
	Create Cap Surface	Creates a dependent surface bounded by a closed parent curve.

Table 6.2 Commands in the NURBS Creation Toolbox *(continued)*

Icon	Tool	Description
	Create U Loft Surface	Creates a dependent surface between parent curves that define its U isoparametric lines.
	Create UV Loft Surface	Creates a dependent surface between parent curves, like a U Loft, except it allows some V lines as well. The ends of the V curves should lie on the bounding U curves.
	Create 1-Rail Sweep	Creates a dependent surface that lofts a parent curve cross-section along a parent curve "rail."
	Create 2-Rail Sweep	Creates a dependent surface by sweeping one parent curve along two other parent curves that act as "rails" for the sweep.
	Create Multisided Blend Surface	Creates a dependent surface blending three or four parent surfaces.
	Create Multicurve Trimmed Surface	Creates a dependent surface that is a copy of a parent surface trimmed by multiple parent curves that form a closed shape.
	Create Fillet Surface	Creates a dependent surface that is a rounded corner between two parent surfaces.

Working at the Sub-object Level

Most of the work you will do in NURBS will be on sub-objects within a single NURBS object. In any given sub-object level, you can click the Plug-in Keyboard Shortcut toggle and use the H key to pull up a Select Sub-Objects dialog box for the sub-objects of that type in your NURBS object. Figure 6.4 shows an example of this dialog box, in this case showing the sub-objects at the surface level. You can also rename these sub-objects in order to organize your work.

NURBS models generally are made with a single object. All the modeling is done at a sub-object level, either directly on the original surface or by attaching or creating new sub-object surfaces.

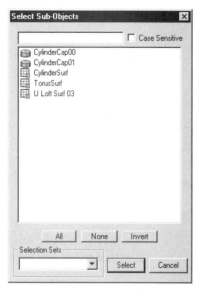

Figure 6.4 *Select Sub-Objects dialog box*

Making a U Loft Surface from Curves

Let's look at one of the tools for generating a surface from curves:

1. Open Curves.max in the CD files for this chapter. It consists of a series of NURBS curves.

2. Click the Create U Loft Surface button. In the front viewport, roll over the bottom curve until it turns blue. Click it, then click the next curve up and the rest of the curves in order. A surface is formed. Right-click to finish. This is how easy it is to use the U Loft tool to make surfaces from curves. Figure 6.5 shows an example.

Capping a Surface

The surface you just created has a hole on either end. Let's use another NURBS tool to cap them:

1. Click the Create Cap Surface button on the NURBS creation toolbox.

2. Roll over the top curve of the object until it turns blue, then click it. The surface is completed. Right-click in the viewport to turn off the tool.

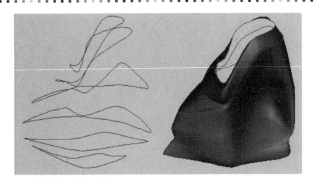

Figure 6.5 *U Loft Surface from NURBS Curves*

3. Arc-rotate so you can see the bottom hole. Click the Create Cap Surface button again, roll over the bottom curve until it turns blue, and click. Right-click in the viewport to turn off the tool. It looks like nothing happened. That's because the cap surface you just created is facing the other way. Let's fix that.

4. In the Modify panel, go to the Surface sub-object level. Click the Keyboard Shortcut Override button at the bottom of the interface. Press H to bring up the Select Sub-Objects dialog box. Choose Cap Surf 02 from the list and click Select.

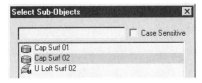

5. In the Modify panel, check Flip Normals. The object looks whole. Return to the object level.

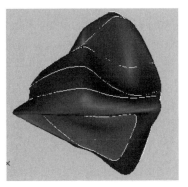

Drawing a Curve on Surface (COS)

Sometimes you will need to trim a NURBS surface. In order to do a trim, you need a curve on the surface to which to trim it. You can generate curves on the surface with several of the tools. The Curve on Surface (COS) tools in the NURBS creation toolbox allow you to draw the curve you want. Let's try it out by drawing one on the surface you just created:

1. Zoom and arc-rotate to find an area of the surface of the object on which you can draw a shape.

2. Click the Create CV Curve on Surface button. As you roll over the surface on which you want to draw, it should turn blue. Draw a closed shape on the surface. If you want sharper curves, create the CVs closer together. If you want sharp points, click three times in the same place. When you get to the first CV again, you should get a prompt asking if you want to close the curve. Click Yes. Right-click in the viewport to turn off the tool. You can draw any closed shape; it doesn't have to look like the one pictured. Note that the curve you made is on the preexisting surface, following the topology of that surface.

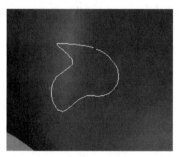

Trimming a Surface

You can trim a curve with any curve on a surface, including, for example, a Normal Projected curve, which projects a curve along a sub-object's normal onto the surface. Let's try trimming the surface you made with the curve you just made:

1. Go to the Curve sub-object level. Select the curve that you drew on the surface. Right-click in the Modify panel and navigate to the CV Curve on Surface rollout. Check Trim. You are left with just the surface within the trim.

2. Check Flip Trim. You have a hole in the surface outlined by your curve.

One thing to keep in mind about trims in NURBS is that they are even more illu-sion than the magic of computer graphics in general. The surface of the "hole" is still there; it's just not displayed. You can even move the CVs of the surface within a "hole." The principle of a calculated geometry being selectively displayed and rendered is also used in the Boolean operations you used in Chapter 4.

Modeling a Vase Using NURBS Tools

In this project, you will use more of the NURBS tools to model a vase. First you will draw the profile of the vase with a NURBS curve, just as you drew a profile curve when you used the Lathe modifier to model the dome in Chapter 4. Then you will use the NURBS lathe tool to generate a surface of the profile revolved around the Z-axis. You will next generate a new surface for the inside of the vase and, finally, use the Blend tool to complete the model.

Lathing a Surface from a Curve

First draw a profile shape of the vase using a NURBS curve:

1. Reset max.

2. Click Create ➜ Shapes ➜ NURBS Curves ➜ CV Curve. In the left viewport, draw a curve similar to the one in Figure 6.6. Start your first CVs at the bottom and click your way around to the top.

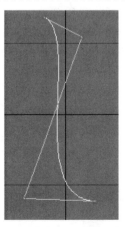

Figure 6.6 *Profile of vase*

3. In the Modify panel, go to the Curve CV sub-object level. Select the middle CV on the lower-left and increase its Weight to about 3.5 to pull the curve closer to this CV. Select the middle CV on the upper-right and set its Weight to 4.4. Save your file as Vase01.max.

4. If the NURBS creation toolbox is not already open, go to the object level and open it. Click the Create Lathe Surface button in the NURBS creation toolbox. Click the CV curve created earlier to create a surface from the curve.

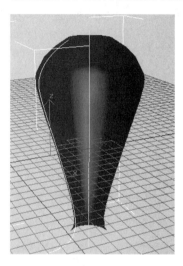

5. At first the surface doesn't look right. In the Modify panel, click the Max button in the Align group of the Lathe Surface rollout. This determines where the axis of rotation is in relation to the CV curve.

6. The overall form looks better now, but the surface is facing the wrong direction. Go to the Surface sub-object level. Click anywhere on the NURBS surface to select it. In the Surface Common rollout, check Flip Normals. Now the correct side of the outside surface is the one drawn.

7. The surface is facing the right direction, but the inside of the top of the vase needs to be visible. The vase also needs some thickness. Click the Create Offset Surface button in the NURBS creation toolbox. In the left viewport, roll your mouse over the surface. Drag very slightly from the edge of the surface toward the middle of the vase to create a new inner surface for the vase. Make sure that you don't drag the wrong way and create an outer surface to the vase facing in the wrong direction.

8. In the Modify panel, change the Offset value if you need to. A value of 50 worked for the sample file on the CD; yours may be less or more depending on how you drew your curve. Right-click in the viewport to turn off the Offset tool.

9. Navigate the view around the vase to see the gap between the two surfaces that must be closed to finish the model.

Creating Curves on the Surface for the Blend

Now you can use the surface you've created to generate the curves needed to finish the model:

1. In the NURBS creation toolbox, click the Create V Iso Curve button.

2. Move your mouse up and down along the surfaces in the left viewport. The blue line represents a curve that can be created along the iso lines in the V direction of this surface. Zoom very close in to the top of the vase in the left viewport. Click the Create V Iso Curve button again. Click the mouse at the extreme top of the inside surface of the vase. Be careful not to click any distance down from the top. The blue line should be superimposed over the top edge of the inner vase surface before you click. This creates a new curve on the surface.

3. With the Create V Iso Curve tool still active, click at the very top of the outer surface of the vase to create the matching curve.

4. Right-click in the viewport to turn off the V Iso Curve button. Save your file as Vase02.max.

Completing the Vase Model with a Blend Surface

To complete the vase model, you need a surface that connects the inside and outside surfaces you have created so far. To do this, you can create a blend from the two curves you created at the boundaries of the surfaces:

1. Zoom in to the top of the vase and arc-rotate so that you can see the edges of the two surfaces.

2. Click the Create Blend Surface button. Move the mouse over the two curves you created on the surface edges. Notice that the curves turn blue to indicate that they are candidates for the Blend tool. Click the outside curve first and then the inside curve. Right-click in the viewport to turn off the Blend tool. You have created a surface connecting the surfaces of the vase. Save your file as Vase03.max.

Vase project by Scott Onstott

Modeling a Character's Head with NURBS

In this exercise, you will model a cartoon character with a NURBS surface. The basis for this model will be a sphere primitive converted to NURBS.

Preparing the Base Form

Starting with the NURBS sphere you created earlier, add curves to the surface:

1. Open Cartoon01.max from the exercise earlier in this chapter or from the CD files for this chapter.

2. In the Modify panel, go to the Surface sub-object level. Select the surface of the sphere in the viewport. Change the viewport display to Wireframe.

3. In the Surface Common rollout, click the Make Loft button. In the Make Loft dialog box, select the From V Iso Lines radio button and click OK. Now there are additional iso lines in the V direction displayed in the viewport.

   Notice that your surface now has Curve and Curve CV sub-object levels for accessing the curves you just created. The Make Loft tool adds CV curves on the NURBS surface along isoparametric lines and makes the surface *dependent* on these curves. The iso lines of the wireframe display were for display only; they could not be altered. Since the surface is now dependent on the curves, you can use the CVs of curves you created to modify the form of the NURBS surface.

4. Return to the object level. Right-click in the Modify panel and navigate to the Display Line Parameters rollout. Experiment with changing the number of U lines and V lines. These parameters control the number of iso lines that this object displays. After you see the effect, set these parameters:

   - U Lines = 0

   - V Lines = 0

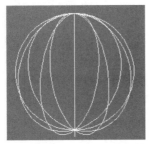

Now the NURBS surface displays only the CV curves you created in step 4. The display iso lines are no longer visible.

Sculpting the Form

You are ready to start sculpting the form of the head using the Curve CVs:

1. Go to the Curve CV sub-object level of the modifier stack.

2. In the left viewport, select the CV on the central CV curve that is in the third row of CVs. Move it to form the shape of the nose. Be careful not to move CVs that belong to neighboring curves.

   You need more CVs on the central curve to form the mouth.

3. Click Refine in the CV rollout. Move your mouse over one of the lattice lines on the central CV curve. Click two points near the mouth to add two additional CVs to the curve. Click Refine again to turn it off.

4. Move the middle one of these mouth CVs inside the volume of the head to create a mouth cavity.

5. Continue to adjust and refine the CVs on the central CV curve until you are satisfied with the profile of your cartoon character's head.

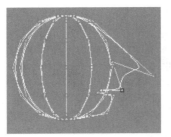

To give further form to the head, adjust the CVs on the curves adjacent to the central curve:

6. To maintain the symmetry of the head, move CVs in pairs. Using the Move tool, select pairs of CVs by holding down the Ctrl key on the CV curves neighboring the central curve. Move these CVs to further define the form of the head.

When you are sculpting, be careful to select outlying CVs in pairs to maintain symmetry. If you lock your selection while moving, there is less chance the symmetry will be thrown off. Switch between views as needed to visualize your model. Change the display from Wireframe to Smooth + Highlights to see what happens to the surface as you move CVs. Sculpting is a trial-and-error experience. Unfortunately when working with a computer, you can't walk around your model or touch it to get the "feel" of what you are doing. You have to arc-rotate a lot to be sure you are seeing the model in three dimensions as you sculpt it on your flat monitor.

7. Sculpt the NURBS surface by moving, rotating, and scaling CVs. Adjust CV Weight settings to pull the surface closer to a CV. Since it is a cartoon head, be as outlandish as you want. Create your own original character.

You can also use soft selection with CVs to move a whole area organically.

8. Return to the object level when you are done sculpting. Save your work as `Cartoon02.max`.

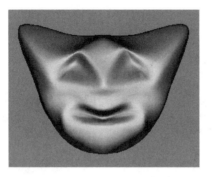

Cartoon project by Scott Onstott

Summary

In this chapter, you learned what NURBS are and how they work. You created and shaped NURBS curves and surfaces. You modeled NURBS surfaces from mesh primitives, used NURBS curves to create surfaces, and used surfaces to generate curves for further modeling. You learned how to set the tessellation of NURBS for the viewport and the renderer and how to tessellate adaptively relative to the camera. You built two models using the NURBS commands in the Modify panel and the NURBS toolbox.

In the next chapter, you will learn about the basic animation tools in max and begin to animate your models.

Part III

Applying Texture Maps and Materials

In This Part

In Part III, you will learn how to simulate complex surfaces by studying some of CG shading theory, learning max's interface for applying materials, and completing a variety of exercises and tutorials. In Chapter 7, you will learn about the structure of max materials, including the various material channels and how these are affected by maps. You will learn how to assign mapping coordinates and will do this in great detail for a low-poly character. In Chapter 8, you will delve more into advanced materials topics and the application of your knowledge of materials. You will complete several complex materials tutorials.

Basic Mapping and Materials

3ds max

Chapter 7

Whenever you see images from a 3D program, you are viewing a simulated three-dimensional reality projected onto a two-dimensional arrangement of pixels. Even in the case of the 3D movies you watch with special goggles so the action appears to jump off the screen, two different 2D images are being projected at the same time, one to your right eye and one from a slightly different vantage point to your left eye, allowing your visual mind to assemble the depth of the scene from the difference in the images. As you learned in Chapters 1 and 2, rendering is the process of calculating these 2D arrangements of colored pixels from the simulated world of the digital file. Every nuance of appearance of object surfaces—their shininess, bumpiness, or transparency, for example—is created through affecting the colors of those pixels in the final rendering. What max does is give you an interface for affecting the calculation of those pixels.

Max calculates the appearance or shading of a surface in the render from many factors, including the object color, the material applied, the shading type and component settings of the material, the maps applied, the mapping coordinates used, the lighting parameters and lighting color, the renderer used, the anti-aliasing settings, and, finally, any post-processing effects. In this chapter, you will learn the basics of color and shading calculations and use max's mapping modifiers and Material Editor to apply colors and bitmaps. You will look at more advanced materials properties and features in Chapter 8, the effect of lighting in Chapter 12, and rendering settings in Chapter 13. Keep in mind that all these aspects of the rendering calculation affect each other. Your lighting will drastically influence the appearance of your materials, for example. These topics are very much related. They are presented in this order due to the typical workflow of an animation project: maps are often applied to characters before animating for games, for example, while lighting is done after the animation is complete. Topics include:

- The structure of materials
- Color models
- Components of surface shading
- Shading algorithms
- Material trees
- The Material Editor
- The Material/Map Browser and the Material/Map Navigator
- Material types
- Map types
- Mapping coordinates
- Unwrapping mapping coordinates for a low-poly character

Understanding the Structure of Materials

In max, how geometry interacts with light is defined by the *material* assigned to it. Rendering calculates the interaction between geometry, material, and light in order to create the resulting image. What you see in a viewport while you're working is not a final rendering —it is a real-time approximation using the interactive viewport renderer. Many effects of materials and lighting cannot be seen in a normal shaded viewport. Max approximates the final rendering as closely as possible within the viewport as far as current technology allows. The level of success max has with this is bound by the performance of your graphics card. As you learned in Chapter 3, max also has a new option called an ActiveShade view that calculates lighting and materials more quickly than the final renderer but allows you to see more of the materials and lighting subtleties updated in the viewport.

What max calls a material, some other 3D programs call a "shader." You can get around the confusion by simply remembering what a material is doing: determining how an object will be shaded.

Meeting the Material Editor

Materials are assigned to objects using the Material Editor, a dialog box that is essentially a whole other program within max. The Material Editor, shown in Figure 7.1, can be brought up by clicking the Material Editor button on the main toolbar, by choosing Rendering ➜ Material Editor in the Menu bar, or by pressing M. As a default, the Material Editor displays six sample slots for materials. You can change the display to 15 or 24 slots. Keep in mind, however, that max has no limit on the number of materials you can use in a scene. The slots are just an interface for making a new material or map.

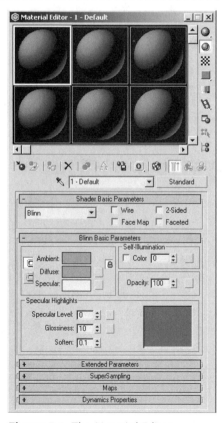

Figure 7.1 *The Material Editor*

A material has to be either in one of the sample slots within the Material Editor or applied to an object in your scene in order to be saved with the `.max` *file. The Material Editor stores 24 sample slots whether or not they are displayed. These are saved with the* `.max` *file.*

You already used the Material Editor a few times in Chapter 4. Let's look at it again:

1. Make a sphere, a box, and a cone in the perspective viewport (Create ➔ Geometry).

2. Select all three objects.

3. Press M to open the Material Editor.

4. Click the first slot on the upper-left of the Material Editor. The active slot is highlighted with a white border.

5. Click the Assign Material To Selection button in the Material Editor.

6. Highlight the name of this material in the pop-up list. Right now it says "1 - Default." Type **Red** for the material name. Save your file as `Materials01.max`.

The objects haven't turned red yet, but you may have noticed that they did change from their original object colors to gray, because the objects now have a material applied to them. So far, your "Red" material only has the name "Red," although it appears gray right now. To make the material red, you need to change one of the color components of the "Red" material. Let's come back to this after learning more about color.

Hot, Warm, and Cold Materials

The white triangles that appear around a sample slot after you assign a material indicate that the material is "hot." A hot material is instanced in the slot and on the selected object. A "warm" material is displayed with gray triangles around the slot, indicating that the material is instanced in the scene, but not on the object currently selected. Changes you make to hot or warm materials in their slots update on the objects to which they are assigned. You use the Material Editor to modify a material on every object to which it is applied. If you want to try out changes without losing your original material, copy the material to another slot by dragging it to the new slot. Then make changes to the new "cold" material slot. When you are sure you like the new material, you can replace the original material in the scene with the Put Material To Scene button.

Understanding Color Models

As you've learned, rendering dramatic and intriguing effects for the eye is essentially a matter of coloring pixels by choosing your materials, lighting, and other settings. Understanding how color works helps in choosing your colors effectively. Color is understood according to various models (also called *color spaces*) invented to describe them. Not all colors that humans perceive in nature are described by any model, nor do the models perfectly translate to each other.

For more depth on color theory and design, check out Principles of Color Design, *2nd ed., by Wucius Wong (John Wiley & Sons, 1997) and* Principles of Color *by Faber Birren (Schiffer, 1987).*

The Subtractive Model

You see color on surfaces because pigments absorb and reflect parts of the spectrum of light. Our eye picks up the light that is reflected and sends this information to the brain for interpretation. Pigments are described by a color model based on the *subtractive* primary colors: cyan, magenta, and yellow. This model is called subtractive because as new pigment is added, the color that pigment reflects is being subtracted from the light you see reflected. When all light has been subtracted, you are, in theory, left with black. In practice, it is difficult to get a true black by mixing cyan, magenta, and yellow pigments, so black is added. This is the CMYK system (K is short for black) used for print.

  The traditional color wheel taught to us since grade school is subtractive in nature, and much of our real-world experience with color involves mixing pigments, so this model is more intuitive to most of us than the additive models. But since this book refers mainly to computer monitors and digital video output, let's stick to the additive models.

Color Perception

The fact that we can see at all is a function of light entering our eyes. Light can enter our eyes directly from a source or can reach our eyes after being affected by reflection off other surfaces, transmission through substances (like the atmosphere), or interference from other light waves. The colors humans perceive are in a very narrow range of the entire electromagnetic spectrum called visible light. Our perception of color is heavily influenced by the vagaries of our visual cortex, and often varies significantly between individuals.

The Additive Models

Light-based transmissions (such as computer monitors, film projections, TV screens, or colored filters on flashlights) can be described by the RGB color model, based on the *additive* primary colors: red, green, and blue. This model corresponds loosely to the system used by the cones in your eye that pick up all the color information you see. Cones are sensitive to either long (red end of spectrum), medium (green area of spectrum), or short (blue end of spectrum) wavelengths of visible light.

The additive colors of light combine to create white light. In the RGB model, red and green produce yellow, which can seem counterintuitive; red and blue produce magenta; and green and blue produce cyan. This gives us a wheel with the three primaries of light and their *complements*. If you open additive_wheel.jpg in the CD files for this chapter, you can see an example of this wheel. Notice the complementary pairs across the wheel from each other: red and cyan, green and magenta, and blue and yellow. In the RGB model, an image is defined solely by the red, green, and blue values of each pixel. You can specify exactly what color you want by entering its RGB values into the Color Selector dialog box brought up by any color swatch in the Material Editor, as shown in Figure 7.2.

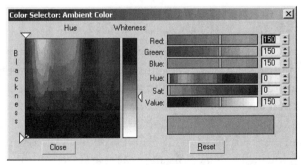

Figure 7.2 *Color Selector dialog box with RGB, HSV, and HWB options*

The RGB color model uses three primaries that can be combined to describe millions of colors. This concept is similar to the XYZ axes of a 3D coordinate system, used for locating myriad points in space. The RGB model is sometimes referred to as a color space, *because the values of the three primary colors can describe a volume mathematically.*

The HSV Model

The hue, saturation, and value (HSV) model, sometimes called hue, lightness, and saturation (HLS), still works with the additive system of the RGB model, but is viewed in a different format. A color in this system is defined by its hue, which is the specific color along the spectrum; its saturation, which is the purity or intensity of the color; and its value, which is the grayscale lightness or darkness of the color. You can specify an exact color by entering these values in the Color Selector.

The HWB Model

A color model related to the HSV model is the hue, whiteness, and blackness (HWB) model. It is based on a system more familiar to painters, where a color is defined by its hue, the amount of white added, and the amount of black added. It can also be used in the Color Selector by adjusting the sliders around the large color plot. It doesn't matter which of the Color Selector models you use to choose your colors. One will probably make more sense to you intuitively, so use that one. You can also get part of the way there with a slider in one model and then adjust it with a slider in another. For example, you might click directly on a color that is close to what you want in the HWB section of the Color Selector, and then turn down the saturation slider in the HSV section.

Components of Surface Shading

How a max material interacts with the CG light in a scene is defined by the material's components. The components of surface shading are part of CG theory that is consistent between programs, although each program may use slightly different jargon or algorithms. Color components—diffuse, ambient, specular, and filter colors—define not the absolute pixel colors rendered but colors that are part of the final rendering calculation. If you are familiar with blend modes in Photoshop, the colors in material components are combined with light colors and other parameters using mathematics similar to that used to calculate layer blending. Other material components define the value of specular highlights, whether an object is opaque, and whether "shading," in the sense of gradations of value relative to a light source, is applied at all.

Diffuse Color

The *diffuse color* component is the color resulting from diffuse light falling directly on a matte surface. This light is called *diffuse* because it is reflected in various directions. Think of diffuse as the ordinary color of an object, as opposed to the color in shadow or highlights. In many materials, the diffuse color is the most important, because it is the strongest material component. However, in a material with strong reflections, you might not see the diffuse color at all. If a texture map is applied to the diffuse color, the pixel colors of the bitmap will replace or add to the base diffuse color, depending on the opacity and settings of the map.

While diffuse color is the most similar to plain object color, they are not the same. Diffuse color is a component of a material applied to an object. An object without any material applied will still have an object color.

Ambient Color

Ambient color is the component used to calculate the color of an object in ambient or background light—the color seen on the darkest areas of an object. This component simulates light that is "all around," not coming from any particular direction. Think of the ambient color as the color in shadow. It is similar to the diffuse color and, as a default, is locked to the diffuse color. Often you want the ambient color to be the same hue as the diffuse color, but a darker value.

Let's change the color of the "Red" material you made earlier:

1. Open `Materials01.max` that you created earlier or from the CD files for this chapter. Press M to open the Material Editor.

2. Click the sample slot for the Red material. In the Blinn Basic Parameters rollout, click the color swatch next to the ambient component. The Color Selector dialog box appears. Select a bright red color. Click the Close button on the Color Selector. Notice that the objects also turned red.

3. The ambient and diffuse color components are locked together by default. Click the Lock button to separate the ambient and diffuse components.

Materials with two identical color components do not look very realistic. Color locking is used as a convenience when you are designing a new material. Unlock the colors and customize each component for the best effect.

4. Click the ambient color swatch to reopen the Color Selector. Darken the color by dragging the Value slider down to about 90. Click the Close button.

Specular Color

Specular color is the color of the specular highlight reflected off an object. Specular highlights appear on objects where the viewing angle is close to the angle of incidence between the ray of light and the surface. Since the specular highlight is a reflection, all the specular components affect reflection calculations. When you are dealing with flat opacity maps or camera-mapping (discussed in Chapter 8) to fake geometry, you generally want to turn the specular to black. When you are dealing with mirrors, you often want to turn the specular closer to white to get a sharp reflection.

Specular Level

Specular level controls the value of the specular highlight in the calculation. If you increase this, more light will be reflected from the object and the specular color component will play a greater role in the overall look of the material.

Other controls of the specular component adjust the size and edges of the specular reflection:

Glossiness controls the width of the specular reflection. Wide specular reflections (low glossiness) simulate rough surfaces, which tend to scatter light at a micro-surface level. Narrow specular reflections (high glossiness) simulate smooth or polished surfaces.

Soften affects the edges of specular highlights, especially those formed by glancing light. Use this control to soften harsh highlights that sometimes can occur with high specular levels.

Let's look at how the specular components affect a material:

1. In your "Red" material, set these parameters:

    - Specular Level = 75

    - Glossiness = 30

    - Soften = 0.5

    The specular highlights graph shows a tall curve that is fairly narrow, corresponding to a high specular level and a surface that will be moderately glossy.

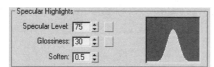

2. Double-click the preview sphere in the sample slot. A separate floating preview window appears. Resize this window to make it somewhat larger. Now you can see your material in greater detail. Save your file as Materials02.max.

Figure 7.3 shows the regions described by the color components on the preview sphere. The preview is lit by two lights—one above and to the left, and another backlight below and to the right. A sphere is ideal for previewing materials because it has smooth curved surfaces that let you see the effect of differential lighting across its surface.

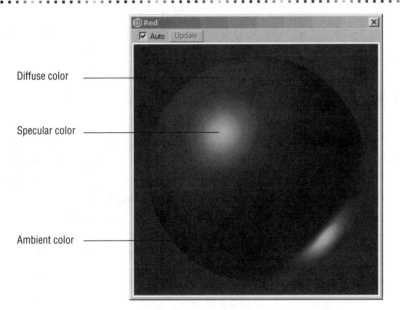

Figure 7.3 *Regions described by color components*

Opacity

Opacity controls the transparency of the object, allowing surfaces behind the object to be added into the calculation of rendered pixels. Opacity is a concept that comes up in many ways in CG. Effects that are not either on or off will often have an intensity value that is essentially a kind of opacity, because you are layering the effect with another effect according to a specified percentage. You will look at the concept of opacity in greater depth in "Masks, Alpha Channels, and Opacity Maps" later in this chapter.

The opacity settings of a material are simply the inverse of transparency settings. An object that is 100% opaque is 0% transparent. Any value less than 100% opaque makes the object translucent. Low values around 0 to 20% make the object look transparent. For glass, it is better to use the Advanced Transparency settings, covered in "Extended Shading Parameters" later in this chapter. The Advanced Transparency settings give you controls for the falloff of transparency that better simulates glass and smoke. These settings are described in more detail in "Extended Shading Parameters" later in this chapter.

Filter Color

The *filter color* component is the color of light transmitted through a translucent or transparent object. This color is in the Extended Parameters rollout. The filter color will affect the color of the shadow of a transparent material. For example, stained glass would filter the light passing through it with this color component, thereby coloring its shadow.

Self-illumination

Self-illumination controls whether the object is "shaded" at all; you can turn down the property of an object to have gradations of value where light hits it in order to simulate an object that sheds light of its own. You might think that if you put a light source inside the geometry of a lampshade, for example, the lampshade would automatically glow, but it would not. The object would be shaded as if no light were coming through its surface until you turned up its self-illumination. This is because CG objects are not real objects made of substances that allow real light to pass through. An object with a CG light inside it does not "know" that it glows until you assign the self-illumination property. This parameter tells the renderer to add extra light to the surface rather than to shade it. You can increase the value in the spinner or put a check in the color check box and select a lighter color—either method can be used for adjusting this component.

Self-illumination flattens the appearance of an object by stripping it of its shading. Observe carefully the effect you want to simulate before using 100% self-illumination.

Compositing Components

Max 4 has a new feature called Render Elements that allows you to render, for example, just the diffuse, specular, or reflection components of a rendering to use in max's Video Post, discreet's combustion, or other compositing program. These compositing programs allow you to tweak the values of that component interactively by adjusting the opacity or blend mode of that layer. Render Elements is covered in more detail in Chapters 13 and 14.

Practical Application of Color Components

Now that you understand what the color components do, you might be interested to know how people use them. Choosing color for your simulated world starts, as with modeling, with carefully observing objects around you while putting aside your preconceptions. Observe the color components of objects in real life—it will help you pick realistic colors for your materials. Table 7.1 describes some practical guidelines for creating realistic-looking color components. Remember that you have to also consider the type of lighting you will be using. Start with these simple guidelines and feel free to break these rules when necessary. You might want to refer back to the `additive_wheel.jpg` on the CD for help in selecting complementary colors.

Table 7.1 Guidelines for Selecting Color Components

COMPONENT	GUIDELINE
Sunlight and spotlights	
Ambient	Complement of specular color
Diffuse	Observed color of object
Specular	Same as color of light
Artificial light in an interior scene	
Ambient	Same as diffuse but with darker value (HSV) or more black (HWB)
Diffuse	Observed color of object
Specular	Close to white

Shading Types

A *shading type* is the algorithm used to determine how objects will appear when light strikes and reflects off their surfaces and where the color components blend at the edges of their regions. Refer back to Figure 7.3 to study the regions described by the color components. Between the ambient and diffuse regions, blending is automatically calculated by the shading algorithm. Between diffuse and specular regions, you set the amount of blending desired by using the specular highlight parameters—then the shading algorithm calculates the quality of the blend.

There are different shading types available for the standard material and the Ray-trace material. Most of the shading types in max are named after pioneers in the history of computer graphics. You will be looking at all the different material types later in this chapter. For now, let's examine the shading types for the standard material:

Phong is the oldest shading type historically. Phong is mostly used for plastic surfaces. The Phong shading type doesn't handle specular highlights very well and should probably be avoided unless you have a good reason to use it.

Blinn is a variation on Phong shading with rounder, more blended highlights. It also handles highlights created by low glancing angles of light better than Phong. It is your general-purpose shading type. Plan on using this type the most.

Oren-Nayar-Blinn is a version of Blinn shading that contains extra parameters for controlling the diffuse component that allow for a matte effect. It is well suited for matte surfaces like fabric or terra-cotta.

Metal is used to create lustrous metallic surfaces such as brushed stainless steel.

Strauss is a simplified version of the Metal shading type.

Anisotropic means that the highlight is directional (as opposed to isotropic, which extends in various directions). It is used for surfaces requiring asymmetrical or elliptical highlights, such as hair, glass, and brushed metal.

Multi-Layer is the most complex shading type. It allows layering of two anisotropic highlights. Use this shading type only in situations requiring exaggerated highlights for special effects.

Figure 7.4 shows the various shading types for the standard material. The blending between color components that shading types perform is subtle—and may be hard to perceive in a printed image. Experiment with these shading types in the Material Editor, and use the enlarged material preview windows to compare and contrast the blending between the components in the different types:

1. Continue working on your file from earlier in the chapter or open Materials02.max from the CD files for this chapter.

2. Open the Material Editor.

3. Select the Red material in the active sample slot.

4. Double-click the preview sphere in the sample slot to open the separate floating preview window. Adjust the size of this window to study your material.

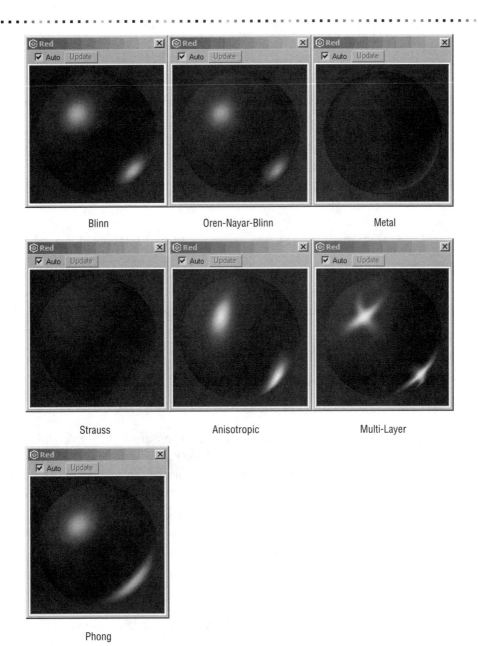

Blinn   Oren-Nayar-Blinn   Metal

Strauss   Anisotropic   Multi-Layer

Phong

Figure 7.4 *Shading types of the standard material*

5. In the Shader Basic Parameters rollout, open the pop-up list that shows the shading types. Select each one in turn and carefully observe the blending effects between the color components of the material.

6. Switch the shading type to Oren-Nayar-Blinn (ONB for short). Notice that the controls in the Basic Parameters rollout are now slightly different.

7. Change the Diffuse Level parameter to adjust the strength of the diffuse color. Change the Roughness parameter to control how matte the surface will appear. Experiment with the parameters.

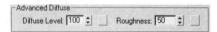

8. Switch the shading type to Metal. Notice that there is no specular color component in this shading type. Change the Specular Level and Glossiness parameters to observe the peculiar shape of the highlights graph. At low glossiness values, the glancing highlight (closer to the diffuse component) grows stronger. At higher glossiness levels, the specular component blends more continuously with the diffuse component. Experiment with the parameters.

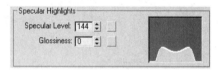

9. Switch the shading type to Strauss. There are only four parameters in the Basic Parameters rollout. There is only one color swatch here—Strauss is the simplest shading type. Glossiness controls the specular component. You can adjust the level of "Metalness" with that parameter. Experiment with the parameters.

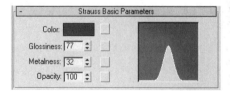

10. Switch the shading type to Anisotropic. Set these parameters:

    • Specular Level = 70

    • Glossiness = 40

- Anisotropy = 75

- Orientation = 20

11. Notice how the highlight graph has two curves shown. The Anisotropy parameter controls how similar the two curves appear—you should be able to see some difference with the setting of 75 set in the previous step. The shape of these two curves determines the shape of the specular highlight. Note that this shading type has a Diffuse Level parameter, similar to ONB. Experiment with Anisotropy and Orientation until you understand their effects.

12. Switch the shading type to Multi-Layer. You can see from the number of basic parameters defining it that this shading type is the most complicated. After experimenting with the other shading types, you should find Multi-Layer somewhat familiar, however. It is nothing more than Anisotropic with an additional layer of anisotropy. The Level parameter in each specular layer controls the strength of that layer. Notice that there is a color available for each specular layer. The other parameters here are similar to ones you've seen before. Experiment with the parameters until you understand their effects.

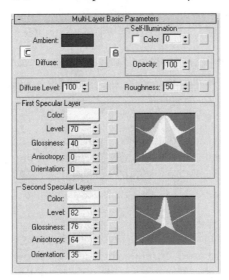

13. Finally, switch the shading type to Phong. Its controls are very similar to Blinn's. Everything here should be very easy to comprehend, compared to the Multi-Layer shading type. Phong shading isn't as good as Blinn at capturing glancing highlights—reflections of light striking an object almost parallel to its surface. You also have to use the Soften parameter more often in order to compensate for overly plastic-looking materials. If you're not looking for a matte plastic look, stick with Blinn as your general-purpose shading type.

Basic Shading Parameters

Every material has a few check boxes in its basic parameters rollout that are the same for all shading types:

Wire   displays objects in wireframe in the rendered image. This check box allows you to show some objects in wireframe (using one material) and other objects fully shaded (by using another material without this parameter checked).

To render all objects as wireframe, you can check Force Wireframe in the Default Scanline rollout of the Render Scene window. To actually build the geometry of a wireframe, use the Lattice modifier you used in Chapter 4.

Face Map   displays the entire material on each face of an object's mesh. If the material is a mapped material, it requires no mapping coordinates. The map is applied to each face in the object's topology. You will learn more about maps in "Understanding Materials and Maps" later in this chapter.

Face Map is often used with particle systems to put a single map on each particle. If you use facing particles and a map with an alpha channel determining opacity, you can fake geometry this way. Particle systems are covered in more detail in Chapter 9.

2-Sided   applies materials to both sides of objects. You used this option already in Chapter 4 when you applied a two-sided material to the guitar in order to be able to see the inside. Use this option sparingly, as it will often double the rendering time because the renderer has to calculate twice as many surfaces from the same number of faces.

Faceted   renders each face as if it were flat, neglecting any smoothing stored in the mesh. This allows you to produce renderings similar to how objects look in viewports shown in faceted display mode—with a blocky and computerized look.

Extended Shading Parameters

The Extended Parameters rollout contains more specialized or advanced parameters for the shading type of the material.

Advanced Transparency gives you controls for refining your transparent materials as well as a more sophisticated form of transparency than that offered by the basic Opacity setting. As you learned in the earlier discussion on color components, filter color controls the transmitted color of light passing through a material. The Falloff settings are used to control the direction that transparency falls off depending on the angle of the surface relative to your point of view. "In" is best for glass, with greater transparency toward the center of the glass than the edges, and "Out" is best for a cloud of smoke, where the outer edges are more transparent than the center of the cloud. The Amount parameter controls the amount of transparency falloff.

For glasslike transparency, it is better to use Advanced Transparency in Extended Parameters with a high "In" Falloff instead of a low Opacity setting in the Basic Parameters rollout.

The Index Of Refraction (IOR) determines how light will be bent through an object with a raytraced refraction map. Raytraced refraction is one of the few rendering calculations that considers the actual volume of an object. The IOR is a property of an object's substance rather than just its surface. Refractions are used for objects like a wine glass or a swimming pool. Raytracing will be covered in more detail in "Reflection and Refraction Maps" later in this chapter. You will use raytraced reflections and refractions in Chapter 8. Table 7.2 gives IOR values of some common materials.

Table 7.2 Common Indices of Refraction

MATERIAL	IOR VALUE
Outer Space	1.0 (exactly)
Air	1.0003
Water	1.333
Ice	1.309
Glass	1.5 to 1.7
Emerald	1.570
Diamond	2.419

Wire   controls the width of the rendered wireframe. These controls only work if Wire is checked in the Basic Parameters rollout.

Reflection Dimming   is used for dimming reflection maps that are in shadow (see "Map Types" later in this chapter for more information on reflection maps).

Understanding Materials and Maps

In max, any color or map other than basic object color is applied to surfaces with a material. Materials are represented in the interface with a blue sphere icon. Materials have standard parameters plus *material channels* to which maps can be applied. Standard materials have a channel for each of the different components described in "Components of Surface Shading" earlier in this chapter, plus several other material channels that will be described in "Maps Rollout" later in this chapter.

Each material channel has a button in the Material Editor, also called a *map slot*, to which maps can be applied. Maps are represented in the interface with a green parallelogram icon. Only materials can be applied to the surfaces of geometry objects. Only maps can be applied to the mapping channels of material or to the map slots for the background, the viewport, or environmental effects (covered in Chapter 13).

In the sample slots of the Material Editor, materials are displayed on 3D objects (a sphere by default), while maps are displayed flat, filling up the whole slot. This is another cue to whether you are dealing with a material or a map. Table 7.3 shows the distinctions between materials and maps.

Table 7.3 Distinctions and Uses of Materials and Maps

	MATERIAL	**MAP**
Interface Icon	● (blue)	▨ (green)
Sample Slot appearance		
Uses	Applying color and maps to geometry surfaces; making sub-materials for compound materials	Applying maps to the material channels of a material; applying as environment, viewport background, environmental effects (e.g., fog), or displacement maps; making sub-maps for compound maps

The Material/Map Browser

The Material/Map Browser allows you to browse through all the materials and maps on your computer. You can browse from your scene, the Material Editor, another .max file, or material libraries of pre-designed materials. You can also create your own material libraries for the organization of materials and maps you design.

Material libraries contain recipes for materials and pointers to maps; they do not contain the maps them-selves. If you want to use your material libraries on another computer, you must take along any maps they reference and use Customize ➜ Configure Paths to ensure that max has a path to those maps.

Let's see how the Material/Map browser works:

1. Open the Material Editor. Click a blank sample slot.

2. Click the Get Material button to bring up the Material/Map Browser.

3. Notice the blue spheres representing materials and the green parallelograms representing maps. Since you will be learning about materials first, filter the list to show only materials by unchecking Maps under Show. Now you only see the blue spheres representing materials.

4. Right now you are browsing from new materials as seen in the Browse From: area of the dialog box. The list shows all the kinds of materials that are available in max.

By clicking different radio buttons, you can browse from:

- Material Library—saved material library (.mat) files containing recipes for materials and maps

- Material Editor—the 24 materials in the Material Editor (whether they are all displayed or not)

- Active Slot—the one material in the current sample slot

- Selected—the material assigned to the currently selected object

- Scene—all the materials applied to objects in the scene

- New—all the material types within max

5. Choose the material library radio button. A long list should appear showing the library materials. Double-click the first material in the library—called Bricks_Bricks_1 (Standard). The material fills the active slot in the Material Editor. By doing this, you are copying a material definition from the library into the Material Editor. You can change this material to suit your project without affecting the original copy in the library.

6. Click the Open button under File. The Open Material Library dialog box appears as a standard file browser. Select the Wood material library (wood.mat).

7. Now the list shows only the materials in the Wood library for you to use. You can save your own libraries from materials listed in the browser by clicking the SaveAs button. You can merge multiple libraries together by using the Merge button. The Save button saves the library that is currently open without prompting you for a new filename. Close the Material/Map Browser.

You can directly import the materials from another max scene file in the Open Material Library dialog box. Change the Files of type from .mat *to* .max. *Then browse to the* .max *file to copy its scene materials as if it were a library.*

Material Trees

Key
Concept

The reason people often get confused when they first start applying materials in max is that they don't understand the concept of max's material tree and get lost between the levels of a material. Max's standard material has the material level and the map levels of each mapping channel. In addition to standard materials, max has compound material types that have whole materials as components. You already used one of these, the Multi/Sub-Object material, in the landscape tutorial in Chapter 4. Max also has compositor map types that have other maps as components. There is no limit, outside of processor power, on the number of levels you can have in a material tree.

The Material/Map Navigator

You can use the Material/Map Navigator to see and navigate the hierarchy of a material tree. The Material/Map Navigator shows the material's hierarchical structure in graphic form, much like Windows Explorer displays your computer's file system. Let's try it out:

1. With the Brick material still selected from the previous section, click the Material/Map Navigator button to bring up the Material/Map Navigator.

The Navigator shows the material tree for the Brick material. The Brick material is a standard material type. This material has a map in the diffuse color channel and a map in the bump channel. Maps placed in material channels are the children of the parent material. This hierarchy is represented by the fact that the parallelograms are indented from the sphere. In addition, one of the maps is shown with a red parallelogram—because it is the one shown in the viewport.

2. Click on the red parallelogram to navigate to the map in the diffuse color channel. Notice that the panel within the Material Editor has changed—you are now in one of the material's child panels. In this case, you are looking at the controls for a bitmap.

3. Click back on the blue sphere within the Navigator. The panel within the Material Editor changes back to the more familiar controls for the standard material.

While you are learning the terminology over the next few sections, keep the Material/Map Navigator open so you can visually grasp the structures of the material trees.

Material Types

Max offers 10 different kinds of materials. Most of the time you will be using the standard material, but there are many occasions when you'll want to use a specialized type of material. Third-party plug-ins offer even more types of materials to choose from.

The Standard Material

The standard material is the default material in max. All the features you've looked at up to this point in the chapter have been those of standard materials. Standard materials offer many options for making realistic-looking surfaces.

Selecting a New Material Type

To select a new material type to replace the default material in the sample slot:

1. Open the Material Editor. Click a blank sample slot.

2. Click the Get Material button to bring up the Material/Map Browser.

3. To simplify matters, keep the Show Maps box unchecked so that you are looking only at material types. Choose the New radio button under Browse From.

4. Double-click a material type. The material you selected replaces the previous material in the sample slot. The new material's panel will also be displayed in the Material Editor.

Replacing an Existing Material

You can replace an existing material's type by clicking the button that states its type in the Material Editor. Changing it this way to one of the compound materials will give you the option of discarding the original material or keeping it as a sub-material of the new material. To change an existing material:

1. In the Material Editor, click the button next to the material's name, which is labeled as that material's type. This also brings up the Material/Map Browser, with only material types available.

    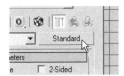

2. Choose a new material type from the list to replace the existing material. If you choose one of the compound materials, the Replace Material dialog box appears.

3. You can make a decision here to replace the old material or keep the old material as a sub-material of the new one. For this example, select Discard Old Material and click OK. Now the new material has replaced the old.

Compound Materials

Compound materials involve a material tree containing more than one sub-material. When you change a material's type to one of the compound types, you can keep the original material (or original material tree) as a sub-material of the new material. Complex trees can result.

Masks, Alpha Channels, and Opacity Maps

For several types of compound materials and maps, you have the option of using masks or alpha channels to determine how materials are blended or composited. These words—"mask" and "alpha channel"—seem to provoke irrational levels of fear in beginning and even intermediate users of CG programs. In reality, if you have ever used any kind of computer application, even to apply boldface to a piece of text, you have used the equivalent of an alpha channel or mask. They are very simple.

When you apply boldface, you first select the text to be bolded. This is what an alpha channel or a mask does: It selects the part of the image for visibility or for the application of an effect. An alpha channel is simply a mask embedded as an extra channel of information in the image file, while a mask or opacity map is generally a separate file. When compositing, the words "mask," "opacity map," "transparency map," and "alpha information" can often be used interchangeably.

If everything in the image is either completely visible or completely invisible, the alpha channel or mask will be pure white (corresponding to 100% opaque) or pure black (corresponding to 100% transparent). Often you want something to be *partially* transparent, such as a glass object against a background or the edges of objects that will be anti-aliased. If you have a grayscale mask or alpha channel, you have 256 levels of transparency corresponding to the 256 levels of grayscale (0 to 255 in value).

As long as you can distinguish between the area you want selected and the area you don't want selected, you have the basis of a mask. Any of the red, green, or blue channels can be used to make a mask. One of the separate elements rendered in Render Elements might be used to create a mask. If the channel is black where you want it white, you can always invert it, either by inverting the grayscale values in Photoshop or by checking Inverted once you bring it into max.

This is where alpha channels *can* be confusing. It's easy to get turned around in your mind as to which way is opaque and which way is transparent, especially if there have been reversals along the way. Fortunately, there are only two choices. If one way is wrong, the other way is probably right. The cardinal rule of masks is this: if it's not doing what you want, try inverting it.

Photoshop Channel Chops *(New Riders, 1998) by David Biedny, Nathan Moody, and Bert Monroy contains in-depth information on creating masks and alpha channels: highly recommended reading for CG artists.*

When is an alpha channel not an alpha channel?

The nomenclature about alpha channels gets a little fuzzy because Photoshop lets you save up to 21 "alpha channels" in a `.psd` file. Only one of these (the first one listed in the Channels palette) will actually determine transparency in a compositing program. Think of all the other "alpha channels" in Photoshop as just extra channels—grayscale images that can be used for selection—rather than as alpha channels in the sense that we mean in compositing. Each pixel can have only one transparency value when composited: *that* is what we mean by its alpha channel information.

The Blend Material

The Blend material mixes two materials together. The amount of the blending is determined by the mix amount parameter. This is equivalent to an opacity setting. Zero means only the first material is seen; 100 means only the second material is seen.

If you prefer, a Mask map can be applied to blend the materials according to the grayscale values of the map. Where the Mask map is black, only the first material is seen; where the map is white, only the second material is seen; where the map is gray, the materials are mixed proportionally to the grayscale value.

If you assign a mask that has gray values, the mixing curve can be used to variably blend materials according to the transition zone parameters. The Upper value determines where in the grayscale values the blend starts and the Lower value determines where the blend ends. If the Upper and Lower values are the same, there is a sharp transition between the materials at a specific grayscale value. If the values are set further apart, the materials are blended across a greater range of the mask grayscale values.

Use a Blend material when you want to mix two materials with fine control over how the materials are blended. Remember to pay attention to the structure of each material type in the Material/Map Navigator. Figure 7.5 shows an example of a Blend material in the Material Editor, the Material/Map Navigator, and the preview slot.

Remember that you will need to render in order to see the complete effect of materials. What you see in the viewport is only a rough approximation of what the image will look like when rendered. The material preview sample slots are more accurate, but they are still not precisely the same as a render. You may want to do test renders to appreciate the full effect of a material.

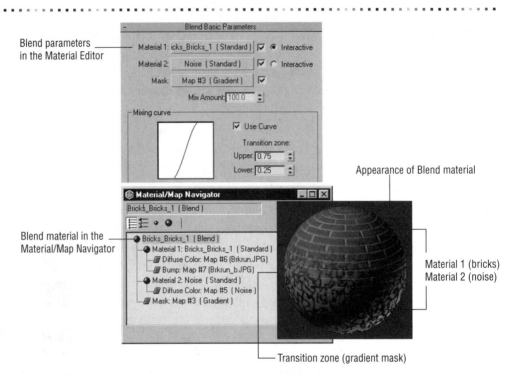

Blend parameters in the Material Editor

Blend material in the Material/Map Navigator

Appearance of Blend material

Material 1 (bricks)
Material 2 (noise)

Transition zone (gradient mask)

Figure 7.5 *Blend material*

The Composite Material

The Composite material mixes up to 10 component materials with three options for the mode of mixing (called *transfer modes* or *blend modes* by Photoshop users): additive, subtractive, or opacity mixing. Opacity mixing works just like the Mix Amount parameter in a Blend material, except without the mask or transition zone options. Additive adds the colors of the component materials, resulting in a material lighter than the base material. Subtractive subtracts the colors of the component materials from the base material, resulting in a material darker than the base material. The materials are composited from top to bottom in the material's rollout. Use Composite materials when you are looking for a layered effect with more than two materials. Use Blend if you are only dealing with two materials and want to use the masking controls. Figure 7.6 shows an example of a Composite material in the Material Editor, the Material/Map Navigator, and the preview slot.

If you want to composite a decal onto an object, you need to use a Composite or Mask map in the diffuse channel of a material rather than a Composite material. Composite and Mask maps are explained in "Map Types" later in this chapter.

Composite parameters
in the Material Editor

Composite material in
the Material/Map Navigator

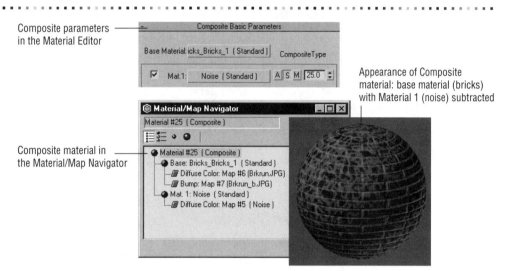

Appearance of Composite
material: base material (bricks)
with Material 1 (noise) subtracted

Figure 7.6 *Composite material*

The Double Sided Material

The Double Sided material applies two component materials to surfaces, one on the side that the normals are facing and one on the reverse side. Translucency defines how much the opposite material will show through. Note that this material allows you to use *different* materials for each side of a surface, unlike the 2-sided check box in the basic parameters of a shading type that applies the same material to both sides of a surface. Use Double Sided materials when you need to assign different materials to the front and back faces of an object.

Applying a double-sided material or checking the 2-sided option in a standard material effectively doubles the number of polygons that the renderer has to calculate for that object. By default a surface is defined as one-sided. Materials that shade both sides force the renderer to calculate an extra set of polygons facing the reverse direction. Use these materials only when you need them.

The Morpher Material

The Morpher material allows you to animate between component materials using the Morpher modifier. The Morpher modifier is covered in Chapter 9. Use Morpher materials only when you are using the Morpher modifier.

The Multi/Sub-Object Material

The Multi/Sub-Object material allows you to assign more than one material to a surface. It assigns any number of component materials based on the material ID values of the surface sub-objects (faces, polygons, patches, or NURBS surfaces). You used a Multi/Sub-Object material in the landscape tutorial in Chapter 4 in order to distinguish the road polygons from the landscape polygons in the Conform compound object. Use Multi/Sub-Object materials whenever you need more than one material to appear on a single object. Figure 7.7 shows the "Landscape and Road" Multi/Sub-Object material from Chapter 4 in the Material Editor, the Material/Map Navigator, and the preview slot.

The Shellac Material

The Shellac material adds the color values of two component materials. The effect is just like a Composite material with two component materials using the additive mode. In fact, this material is really a subset of Composite materials. Use it as a shortcut if you want to composite using the additive color of two materials. Otherwise stick with the more powerful Composite material.

The Top/Bottom Material

The Top/Bottom material applies two component materials to surfaces, one to the top faces of an object and the other to the bottom faces. Top faces are defined as those whose normals point up while bottom faces are those whose normals point down. The transition between them can also be adjusted with the Blend and Position parameters. Curved surfaces give nice transitions while boxes will have one material for an entire face. The World and Local check boxes allow you to define whether the Top/Bottom material is applied consistently regardless of the orientation of the object or if the transition between materials is anchored to the World. Use a Top/Bottom material when you want to blend materials across a curved surface from bottom to top. Figure 7.8 shows an example of a Top/Bottom material in the Material Editor, the Material/Map Navigator, and rendered.

The anchoring of the transition to World coordinates will not display properly in the viewport—sometimes not even in an ActiveShade view. You must render your scene to see the effect.

Multi/Sub-Object parameters in the Material Editor

Multi/Sub-Object material in the Material/Map Navigator

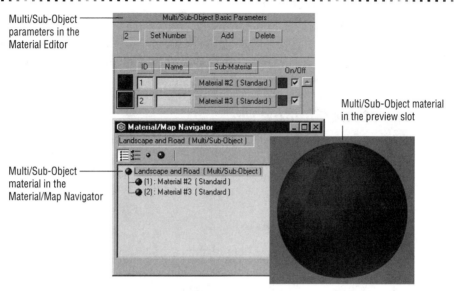

Multi/Sub-Object material in the preview slot

Figure 7.7 *Multi/Sub-Object material*

Top/Bottom parameters in the Material Editor

Top/Bottom material in the Material/Map Navigator

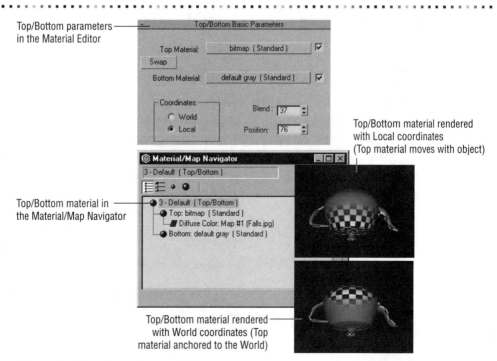

Top/Bottom material rendered with Local coordinates (Top material moves with object)

Top/Bottom material rendered with World coordinates (Top material anchored to the World)

Figure 7.8 *Top/Bottom material*

Special Materials

The remaining materials are only used in special situations. Matte/Shadow is used when you are creating special effects with the environment background image. The Raytrace material is the gateway to a powerful raytracing rendering engine built into max for making beautiful reflections and refractions.

The Matte/Shadow Material

The Matte/Shadow material makes an object invisible, but allows it to receive shadows and affect the alpha channel of the rendering. Use objects with a Matte/Shadow material to project shadows from visible objects onto a 2D environment background or to affect your alpha channel for post-production compositing.

The Raytrace Material

The Raytrace material calculates reflections and refractions based on tracing the path of rays of light that strike the camera, back through the various reflections and refractions in the scene, to the light source. A raytracing algorithm thinks of objects as solids rather than just as surfaces, in order to calculate the refraction of light through their volumes. Raytracing will be covered in more detail in "Reflection and Refraction Maps" later in this chapter. You will use raytraced reflections and refractions in Chapter 8.

Material Channels

So far, you have learned how to adjust the various parameters and color components of different materials and shading types. When you want to create greater variation on a surface than a color component or shading parameter will allow, you turn to the material channels to apply maps to alter the various visual properties of a surface. The channels available within a material vary with different shading and material types.

The term *map* is actually a mathematical term; to map something means to make a correspondence between it and something else. For example, let's say you want to design a material that looks like brick wall. To make this material, you will need to replace the diffuse color component of a standard material with a picture of brick. You do this by applying a map of the brick to the diffuse material channel.

The "Material Channel Mapping" plate in the Color Gallery shows maps applied to various channels of a material. Use this as a guide for applying maps.

Maps Rollout

The Maps rollout in the Material Editor is where you can assign maps to the different material channels. If you are at the basic parameters of a material, you can right-click a blank area of the Material Editor and choose Maps to open up the rollout. Figure 7.9 shows the Maps rollout of the standard material with the Blinn shading type. Let's see how the Maps rollout works:

1. Open the Material Editor. Click a blank sample slot.

2. Set the diffuse color to light green and the ambient to a darker green. Leave specular close to white.

3. Open the Maps rollout. Click the button in the diffuse color channel (it is labeled "None"). The Material/Map Browser appears. Notice that only the maps are displayed in the browser (green parallelograms). This is because only maps can be applied to material channels, not other materials.

4. Select Bitmap from the list of maps. Remember from Chapter 1 that a bitmap means a pixel-based image file.

5. The Select Bitmap Image File dialog box appears as a standard file browser. Browse to the file Brkrun.JPG from the 3dsmax4\Maps\Brick folder. Click Open.

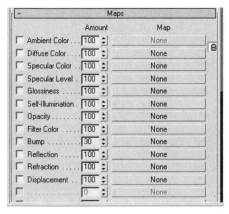

Figure 7.9 *Maps rollout of standard material*

Note that the Material Editor now shows the panel for the map assigned to the diffuse color channel, as shown in Figure 7.10. This is a level below the base material. Watch the Material/Map Navigator if you aren't sure where in the material tree you are.

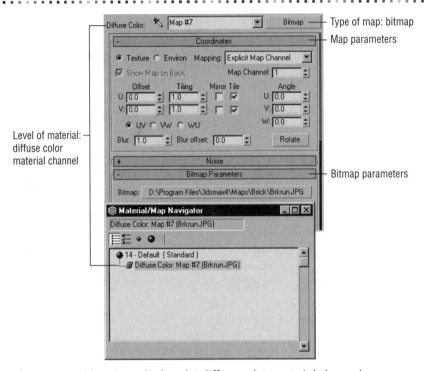

Figure 7.10 *Bitmap applied to the diffuse color material channel*

6. Make a few primitive objects and select them.

7. Click the Assign Material To Selection button. Notice the objects now take on the color of the diffuse component in the viewport.

8. You may be wondering why your objects don't look like brick. Render the scene. They do look like brick in the rendering. Figure 7.11 shows the objects in the viewport and the rendering.

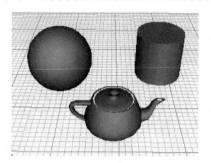 

Viewport shows diffuse color   Rendering shows diffuse map

Figure 7.11 *Diffuse map applied but not shown in viewport*

9. Click the Show Map In Viewport button in the Material Editor. Now you can see the map in the viewport without having to render it.

Only one map can be displayed in the viewport for each material. Only the map itself will show, not the final result of its effect on the material. If you click the Show Map In Viewport button at another map level, that map will become the only one displayed in the viewport. To see the final result of your map on the material, look at the sample slot, use an ActiveShade view, or—for the most accurate version—render your scene.

10. Using the Material/Map Navigator, click the blue sphere to return to the top level of the material tree. Look at the diffuse color component—it is still green.

   What is happening here is that the map in the diffuse color channel is completely replacing the green color, so you see only brick when you render the scene. Look back at the Maps rollout and notice that the amount spinner in the diffuse color channel is set to the default of 100%.

11. Set the amount of the map in the diffuse color channel to 50%. The objects still look like red brick in the viewport, but the sample slot appears with a green tint.

12. Render the scene. Notice that the bricks are rendered with a green tint.

   By adjusting the Amount parameter in the material channel, you are adjusting how much the bitmap is mapping to the diffuse color component. Use the amount spinner to adjust the strength of the map.

Note that the map and the diffuse color are watered down in this way of tinting. An alternate way of tinting a map is to use the Enable Color Map option in the Output rollout. This allows you to apply a control similar to Photoshop Curves to adjust the red, green, and/or blue channels to affect the color and contrast of a map output—without altering the map file itself.

13. In the Basic Parameters rollout, you can now see a capital M in the little box next to the diffuse color component. This is a shortcut button to the diffuse map in the material tree. Make sure the navigator is open and then click the M. You automatically navigate to the bitmap in that channel. The rollout in the Material Editor changes correspondingly.

14. Watch the Navigator as you click the Go To Parent button in the Material Editor. Now you are back in the parent, or top, level of the material (blue sphere in the Navigator).

15. In the Maps rollout, change the amount of the diffuse color map back to 100%. Save your work as `Materials03.max`.

Color Component Channels

The color components discussed earlier in "Components of Surface Shading" have material channels that can be mapped. The Amount parameters of the color components are an opacity setting for the map applied over the base color. The shortcut buttons (in the Basic Parameters rollout, except for Filter Color in the Extended Parameters rollout) all work the same way as you have seen—as shortcuts to their corresponding material channels. You can use these shortcuts or use the larger buttons in the Maps rollout (marked None by default)—they do the same thing.

Opacity Channel

Just like a mask or an alpha channel, a map in the opacity channel determines which areas of a surface are opaque or transparent according to the grayscale values of the map. The Amount parameter determines how transparent a black pixel of the opacity map will be. So a lower Amount will make the surface more opaque. You will use opacity maps in Chapter 8.

Specular Level Channel

The intensity of specular reflections is a very important cue to the eye about the texture and uniformity of a surface. A raised surface will not only be shaded, but will have corresponding variations in the specular intensity. For this reason, a specular level map should generally accompany a bump map, explained in the next section.

There are also subtle variations in specular level that give an object a "realistic" surface. Whether a surface is dirty to the eye or not, flaws and dirt will cause variations in the strength of the specular level across the surface. CG surfaces often look "too clean." To make them look more realistic, apply a specular level map, with a copy composited on the diffuse map, at a low setting.

For a large collection of maps designed specifically for creating realistic surfaces, along with detailed tutorials on how to apply them, check out the dvGarage Surface Toolkit *CD by Alex Lindsay, available at* `http://www.dvGarage.com`.

Bump Channel

Bump maps alter the normals of a surface according to the grayscale values of the map, shading the surface areas corresponding to dark pixels as if they were receded and areas corresponding to light pixels as if they were raised. This creates the illusion of detailed geometry, without the cost of extra polygons. The Amount parameter of a bump map determines the intensity of the effect. Use bump maps to add the appearance of low relief or an etched effect. Figure 7.12 shows an example of how a bump map creates the illusion of extra geometry, alone and in conjunction with an identical specular level map.

People tend to overuse bump maps and underuse specular level maps to create textured surfaces. Try copying the bump map to the specular level channel at a low intensity before upping the bump strength.

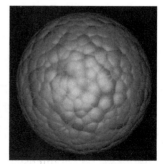

Bump map shown in viewport   Rendered object with bump map only   Rendered object with bump map
and identical specular level map

Figure 7.12 *Bump map on an object affecting the rendered surface*

Reflection Channel

The reflection channel determines how a surface handles light that bounces off it. Three main kinds of maps are applied to the reflection channel: bitmaps that simulate reflections with an image of an environment, automatic reflection maps that take a picture of the scene from the object's point of view and map it back onto the object, and a raytraced map that calculates reflections by tracing each ray of light back from the camera.

Reflection maps work because the map is anchored to the World rather than to the local coordinates of the object. The map therefore doesn't move when the object does, and so simulates the reflection of the surrounding environment. Because the reflection channel describes specular reflections, it is affected by the Specular color component. The higher the value of the specular component, the stronger the reflection. The Amount parameter of a reflection map also controls the strength of the reflection. It generally needs to be turned down to create realistic reflections; otherwise the reflection overpowers the diffuse color or map, making it too strong to look like a reflection.

Refraction Channel

Refraction refers to light that is "bent" as it travels through the boundary between transparent materials. The refraction channel works with the Index Of Refraction parameter in the Extended Parameters rollout. Refraction maps, like reflection maps, are locked to the World rather than to the object. They also involve mapping the view back onto the object. You can use an automatic Reflect/Refract map or a more accurate raytraced refraction map. Use this channel to create more realistic looking glassware, aquariums, gemstones, and swimming pools.

Displacement Channel

The displacement channel allows you to transform part of a surface according to the variation given in a map. It actually creates new geometry, just like the Displace modifier you used in Chapter 4. You could model a piece of terrain from a flat surface using a material with a displacement map. Displacement is a hybrid material/modeling technique. It is computationally intensive and can impact rendering time significantly, so use displacement sparingly.

 The displacement material channel was originally designed for NURBS surfaces and works particularly well with them.

Map Types

As you've learned, maps can be applied in a variety of places in the max interface, from material channels to environmental effects. Maps can be bitmap images, procedurally generated patterns, image filters from Photoshop or Premiere, color modifiers, or ray-tracing algorithms for reflections or refractions. Third-party plug-ins can add other map types to your palette.

Keep in mind that you can't drag a map from one of the sample slots in the Material Editor to an object in the viewport, because maps must be applied to geometry objects using a material with the map in one of its material channels.

You can *drag a map from the Asset Browser or from one of the map buttons in the Material Editor to a geometry object in the viewport. Max assigns a material to the object and automatically places the map in its diffuse color channel.*

Bitmap

As you've already learned, bitmaps are image files from pixel-based graphics applications that can be applied to various material channels. Bitmaps are the most frequently used maps. You can use a scanner or digital camera to collect various bitmaps to use in your materials. You can also buy CDs that contain hundreds of photographed texture maps. The many bitmaps that ship with max are located in the 3dsmax4\Maps folder and its subfolders. You can also apply an .avi or .mov file to create an animated bitmap.

2D Procedural Maps

Procedural maps generate the resultant image using a mathematical algorithm. Maps using a two-dimensional algorithm create flat images that can be placed in any material channel and mapped to surfaces.

Bricks

Bricks generate a tiled pattern between two colors or maps with added noise using a 2D algorithm that simulates bricks. Many predefined architectural brick patterns are included.

Checker

Checker generates a pattern between two colors or maps. Checker always makes an alternating pattern of squares like a checkers or chess board. You can set the tiling and offset of the checker in its map rollout.

Gradient

Gradient creates a smooth variation among three colors or maps in a linear or radial direction.

Gradient Ramp

Gradient Ramp allows you to add as many colors or maps to a gradient as you choose. Use when you desire more control than Gradient allows.

Swirl

Swirl generates swirling spiral patterns between two colors or maps.

3D Procedural Maps

Three-dimensional maps are procedural maps whose effects are calculated for the entire volume of an object. If you cut away part of a surface that uses a 3D map or rotate the mapping, the effect will show all the way through the object. In contrast, 2D maps only show on the surfaces of objects.

Cellular

Cellular generates an organic cellular pattern that can simulate anything from snake-skin to ocean surfaces.

Dent

Dent generates a pattern of two colors or maps that simulates a dented, banged-up surface. This map is often used in the bump channel to simulate realistic dents.

Falloff

Falloff generates a pattern based on the angle between the surface normals of an object and the viewing direction. The pattern fades (or falls off) across a surface. It is good for creating fog effects (using the Distance Blend option) or realistic glass reflections (using the Fresnel option). Falloff is usually used in the opacity channel. It is also some-times used in the self-illumination channel to simulate iridescence.

Marble

Marble generates a marble pattern between two colors or maps. The Vein width and Size of the pattern are adjustable.

Noise

Noise generates a turbulence pattern between two colors or maps. Many maps have a Noise rollout built-in with similar functionality.

Perlin Marble

Perlin Marble generates an alternative marble pattern with noise added. Perlin Marble is more complex than the Marble map.

Planet

Planet generates a contour pattern that simulates a planet's surface as viewed from outer space. Parameters include Continent Size and Island Factor. Use this map to form your own worlds.

Smoke

Smoke generates a fractal turbulence pattern between two colors or maps that simulate smoke and clouds.

Speckle

Speckle generates a speckled pattern between two colors or maps that simulates materials like granite.

Splat

Splat generates a fractal pattern between two colors or maps that simulates splattered paint.

Stucco

Stucco generates a fractal pattern between two colors or maps that simulates the texture of "stucco," a rough masonry product sprayed on exterior building walls.

Water

Water generates a concentric ripple pattern between two colors or maps suitable for the surface of liquids.

Wood

Wood generates a grain pattern between two colors or maps for use in wood.

Compositor Maps

Like materials, maps can be formed into trees with various levels of sub-maps. Compositor maps are to maps what compound materials are to materials. Use compositor maps when you need to combine maps.

Mix Map

A Mix map will blend two colors or maps according to a Mix Amount parameter. This map is directly analogous to the Blend material type between two materials except that it applies only to the material channel you specify. As with the Blend material, the mix amount can be mapped with a mask, and transition zone parameters give you fine control of the blending of the mask.

Composite Map

A Composite map allows you to superimpose multiple maps on top of each other. It is similar to a Mix map, except that the mix amount for each map after the base map is defined by its alpha channel. You can composite as many maps as you like. Use this map to add decals to a diffuse map. To do this, either use a decal map with an alpha channel defining its edges or make one of the sub-maps of the Composite map a Mask map (covered next) with the decal as the Map and the masking image as the Mask. Figure 7.13 shows the structure of a Composite material that uses two decals, one using an alpha channel and one using a Mask sub-map. Review "Masks, Alpha Channels, and Opacity Maps" earlier in this chapter if you are uncertain about using masks or alpha channels.

Mask Map

A Mask map masks the first map according to the grayscale values of the second map. If this is applied to the diffuse channel, it will mask between the first map and the object color; if it is applied as one of the sub-maps of a Composite map, it will mask between the first map of the Mask map and the previous layers of the Composite map. Use this map for sophisticated compositing effects and for composites where the mask information is in a separate file from the rest of the image rather than in the image's alpha channel. Figure 7.13 shows a Mask map (Map 2) being used as a sub-map of a Composite map.

Composite map parameters
in the Material Editor

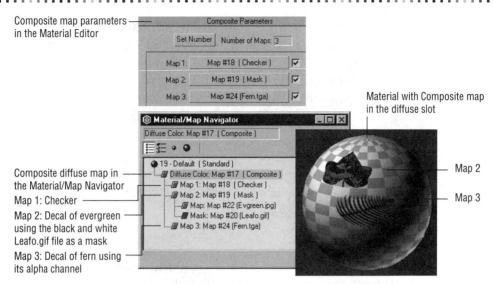

Material with Composite map
in the diffuse slot

Composite diffuse map in
the Material/Map Navigator

Map 1: Checker

Map 2: Decal of evergreen
using the black and white
Leafo.gif file as a mask

Map 3: Decal of fern using
its alpha channel

Map 2

Map 3

Figure 7.13 *Composite map with base map and two decal maps*

Don't let the terminology confuse you. The terms "map" and "mask" can be used generically, yet also refer to specific slots in a Mask map. A Mask map type includes two slots for maps, one called "Map" and one called "Mask." Technically, there are two levels of a Mask map that can be called "Mask map": the lower level is the mask itself; the upper level is the map in the Map slot masked by the map in the Mask slot.

RGB Multiply Map

An RGB Multiply map mixes two maps by multiplying their RGB values and alpha channel values. Use this material in the bump channel to combine two bump maps. In the diffuse channel, if one color and one map are used, the map will be tinted with the chosen color.

Color Modifying Maps

Color modifying maps are used to manipulate the pixel color of other maps. Each map offers a different means of modifying color.

Output Map

Output rollouts are already built into many maps. Apply an Output map for those maps that don't already have these settings. Checking Enable Color Map allows you to adjust the output curve of the image. This allows you to adjust the contrast or hue of a map without changing the map itself.

To apply an Output map, change the type of an existing map to Output and check Keep Old Map As Sub-Map in the Replace Map dialog box.

RGB Tint Map

An RGB Tint map allows you to directly tint a map by using RGB colors. To tint a map change the existing map to the RGB Tint type and check Keep Old Map As Sub-Map.

Vertex Color Map

Vertex colors are a property of vertices in editable mesh and in the Edit Mesh modifier. They allow you to fake lighting and materials very cheaply for games. A Vertex Color map allows you to use vertex colors in a material tree, in a particular mapping channel, or as part of a composited map. You must first assign vertex colors to meshes within their vertex sub-object level.

Vertex Color on Patch Vertices

Max 4 now allows you to assign vertex colors to patch vertices as well as mesh vertices.

Special Maps

Some maps are found under 2D or 3D maps in the Material/Map Browser but have specialized uses.

Combustion Map

Combustion is used to create special effects from discreet combustion. You can paint directly on a bitmap and see the result update in the viewport. This can also be animated. You must have combustion installed on your computer for this map to work.

Photoshop Plug-in Filter Map

A Photoshop filter map is used to manipulate bitmaps with Adobe Photoshop plug-in filters. You must have Photoshop installed on your computer for this map to work. Use this map as a convenience within max instead of having to use filters within Photoshop. You can only use plug-in filters for Photoshop, not the default filters that ship with Photoshop.

Premiere Plug-in Video Filter Map

Premiere video filter map is used to manipulate a video file used as a map with Adobe Premiere filters. You must have Premiere installed on your computer for this map to work. Use this map as a convenience within max instead of having to use filters within Premiere.

Particle Age

Particle Age animates the color or map of particles based on the time since the particle was generated.

Particle MBlur

Particle MBlur adds variable motion blur to particle systems based on their speed.

Reflection and Refraction Maps

As you learned in the Material Channels section earlier, you can fake a reflection with a bitmap. If you don't have much in your scene or environment to reflect, a bitmap will actually be more convincing than calculated reflections. The reflection and refraction maps discussed in this section involve some kind of actual reflection or refraction calculation. Flat Mirror, Reflect/Refract, and Thin Wall Refraction are sometimes called "half-a-ray tracing" because they involve calculation of the scene without tracing every bounce of a light ray; in other words, they trace the light for one bounce from the environment to the object.

Flat Mirror

A Flat Mirror map is used only for surfaces that are completely flat. Flat Mirror should be used only in the reflection channel of a material. You can assign this map to individual objects or to selected coplanar faces within the sub-object level of a larger object.

Reflect/Refract

Reflect/Refract is an all-purpose map used in the reflection or refraction channels. It will generate effects automatically, based on surrounding objects and the environment map. Do not use this map for flat objects—use the Flat Mirror map instead. Reflect/Refract is calculated much faster than the Raytrace map, but it is not as accurate.

Thin Wall Refraction

Thin Wall Refraction is the best map to use to simulate light that is offset when passing through a glass lens or other thin-walled non-opaque substance.

Raytrace

A Raytrace map can be placed in either or both the reflection and refraction channels of a material. This map automatically utilizes the raytrace renderer to calculate reflections and refractions based on the objects and environment of your scene. You will use Raytrace maps in Chapter 8.

Using the Raytrace map can significantly increase rendering time. Use this map only when you want to calculate very accurate reflection and refraction.

Mapping Coordinates

As you learned in Chapter 2, *mapping coordinates* tell max how to assign the texture space of an object. Mapping coordinates use three axes to define texture space: the U, V, and W axes. U and V describe the surface, while W is the axis perpendicular to the surface used to describe rotation of the UV surface.

Mapping coordinates determine the placement of a map and how it is distorted across the three-dimensional geometry by aligning pixel-based maps with vertex-based geometry. Primitives are assigned default mapping coordinates. Lofts can be assigned mapping coordinates in their Surface Parameters rollout by checking Apply Mapping.

Adjusting Mapping Coordinates in the Coordinates Rollout

Most maps have a Coordinates rollout that lets you adjust the default mapping coordinates assigned to an object. Figure 7.14 shows the Coordinates rollout that is part of a typical map.

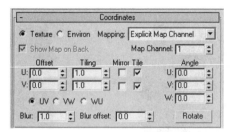

Figure 7.14 *Coordinates rollout of a typical map*

Tiling

Tiling controls how many times a map should be repeated across a surface in either direction. For example, if the tiling of a bitmap is set to 4 in U and 2 in V, the map will be repeated four times in the U direction and two times in the V direction. If the Tile is unchecked with the same values, the map will be the same size as if it were tiled this many times, but it will display only once. This is how you adjust the size of a map on an object.

The Mirror check box will put a mirror copy of the map next to the map and tile that. This can help make an asymmetrical pattern tile better.

Figure 7.15 shows how tiling controls affect the placement of a map on a surface.

Offset

The Offset parameters offset the placement of the map along each axis so that you can align it on the surface exactly as you want. In Figure 7.15, some offsets were used in order to make the tiling values clearer. Figure 7.16 shows examples of offsets.

Using the Coordinates Rollout

Let's try out the Coordinates settings:

1. Open the file Materials03.max that you made earlier or from the CD files for this chapter.

2. Click the M shortcut button next to the diffuse color swatch to go into the bitmap level of the material. Open the Coordinates rollout, if it is not already open.

3. Adjust the amount of Tiling in the U direction by dragging the spinner. Observe how the pattern is repeating more frequently on your objects.

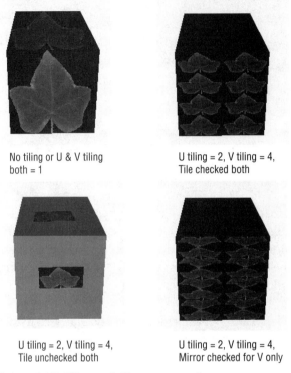

No tiling or U & V tiling
both = 1

U tiling = 2, V tiling = 4,
Tile checked both

U tiling = 2, V tiling = 4,
Tile checked for U only

U tiling = 2, V tiling = 4,
Tile unchecked both

U tiling = 2, V tiling = 4,
Mirror checked for V only

Figure 7.15 *Effects of tiling on map placement*

No offset

Positive U offset only

Negative V offset only

Figure 7.16 *Effects of offset on map placement*

4. Adjust the Tiling in the V direction. See how the pattern is being changed in the vertical direction on your objects.

5. Set both U and V tiling to 0.5 in each direction. Now the brick picture is being repeated half as much in each direction—it looks like you have half as many bricks.

6. Adjust the W angle to 45 degrees. See how the brick pattern now appears rotated on the objects. Save your work as `Materials04.max`.

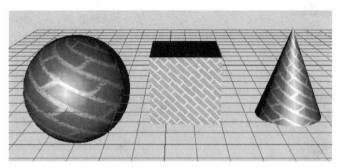

The UVW Map Modifier

You will usually find out that an object is missing mapping coordinates in one of two ways: (1) You go to a map level of your material and check the Show Map In Viewport button, but still don't see the map in the viewport. (2) When you render, you get the Missing Map Coordinates warning.

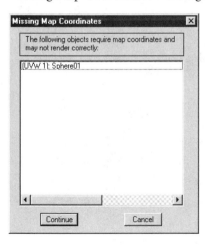

To apply mapping coordinates to a piece of geometry that was not assigned mapping coordinates by default, you need to apply a UVW Map modifier. This modifier offers the options of Planar, Spherical, Cylindrical, and Shrinkwrap for projecting the map onto the geometry. Box projection applies a copy of the map to each side of a box; Face projection applies a copy of the map to each face of the object. The mapping gizmo can be moved and rotated to change the placement of the map.

Third-party plug-ins such as Instant UV can give you more projection options.

In addition to controls over the tiling of the map, the modifier gives you up to 99 mapping channels, for applying more than one set of mapping coordinates with the same gizmo, as well as various alignment options in the sections of the Parameters rollout. The X, Y, and Z radio buttons allow you to choose the axis of alignment. Fit moves and scales the gizmo to best fit the object. Bitmap Fit allows you to choose a bitmap file with an aspect ratio you want the mapping gizmo to match (usually the bitmap you will be applying). View Align aligns the gizmo to the active viewport. Center aligns the gizmo to the center of the object. Normal Align allows you to drag over the normal to which you want the mapping aligned. Region Fit allows you to drag out a region of a viewport where you want the gizmo to be fit. Acquire allows you to pick another object with mapping you want the gizmo to match. Reset puts the gizmo back to its default position.

Applying Mapping Coordinates with UVW Map

Let's use the UVW Map modifier:

1. Open the file `Materials03.max` from your saved files or from the CD files for this chapter. Note that this is the second-to-last file that you saved in this chapter.

2. Zoom in on the Sphere primitive and select it.

3. In the Modify panel, apply a UVW Map modifier from the UV Coordinate modifier set.

   Right now the projection type is set to Planar. This means the Bricks bitmap is being applied onto a plane on the top of the sphere.

4. Open the UVW Map in the stack and go to the Gizmo sub-object level. A yellow gizmo appears in the viewport, representing this projection plane.

5. Rotate the gizmo around its X axis. Observe how the map is projected according to the orientation of this plane. You are dynamically changing the mapping coordinates.

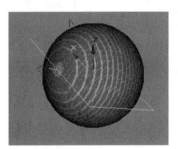

6. Turn off the Gizmo sub-object level in the stack.

7. Change the projection type by clicking the Cylindrical radio button. Observe the cylindrical gizmo that appears around the sphere.

8. Check Cap. The Bricks bitmap is projected along the top, or cap, of the sphere.

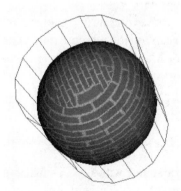

9. Experiment with the other projection types. Go to the Gizmo level and try transforming the gizmo to see the effect. Save your work as `Materials05.max`.

Assigning Different Mapping Channels

In max, geometry objects can have multiple bitmaps applied in different material channels, as well as multiple sets of mapping coordinates. Each set of mapping coordinates resides in its own *map channel* to indicate which map it corresponds to within the material. You tell max which UVW Map modifier to use with which map according to the Map Channel number in the Material Editor. Choose the mapping coordinates to use for a map by setting the Map Channel number to the same number as that of the corresponding UVW Map modifier. Figure 7.17 shows this connection.

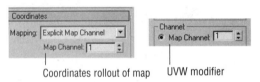

Coordinates rollout of map   UVW modifier

Figure 7.17 *Comparison of Map Channel number as seen in map and in UVW modifier*

Don't confuse material channels *with* map channels, *as they are completely different concepts with similar names. To make the matter even more complicated, materials also have* material effects channels *for applying special post-processing effects, covered in Chapters 13 and 14.*

Using UVW Map Manipulators

Max 4 now has manipulators, like those you saw in Chapter 3 as helper objects, built into the UVW Map modifier. You can use the manipulators to quickly change the size and tiling of the UVW Map gizmo. Manipulators are designed to make editing objects more intuitive. Let's see how it works:

1. Continue working on `Materials05.max` or open it from the CD files for this chapter. Select the sphere.

2. Click the Manipulate button in the main toolbar.

3. Move your mouse over the sphere without clicking. Notice that there are green outlines around the sphere's center. These allow you to change the size of the gizmo. If you look very carefully, you'll notice a green box near the top of the sphere—this is for the height of the gizmo. There are little green circles near the sphere's equator—these are for tiling. The green controls are all *UVW manipulators.*

4. Hold your mouse over a manipulator to see a tooltip appear. Drag the manipulator to change the associated parameter's value. Notice that the value is displayed interactively as you drag.

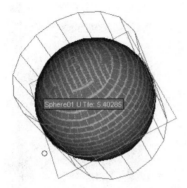

5. Experiment with changing all the UVW manipulators. Save your work as `Materials06.max`.

Using Unwrap UVW to Change Mapping

If you desire even more control over the way your maps are being projected onto your geometry, use the Unwrap UVW modifier. This modifier allows you to assign exactly which pixels of a bitmap correspond to which vertices of the geometry.

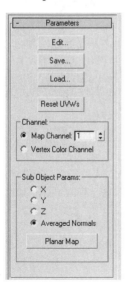

If you click the Edit button in the Parameters rollout, you will bring up the window with a representation of the vertices of your object superimposed on your bitmap. You can then move the points representing the vertices to the pixels of the bitmap you want them to display.

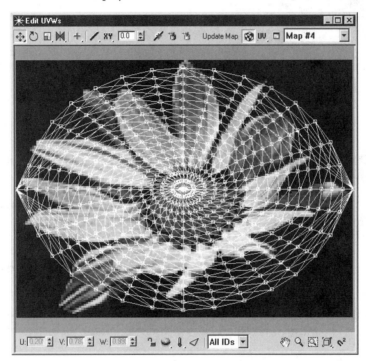

Unwrapping UVW coordinates is crucial to texture-mapping characters in the optimal way for low-poly low-resolution environments like games or Web 3D. The method of using Unwrap UVW is demonstrated in the Pulse Web 3D tutorial in Appendix A. The Hands-on max section later in this chapter demonstrates another method for unwrapping mapping coordinates from a model to a map.

Bezier Vertices in UVW Unwrap

Max 4 now allows you to assign the correspondences of Bezier vertices of patch surfaces in the UVW Unwrap modifier. Thus, you don't have to collapse to mesh to assign texture maps precisely.

Exploring the Material Editor Interface

Now that you understand the concepts used by max's Material Editor, let's take a closer look at that powerful dialog box. Table 7.4 describes its tools.

Table 7.4 Material Editor Tools and Their Uses

Button	Name	Use
	Get Material	Opens the Material/Map Browser.
		Use this to start a new material or map, bring a material or map from a library or other max scene file into the Material Editor, and to make your own material libraries.
	Put Material To Scene	Replaces hot material in the scene with selected sample slot if the materials have the same name.
		When testing changes to a material, copy it to another sample slot by dragging it and make your changes; when you're happy with your changes, click the Put Material To Scene button. Your new version of the material will replace the old one in the scene.
	Assign Material To Selection	Assigns the material in the active sample slot to selected geometry objects.
	Reset Map/Material To Default Settings	Resets both materials and maps to the default values.
	Make Material Copy	Copies the current hot material to itself, thereby "cooling" it.
		The original hot material in the slot will still be applied to objects in the scene, but you won't see it in one of the sample slots.
	Make Unique	Makes an instanced map or material unique.
		You can instance a map from a sample slot to the Environment background or another material, for example. Clicking this breaks the connection between the sample slot and the instance of the map or material.
	Put To Library	Adds the selected material to the currently open material library. If no library is open, a new one will be created. This library will be saved with the .max file until you open a different library.
		To save the new library as a file, use File ➔ Save in the Material/Map Browser.

Table 7.4 Material Editor Tools and Their Uses *(continued)*

Button	Name	Use
	Material Effects Channel	Flyout menu used to assign material effects ID numbers to materials as targets for rendering effects. ID 0 means no material effect is used.
		Rendering effects will be covered in more detail in Chapter 13.
	Show Map In Viewport	Toggle that displays one map of a material in the viewport.
		Navigate to the level of the map you want to display and click the Show Map In Viewport button.
	Show End Result	Shows the result of current changes as they affect the whole material. This toggle is on by default.
		Turn off to see a single material within a compound material or to look at the current map level directly.
	Go To Parent	Moves up one level in the material tree.
	Go To Sibling	Moves across the material tree at the same level to the next material or map.
	Sample Type	Gives you a choice of preview object for the sample sphere: sphere, cube, cylinder, or custom object.
	Backlight	Toggle that adds a light that illuminates the back of the sample object (default is on).
	Background	Toggle that turns on a colorful checker pattern behind the sample object.
		Use background when previewing transparent, reflective, or refractive objects.
	Sample UV Tiling	Flyout menu that contains various tiling settings to preview on the sample object.
		Don't use this unless you have a good reason and know what you're doing. It can fool you since it is not the actual tiling of a map, but changes the tiling in the sample slot.
	Video Color Check	Toggle that checks to see if colors are not safe for video.
		Pixels of "illegal" colors will be replaced with black in the sample slot when the toggle is on.
	Make Preview	Flyout menu that lets you preview the effect of animated maps in the Material Editor.
		The preview file will automatically be opened when complete if you choose the defaults. If you save as a .mov file, use File ➜ View Image File to see the preview.

Table 7.4 Material Editor Tools and Their Uses *(continued)*

BUTTON	NAME	USE
	Options	Controls display options for sample slots. You can change how many sample slots are displayed, load a custom preview object or background, and set other display controls.
	Select By Material	Selects objects in the scene that have the material in the active sample slot applied to them.
	Material/Map Navigator	Opens the Material/Map Navigator. Use this to view the material tree and to move easily between levels through the graphical interface.

True Texture Resolution in Viewports

You've used the Show Map In Viewport button several times. You can also display images as viewport backgrounds, including the environment background image. Max 4 now has the ability to show maps with greater resolution with the interactive renderer in the viewport. Click Customize ➜ Preferences ➜ Viewports, then click the Configure Driver button.

Configure OpenGL

Implementation-Specific Settings
- ☐ Redraw Scene On Window Expose
  - ☐ Full Screen SwapBuffers Destroys Back Buffer
  - ☐ Windowed SwapBuffers Destroys Back Buffer
- ☑ Use Triangle Strips
  - ☐ Display Wireframe Objects Using Triangle Strips
- ☑ Allow Dual Plane Support (OpenGL Extension)
- ☑ Use Incremental Scene Updates (OpenGL Extension)
- ☑ Use BGRA pixel format (OpenGL Extension)
- ☑ Use Generalized Vertex Arrays (Custom Driver Extension)
- ☐ Use Wireframe Faces (Custom Driver Extension)

Appearance Preferences
- ☑ Enable Anti-aliased Lines in Wireframe Views

Background Texture Size
| 128 | 256 | 512 | 1024 | ☑ Match Bitmap as Close as Possible |

Download Texture Size
| 64 | 128 | 256 | 512 | ☑ Match Bitmap as Close as Possible |

Texel Lookup
- ○ Nearest   ● Linear

MipMap Lookup
- ○ None   ○ Nearest   ● Linear

OK   Cancel

To get the best resolution of textures with the interactive renderer, set the following parameters in the dialog box:

- Check Match Bitmap As Close As Possible in Background Texture Size.
- Check Match Bitmap As Close As Possible in Download Texture Size.
- Select Linear in Texel Lookup.
- Select Linear in MipMap Lookup.

You have to reload the scene to get objects already displaying maps to use the new texture size. The interactive renderer will use the new texture resolution for newly created objects.

Hands-on max: Unwrapping Mapping Coordinates for a Low-Poly Character

Detailed mapping work is crucial when creating low-poly models. Good mapping can cover for a lot of missing geometry. The UVW Map modifier gives you nice approximations with cylindrical, box, spherical, and planar mapping, but for characters, the mapping needs to be unwrapped. In this tutorial, you will apply a single diffuse map to the Intrepid Explorer Jim character and unwrap the mapping coordinates in order to get a precise correspondence between parts of the geometry and the single bitmap. In the method used here, you will be using the Texporter plug-in by Cuneyt Ozdas, included on the CD for this book. Programs such as Texture Weapons make this process very easy and quick, but they are expensive, while this technique and the one in the appendix on Pulse 3D are free and yet still offer fine-tune control.

See Cuneyt's other plug-ins for max at `http://www.cuneytozdas.com/software/max`.

To use the Texporter technique, you must break apart the model in order to get flat planes with which to work. Flat planes allow you to make the map seamless and undistorted across the model. Ultimately it is trial and error, but here are some guidelines for breaking apart a model:

- First, detach by body area (head, torso, arms, hands, legs, feet)

- Second, detach by direction (for example, a head may be broken into the front, two sides, the back, and the top)

- Third, detach by map content (for example, an arm may be subdivided between the sleeves of a shirt and the skin)

- Finally, detach any remaining parts (for example, the bottom of the nose, the back of the ears, the crotch)

You detach each part as an element of the same object.

To texture-map the Intrepid Explorer Jim model:

1. With max closed, copy the Texporter3.dlu file from the Plugins\ Texporter directory on the CD to your 3dsmax4\plugins folder. Copy the IEJmaps directory from the CD files for this chapter to your 3dsmax4\Maps directory. Open max.

2. Choose Customize ➡ Configure Paths. On the Bitmaps tab, click Add. Browse to 3dsmax4\Maps and make sure Add Subpaths is checked. Click Use Path and then OK. This can take a while.

3. Open Intrepid_Explorer_Jim04.max in the CD files for this chapter (or open your final optimized character model from Chapter 5 and save it as Intrepid_Explorer_Jim04.max). Using the guidelines explained above, break the model into flat elements by body area, direction, and map content. At the Polygon sub-object level, select the polygons for each section, click the Detach button and check Detach To Element. This detaches the pieces while keeping them within the same object.

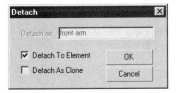

4. As you detach each element, select it and click Hide in the Selection rollout so that you can keep track of what still needs to be detached. When you are done detaching all the parts, click Unhide All in the Selection rollout. Save your file as Intrepid_Explorer_Jim05.max.

If a piece of the model that is intended to be part of a detached section is accidentally left out, it can be detached from the main body and welded back to the intended element.

In order to make the model precisely match the map, you are going to flatten it. But you want to be able to get back your model when you are done. To have your model and flatten it, too, you can use a Morpher modifier. Morpher is usually used in animation to transform models over time from one conformation to another. In this case, you just want to be able to switch between the flattened state and the original state at will, so you will have the original model and one morph target of the flattened model.

5. Holding the Shift key, drag your model to the right. Choose 1 Copy from the Clone dialog box.

6. Apply the Morpher modifier (from the Animation modifier set) to the original model.

7. In the Channel Parameters rollout, click Pick Object From Scene. Then pick the copy of your model in the viewport. The copy should now be listed as Channel 1, your first and only morph target channel for this object. Hide the morph target copy so that it is out of the way.

8. Navigate down the stack to the Editable Mesh and go to the Element sub-object level. Move and rotate the elements you created in step 2 to arrange them so that each element is facing forward.

Be careful to stay at the Element sub-object level and never change the number of vertices. Otherwise you will lose the morph target of the original model.

9. Arrange all the elements in the smallest possible square. A square is best so that there is no distortion in the final map. You want it to be as small as possible to conserve as many pixels of the texture map for the actual geometry as possible. Finding an efficient arrangement is also a trial-and-error process. Apply the same procedure to the hat. Save your file as `Intrepid_Explorer_Jim06.max`.

10. Go to the Vertex sub-object level. Select all the vertices of the model. In the front view, non-uniformly scale along Z until all the pieces are flattened. Do this a few times until they are completely flat.

11. Apply the UVW Map modifier with planar mapping. To make it perfectly square, create a square spline around the mesh and then adjust the gizmo and Length and Width parameters of the UVW Map modifier to make it match the square spline exactly. Save your file as `Intrepid_Explorer_Jim07.max`.

12. Return to the Morpher level of the Stack. Drag the edge of the Modify panel to the left to expand it so that you can see two columns of the panel. In the first morph target channel, spin the percentage up to 100% to return to the original shape of the model. The mesh should look identical to when it started. The difference is that every element now has a set of mapping coordinates that directly correspond to a flat map.

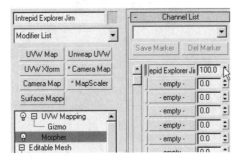

13. Right-click the stack and choose Collapse All.

14. Go to the Vertex sub-object level. Select all the vertices of the model and click Selected under Weld. The default weld threshold should weld all the broken groups back together again. If not, undo and adjust the Weld Threshold or weld each broken piece back together vertex by vertex. Save your file as `Intrepid_Explorer_Jim08.max`.

15. Go to Utilities ➜ More ➜ Texporter. Set Image Size to 1024 × 1024. It is the largest size a map can be for most standard low-poly functions. When the map is completed, it should generally be shrunk to 256 × 256, particularly for Web applications, but it is better to create the art at the larger size and shrink it than have less image resolution than you need. Check Polygon Fill, Edges, and Edges Only. Choose Colorize By: Constant. Click Pick Object and pick your model in the viewport. After a few moments, you should get a rendering of your flattened UV coordinates like that shown in Figure 7.18.

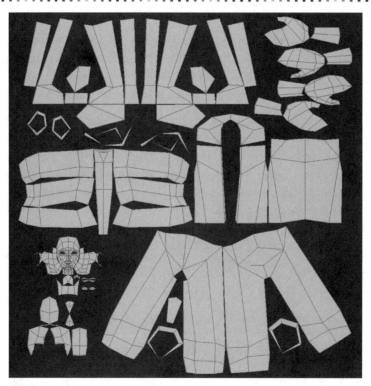

Figure 7.18 *Texporter rendering of flattened UV mapping coordinates*

16. Click the Save Bitmap button in the buffer window. Save the image as a JPEG called UVmap.jpg with the default settings.

17. Open the UVmap.jpg in Photoshop and start painting your character map on a new layer, using the Texporter image as a template. You can scan in images or photos or just paint directly with the drawing tools. Save your painted file as IntrepidEJmap.jpg.

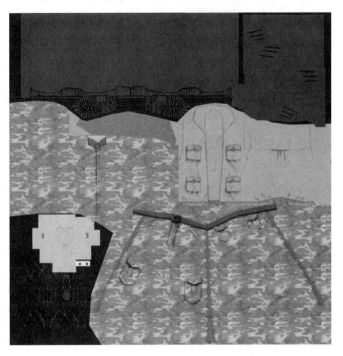

It is important that every color and image go slightly over the lines of the shape in the map; otherwise a seam will show.

18. Open your Intrepid_Explorer_Jim08.max file. Select the model, open the Material Editor, and apply a material to the selection.

19. Name your material. Click the Diffuse map shortcut button, choose Bitmap, and load your IntrepidEJmap.jpg. If you are not satisfied with the map, go back to Photoshop and edit it. Go through the same process for the hat. Save your file as Intrepid_Explorer_Jim09.max.

Intrepid Explorer Jim project by Jason Wiener

Summary

In this chapter, you learned the principles behind surface shading in general and their particular application in max through material trees. You used the Material Editor and its many tools, including the Material/Map Browser and the Material/Map Navigator. You became acquainted with the different shading types, material types, and map types available in max. You looked at the effects of maps on different material channels. You learned about the mapping coordinates of an object's texture space and the ways to change these in max. In the Hands-on max tutorial, you used one method of unwrapping mapping coordinates in order to apply a single map to the Intrepid Explorer Jim model.

In the next chapter, you'll delve in much greater depth into some of the concepts introduced here. You will put all you've learned into practice in advanced materials tutorials.

Advanced Materials

3ds max

Chapter 8

n Chapter 7, you learned the basics of surface shading and applied materials with maps in various material channels. In this chapter you will learn the more advanced settings and applications of materials. You will apply your materials knowledge to several advanced material projects. Topics include:

- Supersampling

- Output curves for maps

- Dynamics properties

- Raytracing reflections and refractions

- Matte/Shadow material

- Composite materials and maps

- Advanced materials projects

- Using the cinematic "cheat" of camera mapping

Advanced Materials Settings

After your glimpse into the depths of materials possibilities in max, you're ready to delve a little deeper into the advanced settings that make it possible to render beautiful and realistic materials.

SuperSampling Rollout

Aliasing is the jagged edges you see in computer graphics due to a smooth edge being described by square pixels. *Anti-aliasing* makes the edges appear smoother by calculating intermediate pixel values along the edges. Max calculates anti-aliasing in several levels: shadows are anti-aliased, for example, as are raytraced reflections, texture maps, and specular highlights. The supersampler, if turned on in the SuperSampling rollout (shown in Figure 8.1), adds another anti-aliasing pass to calculate the best solution for each pixel and relay this information to the renderer.

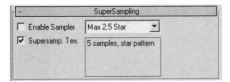

Figure 8.1 *The SuperSampling rollout*

All supersamplers turned on in the SuperSampling rollouts of materials are subject to the global supersampling control in the Render Scene window, discussed in Chapter 13.

If Enable Sampler is not checked, a pixel's color is determined by the center of the area of the scene that it represents, often resulting in aliasing. A supersampler looks at a pixel and takes samples, at a sub-pixel level, of the area of the scene that the pixel represents. Higher sampling rates can mean higher quality anti-aliasing, but they also mean much longer rendering times. Because of this, some supersamplers are adaptive, meaning they only take the extra samples when it is really necessary to improve the anti-aliasing.

Max 2.5 Star   supersampling was the only method available in max 2.5. This supersampler takes five samples—the center of the pixel and four samples around it—and averages them together. It is not adaptive, and the regular sampling pattern can lead to aliasing problems.

Adaptive Uniform   supersampling takes samples in a regular pattern, but the pattern is skewed to improve the anti-aliasing. Adaptive Uniform takes between 4 and

36 samples. It will use the lower sampling rate as long as the change in the pixels is less than the specified threshold. Above that threshold, it will use a higher rate, based on the Quality setting.

If you're still getting aliasing with either of the Adaptive supersamplers, try lowering the threshold rather than unchecking Adaptive.

Hammersley supersampling takes between 4 and 40 samples that are random-ized on the Y axis. Irregular sampling patterns like this can lead to fewer aliasing problems. The sampling rate is based on the Quality setting and is not adaptive, so this rate is applied to all pixels.

Adaptive Halton supersampling offers the best of both worlds: an irregular sam-ple pattern and an adaptive sampling rate. It takes between 4 and 40 samples per pixel. The sampling pattern is randomized along both the X and Y axes, and the higher sampling rate determined by the Quality setting is only used when needed.

Dynamics Properties Rollout

Dynamics is a max utility that detects and emulates real-world collisions. The Dynamics Properties rollout of a material allows you to determine the bounce and friction coeffi-cients of an object based on its material assignment. The Dynamics utility uses these val-ues when calculating collisions. The utility can also override the material settings with ones made within the utility. Because you can use a material with dynamics properties as a component material of a Multi/Sub-Object material, you can use the material to assign dynamics properties of objects at the sub-object level. This provides a level of refinement in which different parts of an object have different levels of elasticity and friction, some-thing you cannot do from within the Dynamics utility itself. Dynamics will be discussed in more detail in Chapter 10. Table 8.1 describes the functions of the dynamics properties.

Table 8.1 Dynamics Properties

PROPERTY	FUNCTION
Bounce Coefficient	Varies from 0 to 1. Use 0 for a steel ball and 1 for a rubber ball, and any-where in between for most objects.
Static Friction	Varies from 0 to 1. Set friction for stationary objects at 0 for ice and 1 for glued objects, and anywhere in between for most other objects.
Sliding Friction	Varies from 0 to 1. Set friction for sliding objects at 0 if they don't slow down, and up to 1 if they come to an abrupt halt while skidding.

Output Curves for Maps

If you check Enable Color Map under the Output rollout for certain types of maps (bitmaps, gradients, Cellular, Falloff, Mix, or Noise), you can access the output curve for the map, as shown in Figure 8.2. You can also apply the Output map as a parent to another map that doesn't have the built-in Output rollout. (You make it a parent by changing the type to Output and checking Keep Old Map As Sub-Map.) This allows you to adjust the contrast and color of the map, as it applies to that particular usage of the map, without changing any of the actual pixels of the map. This is equivalent to taking a single map into Photoshop, adding different adjustment layers to change the curves of the map for different purposes, and telling max which adjustment layer to apply to which particular use of the map—all without opening Photoshop!

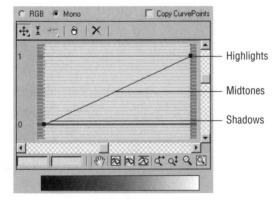

Figure 8.2 *Output rollout with Enable Color Map on*

In Figure 8.2 you can see there are different areas on the color map curve to adjust the shadows, midtones, and highlights of the pixels from the map. The horizontal axis of the color map represents the original intensity of pixels (called *input levels*). The vertical axis represents the new color values (called *output levels*). The default straight diagonal line graph means that all the pixels have the same input and output levels. You adjust the curve by adding vertices in different areas, according to how you want to change the pixels. The color map in max functions similarly to Curves in Photoshop.

The tools for adjusting the output curve are all tools we have seen before in other contexts: Move Point, Scale Point (moves vertically), Add Point (corner or Bezier), and Delete Point. The X icon resets the curve to where you started. If you check RGB, you can set curves for the red, green, and blue channels. The R, G, and B buttons toggle on and off the curve for their respective channels. If you check Mono, you can work just on the grayscale value, to change contrast.

Using this tool, you could use the same map in several levels of a material, applying one version of the map with the highlights emphasized to the Specular level, for example; a different, high-contrast version of the map to the bump slot; and another version of the map with the color de-saturated in the diffuse color channel—without touching a pixel of your map or having to save a single new map file. You could even apply yet another version of the map to the environment background, this time with the color balance shifted. Let's see how it works:

1. Open the file Materials03.max that you saved in the last chapter or from the CD files for this chapter.

2. Open the Material Editor. Select the Brick material sample slot.

3. Click the little M shortcut button next to the diffuse color to go to the diffuse map level.

4. Right-click a blank area of the Material Editor and choose Output to open the Output rollout for this map.

5. Click the ActiveShade button on the toolbar to open an ActiveShade floater. This window will stay on the screen and allow you to see changes you make with Output. The ActiveShade floater automatically updates its render scene every time you make a material or lighting change.

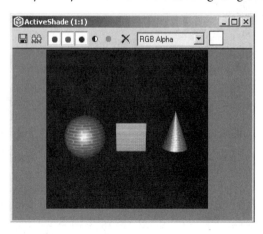

6. To de-saturate the color of the map a bit in the diffuse color channel, change the RBG Level parameter to 0.8.

7. Click the Go To Parent button in the Material Editor. You can use the Material/Map Navigator to change levels instead if you prefer.

8. Open the Maps rollout. Drag the map name from the button in the diffuse color map slot to the button in the specular level map slot. The Copy (Instance) Map dialog box appears. Select the Copy radio button and click OK. Now a copy of the bitmap is placed in this channel.

9. Click the map button for the specular level channel to go to that map level.

10. Open the Output rollout. Check Enable Color Map.

11. To increase the level of highlights in the map, you will need to adjust the curves of the color map. Click the Add Point button.

12. Click the curve about three-fourths of the way up the diagonal line to add a point to the highlights area of the curve.

13. Right-click the point you just added and choose Bezier-Smooth.

14. Click the Move button in the color map controls. Adjust the curve according to Figure 8.3 to increase the level of the specular highlights.

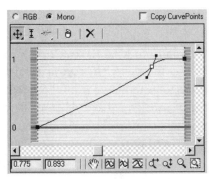

Figure 8.3 *Adjusted color map curve*

15. Click the Go To Parent button. In the Maps rollout, drag the map in the diffuse color channel to the bump channel. Choose Copy.

16. Click the map button for the bump channel to go to that map level.

17. Open the Output rollout. Increase the Bump Amount parameter to 2.0. This will change the amount of bumpiness used without affecting the other material channels.

18. Look closely at the ActiveShade floater to see the rendered results of adjusting Output of several maps. Save your work as `Materials07.max`.

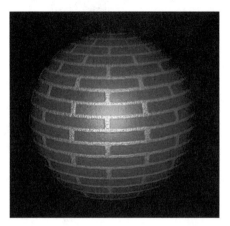

Raytracing

Raytracing is a CG rendering algorithm used to calculate reflections and refractions of light more accurately than the default scanline renderer. Raytracing is named for the process of tracing rays of light back through the scene. The raytracing algorithm starts with the picture plane, the matrix of pixels to be rendered from the viewing point. This way, only the rays that actually reach the picture plane have to be calculated, rather than all rays bouncing outward from the light source. The raytrace engine determines the color of each pixel by treating the pixels as if they were light rays. Then it traces each ray backward through the scene and determines where that ray reflects and refracts off surfaces. Each time a ray is bounced or transmitted, the reflection or refraction affects the color of that ray. Rays can ultimately be traced back to the light source, where the calculation ends. The algorithm can also be stopped before the rays reach their light source with the *ray depth*—the number of times an individual ray can be either reflected or refracted before the calculation ends.

Since raytracing is computationally expensive, use a Raytrace map within a standard material if you are just going to raytrace a single reflection or refraction channel.

The Raytrace map type uses the same raytrace algorithm as the Raytrace material but renders faster. The Raytrace map also has controls for anti-aliasing and attenuation.

Raytracing does not *calculate light that bounces between objects and never reaches the picture plane. In fact, most of the light emitted from a source falls into this category. This kind of bounced light, called* global illumination *or* radiosity, *adds another level of realism to images. There are some renderers designed to simulate this phenomenon: forward Monte Carlo raytracing (in Mental Ray) and radiosity (in Lightscape). See Chapter 13 for examples of alternate renderers.*

Basic Parameters of the Raytrace Material

The Basic Parameters for the Raytrace material, shown in Figure 8.4, include some parameters that should look familiar from standard materials: Ambient, Diffuse, Specular Color, Specular Level, and Glossiness, for example. In a Raytrace material, Ambient is defined as how much ambient color the shadow will absorb. Setting the Ambient color to white is the same as locking it to the diffuse color in Standard materials. Raytrace materials also have special parameters described in Table 8.2. Transparency works like a combination of Opacity and Filter in a standard material, except that Transparency settings are the inverse of Opacity settings.

Table 8.2 Special Basic Parameters of a Raytrace Material

PARAMETER	FUNCTION
Ambient	Controls how much ambient color the shadow will absorb
Reflect	Sets the color of the specular reflection
Luminosity	Replaces shadowed surfaces with the diffuse color
Transparency	Determines the transparency of a material and assigns it a filter color that affects the objects behind it
Index of Refraction	Controls how much a transparent object distorts objects
Environment	Specifies an environment map for reflection and refraction that overrides the scene environment map
Bump	Specifies a bump map that affects the rays traced back to the surface with the bump information

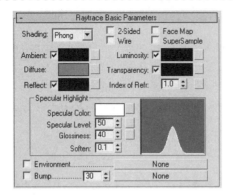

Figure 8.4 *Basic Parameters rollout of Raytrace material*

Unchecking any of the check boxes in front of the color swatches brings up a spinner for adjusting the value from zero to 100 percent. Use this when you want to assign a numerical percentage for the grayscale value instead of a color. The color swatch affects the same control, except it can have hue and saturation as well. Max uses the visible parameter, and ignores the parameter that is not displayed. (They do not update each other.)

Using a Cornell Box to Test Render

Researchers at Cornell University in New York created the *Cornell Box* in 1984 to study rendering algorithms. The Cornell Box is often used to analyze various rendering and lighting effects.

Visit http://www.graphics.cornell.edu/online/box/ *for more information about the Cornell Box and its history in computer graphics.*

1. Open Cornell Box 01.max from the CD files for this chapter. This file contains a simple Cornell Box with one red wall and one blue wall (the other walls are white). All the objects start with Standard materials (or Multi/Sub-Object materials with Standard sub-materials).

2. Do a test render to see how the default scanline renderer handles the scene.

3. Open the Material Editor. Click the Left Sphere material (it starts out being green) to make it the active sample slot.

4. Change the type of the existing material to Raytrace by clicking the button marked Standard on the right side of the Material Editor and choosing Raytrace from the browser.

5. Click the check box next to the Reflect color component. A text box and spinner replace the color swatch. Adjust this spinner to 100%. This makes a perfectly reflective chrome material.

The Reflect parameter overrides the Transparency parameter. If you set the Reflect spinner to 100% or set the swatch to white, the object will be completely opaque, regardless of its Transparency value.

6. Click the Background button to better see the reflective effect in the sample slot.

7. Click the Right Sphere material in the editor. Convert the Right Sphere material to Raytrace type and turn on the Background button. Change the following parameters:

- Transparency = 90%
- Reflect = 15%
- Index of Refraction = 1.5 (glass)

8. Do a test render to see your chrome and glass spheres. Save your work as `Cor-nell Box 02.max`. You can view the results of the raytrace renderer in the "Alternative Renderers" plate in the Color Gallery.

For faster rendering, turn off Raytrace Refractions in the Raytracer Controls rollout.

Extended Parameters of the Raytrace Material

The Extended Parameters rollout for Raytrace materials, shown in Figure 8.5, allows you to simulate extra light, translucency, and fluorescence, giving you finer control over transparent and reflective surfaces. The Density settings allow you to apply a tint to a transparent material based on the object's thickness, and to gradually fill the walls of the object with fog so that it becomes opaque. Table 8.3 describes the function of the extended parameters. Fluorescence shifts the surface color toward a color you select and then illuminates it with white light. Setting the Fluorescence Bias parameter to 1.0 and using a fully saturated color results in an intense, "black light" effect.

You can use the Extra Light setting to simulate a global illumination effect by setting the color swatch to match the color of a nearby object.

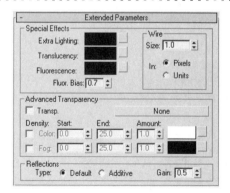

Figure 8.5 *Extended Parameters rollout for the Raytrace material*

Table 8.3 Raytrace Extended Parameters

PARAMETER	FUNCTION
Extra Lighting	Adds extra light and color to a surface evenly, respecting the direction of surface normals.
Translucency	Scatters extra light and color on a surface randomly, disregarding the direction of surface normals; allows shadows cast on the back of the surface to show through.
Fluorescence	Adds or subtracts color from a surface; lights the surface with white light, overriding the current lights in the scene.
Fluorescence Bias	Determines how much fluorescent color is added or subtracted from the surface.
Transparency Environment	Adds an environment map to a transparent surface to appear as a refracted image.
Color Density	Increases the saturation of a transparent surface based on its thickness (similar to tinting colored glass).
Fog Density	Adds opaque color to a transparent surface based on its thickness.
Reflections Type	Allows you to choose whether reflections will be layered with the diffuse color. By default, reflections obscure the diffuse color as they grow stronger. The Additive setting causes the diffuse color to always appear underneath.

Let's refine the parameters for the Right Sphere material to make it look more realistic:

1. Continue working on Cornell Box 02.max or open it from the CD files for this chapter.

2. In the Right Sphere material, open the Extended Parameters rollout. Change the Translucency color to a fully saturated bright magenta. Magenta is good for this situation because it is a blend of the colors on the walls of the Cornell Box.

The Translucency parameter affects only shadow mapping and light distribution. It does not cause the surface to become semi-transparent.

3. Check the box in front of the grayed-out word Color. Click the color swatch on the right side of this row of controls. Change the color density to a light magenta color (such as RGB = 255, 235, 255).

4. Do a test render. Now the translucent sphere looks more realistic. Save your work as `Cornell Box 03.max`.

Environment Mapping

Use environment mapping whenever you want to have an image shown in the background of your rendering. Surfaces rendered with the Raytrace material or the Raytrace map will automatically reflect the environment map.

Let's try using environment mapping:

1. Continue working on `Cornell Box 03.max` or open it from the CD files for this chapter.

2. Click Rendering ➜ Environment to open the Environment dialog box.

3. Click the button labeled None under Environment Map.

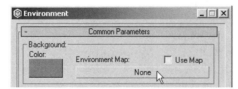

4. Select Bitmap from the Material/Map Browser. In the Select Bitmap Image File dialog box, browse to Lakerem2.jpg in the 3dsmax4\Maps\Reflection folder.

5. Test-render the scene. Observe how the environment map both shows in the background and is visible in the reflections of the objects. The Raytrace material handles this automatically. Save your work as Cornell Box 04.max.

Cornell Box project by Scott Onstott

Raytracer Controls

The Raytracer Controls rollout governs how the raytrace engine renders materials. You can, and should, optimize performance by turning off unnecessary reflections or refractions, and by excluding objects. For greater accuracy you can increase the number of iterations, or "recursion depth," that the raytracer performs. Additional controls include settings for anti-aliasing, blurring, and falloff. Table 8.4 describes the Raytracer controls and their functions.

Table 8.4 Raytracer Controls

CONTROL	FUNCTION
Raytrace Reflections	Turns raytracing of reflective objects on or off.
Raytrace Refractions	Turns raytracing of transparent objects on or off.
Reflect Falloff	Dims reflections to black at this distance (default is 100.0).
Refract Falloff	Dims refractions to black at this distance.
Bump Map Effect	Adjusts the effect of bump maps on raytraced reflections and refractions.
Raytraced Reflection and Refraction Antialiaser	Allows you to blur or de-focus (similar to depth-of-field blurring) raytraced effects using lengthier computations. When you enable Global Antialiasing in the Options dialog box, these settings become available in the Ray Antialiasing drop-down list.
Options	Turns raytracing of various phenomena on or off at the global level (affecting all raytraced materials) or the local level (affecting just the current material).
Global Parameters	Controls the level of recursion and rendering acceleration; also allows you to set the method of global anti-aliasing.
Local Exclude	Excludes objects from being rendered by the current Raytrace material.
Global Exclude	Excludes objects from being rendered by any Raytrace material.

Applying a Matte/Shadow Material

The Matte/Shadow material turns an object to which it is applied into a non-rendering matte object that obscures geometry behind it but reveals the environment background. Matte objects can be set to receive shadows so that a model moving across a flat map background can seem to cast realistic shadows on that background by casting them on the invisible matte object instead. This furthers the illusion that the model is moving within the scene portrayed in the background image. Matte objects can also be set to affect the alpha channel of the rendering so that it can be composited later with other image elements. Table 8.5 describes the settings available for a Matte/Shadow material.

Table 8.5 Matte/Shadow Basic Parameters

PARAMETER	FUNCTION
Opaque Alpha	When checked, the matte object will show as white in the alpha channel of the rendering, like a visible object.
Apply Atmosphere	Allows atmospheric effects such as fog to obscure matte objects.
At Background Depth	Renders atmospheric effects before shadows, so that shadows are unaffected by atmospheric variations.
At Object Depth	Renders atmospheric effects after shadows, so that shadows are affected by atmospheric variations.
Receive Shadows	Allows matte objects to receive shadows from other objects. When checked, the shadows cast on the matte object will be added to the background map. (Note: Lights must have cast shadows checked.)
Shadow Brightness	Sets the transparency of the shadow received. 0 simply replaces the pixels corresponding to the matte object with the color of the shadow. 1 is the same as not receiving shadows. Most of the time you would use a value between these two to add the shadow to the background image.
(Shadow) Color	Sets the color of shadows received by the matte object.
Affect Alpha	Determines whether shadows received by the matte object will also affect the alpha channel of the rendering.
Reflection Amount	Determines the opacity of the reflection map applied to the matte object. 0 turns off the reflection map.
Reflection Map	Adds a reflection map on the matte object to be added to the background image.

Creating Shadows on a Background Using a Matte Object

Let's use a matte object to cast shadows on a background image:

1. Open `matte_shadow01.max` from the CD files for this chapter.

2. Create a camera and check Show Horizon in the Modify panel. Press C to switch to the camera viewport.

3. In Rendering ➜ Environment, assign a Bitmap as an environment map and choose `Chromblu.jpg` from the `3dsmax4\Maps\Reflection` folder.

4. With the camera viewport active, press Alt+B to bring up the Viewport Background dialog box. Check Use Environment Background and Display Background.

5. Move and adjust the camera to align the horizon of the camera to the horizon of the background image.

6. Create a plane in the camera view that matches the ground in the background image.

7. In the Material Editor, create a Matte/Shadow material by clicking the Type button and choosing Matte/Shadow.

8. In the Matte/Shadow Basic Parameters rollout, uncheck Opaque Alpha. Then check Receive Shadows and Affect Alpha. Set Shadow Brightness to 0.2. This makes the shadow more transparent.

9. Assign the material to the plane object.

10. Render the scene. In the Virtual Frame Buffer displaying the rendered image, click the Display Alpha Channel button to see the alpha channel. Figure 8.6 shows the rendered image on top and the alpha channel on the bottom. Notice that the shadow imprinted the alpha channel, so the 3D object and its shadow can be easily composited in another scene.

To reflect the Environment in a matte object, use a Reflect/Refract map or a Flat Mirror map for the reflection map.

Applying a Double Sided Material

All faces have two sides: a front side, determined by the direction of the surface normal, and a back side, facing the opposite direction. By default, only the front side of a face is rendered. This saves rendering time while giving the outside of the object its visible form. To see the inside of an object, or check for flipped faces, you can render both sides. Checking 2-Sided in the Shader rollout of an object's material renders both sides of a face with the same material.

Double Sided materials allow you to apply a different material on each side of an object. These materials can have their own material tree, and they can be blended together as if you are seeing through a translucent wall from one side to the other. Double Sided materials consist of a Facing material for the front faces, a Back material for the back faces, and a Translucency setting determining the blend between them (from zero to 100 percent).

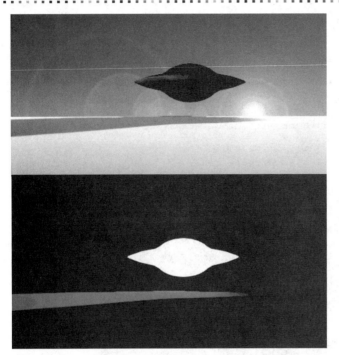

Figure 8.6 *A Matte/Shadow material compositing a shadow on a background image and affecting the alpha channel for easy compositing with other images*

Let's create a Double Sided material:

1. Open the file Bowl01.max from the CD files for this chapter. If you prefer, make a simple bowl yourself—draw a Line and add a Lathe modifier. You may need to adjust the vertices of the Line and Lathe axis to make an acceptable bowl.

2. In the Material Editor, create a Double Sided material by clicking the Type button and selecting Double Sided from the list of materials.

3. Select the bowl object and assign the material to it.

4. Click the Facing Material button to go to the level in the Material Editor.

5. Make the Diffuse color red. Unlock the Ambient color and set it to a darker value.

6. Using the Material/Map Navigator or the Go To Sibling button, go to the Back Material level. Click the shortcut button next to the diffuse color and select a Checker map.

7. In the Coordinates rollout of the Checker map, adjust the U and V tiling to 10 in each direction. Now the checker pattern repeats more often.

8. Render the scene. You have a bowl with the red material on the inside and a checkered material on the outside, as shown in Figure 8.7. Save your work as Bow102.max.

Figure 8.7 *Double Sided material*

Applying a Top/Bottom Material

Top/Bottom materials assign one material to all the faces whose normals point upward, and the other material to the rest of the faces whose normals point downward. Because it is based on the direction of the normals, the Top/Bottom effect does not necessarily correspond to the upper and lower parts of an object. Top/Bottom tends to work better on round objects than on objects like boxes and cones where there is no gradation between the normal directions. The blend amount allows you to blur the edge between the top and bottom materials. The position moves the transition up or down the object. This is based on changing the threshold of the normal direction, so on a geometric object with sudden transitions in normal direction, the boundary will still tend to be at the very top or the very bottom of the object.

Checking World under Coordinates means the orientation of surface normals is calculated relative to World space rather than the coordinate system of the object. If the object is rotated, the material's orientation will stay anchored to the World.

Let's create a Top/Bottom material:

1. Continue working on your `Bowl02.max` file or open it from the CD files for this chapter.

2. Arc-rotate your view until you can see the bottom three-fourths of the bowl.

3. Open the Material Editor. Navigate to the Back material level of the Double Sided material from the previous section. Change its type to Top/Bottom. When you do this step, check Keep Old Material As Sub-Material.

4. Look at the material structure in the Material/Map Navigator. Notice that you now have a Top/Bottom material as the Back material of your original Double Sided material. As a default, the original checkered material is now the Top material of the Back sub-material.

5. Go to the Bottom material level, click the shortcut button next to the diffuse color component, and apply a Dent map.

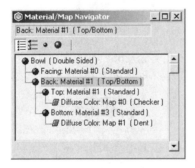

6. Do a test render. At this point, you can't see the Top/Bottom effect.

7. Navigate to the Back material level of the top-level Double Sided material. In the Top/Bottom Basic parameters rollout, set Position to 15 and the Blend to 1. Do another test render. Now the Dent shows in the areas where the normals are pointing down while Checker map is showing in the areas where the normals are pointing up. Note that Top/Bottom does not necessarily mean what it might imply relative to the object. Figure 8.8 shows the Top/Bottom material applied to the bowl. Save your work as `Bowl03.max`.

Figure 8.8 *Top/Bottom Material*

Applying a Shellac Material

The Shellac material blends the colors of two sub-materials according to the amount of light falling on the surface and the amount that you blend the materials together. In the Shellac Basic parameters rollout, Base Material is the starting color and Shellac Material is the material that blends with the base. Shellac Color Blend controls the amount of shellac that blends. The base material shows through more strongly when light on the object is more intense. As the surface gets darker, the Shellac material becomes predominant—it predominates in indirect light. Shellac materials introduce subtle variations to a surface, not unlike real shellac or varnish.

Let's create a Shellac material:

1. Open the file Vase01.max from the CD files for this chapter.

2. Select the Vase object and open the Material Editor.

3. Click the Get Material button and choose Shellac Material. By default, the base Material is red and the Shellac is blue. Apply the material to the Vase.

4. Navigate to the base material level. Click the diffuse map shortcut button and choose Smoke map.

5. Navigate to the Shellac material level and apply a Water map to the diffuse channel.

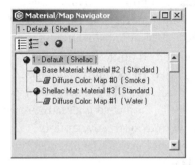

6. Navigate to the top level in the material tree. Set the Shellac Color Blend to 100.

A Shellac Color Blend setting of zero ignores the Shellac effect. This parameter has no upper limit, but values over 100 start to look burned out.

7. Test-render the scene. Try experimenting with different values in the Shellac Color Blend parameter. Do test renders until you are satisfied with your material. Figure 8.9 shows this Shellac material creating a ceramic effect on a vase. Save your work as `Vase02.max`.

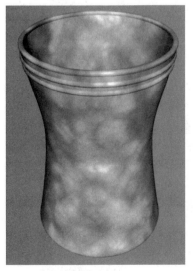

Figure 8.9 *A vase mapped with a Shellac material*

Applying a Composite Material

Composite materials allow you to superimpose up to nine different materials in succession on top of a base material. The final outcome depends on the color and opacity of the component materials, the order in which they are laid down, and the method of compositing.

In the Composite Basic Parameters rollout, shown in Figure 8.10, there are three options for compositing each material. The A button *adds* the color of the new material to what has been laid down previously, excluding areas of transparency. The S button *subtracts* the color of the new material from what is already present, excluding areas of transparency. For both the Additive and Subtractive options, values can range from zero to 200 percent. Above 100 percent the material becomes "overloaded" so that transparent areas of the material become opaque.

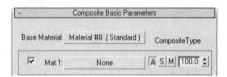

Figure 8.10 *The Composite Basic Parameters rollout*

The M (*mix*) option blends the color and opacity of the current material with the previous state, just as the Blend material does. Values range from zero to 100 percent. At zero, there is no blending and the current material has no effect. When Mix is set to 50 percent, they blend evenly. At 100 percent mixing, the color and opacity of the current material completely override the composite below it. Note that the highest-numbered material is at the top of the composite pile, despite the rollout order.

For complicated materials like the Composite material, it helps to have a bigger view. Double-clicking the material slot in the Material Editor magnifies the display.

Let's create a Composite material:

1. Continue working on your `Vase02.max` file or open it from the CD files for this chapter.

2. Select the Vase and open the Material Editor.

3. Click Get New Material and choose a new Composite material.

4. Apply this material to the Vase.

5. In the base material, apply a Cellular map to the diffuse channel.

6. Navigate to the top level of the material. Click the Mat 1 button, choose Standard, and apply a Speckle map to the diffuse channel.

7. Navigate to the top level of the material. Click the Mat 2 button, choose Standard, and apply a Perlin Marble map to the diffuse channel.

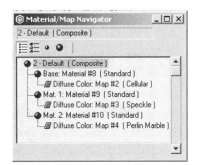

8. At the top level of the material tree, set both Mat 1 and 2 to Mix types within the Composite. Set the amounts of both Mat 1 and 2 to 50.0%.

9. Do a test render. Adjust the parameters of any of the composited materials and mix amounts to get the look you want. Do test renders to see the effects. Use an ActiveShade floater if you want to see the materials changes update without a full render. Save your file as Vase03.max. Figure 8.11 shows the Composite material applied to the Vase.

Figure 8.11 *A vase mapped with a Composite material made up of three different materials*

Applying Maps to Material Channels

In this section you will apply maps to various material channels. The "Material Channel Mapping" plate in the Color Gallery shows the results of maps applied to different channels. You learned the theory in Chapter 7 and saw some of the results. Now you will apply maps to different material channels in order to achieve specific effects.

Mapping the Diffuse Channel with a Composite Map

The Composite map can be used instead of the Composite material to superimpose images. The map version works a bit differently than the material. The Composite map is designed to composite bitmaps based upon their alpha channels. (See "Masks, Alpha Channels, and Opacity Maps" in Chapter 7 for an explanation of alpha channels and transparency information.) The Composite map does not have any parameters to control the amount of blending, because the blending is determined by the grayscale transparency information of the sub-maps. The transparency information of a sub-map can be in an embedded alpha channel or in the mask file of a Mask sub-map.

Let's create a material using a Composite map:

1. Reset max.

2. Copy the Ch8_maps\ folder to your 3dsmax4\Maps directory.

3. Open comp_vase01.max from the CD files for this chapter.

4. Open the Material Editor and apply a material to the Vase. Turn up the Specular Level and turn down the Glossiness to get a ceramic shine that appeals to you.

5. Open the Material/Map Navigator to help you visualize your material as you build it. Apply a Composite map to the diffuse color channel.

6. In the Map 1 slot, place a Perlin Marble map and adjust the colors, tiling, and output of the map to get a ceramic surface you like.

7. In the Map 2 slot of the Composite map, choose Bitmap, and select the file flower01.tif from 3dsmax4\Maps\Ch8_maps. Before you click Open, click View to see the map. Click Display Alpha Channel to see the alpha channel for the file. The image is defined as completely transparent (black alpha) outside of the flower and partially transparent (gray alpha) within the flower itself, as shown in Figure 8.12. Click Open to apply the map as Map 2 of the Composite map.

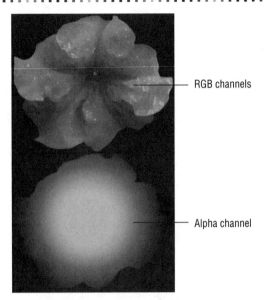

RGB channels

Alpha channel

Figure 8.12 *Image and alpha channel of Map 2*

Only a few image file formats support alpha channels, including .png, .tga, .tif, *and* .psd *formats. Max will recognize these formats, but you will often get errors if you try to use the alpha information of* .tif *files.*

7. Click Show Map In Viewport. Uncheck Tile for both U and V. Change the tiling of the U and V to about 1.5 or 2. Set the U and V Offsets to –0.075 and change the W angle to rotate the image the way you like it on the Vase.

8. Do a test render. Notice that Map 2 is getting burned out (going to white) in places. This is because of premultiplied alpha being turned on, which multiplies the alpha channel with the RGB values. In the Bitmap Parameters rollout, uncheck Premultiplied Alpha. Render again and notice that the spots that were burned to white are now the normal diffuse color that you would expect from viewing the image. Save your files as comp_vase02.max. Figure 8.13 shows the material with the Composite diffuse map so far.

Watch out for the Premultiplied Alpha setting. It's something to be aware of when troubleshooting a composite.

Figure 8.13 Composite diffuse map of cellular base map and bitmap with alpha channel

Adding a Mask Map to a Composite Map

Sometimes your transparency information will be in a separate file rather than an alpha channel of the image. In this case, use a Mask map as a sub-map of the Composite map to mask areas of the image file you wish to designate as transparent. In this exercise, you'll decal another flower on your vase, this time using a separate mask file:

1. Continue working on comp_vase02.max or open it from the CD files for this chapter.

2. Click the sample slot with your Vase material in the Material Editor. Navigate to the top level of the diffuse map, to the Composite Parameters rollout. Click Set Number and choose 3 to add a third map to your Composite diffuse map.

3. Click the map slot for Map 3 and choose a new Mask map. The Mask map gives you two buttons: one for the image to be masked, called Map, and one for the masking image, called Mask. There is also a check box for inverting the grayscale values of the mask file when necessary. Click the Map button and choose a new Bitmap. Browse to flower02.tif file in the 3dsmax\Ch8_maps\ directory. Click View before you open. Click Display Alpha Channel. It is blank, because this .tif file does not have an alpha channel. Click Open.

4. Click Show Map In Viewport. Uncheck Tile for both U and V. Change the tiling to about 1.5 to 2 in U and V. Set the U Offset to 0.5 and the V offset to –0.3.

5. Now you need to add the transparency information to the map slot for the Mask part of the Mask map. Click Go To Parent to return to the Mask map level. Drag the Map button to the Mask button and choose Copy. You are doing this so that you can copy all your UV settings to the Mask sub-map rather than having to enter all the values again.

6. Click the Mask button and open the Bitmap Parameters rollout. Click the long button after the word "Bitmap:" that has the `flower02.tif` file on it. Browse to `flower02_mask.gif` in the `Ch8_maps` directory. Before you open it, click View. It is just a grayscale file.

Not all image files work well for max masks. `.gif` files work well as 8-bit masks; if you are having trouble with a mask file, try switching your image file to a grayscale `.gif` file.

7. Render the scene. The mask file is providing the transparency information for the second decal. Click Go To Sibling and open the Output rollout. Set the Output Amount to 0.8 to make the decal a little more transparent. Figure 8.14 shows the result of the Composite map of three sub-maps and shows its material tree. Save your file as `comp_vase03.max`.

 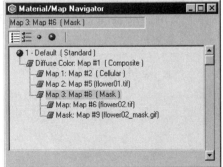

Figure 8.14 *Composite map using Mask map as sub-map*

Mapping the Opacity Channel

As you learned in Chapter 7, maps applied to the opacity channel, often called *opacity maps*, are very similar in concept to alpha channels and masks determining the transparency of an image file in a composite. An opacity map determines the transparency of the surface itself. It essentially composites the rendered image of the geometry with the rendered image of the background and the rest of the scene. Let's apply an opacity map:

1. Open Maps01.max from the CD files for this chapter.

2. Open the Material Editor and click an unused slot. Rename the material "vase." Unlock the Ambient from the Diffuse and set it to a medium blue color. Set the Specular color to a lighter blue.

3. Set these parameters in the Basic Parameters rollout:

    *   Self-Illumination = 38

    *   Opacity = 11

    *   Specular Level = 69

    *   Glossiness = 87

    *   Soften = 0.69

4. In the Shader Basic Parameters rollout, check 2-Sided.

5. Right-click a blank area of the Material Editor and navigate to the Maps rollout. Click the opacity map slot. Choose a Gradient Ramp map.

6. The default Gradient Ramp map has three flags in the gradient from red to green to blue, but you can set as many flags as you want with any colors. Since opacity is determined by grayscale value, you can use all grayscale values for these flags. Add three more flags by clicking in the gradient. Double-click the first flag and set its color to black. Right-click the flag and choose Copy. Right-click each of the other five flags and choose Paste. Double-click each of the five flags to set their values and drag the flags to move them. Create a gradient that looks like Figure 8.15.

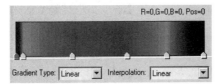

R=0,G=0,B=0, Pos=0

Gradient Type: Linear ▼ Interpolation: Linear ▼

Figure 8.15 *Gradient to create in the Gradient Ramp opacity map*

7. Apply the material to the Vase and render it. The Vase is now transparent with stripes of various degrees of transparency.

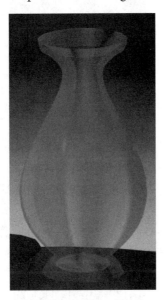

8. Let's make the pattern more interesting by adding a map to one of the flags. Click the third flag, then right-click it and choose Edit Properties. Click the Texture map slot and choose a Checker map. This makes this section of the gradient opaque in places.

9. Navigate to the Gradient Ramp map level. In its Coordinates rollout, change the U tiling to 7 and the V tiling to –17.4. Save your file as Maps02.max.

Mapping the Bump and Specular Level Channels

In Chapter 7, you saw how mapping the bump and specular level channels together creates the appearance of bumps and indentations on a surface without adding geometry. Let's apply this to the pears in this scene:

1. Press W to minimize the viewport. Activate the User viewport zoomed in on the pears and press W to maximize it.

2. Open the Material Editor and choose an empty slot. Name the material "pear." Change the Diffuse color to green. Unlock the Ambient color and choose a darker green. Set Self-Illumination to 10.

3. Click the diffuse map shortcut button. Choose Bitmap and browse to peardiffuse.bmp in 3dsmax4\Maps\Ch8_maps.

4. Assign the Pear material to the three pears.

5. Click Go To Parent to return to the Maps rollout. Open the Maps rollout. Click the bump map button. Choose Bitmap and browse to `pearbump.bmp`. Click View before opening the file. Notice that it is a grayscale image defining the texture of the pear.

6. Click Go To Parent to return to the Maps rollout. Drag from the bump map button to the specular level map button. Choose Instance.

7. Adjust the Amount of the specular level channel to 30 and the Amount of the bump to 53. Render the pears. The pears now have a texture rather than a perfectly smooth surface. Save your file as `Maps03.max`.

Mapping the Self-Illumination Channel

Applying an instance of the diffuse map to the self-illumination channel can bring out the image more. This is best used on flat surfaces or surfaces illuminated from within. Let's try it on the painting in this scene:

1. Press W to minimize the viewport. Zoom in to the painting in one of the viewports.

2. Open the Material Editor and click an empty sample slot. Name the material "painting." Set the Diffuse to a light green color and the Ambient to a darker green. Set Self-Illumination to 12.

3. Assign the material to the Painting object.

4. Click the diffuse map shortcut button, choose Bitmap, and browse to `painting.bmp` in `3dsmax4\Maps\Ch8_maps`.

5. Render the Painting. Click Go To Parent to return to the Maps rollout. You want it a bit brighter, so drag a copy of the diffuse map to the self-illumination channel. Render again. The Painting is less dependent on the lighting of the scene for the image on it to display. Save your file as `Maps04.max`.

Iris Still Life project by Kay Pruvich. The complete project can be seen in the "Materials Projects" plate in the Color Gallery.

Mapping the Displacement Channel

Displacement mapping alters the geometry of the object to which it is applied. Displacement is made according to the grayscale values of a bitmap or a procedural map. Dark values on the map indent the surface; light values raise it in relief. This is in contrast to bump mapping, in which shading simulates low surface relief, but the surface geometry remains unchanged.

Think of mapping the displacement channel as modeling rather than texturing, just as you modeled with the Displace modifier in Chapter 4. Since displacement mapping creates extra geometry, it will slow down rendering, so use bump mapping when you can get away with it. If you will be zooming in close to the edges of the model (where the bump illusion breaks down because it does not alter the shape of the surface), then displacement can be a quick and efficient way to model details. You can displace objects with a map through the displacement material channel, one of the Displace modifiers, or a Displace space warp.

To displace anything other than an editable mesh or NURBS surface, you must first apply a Disp Approx modifier to the object to make the surface displaceable. Displace Approximation works with any surface that can be converted to an editable mesh. Once the surface has been prepared, you simply apply the material with the displacement map. The Amount spinner in the Maps rollout controls the degree of displacement of the surface.

Let's try mapping the displacement channel to model geometry:

1. Create a plane with 10 length and 10 width segments (Create → Geometry → Plane). You must have sufficient topology to support displacement mapping, so you need to use lots of segments.

2. In the Modify panel, apply a Disp Approx modifier to the plane. This makes the plane "displaceable."

3. Open the Material Editor and apply a standard material to the plane.

4. Apply a Cellular map to the diffuse color channel. Turn on Show Map In Viewport. In the Cellular Parameters rollout, set Size to 25.

5. Navigate to the top level of the material tree. Open the Maps rollout. Drag the Cellular map from the diffuse channel to the displacement channel. Choose Instance.

6. Do a test render. The geometry is displaced in the rendering but remains flat in the viewport. Note how displacement is really a modeling technique that can be controlled with materials and maps. Save your work as `Displacement01.max`. Figure 8.16 shows the displacement in the viewport and the rendering. Note that the edges show the difference between a displacement map and a bump map. A bump map would not look much different from the image in the viewport, because it would not change the shape of the surface itself.

Hands-on max: Dining Table Still Life

This tutorial will show you how to apply materials to objects in a still life scene. The still life is of a dinner table setting, without any materials applied. You will create new materials to make the scene appear realistic.

Displacement map
shown in viewport

Displacement map
in render

Edges of surface
show that the
geometry has
actually been
changed rather
than bump-mapped

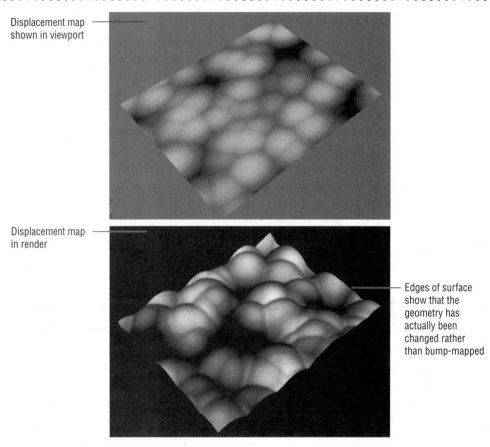

Figure 8.16 *Displacement map shown in viewport and renderer*

Applying a Multi/Sub-Object Material to the Dinner Plate

The plate has a band of decoration and is made of porcelain. The plate was modeled to have two material ID numbers, ID #1 for the porcelain and ID #2 for the checkered decoration. The material ID numbers were set in the Surface Properties rollout of the

Polygon sub-object in the Edit Mesh modifier. To apply a different material to each material ID number, a Multi/Sub-Object material is needed:

You may want to investigate each object in the scene to see how it was made. Many of the objects' modifier stacks are uncollapsed so that you can see their modeling history.

1. Open the file `Dinner Table01.max` from the CD. Press H to open the Select By Name dialog box. Click Plate and click Select.

2. Open the Material Editor. Click the first sample slot in the Material Editor. Open the Material/Map Navigator. Plan to keep this open when designing materials in order to see and navigate your material trees.

3. Click the Get Material button. Choose a new Multi/Sub-Object material. Click Set Number and enter **2**. Name the material "Dinner Plate." Assign the material to the selection.

4. Click the material with ID #1 to navigate to that level. Name this material "Porcelain." Change the shading type to Oren-Nayar-Blinn to better simulate a ceramic surface. Change the Diffuse color to white.

5. Click the Go Forward To Sibling button in the Material Editor. This takes you to the next sub-material. Name this material "Checker Pattern." Apply a Checker map to the diffuse channel. Click the Show Map In Viewport button.

6. In the Checker map, change Color #1 in the Checker Parameters rollout to light green. In the Coordinates rollout, set the Tiling to 2.0 in both U and V directions.

Applying a Bump Map to the Tablecloth

Now give the tablecloth some texture using a bump map:

1. Select the Table object. Click a new sample slot in the Material Editor. Assign the material to the Table. Name the material "Tablecloth."

2. Change the shading type to Oren-Nayar-Blinn to better simulate the fabric. Change the Diffuse color to white and the Ambient color to a light gray.

3. Open the Maps rollout and click the map button for the bump channel. Choose Bitmap and browse to the CARPTTAN.JPG file in 3dsmax4\Maps\ Fabric. Click Open.

4. In the Bitmap Parameters rollout, click the View Image button. A dialog box appears, showing you the bitmap.

5. Notice that this image is in color. Only the grayscale component of this image will be used by the bump channel. Click the Monochrome button in this dialog box to see the grayscale information that will give the appearance of texture to the tablecloth. Close this dialog box.

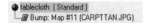

Applying Raytrace Reflections to the Fork and Knife

Now you will give both the fork and knife the appearance of the precious metal silver. Since silver is highly polished and reflective, the Raytrace material is the best choice:

1. Select the Fork and Knife objects.

2. Click a new sample slot in the Material Editor. Name the material "Silver." Assign the material to the selection.

3. Change the material type to Raytrace. Change the shading type to Metal. Change the Diffuse color to a very light gray.

4. Click the Reflect check box and set the value to 25%.

5. Set the Specular Level to 150 and Glossiness to 40.

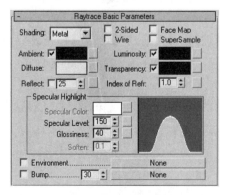

Applying Raytrace Reflections and Refractions to the Wine Glass

The wine glass needs to have a glass material that calculates accurate reflection and refraction. Again, Raytrace is the best choice of material:

1. Select the Wine Glass object.

2. Click a new sample slot in the Material Editor. Name the material "Glass." Assign the material to the selection.

3. Change the material type to Raytrace.

4. Set Reflect to 15%. Set Transparency to 95%. Click the Background toggle button for a better preview of the transparency in the sample slot.

5. Set the Index Of Refraction to 1.5 (for glass). Set the Specular Level to 82 and Glossiness to 50.

Applying Glass and Chrome to the Salt and Pepper Shakers

Each of the meshes for the salt and pepper shakers contains two material ID numbers. ID #1 is for the chrome metal caps and ID #2 is for the glass containers. To apply both materials, use a Multi/Sub-Object material:

1. Select the Salt Shaker and Pepper Shaker objects.

2. Click an empty sample slot and name the material "Shakers." Apply the material to the selection.

3. Change the material type to Multi/Sub-Object. Click Set Number and enter **2**.

4. Navigate to the material with ID #1. Name this material "Chrome."

5. Set Reflect to 50%. Set the Specular Level to 50 and Glossiness to 40.

6. Navigate to the top of the material tree.

7. Since you've already made a Glass material, you can instance it here. While the Shaker material is still the active slot in the Material Editor, drag the Glass material from its slot, down to the button for the second material within the Shaker Multi/Sub-Object material. Choose Instance as the clone type.

```
● Shakers  ( Multi/Sub-Object )
├─● (1) top: Chrome  ( Raytrace )
└─● (2) bottom: Glass  ( Raytrace )
```

Texturing the Salt

The scene contains a separate Salt object representing the salt crystals. It is the child of the Salt Shaker object in the object hierarchy—if you transform the Salt Shaker, the Salt object goes with it. The Speckle map will simulate the variegated crystals.

1. Select the Salt object.

2. Click a new sample slot in the Material Editor. Name the material "Salt." Assign the material to the selection.

3. Apply a Speckle map to the diffuse channel.

4. In the Speckle Parameters rollout, set Color #1 to pure white and Color #2 to a color very slightly darker. Set Size to 3.0.

5. Navigate to the top of the material tree. Open the Maps rollout. Drag the Speckle map in the diffuse channel to the specular color channel. Choose Instance so that changes to one of these maps will update the other. This additional mapping makes the material look a bit more realistic.

Texturing the Pepper

Just as with the Salt object, the Pepper object is the child of the Pepper Shaker object. It needs its own material. You can save a little time and base the Pepper material on Salt.

1. Select the Pepper object.

2. Drag the Salt material to a blank slot in the Material Editor. Rename the copied material "Pepper." Assign this material to the Pepper object.

3. Go into the diffuse color Speckle map. In the Speckle Parameters rollout, set Color #1 to a very dark gray and Color #2 to a color very slightly lighter. The Speckle map simulates the slight variation in peppercorn color.

Applying a Material from Another max File to the Vase

The Vase uses the same material used in another max file. Let's copy this material from the earlier file.

1. Select the Vase object.

2. Click an empty sample slot. Click the Get Material button. In the Browse From area, choose the Mtl Library radio button. Click the Open button. Change the Files Of Type to 3ds max (*.max) to browse the materials of other max files. Browse to the Vase03.max file you saved earlier in this chapter or in the CD files for this chapter.

3. A Composite material appears in the browser. Double-click it to bring it into the Material Editor. Name this material "Ceramic Glaze." Assign this material to the Vase.

Texturing the Ceramic Tiles

The ceramic tiles are the most complex material in the scene. Because of the composition of the camera view, they won't take up many pixels in the final rendered image. However, it is worth learning how to make this material because the process will demonstrate important techniques and the result is a versatile material for use in other projects:

1. Select the Ground object.

2. Click a new sample slot in the Material Editor. Name the material "Ceramic Tiles." Assign the material to the Ground object.

3. Change the shading type to Oren-Nayar-Blinn.

4. Apply a Composite map to the diffuse color channel. Name this map "Grout and Tiles."

5. Apply a Dent map to Map 1 of the Grout and Tiles composite. Name this map "Grout." Set Color #1 to a dark gray and Color #2 to a light gray.

6. Navigate back to the Composite map level. Click the Map 2 slot of the Composite map and choose a Mask map. Name this map "Tiles."

7. The Mask map has two sub-maps: the image part, called Map, and the mask itself, called Mask. Click the Map button and apply a Mix map. Name this map "Tile Color."

8. In the Mix map, make Color #1 dark green. This is the main color of the tiles. Apply a Noise map to Color #2. Name the Noise map "Tile Roughness."

9. In the Noise Parameters rollout, set Size to 1.0.

10. Navigate back up to the Mask map level. Click the Mask button and choose the Bricks map for the mask. Name this map "Tile Pattern." Set the Preset Type in the Standard Controls rollout to Stack Bond.

11. Open the Advanced Controls rollout of the Bricks map. Set the Bricks Setup texture color to white. Whatever is white in a mask is what will show. Set the Mortar Setup texture color to black. The "mortar" will thus mask the grout. Turn on Show Map In Viewport.

12. Set these parameters in the Bricks Setup:

    - Horizontal Count = 1.0

    - Vertical Count = 1.0

    - Color Variance = 0.0

    - Fade Variance = 0.0

13. Navigate to the top of the material tree and open the Maps rollout. Drag the Grout and Tiles Composite map from the diffuse channel to each of these channels:

    - Specular Color

    - Glossiness

    - Specular Level

14. Click the bump map button. In the Browse From area, choose Scene. Select the Tile Pattern map that is masking the Tile color from the grout area. Double-click it to apply it to the bump map level as well. Choose Instance.

You can also instance maps by dragging them from the Material/Map Navigator to an empty sample slot in the Material Editor. In this case you would choose Browse From: Material Editor when you applied the map to another slot. You can instance maps in the Material Editor as background maps and in other places in the interface, allowing you to create complex map trees to apply to single map slots.

15. The ceramic tiles should reflect light, but the grout should not. Create a new Mask map in the reflection channel. Name the map "Shiny Tiles, Matte Grout."

16. Apply a Flat Mirror map to the Map button of the Mask map. This map should only be applied to flat surfaces. Most tiled surfaces are flat, so this is acceptable.

Use the Reflect/Refract map instead of Flat Mirror if you plan to apply the Ceramic Tiles material to curved surfaces.

17. Navigate up the material tree back to the Mask map level. Click the Mask button and again choose the Tile Pattern map from the scene.

18. The still life is complete. Save your work as `Dinner Table 02.max`. Activate the camera view and render the scene to see the result. Figure 8.17 shows the final scene. You can see this image in color in the "Materials Projects" plate in the Color Gallery.

Figure 8.17 *Completed rendering of Dining Table Still Life project*

Dinner Table Still Life project by Scott Onstott

Hands-on max: Texturing a Lamp and Drafting Table Scene

In this tutorial, you will apply materials using a variety of shaders and maps to give a lamp and drafting table a realistic appearance. The model you will use is one that ships with 3ds max 4 on the Learning and Training CD. You can find this CD in the back section of the same CD case that contains your max installation disk. (The CD case opens from both sides, with a disk in each side.)

Creating a Rough Metal Material for the Lamp Arms

Let's start by applying a material to the lamp arms:

1. Open `DraftingTable01.max` from the CD files for this chapter. This is the model from the Learning and Training CD with a camera added to the scene.

The model in the Learning and Training CD also has some odd flipped normals. These are fixed in the version in the CD files for this chapter.

2. Select the Drafting Table object and ungroup it (Group ➜ Ungroup). Press H to bring up the Select By Name dialog box and select Arms01.

3. Open the Material Editor and click an empty sample slot. Name the material "Lamp Arms." Apply the material to the selection.

4. In the Basic Parameters rollout, set the Diffuse color to gray and the Ambient color to black.

5. Set the Specular Level to 150 and the Glossiness to 20.

6. Open the Maps rollout and click the diffuse map button. Apply a Noise map. In the Noise Parameters rollout, set the Noise Type to Fractal and Size to 50. Set Color #2 to a dark gray.

7. Navigate back to the top level of the material. Click the specular level map button and apply another Noise map. Set the Noise Type to Fractal.

8. Navigate back to the top level of the material. In the Maps rollout, click the map button for the bump channel and apply another Noise map. Leave Noise Type as Regular and set Size to 2.0. The Lamp Arms material now has a rough dark metal appearance.

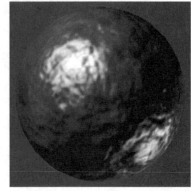

Creating a Shiny Metal Material for the Lamp Base

Next, let's work on the metal base of the lamp to give it a shiny metal appearance:

1. Select the BASE01 object.

2. Click an empty sample slot. Name the material "Metal Base." Apply the material to the selection.

3. To create oval highlights for the reflective silver metal instead of circular ones, change the shading type to Anisotropic. In the Anisotropic Basic Parameters rollout, set the Diffuse color to gray and the Ambient color to black, and check Self-Illumination.

4. Set the Specular level to 180, Glossiness to 30, and Anisotropy to 60. Notice how the Anisotropy affects the shape of the highlight. This is the difference between the size of the highlight as measured from two different directions. If Anisotropy is at 0, it's circular and its size is controlled by the Glossiness level, the same as Blinn or Phong shading.

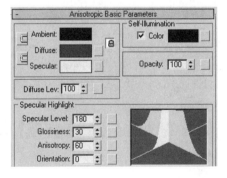

5. Open the Maps rollout. Set the Amount spinner of the diffuse map to 90. Click the diffuse map button and choose Bitmap. Browse to Chromic.jpg in your 3dsmax4\Maps\reflection directory.

6. In the Coordinates rollout of the bitmap, set the Blur offset to 1.

7. Navigate to the top level of the material and open the Maps rollout. Drag the Chromic.jpg bitmap from the diffuse map button to the bump map button. Choose Copy. Set Amount of the bump map to 10.

8. Click the reflection map button and apply a Raytrace map. Turn on the Background toggle button to better show the reflection in the sample slot.

9. Navigate back to the top level of your material. Set Amount of the reflection map to 50. You now have a shiny semi-reflective metallic material.

10. Try rendering your scene. You get a warning that BASE01 is missing map coordinates. The model of the lamp base has not been assigned UV coordinates yet. Click Cancel.

11. In the Modify panel, apply a UVW Map modifier (from the UV Coordinate modifier set) to the BASE01 object. In the Parameters rollout, set the Mapping to Box and click the Fit button in the Alignment options.

Creating a Rough Matte Material for the Drafting Paper

The drafting paper BORDER01 object includes a paper polygon and very tiny guidelines polygons. You will use a Multi/Sub-Object material to apply different materials to the paper and the guidelines:

1. Select the BORDER01 object.

2. You will use a Multi/Sub-Object material to apply different materials to subobject selections based on material ID number assignments. First you need to assign different material ID numbers in the object. In the Modify panel, go to the Polygon sub-object level.

3. Drag the edge of the panel to the left to expand the panel to two columns. This way you will be able to see how many polygons you have selected in the Selection rollout while using the Surface Properties rollout to assign material ID numbers and select by ID number.

4. Press the F2 key to turn on Shade Selected Faces. Select the single polygon that is the whole piece of drafting paper. Notice that the Selection rollout says that you have "2 Faces Selected." These faces are already assigned a material ID number of 1, so leave this selection as is.

5. Choose Edit ➔ Select Invert. Now you have 24 faces selected. These are the tiny faces of the guidelines. In the Surface Properties rollout, enter a **2** in the Material ID rollout and press Enter. Now the guidelines are assigned a material ID of 2.

6. To ensure the guidelines stand out from the paper, type **0.01** in the Extrude spinner and press Enter.

*To check your material ID assignments, click the Select By ID button in the Surface Properties rollout. Type **1** and click OK to select the two faces that have a material ID of 1. Click Select By ID again and type **2** and click OK to select the 100 faces (after extrusion) that have a material ID of 2.*

7. Click Polygon in the stack and return to Object level. Drag the panel back to one column wide.

8. With the BORDER01 object still selected, open the Material Editor and click an empty sample slot. Name the material "Drafting Paper." Apply the material to the selection.

9. Click the Get Material button and choose a new Multi/Sub-Object material. Click the Set Number button and type **2**. Rename the material for ID #1 "paper" and the material for ID #2 "guides."

10. Click the button for the Paper material. Change the material type to Blend. In the Replace Material dialog box, choose Keep Old Material As Sub-Material.

11. In the Blend Basic Parameters, set Mix Amount to 50. Click the button for Material 1 of the Blend. Change its shading type to Oren-Nayar-Blinn. This is a good shader for any matte surface. Set the Diffuse color to white. In the Oren-Nayar-Blinn Basic Parameters, set Roughness to 90.

12. Open the Maps rollout. Set Amount of the diffuse map to 10. Click the diffuse map button and choose a Cellular map.

13. In the Coordinates rollout, set Blur to 5 and Blur offset to 10. In the Cellular Parameters rollout, set Cell Color to white, Variation to 50, and Division Colors to medium gray and dark gray.

14. Click the Go To Parent button to navigate to the Material 1 level of the Blend material. Open the Maps rollout. Drag the Cellular map from the diffuse map button to the diffuse roughness (Diff. Roughness) button. Choose Copy.

Diffuse roughness is specific to the Oren-Nayar-Blinn shader. It adjusts the blend from diffuse to ambient color, increasing the matte quality of the material.

15. Drag the Cellular map from the diffuse map button to the bump map button and choose Copy. Set Amount of the bump map to 10.

16. Navigate to Material 2 of the Blend material. Change the shading type to Oren-Nayar-Blinn. In the Oren-Nayar-Blinn Basic Parameters rollout, set Roughness to 90. Set the Diffuse color to white.

17. Open the Maps rollout. Set Amount of the diffuse map to 80. Click the diffuse map button and choose a Bitmap. Browse to `Carpttan.jpg` in the `3dsmax4\Maps\Fabric` directory.

18. In the Bitmap Coordinates rollout, set U and V Tiling each to 10.

19. Navigate to the top level of Material # 2 of the Blend material Open the Maps rollout. Drag the `Carpttan.jpg` map from the diffuse map button to the bump map button and choose Copy. Set Amount of the bump map to 20. You now have a rough matte surface suitable for paper.

20. Navigate to the other material of the Multi/Sub-Object material. The default Blinn shader will do for a solid opaque black line. In the Basic Parameters roll-out, set the Diffuse color to black, Specular Level to 0, and Soften to 1.0. This will eliminate highlights.

21. In order for the bitmaps to render on the object, it needs UVW coordinates. Apply a UVW Map modifier. Keep the default Planar mapping and click the Fit button under Alignment.

Texturing the Table, Lamp Joints, and Pieces of Tape

Now you will assign materials to the FACE01 object that, oddly enough, includes the three joints of the lamp with the table surface and the four pieces of tape holding the drafting paper in place. To texture this, you will obviously need another Multi/Sub-Object material:

1. Go to the Polygon sub-object level. Click Window Selection to require the entire polygon to be in the marquee for selection. In the top viewport, draw a marquee around the paper, including the four pieces of tape, but without extending the region any farther than necessary. In the left viewport, hold the Alt key to subtract from the selection and draw a marquee around the lamp joint that was also selected. The remaining selection should be of the eight faces of the four pieces of tape. In the Surface Properties rollout, type **2** in the Material ID field and press Enter.

2. In the left viewport, draw a marquee around just the three lamp joints. You should have a selection of 1382 faces. In the Surface Properties rollout, type **3** in the Material ID field and press Enter. Use the Select By ID button to check your assignments.

3. Click Polygon in the stack and return to Object level.

4. With the FACE01 object still selected, open the Material Editor. Click an empty sample slot. Name the material "Face01." Assign the material to the selection.

5. Click the Get Material button and choose a new Multi/Sub-Object material. Click the Set Number button and type **3**.

6. In the Name fields of the sub-materials, enter names corresponding to the material IDs on your object. ID #1 is "tabletop," ID #2 is "tape," and ID #3 is "lampjoints."

Creating a Wood Surface for the Drafting Table

Click the button for the first material for the tabletop. Let's give it a wood surface:

1. In the Basic Parameters rollout, set Specular Level to 40 and Glossiness to 20. Set the Diffuse color to brown.

2. Open the Maps rollout. Click the diffuse map button. Choose a Bitmap and browse to `Walnut3.tga` in the `3dsmax4\Maps\Wood` directory.

3. Click the Go To Parent button to navigate to the top level of the Tabletop sub-material. Open the Maps rollout. Drag the `Walnut3.tga` map from the diffuse map button to the bump map button and choose Copy. Set Amount of bump map to 20. Now you have a semi-glossy wood material.

4. In the Modify panel, apply a UVW Map modifier to the object. Change the Mapping to Box and click Fit alignment.

5. Render the scene to test-render. The wood should be applied to the drafting table only.

Creating a Reflective Translucent Material for the Pieces of Tape

Next, let's apply a sub-material for the pieces of tape at the corners of the drafting paper:

1. Navigate to the Tape material, the second sub-material of the top level Multi/Sub-Object material. Turn on the Background toggle button.

2. Change the material type to Raytrace. In the Basic Parameters rollout, set the Diffuse color to off-white. Uncheck Transparency and enter 30 in the spinner. Set Specular Level to 100 and Glossiness to 80.

3. Open the Maps rollout, click the Reflect Map button, and choose a Falloff map.

4. In the Falloff Parameters, change the Falloff type to Fresnel. The tape now has a reflective semi-transparent material.

Creating a Steel Material for the Lamp Joints

The last sub-objects to texture are the three lamp joints:

1. Navigate to the top level of the Multi/Sub-Object material. Click the Lamp-joints material.

2. Change the material type to Blend. Choose Discard Old Material. In the Basic Parameters rollout, set Mix Amount to 50.

3. Click Material #1 of the Blend material. In the Basic Parameters rollout, change the Shader to Metal. Check 2-Sided.

4. In the Metal Basic Parameters rollout, set Specular Level to 150, Glossiness to 50, and Self-Illumination to 15.

5. Open the Maps rollout. Click the diffuse map button and choose a bitmap. Browse to `Steelplt.jpg` in the `3dsmax4\Maps\Metal` directory.

6. Navigate to the level of Material #1 in the Blend. Open the Maps rollout. Drag the `Steelplt.jpg` map from the diffuse map button to the bump map button and choose Copy. Set Amount of the bump map to 10.

7. Navigate to Material #2 of the Blend. Change the material type to a Raytrace material. In the Basic Parameters rollout, change the Shader to Metal. Check 2-Sided. Set the Ambient, Diffuse, and Reflect colors to white. Set Specular Level to 100 and Glossiness to 60.

8. Open the Maps rollout and click the reflect map button. Choose a Falloff map. Change the Falloff Type to Shadow/Light.

9. Navigate to the top of the Lampjoints sub-material. You now have a reflective steel material.

Creating a Glowing Inside and Shimmering Outside for the Lamp

Finally, you are ready to apply materials to the lamp. Again you need to use a Multi/Sub-Object material:

1. Select the Lampface01 object.

2. Go to the Polygon sub-object level in the stack. In the left viewport, zoom in to the on/off button at the top of the lamp. Toggle to Crossing Selection and draw a marquee around the button from the top to the middle of the bottom polygons. If you arc-rotate, your selection should look like Figure 8.18. Leave these faces as Material ID 1.

3. Go to Edit → Select Invert. In the Surface Properties rollout, enter **2** in the Material ID field. Click Polygon in the stack to return to Object level.

4. With Lampface01 still selected, open the Material Editor and click an empty sample slot. Name the material "lamp." Assign the material to the selection.

5. Click the Get Material button and choose a new Multi/Sub-Object material. Click the Set Number button and type **2**. Rename your sub-materials: ID #1 as "on/off," ID #2 as "lampshade."

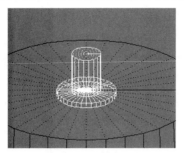

Figure 8.18 *Select these button polygons.*

6. Click the button for the on/off sub-material. Set the Diffuse color to black. Set Specular Level to 90 and Glossiness to 30.

7. The lamp needs mapping coordinates, so apply a UVW Map modifier. Change the mapping to Cylindrical and click Fit alignment.

8. Activate the left viewport and click Zoom Extents Selected. Press P to switch to a Perspective view. Arc-rotate to an angle where you can see some of the inside and some of the outside surface of the lampshade. Right-click the viewport label and choose Views ➜ ActiveShade. Right-click in the viewport and choose Draw Region to draw a marquee around a section of the lamp that includes part of the inside and part of the outside of the lampshade. The viewport will now update changes to the material only within the marquee, allowing for a quicker update.

9. Navigate to the Lampshade material of the Multi/Sub-Object material. Click the Get Material button and choose a new Double Sided material.

10. Click the Back Material button. This material will be the inside of the lampshade. Set the Diffuse color to off-white. Check Self-Illumination and set its color to a light yellow. Set Specular Level to 50 and Glossiness to 20.

11. Navigate to the Facing material of the Double Sided material. Change the shader to Multi-Layer. The Multi-Layer Shader gives two specular highlight layers; this is useful for shiny polished or wet surfaces.

12. Under First Specular Layer, set Level to 40, Glossiness to 10, Anisotropy to 50, and Orientation to 140. Under Second Specular Layer, set Level to 50, Glossiness 50, Anisotropy 0, and Orientation 0.

13. In the Maps rollout, set Amount of the diffuse map to 40. Click the diffuse map button and choose a bitmap. Browse to `Abalone.jpg` in your `3dsmax4\Maps\Misc` directory.

14. In the Coordinates rollout, set Blur offset to 0.05. Your Facing material is now a shiny metal material. Right-click the ActiveShade viewport and choose Close from the upper-left quad. Save your file as `DraftingTable02.max`.

Lamp and Drafting Table texturing project by Blue Bactol

 You will be returning to this project to add lighting in Chapter 12, to render to elements in Chapter 13, and to open the composited elements in combustion for further post-production in Chapter 14.

Hands-on max: Camera Mapping

Camera mapping is a powerful technique that allows you to use a 2D photograph with simple geometry to substitute for very complex geometry and mapping. The beauty of the technique, and the difference between this and sophisticated compositing, is that the camera can move (within limits) within the scene, and the features of the photograph will appear to move as they should relative to the camera, with the parallax that would occur if the camera were really in the 3D scene of the photograph. This can achieve extremely realistic shots with very little work. (*Parallax* is the illusion of background elements moving more slowly than foreground elements, due to the perspective effect that makes background distances appear smaller. Recreating this illusion when using a 2D background makes the difference between a fake-looking composite and a shot that can be mistaken for real film footage.)

Very few people realize how much camera mapping is used in big-budget films. Camera mapping is often used in film to create establishing shots of exotic locales without going to the trouble and expense of a location shot. The groundbreaking subway shot in *The Matrix* also employed a very similar principle to camera mapping. The CG camera was programmed to choose between several photographs of different angles of the subway, based on its position and the angle of incidence to the geometry. Because of this, you got a very realistic shot without every detail of the subway having to be modeled and individually mapped. This is more complex than max's camera mapping, but it is essentially the same "cheat."

How Camera Mapping Works

Camera mapping starts with a photograph of the scene you want to create. What you want to do is map crude versions of the main features of the photograph with the same map as the background, so that when the camera moves, its relation to these features changes realistically.

The difference between camera-mapping your features and just mapping them with regular UVW mapping is that camera maps are projected with the converging perspective lines of an actual camera lens, whereas normal mapping is projected along parallel lines. You can't get the same effect from one photograph with just normal mapping.

 For in-depth information on camera mapping, visit dvGarage at `http://www.dvGarage.com.`

Camera-Mapping an Establishing Shot

In this tutorial, you will camera-map an establishing shot for a movie scene set in Bath, England. To create an establishing shot, a director has three choices: hire a camera crew to fly to the location, set up, and shoot; model the scene from scratch; or use an existing photograph of the scene and camera-map it. In most cases, simple establishing shots get done faster and are cheaper if camera mapping is employed. The camera does not have to fly all around the scene, just subtly track in to bring the audience into the story. Keep in mind that establishing shots generally go by quickly. They usually last only a few seconds, and most audiences only see them once. It is therefore unnecessary to be obsessively perfect about it, even if you start to notice the animation breaking down. As long as it fools you a few times, it is working. If you watch even blockbuster movies carefully and repeatedly, you will notice these "cheats" being used.

This is a complex camera-mapping project, involving a considerable amount of work. If it seems at times not worth the effort, consider how much time, money, and effort it would cost you to fly to Bath and hire a camera crew to take this shot. (Readers from Bath, England, or thereabouts may want to use a different photo in order to appreciate the value of camera mapping.)

Photographing the Scene

The most important resource you need for camera mapping is a good high-resolution photo of your scene in an image file format usable by max. Targa, .bmp, or .tif files are best for camera mapping in max.

Max does not support PICT files (which are native to the Macintosh computer).

If you are taking the photograph yourself, be sure to note the focal length of your camera and the camera's position relative to the ground plane. If you have the photograph taken by a photographer, you need one or the other piece of information (focal length or height of the camera) in order to be able to "fudge" your camera mapping. (With some knowledge of photography and a good eye for it, you might be able to guess the focal length.)

The Bath camera-mapping project uses a single photo taken with a 35mm lens at about five feet from the ground.

Finding the Horizon Line

There are some preparatory steps before bringing the photograph into max. First you need to determine the horizon line. Keep in mind that what you are doing in camera mapping is matching the perspective of the photograph and placing objects based on the determined perspective. Since you know that this photo was taken with a 35mm lens, you only need to determine the horizon line and height of the camera in order to place your objects.

All parallel lines in the photograph should converge toward one point on the horizon. In this example, the natural horizon is obstructed by the buildings, so you'll have to draw one in:

1. Open the original photograph of the scene called `foreground.tga` from the CD files for this chapter in Adobe Photoshop.

    If you study the photograph, you can determine that the building on the right with the columns, labeled in Figure 8.19 as "building D," has several parallel lines that can be used to derive the horizon line. While you only need two lines, you can get a bit more accurate with more. Figure 8.19 shows three lines, two from the top part of the building and one from the base. The place where they all intersect is on the horizon line.

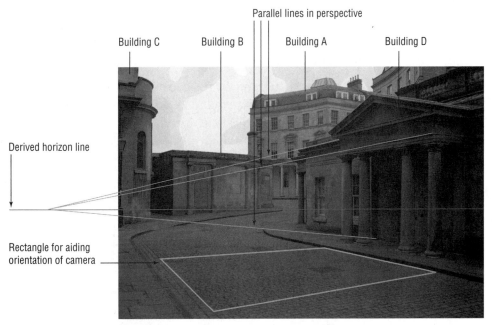

Figure 8.19 *Photograph with derived horizon line*

2. Because the point of intersection in this example is beyond the range of the canvas, you need to change the size. Choose Image ➜ Canvas Size and make the canvas 2000 pixels wide to give yourself a lot of space to work with.

3. Make a new layer and activate the line tool (press N). For each of the three parallel edges you are using for your perspective lines, start at the point of the edge closest to the camera and drag a line along that edge that extends well past the edge of the photo. The point of intersection lies on the horizontal horizon line. Drawing the third line will allow you to check the accuracy of your line drawing. If the third line intersects at the same point as the other two, then you have most likely nailed it. If not, then you need to look at your lines to see where they might have gone wrong.

 It is worth asking yourself at this point how accurate you need this camera map to be. If the camera map is going to serve as an establishing shot, then you don't need to get your calculations down to the hair. Even the pros working on films work only to the level of precision needed for the shot. You don't need to make extra work for yourself.

4. Holding the Shift key to constrain the line to exactly horizontal, draw a line that passes through the intersection point of the first two lines, all the way across the canvas. This is the horizon line of the image that you will match to the horizon line of your camera view in max.

5. In addition to drawing the perspective lines, another helpful device is to find four points in the photo that you know lie on a rectangle and draw lines connecting them. This will aid in orienting the camera in max. In this example, the edges of the street and the perpendicular rows of bricks form a convenient rectangle. Draw lines connecting these points as shown in Figure 8.19.

6. In Image ➜ Canvas size, set your canvas back to the original width of 1200 pixels. Flatten the image and save it as `PerspectiveLines.tga`.

Painting Out the Obstacles

The next step to prepare the photograph is to again open it in Photoshop to separate objects in the photograph into layers where you can paint behind any obstructions the camera will pass. You will apply the original photo to the objects that are closest to the camera (such as the columns in this example) and any objects with no area obscured in the original that will be seen by the camera.

In order for the camera to pass a foreground object and see what is behind it, you need additional images to map to the objects that were obscured by the foreground objects in the original shot. To do this, you make a copy of the original image for each of the objects that will be revealed and paint out the foreground objects. This can be the most time-consuming part of the entire process, but it again depends on what is happening in the shot. If the camera will not move much, then you don't have to do as much painting.

You will make multiple images, each a copy of the original foreground image with different features painted out. You need one of these images to map to each building obscured in the original photo that will come into the view of the camera. You also need one for the ground, one for the sky, and one for any other object you want to build to add accuracy to the shot. In each of these images, you keep the same size and resolution of the original image, but focus only on the part relevant to what it is mapping to.

It is best to work from the background and move toward the camera. If you refer back to Figure 8.19, you will notice that, of the buildings the camera will see, building A is the farthest from the camera. Let's start by making the map for building A:

1. Open the original image file again. Select the image layer in the Layers palette and drag it to the New Layer button to duplicate it. Name the new layer "Building A."

2. Press S to activate the Clone (Rubber Stamp) tool. Set the options to 100% Opacity and check the Aligned check box.

3. Zoom up close on an area of the building obstructed by other buildings. Hold down the Alt key and click to sample from an area of the image where the building is visible that you think looks similar to the obstructed area. Start cloning out the buildings on both sides as well as any smaller obstructions. Since this map will apply only to building A, it doesn't matter what the image looks like outside of the area shown in Figure 8.20. However, it is important to maintain the same image size and resolution for the camera mapping to work. Figure 8.20 shows the altered area of the Building A layer.

 If you want to try camera mapping without doing all the cloning work in Photoshop, you can skip to the "Matching the Camera to the Photo" section. All the images are available in the CD files for this chapter.

4. For building B, you need a map with the side of the building cloned in. Figure 8.21 shows the altered area of the Building B layer.

Figure 8.20 *Building A revealed*

Figure 8.21 *Building B revealed*

5. Building C and the parts of building D that are not directly behind the four columns can be mapped with the foreground image. For the parts of building D behind the columns, you need to make another layer with the columns painted out. Figure 8.22 shows the altered area of the Building D layer. For the columns themselves, you can use the foreground image.

6. You also need a layer for the ground. On this layer, paint out all buildings and other obstacles (such as lamp posts) that obscure areas of the ground that your camera will see. If you have cloned in ground while making the other maps, you can copy and paste those areas to this layer. Figure 8.23 shows an example of the ground painted in as far as needed for this shot.

Figure 8.22 *Building D revealed*

Figure 8.23 *Ground revealed*

7. Finally, you need a layer for the sky. Make a file that is just the sky background to fill any obscure areas of the sky that your camera will see.

For extra realism, you can make a map for building C with the lamp post cloned out.

8. Export each layer as a Targa file. You're done with the Photoshop part of this tutorial, so you can close the program.

Matching the Camera to the Photo

Now you're ready to open up max and set up your camera to match the perspective of the shot:

1. In max, create a camera (Create ➔ Cameras ➔ Free Camera) and orient it so it is facing away from you by clicking in the front viewport. Name the camera Camera_mapping. In the Modify panel, set the Lens parameter to the focal length of the camera that took the photo (35mm). Check Show Horizon.

Name your cameras Camera_description. That way, you can easily find all your cameras grouped together alphabetically, and you can identify the purpose of each.

2. Activate the perspective viewport and press C to switch to a camera view.

3. Click the Render Scene button. You need to set the aspect ratio of the render to match the photo so that your viewport background will also match the rendering output. The photo was scanned in at 1200 × 800. While you could use that as the final output size, you wouldn't be able to track the camera in very far without the image falling apart. You also wouldn't be able to play the animation on most computers. In the Render Scene window, set the output to 300 × 200 and click Close.

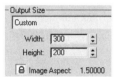

4. With the camera viewport still active, press Alt+B to load your image with perspective lines as your background for this viewport. Click the Files button and browse to `PerspectiveLines.tga` that you made earlier in Photoshop or from the CD files for this chapter. Under Aspect Ratio, check Match Rendering Output. Check Display Background.

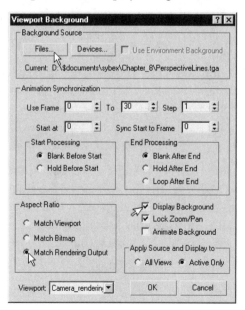

5. In Customize → Preferences → Viewport tab, check Filter Environment Backgrounds. Uncheck Low-Res Environment Background. Click Configure Driver. Check Match Viewport As Closely As Possible.

6. Now you can orbit the X axis of the camera to align the horizon line of the camera with the horizon line in the viewport background. It is also helpful to rotate the camera on its Z so that the grid lines align with the perspective lines in the photo.

When adjusting the rotation of your camera, use keyboard shortcuts for the main camera viewport controls you will be using, Pan and Orbit. The default shortcut for Pan is dragging with the middle mouse button or pressing Ctrl+P. If you assign Rotate View Mode a keyboard shortcut, the key will activate the Orbit tool when you are in a camera viewport. Assign the shortcut in Customize → Customize User Interface → Keyboard.

7. If you knew the exact height of the camera in the scene, you could just put your camera at that height. However, since you have the two other variables—the focal length of the lens and the horizon line—you can figure out the height while aligning simple geometry to the photo.

Matching Simple Geometry to Your Photo

The next step is to model geometry corresponding to the main features of the landscape: the tall buildings, mountains, large bridges, and so forth. These models can be very rudimentary—a box for a building, a box or patch grid edited to fit the curvature for a mountain, and so forth. You need to include the features that the camera passes and those that stand out from the background as it approaches. The first object you place will not only help you establish the height of the camera but will aid in orienting the rest of your scene:

1. In the top viewport, create a plane. This is to align to the rectangle you drew in the PerspectiveLines.tga file. Since you know that the shape you drew in the scene corresponds to a rectangular area, you can align the rectangular plane so it fits. You change the height of the camera and scale the plane until it fits the lines displayed in the viewport background.

2. Create box primitives (Create → Geometry → Box) for some of the buildings. Move and scale the boxes to align them with the buildings. Make sure that you

don't move them off the ground plane. Notice that the base and tops of your boxes will match the perspective of your photo.

3. Repeat this for each of the buildings. Use cylinders for objects like the columns and extrude ngons for forms like the top part of building D. You can even add a Taper modifier to the columns to match their shape. Make a plane with a lot of segments as the ground plane. Name all your objects so they will be easy to find later.

 Because this photo was taken from such an oblique angle it is difficult to get the ground plane to accept the perspective-projected texturing. To aid the projection, increase the segments and the render density parameters of the plane.

4. In Rendering ➜ Environment, load sky.tga as the Environment Background and make sure that Use Map is checked.

5. Once you are done aligning the perspective and placing your models, you can hide the alignment rectangle and turn off the viewport background (press Alt+B and uncheck Display Background). If you need to adjust your models, you can turn the background on again.

Applying the Camera Map Modifier

If you were going to camera-map only a few objects against a photo, you would load your original photo as the environment background. Since you have built objects for everything visible in the scene, this is not necessary.

The World Space version of the Camera Map modifier allows your camera to move in the scene within the range covered by your photograph, because it locks the mapping coordinates to World space rather than local space. This is the version that you want:

1. Apply a Camera Map modifier (World Space type with an asterisk) to each of your modeled features.

 Apply a separate Camera Map modifier to each feature, rather than instancing the modifier between them.

2. For each Camera Map modifier, click Pick Camera and, using Select By Name, select Camera_mapping. Save your file as CameraMap01.max.

Creating Materials to Apply the Images to the Objects

The mapping camera establishes the exact extent of the object relative to the projected image so that the pixels corresponding to the object can be replaced with the pixels of a flat map. The mapping camera must remain still in order to maintain the correct projection of the image. (You will move a separate rendering camera through the scene.) The flat map projected onto these pixels is determined by the diffuse channel of the object's material.

Materials used for camera mapping must have Specular Level and Glossiness set to 0 and Self-Illumination set to 100.

Again, start with the objects in the background and work your way toward the camera:

1. Open the Material Editor. In the first sample slot, name the material "building A." Click Show Map In Viewport. Set Specular Level and Glossiness to 0 and Self-Illumination to 100. In the SuperSampling rollout, choose Adaptive Halton and spin the quality up to 1 and check Enable Sampler.

2. Open the Maps rollout and apply the `buildingA.tga` image to the diffuse channel.

If you completed the earlier part of the tutorial, you will have made all the images for this section. If you didn't, you can find them in the CD files for this chapter.

3. Drag the first sample slot to the second and choose Copy. Name this material "building B." Replace the map in the diffuse slot with `buildingB.tga`.

4. Drag the first sample slot to the third and choose Copy. Name this material "building D." Replace the map in the diffuse slot with `buildingD.tga`.

5. Drag the second sample slot to the fourth and choose Copy. Name this material "ground." Replace the diffuse map with `ground.tga`.

6. Finally, drag the first sample slot to the fifth and choose Copy. Name this material "foreground." Replace the diffuse map with `foreground.tga`.

7. This is where good naming of your models will come in handy. Select the ground plane and assign the ground material. Select all the objects of building A and assign the Building A material. Select the objects of building B and

assign the Building B material. Select the objects of building D behind the columns and assign the Building D material. Select the columns and all the objects of building C and assign the Foreground material.

8. Now the maps should show in the viewport. You can use this to fine-tune the placement of the buildings and see where you may need to adjust your maps. Do a render before deciding whether the ground is skewed, however. The viewport renderer has an even harder time than the renderer with the oblique angle of projection.

Setting Up the Rendering Camera

The camera you have adjusted so far is only for establishing the projection of the map. You must not move it. To move through the scene, you need to set up a second rendering camera:

1. Select Camera_mapping, choose Edit ➜ Clone, and then Copy. Name the new camera Camera_rendering. The rendering camera can move within the scene within limits. The more extreme the camera movement, the more the projection will be distorted.

2. Because of the oblique angle of this photo, you need to start your rendering camera a little forward of the mapping camera. Move the camera slightly forward. You can adjust this later if you get distortions in the render.

3. With the camera viewport active, press C to switch to the view of the selected rendering camera.

4. Click the Time Configuration button in the lower-right corner of the interface. In the Animation area, set the End time to 150 and click OK. This gives you a little more time for the shot. You will learn more about time controls and animation in Chapters 9 and 10.

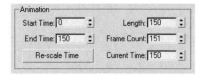

5. Click the Animate button. Drag the time slider to the end of the animation. Move the camera forward in the scene. Remember that the camera can't make

drastic movement or rotation without breaking the illusion. You also can't move it so far that it will see places where the obscuring geometry has not been painted out, such as past the corner of building D.

6. With the Animate button on, adjust the position of the rendering camera at the last frame and maybe one frame in the middle. Adjust the rotation of the camera at these same frames. Be careful not to rotate the camera so as to roll it. Turn off the Animate button. Save your max file as CameraMap02.max.

If you have trouble with this part, read Chapters 9 and 10 on animation and return to this part of the tutorial.

7. Click the Render Scene button. In the Render Scene window, choose Active Time Segment, check Save File, and make sure you are rendering the Camera_rendering viewport. Click the Files button to name a filepath to save the movie. Figure 8.24 shows the settings in the Render Scene window.

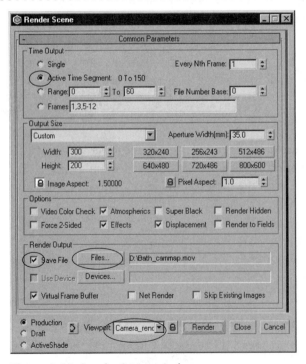

Figure 8.24 *Render Scene window*

8. After clicking the Files button, name the animation file `Bath_cammap.mov`, choose QuickTime Movie as file type, and click Save. In the Compression Settings dialog box, choose Best Quality, and click Save.

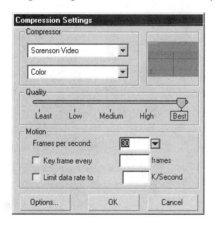

9. Before clicking Render, scroll down to the MAX Default Scanline A-Buffer rollout and choose Blackman from the anti-aliasing settings. (Anti-aliasing algorithms will be discussed in more depth in Chapter 13.) When checking your camera animation, check Disable All Samplers and uncheck Anti-Aliasing. When rendering your final animation, uncheck Disable All Samplers and check Anti-Aliasing. The render time is considerably longer with the super-sampling turned on. Then click the Render button in the Render Scene window. It will take some time to render, so have a break. When you come back, open your animation file in QuickTime to view the file. The rendered Quick-Time movie is also available in the CD files for this chapter. Notice how, starting from a single photograph of the scene, the camera appears to take you into the scene.

Tell max to notify you when your render is done under Customize ➜ Preferences ➜ Rendering. Check Beep under Render Termination Alert or choose a sound file you wish to play when the render is complete.

Bath, England, photo and camera-mapping project by Tom Meade

Trial and Error

Camera mapping takes a bit of getting used to. It also generally takes trial and error even when you're familiar with it. You may find you need to adjust your maps to paint more foreground objects out, your models to better match the scene, and your rendering camera animation to stay within the constraints of the photo. You might also add additional models to catch odd forms in the photo.

If you want to make your render more pristine without the level of supersampling used in this tutorial, you can further alter the maps in Photoshop. When max attempts to anti-alias thin lines in textures, the textures can appear to wobble. One option for fixing this is to open the image in Photoshop and zoom up close to the line. Using the clone tool with a soft 5-pixel brush and 60% opacity, sample from an area near the line and clone across the line. Save the file and click the Reload button in the map's Bitmap Parameters rollout before rendering from max.

Learning camera mapping brings us almost full circle through the development of computer graphics—from 2D images to mapped 3D geometry, back to what might be called 2½D, where 2D images are being substituted for geometry, but in a manner that is educated by the geometry and camera information of your 3D scene.

For other examples of "2 ½ D," check out REALVIZ products at http://www.realviz.com. *The Image Modeler takes the principle of camera mapping a step further by modeling objects for you from photographs of a scene.*

You also animated a camera through the scene and rendered your animation, leading us directly into the three animation chapters that follow.

Summary

In this chapter, you explored max materials options in greater depth. You used your materials knowledge to apply different materials to objects and map various channels of materials. In the Hands-on max sections, you applied materials to whole scenes, and you learned about and applied a tremendously powerful cinematic cheat called camera mapping.

In the next chapter, you will start animating.

Part IV
Animation

In This Part

n Part IV, you will learn how to animate in max. Chapter 9 introduces you to the basic animation tools in max. You will explore transform animation, parametric animation, animating with space warps and particle systems, morphing, and beginning sub-object animation. In Chapter 10, you will use the Track view to fine-tune the timing of animations, use animation controllers and the new animation constraints, link objects to transfer animation information, and use dynamics. In Chapter 11, you will link up a hierarchy, animate with forward kinematics and various kinds of inverse kinematics, and animate with bones and character studio Biped and Physique.

Beginning to Animate

3ds max

Chapter 9

This chapter will provide a foundation of animation concepts and methods. You will learn the basic principles of animation and apply those principles to max. Topics include:

- Animation timing

- Max animation tools

- The Track view

- Transform animation

- Parametric animation

- Space warps

- Particle systems

- Morphing

- Animating sub-object elements

Timing Animated Images

"Animation" literally means imparting life. Animating a character means to give the character lifelike qualities through the way it moves. Much that people interpret as "character" and "personality" is associated with subtle cues of motion. Vitality and exuberant presence—and the opposites of lethargy and vapidity—are conveyed by gait, gesture, and facial expression.

Creating believable characters in this way is an art form of great depth. You need to understand how the timing of movement in real life conveys meaning, and you need to understand how to re-create that effect in your media—in this case, CG.

Reviewing Animation Concepts

As you learned in Chapter 1, animation involves creating the illusion of motion by playing a succession of images, called frames, fast enough to fool the human eye. The smoothness of the perceived motion is affected by how fast the images are played (the frame rate) as well as by the continuity between the images.

You learned in Chapter 2 that animation can be created straight ahead, with each frame being created in order, or pose-to-pose, with significant poses keyframed and the transition frames filled in afterward. Animation in 3D applications uses the keyframe method, with the artist creating keyframes and the computer interpolating or *tweening* between them. Your art as a computer animator, then, is in choosing the right keyframes and giving max the best instructions for interpolating between them.

Studying Motion

Studying motion and how it is timed is very important when tackling an animation task. Pay attention to the timing of ordinary motions in real life. A stopwatch is a very helpful tool for this, and you should *believe* the stopwatch. Yes, it takes that long to sit down or to make a salute.

Studying the masters of traditional cel animation will help you get a ballpark idea of how to break down a motion. It will help your animation greatly to learn the classic principles of traditional animation, such as anticipation, follow-through, ease in and out, squash and stretch, moving holds, and secondary motion. An excellent resource for this is The Illusion of Life, *a book on Disney animation by Frank Thomas and Ollie Johnston (latest of several editions published by Hyperion, 1995; currently out of print, but well worth looking for). Another good starting point is* Cartoon Animation *by Preston Blair (Walter Foster Publishing, 1995).*

Thinking in Frames

To think like an animator, you need to translate all your timing into frames. The number of frames will depend on the frame rate of your output. Frame rates vary from 60 frames per second (fps), the upper limit of what the human eye can perceive, down to 10 fps, currently common on the Internet. The illusion of continuous motion, as opposed to a fast-paced slide show, starts to break down under 12 fps, although this may still work for your purposes. Table 9.1 shows some common frame rates used today.

Table 9.1 Frame Rates of Typical Output Formats

Output Format	Frame Rate
IMAX	60 frames/sec (fps)
NTSC video (North America and Chile)	30 fps
PAL video (rest of world)	25 fps
Film	24 fps
Web	8–30 fps

In traditional cel and stop-motion animation, where each frame was shot separately, the effective frame rate was not always the actual number of frames shot for each second of film. The frame rate for film became standardized at 24 fps. Animators would judge whether a given motion needed to be shot "on ones" or could be shot "on twos." If shot on twos, each frame would be shot twice, making the effective playback rate (in terms of how often the image changed) 12 fps. The timing of an action would still be determined by the number of seconds needed. What changed was how many frames had to be drawn (or in the case of stop-motion, how many different poses needed to be set up) for that motion. For a very swift or intricate motion, the extra frames of shooting on ones could be necessary to keep the continuity. For example, if something flies across the scene in a few frames, having the intermediate frame can help the viewer catch the motion. Or when Mickey Mouse was tinkling the piano keys, the quick finger motions required that the animation be shot on ones. When a motion does not have enough continuity between frames or when its effective frame rate is below 12 fps, it appears jerky.

In CG animation, you don't have to worry about shooting on ones or twos, because you can set a motion to be rendered into as many or as few frames as you choose. It will help you understand animation timing, however, to watch classic animation frame by frame and notice what the animators considered important.

As an example of thinking in frames in your own animations, suppose that you are outputting to 30 fps digital video. You estimate that you need a ball to cross a certain distance in 1.5 seconds, so you animate the motion over 45 frames. If you try this and it seems too slow, that means the ball needs to make the transit in fewer frames, so you need to move the keyframes closer together. What you would do in max is move the *keys*, the values of the animated parameters, from frame 45 to an earlier frame, making the earlier frame the new end keyframe of that motion. You need to become very practiced in thinking in frames and translating a desired change to your animation into how you need to change your keys. Chapter 10 explains the use of interpolation types to control the timing of motion.

Animation skills require a great deal of practice, no matter how much theory you know, so don't lose heart if you get frustrated. The real key to learning animation is persistence.

Max Animation Tools

Max provides a great range of tools for creating animation. This section looks at simple applications of these tools. The interface includes the time control area for segmenting animations and playing back animations in the viewport, as well as a simple on/off button for animating. Max's Track view, almost another program within max, is an exceedingly versatile tool for creating and editing animation as well as for keeping track of everything going on in a scene. The Motion panel gives you alternate access for some of the controls in the Track view as well as the only access for the character studio plug-in covered in Chapter 11.

The Time Slider

You've already used the time slider at the bottom of the interface for simple animations. The time slider allows you to move through the time of a max file by dragging the playback head forward or back through the frames. This is called "scrubbing" your animation. By default a max file has 100 frames at 30 fps, or $1\frac{1}{3}$ seconds.

The Time Control Area

The time control area includes the controls seen in Figure 9.1 and listed in Table 9.2. The central area, which looks and behaves much like VCR controls, is for playing back your animation in the viewport. Additional controls give you options for moving in time through your animation, determining the segment of animation that you wish to work on, and altering the timing of segments of animation.

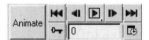

Figure 9.1 *The time control area tools*

Table 9.2 Time Control Area Tools

Button	Tool	Description
◄◄	Go to Start	Moves to the first frame of the active time segment.
◄l	Previous Frame	Moves to the previous frame. If the Key Mode toggle is on, moves to the previous keyframe.
▶	Play/Stop	Plays the animation, by default only in the active viewport. If playing, stops animation.
l▶	Next Frame	Moves to the next frame. If the Key Mode toggle is on, moves to the next keyframe.
▶▶	Go to End	Moves to the last frame of the active time segment.
⚷	Key Mode toggle	When on, will move you to the next keyframe of the selected object. You can change what keys this tool will use under Key Steps in the Time Configuration dialog box.
0	Current Time field	Moves to an exact frame. Type in the frame number and press Enter.
⏲	Time Configuration dialog box	Allows you to set the frame rate, the active time segment, the viewport playback rate, the time display unit, and the steps used by the Key Mode toggle.

The Time Configuration Dialog Box

Much of the Time Configuration dialog box is self-explanatory. Using the Playback and Animation settings, however, requires some explanation.

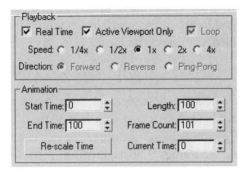

Adjusting Viewport Playback

Playing animation back in the viewports requires a lot of computer memory. Often you will want to determine how this memory is prioritized. Usually you will want the animation to play back in the active viewport only. If you want to see the animation play in real time, check the Real Time box, keeping in mind that the program may have to drop frames to keep the speed in a complex scene. If you need to see every frame, you can either uncheck Real Time or choose one of the slower speeds (¹/₄ or ¹/₂ speed).

If your animation doesn't seem to be playing, check to see whether you are looking at the active viewport.

Displaying Action-Safe Area

If you are outputting to video or broadcast television, you may want to adjust your viewport to display action-safe frames while animating. Television will crop part of your image, and different sets will crop differently. Because of this, there is an area of the screen considered safe for titles and a larger area considered safe for displaying action critical to the shot. While animating a piece for video output, keep all the action within the action-safe area. Right-click the viewport label, choose Configure, and check Action Safe and Show Safe Frames In Active View on the Safe Frames tab.

Setting the Active Time Segment

You can work easily with a long animation by working on one time segment at a time. Only the active time segment appears on your time slider, but the whole animation is still there. If you have an animation of 900 frames and want to skip the first two seconds to work on just the third second, you set the Start Time at 60 and the End Time at 89 (assuming 30 fps). When finished, you could change the active time segment again.

Rescaling Time

The Re-scale Time button rescales the active time segment to the length and position that you choose. If you rescale frames 60 to 89 from a length of 30 frames to 15 frames, the segment plays twice as fast. If you also change the start time from frame 60 to frame 30, this piece of animation is moved to frames 30 to 44, the frames that were previously frames 30 to 44 are moved to frames 45 to 59, and the frames that previously started at frame 90 will now start at frame 60.

The Re-scale Time button changes the timing of your segment. Be sure this is what you want.

The Animate Button

The Animate button, located in the lower-right of the max interface, is a simple, straightforward tool for creating animation keys. It is either on or off. When it is off, any changes you make apply to the whole animation timeline. When it is on, any changes you make create a keyframe at the frame you are on with those changes applied in keys. Keys hold the animation data of a particular track (a parameter or transform track, for example) at a particular frame. The values for that track are interpolated between the keys for the in-between frames. In a CG program, any frame that holds a key is a keyframe. A keyframe can have more than one key.

You can use the Animate button to create most kinds of animation in MAX. An exception to this is particle systems, which animate according to their own parameters, without the use of the Animate button. Other exceptions are plug-ins like character studio footsteps and some inverse kinematics (IK) calculations. In most cases, keys for various parameters are still created, but without the use of the Animate button. The Animate button is just one way to create the keys that make up an animation.

Always remember to turn off the Animate button when you are done animating something. Every change you make with the Animate button on is animated.

The Track Bar

The track bar, just below the time slider, displays the keys of a selected object—with a red box at every frame where the selected object has a key. This is also called a "mini Track view" because it gives you access (via right-clicking a dot) to key properties just as in the Track view. The individual tracks aren't separated the way they are in the Track view, so if you get confused, go back to the Track view.

Let's make a simple animation to demonstrate the use of the track bar and other animation features:

1. Reset max (File ➜ Reset).

2. In the perspective viewport, drag out a box on the left side of the viewport.

3. Give the box three segments each in height, length, and width.

4. Turn on the Animate button.

5. Drag the time slider to frame 100. Move the box to the right, zooming out if you need to.

6. Turn off the Animate button. Play the animation. Save the file as `animation01.max`.

Max created a starting keyframe at frame 0 and an ending keyframe at frame 100. You can see the two red boxes representing the keyframes in the track bar. With the box selected, right-click it and choose Properties. Check Trajectory to display the box's trajectory in the viewport, as shown in Figure 9.2.

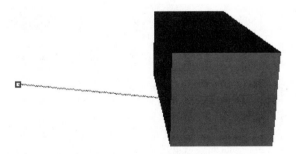

Figure 9.2 *Trajectory of an animated box*

The Track View

The information of a max file is divided into separate areas called "tracks," which track the value of each parameter, setting, or transform over the length of the animation. These tracks can be viewed in the Track view, accessible through the main toolbar button, in the Graph Editors menu, or by right-clicking an object and choosing Track View Selected. You got a glimpse of the Track view in Chapter 2.

Think of the Track view as a kind of office manager for your max file. It organizes all the tracks into a system where you can access almost everything you might need to know about your scene. You can add or delete keyframes, edit timing and transitions, or change animation controllers. You can see all the animatable parameters of an object, its transforms, and its hierarchical linkages.

The Track View Toolbar

The Track view has its own toolbar, with similarities to the main toolbar. Table 9.3 describes some of the more important commands on this toolbar.

Table 9.3 Commands on the Track View Toolbar

ICON	TOOL	DESCRIPTION
	Filters	Filters what types of tracks are shown or hidden in Track view; often used to show only animated tracks.
	Assign Controller	Available here and in the Motion panel; allows change of animation controller (details in Chapter 10).
	Parameter Curve Out-of-Range Types	Tells max whether and how to repeat this animation track (explained in Chapter 10).
	Viewing modes	Toggles between five Track view modes (explained in the next section).
	Add Visibility Track	Adds track determining overall transparency of an object.
	Delete Keys	Deletes selected keys.
	Move Keys	Allows moving of keys; also used to get out of other tools (such as Add Key).
	Add Key	Adds a key at each place (a particular frame of a particular track) that you click.
	Properties	Brings up Key Info dialog box.

Track View Modes

There are five modes of the Track view that change the display of the toolbar and edit window. Generally, you will be editing in either Edit Keys or Function Curves mode.

Edit Keys Mode

In Edit Keys mode you can directly access the keys you've created, create more keys, move them around, and change the tangents between them. You will learn how to do this in Chapter 10.

Edit Time Mode

The Edit Time mode is for working with blocks of time independently of keys. You can use this to copy and paste keys between all valid track types, rather than having to select each type of track separately. The other main use for this mode is the Reduce Keys feature, which allows you to reduce a selection of tightly packed keys (usually motion-capture information) according to a specified threshold.

Edit Ranges Mode

The Edit Ranges mode displays animation data as range bars covering the length of animation, rather than as separate keys. Range bars look as shown in Figure 9.3. This is useful for sliding segments of animation in time. Using the Modify Subtree feature allows you to move animation for an object and all its children at the same time.

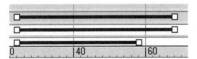

Figure 9.3 *Range Bars*

Position Ranges Mode

The Position Ranges mode allows you to define the range of an animation to be repeated separately from the initial animation. This is used in conjunction with the Parameter Curve Out-of-Range types explained in Chapter 10. By dragging the start and end points of a range, you define the range of the animation used for the out-of-range setting.

Function Curves Mode

The Function Curves mode shows you a graph of the track, with the values of the keys and the tangents in between. The reason the type of timing transition between keys is called a "tangent" is because it refers to the tangent of the function curve going into and out of the key. For example, the animated box you just made will have function curves for the Position track similar to those shown in Figure 9.4. The X, Y, and Z positions are displayed as lines on a graph, with X red, Y green, and Z blue. These curves show the value of the X, Y, or Z position versus time in frames. For position tracks, they are very similar to a trajectory. You will learn how to use these curves in Chapter 10.

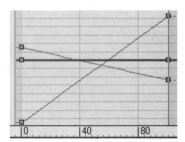

Figure 9.4 *Example of X, Y, and Z function curves*

The Track View Hierarchy

In the Track view hierarchy, the left pane of the Track View window, you can see everything in your scene. Table 9.4 shows how the different types of tracks are indicated by icons in the hierarchy. Click a plus sign in front of a track to reveal more levels within that track.

Table 9.4 Track View Hierarchy Icons

ICON	MEANING
Earth symbol	World track (Scene)
Green cone	Audio track
Lavender cylinder	Generic track
Blue sphere	Material track
Yellow cube	Object track
Green triangle	Controller track (animatable)

Examining an Object's Track View

Let's look at the Track view:

1. Continue working with the file you made earlier (or open `animation01.max` from the CD files for this chapter).

2. Click the Track View button to open the Track view.

3. Click the plus sign in front of the word Objects in the Track view hierarchy to open it up.

4. You can now see the object icon for the box. Open the Box01 track (click the plus sign in front of it).

5. You can now see Transform track and the Object (Box) track. Open this track to see the tracks for Position, Rotation, and Scale.

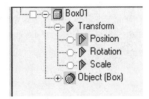

At the very left of the right pane next to the Rotation and Scale tracks, you can see the current rotation and scale values of the box. Rotation is 0 around all axes and scale is 100% in all axes. Position doesn't show a numerical value. This is because the position transform is animated over time and the values are held in the position keys. You can see two circles in the position track, one at frame 0 and one at frame 100. These are the position keys you created when you animated the box.

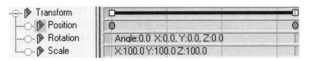

If you open the Object (Box) track, you can see tracks for all the animatable parameters of the box and their current values. If these were animated, you would see keys instead of a single value.

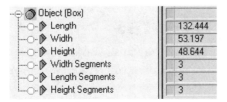

The Track View Edit Window

The right pane of the Track view is the Track view edit window. This is where you can edit keys and the transitions between them, called tangents. It consists of a time ruler showing the active time segment of the animation in white. A vertical line marks the frame at which the time slider is currently set.

You can zoom in and out of the edit window with the zoom tools in the lower-right corner of the Track view. Figure 9.5 shows the zoom tools. These work much like the zoom tools for the viewports.

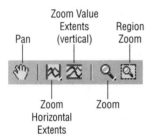

Figure 9.5 *Zoom tools of Track view*

 If you click the Move Keys button and then right-click one of the keys, you bring up the Key Info dialog box for that key. You will work more with the Key Info dialog box in Chapter 10.

The Motion Panel

The Motion panel provides alternate access to some of the same controls available in the Track view, although you can't see all the tracks. You can add keys and change controllers (animation controllers are explained in Chapter 10) for transform tracks. The same key info available by right-clicking a key in the Track view is available here in Key Info rollouts for transform keys. The Motion panel is also the main interface for the character studio plug-in covered in Chapter 11.

Animating Transforms

Transform animation is animation of any of the transforms of an object: move (position), rotate, or scale. This is the kind of animation you created when you animated the box moving from left to right. You also used it when you animated the camera in Chapter 8. It involves animating the transform matrix of the object, which, as you may recall from Chapter 2, is evaluated *after* all changes to the master object and its modifiers. As your animation becomes more complex, the position in the object data flow can become more significant.

Remember that you can always create an equivalent transform animation in the modifier stack by using the XForm modifier and animating transforms of its gizmo rather than the object itself.

Animating Parameters

Parametric animation is the animation of creation parameters, modifier parameters, color values, and many other parameters. You created a parametric animation when you animated the sea surface in Chapter 4. Most parameters in max are animatable, with a few exceptions. To find out whether a parameter is animatable, you can turn on the Animate button, move to a new frame, change a parameter, and see if it animates over time. The other way to check is to look in the Track view. If the parameter has a track with a green triangle in front of it, the parameter is animatable.

Animating a Single Parameter

Let's try a simple parametric animation of the liquid level of a teacup:

1. Open the file tea01.max from the CD files for this chapter.

2. Select the object "tea level." This is simply a cylinder. Click the Animate button on.

3. In the Modify panel, change the Height parameter to 0.

4. Go to frame 60 by typing **60** in the Current Frame field and pressing Enter. Change the Height parameter back to 2.5.

5. Click Play. The tea level now animates from 0 to 2.5. Turn the Animate button off. Save your file as tea02.max.

Max looks in all the configured paths (Customize ➔ Configure Paths... ➔ Bitmap tab) when it is searching for bitmaps. If max is having problems locating the bitmaps used in a .max file, you can either add additional paths under Configure Paths or use the MapPath Editor to remedy the situation. Go to Utilities ➔ More ➔ MapPath Editor to load the simple utility that allows you to re-path bitmaps.

To keep the tea in the cup, you will apply a space warp in "Animating with Space Warps" later in this chapter.

Animating Modifier Parameters

You can also animate the parameters of a modifier. There are many modifiers that provide the ability to deform geometry for animation purposes. Table 9.5 lists those modifiers and the level at which they can be applied, whether object level, sub-object level, or both.

Table 9.5 Animatable Modifiers

MODIFIER	OBJECT DEFORM	SUB-OBJECT DEFORM
Bend	✔	✔
Twist	✔	✔
Taper	✔	✔
Noise	✔	✔
Delete Mesh		✔
Displace	✔	✔
Edit Mesh		✔
Face Extrude		✔
FFD (all)	✔	✔
Flex	✔	✔
Morpher	✔	
Patch Deform	✔	✔
Push	✔	✔
Relax	✔	✔
Ripple	✔	✔
Skew	✔	✔
Skin	✔	
Slice	✔	✔
Spherify	✔	✔
Squeeze	✔	✔
Stretch	✔	✔
Wave	✔	✔
XForm	✔	✔

Animating a Bend Modifier

Let's animate a Bend modifier:

1. Open animation01.max—the file you made earlier or from the CD files for this chapter.

2. Select the box. In the Modify panel, apply a Bend modifier from the Parametric modifier set.

3. Turn on the Animate button and go to frame 30.

4. Turn up the Angle parameter on the bend to 45°.

5. Turn off the Animate button and play the animation. The box bends for the first 30 frames as it is moving.

Notice, as seen in Figure 9.6, that the box doesn't bend very smoothly. It needs more segments in height to bend smoothly. Let's fix this.

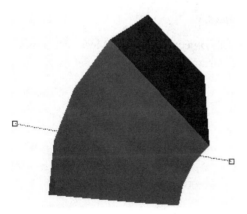

Figure 9.6 *This box has too few segments for a smooth bend.*

Navigating the Modifier Stack

When animating, as when modeling, it is sometimes necessary to navigate the modifier stack to change values lower in the stack. In this case, we need to go to the Box level to change the number of height segments.

1. Select the box and go to its modifier stack.

2. Select Box in the stack.

3. Turn the number of height segments up to 8 and play the animation. The bend is much smoother now.

4. Go back up to the top of the stack (the Bend modifier) and save the file as `animation02.max`.

 When a twisting or bending modifier doesn't seem to do anything, check that you have enough segments. One segment can't bend.

Animating a Noise Modifier

Let's apply some animated noise to the tea surface you made earlier:

1. Open the `tea02.max` file that you made earlier or from the CD files for this chapter. Select the Tea Level object.

2. Apply a Mesh Select modifier from the Selection modifier set. Go to frame 60 in order to see the cylinder. Go to the Vertex sub-object level. In the front view, select the top row of vertices.

3. While still in the Vertex sub-object level of the Mesh Select modifier, apply a Noise modifier from the Parametric modifier set. Set these parameters:

   • Check Fractal

   • Roughness = 0.75

   • Iterations = 6

   • X and Y Strength = 0

   • Z Strength = 1

   • Check Animate Noise

   • Frequency = 0.25

   • Phase = 60

   This applies animated noise to the surface of the tea.

4. Apply another Mesh Select modifier and deselect all the vertices. Save your file as `tea03.max`.

Animating Light Parameters

Lights also have parameters that can be animated to create a sense of mood. An example of this is a scene in the movie *Toy Story* after Buzz Lightyear is confronted with the fact that he is a toy. Over the course of his song, the lighting on his face changes subtly from blue (when he is depressed) to orange (as he pulls himself out of it). Let's animate the multiplier and color values of a light.

1. Reset max.

2. Create a target spotlight from the upper-right corner of the front view, dragging the target to the middle of the viewport.

3. Create a sphere in the middle of the hotspot of the light. You can use the Spotlight view (press Shift+4) to do this.

4. Select the light and go to the Modify tab.

5. Go to frame 100 and turn on the Animate button.

6. Change the spotlight color from white to red. Play the animation. The color of the light on the ball animates from white to red.

7. Stop the animation and go to frame 30. Turn the multiplier of the light up to 2.2.

8. Go to frame 100 and set the multiplier to 0.5.

9. Turn off the Animate button and play the animation. The light becomes brighter until frame 30 and then diminishes.

Animating Material Parameters

Many material parameters can be animated. For example, animating the opacity allows you to fade an object in or out of visibility, and animating a bump map can change the appearance of surface textures over time.

An alternate way to animate visibility is to create a visibility track in the Track view and animate that directly.

In this example, you are going to animate something that you can watch in the viewport, the tiling of a checker map:

1. Reset max. Create a teapot and click the Zoom Extents Selected button.

2. With the teapot selected, open the Material Editor and click Assign Material To Selection.

3. In the diffuse channel, apply a checker map and click Show Map In Viewport.

You will only see the map in viewports that are set to Smooth + Highlights. Make sure the perspective viewport is active.

4. Go to frame 100 and turn on the Animate button.

5. Change the U and V tiling of the checker map to 5.

6. Close the Material Editor, turn off the Animate button, and play the animation. The checker pattern animates from a large to a small check.

Materials can be animated in other ways as well. You can assign an animated map (an .avi *or Quick-Time* .mov *file) in one of the mapping channels. Depending on the mapping channel, it may use the file with its color information or the grayscale values only. If you are using the Morpher modifier, explained in "Morphing" later in this chapter, you can also use a Morpher material to change materials as the object shape changes.*

Animating with Space Warps

Space warps are used in animation to affect objects as they travel through space. This is because space warps are applied in World space rather than local space. This is the same as saying that they are evaluated after the transforms in the object data flow, because it means the object's transform relative to the World has to be calculated before the space warp can be applied. The space warp's effect is defined relative to World space.

There are two main types of space warps: those that affect particle systems and some dynamics and those that affect geometry. The space warps that affect particle systems and some dynamics objects fall into the categories of forces (such as wind or gravity) or deflectors (to simulate collisions and bounces). The kind that affect geometry are categorized as deforming or modifier-based.

For deforming or modifier-based space warps to work well, you often need to apply them to geometry with a lot of segments.

1. Open the tea03.max file that you created earlier or from the CD files for this chapter. Go to frame 60 so you can see the tea level cylinder.

2. Create an FFD (Cyl) space warp about the size of the tea level cylinder (Create ➜ Space Warps ➜ Geometric/Deformable ➜ FFD Cyl). Click Set Number Of Points and set FFD dimensions of 8 side, 4 radial, and 4 height points.

3. Right-click in a blank area of the viewport to turn off the Create Space Warp command. With the space warp selected, click Align, press H, choose the Tea Level object, and click Pick. Align the center of the space warp in X, Y, and Z with the center of the tea level cylinder.

4. Select the Tea Level object. Click the Bind To Space Warp button. (Don't confuse it with the link tools next to it.) Press H to bring up the Select By Name dialog box, choose the FFD space warp, and click Bind. Click one of the select tools to turn off the Bind To Space Warp button. The Tea Level object now shows an FFD binding in its modifier stack.

You can bind an object to a space warp by clicking the Bind To Space Warp button and then dragging from the object to the space warp. You will get a bind to space warp cursor when you have dragged over a space warp. In this case, there are too many objects in the same area to bind the object easily with this method.

5. Select the space warp object again. In the Modify panel, go to the Control Points sub-object level. Selecting different rows of control points in the front viewport, scale them down in the top viewport to get the tea level cylinder to fit within the cup.

6. Play the animation. The tea level now rises within the cup.

7. Hide the FFD space warp. Save your file as tea04.max.

At this point the noise is starting too early and is causing an error in the early frames of the animation. You will fix this in Chapter 10 by adding and adjusting keys. There are other ways you could create this animation without using the space warp. This ongoing animation exercise is to demonstrate a variety of animation tools and methods.

Animating Particle Systems

Particle systems are different from the animated objects you've looked at so far, because they have animation built into the object. Particle systems can be used to create smoke, water, bubbles, a swarm of bees, or anything that behaves as a group of smaller objects flowing. The flow can be affected by various space warps. Different particle systems can be combined to create the overall effect desired. Because particle systems have animation built in, animating a particle system can be as simple as dragging one out in a viewport. Let's use a particle system to create a flow of tea from the teapot.

Creating a Particle System

First let's create a particle system to resemble a liquid:

1. In Create ➜ Geometry, choose Particle Systems from the drop-down menu. Click Super Spray and drag out an emitter in the top viewport about the size of the spout.

2. Activate the front viewport and play the animation. A few particles shoot upward.

3. In the top viewport, region-zoom into the spout of the teapot.

    Move the particle system in the front view into the top of the teapot spout.

4. Arc-rotate in the left view until you are looking straight on at the teapot.

5. Click the Rotate tool. Choose Screen from the Reference Coordinate System drop-down list. Rotate in your user view around Z until it is pointing down from the teapot spout.

   Rotate the particle system 180° around X in Absolute:World and move it above the cup. (You will attach it to the teapot spout in Chapter 10 using an attachment controller.)

6. In the Modify panel, set these parameters for the Super Spray:

   - Percentage = 50

   This is the percentage of the particles that will appear in the viewport. Setting it to a lower number makes the viewport update faster.

   In the Particle Generation rollout, set these parameters:

   - Check Use Rate, set rate to 20

 Use Rate specifies the number of particles to be emitted per frame. This setting is better for continuously flowing particles rather than bursts. Checking Use Total generates the specified number of particles over the life of the particle system. This setting works best for bursts of particles.

   - Speed = 0.5
   - Variation = 5%

   This is the distance the particles travel in a frame.

   - Emit Start = 9
   - Emit Stop = 60
   - Display Until = 100
   - Life = 20
   - Variation = 1

   This means the particles will start emitting at frame 9, stop emitting at frame 60, and display until frame 100. The life span of each particle from the time of creation is 61 frames.

   - Particle Size = 0.7
   - Variation = 3%

- Grow For = 0
- Fade For = 0

Grow For defines how long it takes for the particles to reach full size. Fade For defines how long it takes for particles to diminish to 1/10 their original size.

7. In the Particle Type rollout, check MetaParticles. Metaparticles are particles that cling and regroup based on their distance from each other, creating a more fluid-like effect.

8. Open the Material Editor and apply the tea liquid material to the Super Spray object.

9. Go to frame 40 and render the camera viewport. The particles should be looking more like liquid, as shown in Figure 9.7.

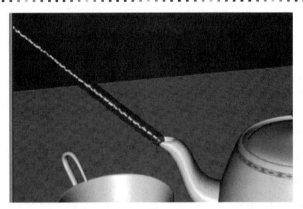

Figure 9.7 *Metaparticles cling to create a fluid-like effect.*

The Super Spray particle system uses more computer resources than Spray particle systems. When you can get away without the extra options of Super Spray, use Spray. In this case, you needed metaparticles, so you needed Super Spray.

Making the Particles Follow a Path

Right now your particles spray upward rather than downward. You want them to follow an arc down to the cup from the teapot spout. To do this, add a PathFollow space warp:

1. Draw a curve from the teapot spout into the cup (Create ➜ Shapes ➜ Line). You will probably need to move the vertices and their Bezier handles in different views to get them where you want them. Name the line "tea path."

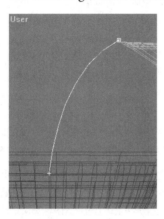

2. Create a PathFollow space warp (Create ➜ Space Warps ➜ Forces ➜ PathFollow) and drag out an icon somewhere in a viewport.

3. With the PathFollowObject01 object selected, go to the Modify panel and click the Pick Shape Object button. Press H, choose the Tea Path object, and click Pick.

4. In the Modify panel of the pathfollow object, uncheck Unlimited range. Set Range to 2.0 and Travel Time to 20. Set Stream Taper to 55% and check Diverge.

5. Select the Super Spray object and click the Bind To Space Warp button. Press H, choose the PathFollowObject01 space warp, and click Bind. Click one of the selection tools to turn off Bind To Space Warp.

6. Play the animation again. Now the particles follow the path down to the cup.

Adding a Deflector Space Warp

If you play the animation, you will notice that the particles are going right through the cup instead of being deflected by it. You need one of the deflector space warps and an object to deflect the particles with.

Particle collision detection isn't exact in max. If you are having problems with particles showing through an object they are deflecting off of, try making a one-sided deflector just above the geometry's surface. The particles will then bounce without showing through.

In the file is a transparent object called liquid deflector. This object is already modeled and positioned to deflect the particles. You tell this object to be a deflector by creating a UOmniFlect space warp and picking the liquid deflector object. You tell the particles to bounce off the deflector by binding them to the UOmniFlect space warp:

1. Create a UOmniFlect space warp (Create ➜ Space Warps ➜ Deflectors ➜ UOmniflect). Draw it anywhere in the top viewport, any size.

2. In the Modify panel of the UOmniFlect, click the Pick Object button. Press H, choose the liquid deflector object, and click Pick. This tells the space warp that the liquid deflector object will have the deflecting properties specified in its parameters.

3. Select the particle system and click the Bind To Space Warp button.

4. Press H, choose the UOmniFlect space warp, and click Bind. To check whether you did this correctly, look at the modifier stack of the particles. On top of the Super Spray should be a PathFollow binding and on top of that a UOmni-Flector binding. Save your file as `tea05.max`.

In Chapter 10, you will correct the timing of the tea level animation so the cup doesn't fill up until the particles reach the bottom. You will then rotate the teapot so that it pours the liquid, and link the particle system to the teapot so that it rotates with the teapot.

Using Animation Modifiers

You may recall that one of the modifier sets available in the Modify panel is called the Animation modifier set. Max has a variety of special modifiers intended specifically for animating. Table 9.6 describes the animation modifiers. You will use some of these in the subsequent sections of this chapter and some of them in Chapter 10.

Table 9.6 Animation Modifiers

NAME	DESCRIPTION
Skin	Allows you to deform a mesh with a linked skeleton. (Example in Chapter 11.)
Flex	Allows you to create secondary animation from movement for cloth, floppy ears, jiggling fat, etc. (Example in "Using the Flex Modifier" later in this chapter.)
Linked XForm	Allows you to move a sub-object selection with another object. Very simple way to deform a mesh. (Example in Chapter 10.)
PathDeform	Allows you to deform geometry along a path.
PatchDeform	Allows you to deform geometry with a patch surface.
SurfDeform	Allows you to deform geometry with a NURBS surface.
Morpher	Allows you to animate transitions between different deformations of a geometry object. (Example in the next section.)
Melt	Allows you to create a melting effect with geometry objects.

Morphing

An exercise given to apprentice animators at Disney was to animate a sack of flour to portray believable personality. A common way to animate such "inanimate objects" in 3D programs is deformation animation. You can do this in max by making copies of a mesh and deforming them (such as with FFD modifiers) to create morph targets and then morphing between them.

In a complex facial morph, you might want to set up a slider manipulator (explained in Chapter 3) for each morph target in the viewport. This would not add any functionality above that of the sliders already in the Morpher Modify panel, but could save considerable time back and forth to the panel.

Morphing in 3D means making a smooth transition between two different forms. The forms, or morph targets, must have the same number of vertices (or control points), because max interprets the morph as one object with its vertices moving around. You already used morphing in Chapter 7 when you used the Morpher modifier to switch between a flattened model and the original model in order to create an accurate texture map template. The only difference there was that you didn't animate between the two states.

You can combine morph targets in a key according to percentages; for example, 10% of this target with 90% of that target. The Morpher modifier provides true weighted morphing. This means that the result is computed using *vertex deltas*, the change in each vertex from the original state. (The original state is the object to which the Morpher modifier is applied. This is sometimes called the base object, the seed object, or the reset morph.) Vertex delta calculation is necessary to create precise controls for facial animation, for example. You want to be able to get just the right eyebrow of one target and just the lips of a second target, rather than have the eyebrows and lips of all the targets averaged together. Vertex delta calculation also means that the morph target percentages can add up to more than 100% without scaling the object. You might want 100% of an eyebrow raise as well as 100% of smirked lips.

An excellent book on making morph targets for lip synch and facial animation is Animating Facial Features and Expressions *by Bill Fleming (Charles River Media, 1998).*

An older type of morphing still available in max is the compound object called Morph. This uses what is called a *barycentric* controller, which averages the values of the vertices of all the morph targets used in a key. With the barycentric controller, if the percentages of the morph targets add up to more than 100%, the resulting object will be scaled up in size. There is no reason to use this kind of morphing anymore. It is only in the program to support files from older versions of max.

Using the Morpher Modifier

The procedure of morphing involves creating morph targets by altering the vertices of object copies, applying the Morpher modifier to the base object state, loading all the other objects as morph targets, and then animating between different target states. Start with copies of one object to ensure that you have the same number of vertices in each morph target.

Let's apply the Morpher modifier to the torch flame of Intrepid Explorer Jim:

If you have not already copied the IEJmaps *directory from the Chapter 7 CD files into your* 3dsmax4\Maps *directory, do so now.*

1. Open torch.max from the CD files for this chapter. This file contains a torch modeled very simply with Surface Tools. The steps are available in the CD files for Chapter 5. In addition, a UVW map modifier has been applied.

2. Open the Material Editor and click an empty sample slot. Apply the material to the torch_wood object. In the diffuse slot, load torch_wood.jpg. Click Show Map In Viewport.

3. Click a new sample slot and apply it to torch_flame object. Click Show Map In Viewport.

4. In the diffuse slot, load flame.jpg. In the opacity slot, put flame_opac.gif.

5. Now you are ready to morph the flicker of the torch. Make three copies of the Torch object.

6. With two of your copies, make dramatically different fire shapes, while staying within the bounds of the diffuse map. With the third copy, make a very small shape for just before the flame dies.

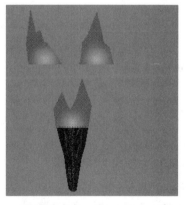

Intrepid Explorer Jim project by Jason Wiener

7. Apply the Morpher modifier to the original object.

8. Click Load Multiple Morph Targets and click each of the three copies. They should load as channels in the Morpher modifier.

To load one morph target at a time, use Pick Object From Scene. The Capture Current State button allows you to create a new morph target from a combination of preexisting ones.

9. Turn on the Animate button. Every few frames, dial up one of the different shapes or a combination of the shapes.

10. Turn off the Animate button and play your animation. You have a simply flickering torch. Save your file as `torch02.max`.

It is possible to detach a section of a mesh, such as a face, and create morphs of just this section, then reattach the body to the morphed piece, thus having morph targets that take up less memory. This works pretty well in cases where the entire animation will stay in max until rendered into a movie, but will break if you are exporting to Web 3D output.

Using the Flex Modifier

Flex is an animation modifier that adds soft-body dynamics to simulate the response of soft flowing objects to motion. (For example, a mold of Jell-O that is moving fast and stops suddenly will jiggle afterward.) The Flex modifier works by using virtual springs between the vertices of an object. You can set the strength and stiffness of the virtual springs to control the dynamics of the object, as you will do in this exercise to control the softness of a tablecloth.

Forces and deflectors will act upon the tablecloth, influencing the way it flexes. You will set the force of gravity to act upon the tablecloth and assign the table itself to act as a deflector. Let's try this technique:

1. Open the file `Tablecloth01.max` from the CD.

2. Create a plane object and place it slightly above the table. Make sure the plane overlaps the tabletop's surface. Name this object "tablecloth." The overlapping tablecloth will eventually hang below the tabletop.

3. Create a Deflector (Create ➔ Space Warps ➔ Deflectors ➔ Deflector). Place the deflector on the table surface. Make the deflector's length and width slightly larger than the tabletop.

4. Set the deflector's bounce parameter to zero. Set friction to 100%. This will make the tablecloth stick to the table surface without bouncing.

5. Create the force of gravity (Create ➔ Space Warps ➔ Forces ➔ Gravity). It doesn't matter where you place this force, as it will act upon the entire scene.

6. Select the tablecloth. Apply a Flex modifier from the Animation modifiers set with the following parameters:

   - Flex = 0.8
   - Strength = 0.0
   - Sway = 7.0
   - Use Chase Springs = Checked
   - Use Weights = Unchecked
   - Sample Type = Euler
   - Samples = 1

7. In the Simple Soft Bodies rollout, set the following parameters:

   - Stretch = 1.0
   - Stiffness = 50.0

8. Click the Create Simple Soft Body button. It will take a few moments to calculate.

9. In the Forces and Deflectors rollout, there are two groups: one for forces and one for deflectors. Click the Add button, and then click the force or deflector object on the screen. Do this for each group.

10. Play the animation to watch the tablecloth fall onto the table and deform. Figure 9.8 shows the completed tablecloth. Save your file as `Tablecloth02.max`.

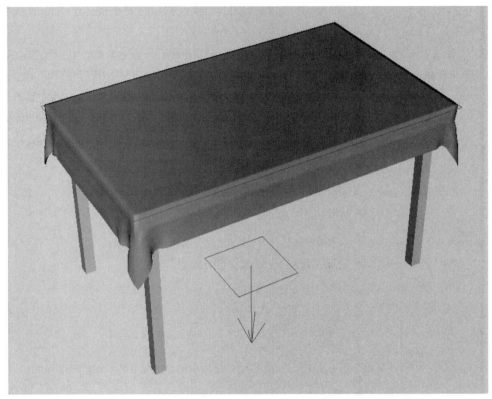

Tablecloth Project by Scott Onstott

Figure 9.8 *Tablecloth made with Flex modifier*

Animating Sub-Objects

Sub-objects can usually be animated, either directly or through the gizmo of a modifier. You can animate vertices directly if you collapse to an editable mesh, but not if you are using one of the Edit modifiers. It's usually better to use an XForm modifier.

Let's try animating vertices different ways. The first method involves animating the vertices directly; the second involves animating the vertices by animating the gizmo of the modifier applied to them.

Directly Animating the Vertices of a Collapsed Object

In this case, you will animate the vertices directly, so you need to collapse the modifier stack from a parametric object to an editable mesh.

1. Reset max.

2. Create a sphere, right-click it, and choose Convert To: Convert To Editable Mesh.

3. Go to the Vertex sub-object level.

4. Open the Soft Selection rollout and check Use Soft Selection.

5. Select the top vertices of the sphere.

6. Turn up the soft selection falloff until the green part of the falloff covers about a third of the sphere.

7. Go to frame 100 and turn on the Animate button.

8. Move the vertices up to stretch the sphere into an oblong shape.

9. Turn off the Animate button and play the animation. The vertices animate upward.

10. Save this file as sphere01.max for reference in the next chapter.

Animating Vertices with an XForm Modifier

Another way of creating the same animation that you created above is with an XForm modifier. As mentioned earlier, direct sub-object animation doesn't work with Edit modifiers, so an XForm modifier is necessary when you don't wish to collapse the stack of your object.

A related modifier, called Linked XForm, is covered in Chapter 10. Linked XForm allows you to link a sub-object selection to a parent object.

Let's make the same animation you just made, using XForm instead:

1. Reset max.

2. Create a sphere.

3. Apply an edit mesh modifier (Modify tab ➜ More ➜ Edit Mesh).

4. Go to the Vertex level and check Use Soft Selection.

5. Select the top vertices of the sphere and turn up the falloff to about the same point as the last exercise.

6. Go to frame 100 and turn on the Animate button.

7. Move the vertices up into the egg-like shape.

8. Turn off the Animate button and play the animation. Nothing happens.

9. Stop the animation and press Ctrl+Z to undo the move.

10. Apply an XForm modifier (Modify tab ➜ More ➜ XForm).

11. Go to frame 100 and turn on the Animate button.

12. Move the vertices up with the yellow XForm gizmo (the wireframe box seen around the upper part of the sphere in Figure 9.9).

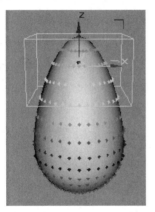

Figure 9.9 *The same vertex animation using the gizmo of an XForm modifier*

13. Turn off the Animate button and play the animation. The sphere animates.

14. Save this file as sphere02.max for later reference.

In Chapter 10, you will compare the results of these two sphere animations in the Track view to evaluate their efficiency for animating.

Summary

In this chapter, you have learned the basics of animation and many of the animation tools in max, including the Track view. You created simple transform and parametric animations, with examples applying to a variety of objects; you animated with space warps and particle systems; you animated with the Morpher and Flex modifiers, and you animated vertex and gizmo sub-objects.

In the next chapter, you will learn about developing your animation skills beyond the beginner level. You will learn about editing keys and tangent types in Track view to translate a desired motion into instructions for max. You will use dummy objects to facilitate animation. You will learn about and use different animation controllers, the movers and shakers of animation in max.

Advancing Your
Animation Skills

3ds max

Chapter 10

n this chapter, you will learn more of the complexities of animating. Animation controllers and the new animation constraints are the mechanism behind animation in max. In this chapter you will learn how to use them, and you'll switch between them to create different animations. Essential concepts presented here will help you develop your ability to analyze a motion and translate it into mouse clicks in max. You will use the Track view to edit the timing of your animation. You will learn the reasons and methods behind the use of dummy objects and will use one to complete an animation you worked on in the previous chapter. You will also learn the basics of max's hard-body dynamics objects and systems. Topics include:

- Animation controllers

- Creating and editing keys in the Track view

- Tangent types for interpolating changes between keyframes

- Parameter curve out-of-range options

- Simple linking

- Using dummy objects

- Using Linked XForm for sub-object animation

- Dynamics

Animation Controllers

Animation controllers are the instructions max uses to create and interpret the keys of an animation. With animation controllers, you are getting closer to the guts of max: why the computer "draws" the frames it does from your settings. In this section you'll look at the more common controllers and how to switch between them.

Some of the features that were "controllers" in previous versions of max, such as the Look At controller, are now called "constraints" in max 4 and are accessed differently. See "Animation Constraints" later this chapter.

Default Controllers

When you use the Animate button, max assigns the default controller for the keys created. Whenever you change the assignment of a controller, you can choose to make the new controller the default for the selected type of track (e.g., for all rotation tracks). Let's look at some of the default controllers. Open the Track view of your `animation02.max` file from the last chapter or from the CD files for Chapter 9.

A quick way to open the Track view for just the selected object is to right-click it and choose Track View Selected.

PRS Controller

Let's look at the animation controllers assigned:

1. Open the box's hierarchy.

2. Click the Filters button. Check Controller Types under Show.

3. Check out the controller types. The default Transform track has three subtracks nested under it: Position, Rotation, and Scale. These are collectively called the PRS controller. You will look at other options for the Transform track later.

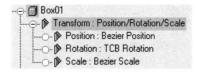

Bezier Controller

The most common default for controllers is the Bezier controller. Notice that the Position track of the box reads Bezier Position. Let's look at what that means:

1. Reset max. (Click No for saving the file and Yes for resetting.)

2. Create a sphere in the upper-left corner of the top view and turn on its trajectory display (Right-click, choose Properties, and check Trajectory).

3. Go to frame 50 and turn on the Animate button. Move the sphere along the X axis to the upper-right corner of the top view. The trajectory is a straight line.

4. Go to frame 100 and move the sphere along the Y axis to the lower-right corner of the top view. Notice that the trajectory curved when you did this. Turn off the Animate button.

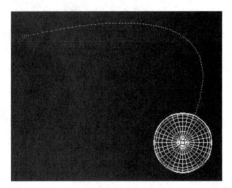

The curve of the trajectory created is the effect of the Bezier position controller: it instructs max to transition from one key to the next with a Bezier curve calculation. This is often very helpful, but it is not always exactly what you want.

TCB Controller

In the original 3D Studio for DOS, the *only* controller available was the TCB (Tension, Continuity, and Bias) controller. TCB is still the default controller for rotation and for many plug-ins. Let's look at the TCB controller for the sphere you just animated:

1. With the sphere selected, go to the Motion panel.

2. Click the Rotation button just above the Key Info rollout.

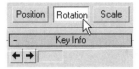

3. In the PRS Parameters rollout, under Create Key, click the Rotation button.

4. When you create a rotation key, its key info appears in the Key Info rollout. This is the same information that is displayed if you right-click the key in the Track view.

This is what the key info looks like for a TCB controller. The crosses in the graph represent transition frames into and out of the keyframe. This graph can be changed with the tension, continuity, and bias settings of the key. Tension changes the curvature around the key, with higher value creating a linear interpolation and more frames around the key. High Continuity adds overshoot before and after the key; low Continuity creates a linear interpolation with even distribution of frames around the key. Bias pushes the curve to one side or other of the key. These settings do the same thing that you will do with function curves in "Shaping Function Curves with Tangent Types" later in this chapter but are less intuitive to understand.

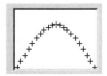

Changing a Controller

It is very easy to change a controller. If max can, it will try to reinterpret your existing keys with the new controller. Sometimes this isn't possible, and you will lose all your keys. It's best to consider what kind of controller you're going to need before you start animating. Max is "smart" about the use of tracks; it will give you a choice of only those controllers appropriate to the type of track selected.

The Linear Position Controller

Since you will be changing a controller on a track for a transform, you can do it from the Motion panel:

1. With the sphere still selected, open the Assign Controller rollout and highlight the Position track.

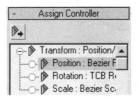

2. This activates the Assign Controller button. Click the Assign Controller button to bring up the Assign Position Controller window.

3. Choose Linear Position and click OK. Notice that the trajectory of the sphere is now straight between the keyframes, the way you might have expected it to be originally. This is the effect of the Linear Position controller. It instructs max to transition between the keys using a linear calculation.

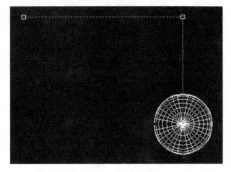

When "blocking out" an animation, animators often use linear position controllers for everything in the first run, to create basic movement that will be refined later.

The XYZ Controller

This time you will change controllers in the Track view:

1. Select the sphere, right-click on it, and choose Track View Selected.

2. Open the sphere's hierarchy to reveal the separate PRS tracks.

3. Highlight the Rotation track, click the Assign Controller button, and choose the Euler XYZ controller type from the dialog box. ("Euler" is pronounced like "oiler.") Notice that you now have a new plus sign in front of the Rotation track.

4. Open the Rotation track to reveal the separate X, Y, and Z Rotation tracks.

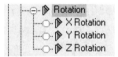

The X, Y, and Z rotations can now be individually controlled. The TCB controller links the rotations around the different axes together, based on an average of the contributions from each axis. The math behind this is complicated, so using the TCB controller to get the precise rotations you want can be counterintuitive. Some people make the Euler XYZ controller the default for rotation, because it calculates the rotation from each axis in order. The averaged rotation of the TCB controller can be better for avoiding gimbal lock problems with hierarchical chains, however. *Gimbal lock* occurs when the rotation doesn't behave as you expect, because the order in which the rotations are calculated causes two of the axes to be pointed in the same direction.

 You can set the order of rotation around axes for an Euler rotation controller in the Euler parameters rollout of the Motion panel. One way to help avoid gimbal lock is to set the axis order to start with the axis around which you wish to rotate (e.g., to rotate only around Z, make the axis order ZXY). To rotate around two axes, make the axes of rotation the first and last axis evaluated (e.g., to rotate around X and Y, make the axis order XZY). To avoid gimbal lock problems in a chain, try linking a dummy object with a TCB controller between nodes.

The Position XYZ controller does the same thing for the Position track: it separates the XYZ position into three separate position tracks. Similarly, Scale XYZ separates the Scale track into three separate Scale tracks, one for each axis.

Nesting Controllers

Controllers can be used in combination to achieve various effects that cannot be easily achieved with a single controller. The common way of combining controllers is to nest them. You encountered examples of nested controllers already when you looked at the PRS controller (which nests Position, Rotation, and Scale controllers under the Transform track), and the Euler XYZ controller (which nests X, Y, and Z Rotation controllers under the Rotation track).

Nested controllers demonstrate a principle that becomes more useful as the motions you animate become more complex: break the motion down into simple components in order to animate. For example, suppose you want to have an object jitter as it follows a simple trajectory. You could accomplish this effect with one controller, but it would require many keys to get both the forward motion and the jittering effect out of the same controller—and a very skilled eye to create those keys. The jittering effect also might not look random enough if completed by hand.

Nesting a Controller under a List Controller

The List controller allows you to combine several controllers together, nested under the list. When you change a track to a List controller, it keeps the original controller and adds a new track available for another controller to refine the effect of the first one. Each time you assign the Available track, a new one is created.

Let's use a List controller to add jitter to a simple trajectory:

1. With the Track view of your sphere still open, assign the position track back to a Bezier position controller to get a smooth trajectory again.

   If you assign a Noise controller to the position track to add noise, you will replace the Bezier controller and lose your trajectory completely. To nest the noise with the forward motion, you need to use a List controller.

2. Highlight the position track, click the Assign Controller button, choose Position List, and click OK. A plus sign appears in front of the Position track.

3. Open the position track to reveal two subtracks: the Bezier position controller you assigned before and an Available track. Note that you still have your position keys in the Bezier track. You will add the jitter to the available track.

Adding a Noise Controller

The Noise controller randomizes the value of the track, with settings for the overall strength and frequency of the noise, as well as a separate animatable Noise Strength track.

Let's add noise to the trajectory by adding the Noise controller to our available position list track:

1. Highlight the Available track and assign Noise Position. In the Noise Controller properties, change the X, Y, and Z strength to 20 and close the window.

2. Play the animation. The sphere now moves along its trajectory but jitters a little along the way.

The Noise Strength track, nested under the Noise Position track, is also animatable. You can nest an XYZ controller under this and animate each strength separately. To do this, highlight the Noise Strength track and assign Point3 XYZ.

5. You can also reduce the Frequency value to make the jitter less frenetic. Right-click the Noise Position track, choose Properties, and adjust the Frequency setting. Save this file as `noise_list.max`.

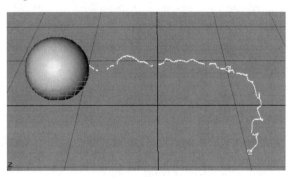

Other Animation Controllers

The possible uses of different controllers are nearly limitless. Table 10.1 describes other controllers available in max and examples of how they might be used.

Table 10.1 Some Controllers and Their Possible Uses

CONTROLLER TYPE	FUNCTION	EXAMPLE
Audio	Bases value on the pulse of an assigned audio waveform.	Movement responding to music.
Block	Groups multiple selected tracks over a range of frames as blocks to be reused at other times.	Repeated walk cycle.
Color RGB	Splits values of a color track into separate red, green, and blue component tracks.	A material with an animated green channel and a glow effect assigned to a specific value of green, creating strange glow effects.
Expression	Programmable: assigns value based on a written expression.	One gear rotating at twice the rate of another.
IK	Use to solve IK for max Bones and other hierarchies (you'll use max Bones in Chapter 11).	A character with a Bones skeleton.
Master Point	Default controller for direct sub-object animation; creates a separate track for each animated sub-object.	Animating control points of an FFD modifier.
Motion Capture	Values controlled by input from external device.	User animates character with mouse movement.
On/Off	Two possible values for track: on or off. Use when you want *no* interpolation between frames.	Blinking light.
Reactor	Similar to Expression, but without the programming; assigns the value of its track to react to the value of another track.	Character smiling whenever a finger pokes his bellybutton.
Script	Similar to Expression, but uses MAXScript.	Fish maintaining certain position relative to rest of school.
Smooth	Gives a pre-set transform with smooth tangents (key info and function curve are not accessible).	Very smooth rocking motion that doesn't need to be tweaked.
Spring	Adds secondary dynamics according to spring tension and dampening values.	Simulation of spring, in conjunction with force space warp such as gravity.
Waveform	Assigns value from a chosen type of waveform.	Evenly pulsing light.

Animation Constraints

In the new max 4 Animation menu, you can assign constraints to selected objects. Some of these were formerly called controllers and some are new. They can still be assigned through the Assign Controller button as well, except that they are listed as constraints. Some have added functionality. You can consider constraints to be a special type of controller with an alternate interface access (the Animation menu) and some peculiarities. For example, when a constraint is applied, it is automatically made part of a List controller with the original controller nested first, the constraint nested second, and an available track.

The Position and Orientation Constraints

You can assign a *position* constraint to constrain an object's position relative to that of a target object or to the weighted average of several target objects. To do this in the previous version of max, you had to use an expression controller. The position constraint has a simpler interface. Assign the position constraint to the object you are constraining, and drag to one of the targets. Then, in the Motion panel's Position Constraint rollout, you can add and delete targets and adjust their relative weights in the constraint.

An *orientation* constraint works exactly the same way, except that it applies to the rotation track rather than the position track.

The Path Constraint

A *path* constraint tells an object to follow a spline or NURBS curve path. It is commonly used for animating cameras—for architectural fly-throughs, "first person" sequences, or typical camera-dolly techniques used in movies—but can be used for any object.

In former versions of max, the path constraint was called a controller, and was limited to one path. In max 4, you can now constrain to a weighted average of multiple spline paths.

The advantage of the path constraint is that you can draw out the desired trajectory with ordinary lines and edit them at any time. The disadvantage is that when you edit the path, all your keys telling the object where it is along the path at what time are altered.

Assigning a Path Constraint

Let's assign a path constraint to a camera:

1. Reset max.

2. Using Create tab ➜ Shapes ➜ NURBS Curves ➜ CV Curve, create a wandering line around the top viewport.

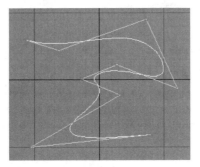

NURBS curves make especially good paths, thanks to their particular smoothness. However, it is fine to use splines instead.

3. Create a target camera in the top viewport near the beginning of the path, dragging the target forward along the path.

4. Select the camera and choose Animation ➜ Constraint ➜ Path Constraint. Drag to the CV curve.

Be sure the camera body, not the target, is selected.

5. Play the animation. The camera automatically moves from the beginning to the end of the path. In the Path Parameters rollout in the Motion panel, you can animate the object's percentage along the path differently (from 20% to 80% and back to 5%, for example). You can also make its orientation follow the path's (check Follow) and have it bank around corners (check Bank and set a Bank Amount).

6. Let's say you plan to use the path for multiple purposes, and for one of these, you want to offset the object toward another path. Draw a second path with different curvature near part of the first path.

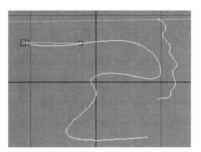

7. Select the camera and go to the Path Parameters rollout. Click Add Path and click on the second path. Click Add Path again to turn it off. Now you have two target paths listed. The Weight parameter is set below the list.

8. What you need is for the second path to influence the first path only for a certain area. Set the weight of the second path to 0. Move to the frame where you want the second path to start influencing the camera. Turn on the Animate button. Set Weight to 0.1.

9. Move to the frame where you want the influence to be the strongest and turn up the Weight. Move to the frame where you want the influence to end and set the Weight to 0 again. Turn off the Animate button. Play the animation. The camera animates from the beginning to the end of the path, but is thrown off by the second path during the time that the weight of the second path was turned up. Save the file as cam_path01.max.

Notice that the target does not move. That is because it is an independent object and is not affected by the camera body's movements. You can animate this manually, apply another path to it, or link it to another object.

The Look-At Constraint

A *look-at* constraint tells an object to always point toward another object. You use a look-at constraint when you want something to follow the motion of something else. You can always combine this with other animations to refine the motion. In max 4, you can assign multiple targets with a weighted influence from each target.

To assign a look-at constraint, select the object, choose Animation ➜ Constraints ➜ Look-At Constraint, and drag to the target object. Add other targets and adjust weights in the Motion panel in the LookAt Constraint rollout.

The look-at constraint was a controller available to the Transform track in previous versions of max. In max 4, it is a constraint available for rotation controllers. The transform version is still the default controller of target cameras and spotlights. It tells the camera or light to always point toward a dummy object, in this case, its target. In the case of target cameras and spotlights, the look-at controller has PRS tracks nested below it.

Be careful when using look-at constraints and animated targets for cameras. Real cameras don't work this way. If you want more realistic camera movement, try animating pan, roll, and tilt, as real camera operators do.

The Link Constraint

The *link* constraint is assigned to the Transform track. It was formerly called a controller, but its functionality is very much the same. The link constraint allows you to link to a parent object, as you would with a hierarchy, but for a specified time period. After assigning the link constraint to the object (Animation ➜ Constraints ➜ Link Constraint), drag to the initial target. In the Motion panel, go to the frame where you want the link to be transferred, click Add Link, and pick the new parent object. Clicking Link To World means that until the frame of the next link, the object will be unlinked. (An unlinked object is a child of the World.) You will use the link controller in Chapter 11 to link Intrepid Explorer Jim's hat and torch to his body while he is walking and to break the link after he falls through the hole.

The Attachment Constraint

The *attachment* constraint attaches an object's position to the surface of a target object. Use this whenever you want an object to remain on the surface of an object regardless of how that surface may change during the animation. For example, you might want an object to heave with the land surface during an earthquake. If you just linked it, it wouldn't move, because the pivot point of land object wouldn't move. You need to have its position be determined by an animated position on the surface of the land.

To use the attachment constraint, highlight the Position track in the Motion panel and click the Assign Controller button. Choose Attachment. Click the Pick Object button and click on the target surface. Uncheck the Align To Surface option if you want the object to maintain its original orientation. Click the Set Position button and drag on the target object until you position your object where you want it. Use the A and B parameters to fine-tune the placement. You can still rotate the object if you have Align To Surface unchecked.

The Surface Constraint

The *surface* constraint allows one object to move over the surface of another. An example might be something rolling over a convoluted surface.

Assign a surface constraint with Animation ➜ Constraints ➜ Surface Constraint and then drag to the target surface. In the Motion panel, check No Alignment to keep the initial orientation or align to U or V. You can animate the U Position and V Position to move the object across the surface.

Using the Track View to Animate

Now that you've created some animations in max, you need to know how to create a specific movement. To do this, you need to break down the key poses of the desired movement, position them on the timeline so they occur at the right time, and instruct max about interpolating between them to get the right timing of your motion. Do you want your motion to accelerate? To pop suddenly? To overshoot the target and then rebound back? All these options are available in max once you know what you want to see and learn how to translate that vision into editing keys in max.

By now, you should be acquainted with the Track view. In this section, you will learn more of the power of the Track view and how to use it. You'll find out how to create keys directly, how to move keys and edit their values, and how to change the transitions into and out of keys. You will learn more about function curves and how to use them, and you will explore options for repeating segments of animation.

Creating Keys

Animating in CG is a matter of creating and editing keys. It can be simple or exceedingly complex. Before discussing the ways to create keys in max, let's consider the more general issue of why it's a good idea to know what you're doing and what keys you're creating.

Planning Your Key Creation

Just because you can animate a certain way doesn't mean it's the best or simplest way. When you go back to edit your keys, you want the process to be as straightforward as possible. Let's look at our animated sphere files from Chapter 9 to see two identical animations with vastly different keys.

1. Open the sphere01.max file you created in the last chapter or from the CD files for Chapter 9. This was created by directly animating the vertices of an editable mesh.

2. Select the sphere and open its Track view.

3. Open its hierarchy under Sphere01 ➜ Object (Editable Mesh) ➜ Master Point Controller. There is a separate track with two keys for every vertex that moved—289 of them in the example on the CD. If you needed to make a small edit to the timing, it could involve a lot of work with all those keys.

4. Now open the sphere02.max file that you created or from the CD files for Chapter 9. This was created using the XForm modifier.

5. Select the sphere and open its Track view.

6. Open up its hierarchy under Sphere01 ➜ Modified Object ➜ XForm ➜ Gizmo ➜ Position. The same animation takes place with just two keys for the Gizmo. This is considerably easier to understand and edit when necessary. Figure 10.1 compares the keys for the two animation approaches.

Animating vertices directly results in two keys for every vertex (578 keys in this case).

Animating vertices through an XForm modifier results in two keys for the whole animation.

Figure 10.1 *Animating sub-objects directly and through an XForm modifier*

The moral of the story is this: Think *about key creation when you animate something. The first method you think of may not be the best way; it may, in fact, take many times longer to animate than spending a little time thinking about what's efficient or, dare I say, elegant.*

Copying a Key in the Track Bar

So far, you have learned two ways of creating keys: 1) going to the desired frame, turning on the Animate button, and making a change; and 2) clicking one of the buttons under Create Key in the Motion panel.

If you already have keys created, you can also create new keys by copying your existing keys in the track bar. Just Shift+drag the key to the frame where you want to create the copy. This will copy all the keys in that keyframe; you can't choose which one to copy.

You will often need to copy a key to bracket the desired change within a certain duration of frames. Say you make a change with the Animate button turned on at frame 30. Max will create a key at frame 30 and, assuming you've created no keys in between, one at frame 0. So your change will occur gradually between frames 0 and 30. If you want the change to occur instead between frames 15 and 30, you need to copy the key at frame 0 to frame 15.

Let's try this to edit the tea level animation from the last chapter:

1. Open `tea05.max` that you created in the last chapter or from the CD files for Chapter 9.

2. Drag the time slider to scrub through the animation. The particles don't hit the bottom of the cup until about frame 36, but the tea level starts rising from frame 0 on. (The particles will hit the bottom a few frames earlier when the particle system rotates with the teapot later in this chapter.) To keep the tea level at zero until frame 33, you need to copy the key for the tea level from frame 0 to frame 33.

3. Select the tea level object. There are two keyframes visible in the track bar (red squares at bottom), one at 0 and one at 60. Click the keyframe at frame 0 and, holding the Shift key, drag it to frame 33.

4. Now scrub through the animation. Now the tea level doesn't start to rise until after the particles reach the bottom of the cup.

Creating Keys with the Create Key Window

Another way of generating keys for a selected object is to right-click the time slider (the part you drag). This will bring up the Create Key window, allowing you to create a transform key for the selected object at that point in time. You can also use this dialog box to copy transform keys from one location (the Source Time) to another (the Destination Time). The default values in Create Key will create a key or keys for the checked transforms at the frame the time slider showed when you clicked it. If you change the source or destination times, you will create keys for the checked transforms *at* the new destination time with values *from* the new source time.

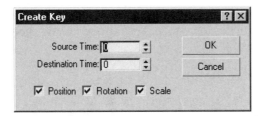

Let's make some rotation keys for the teapot and copy them using this method:

1. Go to frame 20 and turn on the Animate button. Rotate the teapot about –45° around X. Turn off the Animate button.

2. Now you need to copy the key you just made to about frame 56 in order to hold the teapot there while pouring. Still at frame 20, right-click the time slider. Leave the Source Time at 20 and change the Destination Time to 56. Although it's not necessary since you only have rotation keys on the teapot, uncheck Position and Scale. Click OK.

3. Go to frame 0 and right-click the time slider. Leave the Source Time at 0, change the Destination Time to 80, leave only Rotation checked, and click OK.

4. Scrub through the animation. The teapot now rotates upward, holds, and rotates back down. Save your file as `tea06.max`.

You may want to hide the table and teacup while animating the teapot, so that you have better updating in the viewport. You can also turn off Show Map In Viewport on the teapot material.

Adding Keys in the Track View

Another way of creating keys is to add them in the Track view. Of all the methods of creating keys, this gives you the most precise control. Let's use the Track view to add some more keys:

1. Continue working with your teapot file or open `tea06.max` from the CD files for this chapter.

2. Select the teapot, right-click on it, and choose Track View Selected. Open up the teapot hierarchy to see the Rotation tracks. The teapot has already been assigned an Euler XYZ controller.

3. Highlight the parent Rotation track and click Add Keys. Click in the parent Rotation track at frames 13, 17, and 61 to add rotation keys at these frames. (Use the zoom tools to get a good view of what frame you are looking at.) Notice that this adds keys to all three nested tracks. These keys do not change the animation at all, because max captures the in-between data at the point that the key was created. You will edit these keys later in this chapter.

4. Click the Move Keys button to get out of the Add Key tool and avoid creating new keys accidentally. Save your file as tea07.max.

You can switch to the Move Keys tool by right-clicking an empty area of a track.

Editing Keys

Whatever method you use to generate your initial keys, you will need to adjust their values, properties, or timing by editing them afterward. Much of your time animating will be spent editing keys in Track view, changing values and the transitions between keys (called "tangent types") that tell the computer how to interpolate the frames around a keyframe.

Moving Keys

You can move a key in a variety of ways. If it is the only key at a certain keyframe, you can just drag the key in the track bar to the desired location. You can also drag keys using the Move Keys tool in the Track view. With the Move Keys tool, you can marquee-select multiple keys and drag them at the same time (selected keys will be white). You can move a key to a precise frame number by editing the frame number in the Key Info dialog box.

As with the track bar, if you hold down the Shift key while dragging keys in the Track view, you will move a copy of the selected keys.

The Key Info Dialog Box

The main way of editing key values is through the Key Info dialog box. If you are in the Move Keys tool in the Track view, you can bring up Key Info simply by right-clicking a key. You can access the Key Info dialog box for a selected object by right-clicking a key in the track bar and choosing the track. The Key Info for transform keys is also available in a rollout in the Motion panel. Figure 10.2 shows the Key Info dialog box for the Bezier position controller. Table 10.2 describes its functions.

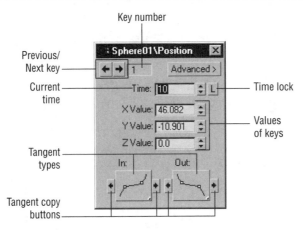

Figure 10.2 *Key Info dialog box for a Bezier controller*

Table 10.2 Tools of the Basic Key Info Dialog box

Tool	Description
Key number	Displays number of the current key.
Previous/Next key	Brings up Key Info dialog box of previous or next key.
Current time	Frame number of key.
Time Lock	Prevents movement of the key along timeline of track.
Values of key	The values of the track at this key.
Tangent types	The tangent of the function curve in and out of keyframe.
Tangent copy buttons	Copies tangent type to the in or out tangent of the adjacent key.

Tangent types are explained in detail in "Interpolating between Keyframes." Also note that the *key* number is not the same as the *frame* number of the key. Key 1 of our animated box is at frame 0. Key 2 is at frame 20. You can move a key by changing its frame number.

The options in the Advanced rollout give you numerical control over Custom tangents through the In/Out velocities (rates of change of parameter). They also allow you to "normalize time," which will average the distribution of selected keys over time, with an additional option of maintaining a constant velocity between them. The net result of normalizing time is to smooth the motion of an object.

Editing a Key's Value

You can edit the value of a key in Track view by entering a numeric value in the Key Info dialog, by entering a numeric value at the bottom of the Track view for a single selected key, or simply by dragging them in Function Curves mode. You will use this method to fine-tune the teapot rotation in "Shaping Function Curves with Tangent Types" later in this chapter.

Interpolating between Keyframes

Even though you may have set keys at the values and frame numbers you want, a 3D application does not necessarily create the rate of change you want in the in-between frames before and after those keyframes.

The typical example of this is animating a window opening between two keyframes (one shut, one open). When the computer interpolates between the keyframes, the window moves slightly in the other direction just prior to the frame when it is supposed to open. In animation terms this is called *anticipation*, but why does it happen? Because the default tangent type assigned to the Bezier position controller is the Smooth type, which includes some anticipation in the calculation.

Changing and adjusting tangent types allows you to refine the effects of the controllers to which they apply.

Ease In and Ease Out

Ease in and *ease out* are terms inherited from traditional cel animators. Animators at Disney discovered that they often wanted to emphasize a key pose, by making the frames before it gradually decelerate the rate of change before the keyframe and the frames after it gradually accelerate the change after. The classic example of this is the peak of a bouncing ball cycle, illustrated in Figure 10.3.

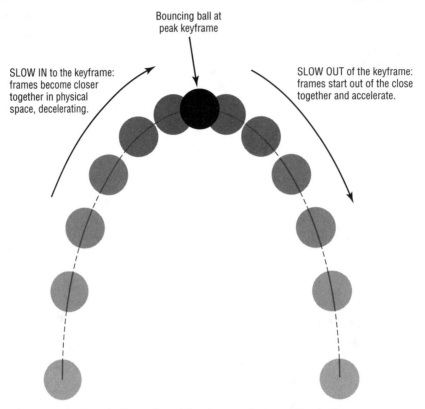

Figure 10.3 *Ease In/Out of peak keyframe of a bouncing ball*

Tangent Types

In max, the ease in/out feature of animation is implemented as the "tangent type" in and out of a key. The tangent referred to is the tangent of the function curve of that parameter. In the case of our unwanted window movement, the solution would be to use a linear tangent leading into the first keyframe of the opening.

Clicking and holding the Tangent Type button in the Key Info dialog box produces a flyout of the tangent options. There is a relation between controllers and the types of tangents they use. The tangent types shown in Table 10.3 and Figure 10.4 are those available for a Bezier controller. A Linear controller would use only the Linear tangent type; an On/Off controller would use only the Step tangent type. The TCB controller, covered earlier in this chapter, gives you a different way of looking at the same animation curve: by altering the tension, continuity, and bias settings, you can see the changes in the distribution of frames around the key.

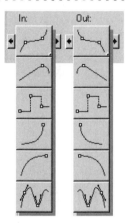

Figure 10.4 *Tangent types in the In and Out drop-down lists*

Table 10.3 Tangent Types of Bezier Controller

BUTTON	TANGENT	DESCRIPTION	USE
	Smooth	The default tangent generates a smooth curve in the values around the key.	Use to get smooth acceleration and anticipation.
	Linear	The Linear tangent, when used as the outgoing tangent of one key and the incoming tangent of the next, generates a straight line in the values between. This is a constant rate of change.	Use to get rid of unwanted anticipation, to hold a value between keys, and to maintain a constant velocity.
	Step	A Step tangent holds the value of one key until the next key. This is an abrupt jump.	Use when you do not want any interpolation between key values.
	Fast In/Out	This rate of change is faster around the key, as in the bottom of a bouncing ball cycle.	Use to accelerate into a key or to pop out of it quickly and then decelerate.

Table 10.3 Tangent Types of Bezier Controller

Button	Tangent	Description	Use
	Slow In/Out	The traditional "slow in/out" of Disney fame; this decelerates the rate of change around the key, as in the peak of a bouncing ball cycle.	Use to decelerate into a key and to gradually accelerate out of it.
	Custom	This type displays the tangents around the key with adjustable handles.	Use to set exactly the curve of motion you want by adjusting Bezier handles. Adjusting a handle while holding the Shift key makes the handles independent.

Shaping Function Curves with Tangent Types

As mentioned before, the word "tangent" refers to the function curve of the track. You were introduced to function curves in Chapter 9. Function curves are a graphic representation of the animated data and are very useful once you understand how to read them. Let's look the function curves of the teapot rotation and edit the tangents to get a precise motion:

1. Continue working on `tea07.max` or open it from the CD files for this chapter.

2. If you don't have the Track view open, select the teapot, right-click on it, and choose Track View Selected. Open up the hierarchy of the teapot.

3. Holding the Ctrl key, highlight the X, Y, and Z rotation tracks, and click the Function Curves button. You will see a graphic display of the rotation values. Notice that the keys you added did not distort the shape of the curve.

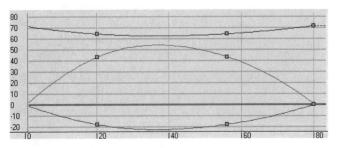

The bottom curve in red is the X value, the middle curve in green is the Y value, and the top curve in blue is the Z value. Note that the line colors of the function curves are a visual mnemonic:

$$XYZ = RGB; X = red, Y = green, Z = blue$$

RGB is the additive color space of all computer graphics, film, and TV.

4. You need to make the curves flat between frames 20 and 56 to hold the teapot still while it is pouring. Right-click one of the keys at frame 20. In the Key Info dialog box, choose Linear as the Out tangent.

5. Click the Copy Tangent button to the left of the Out tangent to copy it to the In tangent of frame 56. Repeat this for the other two curves. You should now have a horizontal line between frames 20 and 56.

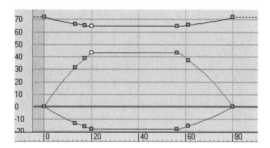

6. Drag the keys at frames 13, 17, and 61 to create curves as shown in Figure 10.5. This creates a motion where there is a very slight overshoot of the hold before staying still and very slight anticipation of the return rotation.

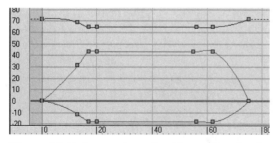

Figure 10.5 Create these function curves for the teapot Rotation modifier.

Animating the Noise Strength and Particle Size

Use the same method to animate the particle size and the strength of the Noise modifier in order to taper off the flow of tea and the turbulence in the teacup as the teapot stops pouring:

1. Select the tea level object and open up its hierarchy in the Track view to see the Strength track under Modified Object ➜ Noise.

2. Highlight the Strength track and assign a Point3 XYZ controller.

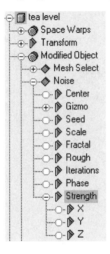

3. You only need Z strength, not X and Y. Click the Add Keys button and add some keys to the Z strength track at frames 0, 25, 26, 70, and 83.

4. You want the noise off until the cup starts to fill; then it abruptly gets very strong and tapers off more gradually after the teapot stops pouring. Using different tangents, make the function curve shown in Figure 10.6 or make your own variation.

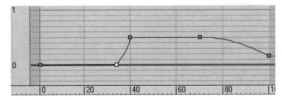

Figure 10.6 *Create this function curve for the tea level Noise modifier.*

5. Select the SuperSpray01 object and open up its hierarchy in the Track view to see the Size track under Object.

6. Add keys to the Size track at frame 55 and 63. Select the key at frame 63 and change its value to 0.337. Save your file as `tea08.max`.

Applying Parameter Curve Out-of-Range Options

Often you will want to loop an animation or part of an animation repeatedly. To do this, use one of the "out-of-range parameter" types. Use these for any animated sequence that is to be repeated throughout the duration of the animation: for example, a spinning windmill or a rotating light beacon.

One out-of-range type can be applied per track. It will automatically apply for the entire duration of the animation. The different out-of-range types can be seen in Figure 10.7 and are described in Table 10.4. Remember from Chapter 9 that the Position Ranges mode allows you to determine which part of an animated sequence will be repeated.

Table 10.4 Parameter Curve Out-of-Range Types

OUT-OF-RANGE TYPE	DESCRIPTION
Constant	Default: plays once, then stops at the last key.
Cycle	Repeats the animation exactly (will jump between last and first frame).
Loop	Repeats the animation exactly, but will interpolate between last and first frame across a designated range.
Ping Pong	Repeats the animation, alternating between forward and backward play.
Linear	Plays the animation once, but projects the rate of change of the last frame linearly afterward.
Relative Repeat	Repeats the animation offset by the value of the last frame, as with climbing a set of stairs.

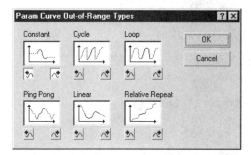

Figure 10.7 *The Out-of-Range Types dialog box assigns animation sequences to loops or cycles.*

Creating a Continuous Animation Cycle

Let's take a closer look at how the out-of-range types work:

1. First you need to create a block of animation to repeat. Open the file windmill01.max from the CD files for this chapter.

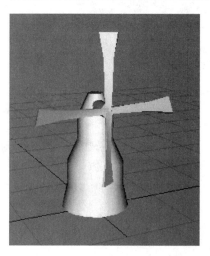

2. Select the windmill blades and lock your selection by pressing the spacebar.

3. Go to frame 20 and turn on the Animate button.

4. Press A to turn on Angle snap. Rotate the blades 90° around the X axis in the perspective view. Press A again to turn off Angle snap. Turn off the Animate button. Play the animation. The windmill turns for 20 frames.

5. You can now use one of the out-of-range types to loop this sequence for the duration of the animation. Select the blade object and open up its hierarchy in the Track view to see its Rotation track. You should see the two keys you just created.

6. Highlight the Rotation track. Click the Parameter Curves Out-Of-Range button.

7. Select the Loop type first by clicking in the Loop window. Notice that this automatically selects both the left and right arrows.

8. Return to the viewport and click the Play button.

Notice that with Loop, the windmill appears to come to a stop before looping the animation. If you watch even closer (watch the axis icon of the rotating object), you will see that the animation is not actually continuing around the remaining 270 degrees. It is resetting itself, popping back the 90° and playing over. You can get the continuous result necessary for a windmill by changing the out-of-range type.

9. Highlight the Rotation track again. Click the Parameter Curves Out-Of-Range button. This time, choose the Relative Repeat type.

10. Play the animation. This time the animation repeats relative to where it ends. This means the second cycle of animation turns the blades another 90° tacked on to the first 90°. At the end of the second cycle, the blades have rotated 180°; the third cycle will add another 90°, and so forth. Save your file as `windmill02.max`.

Simple Linking

You learned the theory behind hierarchical linking in Chapter 2. You need to use this linking technique to complete the teapot animation, because the particle system needs to rotate with the teapot. As the teapot rotates, you want the particle system to inherit the change in rotation and rotate along with it, so you need to link the particle system (the child) to the teapot (the parent):

1. Open the `tea08.max` file you saved earlier or from the CD files for this chapter. Select the Super Spray object.

2. Click the Link tool. Press H, choose the teapot, and click Link.

3. Click one of the selection tools to turn off the Link tool. Play the animation. Now the particles rotate with the teapot. Save your file as tea09.max. The rendered animation of this file is available on the CD as teapot.mov.

Be careful to link correctly. You might want to apply Edit ➜ Hold first. The Super Spray, with its other dependencies (PathFollow, UOmniFlect bindings), may go corrupt if you link it to the wrong object and have to click the Unlink tool. Using the H key to bring up the Select Parent dialog box is wise in this situation.

Using Dummy Objects

Dummy objects (also called "nulls") are a special type of object used in animation and hierarchical chains. You may recall from Chapter 2 that a dummy object is a type of helper object, an object that doesn't appear in the render. Dummy objects are used for a variety of reasons and purposes. They function as reference points for other objects, provide ways of breaking down motion into more easily animatable components, and act as storehouses of information to relay to another link or expression.

Using dummy objects can be very simple in some cases or mind-boggling in a complex hierarchical animation. As with most things in 3D animation, it's best to start with simple cases and work on understanding what is happening in these before building up to the very complex. Let's look at some common uses of dummies.

Providing a Handle

Say you want to animate a character's eye movements. Rather than try to animate the rotation of each eye independently, you could assign look-at controllers to the eyes and assign a dummy as their target. The dummy will then function as a handle to drag the focal point of the eyes around as desired. This is exactly the same function that the target of a target camera or target spotlight has.

Another version of this is linking an object or sub-object to a dummy. The dummy can be used as an "end effector" in an IK chain or as a handle for controlling a sub-object selection.

Almost any object in max can be linked to a dummy object, including lights, meshes, patches, NURBS, and other dummies.

Using Dummies with Linked XForm

Manipulating vertices of a mesh with outside objects is the key to skeletal deformation, often used for character animation. In Chapter 11, you will learn about Skin, the envelope-based modifier that allows you to deform a mesh with bones or other hierarchy. You will also learn about Physique, the more advanced envelope-based modifier that is part of the discreet character studio plug-in for max. The Linked XForm modifier you will work with here is distantly related to these modifiers, in that it allows you to manipulate vertices with outside objects. It is very simplistic in comparison; however, it does illustrate the principle and is useful for certain kinds of manipulations.

You can use the Linked XForm modifier to link sub-object selections to dummies, giving you handles with which to manipulate sub-object selections without having to open the modifier stack or go to the sub-object level each time. Let's try this out on a sphere:

1. Reset max.

2. Create a sphere.

3. Create three dummy objects (Create ➔ Helper Objects ➔ Dummy). Draw them out in the viewport, one above, one to the right, and one to the left of the sphere, as shown in Figure 10.8.

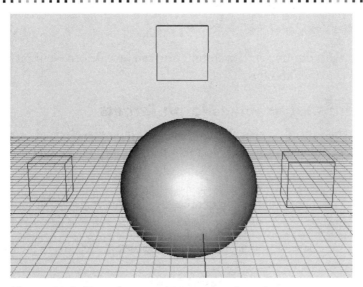

Figure 10.8 *Place dummy objects around a sphere.*

4. Collapse the sphere to an editable mesh. Go to the Vertex sub-object level and turn on soft selection.

5. Select a vertex (or a few) at the top of the sphere and turn up the Soft Selection Falloff until the green area reaches about a third of the sphere.

6. Apply a Linked XForm modifier (Modify tab ➜ Modifier List ➜ Linked XForm).

7. Click Pick Control Object in the Parameters rollout and pick the top dummy object. The tab should now read "Control Object: Dummy01."

8. Apply a Mesh Select modifier.

9. Go to the Vertex sub-object level and turn on soft selection. Select a vertex on the right side and turn up the falloff so the green area covers about a third of the sphere.

10. Apply a Linked XForm modifier.

11. Click Pick Control Object, and this time pick the dummy object on the right.

12. Repeat steps 8 through 11, only this time select a vertex on the left side of the sphere and pick the dummy object on the left as the control object.

13. Apply another Mesh Select modifier on the top of the stack, just to clear the sub-object selection.

14. Choose Edit ➜ Hold.

15. Move the dummy objects around. You can now deform your mesh without going to the sub-object level.

Using Snapshot to Make Morph Targets

You can use this Linked XForm method to deform a mesh with handles and take snapshot meshes of different deformations to make into morph targets. Let's try it:

1. Choose Edit ➜ Fetch.

2. Click the Snapshot tool (under the Array flyout). Choose Mesh as the clone method.

3. Click the Select by Name button and choose Sphere02 from the list.

4. Lock the selection and move Sphere02 to the side. Rename the sphere "Sphere Original."

5. Unlock the selection and select Sphere01 again. Move the dummies around to create a morph target.

6. Repeat steps 2 through 4, this time renaming it "Morph Target 1."

7. Unlock the selection, select Sphere01, and move the dummies to create another morph target named "Morph Target 2." Repeat this step, followed by steps 2 through 4, to create as many morph targets as you like, numbered in order.

8. Select Sphere Original and apply the Morpher modifier.

9. Click Load Multiple Targets and load all the morph targets you've created. Save your file as linked_xfm.max.

Separating Motion Components

The art of animating in 3D involves simplifying movement by breaking it down into simpler components. Dummy objects are often crucial to enacting this strategy.

Consider the motion of a car weaving along a road. As one motion, it is fairly complex to animate, but it can be broken down into two very simple components: the forward motion along the road (which might be defined as a path for an object) and the side to side motion of the weave. In this case, a dummy object would provide the independent axis of motion.

Instead of assigning a path constraint to the car, you would assign it to a dummy object. You would then link the car to the dummy object and position it within or near the dummy. The car will inherit the motion of the dummy, which is following the path. You still retain independent control of the car, however, allowing you to position and turn it independently of the path constraint.

Providing a Second Pivot Point

Dummy objects are often used to provide a rotational pivot other than the pivot point of the object. In Chapter 4, you often moved pivot points in order to rotate an object correctly. If you need a pivot point for a parent's rotation about itself, then if its child objects require different rotation centers, you need to use dummy objects to provide the alternate pivots. For example, say you want an object to rotate around its own pivot but also have a child object that rotates along a point on its periphery. Instead of linking the child directly to it, you would create a dummy object on the parent where you want the child to rotate. Then you would link the child to the dummy and the dummy to the parent.

Dynamics

Dynamics is a simulation of real-world physics by assigning properties of collision and rebound to CG objects. You set up a dynamics system, using the Dynamics utility in the Utility panel, and then add space warps and dynamics objects as appropriate to the simulation. You can also assign dynamics properties in the Material Editor. You can still keyframe objects in the simulation (so that they are not affected by the forces) by checking the This Object Is Unyielding button.

Let's set up a simple dynamics system:

1. Create a thin box as the ground object. Rename it Ground.

2. Create a variety of spheres above the ground object.

3. Create a Gravity space warp.

4. In the left view, create a Wind space warp and move it to the right of the objects.

5. In the Utility panel, click Dynamics ➜ New ➜ Edit Object List. Select all the objects and click the arrow pointing to the right to include them. The objects move to the right pane of the dialog box.

6. Click Edit Object. Choose the Ground object in the drop-down. Check the This Object Is Unyielding button. You don't want the ground to move when the objects hit it.

7. Choose the other spheres from the drop-down. For each one, click Assign Object Effects and include Gravity and Wind, then click Assign Object Collisions and include all the other objects, and then check Calculate Properties Using Surface. Click OK.

8. Click Solve. It takes some time to calculate. When it is done, just play the animation. It is calculated for you. Save your file as `dynamics.max`.

To change the bounce properties of the spheres, either assign a material and change the Bounce Coeffi-cient in the Dynamics Properties rollout or go back into Edit Object, check Override Material Bounce, and change the Bounce value.

Summary

In this chapter, you looked deeper into the mechanics of animating in max. You learned about animation controllers and the new animation constraints. You used the Track view to create keys and edit their values, to move and copy keys, and to change the interpolation between keys. You learned how the different interpolation settings affect the shape of the function curve of a parameter and what this means to the result-ing animation. You explored different uses of dummy objects for animating. You applied your knowledge to a short but detailed animation.

In the next chapter, you will learn about animating characters with hierarchies, using forward and inverse kinematics, max Bones, and the popular character studio plug-in for character animation.

Hierarchical Character Animation

3ds max

Chapter 11

I n this chapter you will learn how to set up hierarchies for the animation of complex characters. You will learn about forward kinematics and several kinds of inverse kinematics, including the new IK solvers in max 4. You will use max Bones and discreet character studio for skeletal deformation of a mesh. You will complete the animation portion of the ongoing Intrepid Explorer Jim project. Topics include:

- Setting up a hierarchy

- Forward kinematics

- Inverse kinematics (IK)

- New IK solvers

- Bones animation

- The Skin modifier

- Character studio's Physique modifier

- Character studio Biped animation

- Importing character studio animations from previous versions

- The Link controller

Using Hierarchies

In Chapter 9, you learned about deformation animation as a common way to animate "inanimate" objects like sacks of flour and bars of soap. For humans and similarly complex structures, this method is insufficient. It's necessary to create a system of hierarchical linkages to animate the character.

The character itself may consist of hierarchical linkages of its separate body parts. This is referred to as a "segmented" model. At one point in the history of 3D computer animation, this was the only type of model available. The more difficult case occurs when the character is a single mesh. You often need this to create the effect of a smooth continuous skin.

Linking Up a Simple Hierarchy

Let's start by creating a very simple segmented hierarchical mode of an upper body:

1. Reset max.

2. Create a cylinder in the top viewport, about 25 radius and 50 height. Name this object Torso.

3. Create a new cylinder in the left viewport at about the position of an arm, about 10 radius and 30 length. Name this Arm Upper L. Position the upper arm to the left of the torso.

4. Shift-drag the cylinder to the left and choose 1 Copy. Name the copy Arm Lower L.

5. In the left viewport, create a sphere positioned over the arm area. Check Base To Pivot in the Create tab. Name this Hand L. In the top viewport, move the hand to the left of the lower arm.

6. Select the three objects of the arm and mirror them to the right side of the torso object, naming the new objects with "R" instead of "L."

7. In the top viewport, create a sphere over the torso area, checking Base To Pivot. Name this Head. In the front viewport, move the head to the top of the torso.

8. Select all the objects, and click Reset XForm (Utilities ➜ Reset XForm ➜ Reset Selected).

9. Right-click the selected objects and choose Convert To: Convert To Editable Mesh. Then choose Edit ➜ Hold.

Mirror is a complex transform that completely rearranges the transforms of the object in World space; this can cause problems when the delta transform is calculated for inheritance through the hierarchy. By resetting the transform, you set the scale and rotation values back to 1, and max places the current rotation and scale information in an XForm modifier. Use this whenever you use complex transforms or non-uniform scale while modeling. When a hierarchy is not transferring the motion as it should, try unlinking all the pieces and resetting all the transforms. Sometimes the extra step of collapsing to mesh helps.

10. Click the Link tool and drag first from the head to the torso, then from the left hand to the left lower arm, then from the left lower arm to the left upper arm, and then from the left upper arm to the torso. Then do the same thing with the right hand and arm, in the same order. Click one of the select tools to turn off the Link tool.

11. Click the Select by Name button and check Display Subtree. The hierarchy in the Select Objects dialog box should now look like Figure 11.1 (left). If it doesn't, choose Edit ➜ Fetch and repeat step 10. Save your file as `hierarchy_linked.max`. The right side of Figure 11.1 shows the model as it currently appears in the viewport.

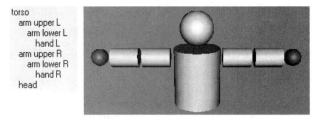

Figure 11.1 *The hierarchy of the upper body*

Forward Kinematics

Forward kinematics is the default animation system for hierarchies. *Kinematics* organizes how motion is inherited through a hierarchy. When you linked up the hierarchy, you linked from child to parent. In forward kinematics, the change in transforms (move, rotate, and scale) is inherited by the child from the parent, so when the parent moves, everything below it moves with it. Let's try it:

1. Select Arm Upper L.

2. Go to frame 100 and turn on the Animate button.

3. In the perspective viewport, rotate the upper arm forward around the Y axis. As you can see, the whole hierarchy below the upper arm rotates with it.

4. Turn off the Animate button and play the animation. Save your file as `hierarchy_fk.max`.

You can refine this animation as much as you like, by rotating the lower arm and hand separately, for instance. In forward kinematics, you are always moving the object and anything below it in the hierarchy.

Inverse Kinematics

Key Concept

In *inverse kinematics* (IK), an inverse relation holds true: the child moves the parents. This is not a simple reversal of the flow of transform information, however. In inverse kinematics, the computer solves the movements of a defined *IK chain*, based on the animated position of the end of the chain, which is called an *IK goal*. In a given animated model, you create a chain with an IK goal anywhere you want to define a point of contact with the floor or outside world. For example, in a leg, you might define an IK chain from the hip to the ankle, allowing you to define the placement of the heel, and then a second chain from the ankle to the toes, allowing you to define the placement of the toes independently of the heel. This better reflects the way arms and legs move, encountering obstacles in the environment to which the whole limb responds, so IK often results in more natural-looking motion for characters.

The software tools that implement IK calculations are known as *IK solvers*, and there are several kinds of IK solvers in max. In any of these cases, IK involves complicated calculations so as to adjust the upper part of the hierarchy as the end effector (the goal) gets to its destination. The quality of the solution depends on the quality of the solver and how appropriate it is to a given animation. Max 4 has new IK solvers to offer better quality IK solutions for character animation.

To get the IK results you want more precisely, adjust the thresholds under Customize ➜ Preferences ➜ Inverse Kinematics. These settings apply to the Applied IK and Interactive IK methods. A lower threshold means greater accuracy at the expense of speed. You will need to experiment to get the best result for your animation.

Using Interactive IK

One straightforward way of using IK on a hierarchy is to turn on the Interactive IK button (Hierarchy ➜ IK ➜ Interactive IK) and animate. If you try this on the model you just created, you will probably get some wild results, because we have not yet set any terminators or IK limits. Undo whatever changes you made, and let's go fix those settings.

Setting a Terminator

To prevent the child from affecting the entire hierarchy, you need to set a terminator. A terminator is the lowest object in the hierarchy unaffected by movements of the end effector.

1. Open the `hierarchy_linked.max` file you created earlier or from the CD files for this book.

2. Select the torso. In the Hierarchy panel, in the IK tab, check Terminator in the Object Parameters rollout.

3. Turn on the Interactive IK button.

4. In the top viewport, move the hand forward. Now you can move the hand and the arm with it without the whole body going all over the place.

Setting IK Limits

Setting IK limits can be laborious. In our example, if we wanted to use IK, we should have set the IK limits of the left arm before mirroring it, because the Mirror tool has an option of mirroring the IK limits. Let's not worry about that and just set some limits for the left arm.

1. Select Arm Upper L and switch to the Parent Reference coordinate system.

2. Open the Rotational Joints rollout.

3. Check Active and Limited for all three axes.

4. Drag the From and To spinners for the X axis up and down and watch the display in the viewport. Use these spinners to set the range of motion you want for this joint around this axis.

5. Drag the From and To spinners for the Y axis to set the range of motion you want around the Y axis. For the shoulder joint, this rotation exists, but be careful not to allow too much.

6. Drag the From and To spinners for the Z axis to set the range of motion you want around the Z axis. The shoulder can't rotate backward on this axis, so one of the constraints should be 0.

7. Press the Page Down key to select the next object down the hierarchy, Arm Lower L. Check Limited in the Y Axis. Use the From and To spinners to set limits for the rotation around Y. Uncheck Active for the X and Z axes, since the arm can't rotate at all in X and only very slightly in Z.

8. Press the Page Down key again to select Hand L. Check Limited in the Y Axis. Use the From and To spinners to set limits for the rotation around Y. Uncheck Active for the X and Z axes. Save the file as `hierarchy_IKlimits.max`.

9. In the Inverse Kinematics rollout, click the Interactive IK button.

10. Go to frame 100 and click the Animate button again. Move the hand to a position in front of the torso. Notice that it is awkward to set the hand where you want it this way. Undo your move. Turn off the Animate button.

11. Create a small dummy object and position it just to the left of the left hand.

12. Link the dummy object to the left hand.

13. With Interactive IK still on, turn on the Animate button. Move the dummy object to a position in front of the torso. Notice that you now have a little more control over the hand rotation.

14. Turn off the Animate button and play the animation. Save your file as `hierarchy_ik01.max`.

Using Follow Objects (Applied IK)

Another type of IK in max involves using a follow object, often a dummy object, to calculate IK for a certain range of frames. This type of IK is considered more accurate than interactive IK. Applied IK is often used for sliding joints in machines, where kinematic accuracy is important. In our example, instead of animating the hand, you would animate a dummy moving from one hand position to another. You then bind the hand to the dummy follow object, not by linking but by clicking Bind in the Hierarchy ➜ IK panel. Then you click the Applied IK button for the range of the animation. The resulting calculation of the IK is different from using the Interactive IK button.

1. Open the `hierarchy_linked.max` file you created earlier or from the CD files for this book.

2. Create a dummy object and position it to the left of the left hand.

3. Select the torso and check Terminator in the IK tab.

4. Go to frame 100 and turn on the Animate button. In the top viewport, move the dummy object to a goal position in front of the model. Turn off the Animate button.

5. Select the hand object. In the Hierarchy ➡ IK panel, turn off the Interactive IK button.

6. Under Bind to Follow Object, click Bind. Press H, highlight the dummy object, and click Pin. Turn off the Bind button.

7. Upper the Apply IK button, choose frames 0 to 100. Save your file as `hierarchy_ik02.max`.

Applied IK is more accurate than the other IK methods for some purposes, but it generates a key for every object in the hierarchy at every frame. This is virtually impossible to edit, so it is not recommended for character animation. Compare your files `hierarchy_ik01.max` *and* `hierarchy_ik02.max`. *Again, keep in mind that "accuracy" is generally only relevant for things like machines, while "natural looking" is more relevant to characters.*

Creating IK Chain Solvers

IK can be calculated either in a way that "remembers" how it was constructed, called history-dependent IK or HD IK, or in a way that does not consider the history, called history-independent IK or HI IK. The new HI IK solvers in max are adjusted in the Motion panel. These are faster and better for longer character animations. The HD IK, interactive IK, and applied IK are set up and modified in this section of the Hierarchy panel. These work best with short animations of less complex hierarchies, such as machines. HD IK gets unwieldy in long animations, because the calculations consider the entire history of the chain.

An additional feature of these new IK chain solvers is that you can have multiple overlapping IK chains on the same object. This allows you to set independent IK goals for a heel and toes, for example, so that you can constrain them to the floor as necessary. In this way, you can ensure that the heel doesn't leave the ground until the leg is fully extended.

If you are going to output to Web 3D, you should use only one IK chain, as multiple IK chains are not supported by these applications.

To create an IK chain, follow these general steps:

1. Select the root of the chain and choose either HI Solver or HD Solver under Animation ➜ IK Solvers.

2. Drag to the end object of the IK chain.

3. Animate the end effector of the chain (in the case of the HI Solver, the IK goal object).

The IK solver will calculate the positions of the objects in the chain to meet the goal with precedence to the objects closer to the end of the chain (called *Child > Parent precedence* in the interface). This is almost always what you want. You can set a different precedence in the Hierarchy ➜ IK panel.

The history-independent method also allows you to toggle between forward and inverse kinematics. By turning off the Enabled button in the IK Solver rollout of the Motion panel, you can switch to keyframing in FK. You can then toggle back to IK for subsequent animation.

Skeletal Deformation with Bones

Key Concept

Max provides a hierarchical system of objects with IK properties assigned, called *max Bones*. Although there are default max Bones objects, the nature of bones lies in the properties assigned to the object, not whether it was originally created as a bone. You can turn bone properties on for any object, but it only makes sense if the object is part of a hierarchy.

If you are familiar with using bones in previous versions of max, be aware that they do not function exactly the same way when you animate them. To make bones behave the way they did in previous versions of max, create a bones chain and assign an HD IK solver from the root to the end bone (you'll see an example later in this section). Bones animations imported from previous versions of max will still work correctly.

In this case, the Interactive IK button and follow objects are unnecessary, because the IK solution is automatically calculated for the system. Bones can be used to deform either a segmented hierarchy or a single mesh. They can also be added to a character studio biped when needed. Bones can be created from the menu bar (Animation ➜ Create Bones) or the Create panel (Create ➜ Systems ➜ Bones).

Volume Fins on Bones

Bones in max 4 have Width, Height, and Taper parameters as well as the options of adjustable fins extending from the sides, front, and back. These allow you to define a volume with your bones. This can help you see what you're doing in the viewport and, if you are going to apply the Skin or Physique modifier, also help the modifier know which vertices of a mesh to assign to the bones. The envelopes of Skin are still symmetrical, however, even if the bone fins are not. You will use Skin in the next section.

Using the Skin Modifier to Deform a Mesh with Bones

In Chapter 10, you used the Linked XForm modifier to deform a mesh. For deformation with envelope control, you can use the Skin modifier. Skin allows you to deform a single mesh skin according to envelopes assigned to bones, whether a max Bones system or other objects used as bones. For more precise envelope control, you can use a third-party plug-in like Digimation's Bones Pro or character studio's Physique instead of Skin.

To deform a single mesh, you make a hierarchical skeleton with an IK chain assigned and apply the Skin modifier to the mesh. In the Modify tab of Skin, you add the bones: a max Bones system or a hierarchy of ordinary primitives. You can alter the assignment of vertices to bones by selecting the bone in the Skin Parameters rollout, clicking Edit Envelopes, and scaling the envelopes with the Move tool in the viewport so that it affects the area of the mesh you want it to deform.

When creating a mesh for skeletal deformation, be sure to give it at least two subdivisions per joint so that it can bend correctly.

Let's use bones and Skin to deform a mesh:

1. Open `tendril01.max` from the CD files for this chapter. This file contains a mesh model with a Morpher animation already applied. (The morph targets are hidden in the file, if you want to examine the morphing more closely.) Also copy the `ch11_maps` directory from the CD files for this chapter into your `3dsmax4\Maps` directory.

2. Choose Animation → Bones. Click slightly below the bottom of the model and then click three places up the tendril, with the last one off mesh for animating. Right-click to stop creating bones. Click one of the select tools to turn off Bones.

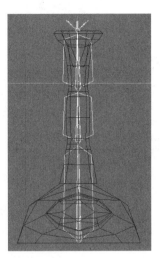

3. Select the root node of the bones (the one at the bottom that you created first) and choose Animation ➜ IK Solvers ➜ HD IK Solver. Roll over the top node until its name pops up, and click on it. This defines your bone chain as an IK chain using HD IK.

4. Select the mesh and apply a Skin modifier.

5. Click Add Bone, highlight all four bones, and click Select.

6. Select the top bone. Move it around. Notice whether any vertices of the mesh are being left behind. Undo the move.

7. If some of the vertices were left behind, highlight the corresponding bone in the Skin modifier and click Edit Envelopes. Select one of the envelope gizmos in the viewport and move it until it includes the correct number of vertices. Test it by moving the top bone again. Save the file as `tendril02.max`.

If you need to adjust the placement of the bones themselves, go to the Hierarchy panel, click Don't Affect Children, and move the bone. Turn the button off when you are done.

8. Turn on the Animate button, go to another frame, and move the top bone to animate it. Do this for a number of frames until you have the animation you want. The mesh should move with the bones. Turn off the Animate button. Save your file as `tendril03.max`.

Tendrilhead project by Jason Wiener
Another sample bones animation by Jason can be viewed in the CD files for this chapter: `viciouslilac.mov`.

Using Character Studio

Of all the plug-ins available for max, the most essential for character animation is character studio. Character studio 3 ships with max 4; you will receive an authorization code for it when you purchase the program. Character studio is the most common way of animating hierarchical characters in max. It is a challenge to master: this section is designed to acquaint you with the essentials to get you started.

Character studio consists of two plug-ins: the Biped system (Create ➜ Systems ➜ Biped), and the Physique modifier (Modify ➜ Modify List ➜ Physique). The overall workflow is to model your mesh; create a biped and fit it to your mesh in Figure mode; apply Physique to the mesh, bind it to the biped, and adjust it to get the envelopes correct; and then animate the biped. The following sections explain these tools in the order of the workflow for animating the Intrepid Explorer Jim character.

You can make morph targets for the facial animation in combination with biped animation. Apply the Morpher modifier below the Physique modifier (this can be done after the Physique has been applied by navigating down the stack if necessary).

Making a Biped

The Biped system is a full skeleton, complete with hierarchical linkages and its own blend of forward and inverse kinematics. It is completely adjustable to your character. It will render, but you turn off its display before rendering your scene. You create a biped by going to Create ➜ Systems, clicking the Biped button, and dragging out a biped in the viewport.

You have to drag out the size of the biped in the viewport. If you just click once, you will create a microscopic biped.

You edit the biped and access the various modes of character studio under the Motion panel. In the Structure section of the tab, you set the number of links you want for the different parts of the body. The most important part of the biped is the center of mass (COM) in the middle of the pelvis, because all the other parts are linked under that. This is the part that is named Bip01 as a default. You can rename the biped and all its respective parts by changing this root name in the Structure rollout, rather than having to rename every part of the body separately.

Create a biped for Intrepid Explorer Jim:

1. Open the textured `Intrepid_Explorer_Jim09.max` file you made in Chapter 7 or from the CD files for Chapter 7. If you did not already copy the IEJmaps directory, copy this directory to `3dsmax4\Maps` from the CD files for Chapter 7.

The best initial position of the mesh depends on how you want the character to move. The posture shown in Figure 11.2 is optimal for most human character animation. From a standing position, rotate the leg from the hip about 15° forward (around X); rotate the knee about 15° back (bent); rotate the leg about 15° around Z (so that the feet point outward); and rotate the leg about 15° around Y (so that the legs are spread). Rotate the arms about 45° up at the shoulder and the elbows about 45° bent. Curve the fingers slightly. All this makes the application of Physique easier, with less distortion.

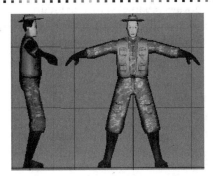

Figure 11.2 *Optimal positioning of mesh for biped animation*

2. In the left viewport, create a plane (Create ➜ Geometry ➜ Plane). This will put the plane at X = 0, making it easy to center the character on that centerline.

3. Select Jim and his hat. Click Align and pick the plane object. Center the models around the X axis only. (The feet should already be at zero. If not, create a plane in the top viewport and then align the minimum of the model with the plane along Z only.) Delete the alignment plane(s).

4. Turn on gridpoint snaps. (Right-click the Snap tool and choose Gridpoints. Press S to turn on snaps.)

5. Create a biped (Create ➜ Systems ➜ Biped) by dragging a biped in the view-port from 0,0,0 to the top of the head.

6. Select by name, choose Bip01 (the center of mass object), and click Select. Open the Structure rollout and rename this object "Jim." This changes the names of all the objects in the hierarchy.

7. Also in the Structure rollout, set the biped to have two fingers of two links each, one toe with one link, and two spine links. You may want to apply Edit ➜ Hold at this point.

Using Figure Mode to Adjust the Biped

Figure mode is for adjusting the parts of the biped to fit your character. It's best to get this just the way you want it before starting to animate. It's possible to make adjustments afterward, but the results aren't always reliable. With the Figure mode button activated in the Motion panel, you can move the center of mass to adjust the overall position of the biped, and then scale the corresponding parts of the biped to fit the segments or areas of the mesh they will affect. Using non-uniform scale is not problematic when scaling biped parts.

You can add a "ponytail," one of the optional body parts on a biped, with sufficient links—like the joints of a finger—to animate things like ears, noses, or hats and other clothing. For a segmented model, you can link the parts directly to the corresponding parts of the biped. For a single mesh, you will have to apply the Physique modifier, as explained later.

Adjust your biped to fit the Intrepid Explorer Jim model:

1. With any part of the biped selected, go to the Motion panel and click the Figure mode button.

2. Rotate and scale the biped parts to fit the mesh starting with the legs to adjust the COM height. The COM should be at the pelvis of the model, about an inch or two below the belly button. You want all the biped objects except the chest to poke through the mesh slightly. The biped fingers, feet, head, toes, and heel should all extend a little further than the length of the mesh.

Press Alt+X to put the mesh in see-through display while you adjust the biped. Select the mesh and press 6 to freeze it so that it is unselectable.

3. After you get one limb scaled and rotated correctly, click the Copy Posture button and then the Paste Posture Opposite button to mirror the posture to the other side of the biped.

4. When you have finished adjusting the biped to the mesh, save your file as Intrepid_Explorer_Jim10.max.

Applying the Physique Modifier

Physique allows a hierarchy to deform a mesh, much like the Linked XForm and Skin modifiers you used earlier.

Apply the Physique modifier while in Figure mode. In the Modify panel of physique, click the Attach to Node button, and then pick the biped. If you link extra bones to the biped, you need to keep the Animate button on while positioning the biped in Figure mode.

Let's apply Physique to the Intrepid Explorer Jim mesh:

1. Select the mesh object.

2. Unfreeze the mesh if you have frozen it (press 7). Select the mesh. Press Alt+X again to turn off see-through display if you have it on.

3. With the mesh still selected, apply the Physique modifier from the Modifier list. It is at the very bottom under Unassigned Modifiers.

4. Click the Attach to Node button, press H, highlight the Jim COM object, and click Initialize.

5. To test the Physique, load a motion capture file. Select the biped, go to the Motion panel, and click the Load File button. Load the Ballet.bip file from the CD files for this chapter. Play the animation. Notice whether any vertices are getting left behind or where the mesh drags or crumples. Press Ctrl+Z to unload the .bip file.

Importing Character Studio Animations from MAX R3

The Physique file format has changed since the last version of max. When you open a file animated with a previous version of character studio, you will get an error message saying that you need to reinitialize Physique. This is very simple and does not involve redoing all your envelopes or animation:

1. Select the Center of Mass object (e.g., Bip01). In the Motion panel, go into Figure mode. The biped and mesh will temporarily revert to their initial position.

2. Select the mesh. Go to the Modify panel and find the Physique layer of the stack (it should be on top).

Initialize   Reinitialize

3. Select the biped again and turn off Figure mode. All your preexisting animation should be intact. Save a new version of the file in the new file format.

Adjusting Envelopes

Envelopes are a sub-object level of the Physique modifier. Each envelope has an outer and an inner envelope. Inside the inner envelope, all the vertices are assigned directly to the corresponding bone link. The vertices between the inner and outer envelopes are affected by a blend of the influence from that bone and any adjacent bone with an envelope overlapping that area. The real work of using Physique is adjusting all the envelopes so that they affect the areas of the mesh they are supposed to affect and *only* those areas. The reason the initial position of the model is spread out is to avoid over-lap between non-adjacent envelopes.

For difficult vertices, assign the vertices to a specific link or links and type in an absolute weight for each link. If you adjust your biped to your mesh very precisely, you will have a lot less envelope work to do.

To adjust the envelopes of the Physique modifier:

1. Go to the Envelope sub-object level of the modifier.

2. Click a bone link in the viewport. An envelope gizmo appears, with a red inner envelope and a violet outer envelope.

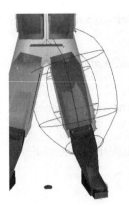

3. In the Blending Envelopes rollout, choose Inner, Outer, or Both and adjust the Radial Scale, Parent Overlap, and Child Overlap parameters to adjust the size of the envelope. Repeat this for each envelope that is having problems.

4. For areas like the face and any special problem areas, go to the Vertex sub-object level of the Physique modifier. Select the vertices, click Assign To Link, and choose No Blending in the Blending Between Links drop-down. Deselect the red and blue crosses in the Selection section so that only Rigid (green) vertices are selected, and click on the bone to which you want to assign them. Click the Lock Assignments button.

5. Test your envelopes with a motion capture file periodically. When the mesh moves with the biped, exit out of Figure mode by clicking the button again. Save your file as `Intrepid_Explorer_Jim11.max`.

Footsteps Mode

Footsteps mode takes care of all the cases where you want the character's feet to be touching the ground: walking, running, or jumping. This has always been a challenging part of character animation: preventing the feet from going through the floor. With max Footsteps, it's taken care of for you. Default footsteps, however, do not make for interesting animation. You start with the footsteps, adjust the weight and stride for your character, and add the motions that make your character distinctive.

To apply Footstep animation to Intrepid Explorer Jim:

1. Open the `Cave.max` file from the CD files for this chapter. Choose File ➜ Merge and choose the `Intrepid_Explorer_Jim11.max` file you created or from the CD files. Click All and Merge. If you created your own cave, merge `Cameras.max` into your file.

2. Select Jim and his hat and move them to a far point in the cave, as shown in Figure 11.3.

3. Select the hat and hide it. You will animate that in the Link Controller section later in this chapter.

4. Select the Jim COM object. Go to the Motion panel and click the Footsteps Mode button.

5. In the Footstep Creation rollout, click the Create Multiple Footsteps button. Create 24 footsteps and click OK.

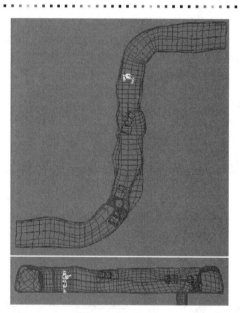

Figure 11.3 *Starting position of character and hat models*

6. Before the biped will use the footsteps, you need to click Create Keys for Inactive Footsteps in the Footstep Operations rollout. Do this and play the animation. The character walks along the footsteps.

7. The character needs to be holding a torch in his left hand. Select the Jim L UpperArm object and delete all its keys in the track bar. Then rotate the arm as if it is holding a torch.

8. In the left viewport, select footsteps 17 through 24 and move them straight down where he falls. Click the Footstep mode button again to turn off that mode. Save the file as `Intrepid_Explorer_Jim12.max`.

Free-Form Mode

Free-Form mode is the mode when none of the other mode buttons are checked. It allows you to create regular animation keys—for all the non-foot objects, and in any frame in which a foot is not touching the ground, for the whole body.

You can go out of Footsteps mode, move the biped around, and click the Set Key button under the Keyframing rollout or just use the Animate button:

1. Select the biped and go to the Motion panel.

2. In Free-Form mode (with no mode buttons activated), animate the character's upper body turning around corners.

3. With the Animate button or with the Set Key button, keyframe the arms and upper body the way you want it to move.

Unlike other objects in max, a biped does not automatically create a keyframe at frame 0 when animated. Use the Set Key button at frame 0 to set your initial key.

4. Go back into Footsteps mode when necessary to adjust the footsteps to fit the motion, using wider steps where appropriate. You can also select footsteps in the viewport and bend the trajectory of the steps or scale the stride over the selected steps with the Bend and Scale parameters in the Footstep Operations rollout.

5. Save your file as `Intrepid_Explorer_Jim13.max`.

Loading Figure and Motion Files

A great feature unique to character studio is that you can save figure files (`.fig`) independently of motion files (such as `.bip`) and apply the same motion to different characters. The Save File and Load File buttons are available in Figure mode for saving figure files and in Footstep mode and Free-Form mode for saving motion files.

Motion Flow Mode

In Motion Flow mode, you can combine your own saved segments of animation with motion capture segments into a unique script. You can then export this script as a `.bip` file, load it, and edit it some more.

If you click the Motion Flow Mode button, and then click Show Graph under the Motion Flow rollout, you will bring up a dialog box that looks like Figure 11.4.

To make icons for clips, click the Create Clip button and then click in the graph area. Switch to the Select Clip tool, right-click the clip icons, and assign motion files to the clips. These can be motion capture files that come with character studio or biped motions that you've saved yourself.

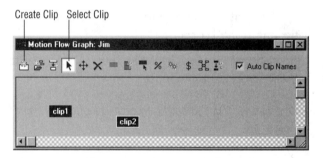

Figure 11.4 *The Motion Flow Graph dialog box*

To make a script, keep the Motion Flow Graph open and click the Define Script button in the Motion Flow Script rollout. Click the clips in the graph in the order you want them to play. You now have a motion script you can simply play in the viewport (while in Motion Flow mode), save out as a script file, or export as a motion file.

Selecting a clip in the script window allows you to click the Edit Transition button to edit the length and type of the transition between the two clips.

To export the whole script as an editable biped motion file, click the Save Segment button just underneath the Mode buttons. You will need to enter the end frame of the animation. This will create a `.bip` file you can load outside of Motion Flow mode and edit.

Layered Motion

Another great feature of character studio is the ability to layer motions. This means that you can have a base motion in one layer with an offset to the animation in a separate layer. For example, you might want to have a character walking and waving at the same time. Rather than keyframe the combined motion, which would be arduous and require a very good eye, you can animate one layer with the walk and a second layer with the wave. You can later collapse the layers into one.

To do this, open the Layers rollout of the Motion panel. Create your first layer of animation normally. Then click the Create Layer button. On this new layer, add keyframes for the second component of the animation.

When you have the combined animation the way you like, you can collapse the layers into a single set of keyframes by clicking the Collapse Layers button.

Adding a Link Constraint

Now you are finally going to link the hat and the torch to Jim using the link constraint you learned about in Chapter 10. Both objects will be linked first to dummy objects that are attached to the biped. They will be switched to other dummy objects as Jim falls down the hole, so that the other dummies can be used to animate the fall:

1. Unhide the hat object.

2. Create a small dummy object at the top of Jim's head. Name this object Hat_Dummyhead. Link the dummy to the biped head object. This is the first object that the hat will be linked to.

If you are using the CD files for this chapter, the dummy for the top of the head is already created and is part of the Physique. In this case, pick the existing dummy object rather than creating a new one.

3. Select the hat. Choose Animate ➜ Constraints ➜ Link Constraint. Press H, choose Hat_Dummyhead, and click Pick. The Hat_Dummyhead object is listed as the first link in the list.

4. Go to frame 249. Zoom in to the Jim character and create a dummy above his head. Name this Hat_Dummy.

5 Click Add Link, press H, choose the Hat_Dummy object, and click Pick.

6. Animate the Hat_Dummy object fluttering to the ground slowly.

7. Go back to frame 0 and zoom in close to Jim again. Merge in the `torch02.max` file hat you made in Chapter 9 or from the CD files for Chapter 9. Choose the Torch_Wood and Torch_Flame objects.

8. Position the Torch_Wood object in Jim's hand.

9. Assign a link constraint to the Torch_Wood object. Press H, and choose Jim L Finger 1.

10. Go to frame 249. Zoom in to the Jim character and create a dummy above the torch. Name this Torch_Dummy.

11. Click Add Link, press H, choose the Torch_Dummy object, and click Pick.

12. Animate the Torch_Dummy object falling to the ground.

13. Select the biped and go to the Motion panel. In the Display rollout, click the Objects button to turn off the display of your biped. Save your file as `Intrepid_Explorer_Jim14.max`.

Intrepid Explorer Jim project by Jason Wiener

Summary

In this chapter, you learned the basics of character animation in max. You learned about forward kinematics and a variety of inverse kinematics methods available in max. You were introduced to the complex hierarchical systems of max Bones and character studio, and you completed animations using these systems. You also used the link constraint to complete the animation for the Intrepid Explorer Jim project.

In the next chapter, you will learn about lighting techniques, the properties of CG lights, and how to apply lighting to your max scenes.

Mastering 3ds max 4

Color Gallery

The *Mastering 3ds max 4* Color Gallery includes full-color images to supplement the grayscale images in the text. Some of them illustrate concepts that can only be seen in full color (for example, the Material Channel Mapping, Anti-Aliasing, and Lighting pages). Some show full-color shots of exercises in the book to better illustrate the projects. Some are samples of work done in 3ds max by various artists to show you a range of what is possible and, we hope, inspire your own new ideas.

MORNING PRAYER

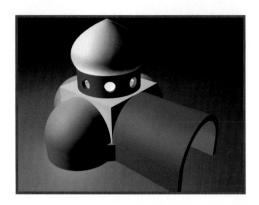

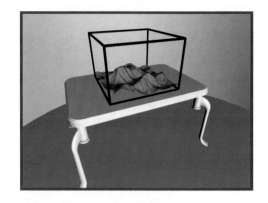

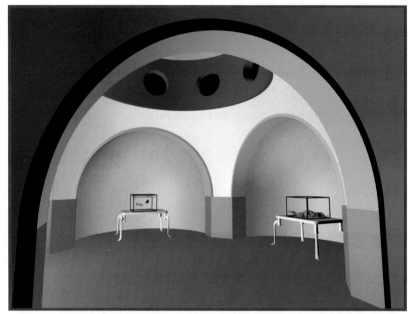

*This museum gallery modeling project was designed by Scott Onstott.
The steps for creating it yourself are in Chapter 4.*

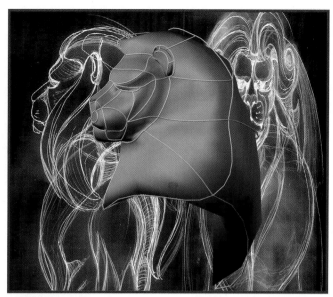

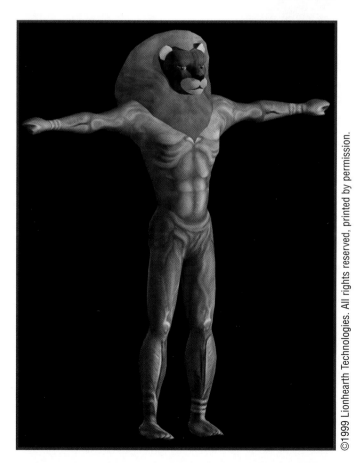

This character was modeled using splines and Surface Tools (see Chapter 5) by Stasia McGehee. Note the use of templates for planning the contours of the splines. Front and side views were mapped onto intersecting planes after registering the drawings in Photoshop.

Diffuse map

Bump map

Specular level map

*Bump and specular
level maps*

Opacity map

*Opacity and specular
level maps*

*Opacity and
specular level maps
with filter color*

*Opacity, specular level,
and filter color maps*

Self-illumination map

MATERIAL CHANNEL MAPPING

Glossiness map

Reflection map

Refraction map

Refraction map with transparency and filter color added

Displacement map

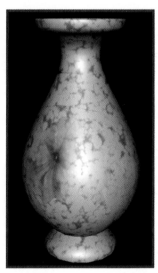

This map composites diffuse channel images using an alpha channel and a separate mask file. See Chapter 8 for the tutorial.

This spread shows the effects of maps applied to the different material channels. Note the effect of adding a matching specular level map with bump maps (making the bump more intense) and opacity maps (eliminating glare in transparent areas). Filter color affects the transparent area and the shadow color when raytraced shadows are used. Self-illumination creates a glowing effect, but it also flattens the appearance of the surface. The map on the glossiness channel uses the Falloff type. The displacement map was applied to a limited area of the object.

The iris still life was modeled and textured by Kay Pruvich. Portions of this project are used in Chapters 8 and 14.

The dinner setting still life was modeled and textured by Scott Onstott. This project is included in its entirety in a "Hands-on max" section of Chapter 8.

The table and lamp texturing and post-production project, by Blue Bactol, is covered in tutorials in Chapters 8, 12, 13, and 14. The top shot is rendered with materials, lighting, and atmospheric effects (volume light) from max. The bottom shot is rendered from combustion with composited text and added glow effects.

These three examples of lighting show the default lighting, perfectly even lighting, and dramatic lighting. The Intrepid Explorer Jim project is by Jason Wiener. Tutorials for creating it are found in Chapters 5, 7, 9, 11, 12, and 14.

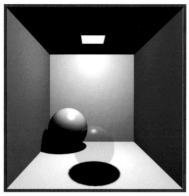

Max scanline rendering

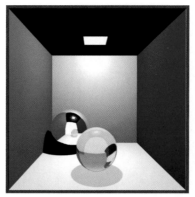

Max Raytrace rendering

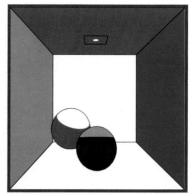

Illustrate cartoon rendering

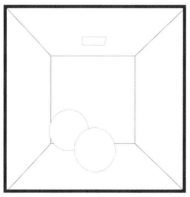

Illustrate outline rendering

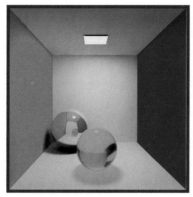

Lightscape rendering

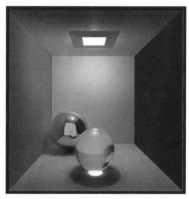

InSight rendering

The Cornell Box project was created by Scott Onstott. These shots show different renderer plug-ins for max, explained in Chapter 13. The exercise for texturing the Cornell Box is in Chapter 8.

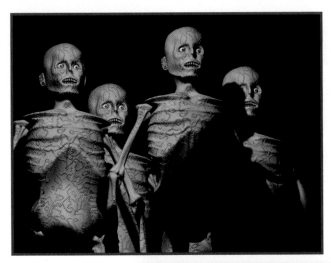

The Hunger scene by Jason Wiener is used here to show different anti-aliasing filters in the renderer. The top image uses the Area filter. The second image uses the Catmull Rom filter, which enhances the edges crisply—too much for this project. (See the iris still life on the Materials Projects page for an example where the edge enhancement helps the image.) The bottom image uses a Blend filter at 0.1. For this image, this results in too much blurring of the faces. Anti-aliasing filters are covered in Chapter 13.

ANTI-ALIASING

The camera mapping project by Tom Meade uses a single photograph (shown above) and simplified models to create an establishing shot for a movie. The illusion starts to break down as you move further into the scene, as you can see in the last frame (below, right), but such shots go by so quickly that they still work for the purposes of the film. The entire camera-mapping project is included in the "Hands-on max" section of Chapter 8. The completed shot is available in the CD files for Chapter 8 as `Bath_cammap.mov`.

Jason Wiener enacted the Intrepid Explorer Jim project in max from his storyboard in Chapter 1. The character is modeled in Chapter 5, textured in Chapter 7, and animated in Chapters 9 and 11. Chapter 12 covers the lighting and Chapter 14 the final shot.

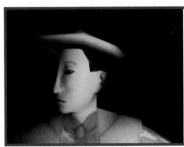

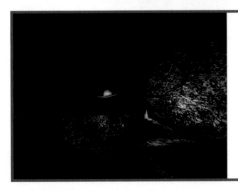

The "Morning Prayer" max project was the collaborative effort of three people, Marc Abraham, Julie Lloyd, and Elizabeth Murray. Marc and Julie modeled and animated the characters and Elizabeth built the environments and texture maps.

TEAPOT

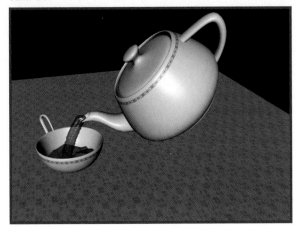

The teapot animation is a tutorial in Chapters 9 and 10.

CAESAR

Articulated (segmented) model created in max by Stasia McGehee.

BUSSTOP

The bus stop scene, inspired by the San Francisco Muni, was created in max by Jason Wiener.

ARTISTS' EXHIBITION

PUNCH

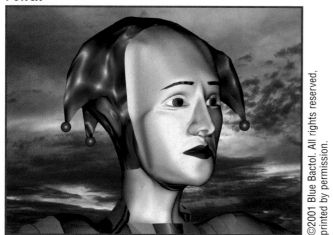

The character of "Punch," featured on the cover and chapter title pages, was designed by Blue Bactol; she created the model in Surface Tools and edited as mesh.

VICIOUS LILAC

The Vicious Lilac cartoon was created in max by Jason Wiener. A segment of animation of this character is also available on the CD as `viciouslilac.mov` *in the files for Chapter 11.*

ALIEN

The alien character was designed and created by John Matsubara.

FETUS

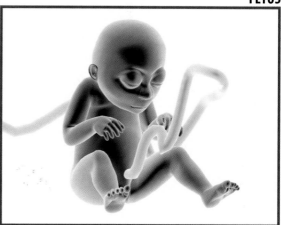

Jason Wiener modeled this fetus in max and then inverted the image in Photoshop.

RATMAN

"Ratman" and "Ogre" are two low-poly characters modeled and animated by Jason Wiener. Note that Ogre's ear is a single polygon with detailed texture-mapping.

OGRE

RAYSHAN

The Rayshan character and fence was built in max by Jason Wiener. He used an opacity map for most of the fence rather than modeling all the links.

Part V

Refining the Rendering

In This Part

Part V focuses on topics that affect the final appearance of the rendering by adjusting pixel colors. While lighting, special effects, and camera work are not similar jobs in the real world, their CG counterparts are very much related. Part V is about the packaging of rendered images for the best presentation. In Chapter 12, you will learn the characteristics of CG lights and apply different lighting setups to dramatically change the appearance of your scene. Chapter 13 covers the many options for rendering, including alternate renderers and network rendering. Chapter 13 also covers the "post-process" effects available in the Environment window. In Chapter 14 you will learn how to cut and cross-fade between cameras and pre-rendered images, how to apply special effects within the Video Post window, and how to composite images within max and in discreet combustion.

Coloring with Light

3ds max

Chapter 12

This chapter discusses the use of lighting and color and their implications in the final rendering of your max scene. You will learn the features of max lights and related tools. You will learn how to use the various settings for each type of light. You will apply lighting to scenes using different approaches. Topics include:

- Principles from masters of painting

- Max light objects

- The light lister

- The color clipboard

- Light and shadow parameters

- A three-point lighting setup

- Volumetric lights

- Mood lighting

The Art of Lighting

Lighting can be very subjective. Not only do no two people light a scene exactly the same way; no two people will see the same result, either. Our sense of sight, which may seem to us such a given—an impersonal input from the world to our eyes and our brains—is in fact something that must be trained to make fine distinctions. While few people who see your final rendered product will be able to make those distinctions consciously, your audience will be affected by the slight differences in light and shadow that create very different moods and meanings.

Moods and meanings? That sounds very subjective; how can you train yourself in this area? The nuances of interplay between lighting and meaning have been studied intensively since films were first made. The meaning of a certain lighting style can never be absolute, since it depends on cultural conventions and precedents for its validity; yet using it can make the difference between effectively conveying your story and leaving your audience yawning.

Lighting is a complex study that takes years of experience to master. In film, teams of people specialize in perfecting just the lighting of scenes. If you are working on your own animation without the luxury of a team of specialists, you have to be your own lighting crew, in addition to being your own writer, director, camera operator, model builder, animator, and editor. It's a challenge to learn all these aspects of filmmaking at once. Any experience you acquire in real-world lighting for photography, film, or video will help you in lighting your virtual set in max. You can also watch movies with an eye for lighting effects, the moods they create, and how they might be produced digitally.

Simulating Light and Color in 2D

As you've learned already, the 3D computer graphics you see are generally 2D arrangements of pixels of different colors. That's it. The magic of a program like max is in calculating the necessary colors of the pixels to simulate reality with all its qualities of light and shading, based on your instructions. The connection between light and color, which exists in the real world as well, is even more intrinsic to CG since the effect of CG light is simply to color pixels differently.

Because your output is a 2D representation of three-dimensional realities, you are striving for the same goal that painters have always pursued: rendering three dimensions in two. Despite the fact that CG methods are so different, the techniques of these masters can still apply. As you learned in Chapter 1, many of these perspective techniques are actually used behind the scenes when 3D software is written. Shaders, for example, calculate how to shade an object based on the angle of the CG light hitting the object; the information on how to do this comes from centuries of cultural experience in drawing and painting. By the same token, the way a 3D program calculates the rendering of objects at a distance is based on conventions of rendering used in Western culture since the Renaissance. Max approximates these rules through intensive calculations that you never see.

Computers can only simulate an illusion of reality, and they do so by calculating approximations of our abstract theories and models of reality. 3D applications have to simplify these approximations in order to render at an acceptable speed. If every ray of light that you would really see were calculated, you would never be able to render a single object. Lighting in the real world is almost infinitely complex. Understanding how artists have rendered 3D realities in 2D images can help you add back what might be lost in approximation. For example, a 3D application will not directly calculate aerial perspective, but by knowing about it, you can add it to a 3D scene. What follows might be considered a "crash" art course in using color and shading to achieve the illusion of depth in 2D images.

Simulating Aerial Perspective

When looking at a landscape in the real world, we see the colors of objects as paler and bluer the farther way they are from us. Blue light is scattered by the moisture and particles in the air of the intervening atmosphere. You can test this by looking at a photograph of a landscape.

1. Reset max.

2. Open the Asset Manager (Utilities ➜ Asset Manager).

3. Select the 3dsmax4\Maps\Backgrounds directory in the left pane of the manager.

4. Double-click the LAKE_MT.jpg image (Figure 12.1) in the right pane.

5. Right-click the image to bring up the eyedropper tool. Drag the eyedropper around the image and notice the red, green, and blue values change. Notice that the blue value increases toward the background.

The colors of the farthest background are lighter and shifted toward blue, because you are looking through more of the atmosphere. Landscape painters make use of this property by painting the farthest mountains a paler, bluer color than the next layer closer to the foreground. You can simulate this effect in max by adding a bluish fog to a scene. For a more sophisticated simulation, apply a Blend material with a Falloff map (using the Distance Blend falloff type) masking between the base landscape material and a foggy bluish material. Using this option, the bluish material will constitute more of the blend in the distance.

Figure 12.1 *Examine the color values in this scene.*

Using Advancing and Receding Colors

The eye can be tricked into seeing certain colors "pop out" toward the foreground while other colors seem to recede. Use red colors to emphasize an object or make it pop forward; use blue in the background for elements that should to recede from the camera. This optical illusion is the result of the differing wavelengths of red and blue light. Using reds and blues in the same scene can accentuate this effect and give your scenes added depth.

Using Contrast and Harmony

Another way to increase the perception of depth in your scene is to employ the *color shift principle*. By shifting the color of a shadow toward the complementary color of the light or the object being lit, you increase the depth of your shadows. The value of the color still needs to be appropriate for the shadow; the complementary hue simply enhances the color contrast to add to the sense of depth. Since you can set a shadow color for max lights, as you will see in "Casting Shadows" later in this chapter, you can use this principle to add punch to your rendered scene. Shadows.tif, in the CD files for this chapter, shows an example of this. The lighting is shifted to a yellowish tint while the shadows have been shifted to a dark purple, to add color contrast to the value contrast.

Refer to additive_wheel.jpg *in the CD files for Chapter 7 to check additive color complements. The complement is the color on the opposite side of the wheel.*

Painting Light and Shadows

You can "paint" light and shadows in CG by using lights to define the values in the scene more precisely than with the simulated illumination of a single light. Since max allows you to use negative lights that serve to "suck light out" of the scene, you can paint with light itself. For example, if you were creating a clearing in a dense forest, streaming with golden sunlight, you might have a brighter, white light illuminating where the light hits the forest floor, with several other negative lights placed to darken the more remote areas of the view. Negative multipliers for lights are explained in the "Multiplier" section later in this chapter.

Only lights of a grayscale color should be used with this technique, because negative lights remove color as well as intensity. Using a negative colored light would shift the remaining light to its complementary color.

Max Light and Color Tools

In addition to understanding the real-world effects you want to imitate, you also need to understand the special characteristics of computer graphics (CG) lights that differ from real lights, so that you know how to adapt your strategy. Let's look at the color and lighting tools available in max.

Default Lighting

A max scene file includes some light by default (so you can see and render a scene without having to create light objects). To have your default lighting include a key light and a fill light, part of a standard lighting setup we will discuss in "A Three-Point Light

Setup" later in this chapter, open the Viewport Configuration dialog box (Customize ➜ Viewport Configuration), check Default Lighting, and choose 2 Lights.

As soon as you create a light object, your scene will get darker, because the default lighting is no longer used once you create a light in your scene. You can toggle the default lights with your created lights in your active viewport by pressing Ctrl+L.

 If you have the active viewport configured with default lighting of 2 Lights, you can add the default lights to the scene (in addition to any other lights you've created) by choosing Views ➜ Add Default Light.

Light Objects

Max has different types of light objects to simulate different real-world lighting effects. Each light object is comparable to a kind of lighting encountered in the real world. There are important differences, however, between a real light and a CG light. For one thing, unless you set an *attenuation* (the lessening of the light as it travels), CG lights go on forever at full intensity. Second, unless you tell a CG light to cast shadows, it will continue shining through objects. Third, you can never see CG lights in the render; you only see objects being lit by them. If you want to see the glare of a light into a camera, you must add a post-process glow or lens effect. Finally, with CG lights, you can control exactly which objects receive illumination or shadow from that light.

Omni

An *omni* light is a point light source, in CG terminology. This is comparable to a light bulb suspended in midair from a thin wire: it throws light in all directions from its center. A single omni is equivalent to six max spotlights arranged around one center, pointing outward. Omni lights can cast shadows and can be attenuated at a distance. They can also be mapped with a projection, as you will see in "Projecting Maps from Lights" later in the chapter. You'll use omni lights in this chapter's portion of the Intrepid Explorer Jim exercise.

Target Spot

Spotlights in max are like the spotlights you see in a Broadway theater. They throw a cone of light, with beams originating from a point and fanning outwards. *Target spots* have two component objects: the light object and the target object. The target, as you learned in Chapter 9, is really a dummy object that the light has been instructed to look at. The cone of a target spot will always point toward the target, no matter where the target is placed. You can link a light or its target to another object, so that light follows the object. When you delete the target spot's light, the target will be deleted with it, but the two parts are technically separate objects.

Free Spot

The *free spot* light has a cone like the target spot, but it does not have a target. You can therefore animate it completely freely, by rotating the light itself and changing its parameters in the Modify tab, rather than by manipulating its target. A free spot will always be created facing into the viewport in which you create it. For example, a free spot created in the front view will shine toward the back until you adjust it.

Target Direct

The *target direct* light also has a target, as its name suggests, but it generates a cylinder of parallel rays rather than a cone of light. Direct light is good for simulating the sun, because the sun's rays, from our distant vantage point on Earth, seem parallel. Parallel rays cast different shadows than the rays of a cone, as can be seen in Figure 12.2, where the same scene is lit by spot and direct target lights of the same intensity, from the same distance, and at the same angle. Notice that the fall of the light on the table and shape of the shadows around the object are different based on the projection of the light. Subtle differences in shadows can make the difference in the believability of your scene.

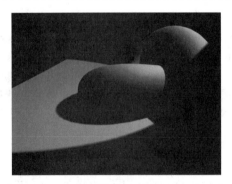 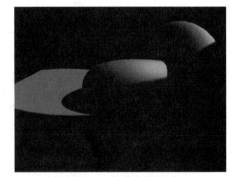

Conical spot light   Direct light

Figure 12.2 *Shadows cast by conical spot light (left) and parallel direct light (right) at the same position, orientation, and intensity*

Free Direct

The *free direct* light is a directional light, with parallel rays, that does not have a target. Like the free spot, it can be adjusted and manipulated directly, rather than through the adjustment of a target object. While free direct lights don't have target objects, they do have a Target Distance setting in the Directional Parameters rollout of the Modify panel that determines the length of the light object.

Changing the Light Type

In max 4, you can now change between the five main types of light objects (omni, target and free spot, and target and free direct) in the Modify panel. This will preserve all your color, attenuation, and shadow settings and apply them to the new light type. You may then need to adjust some of these settings to work with your scene using the new light type.

Sunlight System

A *Sunlight* system, available in Create ➜ Systems, is simply a free direct light along with a compass that allows you to enter the physical location and the exact time of day and year to simulate sunlight realistically for that location and time. The system's parameters are accessible in the Motion panel or through Link Info on the Hierarchy panel.

Using the Light View

As you learned in Chapter 3, lights can be adjusted through the use of the light view and its viewport controls. If you have a spot or directional light selected, Shift+4 will allow you to look through the light in the viewport and position and rotate the light with the light viewport controls. If you have multiple spots or directional lights in the scene but don't have any of them selected, Shift+4 calls up a dialog box where you can select which light to look through in the viewport.

To review from Chapter 3, the Roll tool allows you to rotate the light along the line of light; the Pan tool rotates the light as you would spin a top, moving the target around it; and the Orbit tool rotates the light around the target. (On a free light, Orbit rotates the light around the end of the light object, set by the Target Distance parameter.)

To constrain Pan or Orbit to one axis of rotation, hold the Shift key while rotating.

Using the Place Highlight Tool

The Place Highlight tool in the Align flyout of the main toolbar allows you to position a light by telling it where you would like a highlight to fall on an object. Let's try it:

1. Reset max.

2. Create a sphere.

3. Create a free spotlight (Create ➜ Lights ➜ Free Spot).

4. Select the spotlight and click the Place Highlight tool. You should get a cursor that looks like the tool's icon.

5. Drag the cursor across the surface of the sphere. The light is moved and rotated to place the highlight at that position.

Using the Light Lister

The *light lister* (Tools ➜ Light Lister in the menu bar) allows you to change settings for individual lights in one place as well as to make global changes to all your lights. The Light Lister dialog box shows you every light in your scene, allowing you to select each light, turn it on and off, change the color or multiplier, turn its shadows on or off, and choose the parameters of its shadows—all from one place. Figure 12.3 shows the light settings in the light lister and what they mean. In the Global Settings rollout, you can change these same settings and then click Set All Lights to apply the settings to every light in the scene. You can add additional tint and intensity to all your light objects through the Global Tint and Global Level settings. The Ambient color swatch controls the overall ambient lighting of the scene, affecting the ambient color of all your objects.

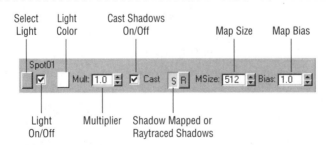

Figure 12.3 *The light lister controls every light in your scene.*

Be careful about changing the Ambient light color. You can lose contrast and easily wash out your entire scene this way.

Using the Color Clipboard

Remember that lighting interacts with the colors of your materials, changing the rendered colors of a surface. A colored light can shift your material colors far from the colors you originally chose, for example. It can be difficult to keep track of subtle variations in color, especially since the eye adjusts and sees the color differently. The color clipboard utility (Utilities ➜ Color Clipboard) is very handy for keeping track of colors and copying them from a rendered image or a color swatch in the interface to other swatches. Let's take a look at it:

1. Reset max.

2. Open your `Vase03.max` file from the Chapter 8 exercise or any max file you can render.

3. Right-click the perspective viewport. Render an image by clicking the Render Scene button. Choose Single, 320×240, and click Render.

4. Right-click the image to get the eyedropper and click a color in the rendering you might want to use again. It will appear in the color swatch in the upper-right of the Render window.

5. In the Utility panel, click Color Clipboard, and then New Floater. This gives you a color clipboard you can save to a `.ccb` file for use anytime.

6. Drag from the swatch in the Render window to a swatch on the color clipboard and choose Copy. You can now take this exact color to the Material Editor or to any other file.

Setting Your Light Parameters

As you saw in the light lister, many light settings are common to all light types. You have access to all these common settings as well as to the settings specific to the type of light selected in the Modify panel. This section covers the various light parameters.

Light Color

The Light Color parameter is like a filter over the light. The grayscale value of the light color affects the light's intensity. You can enter the numerical RGB or HSV values directly on the Modify tab, or you can bring up the Color Selector by clicking the Light Color swatch in the General Parameters rollout of a light object.

Multiplier

The multiplier, beneath the RGB/HSV spinners in the General Parameters rollout, is similar to a dimmer switch that allows you to turn the amount of light up and down. As its name implies, the multiplier increases the light intensity in a linear fashion: a multiplier of 2.0 produces twice the intensity of 1.0; a multiplier of 4.0 four times that of 1.0. The standard of 1.0 does not correspond to a real-life light value (in lumens); you need to acquaint yourself with the results of a light with a 1.0 multiplier and use that as a baseline for comparison. The closest approximation to real-life lighting in lumens is provided by radiosity software, such as Lightscape. These programs (some are plug-ins, some are standalone) produce beautiful results, but require a great deal of processing time. You will learn more about Lightscape's radiosity renderer in Chapter 13.

Increased light multipliers are overused and can burn out parts of your render: a sure sign of amateur work. Try increasing the value of the light color first and increase the multiplier carefully, only as needed. Consider creating additional lights of lower intensity before cranking up a multiplier.

In a feature that's available only in the virtual lighting of CG, the multiplier can also be a negative number, actually removing light from the scene. It has the reverse effect of a positive CG light: darkening rather than lightening the colors of the objects around it. Keep in mind, when using negative multipliers, that they also remove the light color, in effect inverting it to its complement. So a blue light with a negative multiplier will darken the scene *and* shift its rendered colors toward yellow. Any map applied to the light would also be inverted.

Excluding Objects

The Exclude button allows you to use a light for a specific purpose (to provide a slight fill to one object, for example) without affecting anything else in the scene. Used correctly, this can simulate detailed realistic effects. If you have a solid idea of where the light in your scene should be coming from, you can then use different lights specific to each object within the scene to get the exact effect you want. If you do this in a way that creates too many incongruities in the lights and shadows, your audience might not know exactly why, but they won't be convinced of the reality of your scene.

To use this feature, click the Exclude button to bring up the Exclude/Include dialog box. The feature will *either* exclude or include, determined by the radio button setting at the top. (*Include* means you are including only the selected objects and excluding all others.) In the second set of radio buttons, choose whether you are excluding from illumination, shadows, or both. In the left pane, select objects in your scene (Ctrl+click to select multiple objects) and then click the button with the double arrows to move the objects into the right pane.

Attenuating Light at a Distance

As mentioned earlier, a CG light will go on forever unless you specify how it attenuates. All lights in max can be attenuated at a distance. The attenuation settings control how light diminishes relative to the distance from its source. They include the total distance of the light's throw, where the light starts falling off, where the light starts "falling on" (something not possible in a real light), and the type of decay calculation used for the falloff.

If an object is too dark, check whether it is within the attenuation ranges of the light.

Near Attenuation

This setting controls where the light begins to fade in. As mentioned above, this is not comparable to a real-world situation. Imagine that emitted light does not have to start at its source, illuminating everything in its path, but can start somewhere along its path. The End setting of the Near Attenuation parameter is the distance where the light reaches 100% of its intensity. The Start setting is the distance where the light value starts fading in from zero. Checking Show displays the settings graphically in the viewport, giving you interactive feedback on your adjustments. Figure 12.4 shows a spotlight with Near Attenuation settings used.

Remember to always check the Use box when applying attenuation settings.

Figure 12.4 *Near Attenuation settings on this lamp start the effect at a distance from the light source.*

Far Attenuation

The Far Attenuation setting determines where a light begins to fade out at a distance. This is the type of attenuation we are more accustomed to in the real world and is much more common in CG as well. The Start setting is the distance where the light begins to fall off from its full intensity. The End value designates the farthest reach of the light; after that distance, the light has no effect at all.

Decay

The Decay settings determine which mathematical formula max uses to calculate the falloff in light from 100 percent to zero. Table 12.1 describes the effects of the three decay types.

Table 12.1 Effect of Decay Settings of Lights

Decay Type	Effect
None	There is no falloff.
Inverse	The falloff is proportional to the inverse of the distance.
Inverse Square	The falloff is proportional to the inverse of the distance squared. This is real-world falloff, but is rarely necessary and dims the light greatly. To use this setting in max, you will need to either use a lot of lights or crank up the multiplier value.

Adjusting the Hotspot and Falloff

In addition to attenuating at a distance, spotlights and directional lights also diminish along the edges of their cone or cylinder, according to parameters that can be adjusted. The *hotspot* is the angle of the cone of a spotlight (or width of the cylinder of a direct light) within which the light is still at full intensity. The *falloff* is the angle or width at which no illumination is received from the light. You can set these in the Spotlight Parameters rollout of the Modify tab, or use a light view and the viewport navigation controls (the Hotspot and Falloff tools) to adjust them. If you check Show Cone in the Spotlight Parameters, the cone will appear in the viewport even when the light is not selected. The light blue inner cone is the hotspot; the dark blue outer cone is the falloff.

Casting Shadows

All lights in max can cast shadows but, unlike real lights, CG lights have to be instructed to do so. Calculating shadows increases render time, so shadows are turned off as a default. Turn them on by checking Cast Shadows in the General Parameters rollout.

The two types of shadow calculations are shadow map and raytraced shadows. You choose between these in the Object Shadows drop-down list in the Shadow Parameters rollout. The Shadow Map option applies a silhouette image of the object projected along the line of light as a bitmap for shadow images. Ray Traced Shadows calculates the actual fall of light rays around the object. You will look at the benefits and drawbacks of each in the following sections.

Shadow Maps

Shadow maps are bitmaps created during the rendering process and projected in the direction of the light. Specific settings can then be adjusted to control the anti-aliasing of the shadow bitmap. Since shadow-mapped shadows are bitmaps, their resolution relative to the total render size affects how coarse the shadows appear. If your shadows are coarse, the map size may be too small, the camera may be too close, or your falloff may be too wide. (The map size has to cover the entire area within the light's falloff.) If you have two different-sized objects near each other, you may need to use separate lights with different map sizes, excluding the other object from each light.

Here are some of the advantages and disadvantages of shadow-mapped shadows, followed by descriptions of shadow map parameters.

Advantages	Disadvantages
Allows soft edges.	Requires you to fiddle with map size and sampling to control coarseness.
Lets you add color and map to shadow.	Won't apply the transparency or filter color of transparent objects.
Faster to calculate.	Not calculated as precisely as raytraced shadows.
Maps are controllable.	Large map sizes bog down the system.

Bias

This parameter adjusts the distance of the map from the object casting shadows. In the scene below, the sphere on the left has the default map bias of 1, while the sphere on the right has a map bias of 50. Notice that while both spheres are flat on the plane, the distance of the shadow makes the second appear to be floating above the plane.

Size

This parameter determines the dimensions of the map used to make the shadows. As mentioned before, increasing the map size can help get rid of the coarseness (jagged edges) around your shadows. The downside is that this uses more RAM.

Jagged edges on shadows can detract from the believability of your animation. Check some single-frame renders to see if your shadows are aliased.

Sample Range

This parameter affects the softness of the edge of your shadow. A lower value averages a smaller range of pixels, making the edge sharper, with the potential for jagged aliased edges. Higher values average a larger range of pixels, softening the edge.

If you set the sample range too high, you can get banding around the edges and drastically increase your render time. If you have the time and the RAM, you can reduce the streaking by increasing the map size (or by switching to raytraced shadows).

Raytraced Shadows

Raytraced shadows calculate the projection of the light more exactly. This is often called "more accurate," so let's consider what that means. It means that, if lighting in the real world behaved as CG lights do, shadows would look more like raytraced shadows, with exact, crisp edges and dark interiors. Since the raytracing calculation includes transparency, you can get more correct shadows of transparent and translucent objects. Raytraced shadows are also resolution-independent; they can be resized without getting the aliasing problems of shadow maps.

Using raytraced shadows is the only way to get the wire-frame material to cast a wireframe shadow.

The problem with raytraced shadows lies in those exact, crisp edges. In the real world, light is bouncing all around and shadows can have very soft edges. Hard edges, for all the claims of accuracy, are not always realistic. You can improve the realism of raytraced shadows by reducing the Density setting. To summarize the pros and cons of raytraced shadows:

Advantages	**Disadvantages**
Accurate shadows on transparent objects, including filter color (see the Material Channel Mapping plate in the Color Gallery)	No edge softness control
Clean anti-aliased edges	Longer to calculate (render)

You can fake soft edges by rendering your shadows separately, using Render Elements, covered in Chapter 13, or Matte/Shadow materials (covered in Chapters 7 and 8), blurring the shadows, and then compositing them back.

Overshoot

The Overshoot check box for spot and direct lights allows you to cast light outside the volume of the cone or cylinder. This allows you to limit shadows to within the falloff cone without limiting the illumination.

To simulate sunlight, check Overshoot on a direct light to illuminate the entire scene, but only cast shadows within the cylinder of the light.

Shadow Color

As you learned in "Using Contrast and Harmony" earlier this chapter, you can add depth through contrast by making shadow colors complementary to the light or material color. In the Color swatch in the Shadow Parameters rollout, you can set a color for the shadows cast by the light.

Map

You can now apply a map to blend with your shadow color in your shadows. This can be used to simulate refracted light through liquid, like the caustic light a glass of wine casts on a table. You also need to check the box next to the word Map in order to turn it on.

The map applied to a shadow is not the same thing as shadow-mapped shadows. You can apply a map on top of both shadow-mapped and raytraced shadows.

Atmosphere Shadows

The Atmosphere Shadows check box enables a light to cast shadows of atmospheric objects such as fog. The opacity and coloration of the shadow can be set here, too. Atmospherics are covered in more detail in Chapter 13.

Affecting Surfaces

The Affect Surfaces settings adjust how a light affects objects in the scene. Table 12.2 describes the effects of these settings.

Table 12.2 Effects of Affect Surfaces Settings

Control	Effect
Contrast	Controls the difference between the diffuse and ambient areas of the illumination.
Soften Diff[use] Edge	Controls the softness of the actual edge between the diffuse color and the ambient falloff.
Diffuse	Independently affects the diffuse properties of an object's surface.
Specular	Like Diffuse, allows independent control over the specular properties of an object.
Ambient only	Affects only the ambient part of the illumination.

Uncheck the Affect Specular check box to remove white "hotspots" or glares from the specular area of flat surfaces.

Projecting Maps from Lights

The Project Map settings, available for all types of lights in max, allow you to apply any map as a filter to generate interesting lighting effects. This kind of light is commonly called a *gobo*. Using an .avi or QuickTime movie as the map will create a movie-projector effect. Use animated noise maps on a gobo to create caustics on surfaces of water. Project a gobo of leaf shadows onto a wall to simulate light passing through the leaves on a tree without having to model the tree.

Atmospheric Effects

Volumetric lights are lights that shine in the air they pass through, rather than just on the objects they reach. The classic image of sunlight streaming into the Pantheon through the oculus in the dome is an example of volumetric light. You can create this effect in max by using volume lights. Volume lights are essentially lights with fog in their path. The parameters of the fog can be adjusted for different effects, as you will see in Chapter 13.

Lens effects simulate the glows and distortions made when shooting light through a lens (a camera or your eye). An example of this is the glow we see around a light shining straight at us and shooting off into spikes of light. Lens effects are also covered in Chapters 13 and 14. These effects are rightfully considered post-process effects. Volumetric properties can be assigned to lights through the Rendering ➜ Environment window, and lens flares can be assigned through Video Post. However, you can also use the Atmospheres & Effects rollout of a light object. Use the Add button to bring up the Add Atmosphere or Effect dialog box. The Delete button deletes the volumetric or lens effect from the light.

 Deleting an effect from a light doesn't remove it from the scene, even though you may have created it through the light. The effect and its settings are still in the Environment or Effects dialog boxes accessed from the Rendering menu.

Selecting the effect and clicking the Setup button brings up its respective dialog box (ordinarily accessible through the Rendering menu) so that you can adjust the settings of the effect. You will apply a volumetric lighting effect in "Adding Volume Light Atmospherics" later in this chapter.

Designing Your Lighting

Through many decades of study and experimentation with lighting, certain conventions have developed that can give you a starting point for your lighting setup. It's useful to learn these conventions so that you can adapt them to the specific needs of your scene and avoid reinventing the wheel.

A Three-Point Lighting Setup

The *three-point light* setup is a classic arrangement of lights, including a key light, a fill light, and a back or kicker light. You may ultimately have many more than three lights in your scene, yet setting the three basic points can give you a good basis from which to start. Figure 12.5 shows the top and side views of the placement of the lights, explained in more depth in the following sections.

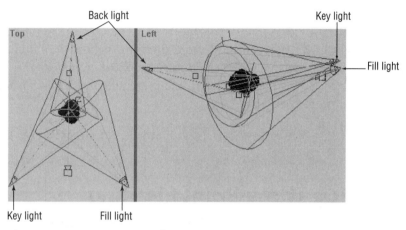

Figure 12.5 *Key light placement, top and side views*

Key Light

A *key* light is the primary light of a particular setup; it's the brightest light and provides the bulk of light for any particular object. Fill and back lights should therefore have lower multiplier values than your key light. A key light is generally placed above the subject and about 45° off the centerline from the camera to the subject, to add depth. The position of the key light may need to be altered based on the number of objects you are lighting, the time of day, whether it is an indoor or outdoor scene, and the mood you're trying to create. You need to experiment to acquire the kind of experience that will help you here. In CG, the key light can also be the sun. You may find that you need more than one light to simulate the sun in your scene.

Fill Light

A *fill* light provides some diffuse light to areas that would be completely dark with only the key light. If you have one key light in the scene illuminating a face, for example, one side of the face will be well lit while the other side will be cast in stark shadow. You want to be able to see the other half of the face, but also keep some of the shadow created by the key light for depth. You use a lower multiplier value (about 40 to 60 percent of the key light) so that you don't wash out the key light, only fill in some shadow areas with light.

The fill light is generally placed lower and opposite to the key light, as you can see in Figure 12.4. Again, you may need to adapt this to fit the needs of your scene. You may need several fill lights.

Back Light

The *back* light, or *kicker*, is generally placed above and behind the object, out of the camera view, as shown in Figure 12.4. Its purpose is to illuminate the top edge or surface of an object, giving the image depth and preventing the lit object from looking like a cutout against the background.

You can examine this three-point lighting setup in `3_point.max` *in the CD files for this chapter.*

Applying Three-Point Lighting

Let's apply a three-point lighting setup, using simple omni lights, to the lamp scene from Chapter 8:

1. Open the `DraftingTable02.max` file you created in Chapter 8 or from the CD files for Chapter 8.

2. Create three omni lights in the top viewport (Create ➜ Lights ➜ Omni): two in the back and one in front.

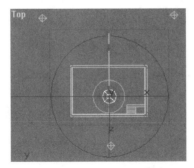

3. For each of these three lights, set the Multiplier to 0.3 and check Ambient Only in the General Parameters rollout.

4. In the left viewport, move these lights up to just below the level of the lamp. Save your file as `DraftingTable03.max`.

You may want to use Draw Region with an ActiveShade viewport to display lighting changes interactively (as you did in Chapter 8 for changes to materials). Note that atmospheric effects do not render in ActiveShade views.

Adding Volume Light Atmospherics

To simulate the light of the lamp, you will use a target spot, to confine the light shed by the lamp to a cone, and then apply a volumetric effect in order to see the cone of light between the light and the table:

1. In the front viewport, click and drag to create a target light pointing down at the table.

2. Position the light in the center of the lamp.

3. In the General Parameters rollout, set the Multiplier to 4.0 and check Cast Shadows.

4. Click the Exclude button. Choose Exclude and then Shadow Casting; then select Lampface01 in the left pane and click the arrow button to move it to the right pane. This prevents the lamp object itself from casting shadows. Click OK.

5. In the Spotlight Parameters rollout, set the Hotspot to 30 and Falloff to 90.

6. In the Atmospheres And Effects rollout, click Add. Choose Volume Light, New, and click OK.

7. Highlight the words Volume Light in the rollout and click the Setup button. This brings up the Rendering ➜ Environment window. In the Volume Light Parameters rollout of this window, set the Density of the fog to 3.0 and Max Light % to 60.0. Close the window.

8. Render the camera view to see the volumetric effect. (You can see the completed render in the Color Gallery of the book.) Save your file as `DraftingTable04.max`.

Zone Lighting

Zone lighting is useful when your character will be moving through a large scene. You create zones of light for the character to move through, with areas of low light providing variety and contrast rather than having a general level of light for a whole scene. This is a bit like spotlighting on a stage; it focuses the attention of your audience in specific areas and can add drama to an unfolding story.

Mood Lighting

You can use lighting to create moods in different ways. You can apply colors or use stark angles, projecting interesting shadows. Consider the story you're telling and how to add drama.

One way to affect mood is through the use of cool and warm lighting. Cool colors are colors that tend toward blue—the colors in the green-blue-violet range. Warm colors are colors that tend toward yellow—the colors in the red-orange-yellow range. Cool colors have been found to slow down viewers' circulation, causing a drop in body temperature, while warm colors stimulate viewers' circulation and a rise in temperature. Consider this when creating peaceful or suspenseful scenes.

Applying Mood Lighting

To look at an example of how lighting can change the mood of the piece, let's try different lighting with the Intrepid Explorer Jim project:

1. Open the `Intrepid_Explorer_Jim14.max` file you created in the last chapter or from the CD files for Chapter 11.

2. Before adding any lights, activate one of your views, press C and choose Camera1_distance. Go to frame 206 and render the scene. This is the scene with just default lighting. (See the "Mood Lighting" plate in the Color Gallery to compare these rendered images.)

3. In the top view, create four omni lights along the tunnel as shown below. Set all the multipliers to 0.5.

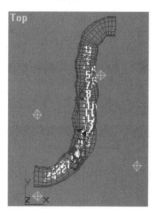

4. Render the scene again. This is completely even lighting. It lights everything and does not contribute to the mood of the scene.

5. Using the light lister, turn off all the omnis you just made and hide them.

6. In the top view, create four new omnis along the tunnel as shown below. Move them up to about chest height. Set all the multipliers to 0.01.

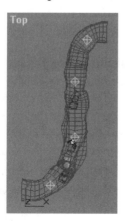

7. Go to frame 0. Zoom in on the torch. Create an omni light to shed the light from the torch and position the light in the flame. Set its multiplier to 1.2 and check Cast Shadows.

8. Click the Exclude button and exclude the torch_flame object from Shadow Casting so that it does not block the light it is supposed to be casting.

9. In Attenuation Parameters, choose Inverse Square decay starting at 0.5m.

10. Link the light to the torch_wood object.

11. Go to frame 206 again and render the camera view. The result is much more dramatic lighting, helping to set the mood of the piece. See the color plates in the Color Gallery to compare the lighting.

12. To make sure that Explorer Jim's hat can be seen in the last shot, make a light that illuminates only the hat. Select omni 4 and rename it omni_hat. Set the Multiplier to 0.97 and set it to include only the hat, and only illumination.

13. Check Use Attenuation and set far attenuation so that the hat falls within the brighter area of the falloff as it falls into the hole. In our example, set Start to about 6 and End to about 8.2.

14. Duplicate omni_hat and name the new light omni_Jim. Set it to include only Intrepid Explorer Jim. Move omni_Jim in front of Jim and down. Set the multiplier to 0.5. Set the far attenuation so that Jim is within the falloff zone when he's part of the way down the hole (frame 252), but not when he's at the top (frame 249). You may want to use the same value for the Start and End attenuation. Save your file as `Intrepid_Explorer_Jim15.max`.

Accent Lighting

Use accent lighting to create the real-world lighting effects needed for specific situations like sconce lighting, neon, or architectural floodlights. For pools of light on a floor or across a table, try using gobos (explained in "Projecting Maps from Lights" earlier this chapter) for faked shadows. If you want to try to simulate the level of ambient bounce light (light reflected between objects) of the real world, you will either have to use hundreds of lights with low multiplier values or get a radiosity renderer such as Lightscape. Radiosity calculates the lighting and colors of bounce light between all your surfaces, as you see in real life. It can create very believable lighting but does take a lot of time to calculate.

Lighting for the Camera

You don't want to spend hours getting all the lights perfect in every room or scene only to have the camera move swiftly through the space without seeing most of it. Leave the lighting and the fine-tuning of scene materials until after the animation and camera movements are correct. Then go back and start adding lights only to those areas that will be seen by the camera. Light only what you see, and make sure your materials and lighting work together to create the style and mood you want. This technique will save you time lighting and will also get you to think about exactly what you want the camera to see.

Using Vertex Colors to Replace Lighting

A technique used in games to reduce the burden of lights on calculating in real time is to simulate shadows on surfaces with vertex colors. You can "paint" your models by assigning colors to different vertices under the Surface Properties rollout of the Vertex sub-object level of an editable mesh. You click the Edit Color swatch and assign a new color.

You can also use the Assign Vertex Color utility to assign vertex colors for you, based on lighting you've already set up. (You can then delete the light.) You need to assign materials to the objects, select them, and check Vertex Colors under Properties. Then open the Assign Vertex Color utility (Utilities ➜ More ➜ Assign Vertex Color) and click the Assign to Selected button. Keep in mind that this will preserve shadows and lighting from one lighting setup only; if a light moves or changes, the shadows will not look right. It's used as a quick fake.

Summary

In this chapter you explored some traditional techniques of artistic rendering and how these relate to max lighting. You learned the features of 3ds max lights; the key settings for each type of light; techniques for using lights in various situations; and the basic three-point lighting setup. You put this into practice by applying a three-point lighting and atmospheric light to a file you made in a previous chapter.

The next chapter covers the Rendering menu. You will explore atmospheric effects in more detail and check out the Render Effects option for lens and filter effects. You will look in detail at different render settings and their results. You will learn how to distribute a render over a network and use the RAM player.

Rendering and Environmental Effects

3ds max

Chapter 13

This chapter presents the 3ds max Rendering menu functions, including the Environment window and atmospheric effects like fog and fire effect. You will learn basic rendering concepts, such as file resolution and output options, as well as more advanced concepts like anti-aliasing filters and motion blur. You will compare the results of different renderers. You will learn how to distribute the rendering of an animated series of images over a network. You will use the RAM player, explore the special effects capabilities of the Render Effects dialog box, and use the new Rendering Elements option. Topics include:

- Understanding rendering
- Environment settings
- Atmospherics (fogs, fire effects, and volume lights)
- Max's rendering tools
- Alternative renderers
- Network rendering
- The RAM player
- Applying Render Effects
- Rendering elements

Understanding Rendering

You have been learning about rendering since the very first chapter, in progressive depth and detail. As you've learned, *rendering* means the representation of three-dimensional information in two dimensions. The question asked by the renderer at render time is, "What color is the scene at this pixel?" This means calculating what objects are in the view of the camera, the effect of material settings on surfaces, and the effect of lighting and other applied effects—all evaluated for each pixel for the rendered image. When you click Render, the renderer converts the information of your scene into the two-dimensional arrays of pixels that are your initial output. This output can be a final product or can be used in post-production as part of a composite of multiple pieces in a final render.

The renderer works in several passes: a pre-render pass (which calculates things like the bitmaps for shadow-mapped shadows), a render pass, and a post-render pass that alters pixels to create effects such as fog and lens effects.

The viewport image is created by a separate renderer, called the *interactive renderer*, using simple shading (such as Gouraud) or no shading in order to maintain real-time performance. The scanline renderer is used in the sample slots of the Material Editor and when you render out your final image. It is also possible to use plug-in renderers within max. In this chapter, "the renderer" means the default scanline renderer.

Creating Environments

The Environment window (Rendering ➜ Environment) provides tools to create the ambience of your scene by affecting the global lighting, setting a background image, and adding fogs, fires, and moody lighting effects.

It may seem odd at first that environmental attributes like fog and ambient light fall within the topic of rendering; after all, using dry ice to make a real fog isn't considered the job of the person who develops the film. It helps to remember again what is happening in a 3D program: information fed to the program is being translated into an arrangement of colored pixels. In CG, ambient light is a shift in the color value of all the rendered pixels; a fire effect or a fog is a shift in the color value of the pixels within the range designated by its parameters.

You encountered the Environment window when you added a volumetric effect to a light and clicked Setup in Chapter 12. Like the Render Scene dialog window, this window is modeless, so you can continue to work on your scene while it is open.

Adding an Environment Background

Using an environment background in your scene is one way of compositing within max. In Chapter 14, you will composite foreground and background plates in a post-production process. By applying a map to the Environment Map button in the Environment window, you can composite the foreground scene against the environment background, also called a *backplate* in your initial render. You could, for example, shoot a character dancing against a backplate of live-action video by loading the digitized video as an environment background.

Make sure you check Use Map so that the environment map is applied.

In Chapter 8, you loaded a viewport background in order to see your perspective lines while modeling in the camera mapping tutorial. You also used a map of the sky as the environment background. Viewport backgrounds are not the same as environment backgrounds, although you can display the environment background in the viewport if you choose. An environment background will render with your scene, whether or not it is displayed in the viewport. If you render an alpha channel, the environment is excluded from that channel, just as a plain background is.

Changing the Environment Mapping

To alter the tiling, coordinates, or mapping type of your environment map, drag it from the Environment Map button to an empty slot in the Material Editor and choose Instance. You can then edit your environment within the Material Editor.

You could also create your map in the Material Editor and drag it to the Environment Map button as an instance. Keep in mind that the Environment Map button will only recognize a map, *not a* material; *the difference between materials and maps is covered in Chapter 7.*

Setting the Global Lighting

The Environment dialog window also has settings to control the global lighting parameters of Tint, Level, and Ambient Light.

The Tint color swatch brings up a standard color picker where you can shift the color values of the lighting in the scene. This is an additive effect, so if you have a blue or a red light in the scene, the tint color is added to the individual light color. Effects of lights in general are added to the diffuse, ambient, and other components of your materials.

Level controls the amount of light in the scene. Raising the level of the light greater than 1.0 is equivalent to raising each light's multiplier value by the same amount.

Ambient Light controls the amount of the base level of light in the scene. In real life, ambient light is the myriad bounced light rays that make objects visible even in low-light situations. This is why when you turn off all the lights in a room, your eyes adjust after a few minutes and you are able to see again—light is not *totally* absent. In CG, you aren't calculating actual ambient light sources and bounces; you are setting a baseline grayscale value for your pixels.

To make your scene "pop" or have extra richness, change the ambient light RGB levels to zero (from the default of 11,11,11). This makes the corners or nooks become a little darker and thus richer in color and depth.

Creating Atmospheres

The phrase "creating atmospheres" is an appropriate pun in CG. You create atmospherics to simulate real-life atmospheric properties like clouds or fog; and you create atmospherics to add a certain ambience or mood to a scene.

All atmospherics amount to the same thing: a shift in color value of the pixels. A volume light is essentially a fog applied to the cone or cylinder of a spot or direct light. A fire effect is essentially a colored fog with some noise parameters designed to emulate different types of flame. The trick is to play with the various parameters of the atmospherics, especially the noise parameters, to create the exact effect, look, or mood you want.

For example, say your shot calls for a clandestine meeting between a dark villain and its cohorts at a wharf on a foggy night. What images come to mind? Dark skies, rolling fog, overhead lights throwing streams of light downward creating pools of light on the docks. These kinds of effects can be simulated with atmospherics. You saw the Atmosphere rollout in Chapter 12 when you added a volume light from the light panel and clicked Setup. You can add volume lights and other atmospherics directly from this rollout by clicking the Add button and selecting a type from the dialog box.

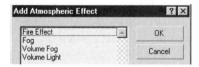

The atmospherics shown in the dialog box are the standard ones that come with max. If you install other atmospheric plug-ins, they will also be available here. Fire effect and volume fog require an atmospheric apparatus, a helper object that contains the atmosphere, defining its extents. For a volume light, the lit area—as defined by the hot spot, falloff, and attenuation settings—determines the extent of the volumetric effect. The extent of regular fog is defined either relative to a camera or through the upper and lower limits of a layer.

Atmospheric effects are calculated at render time, and only when a camera or perspective view is rendered.

If you are stumped as to why your atmosphere won't render, make sure you aren't rendering an orthographic or axonometric user view. Also check that you have Atmospherics checked in the Render dialog box.

Fog

Atmospherics provide you with the ability to generate effects such as a smoke-filled room, a foggy day, or a hanging haze. Choose Fog from the Add Atmosphere window and choose Standard or Layered.

Standard Fog

Standard Fog is defined by the Environment Range settings of the camera you are rendering. Near % sets the density of the fog at the Near Range of the camera, and Far % sets the density at the Far Range. The fog gets thicker the farther it is from the camera, within these parameters. The Exponential setting on standard fog increases the fog density exponentially with distance, rather than linearly. This is usually not what you want. This setting is designed only for rendering transparent objects in a fog.

If you are combining fog with flat opacity maps that are faking geometry, try using a Blend material or a Mix map instead. Blend between the landscape and the fog color with a Falloff map set to the Distance Blend option. Atmospheric fog will turn the transparent parts of the objects white.

Layered Fog

Layered Fog, as its name suggests, is fog parallel to the ground plane. Use this for effects such as dense fog hugging the ground or morning fog low on a lake. A layered fog is defined by the straightforward Top and Bottom settings as well as the Density of the fog between the two heights. You can add more than one layered fog to a scene.

Falloff allows you to fade the density in from zero at the top or the bottom, or to not fade either boundary. Horizon Noise erases back from the horizon line, which gives the effect a feathered edge rather than a very hard, unfoglike edge. Size determines the size of the tendrils of fog made by applying the noise. Angle is the number of degrees below the horizon line that the edge of the fog is feathered to. Phase is for animating the noise: increasing Phase causes the tendrils to move upward; decreasing it moves tendrils downward.

Fog Color and Mapping

You can apply color, a color map, or an opacity map (or combinations of these) to both standard and layered fogs. Since fog shifts the value of the pixels within their parameters, the Fog Color swatch simply shifts the pixels toward another color rather than white. For example, you might use a bluish fog to simulate aerial perspective or an underwater scene. Fog Background applies the fog to the background. The Environment Color Map shifts the pixels' colors toward the colors of a bitmap or procedural map. The Environment Opacity Map shifts the density of the fog effect according to the grayscale values of the map. Both of these maps can also be edited and animated as instances in the Material Editor, as with any other map.

Remember to check Use Map on the maps you apply to your fogs.

Volume Fog

Volume Fog is the same effect as other fogs, except that you define its extent by an atmospheric apparatus (also called an *atmospheric gizmo*), which must be created separately. Drag a gizmo of the appropriate shape (box, cylinder, or sphere) in the viewport (Create ➜ Helpers ➜ Atmospheric Apparatus). In the Environment window, add a Volume Fog, click Pick Gizmo, and pick the atmospheric apparatus in the viewport. The option Soften Gizmo Edges feathers the edges of the fog volume.

In the Volume section of the rollout, Color, Fog Background, Exponential, and Density have the same effect as on a regular fog. Step Size determines the grain of the fog, with a large size being coarser and more likely to be aliased. Max Steps sets a maximum limit for fog sampling, in order to limit render time. In the Noise section of the rollout, you can choose different types of noise to apply to your volume of fog. Noise helps simulate real-world conditions like variations in density, slight wind, or churning.

You can apply your Volume Fog parameters to more than one gizmo in your scene.

Volume Light

Volumetric lights, called Volume Lights in max, are lights that reveal "air" as light passes through them, the way tiny dust particles do in real life. You can use them to create sunlight streaking through a window, a lighthouse beacon on a foggy night, or even sun-like coronas on omni lights. You used a volume light in Chapter 12 to illuminate the cone of light of the lamp.

Like all atmospheric effects, volume lights require considerable processing and increase rendering times significantly. (But they look great!)

In addition to adding the volume light effect in the Modify panel of a light object, you can apply the volumetric effect to a light by clicking Pick Light in the Environment window and then clicking the light. You can apply the same Volume Light settings to more than one light. Just click Pick Light again and pick another light in the scene. To remove the effect from a light, select the light and click Remove Light.

Many of the fog settings for volume light are the same as options you have seen before and work the same way. Attenuation Color allows you to blend gradually from the fog color to the attenuation color in the attenuation ranges of the light. (You must also check Use Attenuation Color.) Atten(uation) Mult(iplier) sets the intensity of the attenuation color. Max Light % sets the maximum glow for the light. Min Light % should usually be zero; it sets the amount of the fog color to be applied outside the light. Filter Shadows determines the quality of shadows in the fog generated when an object passes between the camera and volumetric light. It is this feature that makes the volume light effect so convincing.

Test-render with Filter Shadows set to Low for quicker rendering. Reset to Use Light Smp Range or High for final rendering, but be prepared for render time to triple (or more).

Sample Volume % sets the sample rate of the volume. Attenuation Start % starts the attenuation of the fog at a percentage of the light object's original attenuation; a setting of 80, for example, would start the fog attenuating 20 percent closer to the light than the attenuation of the light starts. Inversely, End % ends the fog's attenuation at a percentage of the light object's. The noise settings for volume lights are very similar to those for volume fogs, except Link to Light, which uses the light's coordinates, rather than the world, as a base for the noise. You generally want to use some noise to break up the density or to add subtle motion.

Fire Effect

The Fire Effect option on the Atmosphere rollout simulates an explosive fireball or licking flames. You can also use it to create smoke and cloud effects. Like Volume Fog, Fire Effect requires an atmospheric apparatus as a gizmo to define its extents. You then click Pick Gizmo to assign the effect to your chosen volume (or volumes).

The Color swatches allow you to select an inner color, outer color, and smoke color. The inner color is where the effect is most intense, comparable to the hottest part of a flame; for cooler areas where the effect is falling off, the outer color is used. The smoke color applies if you check Explosion and then choose Smoke in the Explosion section of the rollout.

The Shape section of the rollout allows you to choose a tendril or fireball shape. Fireballs are more round and puffy; tendrils are directional flames along the local Z axis of the atmospheric gizmo. Long atmospheric gizmos, like elongated boxes or non-uniformly-scaled spheres, lend themselves better to tendril-like effects. Stretch stretches flames along the local Z of the gizmo and can also give an oval shape to a fireball. Regularity determines how much the effect fills the gizmo; a value of 1.0 fills the gizmo completely, while lower values have more irregular shapes that don't reach the gizmo's edges.

The Characteristics section gives you parameters for adjusting the effects within the gizmo. Flame Detail controls the sharpness of the change between the two colors in each flame. The Samples value sets the sampling rate for calculating the effect; a higher Samples value is more accurate but takes much longer to render. The Motion section gives you the ability to animate the agitation and rising of the flames, affecting how quickly they redevelop and how far within the gizmo they travel. The Explosion section allows you to create a beginning and an end to the effect, with or without subsequent smoke. This allows you to simulate violent explosions.

Using max's Rendering Tools

The renderer that ships with max is the Default Scanline A-Buffer renderer, otherwise known as the *scanline renderer* or simply "the renderer." You can also plug in other renderers such as mental ray and Illustrate. This section covers the settings for the scanline renderer. In "Alternative Renderers" later this chapter, you will take a glimpse at other renderers available for max.

Invoking the Renderer

You can invoke the renderer by choosing Rendering ➡ Render or by using the buttons on the main toolbar that you learned about in Chapter 3. The Render Type drop-down list allows you to choose how much of a view to render.

The Render Scene button (or the Shift+R keyboard shortcut) brings up the full Render dialog window.

Render Last (Shift+E) renders the last rendered viewport with the most recent render settings.

Quick Render (Shift+Q) renders the active viewport with the Draft, Production, or ActiveShade render settings.

Using the Virtual Frame Buffer

The *Virtual Frame Buffer*, or VFB, is the window in which your renderings appear. It is also used to display the last rendered image, to display single images when you use View File from the File menu, and to display images in the File Selector dialog box when you click View. You've used the Virtual Frame Buffer in previous chapters, but let's look at it in more detail. Table 13.1 describes the tools in the VFB.

Ctrl+I (the letter "i") brings up the last rendered image in the VFB.

Table 13.1 Tools on the Virtual Frame Buffer Toolbar

ICON	NAME	DESCRIPTION
	Save image	Saves single image (in buffer) to disk, even if you didn't check Save File in the Rendering dialog box.
	Clone Virtual Frame Buffer	Makes duplicate VFB of last rendered image.
	RGB channel toggles	Displays color information for selected channel.
	Display Alpha Channel toggle	Displays just the alpha channel.
	Monochrome toggle	Displays image in grayscale.
	Clear Buffer	Erases image.
RGB Alpha / RGB Alpha / Z / Material Effects / Object / UV Coordinates / Normal	View Channel drop-down	Displays additional grayscale channels when available (as in multi-channel file formats like RLA).
(color swatch)	Selected color swatch	Copies the pixel color where you right-click the image.

When you clone the VFB, the first VFB is overwritten when you next render, while the cloned VFB remains. This is handy for comparing images.

If you hold the Ctrl key, you can zoom into the image in the VFB by clicking and zoom out by right-clicking. The eyedropper tool (right-clicking) also brings up an information display that gives you the RGB values of the pixel as well as information about the image as a whole. This can be useful when viewing bitmaps before applying them.

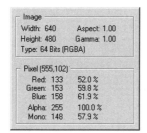

Preview Rendering

Sometimes you want to see a quick render of your animation during the work process without waiting for a full render. One option is to choose Make a Preview from the Rendering menu. This uses the interactive viewport renderer for every frame to quickly create a preview file for real-time playback, but this means that only viewport Rendering Levels are available in the drop-down list (Smooth + Highlights, Smooth, Facets + Highlights, Facets, Lit Wireframes, Wireframes, Bounding Box).

The rest of the Make Preview window is fairly straightforward. Image Size allows you to set the percentage of the current render resolution setting you want to render for your preview. You can also filter types of objects for the render to further speed rendering. If you accept default AVI output, the preview will be opened in the Windows Media Player and played as soon as the preview is complete. Max automatically names this preview `_scene.avi`. You can rename the file by choosing Rename Preview from the Rendering menu. If you choose Custom File Type output, clicking Create brings up a dialog box to choose the file type and name the file. (In this case, view your preview using File ➜ View Image File.)

Choosing Your Render Settings

Rendering is more than just producing an output from a scene file; it is the final bit of control you have before all the information of your scene is committed to pixels. It is like having the film of your movie developed. Think of rendering as the presentation and packaging of your project. You wouldn't take a special gift that you've spent a long time selecting and wrap it in newspaper; you wouldn't wear a dirty T-shirt and jeans to an important job interview; and you want to put some care into the rendering of your animation.

To give your rendering the best presentation, you have to know what effect the various settings have on the end product. This section covers the settings in the max Render Scene dialog box. Let's start with the options at the bottom of the window frame, the ones you always see, no matter which rollouts are open.

Viewport

Use the Viewport option to select which view to render. It consists of a drop-down list of the viewports in your scene, with the active viewport as default. A view has to be in a viewport to be rendered; you can't render a camera that is not given a camera viewport, for example. (You can render any camera from Video Post, however, as you will see in Chapter 14.)

It's a good idea to always check the Viewport setting, just in case. Waiting several hours for a render of the wrong view can be demoralizing.

Production and Draft Renderings

The other choice available in this area of the Render Scene dialog box is the Production, Draft, or ActiveShade radio button. You can use this to assign three different sets of settings. You can switch back and forth among the sets without having to change each setting individually. This is not a "mutually exclusive" radio button in the usual Windows sense. You make your selections for Production while the Production radio button is active, those for Draft with Draft active, and those for ActiveShade with ActiveShade active; max remembers all three set-ups. The Quick Render flyout on the main toolbar contain buttons for Production, Draft, or ActiveShade rendering settings.

Before your final render, the main reason you will use the Render dialog box is to set up test renderings. During this stage of the process you may be concerned with resolution and anti-aliasing filters, and you may be experimenting with many different settings. Or you may be checking animation and not want to render time-consuming things like atmospherics. You probably will not want the renders to be full size. Make these settings on the Draft side. When it comes to the final render, you may be more concerned with pixel size or motion blur, and you will probably want to lock down the settings you discovered in the iterative phase. Make these settings on the Production side.

Use the Production render settings for high-res final work and the Draft render settings for low-res test rendering and experimentation.

Plug-in renderers are another reason you might use the Production/Draft settings. In the Current Renderers rollout, you can assign an available renderer to the Production, Draft, or ActiveShade setting. Then, in the Render dialog box, you can use the Copy Render Params button (the double-headed arrow button next to the radio buttons) to copy the settings between the Production and Draft renderers. You can then switch between your renderers, while using the same settings, by using the radio button or the Quick Render flyout buttons.

Be careful that you don't accidentally *copy settings between Draft and Production settings when only using one renderer.*

The Common Parameters Rollout

Within the scrollable main body of the Render Scene dialog box are four rollouts. The Common Parameters rollout has the basic render settings explained in this section. The Render Elements rollout is explained in "Rendering Elements" later this chapter, the Current Renderers rollout was explained in the previous section, and the MAX Default Scanline A-Buffer rollout is explained in "The Scanline Renderer Rollout" later this chapter. If you have a plug-in renderer loaded, additional rollouts may be available as well.

Let's start with the parameters held in common with all renderers.

Time Output

The Time Output section is where you specify how much of your animation you choose to render: a single frame, a range of frames, the whole project, or just the active time segment. Render nonsequential frames by separating the frame numbers by commas. Use a hyphen to define the endpoints of a range of frames.

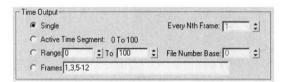

Two additional options are rendering with Every Nth Frame or File Number Base, which are enabled when rendering a time range. Every Nth Frame allows you to skip frames in a sequence. For example, if you are rendering frames 0 to 10 and you render every 2 frames, you will render frames 0, 2, 4, 6, 8, and 10. This is useful for doing quick check renders and special batch renders.

If you are rendering one scene on multiple machines that are not set up for network rendering (discussed later in this chapter), try staggering the starting frame and rendering with Nth frame set to the number of machines. For example, with four machines rendering 900 frames, you would render every fourth frame on each one: frame 0 to 900 on one, 1 to 900 on the next, 2 to 900 on the third, and 3 to 900 on the last. This will ensure that you can view the entire sequence, even if one of the machines fails and every fourth frame is dropped.

File Number Base is for rendering a series of single frames with the filename numbers offset by a given number. For example, if you want to render frames 0–100 but need the filename numbers to start at frame 15 (to merge with another 15-frame trailer, perhaps), set the File Number Base to 15. When the first frame is rendered, it will be named 0015.

You can also use File Number Base to render something in reverse. If you have 100 frames you need rendered backward, set File Number Base to −100. Your sequential files will be reversed in order.

Output Size

The Output Size section is also fairly straightforward, specifying the pixel dimensions of the rendered image. The default is the Custom size option, with the standard preset buttons to the right.

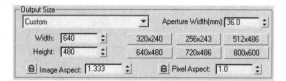

The drop-down list offers many other preset sizes. The main difference between using the Custom output size and using these presets is that Custom has the option of setting a camera aperture width, while the aperture width of the presets is defined by the format type. Table 13.2 describes the use of the various aspect ratios, along with their aperture width.

Table 13.2 Uses of Output Size Options

Output Size	Use
Custom	Standard presets or user-defined; user-defined aperture width
35mm 1.33:1 Full Aperture (cine)	Motion picture film; 24mm aperture
35mm 1.37:1 Academy (cine), 35mm 1.66:1 (cine), 35mm 1.75:1 (cine), 35mm 1.85:1 (cine)	Motion picture film; 20.955mm aperture
35mm Anamorphic (2.35:1) (Squeezed)	Motion picture film, 70mm intended playback shot on 35mm and stretched; 42.57mm aperture
70mm Panavision (cine)	Motion picture film; 48.59mm aperture
70mm IMAX (cine)	IMAX film; 48.59mm aperture
VistaVision	Wide-angle cinematography; 37.719mm aperture
35mm (24mm×36mm) (slide)	Slide film, print graphics; 34.2mm aperture
6cm× 6cm (2 1/4″ × 2 1/4″) (slide)	Slide film, print graphics; 51.6mm aperture
4″ × 5″ or 8″ × 10″ (slide)	Stills or print film; 88.9mm aperture
NTSC	N. America and Chilé broadcast and industrial video; 20.12mm aperture; pixel aspect 0.900
PAL	European broadcast and industrial video; 20.12mm aperture; pixel aspect 1.067
HDTV	High-definition television; 20.12mm aperture

Options

The Options section of the rollout consists of eight check boxes that enable or disable certain options during rendering.

Video Color Check replaces any non-NTSC colors with black in the rendering. Force 2-Sided renders both sides of surfaces, whether or not you have assigned a 2-Sided or Double Sided material. Atmospherics, Effects, and Displacement simply turns on or off the rendering for the atmospherics, Render Effects, or displacement maps you have added to the scene. Super Black is used for compositing to render the background as a pure black and the darkest areas of the foreground a less pure black. Render Hidden renders hidden objects. Render to Fields renders to the two separate fields per frame needed for video.

Render Output

The Render Output section is where you choose the type of file output, the name, and the destination of your file. Click the Files button to bring up the Render Output File dialog box; from the Save as Type drop-down list, choose one of the file output options explained in Table 13.3. You can use all of these file types with animations, but with a still-image file type, you will be outputting a series of stills rather than one movie file. The series will be sequentially numbered (starting with `filename0000`) for easy transfer into Video Post or an external editing or compositing program.

When choosing a file format, consider whether you need an alpha channel. Alpha channels store the transparency information of the pixels for use in compositing. (See Chapter 7 for a detailed explanation of alpha channels.) File formats with a fourth 8-bit channel (described as *32-bit* formats) give you the ability to store an alpha channel. Some formats allow 16 bits per channel, and some allow you to store an alpha channel with less than 24 bits of color information, so your file format may actually be more or less than 32-bit with its alpha channel.

If you want a single movie file with an alpha channel, your only option is a QuickTime movie. Select Animation, Planar RGB, TGA, TIFF, or None for your compressor, and change your color setting to Millions Of Colors+ in the Compression Setup dialog box. Compression is discussed in more detail in the next section of this chapter.

Table 13.3 Output File Formats Available in max

FORMAT	EXTENSION(S)	DESCRIPTION
AVI (Windows Media Player movie)	`.avi`	24-bit, animated
BMP Image (Windows bitmap)	`.bmp`	8- or 24-bit, still image
Kodak Cineon	`.cin`	24-bit still image with printing density options
Encapsulated PostScript	`.eps, .ps`	Encoded still image for PostScript printers
Autodesk Flic Image	`.flc, .fli, .cel`	8-bit, animated
JPEG (Joint Photographic Experts Group)	`.jpg`	Compressed still image
PNG (Portable Network Graphics)	`.png`	8-, 16-, 24-, or 48-bit color plus alpha channel option and interlace option, still image
MOV QuickTime movie	`.mov`	24 or 32-bit with alpha channel, animated
SGI's Image File Format	`.rgb`	8- or 16-bit color plus alpha channel, still image
RLA Image (Run-length encoded version A)	`.rla`	8 or 16 bits per channel, plus alpha and 8 other optional channels, including Z-Depth, still image
RPF Image (Rich Pixel Format)	`.rpf`	8 or 16 bits per channel plus alpha and 12 other optional channels, including all RLA channels and Transparency and Velocity, still image
Targa Image	`.tga`	16-, 24-. or 32-bit with alpha channel, still image
TIF (Tagged Image File Format)	`.tif`	8-bit grayscale or 24-bit color, still image

If you need to use Z-buffer information to take into discreet combustion for 3D compositing, for example, you will need to use a format like RLA. RLA files store extra 8-bit grayscale channels of information, including 3D information like Z depth. This allows for advanced compositing. Remember that the rendering still creates two-dimensional arrays of pixels. An RLA file with a Z-depth channel simply has an additional 8 bits of information that describe each pixel in terms of its distance from the camera. RLA channels are also supported by Adobe After Effects 4.1. RPF files are recognized only by Video Post and combustion.

After choosing your file type, choosing the save location, and typing in your file name, you can click the Save button to return to the Render dialog box with your file output set.

Be sure that Save File is checked, *especially for an animation. Nothing is worse than waiting for a long rendering only to discover that the hours of painstaking work rendered by your processors were not saved to disk. (Only the last frame will remain in the Virtual Frame Buffer.)*

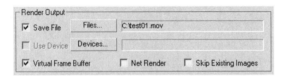

The final settings in the Render Output section are the three check boxes at the bottom. Virtual Frame Buffer renders the frame to the VFB as well as to your saved file. (If it is unchecked, you will have to open the file with File ➜ View File to see your file.) Uncheck the Virtual Frame Buffer box when rendering long animations. Rendering frames takes longer with VFB checked; the time saved per frame may be negligible, but over hundreds of frames it can add up.

The "Network Rendering" section later in this chapter covers the Net Render option in detail.

Skip Existing Images will skip images in your sequence that have already been rendered. As described in "Time Output" earlier, you can break up a rendering using the Nth frame technique in case one of the renders failed. If one did, in fact, fail, you would be missing a quarter of your frames. To quickly render just the missing frames, use the Skip Existing Frames feature. Max will look for breaks in the numerical sequence and render only the missing files.

Video Compression

If you choose an AVI or QuickTime movie file and click the Save button, you will bring up the Compression Settings dialog box. This gives you options for compressing your video to a more compact file size for storage, but more importantly, for better playback on various computers.

If your output is going to be used in a compositing program to create special visual effects, and you have space on your hard drive, use Animation compression or even None. Compression can create artifacts when altering the pixels for the effect, and you will be compressing again after your compositing work.

Video is compressed both spatially (as a still image file is compressed) and temporally, between frames. You need to know what you intend to do with your output in order to estimate the data rate that will be available for playback. For instance, for a 4X CD, your data rate needs to be limited to 350KB/sec. But if you want your video to play back well on a 56Kb modem, your data rate needs to be limited to about 3.5KB/sec. (Data rates, especially as given for internet connections, are often given in *bits*—abbreviated to a small "b"—so you need to divide by 8 to get it in *bytes*—abbreviated to a capital "B" (8 bits = 1 Byte). Keep in mind that you also need to use a figure that is about half of the theoretical data rate.) The first step in finding out your compression needs is to figure out the uncompressed data rate of your file with this formula:

(Resolution of Movie) × (Bit Depth of File in Bytes) × (Frame Rate) = Uncompressed Data Rate

For example, an uncompressed 320 × 240 file with 24 bits/pixel animated at 30 frames/sec is feeding data to the processor at a rate of 320 × 240 pixels per frame, times 3 bytes per pixel, times 30 frames per second, or about 7 MB/sec.

From your uncompressed data rate, you can figure out the compression ratio you need, based on your playback needs. Use this to determine the compression *codec* (the compression-decompression algorithm) and the quality and keyframe settings required to bring your file down to the size you need. (A keyframe for a codec means how many frames you are compressing temporally.) You may need to play with the settings on small pieces of video to see what kind of compression ratio you're getting (by comparing the file size with and without compression). With Sorensen compression for QuickTime, you have the option to set a data rate limit instead. As with any kind of compression, a loss in quality is the price you pay for smaller file size, but keep in mind that if your file is too big for the playback data rate, your video will skip frames and "chunk" along as it plays. This doesn't exactly make for a high-quality experience, either. Table 13.4 shows the video compression codecs available within max, if you have QuickTime installed.

If you are making video for the Web, it is probably worth the investment to get Media Cleaner Pro, which has many more settings for controlling how compression is performed.

Table 13.4 Available Compressors for QuickTime and AVI Movies

QUICKTIME	AVI
Animation	Cinepak Codec by Radius
BMP	Intel Indeo Video R.2
Cinepak	Microsoft Video 1
Component Video	Indeo video 5.10
DV - NTSC	Microsoft MPEG-4 Video Codec V2
DV - PAL	Microsoft MPEG-4 Video Codec V1
Graphics	Full Frames (Uncompressed)
H.261	
H.263	
Intel Indeo Video 4.4	
Motion JPEG A	
Motion JPEG B	
Photo - JPEG	
Planar RGB	
PNG	
Sorenson Video	
TGA	
TIFF	
Video	

The Scanline Renderer Rollout

You have to scroll down the Render dialog box to get to the second rollout (or right-click and navigate to the rollout). This rollout is for settings specific to the renderer. If you use a plug-in renderer, this rollout will have different parameters. This section covers the settings for the default scanline renderer.

Options

The four check boxes in the Options section are self-explanatory. The first three allow you to turn on and off the rendering of Mapping, Shadows, and Auto Reflect/Refract and Mirrors. Force Wireframe will render everything in the scene in wireframe, with a wire thickness you specify in pixels.

Anti-Aliasing Filters

Unlike some 3D programs, max ships without all its bells and whistles turned on, so that beginning users can have fast rendering available without knowing about advanced settings. (Supersampling has to be turned on, for example.) Using different anti-aliasing filters significantly extends the range of rendering qualities and styles available. Each anti-aliasing filter creates a different look and feel for your rendered image. Study these filters carefully and experiment with them. This is an important tool for polishing your rendering by getting the exact look you are after. Table 13.5 describes the use of each filter. The "Anti-Aliasing" plate in the Color Gallery shows renderings of the same max file with three different anti-aliasing settings.

Table 13.5 Attributes of the Anti-Aliasing Filters

FILTER	USE
Area	General sharpen or blur, with a variable-size filter area; this was the original max anti-aliasing filter. (An example of this filter is shown in the Color Gallery.)
Blackman	Sharpen image without edge enhancement, with a 25-pixel filter area.
Blend	Blur with very subtle edge control by blending blurring and sharpening filters at a specified ratio, with a variable-size filter area; can create effects, equivalent to Vaseline on a camera lens, used in film. (An example of this filter is shown in the Color Gallery.)
Catmull Rom	Edge enhancement for creating extremely crisp edges, with a 25-pixel filter area. (An example of this filter is shown in the Color Gallery.)
Cook Variable	General-purpose sharpen or blur, with variable size filter area; Filter Size set above 2.5 blurs.

Table 13.5 Attributes of the Anti-Aliasing Filters *(continued)*

FILTER	USE
Cubic	"Cubic spline" blurring, with a 25-pixel filter area.
Mitchell-Netravali	Uses parameters of blur and ringing to compute anti-aliasing; good for metal reflectivity; decrease blur and increase ringing to bring out detail.
Plate Match/Max R2	Matches camera-mapped, screen-mapped, or matte\shadow material to background image, with a variable-size filter area; seamlessly anti-aliases objects directly onto backplate.
Quadratic	"Quadratic spline" blurring, with a 9-pixel filter area.
Sharp Quadratic	"Quadratic spline" sharpening, with a 9-pixel filter area.
Soften	Gaussian blur, with a variable size filter area.
Video	Blurring slightly for videotape (NTSC or PAL), with a 25-pixel filter area; the effect is not very noticeable when you render, but makes a huge difference when output to video.

The Anti-Aliasing check box turns the anti-aliasing filter on or off. The Filter Maps check box turns the filtering of maps on or off. You would uncheck these in your Draft settings to speed up rendering for test renders.

Global Supersampling

Supersampling is an additional anti-aliasing pass completed at render time to smooth out inconsistencies in the anti-aliasing. It is not calculated at all if anti-aliasing is turned off. With supersampling off, the center of the area represented by the pixel determines the color of the pixel, which can result in jagged aliasing. With supersampling on, the area in and around the pixel is sampled at a certain rate to calculate the pixel color that will best reduce aliasing in the area.

As you learned in Chapter 8, you choose a supersampler and enable it in the Super-Sampling rollout of a material. Checking the Disable All Samplers option turns off supersampling in all materials.

Disable supersampling for test renders to speed up your render; supersampling can drastically increase render time.

Limiting the Color Range

The *Color Range Limiting* option prevents colors from becoming too bright and "blowing out" because of the additive properties of the different color attributes. It also prevents the less common problem of colors being out of range in a negative direction. There are two options: Clamp and Scale. Clamp cuts off any values that fall out of range. In this method, colors that are too bright might wash out or become white. Scale retains the hue information but scales the grayscale value up or down to comply with the ranges. This can cause your Specular highlights to look odd. (It's better to adjust your lighting to avoid out-of-range colors, if possible.)

Object Motion Blur

Object Motion Blur is the simulation of blur without actually blurring pixels. It is set per object in Object Properties. When you apply Object Motion Blur globally (by checking Apply), max renders the object at a sub-frame sampling rate (up to 16 per frame) and offsets the images in the direction the object is moving, creating a "trail" of images. The Duration Subdivision setting represents the number of time intervals the frame is broken into; Samples is the number of these intervals that are sampled. For a very even trail, the Samples value should equal the Duration Subdivision value. For a coarser, more randomized trail, set Samples less than Duration Subdivision. Duration is the number of frames the image is held for. Object motion blur substantially increases render time.

Image Motion Blur

Like Object Motion Blur, the *Image Motion Blur* setting is also assigned to objects in Object Properties. If Apply is unchecked in the Render Scene dialog box, the Motion Blur will not be applied. Image Motion Blur blurs the pixels rather than superimposing a series of images. It is a post-process blur added after the regular render pass. Duration sets the length of the blur. Apply To Environment Map will blur the environment background when the camera moves. Image Motion Blur will not work with objects whose geometry changes over time or those with displacement maps.

Image Motion Blur is generally preferable to Object Motion Blur, creating an effect more similar to an actual camera motion blur.

Auto Reflect/Refract Maps

This setting controls the quality of auto reflection/refraction maps. A higher number will definitely give you a better reflection; it will also significantly increase render time.

Render Statistics

While you are rendering, a status box displays information about your render, including the estimated time remaining to complete the render. This can give you a general idea of how long the animation may take to render. Depending on the relative rendering requirements of different parts of your animation, however, it may be far from accurate. If you check File → Summary Info after the rendering is complete, you can find out how much time it took to complete your last render.

Alternative Renderers

As mentioned earlier, using max does not limit you to the default renderer. There are many ways to calculate raster data (pixels) from vector information (mathematics). In fact, mathematicians and computer scientists continually work toward ever-better "rendering models" for CG images, based on various assumptions about optical phenomenon and simplifications of the natural world. Trying to simulate light in a computer is no easy task; when it is done well, renderings can seem like magic.

As you read this section, you'll want to refer to the "Alternative Renderers" color pages to see the "Cornell Box" illustration for each different renderer. As explained in Chapter 8, a Cornell box is a cube with one red and one blue wall (the other three planar surfaces are white). A chrome sphere is in the back, while a glass sphere is in the front, with one light source. Since all the Cornell boxes have the same geometry, materials and light, this provides a good way to compare renderers.

The Default Scanline Renderer

The renderer that comes with max is called the *default scanline renderer*. The scanline renderer is used in the Material Editor to display materials and maps in its sample slots and is used by default to render a scene. The chief advantage to the scanline renderer is that it is fast compared to higher-quality renderers. (The interactive renderer used to render the viewports is much faster than the scanline renderer in order to maintain real-time response.) As the name suggests, the scanline renderer scans the scene and renders it as a series of horizontal lines. You can watch this in the Virtual Frame Buffer as max renders a frame from the top to the bottom, line-by-line.

The main disadvantage to the scanline renderer is that its results do not look very realistic. The scanline renderer approximates the reflection of light between objects (also called *diffuse inter-reflection*, *global illumination*, or *radiosity*) very roughly using the ambient color. The mental ray, Arnold, and Lightscape renderers all compute global illumination much more accurately, creating more realistic images. The mental ray and Lightscape renderers are explained in the following sections, and sample renders can be found in the Color Section.

The max Raytrace Renderer

Kinetix (now discreet) licensed the Raytrace renderer from Blur Studio in 1997 and made it part of max. This rendering engine now works within the scanline renderer as the Raytrace material and map. (Chapter 8 covers raytracing in depth.)

Blur Studio is always coming up with interesting technology for max; check out what they are up to at http://www.blur.com. *They are currently working on a new renderer that looks promising. Go to their* blurbeta *directory to download free experimental plug-ins.*

Raytracing is good for simulating reflection and refraction of light through materials. If you compare the Cornell boxes with scanline and raytrace rendering in the Color Gallery, you will see a big difference. The Raytracing algorithm traces each light ray back from the viewing plane, through various reflections or refractions, to its light source. These extra calculations take time, sometimes significantly increasing rendering time. In order to limit the number of calculations the renderer has to perform, raytracing does not consider light rays that never hit the viewing plane. The number of calculations required to trace every ray emitted by a light source would be prohibitive.

The Illustrate Renderer

Illustrate, made by Digimation, renders images to look hand-drawn, with a choice of a variety of drawing styles (two styles, Cartoon and Outline, are shown in the Color Gallery). Illustrate also allows you to export to Adobe Illustrator or Macromedia Flash. Illustrate is considered to be the most advanced nonphotorealistic renderer for max.

Check out http://www.digimation.com *for more information about Illustrate and other max plug-ins.*

Illustrate has its own menu in max. Clicking on this menu opens a dialog box where all the controls for this renderer are located.

The Lightscape Renderer

Unlike the other renderers, Lightscape is a stand-alone application. You have to make accurate low-poly models in max and export to Lightscape. Unless you're already accustomed to modeling in low-poly for games or real-time 3D, modeling this way can be a significant task.

In Lightscape, you assign materials to the model and set lighting parameters. Blocks and luminaries may be instanced. Lightscape then calculates a "lighting solution" that stores the lighting information in what is called a *radiosity mesh*.

Information about Lightscape can be found at Lightscape's Web site at `http://www.lightscape` `.com` *and on discreet's site at* `http://www2.discreet.com/support/lightscape`.

Radiosity is an alternate rendering technique that simulates light as if it was thermal (heat) energy. Unlike all the other renderers, Radiosity allows every surface in the model to act as a light source. Light energy is emitted from a source and is passed to various surfaces in the model. The surface with the most energy will act as a source to the rest of the model. Lightscape calculates many iterations of this process until you decide to stop the simulation. All the calculated energy information is stored in the 3D radiosity mesh, which overlays the geometrical mesh.

Lightscape's rendering algorithm effectively records the light that influences the scene but never reaches the picture plane. This effect is sometimes called *global illumination* or *indirect illumination*.

Once the lighting solution is calculated, you can navigate around the scene in what looks like a rendered model. In fact, the model is not rendered—only the diffuse component has been calculated. You must still raytrace the scene in order to calculate reflections and refractions.

The InSight Renderer

The InSight renderer is sold by Integra, Inc. from Japan. This sophisticated renderer is available at a very low cost.

Check out `http://www.integra.co.jp/insight` *for more information on the InSight renderer.*

InSight divides 3D space into *voxels* (fundamental volumetric elements), akin to a pixel, but three-dimensional. A 3D indirect illumination map is calculated and stored in the voxels. An advantage of the voxel system is that the geometry in the scene does not have to be accurately low-poly modeled as it does in Lightscape.

InSight uses a forward Monte Carlo raytracing algorithm. In concept, this rendering algorithm is the opposite of the backward raytracing that is part of max. In forward raytracing, light rays are traced from the light source through the scene to the view plane. In order to calculate the effects of indirect illumination, the program traces a random selection of light rays that will never hit the view plane. Instead these light rays will contribute to the indirect illumination in the scene. The term "Monte Carlo" refers to the random selection of light rays (it's a gamble), which are traced forward through the scene.

InSight also simulates *caustics*, effects caused by the reflection or transmission of the specular component of a material, such as you see on the floor of a pool of water. Just as indirect illumination is determined by inter-reflection of diffuse light in a scene, caustics are determined by the inter-reflection of specular light in a scene.

Look closely at the Insight rendering example in the Color Gallery. Observe the caustic effect at the bottom of the glass sphere. This is the area where the light appears brighter on the floor. Once the InSight plug-in is loaded in the Current Renderers rollout, you can adjust its settings in the InSight Renderer rollout that will appear at the bottom of the Render Scene dialog.

The mental ray Renderer

Mental ray was created by Mental Images GmbH from Germany. It has long been offered as part of the full installation of Softimage. It is now available from discreet as a product that can plug into max. This renderer uses the most sophisticated rendering algorithm currently available for max. Mental ray is able to exploit parallelism on both multiprocessor machines and across networks of machines, making it a good choice for larger animation houses. It may be only the larger houses that can afford mental ray, as it carries a high price tag.

Check out `http://www.mentalimages.com` *for more information about mental ray. Also see discreet's Web site at* `http://www.discreet.com`.

Like Lightscape and InSight, mental ray calculates global illumination. This renderer takes a novel approach by creating what is called a *photon map* to calculate inter-object reflection. The photon map is a three-dimensional map that is created by the mathematics of a particle system.

When mental ray is installed, it adds an Indirect Illumination Params rollout to all lights in max. Set the energy level, decay, and photon emission properties of each light.

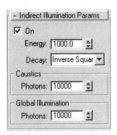

The photons bounce around the scene, reflecting off and refracting through various objects. The history of the photons' interaction is stored in the photon map and becomes the basis for calculating global illumination.

Mental ray is more scalable than the other renderers— in terms of rendering time there's not much of a penalty for using a high-poly model. In addition, the photon map can be saved and reused during the entire course of an animation. Even with this shortcut, mental ray takes longer to calculate an image than any of the other renderers. Mental ray divides each rendered image into *buckets* or small squares. The buckets are rendered starting from the center of the image and continue in a spiral pattern outward from the middle. Buckets can be passed to different processors within a multiprocessor computer or sent to other computers sharing a network for processing. The buckets are then reassembled to form the final still image. In this way, even a single still can be distributed across many processors.

Caustics can also be simulated with a great degree of accuracy. The mental ray plug-in adds a new section to the max Object Properties window. Set each object's parameters for generating and receiving global illumination and caustics in this mental ray Rendering Control section of the Object Properties.

Mental ray adds a number of rollouts to the Render Scene window. Understanding all the options takes quite a bit of practice and experimentation. Be patient; it is worth the effort. Look closely at the Mental Ray rendering in the Color Section. Observe how the red and blue walls' color subtly influences the color of the white surfaces in the Cornell box. Of all the renderers, this one produces the most accurate reflections and reflections as well as the best global illumination and caustics.

Network Rendering

Throughout this chapter, you've seen many references to the time required for rendering and to the tradeoffs between rendering accuracy and speed. Rendering is a "processor-intensive" activity, and one of the best ways to speed it up is to divide the work among multiple computers. *Network rendering*, or *render farming*, is one of the most powerful features of the program, because with one license of max, you are permitted unrestricted multi-machine rendering at no additional cost. For most of us, that means gathering up all the old discarded computers we can find and hooking them up to a network. Setting up network rendering can be simple if you have a functioning Windows 2000 network; it can be as easy as launching the Manager, Server, and max; specifying an output directory; and submitting the job. You can split the render over as few as two computers or as many as hundreds.

How Render Farms Work

Network rendering uses the manager/server principal. One machine is the *network manager*; it takes control of the job and doles out work to other machines called *servers*. The network manager machine can simultaneously be running as a server. Servers are the workhorses; they communicate with the manager and do its bidding. (Don't let max's terminology confuse you if you're used to "client-server" systems. What is usually called a "server"—the central machine directing others—is called a "manager" in max, while the usual "client" is called a "server.") Once you have submitted a job to the manager, the Queue Manager program lets you prioritize, edit, activate, deactivate, and view the progress of your job.

If you don't have a network of computers available and you need to speed up your rendering process, consider using a commercial render farm. Depending on your budget and your deadline, it may be worth the expense.

Setting Up Your Network

Before you can network render, your network setup must meet the following conditions:

- Your machines must be on a stable TCP/IP or DHCP network running Windows 2000 or Windows NT 4.0. (You can't network render on Windows 95 and 98.)

Although it's not officially supported by discreet, you can set up network rendering on mixed Unix/NT networks. These mixed networks often require mapped or mounted drives for shared assets.

- You must have administrator privileges.

- A network adapter or network interface controller (NIC) must be installed on each machine.

- You must have TCP/IP protocols installed and configured on each machine.

The "Configuring TCP/IP" topic in the max User Reference *is an excellent guide for setting up and configuring TCP/IP).*

- For best results, make sure each computer meets the minimum hardware requirements to run max. This is not necessary, however. Machines with less RAM and processor power will simply spend more time rendering the frame than a more robust system would. You can use an older system for rendering that would be too slow for production work.

- You must have an authorized "Typical" installation of max on at least one machine. This is the machine on which you will open the file you are rendering and submit the job to the network renderer.

- All other machines require at least a "Compact" installation and do not need to be authorized.

- All directories containing assets used in the render, including map and output directories, must be available to all rendering servers. If the maps and output directories are not on each local machine, they must be shared over the network. For some Unix and NT networks, you need to map (NT) or mount (Unix) a common drive letter on all server machines. In an NT environment, map a network drive by right-clicking My Computer and choosing Map Network Drive.

Use the Universal Naming Convention (UNC) when you identify paths for files and directories. UNC names begin with a double backslash as in: \\machine_name\directory\subdirectory. *Use UNC names even if the directory is on the local machine. This will prevent rendering errors when remote servers attempt to access the directories.*

Setting Up Network Rendering

Once you have your network set up to meet the above conditions, you can set up network rendering in max. The four applications used in network rendering reside in your 3dsmax4 folder:

- The max application will submit the network rendering jobs.

- ManagerApp communicates with the rendering servers. Any machine on the network can be set up to run the ManagerApp. The machine running the ManagerApp does not require authorization.

- ServerApp receives the frame from ManagerApp, renders the frame, and sends it to the target or output directory. Rendering servers do not need to be authorized and do not require a monitor. It will improve rendering speed if you have sufficient RAM, powerful processors, and more swap space, but display adapters and accelerators make no difference in the render speed.

- QueueManager lets you view and manage the render farm. From QueueManager you can activate, deactivate, reorder or remove the jobs in the queue. You can also add or remove servers from the rendering environment. Any machine on the network can run the QueueManager without authorization, and multiple QueueManagers can run at the same time. Only the first QueueManager connecting to the ManagerApp will be able to make changes. All other QueueManagers that connect to ManagerApp will be in read-only mode unless they obtain queue control.

The functions of network rendering can also be accessed using MAXScript. See Chapter 18 of this book or the "Network Render Interface" in the discreet MAXScript Reference.

Setting Up ManagerApp

Launch ManagerApp from the shortcut in your Start menu (Programs ➜discreet ➜ 3ds max 4 ➜ ManagerApp). When you launch ManagerApp for the first time, the

Network Manager General Properties dialog box appears, displaying the default settings. The default settings will work for most networks. Click OK to accept the General Properties. These configuration settings are stored in a file called maxnet.ini located in the 3dsmax4\network folder. You can access the Network Manager General Properties again by choosing Edit ➜ General Settings from the ManagerApp menu.

Setting Up ServerApp

Launch ServerApp on all other machines, using the Start menu shortcut (Programs ➜discreet ➜ 3ds max 4 ➜ ServerApp).

The machines running the Manager, max, and QueueManager can also be used as servers.

When you launch ServerApp for the first time, the default settings are displayed in the Network Server General Properties window. The Automatic Search option is checked by default, and the default Subnet Mask is 255.255.255.0. The default settings will work for most networks. These configuration settings are also stored in the maxnet.ini file. Click OK to start the Server and register with the Manager.

If you do not want the server to automatically register with the manager, uncheck Automatic Search. This allows you to specify the Manager Name or IP address of the computer running the Manager. You must shut down and restart the ServerApp for these settings to take effect.

If the ServerApp does not automatically connect to the ManagerApp with a screen such as that shown in Figure 13.1, displaying the IP address, check the subnet mask settings in your TCP/IP network. If the subnet mask is different, you need to change the Network Server General Properties (Edit ➜ General Settings) to match your network subnet mask. You must shut down and restart the ServerApp for the setting to take effect. This will overwrite the maxnet.ini file, changing the default settings.

Figure 13.1 *A Server connected to the Manager*

After you set up the Manager and Server applications, you can run them as services by installing `managersvc.exe` *and* `serversvc.exe`. *This means they will run independently in the back-ground as Windows services that are launched automatically upon startup. In order to edit the settings, however, you would still need to launch the ManagerApp or ServerApp application.*

Sending a Network Render

Once ManagerApp is running on one machine on the network and the ServerApp is running on all machines participating in the render, launch max to submit the job to the network rendering queue:

1. On a station that has an authorized copy of max, open the scene file you want to network render.

2. In the Render Scene dialog box, choose all your rendering options, including output file type and path. The file must be saved to a shared directory for the render servers to have access to it. If the directory is on the local machine, you must use UNC naming convention for the servers to find it.

 AVI, FLI, or QuickTime movies can only be rendered on one machine. You can send them to a server machine to be rendered, but the frames will not be divided up among other networked server machines. Only sequential single frame files can be rendered if you want to distribute the work between more than one server machine. These can then be brought into Video Post (covered in Chapter 14) or a video editing or compositing program.

3. Check the Network Render box. For faster rendering, uncheck the Virtual Frame Buffer box.

4. Make sure the desired camera view is being rendered, the output file path is named, and Save File is checked. It doesn't hurt to be extra careful about this, if you'd like to avoid creating your own agonizing war story about a long, wasted render.

5. Click the Render button. In the Network Job Assignment dialog box, click Connect.

6. If Automatic Search is checked, it will automatically look for any managers on the network. If the box is unchecked, enter the name or IP address of the Manager to the left of the Connect button.

7. Upon connecting, the Manager will list any servers available for rendering. As long as ServerApp was launched on the server machines, those machines should appear in the large pane to the right.

8. Select the combination of server machines you wish to use for the render. Names with green icons are ready to render; names with yellow icons are working on another job already. Click Submit. The job is saved and sent to the selected machines to render.

Monitoring the Render Queue

Once your rendering has been sent to the queue, you can monitor it and adjust it using Queue Manager, shown in Figure 13.2.

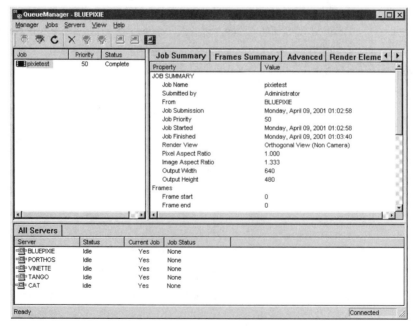

Figure 13.2 *Queue Manager lists all jobs, with information about their status.*

Click the Connect button (or press Ctrl+O) to connect the Queue Manager to the Network Manager. The job list is displayed in the left window in the order of priority from top to bottom. A white icon indicates the job is in the queue waiting for machines to do the work; a gray icon indicates the job is suspended; a black icon indicates the job is completed; and a green icon indicates the job has started and has successfully rendered one or more frames.

To activate, delete, suspend, or reprioritize a job, right-click the job in the list and choose the command. Click the Disconnect button (or press Ctrl+X) to disconnect from the Network Manager.

Servers on the network are displayed in the bottom pane. To display more details, display partial details, or create or delete server groups, right-click in the server pane and choose the command. To add or remove servers from selected jobs, delete servers from the queue, view properties, or create server schedules, right-click on the server icon and choose the command.

A gray icon indicates the server is assigned to the job but is not available or is absent from the network; a green icon indicates the server is assigned and rendering a job; a yellow icon indicates the server is available for assignment; and a red icon indicates the server has responded with a rendering error. Individual servers can fail without affecting the other servers or the job. Select the job in the left pane and view the job log in the right pane for details.

Details for a selected job are displayed in the right pane. The Job Summary, Frames Summary, Advanced, Render Elements and Log tabs give you an overview of the job, its progress, and the servers rendering it.

Troubleshooting a Render

If a render job does fail, you can troubleshoot the problem with the information tabs in the right half of the Queue Manager window. These tabs provide information on what is selected in the queue list on the left.

If a job is selected, you can view its rendering log. If a server fails, look at its render log to find out why. The log will give some indication as to why it failed, such as missing texture coordinates, map errors, and output directory errors. For example, a log may record an error such as that shown in Figure 13.3. The log states the reason for the error as missing texture coordinates. This pane displays the contents of the max.log text file in the 3dsmax4\network directory, which you can also view using any text editor.

Common Network Rendering Errors

This section lists common network rendering errors and the items to check when you see them.

Job Summary	Frames Summary	Advanced	Render Elements	Log	
Property		Value			
2001/05/07 15:54:39		Server BLUEPIXIE failed frame 0. Object (UVW 1): Cylinder01 requires texture coordinate...			
2001/05/07 15:55:46		Server BLUEPIXIE failed frame 0. Object (UVW 1): Cylinder01 requires texture coordinate...			
2001/05/07 15:56:53		Server BLUEPIXIE failed frame 0. Object (UVW 1): Cylinder01 requires texture coordinate...			

Figure 13.3 *Sample error log for failed render*

Server Failure

For server failure, check:

- Paths to bitmap and output directories. If all servers are looking to one machine, make sure the scene is using UNC (Universal Naming Convention) to identify bitmaps, and that the bitmap and output filepaths point to a shared directory. If the bitmaps reside on each individual machine, make sure the location and file structure is identical to the path in the scene. If all servers have a mapped or mounted drive pointing to the bitmap or output directory, make sure the mapped drive letter and path are identical on all machines and match the path in the scene.

- Local disk space. Make sure the rendering servers have adequate space to receive and render the frames.

- Output disk space. Make sure the target location for the rendered frames has adequate space to receive them.

- Mapping coordinates. Make sure all objects in the scene have mapping coordinates.

Only One Server Listed

If the Network Job Assignment dialog box displays only one server for assignment, make sure you are rendering sequential frames. Invalid file formats include AVI, CEL, FLC, MOV, and FLI.

Network Manager Will Not Register

If the Network Manager will not register to a network server:

- Make sure TCP/IP is installed correctly on both machines. If you are not sure TCP/IP is installed correctly, delete the protocol, reinstall it, and reboot the system.

- Check the IP addresses in the DNS Service Search Order, or the Primary and Secondary WINS Server in Microsoft TCP/IP.

- If the network server is installed as a service, make sure the service is started. Go to Control Panel → Services, highlight the Manager service, and click the Start button.

Network Server Will Not Register

If a network server is not registering to the Network Manager:

- Check the settings in the Network Server Properties window. If the Automatic box is checked, the server searches for the Manager using the subnet mask. If multiple managers are running, you must uncheck the box and enter the computer name (DNS Name) or IP address of the Manager machine. If the computer name begins with a number, you must use the IP address.

- If the Network Manager is installed as a service, make sure the service is started. Go to the Control Panel, choose Services, highlight the Manager service, and click the Start button.

The RAM Player

The RAM Player allows you to load images or animations directly into RAM and play them back in real time (RAM permitting). It also allows you to load two clips simultaneously so you can compare them side by side.

The RAM Player has its own toolbar. Table 13.6 describes these tools.

Table 13.6 RAM Player Tools

Icon	Name	Description
📂	Open Channel (A or B)	Loads an image, movie file, or a file sequence into that channel.
🖐	Open Last Rendered Image	Load the last rendered image (whether or not it was saved) into that channel.
✕	Close Channel	Clears the loaded image of that channel from RAM.

Table 13.6 RAM Player Tools (*continued*)

Icon	Name	Description
💾	Save Channel	Save the image in the current channel to a file.
A B	Channel toggles	Toggles display of channel A or B in the RAM player.
A|B	Horizontal/Vertical split screen	Toggles between horizontal and vertical split between channels, when both are displayed.
30 ▼	Frame rate control	Sets the target frame rate for playback (RAM permitting).
⬜	Double Buffer toggle	Synchronizes the frames of the two channels.

The first four buttons occur in two sets, one set for Channel A and one for Channel B. The dual channels allow you to do side-by-side comparisons of the channels by toggling their display with the A and B buttons. You can "scrub" between the images by dragging the split-screen divider back and forth. The A/B button allows you to toggle between a horizontal and vertical split in the display of the A and B channels. Let's compare two images this way:

1. Open the RAM Player (Rendering ➜ RAM Player).

2. Click Open Channel A and browse to `insight.tif` from the CD files for this chapter. Then click Open Channel B and load `mentalray.tif` from the CD files for this chapter. For both files, accept the default settings in the RAM Player Configuration dialog box.

The RAM Player Configuration dialog box allows you to set the resolution used in the RAM Player, to set the maximum RAM to use, to maintain the quality of the original file (by checking Filter Input), and to load the alpha channel into the other channel of the RAM Player.

3. Drag along the image area. You are scrolling the dividing line between the two channels. You can closely examine the differences between different renderings this way. This is a good way to check your anti-aliasing settings.

The playback controls in the RAM Player are identical to those we have seen elsewhere in the interface. The up arrow on your keyboard will play the frames in reverse. Crtl+right-clicking the image or animation allows you to select a color to copy to the color swatch. (Note that this is not exactly the same as in the VFB, where right-clicking brings up an eyedropper tool to do the same thing.) The location and RGB values of the pixel will be displayed in the title bar of the RAM Player.

Even though the RAM Player's performance depends on the amount of available RAM, it will load files greater in size than available RAM. This degrades playback performance. To maintain real time, use discretion in loading files, keeping in mind your available RAM. Synchronizing playback of the two channels with the Double Buffer toggle also reduces the performance of the RAM Player and can degrade real-time playback.

To improve the performance of the RAM Player, uncheck Enable Gamma Correction in the Gamma tab under Customize → Preferences.

Using the Render Effects Dialog Box

Render Effects are applied in a separate post-process rendering pass, which alters the image at the pixel level, although the renderer may use information from the scene such as distance from the camera, normals, and material effects' channel IDs to calculate the effect. Post-production within max is done through the Video Post dialog box. Some Lens Effects that you can apply with Video Post filters are also available through the Render Effects dialog box.

As you learned in Chapter 12, Lens Effects can be added to a light source directly from the light's Modify panel. When you click Setup, you bring up the same Render Effects dialog box that is accessed by choosing Effects from the Rendering menu. Clicking the Add button brings up the Add Effect dialog box.

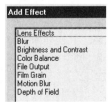

Choosing a Render Effect

Table 13.7 describes the different Render Effects, their general uses, and their settings. Some Render Effects, such as Film Grain, can only be applied to the entire image, while others, like Lens Effects, can be applied selectively to a range of brightness, for example, or to a certain Z depth.

Table 13.7 Render Effects and Their Uses

RENDER EFFECT	USE	NOTES ON SETTINGS
Lens Effects	Special optical effects like lens flares and glows.	Covered in more detail in Table 13.8.
Blur	Softens the scene or individual objects in the scene; can blur a range of brightness and blend back with the original image.	Uniform blurs the whole scene. Directional blurs a selection for a streaking effect to simulate motion; Radial blurs from a fixed point.
Brightness/Contrast	Changes brightness and contrast of image.	Uses a coarse value spinner, not Levels or Curves control. Option to apply the setting to the background.
Color Balance	Shifts colors toward other colors as needed.	Provides sliders to adjust the color values of the image.
File Output	Allows output of just the grayscale values, just the alpha channel, or just the Z-depth channel to a file.	Saves information as a grayscale file in any file format.
Film Grain	Adds randomized noise to image to simulate film grain.	Simple control of grain and option to apply to background.
Motion Blur	Applies image motion blur to the scene (explained in "The Scanline Renderer Rollout" earlier in this chapter).	Duration specifies how long between frames the image is blurred. 1.0 is the entire time.
Depth of Field	Simulates camera f-stop control by blurring elements outside of a specified range of Z depth.	Pick a camera through which you want the effect to happen. Pick the "node" that is the center of focus. Set the range and limits of the effect, horizontally and vertically.

Choosing Lens Effect Settings

Lens Effects provide the ability to add optical effects such as lens flares, solar coronas, and object glows to your scenes. Lens Effects offer so many options, a whole book could be written on them alone. Table 13.8 describes the appearance of some of the Lens Effects options.

Table 13.8 Lens Effects and Their Uses

LENS EFFECT	VISUAL APPEARANCE
Glow	Glow around light, or based on other selections described in Table 13.6.
Ring	Ring offset from glow.
Ray	Small criss-crossed streaks.
Auto Secondary	Colored circles (or shapes) between camera and effect object to simulate lens flares of real cameras.
Manual Secondary	Another lens flare effect that can be added to auto-secondary flares; manual options for creating unique flare.
Star	Very controlled star shape from center of effect.
Streak	Single linear optical effect.

On the Options tab for Lens Effects is an Image Sources section. This selects which parts of the image will be altered by the effect. Table 13.9 describes the different source settings and how these select the pixels to be affected.

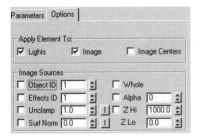

Table 13.9 Image Source Settings for a Glow Lens Effect

IMAGE SOURCE	SELECTION IN IMAGE
Object ID	Any pixels corresponding to an object with that ID in the image. (Object ID is set in Object Properties.)
Effects ID	Any pixels corresponding to a material with that Material Effects ID in the scene. (Material Effects ID is set in the Material Editor.)
Unclamped	Any pixels with values above pure white (RGB 255, 255, 255)—bright areas and highlights.
Surf. Norm	Pixels corresponding to face normals whose angle from the camera is within a set value.
Whole	The entire image.
Alpha	The image's alpha channel.
Z-Hi/Z-Lo	Pixels corresponding to objects selected by their distance from the camera.

Applying Render Effects Interactively

Render Effects can be updated interactively. When you check Interactive, the renderer will open a Virtual Frame Buffer to view the result of the applied Render Effect. It will then re-render just the post-process pass in the VFB as you change the parameters of the effect. You can also move a source object like a light and click the Update Scene button to update the VFB. This saves a lot of time rendering in order to see the effect of your settings.

Rendering Elements

Render Elements is a feature new to max 4 that separates the component information of your file.

Rendering in Layers

The concept of rendering component elements is also called *rendering in passes* or *layered rendering*. It is used in order to fine-tune rendered output in post-production, to composite elements together, and to add special effects.

For example, you can render the diffuse, specular, and shadow layers separately and then take these into Video Post, Adobe After Effects, discreet combustion, or other compositing applications, where you can isolate the effect of each component layer and tweak its value *after* rendering. This eliminates the need for interminable test renders and gives you interactive response for these material properties. Compositing programs also allow you to apply sophisticated image-processing effects to a specific layer: for example, to add "specular bloom" by adding a blurred copy of the specular layer. Most of the filter effects you can apply to still images in Photoshop can be applied to moving images in programs such as combustion and After Effects.

Compositing programs allow you to layer different image elements with fine control over effects that can be applied to each element, or layer, in the composite. You may be familiar with filters and layering in Photoshop—compositing programs take this concept a step further by allowing you to manipulate moving images.

The 3/1 and 3/9/01 weekly tutorials at `www.dvgarage.com` *demonstrate the level of control and sophistication possible in the compositing of rendered layers.*

Using Render Elements

Let's render the elements of the drafting table project:

1. Open the `DraftingTable04.max` file that you made in Chapter 12 or from the CD files for Chapter 12.

2. Press Shift+R. In the Render Scene window, set Time Output to Single and Output Size to 320 × 240, and click Files. Choose a location for your file , choose Targa, and type in **render_elements.tga**. (There will be more than one file, but the file names will all derive from this name.) Make sure Save File is checked and that Atmospherics and Effects are checked under Options.

3. Navigate to the Render Elements rollout and click Add. In the Render Elements, choose Atmosphere. Repeat this procedure for the Diffuse, Reflection, Self-Illumination, and Specular layers.

4. Check that you are rendering the camera view and click Render.

   The first file rendered is the composite; each additional element is rendered as a separate file. As all the elements are rendering, notice that separating the elements does not increase rendering time significantly. The generated files will take up substantially more disk space, however.

Arrange the VFBs of the different elements in the screen and examine them. Notice what is separated out, as shown in Figure 13.4.

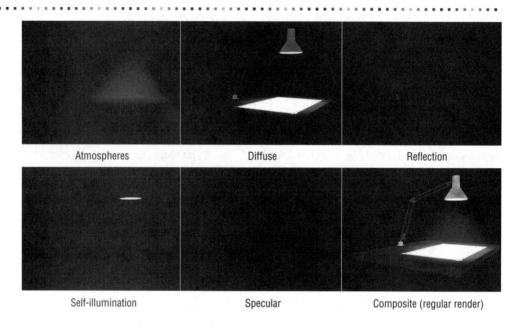

Figure 13.4 *Rendered component elements of lamp and drafting table*

5. Browse to the location of the saved files and view the renders. Note that the full render is given the name you specified in the Render Scene dialog box, while the rest are given that name with an additional tag for the layer. Save the max file as DraftingTable05.max.

- render_elements.tga
- render_elements_Atmosphere.tga
- render_elements_Diffuse.tga
- render_elements_Reflection.tga
- render_elements_Self-Illumination.tga
- render_elements_Specular.tga

Output to combustion

Max 4 also allows you to utput directly to combustion, creating a combustion work-space (.cws) file with the rendered elements arranged as layers. A demo of combustion ships with max4. The demo version is limited only in that you cannot save the work-space files, and there is a red X through the viewport and rendered images.

If you do not have a combustion demo disc, the software can also be downloaded from www .discreet.com.

Chapter 14 contains a simple combustion tutorial. To demonstrate the process of outputting to combustion, let's create the .cws file we will use in that exercise:

1. In the Render Elements rollout, check Enable in the Output To Combustion section.

2. Click Files under Output To Combustion, create a new folder for the file, and name the file render_elements.cws.

3. Click Files in the Common Parameters rollout and choose the folder you just created as the new file path.

4. Click Render. Save your max file as DraftingTable06.max.

Output to combustion will render your normal rendered image file (with all the elements composited), the selected elements and a .cws file containing the workspace, layers, and references to the rendered elements.

Summary

Choosing your rendering options well can make a crucial difference in the final appear-ance of your animation or graphic. The destination of your final output (e.g., com-puter monitor, video, or film), as well as the post-production requirements of your project, will affect how you will need to configure the renderer.

In this chapter, you examined the rendering capabilities of max, including all the rendering settings in the Render Scene dialog box. You learned how max simulates dif-ferent atmospheric effects, including fire effect and various types of fog, and how to use the Environment window to create and adjust these effects and to adjust global set-tings. You explored a variety of alternate renderers and learned how to network render over several computers. You used the RAM Player to compare images and learned how to apply Render Effects interactively. Finally, you rendered component layers with the new Render Elements feature.

In the next chapter, you will learn about post-production, whether done within max or in another program after rendering from max. You will explore the various functions available within the Video Post dialog, including cutting between cameras and pre-rendered sequences and applying image filters. You will explore the editing tools while editing video clips and use alpha channels and to composite rendered images. You will take rendered elements from max into combustion to apply an effect to one surface component and re-composite the elements. You will also composite using the Z-depth information of an RLA file.

Post-Production
and Compositing

3ds max

Chapter 14

n this chapter, you will learn about post-production, the final step in the workflow if you are outputting to digital video, videotape, or film. This includes editing between cameras, compositing, and applying image filters. You will explore the various tools available within Video Post and use them to edit and composite clips. You will complete the Intrepid Explorer Jim animation that you have been working on throughout the book so far. You will also composite and add effects to rendered images from max in discreet combustion. Topics include:

- Camera work as storytelling

- Video Post tools

- Scene and image events

- Video editing with cuts and cross-fades

- Effects filters

- Compositing in Video Post

- Compositing rendered elements and RPF channels in combustion

- Applying effects in combustion

Camera Work as Storytelling

From the start of an animated piece, you need to consider what you want to convey and how to best frame that visually. Your storyboard needs to reflect this. When it comes time to enact your storyboard, you will render different cameras to match the vision of your storyboard. You can do this within Video Post, the post-production tool in max, or take your rendered images into another program such as Adobe Premiere or After Effects or discreet combustion. Although it's something you need to think about early on and throughout your project, let's return here to the subject of camera work in greater depth.

You have been using cameras all along. It is a fairly straightforward thing to create a camera (Create ➔ Camera) and position and orient it. Animating cameras is also usually straightforward, involving simple transform animation, a path controller, or a single linkage. You animated a camera to get a particular shot back in Chapter 8, before you learned much about animating. As you will learn in this chapter, it is also fairly simple to cut between camera views and prerendered image files. Digital editing is very simple to do technically. Editing well and meaningfully, however, is an art form of considerable depth.

Camera work is visual storytelling. If you watch a good film carefully—and you might have to watch it frame by frame—you will see that with good editing, you don't even notice the cuts. The director decided how to position cameras and cut between them so that the story flows naturally. It makes enough sense to us, within the context of film conventions we are used to, that the change of viewpoint fits the unfolding story.

A superb example of visual storytelling is the final shot of the film *The Cradle Will Rock*. This occurs after the preceding action has established the intention of Rockefeller to define the future of art in a direction devoid of meaningful content, so that artists will serve only their corporate masters. The film has also established several touchstones of these visual metaphors for the struggle around whether to sell out one's principles: Diego Rivera's mural being destroyed on Rockefeller's order, actors performing a pro-union play against the dictates of the government and their own union, and a colorful collection of vaudevillian performers holding an impromptu funeral procession for the Federal Theater Project. After cutting between these images very effectively, the last shot cuts again to the funeral procession and then pans up from what has been 1937 to a modern urban street full of glaring commercial neon signs. The effect is both devastating and inspirational, implying both how we got to this point and that it's our struggle now. The message is delivered entirely through the imagery, without a word of dialogue or explanation.

It is well worth the time to study cinematography to learn the conventions of communicating through moving shots—if not in a school or in books, then through your local video store. One thing you should take note of, while studying films, is that the vast majority of the transitions made between shots are normal garden-variety cuts. The beauty of the art is in using cuts well. The bulk of the remaining transitions are fades in or out and cross-dissolves. These transitions have established contexts of meaning in film that modern Western culture has incorporated into its subconscious understanding. A long dissolve, for example, suggests the passage of time, while a fade to black suggests the end of a period of time, creating a sense of distance. The most common thing that amateur editors do wrong is use a lot of fancy wipes (where one image gradually covers another) and other transitions. These have no established context of meaning and can stick out like a sore thumb. They distract the viewer from the story. It's not that you should never use different transitions, but you should learn the conventions first and have a reason for departing from them. That way your departures are more likely to have meaning and less likely to seem tedious and amateurish.

 To learn more about the art of cinematography, check out the Filmmakers Handbook *by Steven Ascher and Edward Pincus (Plume, 1999) and* Digital Cinematography *by Ben De Leeuw (Morgan Kaufmann, 1997).*

The Camera Work of Intrepid Explorer Jim

Most of the cameras of the Intrepid Explorer Jim project were set up for you in the `Cave.max` file you used or the `Cameras.max` file you merged into your own cave file in Chapter 11. These were set up to match the vision and storyboard of the project's creator, Jason Wiener. When conceiving the project and when approaching the camera work, Jason considered how to best introduce the audience to the character, the setting, and the situation. He decided to open with a shot that starts out unresolved—a blur in the distance that coalesces into a character and setting as Jim and his torch move forward. He considered how to build up tension—in this case by shots that bring the audience progressively "closer" to Explorer Jim through a series of successively closer shots. The biggest challenge was how to effect the humor of the last moment. He did this by building the progressively closer shots to a climax at the moment where Jim falls. The audience sees the moment happen on Jim's face before the cut back to see the whole scene.

Table 14.1 describes the five cameras used for the shots. Note that the frame numbers of the animation to be rendered by each camera overlap. A shot from a different angle and distance from the character can "tell the story" of one long trek, even though it is rendering a sequence the audience has already seen. Also note that you will add Camera3_face and link it to the biped's neck, so that the head can move side to side without changing the camera view significantly.

Table 14.1 Camera Shots for the Intrepid Explorer Jim Project

CAMERA	FRAMES TO RENDER	DESCRIPTION
Camera1_distance	0–242	Establishing shot. See Jim from far down the tunnel make his way forward until he passes through the camera.
Camera2_turncorner	30–109	Medium shot of chest and head. Watch Jim navigate a difficult corner from an angle.
Camera3_face	155–254	Close-up of face. See Jim look side to side in increasing trepidation, then forward with wide, startled eyes until he suddenly drops out of frame.
Camera4_full	250–265	Establishing shot of full body, fairly close. See Jim approach and fall into hole, off screen. See torch and hat fall below screen as well.
Camera5_hole	263–350	Medium shot of the hole and a bit around it. Watch the hat flutter and fall into the hole. Watch the torch sputter and die. Fade to black.

Notice that the process of developing your skills in CG is somewhat circular: you need to understand camera work in order to do a good job of storyboarding. In fact, you need to understand all the facets, because they affect each other. You can think of your first read of a book like this as navigating the first spiral of the knowledge required, keeping in mind that you have only begun traveling the road to true mastery. After becoming acquainted with all the topics involved, you are ready to begin anew on a deeper level.

Multi-Pass Depth of Field Camera Option

A real camera focused on a subject has a range of distance from the camera where images appear acceptably sharp. This is called the depth of field. Objects outside of this depth of field (closer to the camera or farther away) appear blurry. In a real camera, the depth of field depends on the aperture, the focal length, and the distance of the subject from the camera. In CG, this is simulated by blurring the image outside a specified range from the camera. Depth of Field has been available as a Render Effect and as a plug-in for Video Post. In max 4, it is available in the Parameters rollout of a camera object in the Multi-Pass Effect drop-down list. Check Enable and then set the Focal Depth parameter—the depth of field around the camera's target—in the Depth of Field Parameters rollout.

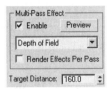

Understanding Video Post

You can do a great deal of editing and post-production work inside max within Video Post. Many beginning max users are afraid of using Video Post and avoid it. To be fair, there are certain mistakes that are easy to make in Video Post that can be frustrating enough to put anyone off. But once you understand how it works—how the Video Post queue "thinks"—you will find it a convenient post-production tool.

Video Post isn't a full video editing package like Final Cut, Premiere, or an Avid Media Composer; it's not a full video compositing package like combustion, After Effects, or Commotion; but for a single window within a 3D program, it's amazing what you can do with it. And since it's built into max, you don't have to go out and buy (and learn) another software package. You can do regular editing, cutting, and cross-fading between cameras and prerendered images; you can also composite between different views or prerendered images, using alpha channels or mask images to define transparency. You can resize images and change their placement in a composite. You can apply any of the various image filters, including all of the Lens Effects filters available in Render Effects, with some options that are available only in Video Post.

Editing in Video Post

When you choose Video Post from the Rendering menu, you bring up the Video Post window. It consists of two panes: the VP queue and the timeline. The left pane is the VP queue, a list of "events" that are read and carried out in order from top to bottom when you "execute" the queue. The events are commands about what to render, what filter or layer effect to apply, and what to do with the information (whether to save it and how). The right pane of the Video Post window is the timeline, which displays the duration of each event in the queue. The Video Post window also has its own toolbar, with many of the same tools you have seen elsewhere in the program.

Let's look at an example of a queue with some events in it, shown in Figure 14.1. Notice that the events are arranged in a hierarchy, like a directory structure on a computer, with the events further to the right nested under events that are above and further to the left. It's vital to understand and pay attention to this hierarchy when using Video Post, so your queue will be executed in the proper order.

Misunderstanding the Video Post hierarchy is the number one thing that screws people up when using the window. If your output event is nested under another event, your output file will contain only the frames of the scene or image event under which it is nested. If your output event is not the last thing in your queue, only the events before it will be saved to disk. In both cases, the other events will be rendered in the buffer, requiring all that processing time, but they will not be saved to disk.

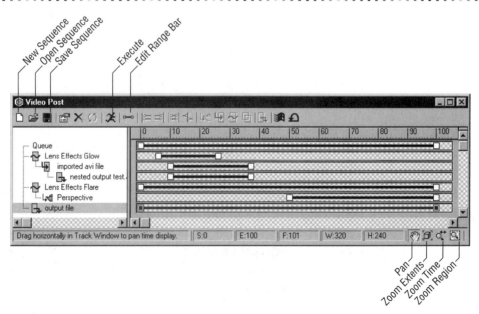

Figure 14.1 *Hierarchy of events in VP queue*

In the timeline in the right pane of Figure 14.1, you can see a bar showing the duration of each event. Obviously, it's similar to the Track View timeline; it's the same as the score or timeline windows of programs like Director, Flash, or Premiere. The Video Post timeline is separate from the scene timeline referenced by individual scene events in the VP queue; the Video Post timeline is used to create a "post-process" rendering different from what would be rendered by the regular rendering tools. In the Edit Range Bar mode (the only one available without multiple events selected), you can slide the range bars horizontally to change their start and end time within the timeline, or move the start and end points to change their duration.

Moving the start and end points changes the spot in the Video Post timeline where the frames of that event will start rendering. It doesn't change which frame of the scene or input image will be the starting point of that event. To change that, you need to double-click the event, then change the Scene Range (for a scene event) or click Options and change Frames (for an image event).

Adding Scene Events

Input events in the Video Post queue can be scene or image events. A scene event can be any sequence of frames from any viewport or camera in your scene. Let's set up a series of cuts between cameras for the Intrepid Explorer Jim animation:

1. Reset max.

2. Open the `Intrepid_Explorer_Jim15.max` that you created in Chapter 12 or from the CD files for Chapter 12.

3. File ➜ Merge and browse to `Facecam.max` from the CD files for this chapter. Click Open. In the Merge List Types, uncheck all except Cameras. Select Camera3_face and click OK.

4. Select Camera3_face and link it to the neck of the biped (Jim Neck).

5. Open Video Post (Rendering ➜ Video Post). Click the Add Scene Event button. In the Add Scene Event dialog box, choose Camera1_distance from the drop-down menu. Uncheck Lock To Video Post Range. Set Scene Start to 0, leave VP Start Time at 0, and set VP End Time to 242. Click OK to close the dialog box. You now have a scene event in your queue.

Notice that Enabled is checked. If you uncheck this box for an event, that event will be grayed out and ignored when the queue is executed.

You can change these settings by double-clicking the event in the queue, bringing up the same dialog box. If you change the range bars interactively by dragging in the window, the VP Start Time and VP End Time will be changed accordingly. The Render Options button brings up the same options that you saw in the Render Scene dialog box in Chapter 13.

6. If the scene event you just created is highlighted, click somewhere else in the VP queue pane to deselect it. If an event is selected, the next event added will be nested with it.

Using the Alignment Tools

You can use the alignment tools to set the correct number of frames in the queue without having to subtract and add frame numbers in your head:

1. Click Add Scene Event. This time choose Camera2_turncorner. Uncheck Lock To Video Post Range and Lock Range Bar To Scene Range. Set Scene Start to 30 and Scene End to 109, set VP Start Time to 30 and VP End Time to 109, and click OK. This means that the range in the queue is the same as the range of frames being rendered.

2. While pressing the Ctrl key, select the new event and the Camera1_distance event. This enables the alignment tools, described in Table 14.2. Click Abut Selected. The second event range is moved to the frame following the first event. Click an empty area of the queue to ensure that no event is highlighted.

3. Repeat steps 1 and 2 for Camera3_face, setting Scene Start to 155 and Scene End to 246 and abutting it to the previous event.

4. To accentuate the moment of the fall, add another event to draw out the expression on Explorer Jim's face when he realizes there is no ground under his feet. Add another scene event for Camera3_face, setting Scene Start to 247, Scene End to 249, VP Start to 1, and VP End to 6. Then abut this to the previous event. This step adds three more frames of the face to accentuate the moment.

5. Go to frame 249. Select Camera3_face and clone a copy of it (Edit → Clone), naming it Camera3b_face. Select Camera3b_face and click the Unlink tool to unlink it from the biped's neck.

6. Create a new scene event for Camera3b_face, setting Scene Start to 249 and Scene End to 254. Set VP range to 1 to 12 to again draw out the moment by doubling the time of it. Abut this event to the previous one.

7. Repeat steps 1 and 2 for Camera4_full, setting Scene Start to 250 and Scene End to 265, and for Camera5_hole, setting Scene Start to 263 and Scene End to 350. Make sure that no event is highlighted before adding a new event. Abut each to the previous event.

Table 14.2 Alignment Tools in Video Post

Icon	Name	Description
	Align Selected Left	Moves the first event selected to align its starting point with the second event selected. If the whole queue is selected (by clicking the word "Queue" in the queue), all the events will be lined up to the earliest starting point.
	Align Selected Right	Moves the first event selected to align its endpoint with that of the second event selected.
	Make Selected Same Size	Changes the duration of the first event selected to match the second event selected. (This does not change which frames are rendered in an image input or scene event.)
	Abut Selected	Moves the start point of the later of two selected events to the frame following the endpoint of the earlier event. When more than two events are selected, the events are made into a series.

Changes in Video Post are not undoable. Do an Edit ➔ Hold if you are at all unsure of your edit.

Adding Image Input Events

For the final shot, you will fade to black. To do this, you will bring in a pure black image as an image input event. An image input event can be any image or movie file or any sequence of frames.

When adding video files as image input events, consider compression. If your file has already been compressed, rendering again with compression will degrade the image substantially through double compression. When bringing prerendered animation into Video Post, render the initial files with minimal compression such as Animation, or even uncompressed (Full Frames for .avi files, None for .mov files, or a sequence of uncompressed still images). Apply compression to the final output from Video Post.

Let's add the black image for the fade:

1. Make sure none of the scene events in your queue are highlighted. If they are, click somewhere else to deselect them.

2. Click the Add Image Input Event button.

3. In the Add Image Input Event dialog box, click Files. Browse to `black.gif` in the CD files for this chapter. Click OK. In the Add Image Input Event dialog box, set the VP Start Time to 495 and the End Time to 540 and click OK.

Input Image Options

Before moving on, let's discuss the options available if you click the Options button in the Add Image Input Event dialog box. If you check Do Not Resize or Custom Size under the Size section, the Alignment options are enabled. If you're bringing in images of different sizes, you can position them with these controls. The Presets give you a visual image of the placement. Coordinates allow you to set an exact X and Y value, in pixels, for positioning the image. Custom Size allows you to set the exact dimensions to which to stretch or compact your image.

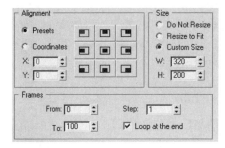

Step is just like Every Nth Frame in the Render dialog window. Step set to 1 means rendering every frame in the range; changing it to 2 would render every other frame, and so on. Loop At The End repeats the chosen series of frames to fill the duration of the range bar (between VP Start Time and VP End Time).

Adding Layer Events

Selecting two events in the queue enables the Add Image Layer Event button. Choose between different types of transitions, including plug-ins for Adobe Premiere, or compositors. You will use the Alpha Compositor in "Compositing in max" later in this chapter. Here you will use the Cross Fade Transition to create a fade.

Cross-Fading between Events

To cross-fade between two events, the events must overlap in the timeline so that there are two images to dissolve between. The period of overlap should be the length of time you want the dissolve to last. Keep in mind that a second is many frames (probably 30 or 15, depending on your time configuration setting). A ⅙-second cross-fade (five frames at 30 fps) is very fast, almost a cut. A slow fade to suggest the passage of time might be three seconds or longer. Make sure that the event you want to cross-fade *from* is above the event you want to cross-fade *to*.

If you put the starting event below the ending event of the fade, your fade will happen in reverse and will make no sense at all. You will have to delete the cross-fade event and start over.

To fade from the fifth camera to black, add a cross-fade layer event:

1. Select both the Camera5_hole and `black.gif` events in the queue.

2. Click the Add Image Layer Event button. In the Add Image Layer Event dialog box, choose Cross Fade Transition from the drop-down menu. Set VP Start Time to 495 and VP End Time to 535. This sets the length of the fade.

You can also close the dialog box and drag the start and end points. To ensure that the Cross Fade Transition is cross-fading between the two events, make the start and end points of the cross-fade event match the period of overlap between your two clips.

Add an Image Output Event!

This one little thing has stumped more people than any interface designer could have anticipated, so highlight the heading of this section in fluorescent orange and put big stars on either side of it. Creating an output event in Video Post is equivalent to checking the Save File box in the Render dialog window: If you don't do it, max will work merrily along, working your processors to capacity to calculate all the pixels of each frame, which will promptly be replaced by the pixels of the next frame until, at the end, only the last frame remains in the Virtual Frame Buffer. You will have just witnessed a piece of performance art in the digital realm, one to remember fondly, perhaps, but not saved to disk.

Add an Image Output Event:

1. Click an empty area of the VP queue pane to deselect any events in the queue. This is an important step. If you have an event selected and then add your

output event, the output event will be nested with the selected event, and only the selected event will be saved to disk.

2. Click the Add Image Output Event button. In the Add Image Output Event dialog box, click Files. Browse to the location to save the file and name the file `Intrepid_Explorer_Jim.mov`. Choose QuickTime movie file type and click Save.

3. In the Video Compression dialog box, choose Sorenson with Quality set to Best. Click Save and then OK.

4. Click the Zoom Extents button. Your queue should now look like this:

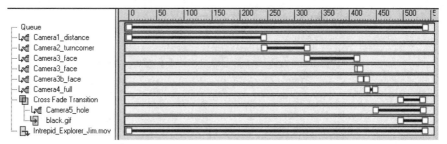

If you add a scene or image input event after adding your image output event, make sure nothing is selected in the queue and add the event. Then drag it above the output event in the queue (or else it won't be saved as part of the output file).

Executing the Video Post Queue

The Execute button is equivalent to the Render button in the Render dialog window. If you remember how Video Post thinks—in a linear progression through the queue, while paying attention to the hierarchy—executing the queue will be just as simple.

1. Before clicking Execute, always check that your output event is enabled (not grayed out). Make sure it is in the leftmost level of the hierarchy. Make sure it is the last item in the queue. Save your max file as `Intrepid_Explorer_Jim16.max`.

2. Click the Execute button. In the Execute Video Post dialog box, choose 320 × 240, choose Range, set the Range from 0 to 540, and click Render. This will take a long time.

Long renders are part of the life when you do CG work. Plan around them. Save your renders until the end of the day to render overnight or plan your errands and the work you can do outside of max for render time.

3. Choose File ➔ View Image File and open `Intrepid_Explorer_Jim.mov`. Play the file a few times. Check out the "Enacting the Storyboard" plate in the Color Gallery that compares the original storyboard panes with the completed shot .

Intrepid Explorer Jim project by Jason Wiener

Image Filters

Image filters are applied to the pixels of the initial render, even though the parameters of the filters may reference information from the 3D scene. This is technically post-production work, equivalent to taking each frame into Photoshop and applying a filter to it. The information from the 3D scene that may determine the range of the effect is essentially a 2D mask selecting which pixels should have the filter applied. Table 14.3 describes the various filters and their uses.

Lens Effects settings are described in more detail in Chapter 13.

Table 14.3 Image Filters Available in Video Post

IMAGE FILTER	DESCRIPTION
Photoshop	Non-animatable third-party filters for Photoshop, if you have Photoshop installed; a mini version of the application is launched, applying the filter to each frame.
Premiere	Animatable third-party filters for Premiere, if you have Premiere installed.
Contrast	Alters contrast and brightness of overall image.
Fade	Fades an image in or out over a series of frames; used for cross-fades as well as fades up from or out to black.
Image Alpha	Uses a channel from a specified file to replace the queue's alpha channel. The channel can be the Object, Materials Effects, or Z Buffer (Z-depth) channels of an RLA or RPF file.
Lens Effects Flare	Creates flares and optical effects.
Lens Effects Focus	Blurs image outside of a specified range to simulate the depth of field of a camera.

Table 14.3 Image Filters Available in Video Post *(continued)*

IMAGE FILTER	DESCRIPTION
Lens Effects Glow	Creates specialized glows based on various selection options.
Lens Effects Highlight	Creates star-shaped glints for metals and liquids.
Negative	Inverts image to its photographic negative.
Pseudo Alpha	Defines an alpha channel as all pixels the same color as the first pixel (the pixel in the upper-left corner of the image).
Simple Wipe	Creates a transition between two events that wipes back the edge of the top event to reveal the underlying event.
Starfield	Generates stars in the background.

Any Lens Effects filter parameter that has a green, double-triangle icon is animatable; if you click the icon, you gray out the icon and turn off animatability for that parameter. While the Lens Effects dialog box is open, you can animate Lens Effects parameters by turning on the Animate button, going to the frame in the scene corresponding to the scene event frame, and changing the parameter. You can also just add keys to the track in the Track view (again, while the Lens Effects dialog box is open). The tracks will be under Video Post in the scene hierarchy.

The inferno portions of Lens Effects Flare and Lens Effects Glow are not part of the Render Effects window. They are only available through Video Post.

Adding Image Filter Events

In Video Post, you can apply filters to an image for a specific duration. In this exercise, you will apply a glow to an object by changing its object ID:

1. Copy Displace.tif from the CD files for this chapter to your 3dsmax4\Maps directory. Then open ghost01.max from the CD files for this chapter.

2. Select the Ghost Morph object. Right-click it and choose Properties. In the G-Buffer section, change the Object ID to 1.

3. Go to frame 50.

4. Open Video Post (Rendering ➜ Video Post) and add a scene event to the queue. Choose Camera 3.

5. Select this Camera 3 event and click the Add Image Filter Event button. In the Add Image Filter Event dialog box, choose Lens Effects Glow from the drop-down list and click OK. The Image Event is nested under the Filter Event.

You can click the Setup button when adding the filter event, but in this case, you can't see the effects of the filter on your actual event. By adding the filter event and then double-clicking it in the queue, the VP Queue button will be enabled when you click Setup. With VP Queue on, the Preview button will show you the result of your filter on your scene or image event.

6. Double-click the Lens Effects Glow event in your queue. This brings up an identical dialog box to the one you just saw, except it is labeled Edit Filter Event. Click the Setup button to bring up the Lens Effects Glow dialog box. Click the VP Queue and Preview buttons just under the preview window, so that you can see the effects of your changes in the window. (Sometimes you also have to click Update to see the effects of your changes.) In the Properties tab, under Source, leave the defaults of Object ID checked and its setting of 1. This selects the ghost morph for the glow.

7. The Filters section determines which of the source pixels you want to glow—for example, those of a particular brightness value or hue. You may want to play with these settings for a while before checking Brightness and unchecking the others. Set the Brightness value to 75. This means pixels brighter than 75 (out of 255) will glow.

8. In the Preferences tab, set Size to 20. This means the glow will spread up to 20 pixels from the object. Change the Color to User, click the color swatch, and select a light cyan color. This changes the glow color from the color of the object's pixels to the color you just selected. Set the Intensity to 50 and click OK.

The User color swatch under Color on the Preferences tab is not the same thing as the Hue color swatch in the Filter section of the Properties tab. What the hue filter does is select the pixels of that hue in the preliminary render for the application of the glow. The user color swatch changes the color of the glow itself.

9. Make sure nothing in the queue is selected and create an image output event. Click Files and save the file as an `.avi` called `ghost_image.avi`. Since you will use this in a composite, choose Full Frames (uncompressed). Click OK twice to close both dialog boxes. Save your max file as `ghost02.max`.

You can save the Video Post sequence as a .vpx *file, but it will not save the parameters of the glow filter. These will be saved with the* .max *file, however.*

10. Click Execute. Check Range and set the range from 0 to 100. Set the size to 320 × 240. Click Render.

Compositing

Key Concept

A typical special-effects film these days includes composites of hundreds of different elements. Within max, you can composite two images at a time. If you want to do composites of many layers, you will probably want to invest in combustion or After Effects to do so. Combustion has the added advantage of letting you use Z-depth, Object ID, Material Effects ID, and other information channels in the composite. For complicated rotoscoping—making traveling masks around moving images—check out Commotion by Puffin Designs (www.puffindesigns.com).

When compositing objects from a 3D program into photographs or live footage, a technique called "light wrap" will make the objects look more realistic in the scene. It involves lightening the pixels of the CG object at the edges where it meets the light of the background image. This can be done using the Light Wrap plug-in (also by Puffin Designs) for Adobe After Effects or by manually compositing and matting in any compositing program. For other detailed techniques for adjusting the appearance of prerendered 3D objects, see the Enhancing 3D bonus tutorial in Creating Motion Graphics with After Effects *by Trish and Chris Meyer (CMP Books, 2000).*

Compositing in max

You've already done some compositing in max. Any time you render a scene with an environment background, you are really compositing the scene with the backplate. In Chapter 8, you used a Matte/Shadow material to composite shadows onto a flat background and a Composite material to composite one map over other maps, using the transparency information in the opacity maps. The opacity map of a material is exactly the same thing to a material as an alpha channel is to a bitmap or movie file. It selects what is visible, what is invisible, and what is partially visible.

The Alpha Compositor

To composite in Video Post, select the two events you wish to composite and click Add Image Layer Event. Choose Alpha Compositor, then click Files and choose the file that has the transparency information of the upper event (usually it's the upper event itself, so you can choose its alpha channel). Then choose the channel of the chosen file that you want to determine the transparency of the upper event; this can be any of the channels in the Mask drop-down list, including the actual alpha channel.

 Think of the file of the alpha channel as a kind of "hole" in the upper event, through which the lower event is showing through. This makes it easier to remember which file should be first in the queue (the one with the alpha channel or mask).

Loading a Sequence of Still Files

In this exercise, you will composite a prerendered sequence of Targa files containing an alpha channel with the .avi file you just rendered. Loading a sequence of files in a max file-selector dialog box requires an Image File List file, or .ifl. An .ifl is a text file listing the files in sequence. If you're the sort of person who enjoys such things, you can create it yourself in a text editor. Normal people can generate it automatically in the file-selector dialog box:

1.   Close Video Post and open the RAM Player (Rendering → RAM Player).

2.   Click the Open Channel A button and browse to iris_alpha0000.tga, the first file of the Targa sequence from the CD files for this chapter. (Make sure you are loading these from where you copied them on your hard drive. Don't try to read them from the CD.) In the file selector window, check Sequence and then click Open.

3.   In the Image File List Control window, accept the defaults and click OK.

4.   In the RAM Player Configuration dialog box, check Load Into Other Channel Under Alpha. Click OK.

5.   After the RGB images load into Channel A and the alpha channels into Channel B, scroll between them so you can see what the "hole" of the alpha channel looks like. It is only the area in the window where there are no reflections or snow. This was created using a Matte/Shadow material and opacity maps. Close the RAM Player.

6. Open Video Post. Click the New Sequence button and click Yes.

7. Add an image input event, click Files, and choose `iris_alpha0000.ifl`. (Note that you could have created the `.ifl` in this file selector dialog box. Since it has been created for the RAM Player, you don't need to create it again.)

Compositing the Layers

Now composite this sequence with the animation you just created. The ghost image will appear in the window behind the reflections:

1. Add another image input event and this time select the `ghost_image.avi` file that you created earlier or from the CD files for this chapter. It comes into the queue after the IFL file. This is correct, because you want to see the image through the "hole" in the iris scene created by the alpha channel.

2. Select the two image events in the queue and click Add An Image Layer Event. Choose Alpha Compositor from the drop-down in the Add Image Event dialog box.

3. Click Files and choose the `iris_alpha0000.ifl` file again. You want to mask the image with its alpha channel, so leave Alpha Channel selected in the drop-down list. Click OK.

4. Click somewhere off of the events to deselect them. Now what do you have left to do? A gold star if you said, "Add an image output event" or even "Save the darn file." Click the Add Image Output Event button. Click Files and save the file as `iris_ghost.mov` with Sorenson compression. Your queue should look like this:

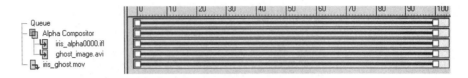

5. Click Execute. After rendering, you should have a QuickTime movie with the "ghost" appearing in the window, with the window reflections still appearing on the surface of the mirror.

Compositing Render Elements in combustion

In this exercise, you will re-composite the elements you rendered in Chapter 13 in combustion, tweak the composite, and add effects. The demo version of combustion that ships with max (in the "3ds max web studio cd set") is limited in that you cannot save workspace (.cws) files and your renders and viewport will have a red X through them. Let's check it out:

1. Launch combustion.

2. Choose File ➜ Open Workspace. Using the left navigation frame, browse to the render_elements.cws file that you exported from max in the last chapter or from the CD files for this chapter. Select the workspace file in the right frame and click OK. The workspace opens with all the rendered elements layered within the composite. From here you can work with the layers to edit the image.

3. Right now the Atmosphere layer is on top, obscuring the rest of the composite. To fix this, double-click the Atmosphere layer in the Workspace panel to make it the current level.

When a layer or operator is selected, an arrow appears to the right of its name.

4. Choose Operators ➔ Keying ➔ Linear Keyer. Click the eyedropper tool and then click on the black area of the image. Turn up the tolerance to about 17%. Notice that you can affect the amount of the atmospheric effect this way. Double-click on the composite layer again ("3ds max - Render Elements") to see the atmosphere composited with the rest of the layers.

The double yellow square icon in front of a layer turns its display on and off in the composite. Turn the different layers on and off and notice their effect on the image.

5. Now you can adjust the effect of just the specular contribution. Click the Specular layer in the Workspace panel. Choose Edit ➔ Duplicate to Duplicate the layer.

6. Double-click the new layer. Choose Operators ➔ Color Correction ➔ discreet CC Curves. On the CC Curves Controls tab, deselect Red, Green, and Blue, so that just the RGB curve is showing. Click on the line in the middle and drag it up slightly to brighten this layer of specular highlights.

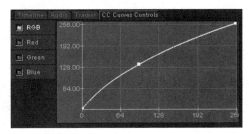

7. Choose Operators ➜ Gaussian Blur. In the Gaussian Blur Controls tab, set the Radius to 2. This blurs the layer to spread out the highlights. Although this example is more exaggerated than you would normally use, this is how you add a "specular bloom" to images.

8. Double-click the composite layer and toggle the display of the new specular layer on and off. Notice that you affected just the specular highlights of the composite. An example of this file is available as `render_elements2.cws` in the CD files for this chapter.

For more information on specular bloom, see the tutorials at `www.dvGarage.com`.

9. Now let's look at applying a stylized effect to a layer. Double-click the Diffuse layer. Choose Operators ➜ Stylize ➜ Emboss. This operator is very similar to the Emboss filter in Photoshop. You can see the result in `emboss.tif` in the CD files for this chapter. The final combustion workspace file is `render_elements3.cws` in the CD files for this chapter.

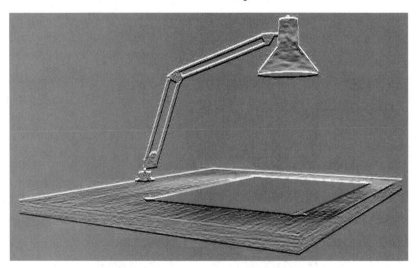

Compositing with RPF Channels in combustion

As you learned in Chapter 13, max supports two kinds of rich pixel rendering: RPF (rich pixel format) and RLA, an older format that supports fewer channels but is recognized by more applications. In this exercise, you will render an .rpf file and edit the layers in combustion:

1. Open the DraftingTable04.max file that you created in Chapter 12 or from the CD files for Chapter 12.

2. Press H, and in the Select Objects window check only Geometry under List Types. Check All and then Select.

3. Right-click the selected objects and choose Properties. In the G-Buffer Object Channel field, type **1** and click OK. This will enable you to select the geometry by its Object Channel ID in combustion.

4. Press Shift+R. In the Render Scene dialog box, render a single frame, output size NTSC D-1. Click Files and save as the .rpf file type with the name table.rpf.

5. In the RPF Image File Format dialog box, choose 8 Bits per channel and check Store Alpha Channel. In the Optional Channels field, check Z, Object, Normal, and Coverage. Table 14.4 describes the optional file channels and the information stored in them.

Table 14.4 Optional Channels of RPF and RLA Files

CHANNEL	RLA	RPF	INFORMATION
Z	✔	✔	Depth of objects relative to the screen
Material Effects	✔	✔	Material Effects ID set in the Material Editor
Object	✔	✔	Object ID set in Object Properties
UV Coordinates	✔	✔	UV mapping coordinates
Normal	✔	✔	Orientation of the face normals
Non-Clamped Color	✔	✔	Pixels that exceeded the valid color range
Coverage	✔	✔	Anti-aliasing data on the edges of the geometry
Node Render ID		✔	Object ID saved as a solid color

Table 14.4 Optional Channels of RPF and RLA Files *(continued)*

CHANNEL	RLA	RPF	INFORMATION
Color		✔	Material color (without transparency)
Transparency		✔	Material transparency in gray values
Velocity		✔	Velocity relative to screen
Sub-Pixel Weight		✔	Sub-pixel information determining pixel color
Sub-Pixel Mask		✔	Sub-pixel information determining pixel transparency

6. Click Render.

7. Open combustion.

8. Choose File ➔ New. In the New workspace dialog box, choose Create A Composite and name the file `rpf.cws`. In Format Options, choose NTSC D-1, the format of the `.rpf` file you saved from max. Click OK to launch your new workspace.

9. Double-click the composite layer in the workspace to make it active.

The active layer has an arrow to the right of its name. The layer you are viewing has a white box to the left of its name.

10. Press Ctrl+I. In the left pane of the Import Footage dialog box, browse to the `table.rpf` file that you rendered from max or from the CD files for this chapter. Click the file in the right pane. The file appears in the queue below and information is displayed about the file at the bottom-left of the pane. Click OK.

11. The file appears on its own layer within the composite. Select the layer that contains the table image.

12. Choose Operators ➔ Selections ➔ G Buffer Object Selection. This allows you to select the pixels corresponding to geometry by Object ID.

13. In the G Buffer Object Selection Controls tab, right-click the Object button and type **1**. Notice that the small preview window in the lower right of the interface displays a marquee around the object with ID #1. Check the Invert button and the marquee selection inverts. If the file contained objects with different object ID numbers, you could toggle through the ID channels here.

14. Choose Operators ➡ Paint. The Paint operator appears above the G Buffer Object Selection operator in the same layer in the composite and the Paint Controls tab now appears in the central control panel.

15. Choose a color to work with in the color picker tab in the small pane to the lower right of the interface. In the Toolbar tab on the lower left, select the Type tool. The options are displayed for the type tool. Type **Mastering 3dsmax 4** in the viewport.

When you are outputting to videotape or television broadcast, be aware of keeping titles within the title-safe area of the frame. In max, you can display areas safe for titles by checking Title Safe in the Viewport Configuration dialog box. In combustion, choose Window ➡ Show Safe Zones or toggle the display on and off by pressing ' (single quotation mark).

16. Click the Picker tool and click the timeline button. Turn on the Animate button. Drag the text off the screen to the left. Move the yellow time indicator about halfway to the right. Move the text to the right. Move the yellow time indicator to the far right. Move the text behind the lamp. Turn off the Animate button.

17. With the animated layer selected, choose Edit ➡ Duplicate. Select the text with the picker tool and change it to an off-white color.

18. Choose Effects ➡ Blur/Sharpen ➡ Box Blur. Set the Radius in the Box Blur Controls to 4.9.

19. Duplicate this layer, change the text color to blue, and change the blur radius to 3.7.

RPF compositing project by Blue Bactol

The CD files for this chapter include an example of this exercise. The combustion file is `pdf2.cws` and the rendered animation is `DraftingTable.avi`. A still image is included in the Color Gallery. These are introductory exercises to the complex application of combustion. For more depth, see the tutorials in the Learning Combustion section of the combustion help.

Summary

In this chapter, you've explored the post-production capabilities within Video Post. You learned how the Video Post queue works and how it interprets the events you enter. You added scene events and image input events, including a sequence of still images. You applied image filter events and looked at the various filters available in Video Post. You cut between a variety of shots, cross-faded between them, and composited them using alpha channel information. You also applied post-production effects to composites in discreet combustion.

In the next six chapters, you will enter the world of MAXScript, max's built-in programming language.

Part VI

Mastering MAXScript

In this part, you will learn about MAXScript: how the language works, and how to use it to streamline working in max. Chapter 15 introduces the basic tools of the language. Then you'll start working with max objects and scenes, learning how to create and manipulate them, including modifiers, materials, and effects. Further ahead you will learn how to create interfaces, like dialog boxes and floaters, and how to use them to help you manipulate the scene.

Once you know how to work with objects and to create your own UI, you'll jump into animation and rendering. You'll learn how to manipulate things like bitmap images, render elements, and even the Network Rendering system. The next step is to learn how to manipulate the different file formats that max supports, and access the menus and quads. At the end, you'll learn how to create your own plug-ins using MAXScript.

All of these chapters show how to apply the language to various aspects of your work, with exercises to help you learn. Throughout this section, you'll see examples of applications created with MAXScript. You'll see that MAXScript is not hard to learn and will save you a lot of time in future projects.

MAXScript Basics

Chapter 15

MAXScript is the easiest way to start programming in 3ds max. You do not need previous programming experience, nor do you need any extra software to work with it. MAXScript can help you in many ways, by automating repetitive tasks, standardizing procedures, importing and exporting data, or even creating your own plug-ins.

Introduced in MAX release 2, MAXScript has gained momentum over subsequent versions, adding features and support, and becoming more fully integrated with MAX. Now in 3ds max 4, MAXScript is responsible for even more important features, and it is also part of the whole user interface, where most icons and options in quad menus are created by scripts. As expected, Discreet has added more functionality to MAXScript and implemented new ways to work with scripts and macros.

MAXScript, as a language, remains the same regardless of the version of 3ds max you are using. In this chapter, we'll highlight all features new to 3ds max 4, making it easier for you to identify them. This chapter has more theory than practice, but it's well worth the time required to understand the foundations of MAXScript. You'll have a better grasp of the basics and the way the language works. Topics include:

- The MAXScript user interface
- Performing math operations
- Using strings
- Using conditions
- Repeating tasks
- Creating functions
- Text file I/O: reading and writing data
- Binary file I/O

The MAXScript User Interface

You can work with MAXScript through different parts of the interface, as seen in Figure 15.1. You will use the Utility panel whenever you have a MAXScript utility. Most of your time will be spent on the Listener, which is the area where you enter command lines.

MAXScript Listener   MAXScript menu

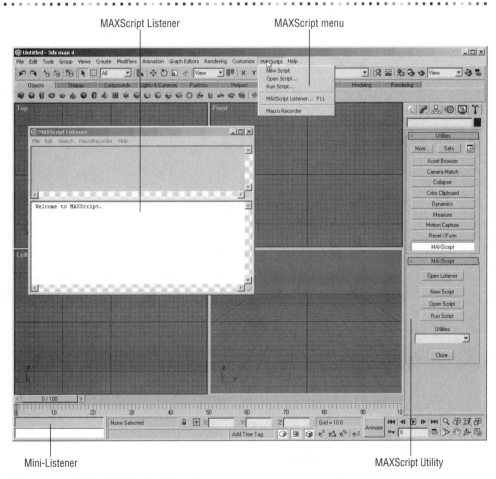

Mini-Listener   MAXScript Utility

Figure 15.1 *The MAXScript interface*

The Utility Panel and Menu Bar

You can work with MAXScript using the Utility panel, as in MAX releases 3 and 2. To access it, open the Utility panel and click the MAXScript button. You will see some buttons and a drop-down list. Listed in Table 15.1, the buttons offer the same actions found in the MAXScript menu.

Table 15.1 Buttons on the Utility Panel

BUTTON	BUTTON NAME	ACTION
Open Listener	Open Listener	Opens the Listener window
New Script	New Script	Starts an empty Script Editor
Open Script	Open Script	Opens a script in the Script Editor
Run Script	Run Script	Runs a script

The drop-down list will display the Utility scripts you have loaded.

Macro Recorder

The Macro Recorder allows you to record every action in max, in the form of a script. This script can also be dragged to a toolbar or Tab, which will automatically create a button for the script.

    The Macro Recorder can be turned on and off using MAXScript ➜ Macro Recorder. When it's on, a checkmark appears in this menu. Most actions you perform in max can be recorded. (See "Using the Macro Recorder" later in this chapter for more information about this feature.)

Listener

The Listener is probably the most important interface item in MAXScript. It's where you type commands, see the output of functions, and view the recorded items. It's divided into two areas, the Macro Recorder pane (pink) and the output/command pane (white).

You can use the Listener as a floating window, as a viewport, or in the Mini-Listener. Besides all the functions in the Listener, the Mini-Listener shows you a list of the latest commands typed or recorded and allows you to select any of them.

Sometimes, when you open the Listener, the Macro Recorder pane is not visible because it's hidden in the top of the Listener window. All you need to do is drag the separating bar and it will appear, or you can turn on the Macro Recorder and the Macro Recorder pane will open automatically.

The Script Editor

When starting a new script or opening an existing one for editing, MAXScript supplies you the Script Editor. This is a standard text-editing program (that is, it creates and works with plain .txt files), with some extra features to help you write scripts:

- Ctrl+D adds color coding to your scripts, separating commands, comments, and strings.

- Ctrl+B highlights the parentheses in your script.

- Ctrl+right-click brings up a shortcut menu you can use to jump directly to commands, functions, and UI (user interface) items.

- Ctrl+R cycles through the last eight cursor positions in the script.

- Ctrl+I tabulates the selected lines, adding one tabulation space in the beginning of the line.

Visual MAXScript

Visual MAXScript is a new addition in 3ds max 4. It provides an easy way to create a script's user interface, similar to the tools provided by Visual Basic, Visual C++, and other visual languages.

Like those tools, Visual MAXScript is a sort of "interface for creating interfaces." Many scripts you write will be interactive, asking the user for information in order to do their job. To get this information, your script will display text input boxes, spinners or sliders for selecting values, and so on. Writing code to display all these UI elements—precisely defining the size, position, etc., of each item—is tedious. Visual MAXScript instead displays its own set of windows where you can "visually" create your script's interface elements and assign events to them. Figure 15.2 shows a script's interface being created in Visual MAXScript. On the left is the interface under construction; on the right is the input area for defining the properties of the current UI element. In this example, we are defining the spinner selected on the left.

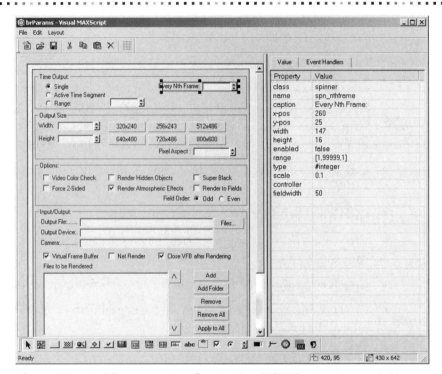

Figure 15.2 *Building a user interface in Visual MAXScript*

You can start Visual MAXScript by selecting it in the Utilities Panel or by opening the Script Editor and choosing Edit ➜ Edit Rollout or Edit ➜ New Rollout. You'll learn how to use Visual MAXScript in Chapter 17.

Plug-in Scripts

Plug-in scripts are simply scripts that act like regular plug-ins. They can be objects, modifiers, render effects, helpers, etc. A plug-in script does not require its own interface, because it is incorporated into the max interface, as new plug-ins would be. See Chapter 20, for more information.

Working in MAXScript

Let's create a simple script, illustrating how you can work in MAXScript. You'll start creating a bent torus, which is the character's mouth seen in Figure 15.3. First you'll record an action and save it using the Macro Recorder, and then you'll write a script that enables max to create the mouth object automatically. You can use this example with any other object, modifier, material, or Render Effect in max.

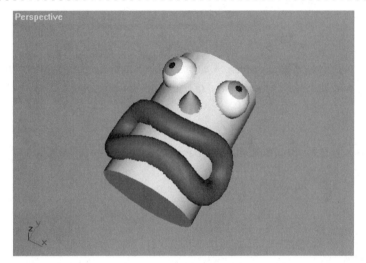

Figure 15.3 *A character whose mouth is formed from a bent torus*

Follow the steps below to record the creation of the torus:

1. Open the Listener in one of these ways:

   - Select MAXScript ➜ MAXScript Listener.

   - In the Utility panel, open the MAXScript rollout and select Open Listener.

   - Right-click the Mini-Listener and select Open Listener.

   - Press F11

2. In the Listener, select Macro Recorder ➜ Enable.

3. Turn on 3D Snap.

4. In the top view, create a Torus object.

Now you'll set some parameters for the torus object.

5. Go to the Command Panel ➔ Modify panel and specify the following values:

Parameter	Value
Radius 1	90
Radius2	20
Segments	36
Sides	20

If you do not switch to the Modify panel, all options will be recorded in a single MAXScript line. The final result is the same, but it will be more difficult to edit the script in the future.

6. Go to the Modifiers tab and click Bend.

7. In Bend, specify the following parameters:

Parameter	Value
Angle	340
Direction	90
Bend Axis	Y

8. In the Macro Recorder pane, select the lines you have just recorded and drag them to the Objects tab, as shown in Figure 15.4. This automatically creates the button for you. Note that your script has been sequentially named (Macro1, Macro2, etc.).

9. Reset max using File ➔ Reset.

10. Click the button you just created, and max will create the same object you did before.

Everything that you type in the Listener or record using the Macro Recorder can be dragged to a toolbar or to a tab, where it will automatically create a button. This button makes it easier to use the script because you can just click it to repeat the action. The script created from a drag-and-drop operation will be stored in the \UI\Macroscripts *folder.*

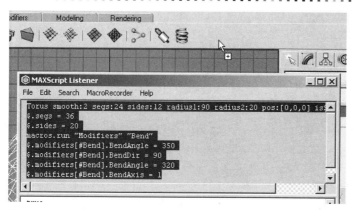

Figure 15.4 *Dragging a script to the Objects tab*

The script repeats the exact steps used for this object, which means the object will always be created in the same position. You might want to create the object and insert it anywhere, just like any other new object in max. Let's do that, editing the script and adding some options to do this.

1. Right-click the new button and select Edit Macro Script, bringing up a MAXScript editing window.

2. Add this line just before the `torus` command:

```
pt = pickpoint prompt:"\nSelect Position:"
```

Your script window should now look like the one in Figure 15.5.

```
DragAndDrop-Macro3.mcr - MAXScript                           _ □ x
File  Edit  Search  Help

macroScript Macro3
    category:"DragAndDrop"
    toolTip:""
(
    pt = pickpoint prompt:"\nSelect Position:"
    Torus smooth:2 segs:24 sides:12 radius1:90 radius2:20 pos:pt isSelected:on
    $.segs = 36
    $.sides = 20
    macros.run "Modifiers" "Bend"
    $.modifiers[#Bend].BendAngle = 350
    $.modifiers[#Bend].BendDir = 90
    $.modifiers[#Bend].BendAngle = 320
    $.modifiers[#Bend].BendAxis = 1
)
```

Figure 15.5 *Editing the macro script*

The pickpoint command asks for a point to be clicked on screen, or a location to be typed in X, Y, Z format. The position will be assigned to the pt variable.

When using strings, add \n to start in the next line.

3. Locate the pos:[...] statement in the torus line, and change it to pos:pt.

4. Evaluate the script, selecting File ➜ Evaluate All in the Script Editor menu, and save it. Nothing will happen here, but you will see the difference the next time you insert the object. Click the button and create more torus objects. Notice that now you have the option to select where you want each object.

5. Close the script.

6. Right-click the button and select Edit Button Appearance.

7. Select Text Button and type **Mouth** as in Figure 15.6.

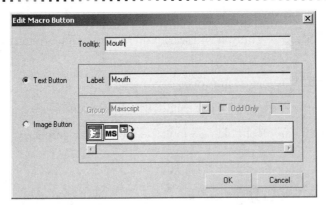

Figure 15.6 *Editing the button appearance*

8. Type the same text in the Tooltip, and click OK. Notice that you now have a text button, and it has a tooltip.

Using this exercise, you learned how simple it is to record an action and create a script with it. You also learned how to interact with the script and wait for user input.

You can also select an image icon for the button. Max comes with a huge number of button icons already created, one for each object and modifier; a small sample is shown in Figure 15.7.

Figure 15.7 *Preinstalled button icons*

Using the Macro Recorder

The Macro Recorder is one of the most important features in 3ds max. It records all scriptable actions you perform and outputs them in the script format. You can use it not only to create scripts directly using drag-and-drop, but also to create scripts using the commands you need without the need to memorize those commands.

You can configure the Macro Recorder by selecting the Macro Recorder menu in the Listener. You can configure MAXScript to record actions *absolutely*, which means in real-world PRS (Position, Rotation, and Scale) to a specific, named object; or *relatively*, which means relative to the PRS of the active selection. As an example, if you had all options as absolute, moving an object called Sphere01 would record the following line:

```
$Sphere01.pos = [10,10,10]
```

If you had all options as relative, it would record the following line:

```
move $ [-10,0,0]
```

If you used `$sphere01` in a script, it will only work if an object exists with that specific name. This is not a common situation in scripting, since you want the flexibility to apply the script to many different objects and situations.

 Always have the Macro Recorder configured for Relative and Selections. This way you can reuse your scripts, independent of the name of an object and its location in the scene. If you configure for Absolute, you will not be able to reuse your scripts for other objects, but only for the objects you had when you recorded the script.

In the Macro Recorder area of the Listener, you can save what has been recorded. When this file is loaded using the File ➜ Run Script command, it will repeat all the steps you have recorded. This way you can record information to be used in other scripts, as we will do in many exercises in Chapter 16.

Macro Recorder Limitations

The Macro Recorder records only actions that are exposed to MAXScript. Here's a list of some objects and functions that are *not* exposed:

- Compound objects, except Shapemerge and Terrain (which have limited support)
- NURBS curves and surfaces
- Line Shape
- Systems
- Anything in the Command Panel's Hierarchy panel
- Anything in Track View, except Controllers and Keys manipulation
- Anything in Video Post
- Render Scene dialog changes
- Array, Align, Spacing, Place Highlight, Mirror, Snapshot, etc.
- Anything in the Utility panel
- Commands in Editable Mesh, Poly, Spline, Patch, and NURBS (Position, Rotation, and Scale are recordable)
- Controller dialogs (like Noise Controller, Waveform Controller)
- Changes made to keys in Motion/Trajectories
- Hide/Freeze by Name and Hide/Freeze by Hit
- Display Color, Hide by Category, and Link Display
- Most rollout items in the Display Properties rollout in the Display panel
- Linking/unlinking in Schematic view

Many plug-ins are available for 3ds max 4. Some of them are recordable, and others are not, depending on how the developer created the plug-in code. It's a good idea to ask the developer about recordability and to request MAXScript capabilities in plug-ins.

Key Concept

Working with Variables

Variables are simply containers that hold a value, property, etc. Why do you need variables? To make scripting fluid and customizable. For instance, you can create a script to find out whether the current temperature is hot or cold. This script would compare the current temperature with a certain value. If the current temperature is below, say, 30 (Fahrenheit), it is cold. Your script would have a variable, called `temperature`, which you would compare to another variable, named `cold`, and this comparison would tell you if it is cold or not. Using this method, you can easily change the values of either variable and rerun the script over and over.

Variables are also useful because they allow you to know what property you are using, which is convenient when you are working with the name of the property, rather than the property itself. Suppose you need to access a property in a diffuse map of an object. To do it in MAXScript, you would need to use

```
object.material.diffusemap.property
```

If you assign a *variable* = `object.material.diffusemap`, you will save time using just *variable*.`property` in the future.

In MAXScript, the equal sign (=) acts as an assignment operator; it tells max to make the item on the left equal to the item(s) on the right. To find out whether two things are equal, we use a double equal sign (==), which is described in "Comparing Variables" below.

Compared to other programming languages, MAXScript makes it very easy to assign variables. Almost every programming language requires you to declare variables, variable types, and even the amount of memory to be used. In MAXScript, you don't need to do anything like this.

Assigning Variables

You assign a variable by simply entering a value for the variable. And you can use any kind of value—a number, a property, a string of text, etc.

You can use any name for a variable, excluding some names used by MAXScript commands, special characters, and spaces. A variable name can also have numbers, but it must start with a letter. Here are some of the most common types of variables you can assign in MAXScript.

Type of Variable	Description	Example
Integer	Integer number	`x = 1`
Float	Decimal number	`x = 1.2345`
String	Any text	`x = "celsius"`
Point2	Any XY position	`x = [12,-25]`
Point3	Any XYZ position, color, etc.	`x = [12,-25,8]`
Time	Time, in max formats (frames, SMTPE, seconds)	`x = 3m18s7f` (min, sec, frames)
Array	Array of variables	`x = #(8,"text",5f)`

You can assign an integer value to a variable, and later in the script you can assign a different value, which doesn't need to be an integer. This is different from many programming languages, where you can't automatically change a variable's type once it's assigned. However, very few max operations can be done mixing variable types.

Now you will assign some variables so you can see how it's done in MAXScript:

1. Open the Listener.

2. Type **x = 1** and press Shift+Enter.

 Pressing Shift+Enter processes the line and displays the result on the subsequent line in the output/command pane. (Pressing Enter alone moves the cursor to the next line, but it does not process the command unless the cursor is in the last line.) The numeric keypad Enter key processes the line the same way as Shift+Enter. This process step is called evaluating, and we'll refer to it this way in the book.

3. Type **y = 2.5** and evaluate.

4. If you type **x** and evaluate, MAXScript will display the value of the x variable.

Performing Math Operations

Math operations are performed the same way variables are assigned, simply by typing the math formula, for example, z = x + y.

All basic math rules are respected in MAXScript, which means that you can use parentheses and the precedence rules. That is, operations in parentheses will be evaluated first, followed by exponential operations; then multiply and divide, and finally addition and subtraction. Suppose you have the two following examples: 2 * 3 + 4 and 2 * (3 + 4). In the first instance, MAXScript will first calculate 2*3 and then add 4. In the second one, MAXScript will first calculate 3 + 4 and then multiply the result by 2.

Performing Basic Math Operations

Let's work with some variables and basic math operations to get a feel for how 3ds max handles these functions.

In the Listener, type and evaluate each line below. Check to see if the result you get matches the one in the following list.

Formula	Result
x = 2 + 3.5	5.5
x = 2 * (3 + 5)	16
x = 2 * 3 + 5	11
x = "abc" + "def"	"abcdef"
x = 3 ^ 2 * 4	36
x = 3 ^ (2 * 4)	6561
x = 16 * 2 / 5	6 (all numbers were integers)
x = 16.0 * 2 / 5	6.4 (at least one number is a float)
x = 27.0 / 5 * 3	16.2
x = 27.0 / (5 * 3)	1.8
x = [1,2,3] * 2	[2,4,6]
x = [1,2,3] + 5	[6,7,8]
x = [10,5,-8] + [3,8,2]	[13,13,-6]
x = [3,4,-2] * [4,1.5,-1]	[12,6,2]

You cannot perform math functions mixing numeric and nonnumeric variables. But you can add (concatenate) string variables. Also, notice in the examples in the table that you can perform simple operations using point2 and point3 variables, and even mix them with integers and floats.

When you are using the same variable on both sides of a simple equation, you can use a different syntax that is easier to manipulate: move the operator in front of the equal sign and omit the second variable. This is very useful, for example, when incrementing a variable: x += 1 is the same as x = x + 1. This rule is valid only for the four basic operations (addition, subtraction, multiplication, and division).

Performing Advanced Math Operations

Besides the basic operations, MAXScript supports all extended math functions like logarithms and trigonometry, and has a random number generator. Here are some examples.

Function	Description	Example	Result
abs	Absolute value	abs(-15)	15
mod	Remainder of a division	mod 20 3	2
sin	Sine	sin 45	0.707107
asin	Arcsine	asin 0.707107	45.0
sqrt	Square root	sqrt 196	14
random	Creates random values	random 0.0 1.0	0.318949
pi	π constant	pi	3.14159
e	Exponential Constant	e	2.71828
degtorad	Converts degrees to radians	degtorad 45	0.785398
radtodeg	Converts radians to degrees	radtodeg pi	180.0

These functions are extremely useful when dealing with math. For example, some controllers output values in radians, and they will require conversion to be manipulated in the UI.

There are many more math functions in max that are rarely used and not listed here. Check the online Help for a complete list.

We need math functions to create almost any script in max. In the following chapters we will use math functions in many scripts, to calculate positions and texture sizes and to manipulate bitmaps; and we even use trigonometry to create plug-in scripts. For instance, on Chapter 20, we'll create a plug-in script, and it requires us to use trigonometry to calculate the vertices coordinates.

To start, however, we'll try some very simple exercises that are not related to max but will teach you how to use math operations. In this exercise you'll create a simple script to convert Centigrade to Fahrenheit:

1. In the Listener, type C = 10 and evaluate.

2. Type F = (C/5 * 9) + 32 and evaluate. The result displayed will be 50.

3. Now type C = 0 and evaluate.

4. Scroll back to the end of the F = line and evaluate again. The result is now 32.

Notice that using the main keyboard's Enter key to evaluate this line will not work. You need to use the numeric keypad Enter or Shift+Enter now, as explained previously.

5. Repeat the steps above for C = 20, C = 30, and C = –5. The results should be 68, 86, and 23 respectively.

Key Concept

Using Strings

Every text variable is a *string*. Strings are used to format data output, add prompts for commands, and indicate file paths.

Any variable can be converted to a string simply by using

```
new_variable = old_variable as string
```

(You can convert to any variable type using this "as" method, except you cannot convert a string to a number, unless it's a numeric string such as *"2"*.)

You can also add a string variable to an existing string to create a larger string and to format data output. For instance, suppose you have the variable T = 30 and you want to write a script to output it, just like `Temperature` = T, but substituting the variable value for T. You can do it this way:

```
"Temperature = " + T as string
```

which will return `"Temperature = 30"`.

Outputting String Variables

All string variables can be output to the Listener. This is useful either to show the result of script calculations or to prompt the user for input. The `print` and `format` commands are used to output strings.

The `print` command simply prints the string to the Listener, to a new script window, or to a file. For instance, in our script that checks whether it's hot or cold, you could output the result using the `print` command this way:

```
print "It is hot."
```

For more information on printing to a new script or to a file, see "Text File I/O" later in this chapter.

The `format` command does the same as the `print` command, but it's easier to use when printing a series of variables and results. To use the `format` command, type the % character in the middle of the string, and it will be replaced by the variable results. For example, in

```
format "If it is below % it is cold. Above % it is hot." cold hot
```

the first % character will be replaced by the value of the `cold` variable and the second will be replaced with the value of the `hot` variable.

Using Special Characters in String Values

Some symbols and characters have special meanings when used for string values and must be used in a different format to differentiate these uses from the actual symbol or character. For instance, in the `format` command, the % symbol represents a variable value that will substitute for it, but if you need to display the actual % symbol in a string, you can use \% to represent it.

The next list presents some of the commonly used symbols and characters and their special formatting, and the results you'll see when you use that format:

Character	Result
\"	"
\n	New line
\\	\
\%	%
\?	?
\x*hex_number*	Character represented by the hexadecimal value

In particular, \\ characters are very important for defining file paths.

 3ds max uses the extended ASCII table available in Windows. To find a character's decimal value, use the Character Map.

Special Characters in Strings

When using \x*hex_number*, make sure you have a space after it, or any following text will be understood as part of the hex value. For instance, `print "35\xb0C"` will not return the degree symbol (decimal 176 in the character set max uses), but instead will attempt to evaluate b0c as the hexadecimal character. To get the degree symbol, you will need to separate the strings and add them, this way:

```
print ("35" + "\xb0" + "C")
```

This will return "35°C".

Use \n (for a new line) at the end of a string, to make the interface look cleaner in the Listener. As an example, when you create an error message, you can have multiple lines to show the user what the error was, as in this example:

```
print "Error!\nSelect a 3D Object."
```

This will return:

```
"Error
Select a 3D Object."
```

Manipulating Strings

Sometimes you might need part of a string, or you might need to search for words and characters inside strings. MAXScript provides you a series of commands that allow you to do it.

Searching for Text

The `findstring` command searches for a string inside another string, and returns the character position of the match. If there is more than one match, it returns only the first. For instance,

```
findstring "It is hot here." "h"
```

will return 7.

All strings have an option that shows how many characters are in the string. Simply type `string_variable.count` and you'll get the number of characters in that string variable.

Cropping Text

The `substring` command crops part of a string and returns it as a new string. It works by defining the character position and the number of characters to copy. For instance

```
substring "It is hot above 80F." 7 3
```

will return `"hot"`.

Findstring is very useful when used together with `substring`, to search and filter the string portion you want. For instance, you can use

```
str = "It is hot above 80F."
substring str (findstring str "h") 3
```

This line will search for and copy the letter "h" and the next two letters in a single command.

Transforming Text into Commands

The `execute` command executes the string as a command. It's very useful when you need to use an object name in the scene or read some information from a file.

For instance, `execute "temperature = 25.9"` would set the value of the variable `temperature` to 25.9. This value could have been read from a file or entered as text in any field.

You can use the \ " *special character to insert string variables or values inside an* execute *command. For instance,* execute "a = \"temperature\"".

Entering Data

Sometimes you might need the user to type a value or text in the Listener—an object name, a function value, a position, and so on. MAXScript provides functions for these types of tasks.

Entering Text

Using the getkbline ("get keyboard line") command you can ask the user to type text in the Listener. It may or not use a prompt to ask the user to type something. For example, you can use

```
user_name = getkbline prompt:"Enter your name:"
```

The user name will be stored in the user_name variable.

Entering Values

Using the getkbvalue ("get keyboard value") command you can ask the user to type a numerical value in the Listener. It works exactly the same way as getkbline, except that it returns a float or an integer variable.

Both getkbvalue *and* getkbline *can be used to ask the user to enter numeric values, but when using* getkbline, *the script must convert the variable to float or integer, using the command* variable = variable as float *or as* integer. *If the user entered a letter instead of a number, the conversion will return undefined.*

Using Conditions

Conditional commands are essential for any programming language. They allow your program to test values and perform different actions, based on the result. Conditions make the script "think" and react the way you want it to. We use conditions in 3ds max to drive the programs' direction. For instance, you may want to select a specific type of object in the scene. To do that, your script would search all objects in the scene and then use conditions to verify if an object matches your criteria. If it does, you store it in a variable. If not, you discard it and move on until all objects have been searched. We'll do that in an exercise later in this chapter.

If...

The if command is *very* powerful. It can test and check for values and perform the selected actions if the comparison is met.

Comparing Variables

First, you need to learn how comparisons work in MAXScript. You can check for basically four conditions: whether two variables are equal or different, or whether one is greater or smaller than the other. The syntax to do this is simple:

```
variable1 comparison_operator variable2
```

This expression will return True if the comparison is true, or False if it fails.

If a comparison is entered in the Listener, MAXScript will output True or False. If it's part of a scripted command, no value will be printed, but the script will read the True/False and will act as needed.

These are the comparisons that can be made in MAXScript:

Symbol	Comparison
==	equal to (*two* equal signs; remember, this is different from =)
!=	different from
>	greater than
<	less than
>=	greater than or equal to
<=	less than or equal to

Equal to and *different from* can be used in all variable types or functions, and the remaining comparisons can be used only with numerical values or functions.

Actions Based on Comparisons

Using the if command and comparisons, you can make the script react the way you want it to. We will use a simple example here to illustrate how conditions work, but you will see that we use conditions in all scripts we write, like checking whether the user selected a valid object, if the object has a material applied, if the value is a valid color value (color values must be in the range 0–255), etc. The next few chapters are full of practical examples of conditions and comparisons.

In this example you can check the current temperature to see whether it's cold or hot. Then, if it's cold, the script will output a sentence telling you it's cold. If it's hot, the script will tell you so. This is a simple example of comparisons and actions based on comparisons.

The if command requires two keywords to define which action to take: then and else. It works by making a comparison; then, if the comparison is true, it runs a series of actions; else, if the comparison is false, it runs a different set of actions. The else statement can be omitted if a False result means the script just doesn't do anything.

The IF command always waits for an else *to output all results. To see the result on screen after the latest* if, *type something, and you'll see the result being evaluated. Instead of* if... then... else, *you can use* if... do, *which will not wait for an* else; do *will evaluate the result automatically.*

For instance, let's write a small script to test whether the current temperature (30ºF) is hot or cold:

```
cur_temperature = 30
if cur_temperature > 80 then print "It is hot."
if cur_temperature < 40 then print "It is cold."
```

In our example, the temperature will be checked, and the result will be output on the screen. If you want to go a bit further and allow the user to interact with the script, you can change the first line to

```
cur_temperature = getkbvalue prompt:"Enter current temperature:"
```

Now, the script works by itself and allows you to test for different temperature values.

Multiple Comparisons

Sometimes a script might need to make more than one comparison. You can do this using Boolean expressions, such as and and or. The and Boolean will return True *only* if all comparisons are true; or will return True if at least one is true. For instance, (2 < 4) and (sin 45 < 1) will return True, because both conditions are met. The expression (2 < 4) or (sin 45 > 1) will also return True, because at least one of the conditions is true.

The Boolean expression not inverts the expression being checked. For instance, not (2 > 4) will return True, because you're checking to see if 2 is not greater than 4, which is true.

Using Boolean expressions makes it easier to create multiple comparisons, instead of creating a series of comparisons and commands. Let's redo the temperature example, now using Boolean expressions and else:

```
cur_temperature = getkbvalue prompt:"Enter current temperature:"
if (cur_temperature <= 80) AND (cur_temperature >= 40) then
    print "It is warm"
  else
    if cur_temperature > 80 then
      print "It is hot"
    else
      print "It is cold"
```

It's useful to tabulate a script (that is, indent it with spaces or tabs like the example code above) so you can keep track of the organization of the comparisons. The Script Editor makes it easier to create this formatting, inheriting the same tabulation when you break lines.

This script will return the result immediately because you used if... then... else, covering all conditions. It also demonstrates that you do not need to make a comparison for a temperature lower than 40, because it's the only option that remains after all other comparisons.

Now select all the lines in this script and drag them to a toolbar, creating a Macro Script. Edit the button so it reads "Temperature." Once you press this Temperature button (see Figure 15.8), max will ask you the temperature, you type it, and you'll be told whether it's hot or cold.

Key
Concept

Repeating Tasks

The biggest advantage of any programming language is the ability to repeat tasks automatically. MAXScript provides tools for repetition, which will be useful when you're dealing with objects, materials, etc.

In max, you never deal with just a single object, a single material, etc. Once you have a selection set, you have many objects. If you want to classify them, or filter the selection to contain, say, only light objects that are on, you'll use a command that provides you a way to repeat the same task over and over. This will save you time, and it will make your scripts flexible, so that they work regardless of the number of interactions you need them to run.

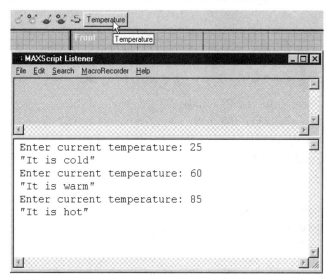

Figure 15.8 *Temperature script*

Arrays

To know more about repeating tasks, you need to learn about arrays. An *array* is a variable made of a series of nested variables. When you want to repeat the same action on a series of max elements, you'll represent those elements as variables within an array. Arrays can hold any type of variables and can even mix types.

You define an array variable by assigning it and the values of its members, all at once. For instance, a = #(10,20,30) will create an array of three variables, and will set 10, 20, and 30 as the value of each member of the array. Then, to access any element of this array, you use *array[i]*, where *array* is the array name, and *i* is the index of this element. For instance, a[1] will return 10, a[2] is 20, and a[3] is 30.

Arrays, like strings, have a count property you can use to see how many elements are in an array. To do this, type *array*.count.

Adding Elements to an Array

To add elements to an array, simply type *array[i]* = *value*. This index can be any integer number. For instance, if you create an empty array a, using a = #(), and add the third element of this array using a[3] = 5, you will create an array with two undefined values, a[1] and a[2].

To automatically add a value to the next available element of an array, you can use the append command. Continuing from the example above, you could use the command append a "hot" and "hot" would be added as the fourth element of this array.

Sequential Tasks

By using the for command, you can make the script repeat the same steps *for* as long as you want. for is essential when manipulating objects, as you will see in Chapter 16.

The for command counts from one number to another and repeats a series of commands within this interval. For instance,

```
for x in 1 to 6 do print x
```

will repeat the print command six times, printing "123456".

For is often used with arrays, accessing the different elements of an array. For instance,

```
for i in 1 to a.count do print a[i]
```

will step through all elements of the array and print them.

Nonsequential Tasks

Sometimes you don't know how many times you will need to repeat an action; it must be repeated until you meet a condition, and then the script can move on to something else. This can be done using while.

The while command will run *while* a particular condition is true, and will stop running when that condition has changed. For instance, you can use while to ask the user to enter data to be used in a script; when the user types **Exit**, the script stops entering data. You can do that easily, like this:

```
test = 0
data = #()
while test != "Exit" do
    (
    test = getkbline prompt:"Enter data (type Exit to stop): "
    if test != "Exit" then append data test
    )
```

This example shows how parentheses define a series of commands to be executed inside the while command. You can use parentheses every time an action needs more than one command, in `if... then... else` or in `for` statements. The parentheses also help you organize and understand the script better.

The `while` command evaluates all lines before it checks for the condition again. That's why you added `if test != "Exit"`, because the `while` will only exit the loop after the loop ends. This way you will not append "Exit" to the array.

Use the `while` command with caution because it may freeze a script. If you ask the script to check for a variable and forget to change the result of this variable after each check, `while` will loop infinitely. To exit this loop, you must press the Esc key, which will interrupt any script being processed.

Key Concept

Creating Functions

Functions are your tool for creating new commands in MAXScript. These commands will process some data and return an answer. Functions are useful when you need to repeat actions frequently in a script; instead of repeating a series of commands, you create a function and use it, making the script smaller and faster.

To define a function, you first need to define what data will be needed by the function. For instance, let's create a function to convert integer numbers to four-digit string numbers, like "0001" for 1 and "0100" for 100, used when you add a suffix to a bitmap that will be saved to disk. This function will take the number and return the converted string.

First, let's define the function:

```
function nth_number number =
  (
  if number < 10 then
    return_value = ("000" + number as string)
   else
    if number < 100 then
      return_value = ("00" + number as string)
     else
      if number < 1000 then
        return_value = ("0" + number as string)
       else
        return_value = number as string
  return_value
  )
```

In this case, the function is named `nth_number`, and it requires one argument, `number`, that will be processed. This number will be checked within the function and a `return_value` variable will be created. This variable will return the formatted number; this function can be used as

```
formatted_number = nth_number number
```

where you would substitute any integer for `number`.

You can test this script by typing `a = nth_number 27`; it will return `"0027"`.

Organizing Complex Data

To organize complex data in MAXScript you can use *structures*. Structures are useful to help you understand variables and their properties. A structure is a compound variable where you can define properties; to define a structure, simply type

```
struct variablename (property1name, property2name, ...)
```

For instance, you can create a structure to manage a project. This structure will have three properties: the name of the person who is working, starting time, and end time. The following code defines a structure type and then creates one variable using that type:

```
struct project (name, start, end)
oct2599 = project (name:"John", start:11.5, end:14.25)
```

To access this data later, all you would need to do is type *variable.value*; for example, `oct2599.name` will return "John". The same applies to all other properties.

Below is a sample script that will convert the local time to a structure variable storing the date and the number of seconds. It shows you almost all the concepts taught in this chapter. We will use this script later, in Chapter 19.

```
struct clock (day, month, year, sec)
fn right_now =
(
ctime = clock()
l = localtime
l_tmp = filterstring l " :/"
m = l_tmp[1] as integer
d = l_tmp[2] as integer
if m > 12 do (tmp = d; d = m; m = tmp)
y = l_tmp[3] as integer
```

```
h = l_tmp[4] as integer
mm = l_tmp[5] as integer
s = l_tmp[6] as integer
if l_tmp.count > 6 then
    (
    if h == 12 then h = 0
    if l_tmp[7] == "PM" do h += 12
    )
ctime.day = d
ctime.month = m
ctime.year = y
ctime.sec = s + mm * 60 + h * 60 * 60
return ctime
)
```

This script will check to see whether the time configuration in your system is
A.M./P.M. or 24-hour, but it will not accept dates in dd/mm/yyyy format. It works by
filtering the localtime string, outputting the date and time as integer values. This filtering is handled by filterstring, which removes the specified characters from the
string and outputs an array of the elements.

Then the script converts the hour, minute, and second values to seconds only.
Manipulating only the seconds and converting the output result to hours, minutes, and
seconds later saves script code and processing time.

All the result values are placed in a structure variable, which separates the data to
be reused easily later.

To execute it, simply assign a new variable to the function right_now. This will
assign the current time to this variable. This script is useful for calculating how long a
certain function takes to process. For instance, start = right_now() will return
#clock(day:27, month:4, year:2001, sec:23119). You can later assign a new
variable and compare it with this one, calculating the time lapse.

Text File I/O: Reading and Writing Data

You can read data from and write data to a text file, adding further flexibility to your work
in MAXScript. This file can contain initial settings for a script, data to be imported and
processed, or simply the results of any calculation made in any script.

Managing Files

As in any programming language, files must be opened or created before you can manipulate them in MAXScript.

Creating Files

The `createfile` command creates a new file and allows you to write to it. For instance,

```
fname = createfile "c:\\3dsmax4\\scripts\\test.dat"
```

creates a `test.dat` file. The value assigned to this variable is a *filestream* value. Filestream is a File I/O class, which means this variable represents a file opened for input/output.

Notice that you've used \\ instead of \, because \\ is the special character that is used to represent a single \ in strings.

Later, when you start writing to this file, you can simply use the `print...to` command, like this: `print "Sample text" to:`*fname*, which will write this string into the destination file. (If the destination file isn't empty, `print...to` adds the string to the end of the file.)

If you want to write data to a file and you want it to create a line break, make sure you add \n to the string.

Opening Existing Files

The `openfile` command will open existing files for reading or appending. It works exactly like `createfile`, except that you can specify the mode in which you opening the file: a is for appending and r is read-only.

If the file does not exist, `openfile` will return undefined. For instance,

```
fname = openfile "c:\\3dsmax4\\scripts\\test.dat" mode:"r"
```

will open the `test.dat` file as read-only.

All files must be closed after they are used (whether they were created or opened), using the syntax `close` filename. If you do not close the file, you will not be able to access it outside MAXScript, and you will be wasting memory.

Reading and Writing Data

Once you open a file or create one, you can read or write data to it. All data read from a file is in string format and must be converted to integer, float, or another format if needed.

Writing Data

Writing data to a file is as simple as outputting data in the Listener. The `print` and `format` commands have an option that allows their output to be directed to a file. Simply add TO:*filestream*, where *filestream* is the variable you assigned the file to, using either `openfile` or `createfile`. For instance, you could have:

```
fname = createfile "C:\\test.dat"
format "This is sample text.\nThis is the second line." to:fname
close fname
```

This would create a file and write two lines of text in it. After creating the file, open it in Explorer, and you will see the data written to it. Notice you've closed the file after printing data to it. If you hadn't closed it, you would not be allowed to open it in Explorer.

Reading Data

Reading data from a file is similar to writing it. You can use a series of commands to locate text, position the file, etc. Let's see some of these.

The `readline` command allows you to read one line of the file. For instance, continuing to work on the file you created before:

```
fname = openfile "C:\\test.dat" mode:"r"
str = readline fname
close fname
```

`str` will be the first line of the file, which is "This is sample text."

The `readchar` command allows you to read a single character of the file and works the same way as `readline`.

The `eof` condition will tell you if your script has reached the end of the file or if there is still data to be read. It's useful in a `while` command that reads all the data in a file. For instance, the script below will read all lines of the file and store them in the `str` array:

```
fname = openfile "C:\\test.dat"
str = #()
count = 1
while not eof fname do
```

```
(
str[count] = readline fname
count += 1
)
close fname
```

There are more commands to read and manipulate data from a text file, like reading encrypted files, reading delimited strings, seeking data, and so on, but these more specialized commands are not commonly used. You can learn about them on the online Help.

INI Files

MAXScript has implemented special read/write commands to manipulate INI files. INI files are special files with the following syntax:

```
[Section1]
key1 = string_value1
key2 = string_value2
[Section2]
...
```

It's easier to manipulate these files through MAXScript because you don't need to worry about opening or closing files. All you need to do is define a useful format. Their only limitation is that the value stored will always be a string.

You can store numerical data in INI files, but this data will have to be converted to a number, using as integer *or* as float.

Let's create a single file that will be manipulated later:

```
fname = createfile "c:\\test.ini"
print "[Objects]" to:fname
print "\nGeometry=" to:fname
print "\nLights=" to:fname
close fname
```

After the file is created, you can manipulate it using getinisetting or setinisetting. Getinisetting will read the value stored in a keyword in a given section, and setinisetting will write a new value to a keyword.

For instance, in our example, type:

```
setinisetting "c:\\test.ini" "Objects" "Geometry" "Box"
```

This will write the "Box" string to the Geometry keyword. If the keyword or the section does not exist, it is created. If you want to read this value, simply use `getinisetting`:

```
getinisetting "c:\\test.ini" "Objects" "Geometry"
```

If the INI file is blank or nonexistent, `setinisetting` *creates it and also creates the structure for you.*

Working with Binary Files

3ds max 4 also allows you to work with binary files. The commands are very similar to text file I/O, and the same rules of opening, creating, and closing the file apply. For example, you can create a game engine Import/Export plug-in using binary file I/O.

Managing Binary Files

To create or open binary files you can use `fopen`. Fopen will need a string mode, which can be either `"wb"` for writing or `"rb"` for reading. For instance,

```
binfile = fopen "c:\\test.bin" "wb"
```

will open or create the file `test.bin` for writing.

To close the file you can use `fclose`. To move to a specific position in the file, you can use `fseek`, and to see which position you are in the file, use `ftell`. For instance, `fseek binfile 0` will return to the beginning of the file.

Reading and Writing Binary Data

You can read and write five different types of binary data: String, Short Integer, Long Integer, Float, and Byte. For instance, to write a long integer you would use the `writelong` command. To read a short integer you would use `readshort`, and so on.

The following example creates and writes binary data to a file:

```
binfile = fopen "c:\\myfile.bin" "wb"
writelong binfile 1838
writestring binfile "test"
writebyte binfile 65
fclose binfile
```

Summary

The concepts in this chapter have helped you understand better the way MAXScript works. You've learned also a bit of programming logic, which is the way the computer "thinks."

   In the next chapter, you'll learn how to manipulate scene elements, how to interact with objects, and how to create materials, using several concepts learned in this chapter.

Manipulating Scenes with MAXScript

3ds max

Chapter 16

One of the primary uses of MAXScript is to work with scene objects, creating, modifying, and automating any task that can be done with the objects.

In this chapter you will learn about some of the MAXScript tools you can use to manipulate scenes and work with objects. Throughout the chapter you will have an opportunity to try out what you've learned by creating real, working scripts.

- Scripting objects

- Accessing global object properties

- Replicating objects

- Creating materials

- Scripting modifiers and options

- Creating and managing a hierarchy

- Using environment and render effects

- Working with splines

- Working with meshes

- Working with editable poly objects

- Working with patches

Scripting Objects

Using MAXScript you can create and modify almost everything in max. There are some restrictions, which are the same restrictions that apply to the Macro Recorder (see the section "Macro Recorder Limitations" in Chapter 15).

Working with objects in MAXScript takes advantage of the object-oriented behavior of 3ds max 4. Let's see how.

Creating an Object and Accessing Its Properties

You can create objects in MAXScript by just assigning an object to a variable. It's as simple as typing a = box(). If you do so, a default-size box (25×25×25) will be created. In the same way, you can create every primitive, helper, camera, light, and so forth. Complex objects, such as editable meshes, splines, patches, NURBS, and compound objects, require different commands.

As soon as you assign an object to a variable (or create an object and then assign it to the variable), you can access any object property using this variable. The property will be valid until the object is deleted, the variable is redefined, or 3ds max is restarted.

If you want a variable to be saved with a scene, you need to use persistent global variables. See Chapter 19 for more information.

When you create a simple object, as in the box example above, it's created with a default size, position, etc. You will most likely want to access and change this data. But in order to do so, you need to know which data is available for you. Why? Because every object has different properties. For instance, a sphere has a radius, but a box has height, length, and width. To list an object's properties, you use the showproperties command. Once you have typed **a = box()**, then if you type

```
showproperties a
```

MAXScript will list the properties in the Listener, as shown in Figure 16.1.

You can access any of this box's properties by typing a.*property* (for example, a.height would display 25). You can also change the values of each property, typing a.*property* = *value* (for example, a.height = 60).

You can set an object property at the time of creation, specifying the properties and their values:

```
a = box height:60 width:30 length:40
```

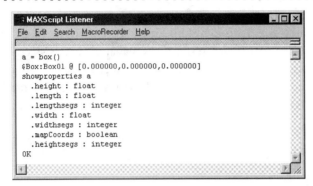

Figure 16.1 *Displaying an object's properties with* `showproperties`

There's no limit to the number of properties you can define, and if any property is not listed, it will be set to its default value. If a property is listed but does not relate to that object, it's discarded.

Besides using `showproperties`*, you can also record an object creation and its parameter changes as a macro. This makes it easier for you to manipulate objects, and keeps you from having to memorize hundreds of commands and properties.*

Key Concept

Accessing an Object by Name

Sometimes you do not create objects in MAXScript, but you need to process objects already created. To do so, you need to learn how to select objects and manipulate selections, and how to refer to objects by name.

You can access any object by its name simply by adding the $ symbol before the object name. For instance, if you have an object named "Wall," you can access it using $wall.

Object names in MAXScript are not case-sensitive. If you have two objects, one named "Ball" and another named "ball," MAXScript will not distinguish between them even if you use $ball *or* $Ball*. (And 3ds max, unfortunately, allows you to name as many objects as you wish with the same name.)*

You can also assign variables that point to named objects in the scene, like a = $wall. From then on, you can access the object as a or as $wall.

If the object is renamed, you cannot use $name any more. But if you assign $name to a variable and later rename the object, this variable can be used. For example, you could create a box named "Box01", type var = $box01, *and then rename "Box01." If you type* var, *MAXScript shows you the box properties; if you type* $Box01 *it returns undefined.*

If your object name has spaces, you will need to surround the name with single quotes. For instance, to refer to an object called "box object" you would use $'box object'.

Working with Selections

Sometimes you don't know a specific object name in advance, or you do not want to use a specific object, but you want to use an object that the user will select while running your script. You can refer to selections in two ways: using selection, which is an array of all selected objects, or using the $ symbol.

There are some peculiarities in selections that need to be addressed. First, it is very important to know how many objects have been selected, using $.count or selection.count. This is important because if selection.count returns only one object selected, this object can be accessed simply using $. On the other hand, if it returns more than one object, you must use selection[i], where i is the index number, to access each object in the selection array.

Manipulating Selections

You can add or remove objects from a selection. To remove an object from the selection, use the deselect command; to add objects to a selection, use the selectmore command. To simply discard any selection and select a specific object, you can use the select command.

You can use wildcards when specifying object names. For instance, if you want to select all objects that start with "B", you can use select $B*. *If you want to select all objects that end in "01" you can use* $*01. *You can also use the "?" wildcard to represent a single character.*

Using Built-in Selections

Max has built-in selections based on the object type. This makes it easier for you to select all 3D objects in the scene, or all lights, etc. These built-in selections are:

Selection	Objects Selected
objects	All objects in the scene
geometry	All 3D objects
shapes	All 2D objects
lights	All lights
cameras	All cameras
spacewarps	All space warps

You can combine these selections with the previous commands to create any selection you need. For instance, these three commands select all cameras and 3D objects, and then remove some specific objects:

```
select cameras
selectmore geometry
deselect $*02
```

The last command removes from the selection every object that has "02" at the end of its name.

Identifying Objects with Object Classes

MAXScript identifies each different object type as a *class*. For instance, spheres are from the Sphere class and boxes are from the Box class. This helps you filter objects and know exactly which objects you want to select or manipulate.

Classes aren't valid only for objects. Classes are a way to identify each and every object, modifier, material, or effect in 3ds max.

In order to know which class an object belongs to, use the classof command. To try an example, create and select a sphere in your scene. Now type **classof $**. MAXScript will return the class of that object, sphere.

Besides the class, MAXScript has a property called *superclass*, the general category the object type belongs to. For spheres and boxes alike, typing **superclassof $** will return geometryclass, since both classes are 3D objects.

You can now build a simple script to select all spheres in the scene:

```
clearselection()
for i in 1 to objects.count do
  (
  if classof objects[i] == sphere then selectmore objects[i]
  )
```

In this script, `clearselection` is a new command; all it does is remove all selections. The `for` command steps through each object in the scene. The `if` command checks to see whether the object is a sphere and, if it is, adds the object to the selection.

Accessing Global Object Properties

Some properties, like name and class, are valid for all objects in the scene. You'll address them often in your scripts, so let's examine them.

You can access all the properties listed in the Object Properties dialog box (Figure 16.2) in MAXScript. These properties include the name, wireframe color, and cast and receive shadows. Other properties, valid for almost all objects, will define the hierarchy, the material, whether the object is hidden or frozen, whether it is a target or is looking at one target, and more.

All properties in the Object Properties dialog box can be accessed through MAXScript. Just type **object.property = value** and you will set its value. If the property is represented by a check box, the value will be either True (checked) or False (unchecked). Other properties require a different value; Object Channel, for instance, is an integer number. Here are a few of the properties that can be accessed:

Property	Description
.name	Object name
.wirecolor	Viewport color
.ishidden	Returns True if the object is hidden
.gbufferchannel	Object channel ID
.visibility	Controls the object's visibility track
.renderable	Controls whether the object renders
.boxmode	Display as box

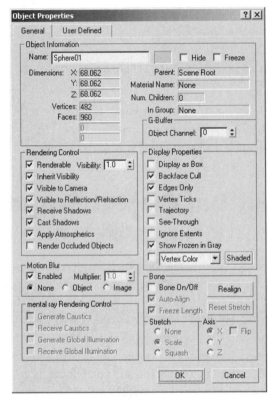

Figure 16.2 *The Object Properties dialog box*

You do not need to memorize all the properties. Just turn on Macro Recorder and change any number of object properties. All changes will be recorded.

Spline Properties

MAXScript has some properties that are valid only for splines. These properties control the General Properties for splines, which are shown in Figure 16.3. Max 4 has implemented some new features in splines, giving you more control over the spline visibility and also allowing animation.

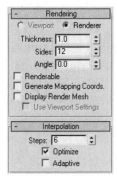

Figure 16.3 *The Spline general properties rollout*

The MAXScript spline properties are `.steps`, `.optimize`, `.adaptive`, `.renderable`, `.thickness`, `.sides`, `.angle`, and `.mapcoords`, controlling exactly the same properties displayed in Figure 16.3. Thickness, sides, and angle are the only ones that support animation.

Notice that Spline objects have two `renderable` *properties: one for the spline itself and one as an object. When you access the* `renderable` *property, you're reading the max object property. If you want to access the spline's property, you need to use* `.baseobject.property`*. For instance, to access the* `renderable` *property in the spline object named "circle," you would use the command* `$circle.baseobject.renderable`*. Unfortunately, these properties are not macro recordable.*

Replicating Objects

Sometimes you might need to create copies of an object, maintaining or not maintaining a relationship with the original. You can do so using any of three commands: `copy`, `instance`, or `reference`. They produce exactly the same result as the Copy, Instance, and Reference operations in max. For example, if you create a box using `b = box()` and want to copy it, use `c = copy b`. The `reference` and `instance` commands work exactly the same way.

Another interesting way to create a copy is the `snapshot` *command. It copies the object, converting it to an editable mesh, but it considers all space warps and effects applied to the object.*

Accessing an Object's Position, Rotation, and Scale

It's very important to know where an object is in space and which transformation has been applied to it. You might access a box object in MAXScript and read its height, but this will not serve for anything if you don't read which Z scale was applied to it.

All transformations depend mainly on which controller has been assigned to an object. Usually, you access position, rotation, and scale simply by adding `.position`, `.rotation`, and `.scale` to an object.

Position and Scale

Position is the easiest to work with. Simply adding `.pos` or `.position` will usually access the object's position. A position's value is a point3 variable, where you can access independently `.x`, `.y`, and `.z`.

Position values can also be specified when the object is created (as in the statement `b = box pos:[10,20,10]`), just like any other object option.

Some objects may not allow you to access position data using `.pos`, because they have a special controller. For example, because bone objects have an IK controller, using `.pos` may return invalid or undefined. Bones with end effectors or without the IK controllers will allow `.pos`. To find their position in space, you can use the command `.transform.translation`, which will read the current translation of the object in 3D space. This command works for all objects in max, no matter which controller has been applied. As a rule of thumb, use `.pos` to access PRS controllers and `.transform.translation` for all others.

Scale works exactly the same way as position. In some cases, if `.scale` fails, you can use `.transform.scale`.

Rotation

Rotation might be a little bit difficult to understand. This is because max uses TCB (Tension, Continuity, and Bias) rotation by default. TCB rotation uses a quaternion algebra (or *quats*) to calculate the rotation. TCB rotations are smooth for animation, but it's a little hard to manipulate TCB values in MAXScript, since the quaternion doesn't show us directly the rotation of the object. For more information on quats and TCB rotation, refer to the MAXScript online Help.

We'll make rotation simple and use a different rotation method, called *eulerangles*. These are X/Y/Z rotation vectors that work the same way as position and scale. In order to access the rotation without using quats, you need to access each axis independently, using *object*.`rotation.`*axis*`_rotation`, substituting x, y, or z for `axis`.

You cannot access the Euler rotation using `.transform.rotation`. *A workaround is to convert it to Euler using* `as  eulerangles`. *Then you can read each axis separately.*

For instance, to access a box's Z rotation for an object assigned to the b variable, you can use b.`rotation.z_rotation`.

Hands-on MAXScript: Creating an Array and Changing the Rotation

Let's create a script that creates an array of objects and changes their rotation across the array, as in Figure 16.4.

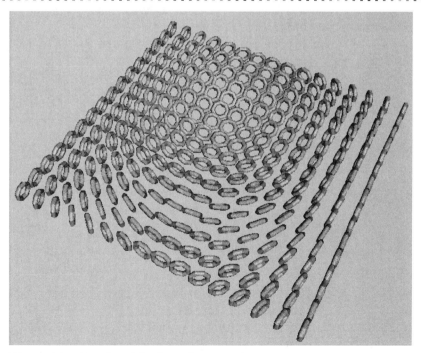

Figure 16.4 *Results of the Array Rotate script*

The `array` command can create a 2D array but does not allow you to rotate the objects in two axes in the array. This script enables you to assign a different X and Y rotation.

To work with this script, you first will need to select an object. Then, the script will ask you how many rows and columns you want in the array. Finally, you define the position of the first object in the bottom left of the array.

Start a new script and type all the commands shown in Listing 16.1. If you prefer, open this code, using MAXScript ➜ Open Script, from the CD-ROM that accompanies this book, in the file named `array_exercise.ms`.

LISTING 16.1: THE ARRAY ROTATE SCRIPT (ARRAY_EXERCISE.MS)

```
if selection.count == 0 then
    format "Select at least one object.\n"
    else
    (
    obj = $
    size_x = abs(obj.min.x - obj.max.x)
    size_y = abs(obj.min.y - obj.max.y)
    nx = getkbvalue prompt:"Enter number of objects in X:" \
        as float
    ny = getkbvalue prompt:"Enter number of objects in Y:" \
        as float
    pt = pickpoint prompt:"Select Start Position:"
    start_x = -90
    start_y = -90
    end_x = 90
    end_y = 90
    for j in 0 to ny do
        (
        for i in 0 to nx do
            (
            s = copy obj
            s.wirecolor = obj.wirecolor
            s.pos = [pt.x + size_x * i, pt.y + size_y * j, pt.z]
            s.rotation.x_rotation = \
                start_x + (end_x - start_x) * i/nx
            s.rotation.y_rotation = \
                start_y + (end_y - start_y) * j/ny
            )
        )
    )
```

Notice that we added a backslash (\\) character at the end of the physical line to indicate that the script continues on the next line. Although you can do this in your code, you do not need to add a backslash when writing scripts, because the MAXScript Editor allows very long lines, but we need to break lines so they fit the book's format.

Select all lines and drag them to the Compounds tab, or to any toolbar of your choice. Edit the icon and rename it to "Array Rotate." Now let's examine how the script works.

First, it checks to see if there's an object selected. If not, the script returns a message asking the user to select an object before using the script, then the script ends.

If there are objects selected, `abs (obj.max - obj.min)` tells us how large the object or the selection is in X and Y. Using `getkbvalue` and `pickpoint`, we ask the user for the information the script needs: the number of copies in X, Y and the position of the first object.

The `start_x` and `snd_x` variables define the initial and final rotation of the object around the X axis, and this rotation will be progressive, which means that any object between the first and the last in X will be rotated until it reaches the final rotation value. The same happens in Y.

We used nested `for` commands here, one to copy the object in X and other to copy the object in Y. This is possible because we're multiplying the size and the `i` or `j` value, which will make it possible to calculate the position of the object in the array. The math is simple: initial position in X added to the distance in X multiplied by the number of the copy (`i` or `j`).

Next comes the rotation part. The rotation is incremental, and we have the start and end values, so the script makes this calculation:

start + (end − start) × object number / total number of objects

This way, we will increment the rotation for each copy that's done. Since we're doing the same in X and Y, we will be able to apply rotation to the objects in the two axes.

You could enhance the script by asking the user for the initial and final rotation, and you could also add a user interface, which you will learn to do in Chapter 17.

Creating Materials

Materials are essential to any scene you develop in max. And of course, MAXScript can access every parameter in any material. To assign or access a material in one object, use the form *object.material*. This will return the material assigned to an object. You can also assign a material to a variable and later assign it to an object, using the syntax forms *variable = material* and then *object.material = variable*.

The same rules apply to MAXScript as elsewhere in max: if you modify a material that has been assigned to an object, all other objects that have this material will be modified, unless you clone it before modifying.

Standard Materials

Materials work the same way as objects. If you assign a standard material to one object, it will be assigned with default values, until you change them.

You can create a blank standard material by simply typing

```
variable = standardmaterial()
```

or

```
variable = standard()
```

Then, you can assign this material to an object using

```
object.material = variable
```

You can assign the material directly to the object. It's just easier to manage the material when you have it assigned to a variable first.

Each material has a series of properties, which can be listed by the showproperties command. For instance, type **m = standardmaterial()**. Now enter the command **showproperties m**. You will see all properties of this material. Note that you need to have the material assigned to a variable before using showproperties. The command showproperties standardmaterial() does not work.

Defining Colors

The first thing you need to adjust in a material is the color. One of the ways to define colors in MAXScript is using a point3 variable, similar to position or scale.

You can define any color in any material using

```
material.color = [red,green,blue]
```

The property will vary depending on which color will be defined. Using the example above, you'd set the diffuse color to red with m.diffusecolor = [255,0,0].

Defining Shaders

In 3ds max, materials can be made using different shaders. Each shader will define a series of properties to the material.

You can define the shader using two different properties: .shadertype, which will require an index number of the shader; or .shaderbyname, which will require a string with the name of the shader. Figures 16.5 and 16.6 show examples of two different shaders.

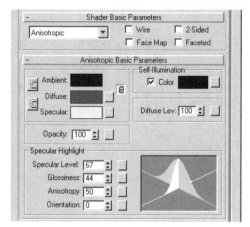

Figure 16.5 *Anisotropic shader options*

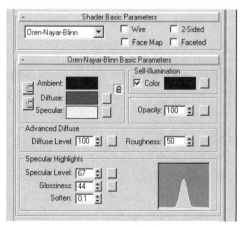

Figure 16.6 *Oren-Nayar-Blinn shader options*

As soon as you change a material shader, the properties of that material will also change. For instance, if the shader is Strauss, you will not be able to set the `.ambientcolor` *property, because ambient color does not exist in that shader.*

Using the same example you used above, let's set a different shader and some properties. Type **m.shaderbyname = "Strauss"**.

Working with Maps in Materials

Besides working with materials, you also need to work with maps. MAXScript can access any information within any map in max. Let's look at some maps and see how you can work with them in materials.

Texture Maps

The first, and possibly the most used, type of map you will see is the *bitmap*. To create a bitmap you simply use *variable* = `bitmaptexture()`. Since it works the same way as `standardmaterial()`, you can assign it directly to the material, for instance

```
m = standardmaterial()
m.diffusemap = bitmaptexture()
```

Using `showproperties` you can list all options in a bitmap. The most important one, and possibly the most used one, is `.filename`, which allows you to assign a filename to the bitmap. For instance, using the example above, you can set the bitmap filename using

```
m.diffusemap.filename = "c:\\3dsmax4\\maps\\chromic.jpg"
```

Notice that your commands are getting bigger as you nest properties. This is why it's better to assign variables instead of using the nested properties. If you had assigned a variable named b *to the bitmaptexture, all you would need is* b.filename = "c:\3dsmax...".

Remember to use \\ instead of a single \ in a string to specify the bitmap file path.

Using selectsavebitmap *to Script User Interaction*

It's very difficult to memorize filenames and paths. Fortunately, you can use a MAXScript command, `selectsavebitmap`, that will ask the user to select a file and will assign the complete path to a variable. When executed, this command displays a dialog box asking the user to select a bitmap to be saved (Figure 16.7).

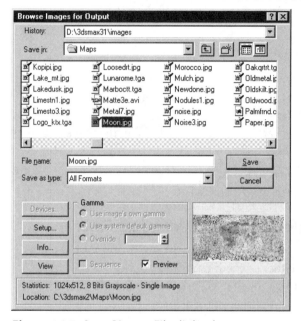

Figure 16.7 *Save Bitmap File dialog box*

You can use it to assign a bitmap file directly to a texture map, like this:

```
bmp = bitmaptexture()
bmp.filename = selectsavebitmap()
```

Showing a Material in the Viewport

In 3ds max 4 you can show the materials in the viewport. The .showinviewport property allows you to turn a material on or off. Alternatively, you can use showtexturemap, which will require you to specify the material and optionally a map that will be shown. Using the examples above, you would have

```
showtexturemap m bmp on
```

or

```
showtexturemap m on
```

The Material Editor

In 3ds max, all the work done with materials happens in the Material Editor. In MAXScript, you usually can use the Material Editor to display a material to the user. MAXScript has several commands to read or display a material in any of the Material Editor slots.

Reading Materials

You can read a single material from any of the 24 slots of the Material Editor, by using getmeditmaterial. You also can use meditmaterials[*index*], where *index* will represent the number of the slot you want to access.

For instance, if you want to assign the material in the first slot to the selected objects, you can use *either* of these lines:

```
$.material = meditmaterials[1]
$.material = getmeditmaterial 1
```

Displaying Materials in the Materials Editor

To display any material in the Material Editor, use the opposite process from reading a material. You can use either setmeditmaterial or meditmaterial[*index*]. For instance, if you want to set the first Material Editor's slot with the material of the selected object, you can use either of these lines:

```
meditmaterials[1] = $.material
setmeditmaterial 1 $.material
```

Material Libraries

MAXScript can access the current material library or any other material library as an array of materials. Use currentmateriallibrary to return all materials in the current library indexed as an array.

Since it is an array, you can use append to add materials to the library. You can also use

```
currentmateriallibrary.count
```

to find out how many materials are in the library, and

```
currentmateriallibrary[index]
```

to read any material from the library.

You can use `loadmateriallibrary` and `savemateriallibrary` to load and save the current material library. These two commands will require you to specify a file-name string to load or save the file.

If the Material/Map Browser is opened, the material library is not updated automatically. You must either close and reopen the browser or choose another filter and re-select the material library.

If you do not know the name and path of the material library, you can use `fileopenmatlib`, `filesavematlib`, and `filesaveasmatlib` to display a dialog box where you can choose the material library file to open or save, as shown in Figure 16.8.

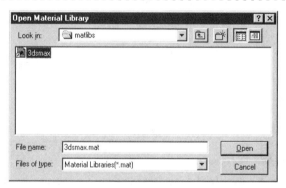

Figure 16.8 *The Open Material Library dialog box*

Other Materials and Maps

MAXScript allows you to create and manipulate all materials and maps. Each one has different options, along with different sub-materials or maps. For instance, the Multi-Sub object material is created in MAXScript using `multimaterial`, and since it is made of sub-materials, you can access each of them as an array index, using `multimaterial [index]`. You can also access the Multi-Sub material ID using the `.materialidlist` array, which is a new feature in 3ds max 4.

Some maps, like composite, mix, and mask, also require sub-maps and work either using an array variable or through the different map options.

You can use the Macro Recorder to record changes and parameters in different materials. These recorded lines can then be copied and pasted into any script, so you won't have to memorize lots of commands and their different options.

Recording Materials

The Macro Recorder can record all options in a material or map, when you work with them in the Material Editor. You can use it to help you create materials in scripts, which will save you a lot of time.

The actions are recorded based on the selected slot in the Material Editor. Setting the diffuse color creates, for instance,

```
meditMaterials[1].diffuse = color 50 149 181
```

The recorded line must then be adjusted in your script, manipulating the material you want. For instance, if this material belongs to a specific object named "box" you should use

```
$box.material.diffuse = color 50 149 181
```

If you want to manipulate the current object's material, you can read it in the Material Editor, using the Pick Material From Object button, and then manipulate the material using the Recorder. At the end, you can set the material to the object again using the Assign Material to Selection button.

Hands-on MAXScript: Adding a Noise Bump Map to a Material

In this exercise you will make a script that adds a noise bump map to an object's material and then make some adjustments in the material.

This script will read the material of the selected object, change the shader to Oren-Nayar-Blinn, and then add the noise map to the bump map. The script also will ask the user how much bump they want. At the end, you turn this script into a Macro Script and assign this macro to a button in any toolbar.

Start a new script and type these commands (or open the file bump_exercise.ms on the CD-ROM):

```
if selection.count != 1 then
format "Select a single object first."
else
(
obj = $
if obj.material == undefined then
format "Selected object has no material applied.\n"
else
(
meditmaterials[1] = obj.material
```

What we did here was test how many objects were selected, and warn the user that one and only one object must be selected. Then, if only one object was selected, we checked to see if it had a material applied. If so, the script copies this material to the first Material Editor slot.

Now turn on the Macro Recorder and edit the following values in the material:

- Shader = Oren-Nayar-Blinn

- Roughness = 30

- Specular Level = 43

- Glossiness = 35

- Soften = 0.5

- Bump Map Amount = 40

- Bump Map = Noise Map

- Noise Size = 15

This is the result of what was recorded:

```
meditMaterials[1].shaderType = 4
meditMaterials[1].adTextureLock = on
meditMaterials[1].adTextureLock = on
meditMaterials[1].diffuseRoughness = 30
meditMaterials[1].specularLevel = 43
meditMaterials[1].glossiness = 35
meditMaterials[1].Soften = 0.5
meditMaterials[1].bumpMapAmount = 40
meditMaterials[1].bumpMap = Noise ()
meditMaterials[1].bumpMap.size = 15
```

Let's add the user interaction part to the script, continuing the script you started:

```
bump_amount = getkbvalue prompt:"Enter Bump amount: "
bump_size = getkbvalue prompt:"Enter Bump size: "
```

Copy the recorded lines to the script, and edit the following lines:

```
meditMaterials[1].bumpMapAmount = bump_amount
meditMaterials[1].bumpMap.size = bump_size
```

Remember to close the two parentheses that were opened, and the script is ready! If you want, you can drag it to the toolbar and create a Macro Script button. Also remember that the Listener must be opened, so the user can type the values requested with getkbvalue. (Unfortunately, the Mini-Listener does not work in instances like this.)

Listing 16.2 shows the final complete script.

LISTING 16.2: THE NOISE BUMP MAP SCRIPT (BUMP_EXERCISE.MS)

```
if selection.count != 1 then
format "Select a single object first."
else
   (
   obj = $
   if obj.material == undefined then
   format "Selected object has no material applied.\n"
   else
      (
      meditmaterials[1] = obj.material
      bump_amount = getkbvalue prompt:"Enter Bump amount: "
      bump_size = getkbvalue prompt:"Enter Bump size: "
      meditMaterials[1].shaderType = 4
      meditMaterials[1].diffuseRoughness = 30
      meditMaterials[1].specularLevel = 43
      meditMaterials[1].glossiness = 35
      meditMaterials[1].Soften = 0.5
      meditMaterials[1].bumpMapAmount = bump_amount
      meditMaterials[1].bumpMap = Noise ()
      meditMaterials[1].bumpMap.size = bump_size
      )
   )
```

Key Concept

Working with Modifiers and Modifier Options

Modifiers are essential for modeling in 3ds max. You also need modifiers for material and surfaces manipulation. In this section you will look at how to add modifiers and use modifier options.

Adding Modifiers

You can add a modifier to any 3ds max object, if the modifier is valid for the object type. For instance, you can add a Bend modifier to a cylinder. First, create a cylinder using

```
c = cylinder height:60 radius:12 heightsegs:15
```

Then add the bend using `addmodifier c (bend())`. Notice the `()` after `bend`. This is because we have no parameters assigned to the modifier. If we wanted, we could directly specify the angle, using `addmodifier c (bend angle:30)`.

If the modifier added to the object is not compatible, 3ds max will return an error message. You can check the object's class to see if it's compatible with the modifier, or you can use the `validmodifier` command, which will return True if the modifier can be added to the object. Using the cylinder above, you could check to see whether it allows you to use the Normalize Spline modifier by means of

```
validmodifier c (normalize_spline())
```

Using Modifier Options

The modifier options are accessed the same way you access all properties in MAXScript. Continuing to use the cylinder example, you can see the properties of the bend modifier by using `showproperties c.bend`. You can then change the angle of the bend with `c.bend.angle = `*`value`*, as in Figure 16.9.

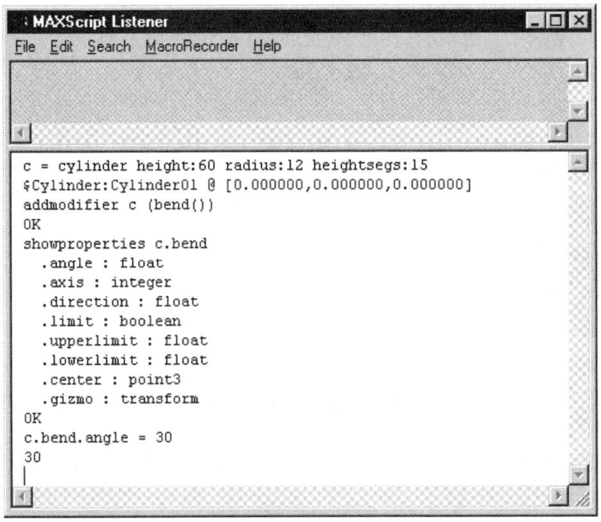
MAXScript Listener
File Edit Search MacroRecorder Help
c = cylinder height:60 radius:12 heightsegs:15
$Cylinder:Cylinder01 @ [0.000000,0.000000,0.000000]
addmodifier c (bend())
OK
showproperties c.bend
.angle : float
.axis : integer
.direction : float
.limit : boolean
.upperlimit : float
.lowerlimit : float
.center : point3
.gizmo : transform
OK
c.bend.angle = 30
30

Figure 16.9 *Bend Modifier properties*

You can access any property of any modifier this way. Some modifier values are check boxes, which will be enabled or not. In MAXScript, these usually use True (on) or False (off).

When a modifier has radio buttons, the value exposed is an integer, specifying which of the buttons is active.

Global Options

A modifier can be enabled or disabled, either globally or in the viewports only. You can also change its name, and even remove the modifier or collapse the stack. These properties are global to all modifiers.

- To change a modifier name, simply add .name to the end of it and change its name.

You can access any object modifier in several ways:

- *obj*.modifiers[*index*], where *index* is the number of the modifier in the stack, counting downwards as they appear in the stack list
- *obj*.modifiers["*name*"], *obj*.modifiers[#*name*], or *obj*.*name*, where *name* is the modifier name

To enable or disable the modifier, type *obj*.modifier.enabled = true or false. This will enable/disable the object in both the viewport and the renderer. To enable/disable the modifier in viewports only, you can use .enabledinviews.

It's useful to disable, in viewports, modifiers that take time to process. This will make your work in 3ds max faster. Some examples are Optimize or MeshSmooth.

To remove a modifier from an object, you can use deletemodifier, which works the same way as addmodifier. For instance, deletemodifier c c.bend will remove the Bend modifier applied to our cylinder.

If you want to collapse the stack, as if you were using the Edit Stack button, you can use the collapsestack command. The statement collapsestack c will collapse all modifiers applied to the cylinder.

Working in Sub-Object Level

Most of the modifiers have sub-objects. You can access them and change their parameters through MAXScript.

For instance, the Bend modifier has two sub-objects: Gizmo and Center. You can change their position, rotation, and scale through MAXScript by simply accessing `object.bend.gizmo` or `object.bend.center`. All position, rotation, and scale information for the modifiers is calculated in object space, which means that the XYZ coordinates' origins are the object's local coordinate system.

Usually, gizmo sub-objects allow you to change their position, rotation, and scale. Center sub-objects allow only position changes.

Some modifiers have different sub-objects and require different methods to access their properties.

Space Warps

You can create space warps as normal 3D objects; all their properties are easily adjustable, as with any 3D object.

You cannot add a space warp the way you add a modifier, and you cannot link one to an object, because a space warp requires the Bind tool. To do so, you can use the `bindspacewarp` command to associate objects and space warps.

Some space warps—Path Follow, for instance—require several adjustments to be made not on the space warp object itself, but on the binding. These options can be accessed as normal modifiers.

For instance, let's create a rippled surface, using two space warps:

```
c = cylinder radius:300 height:1 capsegs:40 sides:80
sw1 = spaceripple pos:[200,200,0]
sw2 = spaceripple pos:[100,-50,0]
bindspacewarp c sw1
c.ripple_binding.name = "Ripple1"
bindspacewarp c sw2
c.ripple_binding.name = "Ripple2"
c.ripple1.flexibility = 0.25
c.ripple2.flexibility = 0.4
```

This script creates a surface and two ripple space warps. Then it associates each of them with the surface and renames them. At the end, the code adjusts their flexibility, which is a property that exists when this space warp is associated with an object. You can see it by selecting the cylinder and then selecting the space warp in the Modify tab.

Hands-on MAXScript: Creating a Material and Applying It to a Selected Object

Let's create a script that will create a brick material and apply it automatically to the selected object, such as the wall in Figure 16.10. Because it's brick, the object will need UVW mapping coordinates. The only parameter that will be requested from the user is the size of the brick. This script has no requirements, except that an object needs to be selected.

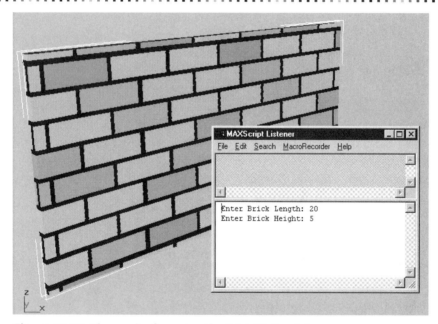

Figure 16.10 *The result of running the Brick Wall script*

Start a new script and type the commands shown in Listing 16.3. (This code is available as brick_exercise.ms on the CD-ROM that accompanies this book.)

LISTING 16.3: THE BRICK WALL SCRIPT (BRICK_EXERCISE.MS)

```
if selection.count == 0 then
format "Select an object first.\n"
else
```

```
(
obj = $
m = standardmaterial()
bmp = bricks()
m.diffusemap = bmp
showtexturemap m bmp on
obj.material = m
max modify mode
brick_size = getkbvalue prompt:"Enter Brick Length:"
brick_height = getkbvalue prompt:"Enter Brick Height:"
addmodifier obj (uvwmap name:"UVW")
obj.uvw.maptype = 4
obj.uvw.length = brick_size * 3
obj.uvw.width = brick_size * 3
obj.uvw.height = brick_height * 8
)
```

You will notice that you've created a standard material and a default brick map. Then this material was assigned to the selected objects and the Show Map In Viewport option was turned on.

`max modify mode` *is a command that will switch to the Modify Panel. It's just a cosmetic option in the script, one that will make it easier for the user to adjust the brick size later.*

You asked the user to enter the brick size, applied a UVW map modifier, specified Box type, and then defined the length, width, and height of the UVW map according to the values specified by the user.

You can enter information when adding a modifier. We didn't need to separate the UVW command into four lines; it could have been done the same way as with the `name:"UVW"` *property, but it's better to split the command into several lines, because that makes it easier to organize and debug the script.*

Creating and Managing a Hierarchy

You can create and manage hierarchies in MAXScript. It's the same as using the Link and Unlink tools, but you can also list and check the object relations in MAXScript.

You can link objects the same way you do manually in the viewports, selecting the children and linking them to a parent. In MAXScript, it's done using the `.parent` property, which is valid for all objects.

For example, let's create two objects and link them:

```
b = box pos:[100,0,0]
c = cylinder pos:[50,0,0]
c.parent = b
```

In this example, b is the parent and c is the child. Of course you could use any means you wish to specify the objects: $name, selection[*index*], etc.

You can use .children to see which objects are linked to one object, and you can also append child objects. For example, let's create a sphere and link it to the box, continuing the previous example:

```
s = sphere()
append b.children s
```

To simply list the child objects, use b.children. If you want to know how many child objects you have, use b.children.count. Since the index of children is an array, you can also use b.children[*index*] to access each child object.

Using Environment and Render Effects

You can adjust environment options and assign environment effects and render effects using MAXScript. Using environment options, you can create special effects and enhance your scenes, adding more realism.

Accessing Global Environment Variables

Global environment variables, such as background color and environment map, control the Common Parameters, displayed in the rollout in Figure 16.11.

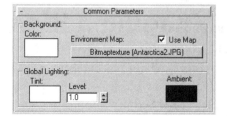

Figure 16.11 *Global environment parameters*

Adding a Background to a Scene

There are two ways to add a background to a scene: using a plain background color or using a map. You can set both of them in MAXScript.

The backgroundcolor command sets the background color. For instance, backgroundcolor = [255,255,255] will set the background color to white.

Using environmentmap allows you to place any map in the background. To do this, you also need to enable useenvironmentmap. For instance:

```
fname = selectsavebitmap()
bmp = bitmaptexture filename:fname
bmp.coords.mappingtype = 1
bmp.coords.mapping = 4
environmentmap = bmp
useenvironmentmap = true
```

This will ask the user to select a bitmap to be used in the background. The bmp.coords.mappingtype and .mapping commands will set the mapping type to Screen.

Setting Illumination Parameters

The three parameters in the Common Parameters rollout that control the overall illumination of the scene are ambientcolor, lighttintcolor, and lightlevel. Note that ambientcolor and lighttintcolor are color values, while lightlevel is an integer.

Be careful when adjusting any of these values, because they can mess up all illumination in a scene.

Creating Environment Effects and Atmospheric Gizmos

To use certain environment effects you will need to create atmospheric helpers, also called atmospheric gizmos. They're needed for Fire Effect and Volumetric Fog effects. There are three gizmos, and they all work exactly the same way:

```
a = spheregizmo()
b = cylgizmo()
c = boxgizmo()
```

Since they're sphere, cylinder, and box, they have the same basic options as the regular 3D objects, plus a Seed option, which is the number that will generate a unique, random volumetric effect.

Environment effects are similar to materials. You will first create the effect you want, and then you will add it to the Atmosphere Effects queue, shown in Figure 16.12.

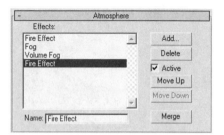

Figure 16.12 *Atmosphere effects*

You have four built-in atmospheric effects in 3ds max: Fire Effect, Fog, Volume Fog, and Volume Light. All of them are used the same way:

```
eff = fire_effect explosion:1
eff2 = volume_light density:10
```

In this example, `eff` is a Fire Effect, and the property that defines the explosion effect is on (`explosion:1`). `eff2` creates a Volume Light and sets its density to 10%.

Once the effects are defined, you need to add them to the Atmosphere rollout, using `addatmospheric` *effect*. Using the examples above, you can add both effects to the atmospheric effects list:

```
addatmospheric eff
addatmospheric eff2
```

You've seen that you need the gizmos for the effects to work—or, for Volume Light, you need a light. But you also need to tell 3ds max which gizmo or light relates to which effect. This is done by the `appendgizmo` command, which will associate an object with an environment effect. For instance, let's create a gizmo and a light, to be associated with the effects in the previous example:

```
l = omnilight pos:[100,0,0] farattenend:50 farattenstart:0
g = spheregizmo pos:[-100,0,0] seed:3413
appendgizmo eff g
appendgizmo eff2 l
```

You cannot associate a light with a fire effect or a volume fog, and you cannot associate a gizmo with a volume light.

Each effect has a `.numgizmos` property that will list the number of gizmos associated to it. You can use `getgizmo` to retrieve any associated object. For instance, `getgizmo eff 1` will list the first gizmo associated with this effect. To remove any gizmo you can use `deletegizmo`.

In older versions of max, the fire effect was called combustion. *In 3ds max 4, combustion is a texture map. If you have older scripts that use the combustion atmosphere effect, you'll have to rename them so that the script works in 3ds max 4.*

Creating Render Effects

Render effects are post-processing filters applied to a rendered image. Several render effects can be applied, and you manipulate them the same way you manipulate environment effects.

You create a render effect the same way you do an environment effect. 3ds max has several render effects; let's use the Brightness and Contrast render effect as an example:

```
bc = brightness_and_contrast()
```

You can list its parameters using `showproperties`. Let's change the brightness and contrast level:

```
bc.brightness = 0.8
bc.contrast = 0.6
```

Now, let's add it to the render effects list, using `addeffect`:

```
addeffect bc
```

As with environment effects, you can use `numeffects` to list the number of effects you have in your scene. You can use `geteffect` to read an effect in the list and `deleteeffect` to remove any of them.

Hands-on MAXScript: Creating an Explosion

Let's create a script that will create an object explosion. This script will create a Particle Array object and a Fire Effect and will synchronize these effects for the explosion. All information the user will need to enter is at the start and end of the explosion.

To make this exercise easier to understand, first open the file on the CD-ROM named asteroid_explosion.max. This file consists of an animated asteroid, which will be exploded using the script you will now create.

Now create the script. Start a new script and type the commands shown in Listing 16.4 (or access the code on the CD-ROM in the file named explosion_exercise.ms).

LISTING 16.4: THE ASTEROID EXPLOSION SCRIPT (EXPLOSION_EXERCISE.MS)

```
if selection.count != 1 then
format "Please select a single object.\n"
else
(
obj = $
size = (distance obj.min obj.max)
clearlistener()
start = getkbvalue prompt:"Enter Explosion Start Time:"
end = getkbvalue prompt:"Enter Explosion End Time:"
p = parray emitter:obj wirecolor:obj.wirecolor
p.particletype = 2
p.fragmentmethod = 1
p.fragchunkminimum = 30
p.speed = 2
p.Fragment_Thickness = size/8
p.emitter_start = start
p.life = (end - start)
p.display_until = end
g = spheregizmo pos:obj.pos radius:size
g.parent = obj
eff = fire_effect explosion:1 name:"Explosion"
appendgizmo eff g
addatmospheric eff
st = animationrange.start
ed = animationrange.end
if end > ed then animationrange = (interval st end)
with animate on
(
at time start eff.phase = 0
at time end eff.phase = 300
at time 0 obj.visibility = on
at time start obj.visibility = on
at time (start + 1) obj.visibility = off
)
)
```

As always, you can use the Macro Recorder to make it easier to design the script. All Particle Array properties could have been recorded and adjusted to the variable names in the script. We used `clearlistener()` to clear the Listener window, as a precaution, in case you had any previous script output on it.

We introduced some animation techniques in this script. `Animationrange` controls the number of frames in the scene. Using `with animate on` is the same as turning on the Animate button. Then, `at time` is the same as going to that frame to adjust an object's value.

Like all other exercises, you can drag this script to the toolbar and create a Macro Script. After that, select the Asteroid object and run the script. The explosion starts on frame 50 and ends on frame 100.

You can load the file `asteroid_explosion_final.max` from the CD included with this book to see the result.

Working with Splines

Splines are essential for modeling. Most of what you do starts with spline modeling. You can create shapes in MAXScript the same way you create primitives or other objects, and you also can create splines by creating each vertex and segment.

Creating Shapes

You can create any Shape object in MAXScript, except the Line object. For instance, you can create a circle using `c = circle radius:30`.

2D objects can only have certain modifiers applied, like Extrude, Bevel, or Lathe. MAXScript allows you to check whether the object is a spline before adding these modifiers. This can be done using `validmodifier c (extrude())`, for instance. If it returns True, this modifier can be applied to the object.

Converting Shapes to Splines

Like 3D objects, shapes can have their modifiers collapsed, converting them to editable splines. You can use `converttosplineshape` to convert any shape to an editable spline. The advantage of working with editable splines is the ability to animate each vertex and the advantage of manipulating its vertices, segments, and splines. Many MAXScript commands require an editable spline to work.

The Editable Spline object, which can be created through the Line command or by converting a Shape object, has no options except the Global Spline options (steps, adaptive, renderable, etc).

Understanding Splines

To better understand shapes and splines, let's review a few terms. The *shape* is the entire 2D object. The *spline* is each element, closed or not, in the shape. A *vertex* or a *knot* is each control point of the spline. A *segment* is an interval between two vertices. You can see this in Figure 16.13.

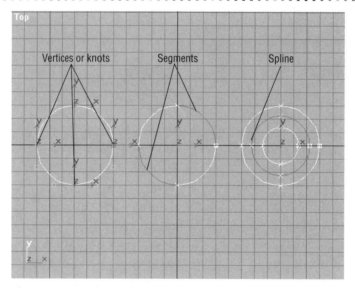

Figure 16.13 *Shape elements*

You can find out how many vertices are in one shape or spline using the numknots command. This works in any shape; for instance, using the previous example, numknots c will return 4, the number of vertices present in a Circle shape.

However, to use numknots in a specified spline, the object must be an editable spline, and you must specify the number of the spline in the shape. To know how many splines a shape has, use `numsplines`, which is also valid only in editable splines. Follow this example to understand how `numknots` and `numsplines` work:

```
d = donut()
d = converttosplineshape d
numsplines d
numknots d 1
```

A Donut shape has two splines, so `numsplines` d will return 2. Then, each of these splines has four vertices, which means `numknots` d 1 will return 4. In a Donut shape, the first spline is the one related to Radius 1. On other shapes it will vary, but as a rule, splines are numbered according to their creation order. Another way to know the number of splines is using the object's `.numsplines` property.

The `curvelength` command returns the length of a spline and is valid in all shapes. For example, let's calculate the length of the circle. First, create it using the command `c = circle radius:30`. Now, `curvelength` c will return 188.494, which is the length (in this case, the circumference) of a circle with radius 30.

You can read any coordinate in the spline by specifying its position relative to the start. To do so use `lengthinterp` or `pathinterp`. Both work the same way, but they differ in their calculation methods. `pathinterp` calculates the points based on the segment's length; `lengthinterp` calculates them based on the overall length of the spline. This is the same difference as when you animate an object through a Path and turn Constant Velocity off or on.

For instance, if you want to know the position of the point that is 25 percent from the start of the circle in your example, you could use `lengthinterp c 0.25`. If you use it in an object that has more than one spline, you need to indicate which spline you're looking at, using `lengthinterp c 1 0.25`.

Editing Splines

MAXScript has commands that are useful for editing spline sub-objects in scripts. For instance, using MAXScript, you can change all vertices of a shape to "Corner." You can also reverse the direction of a spline, etc.

Editing Vertex Data

You can edit almost all vertex parameters and properties—the vertex position, its tangent, etc.—with MAXScript. All the commands you will see here will only work in Editable Spline objects, so if you need to work on any other shape, it first must be converted to a spline.

To find out the type of a vertex (corner, Bezier, smooth, or Bezier-corner), you can use getknottype. To change it, use setknottype. To use both commands, you need to specify the spline number and the vertex number. For instance, let's set the second vertex of a circle to corner. Since this object has only one spline, the spline index will be 1 in all commands.

```
c = circle radius:30
c = converttosplineshape c
getknottype c 1 2
setknottype c 1 2 #corner
updateshape c
```

Every time you make changes to a shape or spline and want to see it on screen, you need to use the updateshape *command.*

You can use getknotpoint and setknotpoint to change the position of a vertex. Let's edit the position of vertex 2 and move it, creating a droplet shape, like in Figure 16.14. First, use getknotpoint c 1 2 to see the actual position of the vertex. It will be something close to [0,30,0]. Move it 30 units up, using setknotpoint c 1 2 [0,60,0].

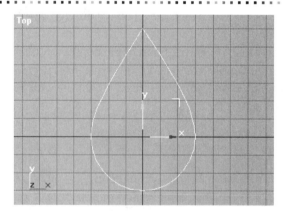

Figure 16.14 *A droplet shape*

You can use setknotselection and getknotselection to select vertices or to read the vertex selection. Both commands will use an array containing the indexes of the vertices that are selected, but setknotselection also has the option to retain the previous selection, adding the new selection to it. For instance, select vertices 1, 2, and 3 in your example, using `setknotselection c 1 #(1,2,3)`. To enable the selection, you must enter sub-object mode. This is done using `subobjectlevel`. In your example, just type `subobjectlevel = 1`, and you will see the vertices selected.

Editing Segment Data

The options available for working with segments are almost the same as those for working with vertices. Of course, you cannot set the segment position, but you can select a segment and set its type (curve or line).

Besides these options, you can also refine a segment. The `refinesegment` command will require you to indicate which spline and segment you want to work with, and then where you want to refine it, using a position index from 0 (the start of the segment) to 1 (the segment's end). For example, a setting of 0.5 would mean you want to refine the segment at a point exactly in the middle (50 percent of the way along the segment).

Let's refine the droplet, creating two more vertices in the pointed portion of the shape:

```
refinesegment c 1 1 0.5
updateshape c
refinesegment c 1 3 0.5
updateshape c
```

Remember that when you refined the segment, a new vertex was added, so the number of the segments changed. That's why you refined segments1 and 3 instead of 1 and 2.

Editing Spline Data

To see how many segments or vertices you have in a spline, you can use `numsegments` and `numknots`. Continuing the above example, `numsegments c 1` and `numknots c 1` will now both return 6.

You can use `isclosed` to check whether a spline is closed. The `open` command opens a spline, disconnecting the first and the last vertices; you can use `close` to do the opposite, joining those vertices. Using `isclosed c 1` in our example will return True, since the drop is closed. Using `open c 1` will disconnect one segment and `close c 1` will return it to its original state.

The `reverse` command will invert the order of the spline. It's useful when you have lofts, animation paths, or surface sections that are going in the wrong direction. You will not see any change in the spline in the screen, except the vertex numbering.

Also, `setfirstknot` allows you to select which vertex is the first one. It's also very important for modeling. Using `setfirstknot c 1 3` will set the first vertex to the vertex on the point of the droplet shape.

Don't forget to use `updateshape` *in the commands above to see the changes on screen.*

Creating Splines from Scratch

You can create splines manually in MAXScript, specifying each vertex and spline position. It's not simple, but sometimes it's the only way it can be done.

You can create splines by creating and connecting vertices (using `addknot`) and also by creating splines in the same shape (using `addnewspline`). This way you can create splines and vertices, which will be connected sequentially.

Let's create a rectangle as an example:

```
ss = splineshape()
addnewspline ss
addknot ss 1 #corner #curve [0,0,0]
addknot ss 1 #corner #curve [10,0,0]
addknot ss 1 #corner #curve [10,10,0]
addknot ss 1 #corner #curve [0,10,0]
close ss 1
updateshape ss
```

The first command, `ss = splineshape()`, creates an Editable Spline object, with no vertex or spline. Then, manually you create the spline and the vertices, which are automatically connected in sequence.

The Edit Spline Commands

MAXScript allows you to access a series of commands in Edit Spline. Most of these commands will start one action and wait for the user input. Some of them, like `weld`, will go ahead and perform the action on the selected elements.

The Edit Spline commands are all present in the quad menus shown in Figure 16.15, and in MAXScript all of these commands start with `splineops`. For instance, you can delete the selected vertices, segments, or splines simply by positioning the sub-object in that level and using `splineops.delete`.

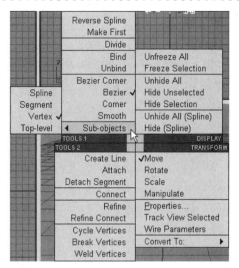

Figure 16.15 *Splines quad menu*

Hands-on MAXScript: Copying and Editing a Spline

Let's create a script that will create a copy of a spline, dividing it into a series of segments of equal size. Using the Normalize Spline modifier allows you to subdivide a spline in segments with the same length, but does not allow you to subdivide a spline in a defined number of segments.

Start a new script and put in the commands from Listing 16.5 (or access the sample code on the CD-ROM, in the file named divide_exercise.ms).

LISTING 16.5: THE NORMALIZE SPLINE SCRIPT (DIVIDE_EXERCISE.MS)

```
if selection.count != 1 then
format "Please select a single object.\n"
else
if superclassof $ != shape then
format "Selected object must be a Shape.\n"
else
(
```

```
tmp = copy $
obj = converttosplineshape tmp
ns = numsplines obj
nv = numknots obj
size = getkbvalue prompt:"Number of segments per spline:"
if size < 3 then size = 3
size = size as integer
ratio = 1.0/size
ss = splineshape()
for i in 1 to ns do
(
addnewspline ss
for j in 1 to size do
(
pt = lengthinterp obj i (ratio*(j-1))
addknot ss i #smooth #curve pt
)
if (isclosed obj i) then close ss i else
(
pt = lengthinterp obj i 1.0
addknot ss i #smooth #curve pt
)
updateshape ss
)
delete tmp
)
```

This script checks to see if there's an object selected, and then checks to see if the selected object is a spline, using the superclassof command. Then, the script creates a copy of the selected object and converts this copy to an editable spline, so you can have access to all commands.

The script needs to know how many segments the user wants to divide the object into, so we've added a user input option for this. After that, it's all math and scripting. The ratio variable will be used when you calculate the position of every new segment, based on a percentage of the length of the spline. That's why you use lengthinterp later.

Two nested for commands are needed, one to step through each spline in the object and other to step through each segment that will be created. There is a check to see whether the original spline is closed, and if it was, the new spline will also be closed. If not, the new spline will be open, and the final vertex is calculated. The end of the script updates the shape and deletes the temporary shape.

The only problem in this script is that all vertices are #smooth. You could check for the tangents, but it would add a bit more work to the script.

Feel free to create a Macro Script of this script. We will return to it in Chapter 17, where we enable the user to adjust the number of segments even after the spline was created.

Working with Meshes

As you did with 2D objects, you will also need to manipulate 3D objects using the editable mesh object. It is the only way to access and manipulate vertex and face information.

Creating Editable Meshes

3ds max 4 allows you to create mesh objects from scratch. You will need a vertex array and a face array, just like those we will use when creating plug-in scripts. The easiest way to work with editable mesh objects is to convert objects in one of two ways: using the `collapsestack` or the `converttomesh` commands.

When you convert an object to an editable mesh, either using MAXScript or the Edit Stack button, if the object was modified by space warps or world space modifiers, their effects will be discarded. To convert an object to an editable mesh and consider the effects of the space warps, you can use the Snapshot tool or the `snapshot` command in MAXScript.

Let's say you have `b = plane()`; these are the three ways you can convert it to an editable mesh:

```
b = converttomesh b
b = snapshot b
b = collapsestack b
```

Or you can create it directly specifying vertices and faces:

```
v = #([-10,-10,0],[10,-10,0],[10,10,0],[-10,10,0])
f = #([1,2,3],[3,4,1])
b = mesh vertices:v faces:f
```

Note that the `collapsestack` command only converts the object to an editable mesh if the object has modifiers applied to it.

Mesh Properties

It's important to know certain information about meshes (such as the number of faces and vertices, which ones are selected, etc.) so you can manipulate a series of vertices, edges, or faces. Some of these properties are:

Property	Description
.numverts	Number of vertices
.numfaces	Number of faces
.numtverts	Number of texture vertices
.numcpvverts	Number of vertices that have Color per Vertex applied
.selectedverts	Vertices that are selected
.selectededges	Edges that are selected
.selectedfaces	Faces that are selected

You can use simple commands to attach objects, create Booleans, and adjust simple parameters in editable mesh objects.

To attach objects, use the `attach` command; you need an editable mesh and any other object. If it's a 2D object, NURBS, or patch, it will be converted to editable mesh and attached. For instance, to create two objects and attach them:

```
a = sphere()
b = box pos:[30,0,0]
c = converttomesh a
attach c b
```

Creating Simple Booleans

You create simple Booleans using simple math formulas (addition, subtraction, and intersection) on nodes, but the resulting object will be an editable mesh, as seen in Figure 16.16. To use the Boolean compound object and retain all sub-objects, use `boolobj.createbooleanobject`.

`boolobj` *has lots of commands. Take a look at the max online Help to learn more about them.*

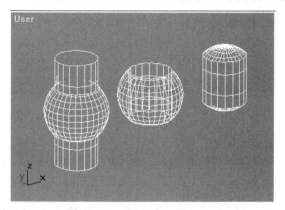

Figure 16.16 *An editable mesh created from Booleans*

To use simple Booleans, treat objects as part of a math operation. For instance:

```
a = box pos:[-10,10,0]
b = sphere radius:20
c = a + b
delete b
```

When the Boolean is processed, the first operand is deleted and any others remain. That's why we've deleted b.

The other two operations, subtraction and intersection, can be made with the use of the minus (–) and the multiply (*) symbols. You can perform more than one operation in a single command:

```
a = box pos:[-10,0,0]
b = sphere radius:15
c = box pos:[0,15,0]
d = a * b - c
delete b
delete c
```

You can also create compound Booleans using MAXScript:

```
a = box pos:[-10,0,0]
b = sphere radius:15
c = boolobj.createbooleanobject a b 1 1
boolobj.setboolop c 1
delete b
```

In createbooleanobject, you need to specify two objects:

- How the second operand—here, b—will be treated (1 = instance, 2 = reference, 3 = copy, 4 = move)

- How the materials will be treated (1 = combine, 2 = match ID, 3 = match materials, 4 = use new node, 5 = use original)

In setboolop, you specify which Boolean operation will occur (1 = Union, 2 = Intersection, 3 = A-B, 4 = B-A, 5 = Cut).

Note that after changing the Boolean operator, the object will only update on screen when you click it, or when it redraws. You can use max views redraw to force a redraw.

Accessing Vertex, Face, and Edge Information

Sometimes it's useful to have access to and manipulate Vertex, Face, and Edge information. Let's look at some of these commands and some examples.

Getting Vertex Data

Some vertex commands are replicated from properties in an editable mesh. These commands are: getnumverts, getvertselection, and getnumtverts. You can use either object.numverts or getnumverts obj. You can read several other types of information from vertices, including these:

Command	Description
getvert	Returns the vertex position
getnormal	Returns the normal related to the vertex
gettvert	Returns the UVW coordinate of the vertex
getvertcolor	Returns the color of the vertex
getvertselection	Returns an array of the selected vertices

This information is very useful for writing scripts. All these commands have a set command related to them that will write new data to each property. For instance, if you want to move a certain vertex [10,2,4], you can do it this way:

```
s = sphere()
s1 = converttomesh s
```

```
pt = getvert s1 1
setvert s1 1 (pt + [10,2,4])
update s1
```

 Mesh operations also require an update in order to be seen on screen.

Getting Face Data

Basically, all Vertex commands have similar commands in Face. For instance, instead of getvert, you would use getface for a face. (But of course, faces do not have Color Per vertex, and vertices do not have Material ID.) Some of these commands are:

Command	Description
getface	Returns the face's adjacent vertex
getfacenormal	Returns the face normal
getfacematid	Returns the Material ID of the face
getfacesmoothgroup	Returns the Smoothing Group index

As with vertices, all get* commands for faces have a related set* command. For instance, you can change the material ID of the faces of an object, setting it to 2 if the face is even, or 1 if it's odd. Let's continue using the previous example:

```
for i in 1 to s1.numfaces do
(
if (mod i 2) == 0 then
   setfacematid s1 i 2
   else setfacematid s1 i 1
)
update s1
```

You can now create a Multi-Sub material with one submaterial red and the other green. Then, you can apply this material to the object, so you can see the material ID of the faces:

```
meditMaterials[1] = Multimaterial ()
meditMaterials[1].materialList.count = 2
meditMaterials[1].materialList[2].diffuse = color 255 0 0
meditMaterials[1].materialList[1].diffuse = color 30 255 0
s1.material = meditMaterials[1]
```

Other Face and Vertex Commands

Other commands, beyond `set` and `get`, will also affect faces and vertices. You can extrude faces using `extrudeface`. Let's extrude the faces of the middle of the sphere:

```
setfaceselection s1 #{81..144}
extrudeface s1 #selection 20 80
update s1
```

This example demonstrates a new way of specifying an array: a *bitarray*. The syntax `#{a..b}` specifies all numbers in the range from *a* through *b* as an array. See information about bitarrays in "Operations on Meshes" later in this chapter.

You can use `deleteface` or `deletevert` to delete a face or vertex in an editable mesh. You can also use `collapseface`, which will weld all three vertices of a face in one single point at its center.

All of these commands change the number of faces, therefore also changing the faces' sequential numbers.

Getting Edge Data

You cannot set an edge's position, or any other edge property except visibility and selection.

To read and set an edge's visibility, use `getedgevis` and `setedgevis`. For instance, you can check whether one of the three edges of one face are visible or not:

```
getedgevis s1 40 1
```

You need to specify the face number (40) and the edge number (1, 2, or 3). The command will then return true or false. `setedgevis` works the same way.

Operations on Meshes

New

Several new commands were introduced in 3ds max 4 to manipulate mesh objects. These commands resemble the options available in the Editable Spline rollouts in the Command Panel, such as Weld, Bevel, Break, and Cut among others. Each of these options operates on different sub-object levels. These new commands are part of the `meshop` structure.

For instance, on an editable mesh object assigned to b,

```
meshop.weldvertsbythreshold b #{1,3..8} 1.0
```

will attempt to weld vertices 1 and vertices 3 to 8 using a threshold value of 1.0 units.

Most meshop *commands require sub-object lists. These can be passed in many ways, such as* #selection, #all *or a bitarray. A bitarray is similar to an array, but it can contain separate elements and ranges. For instance, the bitarray* #{1..5,8} *contains all numbers between 1 and 5 plus the number 8.*

Another mesh command is meshop.detachfaces, which executes the same command as Detach in the UI, separating the faces as another element or object.

See the online Help for a complete list of meshop commands.

Working with Editable Poly Objects

Editable poly objects can be created only by converting or collapsing objects. This is done using convertto or collapsestack, but collapsestack will only work if the topmost modifier on stack outputs an editable poly object.

An easy way to create an editable poly object is applying the Turn to Poly modifier on the object and then collapsing it. The example below shows how to do it:

```
b = box()
addmodifier b (turn_to_poly())
collapsestack b
```

Operations on Editable Poly Objects

You can operate in editable poly objects the same way as meshes, using polyop struct. Several commands are identical to the mesh commands, but some of them are poly-specific.

For instance, you can apply meshsmooth on vertices 1 and 2 of the previous example using polyop.meshsmoothbyvert b #{1..2}.

Working with Patches

You can now create and manipulate editable patch objects in 3ds max 4. The easier way to create a patch object is by converting an editable mesh or editable poly object, or by collapsing the stack when a Patch modifier is on top (Surface, Edit Patch or Turn to Patch).

Operations on Editable Patch Objects

As you can with editable poly and editable mesh objects, you can work with patch objects using the patch structure.

For instance, you can use `patch.getvert` to read a vertex position and `patch` `.setvert` to define it. The following example illustrates the use of these commands:

```
s = plane lengthsegs:1 widthsegs:1
convertto s editable_patch
patch.setvert s 1 ((patch.getvert s 1) - [5,5,0])
patch.update s
```

Working with Edit Mesh, Patch, and Spline

It's possible to work with Edit Mesh, Edit Patch, and Edit Spline in MAXScript. These commands are the same ones that are displayed for you when you right-click an object. They will work the same if you're in the modifier level, with an Edit Mesh modifier applied, or if you have an editable mesh object. The same is valid for the remaining objects, except for editable poly objects that do not have a modifier.

Working with them is the same as working with Edit Spline. Edit Mesh commands will start with `meshops`, Edit Poly commands with `polyops`, and Edit Patch commands with `patchops`.

The intent of these commands is only to start actions, and they require a previous sub-object selection. For instance, if you want to delete the selected faces of an object, you can use `meshops.delete object`. In this case, the script will display a dialog box to confirm whether it should delete the isolated vertices.

These commands require 3ds max to be in the Modify panel, with one of the sub-objects selected. To change to the Modify panel, type **max modify mode**; to select the sub-object you want, use `subobjectlevel`.

In an editable spline, sub-object levels are:

Sub-Object Level	Level
1	Vertex
2	Segment
3	Spline

In an editable mesh, sub-object levels are:

Sub-Object Level	Level
1	Vertex
2	Edge
3	Face
4	Polygon
5	Element

In an editable poly, sub-object levels are:

Sub-Object Level	Level
1	Vertex
2	Edge
3	Border
4	Polygon
5	Element

In an Editable Patch, sub-object levels are:

Sub-Object Level	Level
1	Vertex
2	Edge
3	Patch
4	Element

You can make some commands work directly, if you are in the correct sub-object level and if you have a selection. For instance, you can weld vertices using `meshops.weld`, but this will only use the options provided in the UI. If you wish to specify the threshold via scripting, you will need to use `meshop.weldvertsbythreshold`, as shown before.

Hands-on MAXScript: Creating a Scatter and Adjusting Vertex Color

This section features two exercises. In the first you will make a script that works similar to Scatter. The second script will adjust the hue, saturation, and value of the vertex color of an object.

Creating a Scatter

Scatter only allows 3D geometry to be selected. You will do a simple scatter that will copy any object and position each copy to the center of each face.

Start a new script and type the commands found in Listing 16.6. (You can access this code from the CD-ROM, in the file named `scatter_exercise.ms`.)

LISTING 16.6: THE SCATTER SCRIPT (SCATTER_EXERCISE.MS)

```
if selection.count != 1 then
format "Select an object first.\n"
else
if superclassof $ != GeometryClass then
format "Select a 3D Object first.\n"
else
(
scatterobj = omnilight()
obj = $
obj2 = snapshot obj
nfaces = obj2.numfaces
f = #()
n = #()
for i in 1 to nfaces do
(
scat2 = instance scatterobj
f[i] = getface obj2 i
for j in 1 to 3 do n[j] = getvert obj2 f[i][j]
scat2.pos = (n[1] + n[2] + n[3])/3
scat2.parent = obj
)
delete #(obj2,scatterobj)
)
```

Just like the other exercises in this chapter, this one checks to make sure there is a selected object and that it's a 3D object. After that, the object to be scattered is created. If you want to scatter different objects, you simply change the object created through the variable scatterobj.

The script then creates a copy of the selected object, using snapshot. This way, if the object has any space warp or any world space modifier, it will be considered on the copy. If any other copy method is used, all space warps and world space modifiers will not be considered.

Using a for command, you create instances of the scattered object, get each face's vertices, and read their positions. The omnilight is then positioned in the average position of the three vertices. At the end of script, you need to delete the copied object and the original light, which were only created so you could manipulate and clone them.

Adjusting the Vertex Color of an Object

This exercise will adjust the hue, saturation and value of the vertex color of an object. It will ask the user to type how much to add in Hue, Saturation, and Value. Then, the script will add these values to the vertex color of each vertex.

Let's begin. Start a new script with the commands from Listing 16.7 (or access the code from the file named cpv_exercise.ms on the CD-ROM).

LISTING 16.7: THE VERTEX COLOR SCRIPT (CPV_EXERCISE.MS)

```
if selection.count != 1 then format "Select an object first.\n"
else
if superclassof $ != GeometryClass then
format "Select a 3D Object first.\n" else
(
obj = $
if classof obj.baseobject != Editable_mesh then
obj = converttomesh $
collapsestack obj
if getnumcpvverts obj == 0 then
format "Object must have Color per Vertex information." else
(
hue2 = getkbvalue prompt:" Amount to be added to the Hue:"
sat2 = getkbvalue prompt:"Amount to be added to the Saturation:"
val2 = getkbvalue prompt:"Amount to be added to the Value:"
for i in 1 to obj.numcpvverts do
(
tmp_col = getvertcolor obj i
if (tmp_col.hue + hue2) > 255 then
   (tmp_col.hue = tmp_col.hue + hue2 - 255)
else
(
if (tmp_col.hue + hue2) < 0 then
   (tmp_col.hue = tmp_col.hue + hue2 + 255)
else (tmp_col.hue = tmp_col.hue + hue2)
)
if sat2 + tmp_col.saturation > 255 then
   tmp_col.saturation = 255 else
if sat2 + tmp_col.saturation < 0
   then tmp_col.saturation = 0
   else tmp_col.saturation += sat2
```

```
if val2 + tmp_col.value > 255 then
    tmp_col.value = 255 else
if val2 + tmp_col.value < 0 then
    tmp_col.value = 0
    else tmp_col.value += val2
setvertcolor obj i tmp_col
)
)
update obj
)
```

Once an object is selected, the script checks to see whether it has vertex color information. If it does not have vertex color information, the script stops. Then it checks whether the base object is an editable mesh, using the `.baseobject` property. If the object is not an editable mesh, it's converted to one. If it's an editable mesh, its stack is collapsed. All this is done so you can edit the vertex color. If the object is not an editable mesh, or if it has any modifier on top, it will not allow you to edit vertex color.

You ask the user to enter the hue, saturation, and value of the color. This value will be added to each vertex's color. To step through each vertex, we use the `for` command, which tests all vertices that have Color Per Vertex information, from 1 to `.numcpvverts`.

Now you read the color of each vertex and manipulate it. First, you adjust the hue. Since the hue is cyclic, we need to make sure it's between 0 and 255. You add two conditions: if the adjusted hue is bigger 255, the script adjusts it, subtracting 255. If it's negative, the script adds 255.

The same happens for saturation and value, except that if the value is negative, it's rounded to 0, and if the value is bigger than 255, it's rounded to 255. After the calculations are done, you simply need to set the adjusted vertex color to the object using `setvertcolor`.

Now the script is done. Save it, because you will use it in a later chapter to make it interactive.

Summary

In this chapter you learned different ways of using MAXScript to manipulate objects and materials, which is one of its most common uses. All this information will be used in future chapters, when you start working with animation.

In the next chapter you will build on the skills you learned here and on the scripts you created by adding a user interface to the scripts.

Creating a
User Interface

3ds max

Chapter 17

None of the scripts we have created so far look like any sample script that comes with 3ds max. That is because those scripts each have a user interface. This interface makes the script look like a 3ds max command, dialog box, or any 3ds max interface item.

Using a user interface (UI) allows us to make our scripts easier to use and understand, and more intuitive also. Let's learn how to implement one, and enhance the scripts we have done so far.

- Designing utilities and UI items

- Using alert messages

- Building rollouts

- Floaters and dialogs

- Using Visual MAXScript

- Macro scripts

- Making scenes interactive

Designing Utilities

The simplest type of script that has an interface is the utility. Utilities appear as new rollouts in the MAXScript area of the Utility tab, as seen in Figure 17.1.

. . . .

Figure 17.1 The MAXScript area in the Command Panel

To run any utility, simply choose Run Script and select a Utility Script file. It'll appear in the drop-down list. When you select it, 3ds max will start the script and add a rollout under the MAXScript rollout. All options from this script can be found in this new rollout. An example of a utility is the Custom Icon Maker sample script that comes with 3ds max.

Creating a Utility

A utility is very similar to a Macro Script, but it has a defined space for an interface. By contrast, when we need an interface in a Macro Script, we need to use floaters, which we'll see later in this chapter.

Let's create a utility as an example. You will need to use interface items, such as buttons or spinners, to make this script work. Start a new script and write:

```
utility example "Utility Example"
(
)
```

This is the basic format of a utility script. It requires a variable name and a text name, which will be displayed in the Utilities drop-down list. It also requires brackets that define where the utility starts and ends.

Using File ➜ Evaluate, evaluate this script and notice that it appears in the list of utilities. Select it from the list and it becomes a rollout:

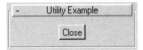

As you see, it has nothing but the Close button. All utility rollouts have a Close button at the end.

Buttons

Let's start adding content to this script. The first UI item we'll use is the button. When a button is pressed, it performs a specific action or set of actions. To add a button to our script, add this line inside the brackets:

```
button go "Start"
```

Now evaluate your script and notice that, with no more code than this, we already have a button.

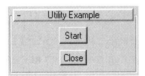

Now that we have a button in the script, click it. Did anything happen? Of course not, because we haven't added any commands to this script yet. Let's do so. Here's the whole script:

```
utility example "Utility Example"
(
button go "Start"
on go pressed do
(
pt = pickpoint()
c = cylinder pos:pt radius:15 height:60 heightsegs:15
)
)
```

Now the button has a series of actions to perform when it is pressed. The syntax is simple: on *button_variable_name* pressed do etc.

We can enhance the button appearance by specifying its width, height, and a tooltip. To try that, let's add a second button that will bend the cylinder, and let's adjust the buttons' appearance (specifically, their widths and tooltips). Here's the script again:

```
utility example "Utility Example"
(
button go "Start" width:120 tooltip:"Start Object Creation"
button bend_it "Bend" width:120 tooltip:"Bend the Object"
on go pressed do
(
pt = pickpoint()
global c = cylinder pos:pt radius:15 height:60 heightsegs:15
)
on bend_it pressed do
(
addmodifier c (bend angle:30)
)
)
```

Evaluate the script and test each button. You will notice we've put both button definitions at the top of the script and both actions below. There's no specific requirement for all the buttons to be defined first; doing so just makes it easier to organize the interface. Notice also that we've specified a 30-degree bend directly in the addmodifier command.

You need to declare c *as a* global *variable, or MAXScript will erase it after finishing the sequence of commands it's working with. See more about local and global variables on Chapter 19.*

Spinners

Spinners are UI items used to specify values. They are the same controls we use in the max UI to specify the radius of a cylinder, the size of a box, and so forth.

Continuing our example, let's add a spinner to control the bend angle. Listing 17.1 presents the complete script at this point.

LISTING 17.1: THE SPINNER SCRIPT (UTILITY_BEND.MS)

```
utility example "Utility Example"
(
button go "Start" width:120 tooltip:"Start Object Creation"
button bend_it "Bend" width:120 tooltip:"Bend the Object"
```

```
spinner bend_ang "Angle"

on go pressed do
(
pt = pickpoint()
global c = cylinder pos:pt radius:15 height:60 heightsegs:15
)

on bend_it pressed do
(
if c != undefined then
addmodifier c (bend angle:30)
bend_ang.value = 30
)
on bend_ang changed val do
(
if c != undefined then
for i in 1 to c.modifiers.count do
(
if classof c.modifiers[i] == Bend then
(
c.modifiers[i].angle = bend_ang.value
exit
)
)
)
)
```

After evaluating the script, you will see the interface with the spinner added as in Figure 17.2.

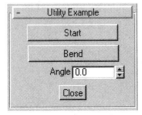

Figure 17.2 *The Utility Example script, with a spinner*

This version of the script adds a couple of checks before adjusting the bend value. It needs to check whether the Bend modifier was applied to the object. First, it checks to see if c exists in the scene. After that, the script scrolls through all modifiers in the object to see if any of them is a Bend. If so, the angle is modified. Notice that we've used an Exit command. It stops the loop and exits, so that only the first Bend of the object will be edited, if there is more than one bend.

We can add a similar check to the button so that it does not apply another bend to an object that already has a bend applied. You can see the complete code of this script on the CD, in the file `utility_bend.ms` under the Chapter 17 directory.

Let's adjust the spinner properties. You noticed that the spinner goes from 0 to 100. We might want a different range. To choose one, simply specify:

```
spinner bend_ang "Angle" range:[-180,180,0]
```

This will set the spinner range from −180 to 180, with 0 as the default. (If the user right-clicks a spinner, it resets itself to the default value.)

We can set more properties in a spinner. For instance, the spinner values in this script are floating-point. Sometimes we might need integer values. We can specify the type using `type:#integer` or `type:#float`. We can also set the stepping of the spinner, defining its precision. This is done using `scale:0.01`, for instance. In this case, the spinner will always step in multiples of 0.01.

Let's edit our script, adjusting the spinner one more time. Set the spinner type to float, and also make it snap in multiples of 2.5:

```
spinner bend_ang "Angle" range:[-180,180,0] type:#float \
    scale:2.5
```

Evaluate the script and notice the spinner jumps only in values that are multiples of 2.5. You can enter any value by typing, but using the mouse will always provide the restricted values.

Global Properties

We can adjust several global properties of a UI item. Properties are used to organize UI elements in the script and to allow easier manipulation. We can turn items on or off, or position and align any UI item.

An item can be enabled or disabled very simply. At creation time, specify `enabled:true` or `enabled:false`. To change this later in the script, just attach the `.enabled` property. For instance, we can create a button that is initially turned off, using:

```
button create "Button Example" enabled:false
```

Later in the script, if we want to enable this button we can use:

```
create.enabled = true
```

We can specify the position of each item using pos:[x,y]. Sometimes we might want one spinner beside another, and only changing the position of the spinner in the UI will allow us to do it. An easier way is using offset:[x,y], which will specify the position based on the actual position of the object.

An easier way to specify the position of an item is aligning it to the left, right, or center, using align:#left, align:#right, or align:#center.

Other Interface Items

There are many more interface items besides spinners and buttons. Some will be demonstrated in other chapters, but let's look at the most common ones here.

Sliders

Sliders are similar to spinners but use a different visual metaphor. They work the same way, except they can be horizontal or vertical. Sliders do not allow us to specify the stepping using the scale property. Instead, they allow the user to select a position from a continuous range, like an old analog thermostat.

Let's change the spinner from the example we used before to a slider. First edit the spinner line, changing the word "spinner" to "slider" and removing the scale definition:

```
slider bend_ang "Angle" range:[-180,180,0] type:#float
```

Evaluate the script and play with the slider, as in Figure 17.3.

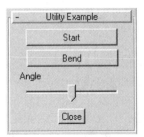

Figure 17.3 *The Utility Example script, with a slider*

We can orient the slider horizontally (the default) or vertically, using the `orient` property: `orient:#vertical` or `orient:#horizontal`. We can also add a series of ticks to indicate the stepping of the slider, specifying `ticks:number`, where *number* is the number of ticks to be added. For instance, let's change the slider to vertical and add five ticks to it:

```
slider bend_ang "Angle" range:[-180,180,0] type:#float \
    orient:#vertical ticks:5
```

Evaluate and see the difference.

Notice that we added a backslash (\) character at the end of the physical line to indicate that the script continues on the next line. We did this simply because the printed page allows fewer characters per line than a monitor screen. Although you can do this in your code, you do not need to add a backslash when writing scripts, because the MAXScript Editor allows very long lines.

Use sliders when you don't need the user to specify an exact value. It's not possible to adjust a value the same way as with spinners, and it's also not possible to reset a slider as we can by right-clicking a spinner.

Check Box

A *check box* is an On/Off control. It's useful for many actions in MAXScript. For example, all the options in the Object Properties dialog box, are check boxes. Another example can be seen in Figure 17.4.

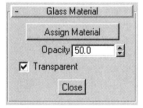

Figure 17.4 *A sample check box*

Check boxes can be used to control many options within objects. Let's write a script that will add a default material to an object and will allow us to specify whether the material is or is not transparent. Start a new script and type:

```
utility glass "Glass Material"
(
button go "Assign Material" tooltip:"Assign Material" width:120
```

```
spinner opac "Opacity" range:[0,100,50] type:#float
checkbox onoff "Transparent" checked:true

on go pressed do
    (
    if selection.count == 0 then
    format "Select an object first.\n"
    else
        (
        global mat
        mat = standardmaterial()
        if onoff.checked == true then
            mat.opacity = opac.value
        else
            mat.opacity = 100
        $.material = mat
        )
    )
on opac changed val do
    (
    if mat != undefined then
    if onoff.checked == true then
        mat.opacity = opac.value
      else
        mat.opacity = 100
    )
on onoff changed state do
    (
    opac.enabled = state
    if mat != undefined then
    if onoff.checked == true then
        mat.opacity = opac.value
      else
        mat.opacity = 100
    )
)
```

This script allows the user to select an object and assign a default Standard material to it. Then, it checks to see if the onoff check box is turned on, using the checked property. If it's on, the slider's opacity value will be used; if it's not, the object will not be transparent, and the slider will be disabled.

When adjusting the properties of the spinner and the check box, we first need to check whether the material has been created and assigned. This is done using

```
if mat != undefined
```

The script will only change the transparency of the material that has just been assigned to the object. You will learn later how to adjust properties on selected objects, and how to ask the user to select objects.

This script would be a great place to use *functions*. If we defined several commands into a function here, we would save a lot of code, since `if onoff.checked` is called three times in the script. We'll use functions in future examples so you can see the difference.

Colorpicker

A *colorpicker* is a max UI item that allows us to choose one color. It displays the Color Selector dialog and returns the selected color value. Let's add one to our example script, as in Figure 17.5, and let's adjust some values.

Figure 17.5 *A sample colorpicker*

You can find the final script on the CD as `utility_transparency.ms`. Between `button` and `spinner`, add:

```
colorpicker mat_col "Material Color" color:[255,255,255]
```

This will create the colorpicker and set its default color to white.

Now let's add the events that will change the color of the object in the scene. Below `checkbox`, add the following code:

```
on mat_col changed val do
    (
    if mat != undefined then
        (
        mat.diffusecolor = mat_col.color
        mat.filtercolor = mat_col.color/2
```

```
          mat.ambientcolor = mat_col.color/4
          )
    )
```

In addition, we need to edit the on go pressed loop, so it reads the colorpicker color and uses it in the material. After mat = standardmaterial() add:

```
mat.diffusecolor = mat_col.color
mat.filtercolor = mat_col.color/2
mat.ambientcolor = mat_col.color/4
```

The changes we made will set the ambient, diffuse, and filter colors; all three are based on the colorpicker color we created. Evaluate the final script and test it on any object you wish. Notice that the color adjusted through the Color Selector dialog is interactive and displayed on screen.

As an exercise, create a separate colorpicker for each color, create different spinners, and adjust the script as you wish.

Pickbutton

A *pickbutton* is a button that will be used to select an object. It's similar to the Pick Operand button in ShapeMerge, Conform, Boolean, and other max UI windows.

Let's edit the script we just wrote and add a Pickbutton, to select the object before assigning the material, as in Figure 17.6:

Figure 17.6 *A sample pickbutton*

Open a new script and type all the code shown in Listing 17.2. You can access this code on the CD that accompanies this book, in the file named utility_glass2.ms.

LISTING 17.2: THE PICKBUTTON SCRIPT (UTILITY_GLASS2.MS)

```
utility glass "Glass Material2"
(
pickbutton pick "Select Object" tooltip:"Select Object" width:120
button go "Assign Material" tooltip:"Assign Material" \
   width:120 enabled:false
spinner opac "Opacity" range:[0,100,50] type:#float
colorpicker mat_col "Material Color" color:[255,255,255]
checkbox onoff "Transparent" checked:true

fn check_onoff =
   (
   if onoff.checked == true then
       mat.opacity = opac.value
     else
       mat.opacity = 100
   )
fn mat_color =
   (
   mat.diffusecolor = mat_col.color
   mat.filtercolor = mat_col.color/2
   mat.ambientcolor = mat_col.color/4
   )

on pick picked obj do
   (
   if superclassof obj != GeometryClass then
      format "Select a 3D Object.\n"
   else
      (
      global sel_obj = obj
      pick.text = obj.name
      go.enabled = true
      )
   )
on go pressed do
   (
   global mat = standardmaterial()
   mat_color()
   check_onoff()
   sel_obj.material = mat
   )
```

```
on mat_col changed val do
    (
    if mat != undefined do mat_color()
    )
on opac changed val do
    (
    if mat != undefined do check_onoff()
    )
on onoff changed state do
    (
    opac.enabled = state
    if mat != undefined do check_onoff()
    )
)
```

The pickbutton will ask the user to select an object. When an object is selected, the script checks to see if it's a 3D object (because we can't assign materials to lights, dummies, and so on). If so, the Assign Material button will be enabled, and the pickbutton will display the object's name. The rest of the script works just like previous versions, but it doesn't need to have an object selected before it is used; that's why the user selects an object through the pickbutton. Notice that we also used functions, which saved us a lot of code.

Radio Buttons

Radio buttons allow users to choose one from among several options. Examples of radio buttons in the max UI include the choice between Chop and Squash in Spheres, or the choice of Particle Type in any of the Particle Systems windows.

We can use radio buttons to choose which type of bump map to apply to the object, using the script we created to apply a bump map in Chapter 16 (some sample radio buttons are illustrated in Figure 17.7).

Figure 17.7 *Sample radio buttons*

Start a new script and type all the commands shown in Listing 17.3. You can access this code on the CD that accompanies this book, in the file named utility_bump.ms.

LISTING 17.3: THE RADIO BUTTON SCRIPT (UTILITY_BUMP.MS)

```
Utility add_bump "Add Bump Map"
(

pickbutton pick_obj "Select Object"
radiobuttons type "Type" \
labels:#("Noise","Smoke","Speckle","Splat","Stucco") columns:2
spinner amount "Bump Amount" range:[-1000,1000,30]
spinner size "Bump Size" range:[0,10000,25]

fn upd_material =
    (
    case type.state of
        (
        1:    m.bumpMap = Noise ()
        2:    m.bumpMap = Smoke ()
        3:    m.bumpMap = Speckle ()
        4:    m.bumpMap = Splat ()
        5:    m.bumpMap = Stucco ()
        )
    m.bumpMapAmount = amount.value
    m.bumpMap.size = size.value
    )

on pick_obj picked obj do
    (
    if obj.material == undefined then
        format "Selected object has no material applied.\n"
    else
        (
        global m
        m = obj.material
        m.shaderType = 4
        m.diffuseRoughness = 30
        m.specularLevel = 43
        m.glossiness = 35
        m.soften = 0.5
```

```
                    meditmaterials[1] = m
                    max mtledit
                    upd_material()
                    )
            )
    on type changed state do if m != undefined do upd_material()
    on amount changed val do if m != undefined do upd_material()
    on size changed val do if m != undefined do upd_material()
    )
```

As you can see when you evaluate this, two columns of radio buttons will be created. We added five labels to the radiobutton object, so five buttons appear. MAXScript will return the index number of each button as soon as it's selected. That's what calls on type changed state. To know which radio button is selected, we can use the .state property.

Another enhancement we added in this script is the use of **case**. This conditional branching statement tests a series of values, performing a different action for each result.

We also created a function (with **fn**) that will be called whenever one of the parameters is changed. Since the action is always the same, by creating a function we avoid the need to repeat it each of the many times it's used in the script.

Labels

A *label* is used to place text in your UI. The user cannot interact with this text, but the script can change the text as a way of outputting results. To demonstrate this feature, let's add a label that will show us some information about the previous example, like the credits for the script, as in Figure 17.8.

Figure 17.8 *Sample labels*

After the second spinner, add:

```
label a01 "Auto Bump Utility"
label a02 "Made by"
label a03 (put your name here between quotes)
```

Now evaluate the script and notice your credits there. We can also change the text in a label within a script. For instance, we can have the script calculate a value and output it in the UI. This is done by using the `.text` property, as in `a02.text = "Designed by"`.

Using Alert Messages

Key Concept

Sometimes we need to show messages to the user. There are three ways to do that with MAXScript, using dialog boxes. You can display a box that simply alerts the user, a more complex dialog that asks for user input, and a third box that allows the user to cancel the action.

Messageboxes

A *messagebox* is a dialog box that alerts the user, who will be required to click OK in it. There's no other option, and the script is halted until the user clicks OK. It's useful for error messages and important instructions.

Use the messagebox with care, because it halts the script until dismissed.

In our previous exercises, we could have used a messagebox to alert the user about picking a wrong object, or when he picked an object when none was required, instead of using `print`. Let's edit `utility_bump.ms` and add a messagebox alerting the user that the object needs a material on it, as in Figure 17.9.

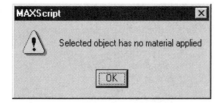

Figure 17.9 *A sample messagebox*

Locate this line and edit it, replacing the current `format` with `messagebox`.

```
if obj.material == undefined then
    messagebox "Selected object has no material applied"
else
```

Evaluate the script and test it on an object with no material assigned. This script is saved as `utility_bump2.ms` on the CD.

Queryboxes

Sometimes we might need a more complex alert box. We also have a way to ask the user which direction to follow, using a Yes or No alert box. This type of control is called a *querybox*.

Continuing the previous example, we can ask the user whether to assign a standard material to the object if it has no material. Let's do that, as in Figure 17.10.

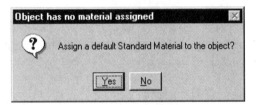

Figure 17.10 *A sample querybox*

Substitute the line we edited previously with the following ones:

```
query = false
if obj.material == undefined then
(
query = querybox "Assign a Standard Material to the object?"
    title:"Object has no material assigned"
if query == true then obj.material = standardmaterial()
)
else query = true
if query == true then
```

Here we created a variable called `query`. If the object has no material, we ask the user if we should assign a default material to it. If the user chooses Yes, the variable value will be True. Then, we'll assign the material and the script will process the rest.

If the user chooses No, the variable value will be False, and the script will not proceed. In case the object already has a material assigned, the script will skip the querybox and will assign true to the variable, so it can proceed.

This version of the script is saved as `utility_bump3.ms`.

Yesnocancelboxes

A *yesnocancelbox* is the same as a *querybox* but also has a Cancel button. Instead of returning True or False, it returns `#yes`, `#no`, or `#cancel`.

Building Rollouts

Rollouts are used when we have too much information to display all at once and we want to organize it better. A good example in the max UI is SuperSpray; its parameters are organized through rollouts, grouping like items together and rolling them up to save space.

A rollout is self-contained. All actions related to all items must be performed for each rollout, but there are ways to access other rollouts' items values also. For instance, suppose you have the following rollouts:

```
rollout rollout1 "Rollout 1"
(
button button1 "First Button"
)

rollout rollout2 "Rollout 2"
(
button button2 "Second Button"
)
```

You could not use `on button1 pressed do` while in the second rollout (rollout2), because this button only exists in the first rollout (rollout1). On the other hand, you can enable or disable it using `rollout1.button1.enabled = false;` by adding the rollout name before the UI item, you can access and change its properties.

Adding and Removing Rollouts

Every utility has a rollout automatically, but we can add as many more rollouts as needed to each utility. The rollouts we add work exactly the same as the utility's main rollout, but more rollouts only appear when explicitly added to a utility or a floater. To add or remove rollouts we can use `addrollout` and `removerollout`. The following script is an example of adding and removing rollouts; its output is shown in Figure 17.11.

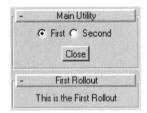

Figure 17.11 *Multiple rollouts*

```
rollout first "First Rollout"
    (
    label f "This is the First Rollout"
    )
rollout second "Second Rollout"
    (
    label s "This is the Second Rollout"
    )

utility main "Main Utility"
(
radiobuttons menus labels:#("First","Second")

on main open do addrollout first
on main close do
    (
    removerollout first
    removerollout second
    )
on menus changed state do
    (
    case state of
        (
        1: (
```

```
        removerollout second
        addrollout first
        )
    2: (
        removerollout first
        addrollout second rolledup:true
        )
    )
  )
)
```

In the second rollout, we added the `rolledup` option. It will define whether the rollout starts out opened or not.

Notice that we also used two more events: `on main open` and `on main close`. These are events to be executed when the utility is opened and closed. You can use them with utilities and rollouts.

Floaters

Besides using rollouts in utilities, we can use them in floaters. *Floaters* are dialog boxes that contain several rollouts; they look like areas from the Command Panel but "float" separately in the max window. An example is the Render Scene floater.

We can create a floater using `newrolloutfloater` and close any floater using `closerolloutfloater`. The `newrolloutfloater` command requires a caption string and the floater's width and height values (see Listing 17.4 for an example of this command). Let's adjust the Normalize Splines script we created in Chapter 16 and make it a rollout floater script. We'll need two UI items: a pickbutton to select the object and a spinner to specify the number of segments (the final result is shown in Figure 17.12).

• •

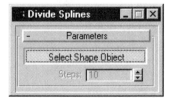

Figure 17.12 *A sample floater*

Open a new script and type all the commands shown in Listing 17.4, or access this code on the CD that accompanies this book, in the file named floater_ divideshape.ms.

LISTING 17.4: THE FLOATER SCRIPT (FLOATER_DIVIDESHAPE.MS)

```
rollout divide_params "Parameters"
(
pickbutton pick_shape "Select Shape Object" width:160
spinner steps "Steps: " range:[3,1000,10] type:#integer \
    enabled:false

fn convert_it shp =
    (
    x = shp
    tmp = copy x
    pick_shape.text = shp.name
    obj = converttosplineshape tmp
    ns = numsplines obj
    nv = numknots obj
    size = steps.value
    ratio = 1.0/size
    if ss != undefined do delete ss
    ss = splineshape()
    ss.name = x.name + "_Divided"
    ss.wirecolor = x.wirecolor
    ss.pivot = x.pivot
    for i in 1 to ns do
        (
        addnewspline ss
        for j in 1 to size do
            (
            pt = lengthinterp obj i (ratio*(j-1))
            addknot ss i #smooth #curve pt
            )
        if (isclosed obj i) then close ss i else
            (
            pt = lengthinterp obj i 1.0
            addknot ss i #smooth #curve pt
            )
        updateshape ss
        )
```

```
        delete tmp
        )

    on pick_shape picked shp do
        (
        global ss,x
        ss = undefined
        x = shp
        convert_it x
        steps.enabled = true
        )
    on steps changed val do
        (
    convert_it x
        )
    )

    try (closerolloutfloater divide) catch()
    divide = newrolloutfloater "Divide Splines" 200 116
    addrollout divide_params divide
```

Basically, the spline creation is defined as a function that will be called from either the pickbutton or the spinner. When we pick a new shape, we define `ss = undefined`, resetting the function and creating a new spline. In addition, when selecting an object, we enable the spinner so that the number of segments can be adjusted.

As usual, some new concepts were introduced here. We used `try` and `catch` to make sure the floater was closed before opening a new one. The `try` command tests the function; `catch` will execute another function if the one that was tried didn't work. In our situation, we have no function inside `catch`. If we did not use this, executing the script would create many floaters, one on top of the other.

A Pickbutton Filter

The script we just wrote has a problem. If we select a 3D object, a helper, or anything that's not a shape, it will crash. To fix this, we can implement a filter in the pickbutton that will select only shapes. This filter is a function that will test an object under the cursor and return True if it's a shape. Before the pickbutton definition, type:

```
    fn isshape obj =
        (
        superclassof obj == shape
        )
```

This function will return True if the object is a shape, so the object can be selected. (If the object is not a shape, the script simply stops.) We now need to implement it in the script, telling pickbutton to use this function:

```
pickbutton pick_shape "Select Shape Object" width:160 \
    filter:isshape
```

Opening Floaters

This script executes automatically when evaluated. It would be interesting if we could have a utility that could call this script when started, and would have a button to open this floater when it's not available anymore. This is very simple to do. All we need to do is include the rollout floater commands as an on open utility action and as an on pressed button action.

Edit your script, removing the lines that open the floater (try, divide=, and addrollout). Now let's create a utility to call the floater:

```
utility divide_utility "Divide Shapes"
(
button go "Open Floater" width:120

on go pressed do
    (
    global divide
    try (closerolloutfloater divide) catch()
    divide = newrolloutfloater "Divide Splines" 200 116
    addrollout divide_params divide
    )
on divide_utility open do
    (
    global divide
    try (closerolloutfloater divide) catch()
    divide = newrolloutfloater "Divide Splines" 200 116
    addrollout divide_params divide
    go.enabled = false
    )
)
```

Always make the rollout variable global, so closerolloutfloater *can close it later. See Chapter 19 for more information on global variables.*

Evaluate this script now, and open this utility. The button is always active, even if the floater is opened. We can adjust this by disabling the button when the floater opens and enabling it when it closes. In the rollout code, add:

```
on divide_params open do divide_utility.go.enabled = false
on divide_params close do divide_utility.go.enabled = true
```

This will disable the button in the utility when it's opened and enable it again when it's closed.

Notice how we access this button. We need to use `rollout.button.property` *to access it. In this case, it's not a rollout, but a utility, and the process is the same.*

Creating Dialog Boxes

Besides working with floaters, 3ds max 4 also allows you to create dialog boxes, using the `createdialog` command. Dialog boxes look cleaner and have the same look and feel as built-in max dialog windows, like Select By Name and others. Dialog boxes, unlike floaters, can each have only a single rollout.

To create a dialog box for the script in Listing 17.4, you would add the following line at the end, after the rollout is declared:

```
createdialog divide_rollout 170 46
```

The dialog box is smaller than the floater because it does not include the floater's borders and header. As a rule of thumb, floaters are 30 × 70 pixels larger than dialog boxes.

If you're using dialog boxes, you won't need to use floaters or add the rollout to a dialog. Thus, `Createdialog` *substitutes for the* `newrolloutfloater` *and the* `addrollout` *commands.*

When creating a dialog box, you can specify `modal:true`, and it will block the access to the rest of the interface until the user closes the dialog box. This very useful feature helps you make sure the user has input all needed data.

To remove a dialog box, you should use the `destroydialog` command.

Creating Rollouts with Visual MAXScript

Visual MAXScript makes it a lot easier for you to create rollouts and utilities. You can place several UI items, configure their appearance and also write the events associated with them.

You can start Visual MAXScript in any of several ways:

- By selecting Edit Rollout or New Rollout in the Script Editor
- By pressing F2 while in the Script Editor
- By selecting Visual MAXScript among the utilities in the Utility Panel

Once you load Visual MAXScript, it will look like Figure 17.13.

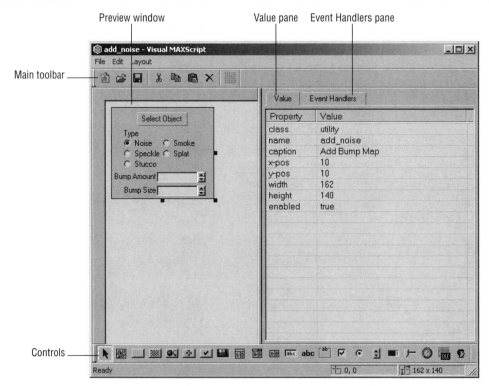

Figure 17.13 *The Visual MAXScript window*

The workflow in Visual MAXScript is quite simple. You either open an existing rollout or create one from scratch. Then you add the controls you need, picking them among the bottommost toolbar. On the right pane, you can specify the properties of the selected control, or its events. Once you're done, clicking Save will update the Script Editor.

Let's see how it works using a step-by-step exercise to recreate the script in Listing 17.3.

Hands-on MAXScript: Using Visual MAXScript

This exercise will re-create the script in Listing 17.3, showing how to use Visual MAXScript to create and edit utilities and rollouts. You will start from scratch and create the script. Then you will make some changes to the existing code, to see how you can use Visual MAXScript to edit existing utilities.

1. Start a new script and type:

   ```
   utility add_noise "Add Bump Map"
   (
   )
   ```

2. Select Edit ➜ Edit Rollout to open Visual MAXScript.

3. Expand the preview window until it is 150 pixels in height.

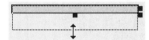

4. Turn on the Grid by clicking the Grid/Snap icon on the toolbar.

5. Select Pickbutton on the Controls toolbar and draw the pickbutton on the window.

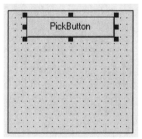

6. With the Pickbutton selected, enter the following information on the Value pane:

Property	Value
Name	pick_obj
caption	Select Object

7. Select the Event Handlers pane and check Picked. This will assign an on picked event to the pickbutton.

8. Click the word "picked" and enter the following code in the dialog:

```
if obj.material == undefined then
format "Selected object has no material applied\n"
else
(
global m
m = obj.material
m.shaderType = 4
m.diffuseRoughness = 30
m.specularLevel = 43
m.glossiness = 35
m.Soften = 0.5
meditmaterials[1] = m
max mtledit
upd_material()
)
```

9. Click OK to dismiss the dialog.

A pickbutton can have only one possible event associated. Some items allow various events to be associated. Notice that you can navigate among the events for the different elements using the two drop-down lists at the bottom of the Edit Event Handler dialog box, as in Figure 17.14. This makes it easier to copy and paste blocks of code from one event to the other.

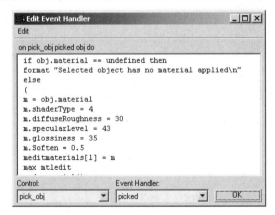

Figure 17.14 *The Edit Event Handler dialog box*

10. Select Radiobuttons in the Controls toolbar and drag a radiobutton control on the window.

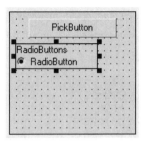

11. With the Radiobutton control selected, enter the following information on the Value pane:

Property	Value
Name	Type
Caption	Type
Columns	2

12. Click the Labels property, so you can edit the array of labels.

13. Select Radiobuttons in the dialog and press the Del key to remove it.

14. Type **"Noise"** and press Enter to add it to the list. Do the same for **"Smoke"**, **"Speckle"**, **"Splat"**, and **"Stucco"**. Click OK when you're done. You need to include quotes around these items so that MAXScript recognizes them as string values inside the array.

15. Select the Event Handlers pane and check the Changed pane

16. Click the word *changed*, enter the following code in the dialog, and click OK when done:

```
if m != undefined then upd_material()
```

17. Create two spinners and assign their values as follows:

Property	Spinner1 Value	Spinner2 Value
name	amount	size
caption	Bump Amount	Bump Size
range	[−1000,1000,30]	[0,10000,25]

18.   On both spinners, assign the following code to the changed event, and turn it on:

```
if m != undefined then upd_material()
```

 You can use copy-and-paste to duplicate the spinners. The copied spinner will be offset 10 × 10 pixels, and you can then reposition it. All events and properties are copied, and it is automatically assigned a new name.

19.   Save the script and exit Visual MAXScript.

Your script is now ready. There's only one missing piece: the upd_material function. Enter it right after the spinners in the script, and before the events:

```
fn upd_material =
  (
  case type.state of
    (
    1:    m.bumpMap = Noise ()
    2:    m.bumpMap = Smoke ()
    3:    m.bumpMap = Speckle ()
    4:    m.bumpMap = Splat ()
    5:    m.bumpMap = Stucco ()
    )
  m.bumpMapAmount = amount.value
  m.bumpMap.size = size.value
  )
```

Once you evaluate the script, the rollout should look similar to Figure 17.15.

Figure 17.15 *Add Bump Map Utility*

As you can see, the spinners are not well aligned. This is because Visual MAXScript considers the width of the spinner as a single number, including the width of the spinner itself and the caption. You can fix it by adding the `fieldwidth:45` property to the spinners, which will then define the width of the spinner box.

In our previous examples, you enhanced the script code, adding a querybox to it and adding your credits to the script. Let's make those changes in Visual MAXScript now.

20. Select Edit➜ Edit Rollout in the Script Editor.

21. Expand the Rollout size.

22. Add three labels and change their captions to Auto Bump Utility, Designed by, and your name.

```
     Auto Bump Utility
        Designed by
Alexander Esppeschit Bicalho
```

23. Select the pickbutton, go to the Event Handlers pane, and click Picked.

24. Change the event code to the following:

```
query = false
if obj.material == undefined then
(
query = querybox "Assign a Standard Material to the object?" \
    title:"Object has no material assigned"
if query == true then obj.material = standardmaterial()
)
else query = true
if query == true then
    (
    global m = obj.material
    m.shaderType = 4
    m.diffuseRoughness = 30
    m.specularLevel = 43
    m.glossiness = 35
    m.soften = 0.5
    meditmaterials[1] = m
    max mtledit
    upd_material()
    )
```

Feel free to reposition the controls on the dialog as you wish.

Macro Scripts

Macro Scripts are scripts created by recording actions with the Macro Recorder and dragging and dropping the code on a toolbar, or by typing MAXScript code manually. Macro Scripts are used so you can add scripts to menus, quads or toolbars.

Their file extension is `.mcr`, but they are actually the same file type as scripts you write in MAXScript (`.ms`). You were introduced to Macro Scripts in Chapter 15, but we can take a closer look now.

There are several properties we can add to a Macro Script: the `category` where the Macro Script will be added; the `buttontext` that will appear when using a text button; the `tooltip` of the button; and the bitmap `icon` (which is explained below).

When you drag and drop, max automatically fills these properties in for you, auto-numbering the Macro Script and defining it as the Drag&Drop category.

This is an example of a Macro Script:

```
macroscript example
    category:"Mastering 3ds max"
    buttontext:"Example"
    tooltip:"Macro Script Example"
    icon:#("example",1)
(

script commands...

)
```

Using Icons

You can use a bitmap icon to define your Macro Script button. It can be automatically defined using the `icon` property. To create these icons, use any painting program.

This bitmap is nothing more than a BMP file with two different resolutions (for large and small icons) and a mask file. You can use more than one icon in the same BMP file, simply placing them side by side (see Figure 17.16).

Figure 17.16 *Sample bitmap icons*

When specifying the icon property, you need two parameters: the filename (without path or extension) and the icon number. Icons are numbered left to right, starting at 1. For instance, in the previous Macro Script, we used icon:#("example",1) where example would be the BMP file with the icon and we want to use the first icon in this file.

Macro Script Events

You can assign events to Macro Scripts in 3ds max 4. This allows you to specify when a Macro Script is visible, enabled, and checked. This is useful when you create Macro Scripts that you want placed in Menus or Quads, but you want control over when they are visible and available.

If you use any of these events, you will need to place the main Macro Script code inside an on execute *event.*

For instance, this macro turns on or off one light object, but its button is only visible when a light is selected and will be checked if the light is on:

```
macroscript lightonoff
category:"Mastering 3ds max"
buttontext:"Light On/Off"
(
    on isvisible return
    (selection.count == 1 and superclassof selection[1] == light)
    on isenabled return
    (selection.count == 1 and superclassof selection[1] == light)
    on ischecked return
    (try (selection[1].on == true)catch (false))
    on execute do
    (selection[1].on = not selection[1].on)
)
```

Evaluate this macro and place it on a Menu or Quad. You will notice it appears only if you have only one light object selected. This is because of the isvisible and isenabled events. If it is on, a check will appear besides the menu, because of the ischecked event. Notice that we used the try/catch construction, introduced earlier in this chapter. It's needed because you may have different light plug-ins, and they may not have the on property.

At the end, the main code of the script inverts the state of the on property, and it is called in the on execute event.

You do not need the `on isenabled` event if you plan to add this macro to a menu or quad, but it if you add this macro to a toolbar, `isvisible` does not work, and it may crash the script. This is why you added both `isvisible` and `isenabled` even though both perform the same verifications.

Adding Macro Scripts to Keyboard Shortcuts, Toolbars, Menus, and Macros

There's no need to load a Macro Script file. Just place it in the `UI\Macroscripts` folder, or evaluate it (MAX automatically copies it to the correct folder), and it will be loaded automatically when MAX starts.

Once the Macro is loaded, it appears as an Action Item in the Customize User Interface dialog. You can now assign it to a keyboard shortcut or to any toolbar, menu, or quad. See "Customizing the max Interface" in Chapter 3.

If you remove an `.mcr` file from the `Macroscripts` folder, MAX will not load it in the UI, since it will not find the related script. The opposite does not happen; if you remove a button from the UI, the script file will not be removed.

Macro Script Floaters and Dialogs

It's very easy to incorporate floaters and dialog boxes that you've already created into Macro Scripts. We can do this in two different ways: by dragging and dropping or by writing code manually.

First, let's use drag-and-drop. Open the file `macro_divideshape.ms` from the CD, or use the script shown earlier as Listing 17.4. Then select the entire script and drag it to any toolbar. The Macro Script will be created automatically.

Now let's do it manually. Before the rollout declaration, we'll add the Macro Script header. Just type:

```
MacroScript Divide_Shape category:"Tools" tooltip:"Divide Shape"
(
```

Don't forget to close the parenthesis at the end of the script. Evaluate this script and customize the toolbar to add it as a button.

This script must be saved in `UI\MacroScripts` to be loaded automatically when max Starts. If it's not placed in this folder, max will create a copy of it there when it's evaluated.

Making Scenes Interactive

Using scripts can help the animation process tremendously. We can use scripts to manipulate objects and easily adjust their position, rotation, scale, material, etc., making it easier for us to animate.

Key Concept

Animating With Scripts

Let's create a simple script that will help us animate a series of objects. In our example, we'll animate a hand, by animating the fingers using a script, as in Figure 17.17. Open the dummy_hand.max file from your CD. It contains the hand model to be animated.

Figure 17.17 *The Hand Controller script*

The script we'll create will be able to use any hand hierarchy, not only this one. We'll need to name the objects according to a certain convention: the fingers are named *name*A_01,*name*B_01, etc, where *name* is the hand object name. In addition, the fingers are named A_01 to E_01 from Thumb to Little. They're all linked to the hand also. The thumb has only two finger links, and the other fingers have three links.

Open the hand_controller.ms script from the CD, or type all the commands shown in Listing 17.5.

LISTING 17.5: THE HAND CONTROLLER SCRIPT (HAND_CONTROLLER.MS)

```
rollout hand_rollout "Parameters"
(
local A1,A2,B1,B2,B3,C1,C2,C3,D1,D2,D3,E1,E2,E3,F1,F2,F3
local S1,S2,amount
```

```
Pickbutton sel "Select Hand Object" width:120 align:#left \
    offset:[25,0]
checkbox inv "Invert Rotation" align:#right offset:[-25,-20]
slider A "Thumb" orient:#vertical align:#left range:[0,180,0] \
    ticks:9 width:50
slider B "Index" orient:#vertical align:#left range:[0,270,0] \
    ticks:9 offset:[60,-101] width:50
slider C "Middle" orient:#vertical align:#left range:[0,270,0] \
    ticks:9 offset:[120,-101] width:50
slider D "Ring" orient:#vertical align:#left range:[0,270,0] \
    ticks:9 offset:[180,-101] width:50
slider E "Little" orient:#vertical align:#left range:[0,270,0] \
    ticks:9 offset:[240,-101] width:50
slider AA width:50 offset:[-5,-8] range:[-60,60,0]
slider BB width:50 offset:[55,-39] range:[-15,15,0]
slider CC width:50 offset:[115,-39] range:[-15,15,0]
slider DD width:50 offset:[175,-39] range:[-15,15,0]
slider EE width:50 offset:[235,-39] range:[-15,15,0]
button RA "Reset" align:#left offset:[-2,0]
button RB "Reset" align:#left offset:[58,-26]
button RC "Reset" align:#left offset:[118,-26]
button RD "Reset" align:#left offset:[178,-26]
button RE "Reset" align:#left offset:[238,-26]

on sel picked obj do
    (
    global objname
    objname = obj.name
    sel.text = objname
    A1 = execute ("$" + objname + "A_01")
    B1 = execute ("$" + objname + "B_01")
    C1 = execute ("$" + objname + "C_01")
    D1 = execute ("$" + objname + "D_01")
    E1 = execute ("$" + objname + "E_01")
    A2 = A1.children[1]
    B2 = B1.children[1]
    C2 = C1.children[1]
    D2 = D1.children[1]
    E2 = E1.children[1]
    B3 = B2.children[1]
    C3 = C2.children[1]
    D3 = D2.children[1]
```

```
    E3 = E2.children[1]
    )
on a changed val do
    (
    if inv.checked then val = -val
    A1.rotation.x_rotation = val/2
    A2.rotation.x_rotation = val
    )
fn rotate_fingers f1 f2 f3 amount =
    (
    if inv.checked then amount = -amount
    f1.rotation.x_rotation = amount/3
    f2.rotation.x_rotation = amount/3*2
    f3.rotation.x_rotation = amount
    )
on b changed val do rotate_fingers B1 B2 B3 val
on c changed val do rotate_fingers C1 C2 C3 val
on d changed val do rotate_fingers D1 D2 D3 val
on e changed val do rotate_fingers E1 E2 E3 val
on aa changed val do A1.rotation.z_rotation = val - 90
on bb changed val do B1.rotation.z_rotation = val
on cc changed val do C1.rotation.z_rotation = val
on dd changed val do D1.rotation.z_rotation = val
on EE changed val do E1.rotation.z_rotation = val
on RA pressed do
    (
    A1.rotation.z_rotation = -90
    A1.rotation.x_rotation = 0
    A2.rotation.x_rotation = 0
    A.value = 0
    AA.value = 0
    )
fn reset_rotation f1 f2 f3 s1 s2=
    (
    f1.rotation.x_rotation = 0
    f1.rotation.z_rotation = 0
    f2.rotation.x_rotation = 0
    f3.rotation.x_rotation = 0
    s1.value = 0
    s2.value = 0
    )
```

```
on RB pressed do reset_rotation B1 B2 B3 B BB
on RC pressed do reset_rotation C1 C2 C3 C CC
on RD pressed do reset_rotation D1 D2 D3 D DD
on RE pressed do reset_rotation E1 E2 E3 E EE
)

try (closerolloutfloater hand_floater) catch()
hand_floater = newrolloutfloater "Hand Controller" 330 251
addrollout hand_rollout hand_floater
```

You can make this script either a Macro Script or a utility. If you make it a Macro Script, it will be more accessible to the user. If you make it a utility, it will require the user to navigate to the Utility Panel to use it. Simply evaluating it will open the floater.

Let's look at some of the features used in this script. First, we used offset to specify the position of the UI items. This makes the script more compact and easier to use. We used execute to define the finger names. This is done so we can pick the exact object, named according to the rules we defined earlier. Then we define each finger link, selecting the finger's children.

We also used many functions. Since the rotation of the fingers will occur similarly in all fingers with three links, using functions makes the script easier and faster. We don't need to repeat all the code everywhere; we just use the functions and define the correct parameters.

One interesting feature we added to the script is the Invert button. This allows the user to re-use this hand as a left or a right hand, or even to add some strange movements to the hand.

Feel free to modify this script and add other features.

Summary

Adding a user interface to a script is essential to making it interactive and easy to use. This chapter laid out the most important techniques to include UIs with your scripts.

Make sure you have in mind all the features you want in your script before starting. Some people prefer to start from the UI, some prefer to start from the "engine" of the script (the actions). Do it the way you feel comfortable, but it will be easier to build the code if you think out the requirements first, creating a "storyboard" of the script the same way that moviemakers do.

In Chapter 18 you'll learn how to use MAXScript with keyframes, controllers, and everything related to animation.

Animating with
MAXScript

3ds max

Chapter 18

MAXScript can be used to edit and adjust animation parameters. You can also use scripts as custom animation controllers and to change controllers. In addition to all these features, MAXScript can control rendering and manipulate bitmap files. Let's examine these features in this chapter.

- Working with animation controllers

- Working with animation constraints

- Manipulating rendering results

- Manipulating bitmaps with MAXScript

- Using render elements

- Managing network rendering

Working with Animation Controllers

You can assign and change the animation controllers to all tracks of an object through MAXScript. You can also assign and change keyframe information and adjust many animation parameters.

Every animated parameter in 3ds max requires a different animation controller, which can be assigned in MAXScript. The controller will define how the keyframes will be interpolated, which means how the animation will be built between the keyframes. You can use MAXScript to adjust the information about each controller and keyframe.

Assigning Controllers

Access each property's controller simply by adding `.controller` to the property. For instance, `obj.position.controller` will show us which controller is assigned to the object's position.

All controllers can be assigned through MAXScript. Among them are these controllers:

- Bezier
- Linear
- Noise
- TCB
- Euler_XYZ

Let's assign a noise controller to the scale of an object and adjust its parameters:

```
obj = sphere()
obj.scale.controller = noise_scale()
obj.scale.controller.noise_strength = [2,2,0]
obj.scale.controller.frequency = 0.2
obj.scale.controller.fractal = false
```

You can use `showproperties obj.scale.controller` *to list the Noise Scale options.*

Track View Properties

Your script can access object properties as they appear in the Track View. To do so, you need to add [*index*] after the object name. For example, obj[3] is the Transform track and obj[4] is the Node track (called the Object track in Track View). These properties are called *subanims*.

These are the subanims an object can have:

Index	Subanim
1	Visibility track
2	Space warps
3	Transform
4	Node (Object) track
5	Material
6	Image Motion Blur Multiplier
7	Object Motion Blur On Off

Some objects will not use all subanims, if the property in a subanim cannot be assigned to that object—for instance, lights will not have materials assigned. However, even when a subanim is unused, the numbering stays the same.

To find how many subanims you have in a node, use the .numsubs property. To learn the names of the subanims you can use getsubanimname and getsubanimnames. The getsubanimname command requires the index of the subanim, while getsubanimnames returns an array of all the properties, listing them in the Listener and making them available to searches such as FOR loops.

You can change the controller of any subanim, and any of its properties. You can also learn whether the subanim is animated or not, by using the .isanimated property.

The .value property will list the value of a subanim. If an object is animated, the .value property will show the subanim value at the current frame.

Figure 18.1 shows the Track view of a sample object—a sphere. To create the sphere and access its subanims, type:

```
obj = sphere()
obj.numsubs
getsubanimname obj 3
obj[3].numsubs
getsubanimname obj[3] 1
obj[3][1].value
```

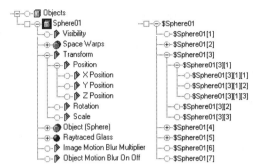

Figure 18.1 *Track View of the subanims, and their syntax in MAXScript*

Notice that `obj.numsubs` returns 7, which is the number of subanims an object has. Then, `getsubanimname obj 3` will list the name of the third subanim, in this case `#transform`.

Then we checked to see how many subanims Transform has, using `obj[3].numsubs`. It returns 3, which is expected since the sphere has a PRS Transform controller.

Finally, we asked for the name of the first subanim in Transform, and for its value. Notice we used `[3][1]`, which means we're accessing the first subanim of the third subanim. An XYZ Position controller also has three subanims, where the Y axis is `obj[3][1][2]`.

Managing Keyframes

The main idea of MAXScript's access to controllers is to manage keyframes. You can adjust keys, change their values, move them in time, and add and delete them.

To access keys, simply use the `.keys` property, calling it in `obj.parameter.keys` or `obj.parameter.controller.keys`. These return an array of keys. Like any array, its elements are accessible using `[index]`, and you can find how many keys exist using `.count`. Let's look at a small example to see how it works:

```
obj = sphere()
animate on (
at time 40 obj.radius = 50
at time 60 obj.radius = 25
)
k1 = obj.radius.keys[1]
```

There are two new commands here. First, `animate on` affects actions in the same way as if the Animate button was turned on. In addition, `at time` changes the selected values at the specified time.

This code also assigns the first key to the variable k1. You can now adjust several parameters in this key using this variable. First, you can adjust any key value with the `.value` property. To change it to 30, in our example, you'd type `k1.value = 30`. To move this key to frame 10, use the `.time` property as in `k1.time = 10`.

Select the object in the viewport and observe the Track Bar. All changes made to the keyframes and to the animation will appear instantaneously.

Some controllers allow many more options for a key. Bezier controllers allow us to adjust the tangent type of a key and change it to linear, smooth, etc. This is done using `.intangenttype` and `.outtangenttype`. You can specify the following tangent types: `#smooth`, `#linear`, `#slow`, `#fast`, `#step`, and `#custom`.

Using Functions to Manipulate Keys

Several functions can be used to manipulate keys. These functions add, remove, select, and move them. You can create keys with `addnewkey controller time`. This command adds a new key to the specified time, with the value found at that time. Using the previous example, you can add a keyframe at frame 30 using the command `addnewkey obj.radius.controller 30`.

Notice that this addition changes the number of keys, which means the index of the keys will also change. Thus, `obj.radius.keys[2]` is now the keyframe you just created at frame 30, instead of the key at 40. In addition, its value is automatically assigned by the animation curve, but you can change it at any time using the tools you have already learned.

To select keys, you can use two commands: `selectkey` and `selectkeys`. Both commands are additive. The `selectkey` command selects a single key and add it to the previous selection, and `selectkeys` selects keys in a given interval (and adds them to any already selected). In the previous example,

```
selectkeys obj.radius.controller 0 30
```

will add all keys from frame 0 to 30 (inclusive) to the selection. `Selectkey obj.radius.controller 3` will select the third key, adding this key to the previous selection.

If you want to deselect keys, the process is the same as selecting but the equivalent commands are `deselectkey` and `deselectkeys`.

To delete keys, you can use two commands: `deletekey` and `deletekeys`. The first deletes a specified key, and doesn't work for multiple keys, which means you need to do it one key at a time. Let's delete the key at frame 40, which is key 3, using the command `deletekeys obj.radius.controller 3`. The `deletekeys` command works on a selection of keys (`deletekeys #selection`) or on all keys (`deletekeys #all`).

To move keys, use `movekeys`. If `#selection` is specified, it moves the selected keys. If not, it moves all keys. Let's move the key in frame 60 to frame 80 in the previous example:

```
deselectkeys obj.radius.controller 0 60
selectkey obj.radius.controller 3
movekeys obj.radius.controller 20 #selection
```

This `movekeys` command will move the selected keys 20 frames ahead. To move a key back in time, use a negative number.

Controller Operations

Some of the most important controller features in MAXScript are the time features. They allow us to access the Edit Time options in Track View.

Many time operations can be performed through MAXScript. Some controllers will not support these features, so you need to check to make sure the controller can be accessed by using `supportstimeoperations`. If it returns True, you'll be able to edit the keyframe timing.

You can scale the time in a specified interval of a controller. This works similarly to the Scale Time option in Track view. To do so, you need to use the `scaletime` command. It requires a time interval and a scale float. Let's look at a simple example of this:

```
s = sphere()
select s
animate on
(
at time 0 s.scale = [1,1,1]
at time 20 s.scale = [1,1,2]
at time 50 s.scale = [2,2,1]
)
supportstimeoperations s.scale.controller
scaletime s.scale.controller 0 1s20f 1.5
```

Notice that the keyframes were scaled and moved from 20 to 30 and from 50 to 75.

Another important time operation is `reversetime`. It allows us to reverse the time, thus making it easier to render an animation backwards. Let's reverse the time in our previous example:

```
reversetime s.scale.controller 0 75 #incleft #incright
```

This will reverse the animation in the given interval—including the keyframes at the beginning (#incleft) and end (#incright) of the interval.

You can also delete all key information in an interval, using deletetime. Besides #incleft and #incright, you can use #noslide, which will delete the keys but maintain the remaining keys in their positions. If #noslide is not specified, all remaining keys to the right of the deleted interval will be slid to the left, filling the gap.

Let's create a Macro Script that will reverse the time of all objects in the scene. This will allow us to render the animation directly, without needing to use the Video Post or any editing software to reverse it. Open the reverse_time.mcr file from the CD, or start a new script and type all the commands in Listing 18.1.

LISTING 18.1: THE REVERSE KEYS SCRIPT (REVERSE_TIME.MCR)

```
macroscript Reverse_Time category:"Tools" tooltip:"Reverse Time"
(
objtracks = objects as array
count = 1
while count <= objtracks.count do
    (
    n = objtracks[count].numsubs
    for i in 1 to n do append objtracks objtracks[count][i]
    count += 1
    )
revtracks = #()
for i in 1 to objtracks.count do
    (
    if objtracks[i].controller != undefined \
    and objtracks[i].numsubs == 0 and objtracks[i].isanimated \
    then append revtracks objtracks[i]
    )
for i in 1 to revtracks.count do
    (
    reversetime revtracks[i] animationrange #incleft #incright
    )
)
```

(Again, the backslash at the *end* of a printed line means that statement continues on the next line.) This script creates an array of all objects and appends all subanims to it. Then it creates another array, using only the tracks that have a controller assigned, are animated, and have no subanims. This array will contain all the controllers that will be reversed; the reversal happens in the last loop.

This script may not work correctly with expression controllers, script controllers, TCB rotations, and reactors, because of the way their keyframes and parameters are stored.

Reducing Keys

You can also remove unnecessary keys in an animation using MAXScript. This is done using reducekeys, which reduces the keys in a given controller, based on a specified threshold. It can reduce keys in the active animation range or in a specified interval. For instance, to reduce the keys in the previous sphere example, you would use the command reducekeys s.scale.controller 3 1, where 3 is the threshold of the reduction and 1 is the frame step that will be used to sample the reduction.

Hands-on MAXScript: A Collapse Position Floater

Let's create a script that collapses all position controllers, substituting for them a Bezier controller, and reducing keys through a specified threshold (the interface for this script is illustrated in Figure 18.2).

3ds max 4 has a feature that collapses controllers to the default controller, by sampling keys similarly to this example. This script illustrates how you can write it on your own, and still add a keyframe reduction option to it. If you had to do this in max, you would need to use the Motion Panel to collapse the controller and Track View to reduce the keys. Here you'll have these two options in a single script.

Figure 18.2 *The Collapse Position floater*

Open the `collapse_position.ms` script from the CD-ROM that accompanies this book, or start a new script and type all the commands in Listing 18.2.

LISTING 18.2: THE COLLAPSE POSITION SCRIPT (COLLAPSE_POSITION.MS)

```
rollout collapsePRS_rollout "Parameters"
  (
  pickbutton sel "Select Object" width:120
  spinner sample "Interval (frames):" enabled:false \
    range:[0,10,1]
  checkbox reduce "Reduce Keys" enabled:false
  spinner threshold "Threshold:" enabled:false range:[0,10000,3]
  button apply "Apply Reduction" width:120 enabled:false
  button go "Start" width:160 enabled:false
  on sel picked obj do
    (
    sel.text = obj.name
    global s_obj
    s_obj = obj
    p = s_obj.position.isanimated
    apply.enabled = false
    if p then
      go.enabled = reduce.enabled = sample.enabled = true
    )
  on reduce changed state do
    (
    threshold.enabled = state
    if go.enabled == false then apply.enabled = state
    )
  on go pressed do
    (
    values = #()
    st = animationrange.start
    ed = animationrange.end
    num_steps = (ed - st) / sample.value
    num_steps = (num_steps as integer)/160
    for i in 1 to num_steps do
      (
      f = (i*sample.value) as time
```

```
      at time f append values s_obj.position.controller.value
      )
   s_obj.position.controller = bezier_position()
   for i in 1 to num_steps do
      (
      f = (i*sample.value) as time
      animate on
         (
         at time f s_obj.position = values[i]
         )
      )
   if reduce.checked == true then apply.enabled = true
   go.enabled = false
   )
on apply pressed do
   (
   reducekeys s_obj.position.controller threshold.value \
     (sample.value as time)
   )
)
try (closerolloutfloater collapsePRS_floater) catch()
collapsePRS_fl = newrolloutfloater "Collapse Position" 210 210
addrollout collapsePRS_rollout collapsePRS_fl
```

Once you evaluate this script, a floater appears, with a pickbutton to select an object. As soon as the user selects the object, the script will test to see if this object has position animation. If it does, all UI controls will be enabled, and the user will be able to start the script.

When Start is pressed, the script reads the position of the object at intervals specified by the spinner value. After reading all these values, the script will assign a Bezier controller to the position and assign all these values to the corresponding times.

If the user chooses to reduce the keys, they will be able to specify the threshold. When the user presses Apply Reduction, the keyframe reduction will be calculated.

Try this script on an object with a noise controller assigned to the Position, and notice the results.

You will find another script called collapse_PRS.ms on the CD that accompanies this book. This script will do the same thing as collapse_position.ms, but will allow the user to pick the Position, Rotation, or Scale controllers.

Using Constraints

Constraints are a new feature of 3ds max 4. They replace some old controllers and add new functionality. Their plug-ins were created using a new SDK (Software Developer's Kit) system called Function Publishing. This allows the developer to easily add the MAXScript functionality to the code. Plug-ins that use Function Publishing appear as interfaces in MAXScript.

First, let's see how interfaces work, and then you will be able to learn how constraints work.

Using Interfaces

Interfaces are new in 3ds max 4. As noted above, they derive from the new Function Publishing system, designed to give access to a third-party plug-in's information. An *interface* in MAXScript is an object-oriented programming tool consisting of a set of methods and properties designed specifically for working with a particular max feature or plug-in.

There are several interfaces in MAXScript. 3ds max has several built in interfaces, which handle menus, the renderer, parameter wiring, etc. These are called *core interfaces*, and they are not usually associated with nodes. If you want to list all core interfaces, getcoreinterfaces() will return an array containing all of them. Because they're not associated with nodes, showinterfaces wouldn't list them.

If you use showproperties on a node and it returns nothing, use showinterfaces to see if it has any interface associated. There's no rule to say if an object will have an associated property or interface.

Among the core interfaces, we have the medit interface, which manages the Material Editor. To list the commands and properties for this interface, you can use the showinterface command. As an example, showinterface medit would list:

```
Interface: medit
 Properties:
 Methods:
  <maxObject>GetCurMtl()
  <void>SetActiveMtlSlot <index>slot <boolean>forceUpdate
  <index>GetActiveMtlSlot()
  <void>PutMtlToMtlEditor <maxObject>mtl <index>slot
  <maxObject>GetTopMtlSlot <index>slot
  <boolean>OkMtlForScene <material>mtl
  <void>UpdateMtlEditorBrackets()
 Actions:
```

The values within < > show what those commands and properties expect. For instance, *index* means the command will require or return an integer value that is an array index, and *void* means it is a function and returns no value. Using the commands in this extension, `medit.getcurmtl` will return the material in the current Material Editor slot. Similarly, `medit.getactivemtlslot()` will return the index number of the current Material Editor slot. To set the current Material Editor slot to 10, you would use `medit.setactivemtlslot 10`.

Assigning Constraints

Assigning constraints in 3ds max through MAXScript requires you to perform a series of steps:

1. Assign the constraint to the required transform controller.

2. Add the target nodes to the constraint.

3. Set each target node's weight.

4. Set the remaining parameters for the constraint.

As an example, let's assign a path constraint to an object. The other constraints work in a similar way, with slightly different properties available.

We need to set up a scene first. To do so, execute the following commands:

```
s = sphere pos:[10,10,0] radius:15
c = circle pos:[-30,-50,0] radius:100
h = helix pos:[-50,0,0] radius1:50 radius2:80
```

Now let's assign the path constraint using

```
s.pos.controller = path_constraint().
```

You can query the properties of the path controller using the command `showproperties s.pos.controller`, and you can also query the interfaces using `showinterfaces s.pos.controller`.

In this example, you want to assign both the helix and the circle as targets to the path constraint. The following code will do that:

```
s.pos.controller.appendtarget c 0
s.pos.controller.appendtarget h 100
```

The value you're setting is the weight of the node. For example, you can animate the weight of the nodes using:

```
animate on
(
```

```
slidertime = 100f
s.pos.controller.setweight 1 100
s.pos.controller.setweight 2 0
)
```

If you want to set the remaining properties in the path constraint, you can access them as you would any regular node property. For instance, you can turn on `follow` using this command:

```
s.pos.controller.follow = true
```

 Notice that the path constraint also has a `.path` *property. This property lists the first target assigned to the path constraint, and only exists to maintain backward compatibility with scripts that used the path controller in previous versions of 3ds max.*

All remaining constraints work the same way as the Path constraint. You can list their properties and interfaces to check how you can work with them.

Hands-on max: Expression Controller

Expressions aren't scripts, but they are very useful and sometimes easier to use than scripts. Expression controllers allow the user to assign math formulas to any parameter. These math formulas can depend on any other object's parameters; for instance, you can change an object's color depending on another object's position. We'll illustrate both expression controllers and script controllers so you can see the advantages of each.

You can assign an expression controller to any parameter in 3ds max. To do so, select the parameter in the Motion tab or in the Track View and assign a float, position, scale, or point3 expression to it.

Right-click the Track View and select Properties as in Figure 18.3. This will open the Expression Controller dialog box (Figure 18.4). It's a modeless window, which means you can manipulate objects and properties in the scene while still accessing this dialog box. You cannot close the Track View.

Figure 18.3 Defining the position expression

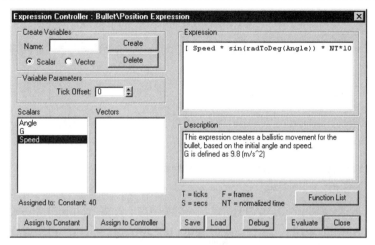

Figure 18.4 *Expression Controller dialog box*

To define an expression, you need to know how you want the object to behave. For instance, let's create an expression using a previously modeled example. Open the file `wheel_expression.max` from the CD. It contains a box and a cylinder, which is attached to the box. What you want is to have the wheel rotating according to the box movement. Let's create an expression for it:

1. Open the Track View and locate the wheel's Rotation track.

2. Change the rotation controller to Euler XYZ.

3. Expand the Rotation and select Y Rotation.

4. Assign a Float Expression to the rotation.

5. Right-click the Track View and select Properties.

6. Type **Car** in the Name field, select Vector, and click Create. This creates a variable that will be defined by the car's position. The wheel rotation will be based on this variable.

7. Select Car from the Vectors list and click Assign to Controller.

8. In the Track View, select Car → Transform → Position.

9. Create a new Scalar variable named Radius.

10. Select it and click Assign to Controller.

11. Try to select Wheel ➜ ModifiedObject ➜ Object ➜ Radius.

You will not be allowed select this property, because it needs to have a Bezier float controller assigned to it:

12. Close the Expression dialog box.

13. Assign a Bezier float controller to the Radius of the cylinder.

14. Reopen the Expression dialog box and repeat steps 10 and 11.

15. Now type this expression:
    Car.x/Radius

Car.x is the X position of the Car, and Radius is the radius of the wheel. This expression will return the number of radians of the curve length, which will rotate the object accordingly. If it rotates in the wrong direction, just add a minus sign (-) to the expression. You can see the whole expression in Figure 18.5.

Rotations are always calculated in radians in an expression controller.

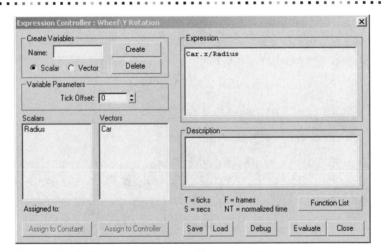

Figure 18.5 *The car wheel expression controller*

The file Wheel_expression_ready.max on the CD contains the finished expression and a small animation example. There's another example, Bullet_expression.max, which shows an example of ballistics movement applied as an expression.

Script Controllers

A script controller works the same way as an expression controller, with a small difference: it's a script. There's no need to learn new techniques or formulas—just write it as a regular script. Script controllers are very useful because you can access and modify any property in any object, not only in the local object. You can even call functions and read and write files from script controllers.

Creating Script Controllers

To create a script controller, use the same process as for an expression controller. Simply select any object track and assign a position, rotation, scale, float, or point3 script controller. Right-click the Track View and select Properties; it will display the Script Controller dialog box (Figure 18.6).

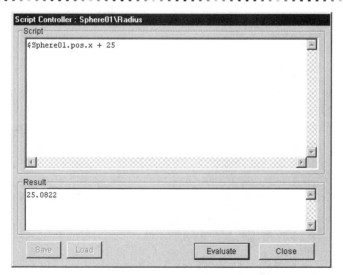

Figure 18.6 *The Script Controller dialog window*

The script controller must return a result to the script, which is different from the scripts you've written, because so far you have always used variables to store values.

Let's repeat the expression controller example, this time using a script. Open file `wheel_script.max` from your CD and follow these steps:

1. Locate the Rotation track of the wheel and assign an Euler XYZ controller to it.

2. Locate the Y Rotation track and assign a float script controller to it.

3. From the Track View shortcut menu, select Properties. In the script area, type
   `$Car.pos.x/$Wheel.radius`

4. Animate the car moving from left to right and notice the wheel animation.

   Note that the script controller does not update automatically in the screen when you change a parameter. Objects update when you move the time slider or change the current frame.

The file `Wheel_script_ready.max` contains the finished expression and a small animation example.

To update the objects from the script controller easily, move to the next frame and then move back to the current frame.

Conditions

The great advantage of the script controller is that you can actually write any script in it, using conditions and making decisions about what action to take.

In this section you'll create a script that will automatically increase the optimize strength according to the distance of the object; if the object is farther than a certain distance, it will retain its value. Open `auto_optimizer.ms` from your CD, or start a new script and type all the commands in Listing 18.3.

LISTING 18.3: THE AUTO OPTIMIZER SCRIPT (AUTO_OPTIMIZER.MS)

```
utility optimizer "Auto Optimizer"
   (
   local opobj,cam
   pickbutton pcam "Pick Camera" width:120
   pickbutton pobj "Pick Object" enabled:false width:120
   spinner cdist "MIN Distance" enabled:false range:[0,10000,0]
```

```
spinner mdist "MAX Distance" enabled:false range:[0,10000,0]
spinner opfar "Face Thresh." enabled:false
on pcam picked obj do
   (
   cam = obj
   pobj.enabled = true
   )
fn opt_calc obj c =
   (
   txt1 = "d = distance $" + c.name + " $" + obj.name + "\n"
   txt2 = ("if d > " + cdist.value as string + " and d < " + \
      mdist.value as string + " then\n")
   txt3 = ("f = " + opfar.value as string + "*pi*2*" + \
      "((distance $" + c.name + " $" + obj.name + ")- " + \
      cdist.value as string + ")/(" + \
      (mdist.value - cdist.value) as string + ")/360\n")
   txt4 = ("else if d < " + cdist.value as string + \
      " then f=0 else f = " \
      + opfar.value as string + "*pi/180\nf")
   obj.optimize[1].controller.script = \
      (txt1 + txt2 + txt3 + txt4)
   )
on pobj picked obj do
   (
   opobj = obj
   addmodifier opobj (optimize())
   d = distance cam opobj
   cdist.enabled = true
   cdist.value = d
   mdist.enabled = true
   mdist.value = d + 10
   opfar.enabled = true
   opobj.optimize[1].controller = float_script()
   opt_calc opobj cam
   )
on cdist changed val do opt_calc opobj cam
on mdist changed val do opt_calc opobj cam
on opfar changed val do opt_calc opobj cam
)
```

This script allows the user to select a camera and an object. Then, the user can specify the distance where optimizing starts and where it reaches the higher value. Closer than the minimum distance, the optimize value will be zero; beyond the maximum distance, it will be constant and equal to the higher value.

The Auto Optimizer script creates a script controller and writes the following script (if the camera is named $Camera01 and the object is a sphere named Sphere01):

```
d = distance $Camera01 $Sphere01
if d > min and d < max then
f = threshold * pi * 2 * ((distance $Camera01 $Sphere01)-min) /
   (max-min) / 360
else if d < min then f = 0 else f = threshold * pi / 180
f
```

First, it checks the distance between objects. If it's between Min and Max, it calculates the face angle threshold. This value is interpolated from 0 to Threshold, and it's calculated in radians (this explains *2*pi/360).

If the distance isn't between those two values, the script checks whether it's above or below them, and will set the correct values.

Animate an object moving outwards the camera. Then, using this script, specify the optimize value and the distances. Play the animation and notice how it gradually reduces the number of faces.

Dependencies and Setup

The biggest limitation of the script controller in previous versions of MAX is that it did not allow interactive updating if the script depended on other properties or nodes. In 3ds max 4 you can specify which nodes the script controller depends on; it will watch those nodes, and whenever any property changes, it will interactively change.

A simple example is to create three spheres, side by side. Then assign a script controller to Sphere02 Position and use the following script:

```
($sphere01.pos + $sphere03.pos)/2
```

This script will center Sphere02 between Spheres 01 and 03. Now if you move either Sphere01 or 03, Sphere02 won't update on screen. If you drag the time slider, then it will update.

Now, go back to your Script Controller window and add the following line before the existing code:

```
dependson $sphere01 $sphere03
```

From now on, if you move Sphere01 or 03, Sphere02 will interactively be affected.

Notice that this script relates to objects by their name. This will make the script fail if an object is renamed or deleted. It is a good idea to create a persistent global variable that stores the object, and then reference this variable on the script controller. See Chapter 19 for more information on persistent global variables.

If you have many script controllers on a scene, they can slow down the interactive display. One option is to turn off the script controllers using the MAXScript tab of the Preference Settings window (Figure 18.7). This may also be helpful when you have script controllers crashing and many error messages popping up. Just disable Load Controller Scripts and they will not be executed.

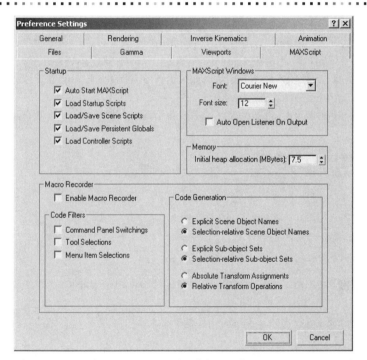

Figure 18.7 *The MAXScript tab of the Preference Settings window*

Animating Vertices

If you look at the tracks of an editable mesh object in Track view, you will notice that there are no tracks for vertices, but there is a Master Point controller. However, as soon as you animate any vertex, it appears in Track view as a new track.

The same happens in MAXScript. There's no way to animate vertices until you tell MAXScript you want to animate them. This is done using `animatevertex`, which works with editable meshes, editable splines, and FFD (free-form deformation) modifiers, allowing us to access the vertex tracks and animate them. To use `animatevertex`, you need to specify which vertices you want to animate so 3ds max will create the tracks and you can access them through a script.

For example, if you want to animate vertex 3 in the selected object, use the command `animatevertex $ 3`. If you're unsure of which vertices you'll animate, you can use `animatevertex $ #all`, which will allow you to animate all vertices, but this is memory-intensive and *very* hard to track in Track view later.

Editable Mesh

You can access the editable mesh vertex position in two ways: using `obj.vertex_n` or `obj[4][1][n].value`. In either case, *n* is the number of the vertex.

The vertex position is in the object's local coordinate system. To find the position of the vertex in the world coordinate system, you simply need to multiply it to `obj.objecttransform`. Let's look at a simple example to understand this.

```
b = box()
c = converttomesh b
animatevertex c #all
v1 = c.vertex_1
```

This will return the first vertex position, which will be [–12.5,–12.5,0].

```
c.pos = [20,20,5]
v1 = c.vertex_1
```

After moving the object, `c.vertex_1` still returns [–12.5,–12.5,0], which proves that the vertex position is in object space, not in world space.

```
v1a = c.vertex_1*c.objecttransform
```

This will return [7.5,7.5,5], which is the vertex position in world space.

```
c.vertex_1 = [0,0,0]
```

This will move the vertex to [0,0,0], but in object space, which will move it to the center of the base. If you want to move it to [0,0,0] in world space, you'll need:

```
c.vertex_1 = [0,0,0]*(inverse c.objecttransform)
```

Editable Splines and FFDs

All rules valid for editable meshes are valid for FFDs and editable splines. The only difference is in the way to access the vertex information.

In editable splines, you can use `obj.spline_n___vertex_m`, where *n* is the spline number and *m* is the vertex number. (Yes, there are three underscores between `spline_n` and `vertex_m`.) Alternatively, you can use `obj[4][1][2]`. Since the editable spline allows animation of the vertices and the tangents, the vertices will be every third index, starting on 2. To understand it better, look at the Master track in an editable spline (such as the one in Figure 18.8).

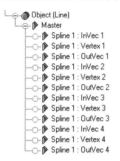

Figure 18.8 The tracks of an editable spline's vertices

In FFDs, you can use `ffd.control_point_n`, where *n* is the vertex number. You can also access it using indices, but each FFD will have a different index for the Master track. To know which is the Master track, you can run a script and use `getsubanimname` to check it. Here's an example:

```
f = ffd_2x2x2()
for i in 1 to f.numsubs do
if getsubanimname f i == #Master do
    format "FFD 2x2x2 Master is %\n." i
f2 = ffdbox()
for i in 1 to f2.numsubs do
if getsubanimname f2 i == #Master do
    format "FFD Box Master is %\n." i
```

These will show us that the FFD 2x2x2 Master Track is in subanim 3 and FFD Box Master Track is in subanim 6.

Manipulating Rendering Results

One important advantage to using MAXScript is its ability to manipulate the rendered result. MAXScript also accesses the G-Buffer (Geometry Buffer, which includes Z-Buffer, Object ID, etc.) channels, allowing you to manipulate them or output them to disk as bitmap masks.

The first step in working with the renderer is to adjust the parameters in the Render Scene dialog box. You can adjust the width, height, output file, anti-alias filter, and some other options.

The `renderer` command allows you to define whether the renderer is the Production or the Draft renderer. To define which one will be used, you need to specify `renderer = #production` or `renderer = #draft`.

You can use `renderwidth`, `renderheight`, and `renderpixelaspect` to adjust these characteristics of the renderer. As an example you can use:

```
renderwidth = 752
renderheight = 480
renderpixelaspect = 0.85
```

The `renderdisplacements` and `rendereffects` commands enable or disable Displacements and Render Effects. This is the same as turning these options on or off in the Render dialog window. You can use them as follows:

```
renderdisplacements = false
rendereffects = true
```

The `rendoutputfilename` command defines the filename and path to save the rendered image in (note that this is "rend…", not "render…"). The extension specified in the filename will define the file type, and the default settings will be used for that file. If you want to specify different settings, you can use `selectsavebitmap()` to select a filename:

```
rendoutputfilename = selectsavebitmap()
```

And remember to use the \\ symbol correctly, as in this example:

```
rendoutputfilename = "d:\\3dsmax4\\images\\proj01.tga"
```

If the renderer is the 3ds max default Scanline Renderer, you can also set the anti-alias filter. This is done using `scanlinerender.antialiasfilter = filter`, where *filter* can be any anti-alias plug-in filter. As an example:

```
scanlinerender.antialiasfilter = catmull_rom()
```

Using all the commands above, together with the render() command, it's almost possible to rewrite the entire Render Scene dialog box using MAXScript.

Rendering Images

You can use the render() command to render images. This command has many options. Let's see some of these options in our examples.

For instance, you can make a script to render a series of 3ds max files with each anti-alias filter, for comparison:

```
aa = #("area","blackman", "blendfilter","catmull_rom", \
     "cook_variable", "cubic", "mitchell_netravali", \
     "quadratic", "sharp_quadratic","soften", "video")
for i in 1 to aa.count do
  (
  scanlinerender.antialiasfilter = execute (aa[i] + "()")
  render outputfilename:(aa[i] + ".tga") outputwidth:320 \
  outputheight:240 vfb:off
  )
```

The outputfilename option defines the name of the rendered file. The outputwidth and outputheight options define the image size. The vfb:off option turns off the Virtual Framebuffer (the dialog box that contains the rendered image after you've rendered).

Manipulating Bitmaps with MAXScript

You'll need to use bitmaps to store the rendered information. MAXScript also allows us to manipulate the bitmap, and even to manipulate animated files such as AVIs or FLCs.

You can create a bitmap using *variable* = bitmap *width height*. This command must include the width and height parameters. For instance, you can create an empty bitmap using empty = bitmap 640 480.

You can create bitmaps to store the rendered image. This can be done in two ways, the first being:

```
b = bitmap 640 480
render outputwidth:640 outputheight:480 to:b
```

The option to: will specify that the rendered output will be stored in the specified bitmap.

You can also use:

```
b = render outputwidth:640 outputheight:480
```

This will render the bitmap and automatically output it to the variable b.

Bitmaps have several properties, such as .height and .width to return the height and width of a bitmap. The property .numframes will show how many frames exist in an animated bitmap, such as an AVI, MOV, or image sequence bitmap.

Bitmap I/O

Bitmaps have a .filename property that allows us to specify the filename associated with them. You can save bitmaps by defining the .filename property and using save. For example,

```
b = render()
b.filename = "save_example.tga"
save b
```

will render with the default values and save the rendered image to the file specified.

You can read bitmaps using two commands: openbitmap and selectbitmap(). The first command opens a specified bitmap and loads it into memory. The command b = selectbitmap()displays a dialog box (Figure 18.9) that allows the user to select a bitmap file.

You cannot directly manipulate or save bitmaps that were read from a disk; you must first make a copy of a bitmap using the copy command. Suppose you wanted to save the bitmap loaded previously. You'd need to do it this way:

```
c = copy b
c.filename = b.filename
save c
```

You can use display to show a bitmap on screen and undisplay to close it when displayed.

After using bitmap files that were loaded or saved, it's very important to close them. This will remove them from memory, which usually helps a lot, because many bitmaps take large amounts of RAM. To do so, just use close bitmap, where bitmap is the bitmap variable. This command will close this bitmap and free the allocated memory.

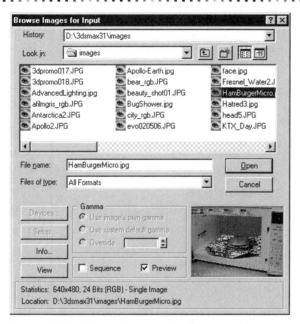

Figure 18.9 *The dialog box displayed by* selectbitmap()

When working with bitmaps, MAXScript usually requires a lot of memory, and part of this memory will not be reclaimed automatically. To reclaim this memory you can use gc(), *which will invoke the garbage collector and get rid of all the garbage you might have in memory.*

Configuring Bitmaps

You can configure the settings for the BMP, JPEG, PNG, and TARGA file formats using MAXScript. Because each bitmap format has different options, each will have different commands and properties. For example, jpeg.setquality 100 will set the JPEG quality to 100. You can query which commands are available using showinterfaces.

Table 18.1 lists the commands available for these interfaces and their options.

Table 18.1   Bitmap I/O Interfaces

COMMAND	DESCRIPTION	OPTIONS
JPEG File		
jpeg.setquality	Sets the quality	0–100
jpeg.setsmoothing	Sets the smoothing	0–100
PNG File		
png.settype	Sets the file type	#paletted, #true24, #true48, #gray8 or #gray16
png.setalpha	Turns alpha on/off	true or false
png.setinterlaces	Turns Interlaced on/off	true or false
BMP File		
bmp.gettype	Sets the file type	#paletted or #true24
TARGA File		
targa.setcolordepth	Sets the color depth	16, 24 or 32
targa.setcompressed	Turns compression on/off	true or false
targa.alphasplit	Turns alpha split on/off	true or false
targe.premultalpha	Turns Premultiplied on/off	true or false

For each set command there's a corresponding get command, which will read the current state. For instance, png.gettype() will return the current PNG file type.

Pixel Manipulation

You can manipulate the bitmap pixel color. It can be useful to read this information and process it, to adjust any bitmap parameters or attach any information to it.

Two commands are used to perform these operations: getpixels and setpixels. Both of them work in the same way: getpixels returns an array of colors, starting at a given coordinate with a specified length, and setpixels writes an array of colors starting at the specified coordinate. Usually, both of these are used in loops, to automate the process.

As an example, let's create a script that reads a bitmap and embeds it as a watermark in the rendered image. Open add_watermark.ms from the CD, or start a new script and type all the commands in Listing 18.4.

LISTING 18.4: THE ADD WATERMARK SCRIPT (ADD_WATERMARK.MS)

```
rollout add_watermark "Parameters"
(
local img, big, big2, logo, base, side, bmp
button sel_bmp "Select Logo Bitmap" width:150
button sel_img "Select Rendered Image" width:150 enabled:false
button config  "Configure Renderer" width:150
button go "Render" width:150 enabled:false
spinner bottom "Distance from Base: " type:#integer \
    range:[0,30,10] fieldwidth:35
spinner right "Distance from Right: " type:#integer \
    range:[0,30,10] fieldwidth:35
on sel_bmp pressed do
    (
    bmp = undefined
    bmp = selectbitmap()
    if bmp == undefined then
        sel_img.enabled = go.enabled = false
        else sel_img.enabled = go.enabled = true
    )
on config pressed do max render scene
fn add_it big2 logo base side =
    (
    if big != undefined do undisplay big
    big = copy big2
    bh = big.height
    bw = big.width
    lh = logo.height
    lw = logo.width
    if (lh + base) > bh and (lw + side) > bw then
        print "Logo too large for image"
    else
        (
        start_left = bw - side - lw
        start_top  = bh - base - lh
        for i in 0 to lh do
            (
```

```
                    tmp_color = getpixels logo [0,i] lw
                    setpixels big [start_left,start_top + i] tmp_color
                    )
                display big
                )
            )
        on sel_img pressed do
            (
            img = selectbitmap()
            if img != undefined then
                add_it img bmp bottom.value right.value
            )
        on go pressed do
            (
            img = render vfb:off
            if img != undefined then
                add_it img bmp bottom.value right.value
            )
        on bottom changed val do
            add_it img bmp bottom.value right.value
        on right changed val do
            add_it img bmp bottom.value right.value
        )
    try (closerolloutfloater watermark_floater) catch()
    watermark_floater = newrolloutfloater "Add Watermark" 220 215
    addrollout add_watermark watermark_floater
```

You can create a Macro Script or a utility from this script. When this script is evaluated, a floater appears and allows the user to select a logo bitmap (Figure 18.10). The user will have two choices, to render a scene or to select a rendered scene.

Figure 18.10 *The Add Watermark floater*

The Configure Renderer option allows the user to adjust the render parameters, because otherwise the render will use default values.

Right after rendering or selecting an image, the logo will be pasted in the image, using `getpixel` and `setpixel`. Notice that you used loop commands to paste each row of the logo into the bitmap.

Rendered Channel Information

3ds max renders various channels besides the colors you see on the screen. It renders the Object IDs, Material IDs, UVW Map, Normals, Z Depth, and more. This information is useful for post-processing in 3ds max or in any external program. These channels are enabled when you render RLA or RPF files.

MAXScript has full access to these channels, allowing us to read their information directly or as grayscale images. Then you can output these images and use them as masks inside or outside 3ds max. You can access these channels by rendering an image and asking the renderer to calculate these channels, or by loading an RLA or RPF file.

To render the channels, you need to add `channels:#(channel array)`, where *channel array* is an array of the channels you want to render. The channels you can list in this array are: `#zdepth`, `#matid`, `#objectid`, `#uvcoords`, `#normal`, `#unclamped`, `#coverage`, `#node`, `#shadercolor`, `#shadertransparency`, `#velocity`, and `#weight`.

To read channel information, use `getchannel`, which returns the channel parameters for the specified pixel. This information is extremely technical and differs for each channel. If the bitmap does not have that channel, it will return undefined.

To read the channel information as a grayscale bitmap, you can use `getchannelasmask`. The grayscale is similar to the images you see in the VFB when you select these channels. This bitmap can be saved and used anywhere in MAX, or in external post-processing software.

Let's create a script that will render an image (or load a rendered bitmap) and save the channels in separate bitmaps. Open the file `render_channel.ms` from your CD, or start a new script and type the commands in Listing 18.5.

LISTING 18.5: THE RENDER CHANNEL SCRIPT (RENDER_CHANNEL.MS)

```
rollout render_channel "Parameters"
  (
  button sel_bmp "Select a Bitmap File" width:150
  button rend_it "Render Image" width:150
  dropdownlist channel "Select Channel" enabled:false \
    width:150 align:#center
```

```
button save_it "Select Bitmap to Save" enabled:false \
   width:150
fn enable_list bmp =
   (
   if bmp != undefined then
      (
      list_items = #("RGBA_Channel")
      chan_list = #(#Zdepth, #MatID, #ObjectID, #UVCoords, \
       #Normal, #Unclamped, #Coverage, #Node, #ShaderColor, \
       #ShaderTransparency, #Velocity, #Weight)
      for i in chan_list do
         if getchannel bmp [0,0] i != undefined do
            append list_items (i as string)
      channel.items = list_items
      channel.enabled = true
      )
    else
      (
      channel.items = #()
      channel.enabled = false
      )
   )
on sel_bmp pressed do
   (
   global img
   img = undefined
   img = selectbitmap()
   enable_list img
   )
on rend_it pressed do
   (
   img = render vfb:off channels:#(#zdepth, #matid, \
      #objectid, #uvcoords, #normal, #unclamped, #coverage, \
      #node, #shadercolor, #shadertransparency, #velocity, \
      #weight)
   enable_list img
   )
on channel selected i do
   (
```

```
        execute ("bmp_channel = #" + channel.selected)
        save_it.enabled = true
        )
    on save_it pressed do
        (
        if img2 != undefined then (close img2)
        if bmp_channel == #RGBA_Channel then img2 = copy img
            else img2 = getchannelasmask img bmp_channel
        img2.filename = selectsavebitmap()
        save img2
        display img2
        )
    )
try(closerolloutfloater channel_floater)catch()
channel_floater = newrolloutfloater "Render Channel" 200 195
addrollout render_channel channel_floater
```

This script uses a new UI item, the *listbox*, which allows the user to pick one option among several options in a list.

This script allows the user to select or render an image. Then it checks to see which channels exist in this bitmap, and builds a list to be displayed. The user will select the channel they want to save, and can select a bitmap to save it to.

Bitmaps in the UI

You can add bitmaps to your script's UI, to enhance it and make it easier to understand. You can use a bitmap in a button, checkbutton, materialbutton, or mapbutton. This is done using the .images property.

Buttons allow up to four different images: two that will be displayed when the button is not pressed (enabled or disabled), and two that will be displayed when the button is pressed (also enabled or disabled). The images must all be the same size, part of the same bitmap file, and placed side by side like the schematic in Figure 18.11.

Button Image	Button Image	Button Image	Button Image
Not Pressed Enabled	Pressed Enabled	Not Pressed Disabled	Pressed Disabled

Figure 18.11 Schematic of a bitmap file for a button

3ds max accesses a bitmap file by dividing the overall image into four even pieces; each button state is represented by one piece of the file. Thus, when a button is enabled and pressed, 3ds max displays the second quarter of its bitmap file. Let's create a small script that illustrates this. It uses the sample bitmap shown in Figure 18.12 and shows the button image when it's enabled or disabled, and when it's pressed or not. This bitmap file (`button_test.jpg`) is supplied in the CD. You may need to copy it to any map path, or to the scripts path, to allow the script to work.

Figure 18.12 *The Render Channel floater with a bitmap preview*

```
rollout imagebutton_rollout "Test"
  (
  button test width:200 height:80 \
     images:#("button_test.jpg",undefined,4,1,2,3,4)
  checkbox en "Enabled" checked:true
  on en changed state do test.enabled = en.checked
  )
try(closerolloutfloater ib_floater)catch()
ib_floater = newrolloutfloater "Image Button" 240 180
addrollout imagebutton_rollout ib_floater
```

(Actually, you can never see the Image Button Pressed Disabled with this example. It's only visible with a checkbutton, or if you disable and press it through the code. But this demonstration should suffice.) Bitmaps can also be specified directly in rollouts. Instead of using a button with images, you can use a bitmap directly. Simply use the `bitmap` command and specify this bitmap the same way as spinners or buttons.

A bitmap has two properties: `.filename` and `.bitmap`. The first allows us to specify directly a filename, and the second allows us to use a bitmap variable that has been declared.

Bitmaps are useful because they allow us to show things like render previews, materials, maps, and colors in the UI. Let's edit the Render Channel script and display a window with a preview of the channel you've selected, as shown in Figure 18.12.

You can load the script from the CD—it's named `render_channel2.ms`—or you can follow the instructions below and edit the original Render Channel script yourself.

Between `dropdownlist` and `button`, add:

```
bitmap preview width:150 height:90
```

In the `enable_list` function, after `channel.enabled`, add:

```
bmp_small = bitmap 150 90
copy bmp bmp_small
preview.bitmap = bmp_small
gc()
```

In `on channel i selected`, after `save_it.enabled = true`, add:

```
if img2 != undefined then (close img2)
if bmp_channel == #RGBA_Channel then img2 = copy img
    else img2 = getchannelasmask img bmp_channel
bmp_small = bitmap 150 90
copy img2 bmp_small
preview.bitmap = bmp_small
gc()
```

Change `on save_it pressed` to:

```
on save_it pressed do
    (
    img2.filename = selectsavebitmap()
    save img2
    display img2
    gc()
    )
```

Also, let's edit the height of the floater, so the new UI fits within it:

```
channel_floater = newrolloutfloater "Render Channel" 200 292
```

You're done now. Evaluate this script and notice the previews showing in the UI.

Notice that you've used the command `gc()`, mentioned earlier. It's a command ("garbage collection") that frees the memory by cleaning up unused items.

Using Render Elements

Render Elements is a new feature in 3ds max 4, discussed in Chapter 13. You can use MAXScript to assign Render Elements and set their properties. 3ds max has 11 Render Elements. They are: SpecularRenderElement, DiffuseRenderElement, Self_Illumination, ReflectionRenderElement, RefractionRenderElement, ShadowRenderElement, AtmosphereRenderElement, BlendRenderElement, Z_Depth, AlphaRenderElement, and BackgroundRenderElement.

To manage the Render Elements, you will use the

```
maxops.getcurrenderelementmgr()
```

command. It returns an interface that will give you access to the Render Elements Manager.

For example, you can access the Render Elements Manager and list its commands using:

```
rel_mgr = maxops.getcurrenderelementmgr()
showinterface rel_mgr
```

This interface will give you access to all properties shown in Figure 18.13.

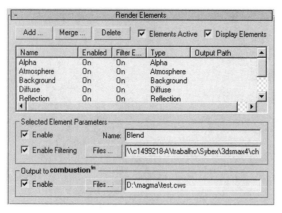

Figure 18.13 *Render Elements rollout*

Now you will need to add the Render Elements you want to render. The following example adds the Z_depth elements and sets some properties:

```
rendoutputfilename = "c:\\3dsmax4\\images\\sample.tga"
rendsavefile = true
```

```
re = z_depth()
re.zmin = 100
re.zmax = 1000
rel_mgr.addrenderelement re
```

Setting the Render Output File Name before setting the Render Elements will automatically set their file-name and path.

You cannot set any Render parameter while the Render dialog is opened.

In this example, you specified the file name to be saved by the renderer, and you turned it on. Then you created a z_depth render element, set some properties, and added it to the Render Elements.

General Render Elements Properties

Besides adding and removing Render Elements, MAXScript also gives access to the remaining properties in the Render Elements rollout. Table 18.2 shows some of the commands that will do so.

Table 18.2 Render Elements Interface

COMMAND	DESCRIPTION
setelementsactive	Turns Elements Active on/off
setdisplayelements	Turns Display Elements on/off
setcombustionoutputenabled	Turns Combustion Output on/off
setcombustionoutputpath	Sets the output path for the combustion file

For each set command we have a get command. For instance, continuing the example above, you can set the combustion output using:

```
rel_mgr.setcombustionoutputenabled = true
rel_mgr.setcombustionoutputpath = "c:\\3dsmax4\\images\\samp.cws"
```

To render the scene and output the render elements, you will need to use the max quick render command, or then manually use the renderer. Using the render() command will not output Render Elements.

Managing Network Rendering

The Network Rendering engine has been completely redone in 3ds max 4. It is now entirely accessible through MAXScript, allowing you to connect to the Network Rendering Manager, retrieve a list of computers, jobs, and their status, and also submit your own jobs to the queue.

Accessing the Manager

The first step in working with Network Rendering is to connect with the Manager. To do so you have to use `netrender.getmanager()` to access the Manager Interface. Then you connect with the manager, specifying its IP address or the computer name, or by having 3ds max search the given subnet.

For instance, you can access the server named "`my_server`" using:

```
mgr = netrender.getmanager()
mgr.connect #manual "my_server"
```

If the connection was successful, it returns True.

Once you have connected to the Manager, you can access its properties and access servers and jobs assigned to that Manager.

Table 18.3 lists some of the Manager properties.

Table 18.3 Manager Interface Properties

PROPERTY	DESCRIPTION
.connected	Returns true if you are connected to the manager
.havecontrol	Returns true if you have control over the queue
.numjobs	Returns the number of jobs assigned
.numservers	Returns the number of servers
.numgroups	Returns the number of groups

Accessing Jobs

Once you are connected to the Manager, you can either submit new jobs or modify existing jobs in the Queue.

To submit a new job, you can use `newjob`. If we extend the previous example, `myjob = mgr.newjob()` submits the current scene to the queue. After creating the job, you submit it to all servers in the queue using `myjob.submit servers:#()`. If you want to specify which servers you want to submit to, you just list them in the array. You'll learn how to work with servers in the next section.

Make sure you have set all rendering parameters before submitting a job to the queue, especially File Save and File Path. Note also that the file path needs to be a UNC file path, using the `\\computer\share\folder` *format.*

To manage existing jobs, you will first need to get control over the queue. This is to prevent two users to manage the queue at the same time. In our example, `mgr.getcontrol()` gives you control over the manager.

After you get control over the queue, you can read the list of jobs using `getjobs`. If you do not want to get a list of all jobs, you can filter the type of job you want. The available types are listed in Table 18.4.

Table 18.4 Job Type Filters

TYPE OF JOB	DESCRIPTION
#suspended	Returns a list of suspended jobs
#complete	Returns a list of completed jobs
#waiting	Returns a list of jobs that are waiting or being rendered
#started	Returns a list of jobs that are current being rendered

Continuing our example above, you can use `jobs = mgr.getjobs()` to get a list of all jobs in the manager's queue, or you could use

```
completed = mgr.getjobs filter:#completed
```

to get a list of the finished jobs in the queue.

`getjobs` returns an array with several job interfaces. You can then access these Jobs properties and change them. Table 18.5 lists some of the properties you can access.

Table 18.5 Job Interface Properties

JOB PROPERTY	DESCRIPTION
.fromframe	Defines the initial frame
.toframe	Defines the final frame
.nthframe	Defines the frame interval

Table 18.5 Job Interface Properties *(continued)*

`.outputwidth`	Defines the width of the rendered frame
`.outputheight`	Defines the height of the rendered frame
`.priority`	Defines the job priority
`.renderpixelaspect`	Defines the pixel aspect
`.rendercamera`	Defines the camera being rendered
`.renderfields`	Turns on/off Render Fields
`.renderdisplacements`	Turns on/off Render Displacements
`.force2sided`	Turns on/off Force 2 Sided
`.renderhiddenobjects`	Turns on/off Render Hidden Objects
`.renderatmosphericeffects`	Turns on/off Atmospherics
`.rendervideocolorcheck`	Turns on/off Video Color Check

These are only a few of the properties for jobs. You can use `showinterface` to list all of them.

You can change the state of a job using one of the following commands: `delete`, `suspend`, or `resume`. In our example, `myjob.suspend()` will suspend this job in the queue.

Accessing Servers

You can access network servers the same way you access jobs. This is done using `get-servers`. In our example, `servers = mgr.getservers()` returns an array with all servers. Table 18.6 lists some of the filters you use to get the server's list.

Table 18.6 Server Type Filters

FILTER	DESCRIPTION
`#idle`	Lists idle servers
`#busy`	Lists busy servers
`#absent`	Lists servers that are not online
`#suspended`	Lists suspended servers
`#job`	Lists all servers assigned to a specific job

In our example, `mysrv = mgr.getservers filter:#job key:myjob` would list all servers assigned to `myjob`.

Servers also have properties. Some of these properties are listed in Table 18.7.

Table 18.7 Server Interface Properties

PROPERTY	DESCRIPTION
.state	Returns the state of the server (#idle, #absent, or #busy)
.name	Returns the name of the server
.performance	Returns the performance index
.netstatus	Returns the Netstatus Interface for this server

Using our example, `mysrv[1].name` returns the name of the first server assigned to `myjob`.

The Netstatus interface is very useful, because it lists the hardware properties of the server. Table 18.8 lists some properties available in Netstatus.

Table 18.8 Netstatus Interface Properties

PROPERTY	DESCRIPTION
.disks	Returns a bitarray of the existing disks
.workdisk	Returns the disk where 3ds max is set up
.spaceondisk	Returns the space on disk for the specified drive
.memorysize	Returns the amount of RAM in bytes
.numprocessors	Returns the number of processors
.boottime	Returns the time the Server process was started

In our example, `netstat = servers[1].netstat` will assign the Netstatus of the first server in the array to `netstat`. Then we can use `netstat.memorysize` to query how much RAM that server has.

You can see a complete list of properties and commands available to manage Network Rendering in the online Help, or by querying `showinterface` *for each of the explained interfaces.*

Summary

You can now write complex and useful scripts, which will help you tremendously on a daily basis.

In the next chapter, you will learn some more advanced tools that will make scripting easier and will allow you to manipulate files, Xrefs, viewports, and much more.

Advanced Scripting

3ds max

Chapter 19

You have seen many ways to use MAXScript in 3ds max. You will now see some features and tools to improve scripting. In this chapter we'll examine scene management tools, Xrefs, callbacks, and more. What all these commands have in common is that they are not connected to a specific object or function; they're usually related to the scene or to 3ds max in general. Topics include:

- Declaring global and local variables

- Preparing startup scripts

- Using scene scripts, callbacks, and handlers

- Working with 3ds max files (including Xrefs)

- Customizing viewports

- Accessing global functions and properties

Declaring Global and Local Variables

When you declare variables in a script, you need to define whether they are local or global. If they are local, they will be deleted after the script ends. If they are global, they will remain in memory after the script ends. In addition, when you're using multiple rollouts, if the variable is local, it is valid only inside the rollout in which you defined it. When you need to work with variables among rollouts, make sure you declare them as global.

In older versions of MAX, any time you declared a variable, it was assumed to be global unless you specified it to be local. 3ds max 4 reverses this scenario, so that whenever you declare a variable, it is assumed to be local and will not exist anymore when the block of code ends.

As an example, start a new script and type:

```
for i in 1 to 3 do
(
p = i*10
format "Internal: %\n" p
)
format "External: %\n" p
```

Notice that the Internal values are correct, but the External value is undefined. This is because the variable p is local and is deleted right after the for command ends.

Repeat the script, now declaring p as global:

```
global p = i*10
```

Notice now that p will return a value after it ends.

When declaring variables as global, make sure you use a unique name that will not be used in other scripts, to avoid possible conflicts. (The only names you cannot use are commands in MAXScript. For instance, you cannot use "function" as a variable name.)

Preparing Startup Scripts

You can set up scripts to execute automatically. There are a few ways to do so. MAXScript searches for a file called startup.ms, and executes it automatically when max is loaded.

You can also put the script in the `Startup` folder, under `Scripts`. When launched, MAXScript will search all files in all subfolders inside `Startup`.

Another way to call a script when max starts is using the command line, through the startup shortcut or using a DOS prompt. Simply type

```
3DSMAX -U MAXSCRIPT script.ms
```

where `script.ms` is the name of the script you want to call.

If you put all your utilities in the `Startup` *folder, they will be automatically listed in the MAXScript Utility tab.*

Plug-in Scripts

Plug-in scripts can be placed in the `Startup` folder or in any `Plugins` folder. MAXScript will search for them there and will load them automatically, like regular plug-ins. You will learn about plug-in scripts in detail in Chapter 20.

Using Scene Scripts

You can save scripts and variables inside a scene. You also can define scripts that will monitor the scene and perform actions in defined situations, such as prior to rendering, prior to saving, when an object is deleted, when a selection changes, and so on.

Key Concept

Persistent Variables and Functions

Persistent variables and functions are those that will be saved with the scene. You can create as many persistent functions or variables as you need; just make sure you use unique names so they do not conflict with other variables in other scripts.

For instance, you can create a set of functions and variables that will calculate how much time one person takes working on each scene in max. This script can be defined as a startup script and will manipulate information saved with the scene. Then, using handlers, you will be able to define when this script will be called and how the result will be output.

You will start by defining some variables as persistent. Open the Listener and type:

```
persistent global time_working
time_working = 0
```

This will create a variable that you will use in the script.

Manipulating Persistent Variables

You can list and remove persistent variables. To list all persistent variables (and their values), use the `persistents.show()` command.

To delete persistent variables you can use `persistents.remove`, listing the name of the variable, starting with #. For instance, to remove the persistent variable `part_time` you would use `persistents.remove #part_time`. To remove all persistent variables, simply use `persistents.removeall()`, and all persistent variables will be removed.

Change Handlers

Change handlers are scripts that will be called on the occurrence of some event, such as when the time slider is scrolled, when a viewport is redrawn, when a property is changed, or when some predefined action happens, such as File Open or Render.

General Callbacks

General callbacks are called when certain max events happen, such as Render, File Open, File Reset, etc. These events can be called usually before and after these events. Table 19.1 provides a list of the most commonly used events.

Table 19.1 Common Events for General Callbacks

EVENT	DESCRIPTION
#viewportchange	The viewport layout is changed
#systemprereset	Before max is reset
#systempostreset	After max is reset
#systempresave	Before saving a file
#systempostsave	After saving a file
#filepreopen	Before opening a file
#filepostopen	After opening a file
#prerenderframe	Before rendering a frame
#postrenderframe	After rendering a frame
#presystemshutdown	Before exiting 3ds max
#postsystemstartup	After 3ds max has been started

Usually callbacks call functions. To add callbacks, you use `callbacks.addscript`. You must specify `callbacks.addscript` *event string id*, where *event* is the event at which you want the callback to execute; *string* is the script itself in a string format; and *id* is the callback identification, which is its name.

You will write a script that will tell us how many objects are selected. In the Listener, type:

```
callbacks.addscript #selectionsetchanged \
"format \"There are % objects selected.\\n\" selection.count" \
id:#test
```

This will create a callback; whenever you click in the screen, it will list how many objects are selected.

To remove a callback, use `callbacks.removescript`. You then specify the ID or the event you want to remove. You can use `callbacks.show()` to list all callbacks.

Hands-on MAXScript: Creating a Timer

Let's create a script that will count the time you take working in each scene. It will use a persistent global variable that will store the number of seconds you worked. This variable will be incremented using a `#filepresave` callback.

Locate the file `timer_functions.ms` on the CD that accompanies this book. Run it and copy it to your startup scripts folder. This file defines two functions that will store the time and calculate the elapsed time between two intervals. It's very similar to the one you created in Chapter 15.

Now we will create another script file that includes the callbacks. Either open the file `timer_callbacks.ms` from the CD that accompanies this book, or start a new script and type everything shown in Listing 19.1. (Remember, the backslash at the end of a line means that the line is continued.)

LISTING 19.1: THE TIMER CALLBACKS SCRIPT (TIMER_CALLBACKS.MS)

```
fn calculate_time_working =
(
end_max_working = right_now()
session_time = elapsed_time start_max_working end_max_working
time_working += session_time
start_max_working = right_now()
)
fn reset_time_working =
```

```
(
global start_max_working
start_max_working = right_now()
persistent global time_working = 0

callbacks.removescripts id:#start_max_working
callbacks.removescripts id:#end_max_working

callbacks.addscript #systempostnew "reset_time_working()" \
   id:#start_max_working
callbacks.addscript #systempostreset "reset_time_working()" \
   id:#start_max_working
callbacks.addscript #systemprenew "calculate_time_working()" \
   id:#end_max_working
callbacks.addscript #filepreopen "calculate_time_working()" \
   id:#end_max_working
callbacks.addscript #systemprereset "calculate_time_working()" \
   id:#end_max_working
callbacks.addscript #filepresave "calculate_time_working()" \
   id:#end_max_working
)

reset_time_working()
```

First, we defined two functions. One resets the system and restarts all variables; the other calculates the elapsed time and adds it to the persistent variable.

The first function (`calculate_time_working`) simply calculates the elapsed time since the last time it was called and adds this value to the persistent variable `time_working`. Since this variable is persistent, it will be stored and saved with the program, and it can be restored the next time this file is opened.

The second function (`reset_time_working`) creates the persistent global variable and resets it to zero. Then, it removes all previous callbacks and defines them again. Notice that when we create a new max file, some callbacks (`#systempostnew` and `#systempostreset`) will reset the timer and restart themselves. Before saving the file, other callbacks (`#systemprenew`, `#filepreopen`, `#systemprereset`, and `#filepresave`) will call the `calculate_time_working` function, which will update the timer.

Place this script in the `Startup` folder, so it will be automatically loaded. To extend this exercise, you can create a script to display the `time_working` variable value, and even display it in hours, minutes, seconds format, or have it placed in the Scene Properties.

When

The when command is a change handler that also responds to an event, but this event is a scene node event. You can define actions to happen when objects are deleted, when objects are modified, when parameters are changed, and so on.

For example, create a sphere and name it Ball. In the Listener, enter the following line, which will create a handler that will warn you if this object is deleted:

```
when $Ball deleted do messagebox "Object Ball has been deleted."
```

Now, delete the object and see the message displayed.

The when handler is capable of much more. You can define very complex handlers that can be driven by almost any parameter in max. However, when handlers are not persistent and will be discarded when the file is closed.

Working with .MAX Files

MAXScript allows you to work with .max files and all other supported file types. You can open, save, merge, import, export, and cross-reference (Xref) files within MAXScript.

These operations are useful for automating tasks, such as rendering queues and batch file conversions; they save tremendous amounts of time.

Opening and Saving

Key Concept

You can open .max files using loadmaxfile. All you need to specify is the filename and path. If no path is specified, MAXScript will use the default Scenes Path in max.

It is necessary to specify the extension when using loadmaxfile. *Also remember to use* \\ *instead of a single backslash.*

You can save .max files using savemaxfile; for this command it is necessary to specify both the filename (with extension) and path. If you want to know the current filename and path, you can use maxfilename and maxfilepath. For instance, to save the current file in the current folder you should use savemaxfile (maxfilepath + maxfilename).

Partial Loading and Saving

You can save a file partially—that is, save selected elements of a scene—using Save Selected. To do so in MAXScript, you can use savenodes. To use this command you need to specify the objects you want to save, using an array of objects or a built-in array, like selection, objects, lights, etc. For instance, you can save the active selection using

```
savenodes selection "saved_selection.max"
```

You can also merge files, loading objects from other scenes. You can do that in two ways, either by pointing at the objects you want to merge or by calling up the Merge Objects dialog box. You also have options that will define how the merge will work, either by deleting old duplicated objects, by ignoring duplicates, or by displaying a dialog window asking what to do when duplicates are found.

To merge files use `mergemaxfile`. For instance, to merge the file you just saved with `savenodes`, use

```
mergemaxfile "saved_selection.max" #prompt
```

This will display the Merge Objects dialog box, and the script will continue to run after the merge ends. If you want the old duplicated objects to be deleted, use `#deleteolddups`. If you want to ignore them, use `#mergedups`. And if you want the user to decide, using a dialog box, use `#promptdups`.

You can specify which objects are to be merged. To do so, you need to know which objects are present in the scene you want to merge; use `getmaxfileobjectnames` to find out. It will return an array containing all objects in the file, so you can use it with the `mergemaxfile` command. For instance, if you want to merge the `arm` object in the `creature.max` file, deleting the old one if it exists, you would use

```
mergemaxfile "creature.max" #(#arm) #deleteolddups
```

Importing and Exporting Files

To import and export files, you can use `importfile` and `exportfile`. The exporter will be defined by the extension of the file. By default the Exporter Options window will be displayed, but you can skip this using `#noprompt`, and the exporter will use default options.

For instance, to export the current scene as an STL file, you would use `exportfile "exported.stl"`. To import it back, use `importfile "exported.stl" #noprompt`, skipping the Import Options dialog window.

Other File Commands

You can hold and fetch files through MAXScript, using `holdmaxfile` and `fetchmaxfile`. No parameters are needed for these commands.

You can also reset max using the MAXScript `resetmaxfile` command. You can also skip the dialog boxes that would appear, by using `#noprompt`.

Use `resetmaxfile #noprompt` *with caution. If your max file has not been saved, all changes will be lost.*

Sometimes you might need to know whether a file has been saved or not. You can use `checkforsave()` to do so. It brings a dialog asking you to save the file, in case changes were made since the last save. It will return True if the file has been saved and False if changes were made and not saved.

You can also quit max through scripts with the command `quitmax`. This is useful if you are batch-processing files for render, import, etc. Like `resetmaxfile`, `quitmax` also has a `#noprompt` option.

Hands-on MAXScript: Batch Converting 3DS Files

We'll create a script that converts all 3DS models from a selected folder into `.max` files. It is a Macro Script with a rollout and a button, which will ask the user to select a folder containing the 3DS files, as in Figure 19.1.

Figure 19.1 *The window displayed by the Batch 3DS Convert script*

Then, the script will search and list the number of files found. If it finds any 3DS files, the Convert button will be enabled, allowing the file conversion. Either open the file `convert_3ds.mcr` from the CD that accompanies this book, or start a new script and type everything shown in Listing 19.2.

LISTING 19.2: BATCH CONVERTING 3DS MACRO SCRIPT (CONVERT_3D.MCR)

```
macroScript Convert_3DS
    category:"Tools"
    tooltip:"Convert 3DS Files to MAX"
```

```
   (
rollout convert_3ds_params "Parameters"
   (
   local f,f_name, f_ext, f_path

   button folder "Select Directory" width:120
   label status "0 files found"
   button go "Convert!" width:120 enabled:false
   on folder pressed do
      (
      f_path = getsavepath caption:"Select 3DS Directory"
      f = getfiles (f_path + "\\*.3ds")
      status.text = (f.count as string + " files found")
      if f.count > 0 do go.enabled = true
      )
   on go pressed do
      (
      resetmaxfile()
      for i in 1 to f.count do
         (
         resetmaxfile #noprompt
         importfile f[i] #noprompt
         f_name = getfilenamefile f[i]
         f_path = getfilenamepath f[i]
         savemaxfile (f_path + f_name + ".max")
         )
      go.enabled = false
      )
   )
global convert_3ds_floater
try(closerolloutfloater convert_3ds_floater) catch()
convert_3ds_floater = newrolloutfloater "3DS Convert" 200 140
addrollout convert_3ds_params convert_3ds_floater
)
```

Evaluate the script and create a button in any toolbar for it. Test the script, asking it to convert a series of 3DS files in any folder. (If you do not have any 3DS files, export some from your scenes.)

Now you will see what is new in this script. We've used a couple of commands that were not discussed earlier. Among them is getsavepath. It displays the Browse For Folder dialog box (illustrated in Figure 19.2) and returns the selected folder path as a variable.

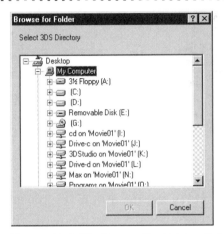

Figure 19.2 *The Browse For Folder dialog box*

Right after that command, we have `getfiles`, which searches for files and lists all of them as an array. This allows us to see whether there are files in the selected folder.

In the next action, we used `getfilenamefile` and `getfilenamepath`. These commands filter a filename and display only the name (without the extension) and only the path, respectively. These are used when you need to specify a different filename extension, or to change filenames or paths.

Try variations of this script, using radio buttons to select the converted file type. You can also select another folder for the output files. You can also play with `getdirectories`, which is a command that will list all folders inside the selected folder, and make your script convert all 3DS files in a directory structure.

Xref

As discussed in Chapter 4, external references (Xrefs) allow you to incorporate objects from one file into another file and thus provide a convenient way for members of a team to work independently on different aspects of a complex project. You can Xref scenes and objects using MAXScript. You will be able to load, unload, and merge Xrefs. You can even access properties in an Xref scene.

Xref Objects

To load an Xref object, you can use `xrefs.addnewxrefobject`. It requires two parameters, the filename and the object name.

The Xref object has several properties. For instance, you can select a proxy object and file to the Xref objects using `.proxyfilename` and `.proxyobjectname`. By default, Use Proxy is off unless you enable it with `.useproxy`.

For instance, if you have a object named Arm in a scene named Creature and you wanted to Xref that object in, you'd use `p_arm = xrefs.addnewxrefobject "creature.max" "arm"`. If you wanted to use a proxy object Box in the same file, you could type:

```
p_arm.proxyfilename = "Creature.max"
p_arm.proxyobjectname = "Box"
p_arm.useproxy = true
```

To update the Xref object, you simply use `updatexref obj`, where *obj* is the proxy object name. This will load the Xref file and update the mesh on screen if any change has occurred to the original.

Xref Scenes

An Xref scene works just like the Xref object, except that it is not an object you can select.

To add Xref scenes, use `xrefs.addnewxreffile`. The only parameter required is the filename. To access the scenes' parameters, you can assign them to variables at the creation time, or you can read their values later, using `xrefs.getxreffile index`, where *index* is the number of the Xref. To find how many Xref scenes you have loaded, you can use `xrefs.getxreffilecount`.

For instance, you could Xref the Creature scene. To do so, you'd use

```
creature = xrefs.addnewxreffile "Creature.max"
```

You can access and set all properties that appear in the Xref Scene dialog box. For instance we'd create a dummy and bind the Xref to it using

```
d = dummy()
creature.parent = d
```

We can also turn on Automatic Update using

```
creature.autoupdate = true
```

MAXScript can also access all objects inside an Xrefed file. This is read-only access, so you will not be able to change any information.

Hands-on MAXScript: Copying Xref Materials

As an example, we will now write a script that will copy all materials in an Xref scene to the Material Editor Samples (see Figure 19.3).

Figure 19.3 *The window displayed by the Xref to Medit script*

Open the copy_xref_materials.mcr file from the CD, or start a new script and type all the commands shown in Listing 19.3.

LISTING 19.3: THE XREF TO MEDIT SCRIPT (COPY_XREF_MATERIALS.MCR)

```
Macroscript Read_Xref_Materials
    category:"Tools"
    tooltip:"Copy all Xref Scene Materials to Medit"
(

Rollout read_xrefmat_rollout "Parameters"
    (
    Listbox xref_list "Xref Scenes" width:280 height:10 \
        align:#center
    button go "Copy Materials" width:280 enabled:false \
        align:#center

    on read_xrefmat_rollout open do
        (
        n = xrefs.getxreffilecount()
        l = #()
        for i in 1 to n do
            append l (xrefs.getxreffile i).filename
        xref_list.items = l
        )

    on xref_list selected x do
        (
```

```
        selected_xref = x
        go.enabled = true
        )

    on go pressed do
        (
        yn = false
        yn = querybox "Overwrite the Materials Editor?" \
            title:"Overwrite Alert!"
        if yn then
            (
            xref_scene = xrefs.getxreffile xref_list.selection
            n = xref_scene.tree.children.count
            lib = materiallibrary()
            for i in 1 to n do
                (
                curmat = xref_scene.tree.children[i].material
                if curmat != undefined do append lib curmat
                )
            nmat = lib.count
            if nmat > 24 do nmat = 24
            for i in 1 to nmat do
                meditmaterials[i] = lib[i]
            )
        )
    )

try (closerolloutfloater read_xrefmat_floater) catch()
global read_xrefmat_floater
read_xrefmat_fl = newrolloutfloater "Copy Xref Mtl" 330 253
addrollout read_xrefmat_rollout read_xrefmat_fl

)
```

The script uses a listbox that will list all Xrefs available in the scene. The list is created in the on open action and added to the UI. Then the user is asked to select an Xref in the list. Notice that if an Xref is not selected, the go button is not enabled.

When the user clicks Go, the script uses a querybox to make sure they know that all slots in the Materials Editor will be overwritten. If the user clicks yes, the script creates a temporary material library with the materials from the Xref scene and copies it to the Materials Editor.

It is important to keep in mind that you need to test to see if the object has a material, before it is copied; and how many materials are in the created library before you copy its contents to the Material Editor. Otherwise, if you had more than 24 materials, you would have crashed the script, since there are only 24 slots in the Material Editor.

Customizing Viewports

You can control the viewport layout and the viewport type using MAXScript. It is also possible to adjust several parameters in each viewport.

Viewport Layout

You can set 14 different viewport layouts using MAXScript. This is done using `viewport.setlayout` *layoutname*. Layouts are named as shown in Table 19.2.

Table 19.2 Viewport Layout Names

NAME	LAYOUT	NAME	LAYOUT
#layout_1		#layout_3ht	
#layout_2v		#layout_3hb	
#layout_2h		#layout_4	
#layout_2ht		#layout_4vl	
#layout_2hb		#layout_4vr	
#layout_3vl		#layout_4ht	
#layout_3vr		#layout_4hb	

Adding Viewport Layouts to the Quad Menu

You can add options to set the viewport layout using the Quad menus, shown in Figure 19.4.

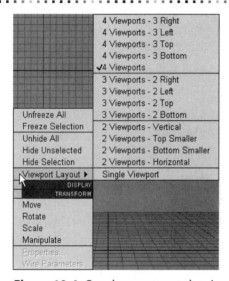

Figure 19.4 *Quad menu to set the viewport layout*

1. Start a new script and enter the following code:

```
macroscript mi_layout1
    category:"Viewport Layout"
    buttontext:"Single Viewport"
    (
    viewport.setlayout #layout_1
    )
```

2. Now repeat the same code block, changing the Macro Script name, the button-text, and the layout name each time as in Table 19.3. If you prefer you can open the file macro_viewport_layout1.mcr on the CD-ROM.

3. Once you're done, evaluate this file.

4. Now open the Customize User Interface dialog box using Customize ➔ Customize User Interface.

Table 19.3 Viewport Layout Macroscript data

MACROSCRIPT NAME	BUTTONTEXT	LAYOUT NAME
mi_layout2v	2 Viewports - Vertical	#layout2v
mi_layout2h	2 Viewports - Horizontal	#layout2h
mi_layout2ht	2 Viewports - Top Smaller	#layout2ht
mi_layout2hb	2 Viewports - Bottom Smaller	#layout2hb
mi_layout3vl	3 Viewports - 2 Left	#layout3vl
mi_layout3vr	3 Viewports - 2 Right	#layout3vr
mi_layout3ht	3 Viewports - 2 Top	#layout3ht
mi_layout3hb	3 Viewports - 2 Bottom	#layout3hb
mi_layout4	4 Viewports	#layout4
mi_layout4vl	4 Viewports - 3 Left	#layout4vl
mi_layout4vr	4 Viewports - 3 Right	#layout4vr
mi_layout4ht	4 Viewports - 3 Top	#layout4ht
mi_layout4hb	4 Viewports - 3 Bottom	#layout4hb

5. Go to the Menus tab and click New to create a new menu. Menus are created to be used on the Main menu or in Quad menus.

6. Name it Viewport Layout.

7. Select it from the drop-down list.

8. On the left side, select the Viewport Layout category.

9. Drag mi_layout1 to the menu.

10. Add a separator to the menu.

11. Drag all layouts for 2 Viewports and add a separator after them.

12. Do the same for 3 and 4 Viewport layouts.

You should have the same result as shown in Figure 19.5.

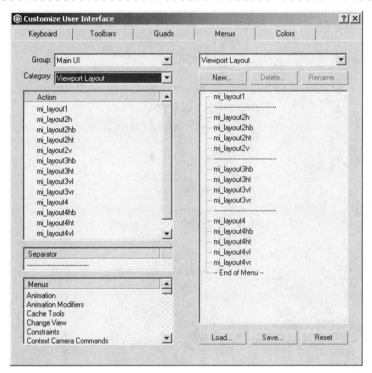

Figure 19.5 *Creating the Viewport Layout*

13. Go to the Quads tab.

14. Select the Default Viewport Quad.

15. Select the Top/Right quad, which is the Display Quad.

16. Drag the Viewport Layout menu from the bottom left pane to the Quad pane. The Customize User Interface window should now be similar to Figure 19.6.

17. Now all your viewport options appear in your Display Quad as a Sub-Menu, similar to Figure 19.4.

If you want to enhance your script, you can add an ischecked *event, which will add a checkmark to the current viewport layout. See* `macro_viewport_layout2.mcr` *on the CD-ROM.*

Figure 19.6 *Adding Viewport Layout to the Quad menu*

Viewport Type

MAXScript allows you to control the 3D viewports. You can set any type of viewport, but once you change to a 2D viewport (Track View, Schematic View, Asset Browser, or MAXScript Listener), you will not be able to change it again.

To get and set viewport types, you can use `viewport.gettype` and `viewport.settype` respectively. The supported viewport types are shown in Table 19.4.

When setting Camera or Spot view, if there is no camera or spot selected, the Select Camera or Spot dialog window will be shown.

You can set the active viewport using `viewport.activeviewport`. It will require an index number that will identify the viewport. You can use `viewport.numviews` to inquire how many viewports you have.

Table 19.4 Viewport Names

NAME	VIEWPORT
#view_top	Top view
#view_bottom	Bottom view
#view_right	Right view
#view_left	Left view
#view_bront	Front view
#view_back	Back view
#view_persp_user	Perspective view
#view_iso_user	User view
#view_camera	Camera view
#view_spot	Spot view
#view_shape	Shape view
#view_grid	Grid view
#view_track	Track view

Remember that Track View, Schematic View, Asset Browser, and MAXScript Listener will not be considered in any of these commands. Once you change a viewport to any of them, you cannot change it back using MAXScript.

Camera Views

You can manipulate Camera views, to define which camera will be used and also to find out which camera is being used in a viewport. The getactivecamera or viewport.getcamera() command will list the camera that is used by the current camera view.

The viewport.setcamera command will allow us to set a camera in the current camera view. For instance, viewport.setcamera $Camera02 will set the current camera view as Camera02. If the current view is not a camera, it will return undefined.

Miscellaneous Viewport Manipulation

You can also set various viewport characteristics through MAXScript, such as redraw, safe frames, and wait cursors.

Redrawing

Some actions require us to force a redraw on screen. There are three ways to do so: `redrawviews()`, `completeredraw()`, and `max views redraw`.

The `redrawviews()` command will redraw only what has been changed on screen, providing a fast, but not so accurate redraw. By contrast, `completeredraw()` and `max views redraw` will redraw the entire screen, regardless of what was or was not changed, which will be slower but more accurate.

Safe Frames

You can turn the safe frames features on or off. To do so you can use two commands, `displaysafeframes` or `max safeframe toggle`. The latter will toggle the status of the safe frames (if they were off, they will be turned on, and vice versa). The viewports with safe frames are automatically redrawn.

To use `displaysafeframes`, you need to say whether it is true or false; for instance, `displaysafeframes = true` will turn it on for the active viewport. The viewport is not redrawn automatically, so you will need to use `completeredraw()` or `max views redraw` to refresh the viewport and display the safe frames.

Cursors

When the script is processing, nothing happens on the screen, so you might want to let the user know that max hasn't frozen. A way to do so is to change the cursor to the system wait cursor (usually an hourglass) until the process is over, and then switch it back to normal. To do so you can use `setwaitcursor()` and `setarrowcursor()`. They will set the cursor to the wait cursor and back to the normal arrow, respectively.

Adding a Rollout to a Viewport

3ds max 4 allows you to place a rollout in a viewport. To do so, you need to create a dialog box using this rollout and then use the `registerviewwindow` command.

As an example, let's use the Hand Controller script you created in Chapter 17. You will make it a dialog and register it as a viewport.

Open the file `hand_controller.ms` from the CD-ROM. Then remove the last three lines and add the following code:

```
createdialog hand_rollout 330 250
registerviewwindow hand_rollout
```

Evaluate the script, and then right-click the viewport and select Extended ➜ Parameters, as in Figure 19.7. You will then see the dialog moving to the viewport, as in Figure 19.8.

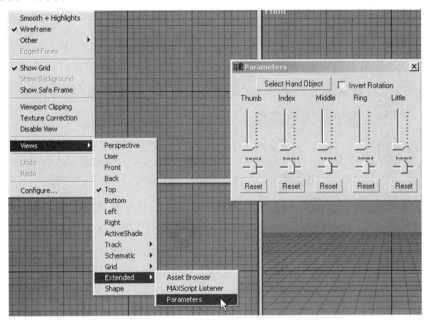

Figure 19.7 *Extended viewport options*

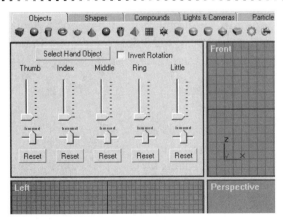

Figure 19.8 *The Hand Controller rollout in the viewport*

If you change the viewport to any different type, the dialog will be displayed again. Also, closing the dialog removes the rollout from Extended Views.

Accessing Global Functions and Properties

3ds max has several configuration properties and commands that control the interface, turn buttons on or off, change Preferences options, and access scene properties. We'll now see some of these functions and properties.

Controlling the max Interface

There are several commands that can control max Global Properties or that can control the way max behaves. Some of them allow us to activate certain items; some turn on buttons; some change the UI configuration, etc. Let's examine some of these helpful commands.

Key Concept

Controlling the Command Panel

You can use `setcommandpaneltaskmode` to control which one of the tabs is opened in the Command Panel. Similarly, you can use `getcommandpaneltaskmode` to know which panel is activated. This is useful because some options—sub-object level, for instance—will not run if a specified Command Panel tab isn't activated. (See the section "Working with Edit Mesh, Poly, Patch, and Spline" in Chapter 16 for details on how to turn on sub-object mode with a script.)

To set any panel active, you simply need to specify

```
setcommandpaneltaskmode #panel
```

where *panel* is one of the six Command Panel tabs: Create, Modify, Hierarchy, Motion, Display, or Utility. Instead of using `setcommandpaneltaskmode`, you can use `max mode panel`, substituting the panel name for `panel`, just like the previous example.

Transform Tools

You can activate all transform tools using scripts. See Table 19.5 for a list of the commands you can use to activate each transform tool.

Table 19.5 Transform Tool Commands

COMMAND	TRANSFORM TOOL
max move	Move tool
max rotate	Rotate tool
toolmode.nonuniformscale()	Non-Uniform Scale tool
toolmode.uniformscale()	Uniform Scale tool
toolmode.squashscale()	Squash tool
max select	Select tool

The toolmode commands also allow us to set the active coordinate system and which pivot point will be used. The command toolmode.coordsys will set the active coordinate system, which you need to choose from among #view, #screen, #world, #parent, #local, or #grid.

To set the coordinate system center, you can use the properties of toolmode: .pivotcenter(), .selectioncenter(), or .transformcenter(). These will set the coordinate system center to each object's pivot, to the center of the selection, or to the origin of the coordinate system, respectively.

Prompt Line

Various max commands use the prompt line to ask the user to perform certain actions and to display the result of actions. You can also use the prompt line in MAXScript.

You can use pushprompt to add a string to the prompt line. The previous string will be stored in a temporary buffer. To restore the previous string, you can use popprompt(). For instance, type:

```
pushprompt "Select Shapes to be trimmed:"
```

The text string will be displayed in the prompt. If you enter popprompt(), the previous prompt will be restored.

You can use pushprompt as many times as needed, and the previous prompts will be stored in memory. popprompt() can restore each of them, moving backward one at a time, until the first prompt is reached.

The replaceprompt command will substitute the actual prompt with a specified string, regardless of the usage of pushprompt and popprompt. The only drawback is that the old prompt cannot be restored; essentially, the popprompt buffer is cleared.

Displaying Calculation Progress

Some plug-ins display a progress bar in the status bar, as in Figure 19.9, to show the user that some processing is taking place. You can do this with scripts also.

Figure 19.9 *Sample progress bar*

The `progressstart` command creates a progress bar and sets it to 0%. Its only argument is the title of the progress bar. Then, you need `progressupdate` to update the progress bar, specifying the actual percentage as an integer number. At the end of the process, you need `progressend()` to remove the progress bar.

Do not enter `progressstart` *in the Listener, because it may lock max and you will not be allowed to cancel the command.*

Hands-on MAXScript: Displaying a Progress Bar

Here is an example script that uses a progress bar to show its progress. This script will create Editable Mesh vertex animation, moving the vertices sequentially. For instance, it moves vertex 1 in frame 1, vertex 2 in frame 2, and so on. The offset is specified, so you will have the whole object shifted after it ends.

Open the `offset_vert.ms` file from the CD, or start a new script and type all the commands shown in Listing 19.4.

LISTING 19.4: THE PROGRESS BAR SCRIPT (OFFSET_VERT.MS)

```
utility move_vertex "Move Vertex"
(
local obj2, offset_vert
pickbutton sel "Select Object" width:120
button go "Process" width:120
```

```
label verts ""
spinner nov "# verts/frame" type:#integer range:[1,100,1]
label fr ""
spinner x "Offset X"
spinner y "Offset Y"
spinner z "Offset Z"
fn offset_vert sel_obj ox oy oz nov =
   (
   local obj = sel_obj
   n_frames = (obj.numverts/nov)
   if animationrange.end < n_frames then
   animationrange = interval animationrange.start n_frames
   local c_frame = 1
   progressstart "Moving Vertices..."
   setwaitcursor()
   for i in 1 to obj.numverts do
      (
      str3 = ("deletekeys $" + obj.name + ".vertex_" + \
         i as string + ".controller #allkeys")
      execute str3
      local p = execute ("$" + obj.name + ".vertex_" + \
         i as string)
      local p2 = p + [ox,oy,oz]
      local str = "$" + obj.name + ".vertex_" + i as string + \
         " = " + p as string
      local str2 = "$" + obj.name + ".vertex_" + i as string + \
         " = " + p2 as string
      animate on
         (
         at time (c_frame-1) (execute str)
         progressupdate ((i*100/obj.numverts))
         at time c_frame (execute str2)
         )
      if (execute ("numkeys $" + obj.name + ".vertex_" + \
         i as string + ".controller")) > 2 then
         execute ("deletekey $" + obj.name + ".vertex_" + \
            i as string + ".controller 1")
      if (mod i nov) == 0 then c_frame += 1
      )
```

```
      progressend()
      setarrowcursor()
      )
  on sel picked obj2 do
      (
      global move_vertex_object = undefined
      move_vertex_object = snapshot obj2
      delete obj2
      animatevertex move_vertex_object #all
      verts.text = (move_vertex_object.numverts as string + \
          " vertices")
      fr.text = ((move_vertex_object.numverts/nov.value) as string \
          + " frames")
      )
  on nov changed value do
      (
      try
          (
          fr.text = ((move_vertex_object.numverts/nov.value) \
              as string + " frames")
          )
      catch()
      )
  on go pressed do
      try(offset_vert move_vertex_object x.value y.value z.value \
          nov.value) catch()
  )
```

To use this script, create a cone and select it in response to the prompt. Then, enter **10** in Z, and press Start. After the script is done, play the animation. You will see the vertices moving systematically.

Notice that we used `execute` several times in this script. This is because we need to access the different vertices, and they were accessed using `.vertex_n`. Notice also the use of the progress bar and the wait cursor. They both let us know that the script is working.

To ensure that the script will work correctly, we also used `try/catch` to call the function when the spinner values are adjusted. This is to prevent failure due to missing objects.

Working with Menus and Quads

3ds max 4 introduced a new way to customize menus and quads. All these new options are also available through MAXScript through the menuman interface.

Using this interface you can create your macros and automatically assign them to the correct menu or quad, without worrying about whether the user knows how to customize max.

Menu Files

Using the Menu Manager, you can load and save menu files. The menu file will contain all configurations for the menus and quads.

You can use menuman.loadmenufile and menuman.savemenufile to load and save menu files respectively. To find out which menu file is current, you can use menuman.getmenufile().

Menu files are saved in the current UI folder with the MNU extension.

Be careful when working with menu files, and make sure you create a backup of the original MNU files, so you can always come back if something goes wrong.

Creating Menus

To create a menu, you follow these general steps:

1. Create a menu.

2. Create a submenu item.

3. Add action items and separators.

4. Place this menu in a quad or menu.

Let's do an exercise that will add all the viewport macros created earlier in this chapter to a menu in the Main Menu bar. When finished, your menu should look like Figure 19.10.

Open menu_viewport_layout.ms from the CD, or start a new script and enter the code in Listing 19.5.

Figure 19.10 *A Viewport Layout menu*

LISTING 19.5: THE VIEWPORT LAYOUT MENU (MENU_VIEWPORT_LAYOUT.MS)

```
if menuman.registermenucontext 0x4a5b689 do
(
    vp_macros = #("mi_layout1", "mi_layout2v", "mi_layout2h", \
    "mi_layout2ht", "mi_layout2hb", "mi_layout3vl", \
    "mi_layout3vr", "mi_layout3ht", "mi_layout3hb", \
    "mi_layout4", "mi_layout4vl", "mi_layout4vr", \
    "mi_layout4ht", "mi_layout4hb")
    vp_menu = menuman.createmenu "Viewport Layout"
    vp_sub = menuman.createsubmenuitem "VP Layout" vp_menu
    vp_submenu = vp_sub.getsubmenu()
    for i in vp_macros do
        (
        vp_item = menuman.createactionitem i "Viewport Layout"
        vp_submenu.additem vp_item -1
        )
    main_menu = menuman.getmainmenubar()
    help_menu = 0
    for i in 1 to main_menu.numitems() do
        (
        tmp_menu = main_menu.getitem i
        if tmp_menu.gettitle() == "&Help" do
```

```
        (
        help_menu = i
        exit
        )
    )
    main_menu.additem vp_sub help_menu
    menuman.updatemenubar()
)
```

We started by using `menuman.registermenucontext`. This command registers the new menu and saves it in the MNU file, using the hexadecimal number supplied. If you run this script twice, `menuman.registermenucontext` will fail and will not create the menu again. This allows us to place this code, and you'll be sure the menus aren't being created many times.

Then we create an array containing all the macros we want to add to the menu. This is just to simplify the work and to save time.

Moving ahead, we create a menu using `menuman.createmenu`. This is the menu title that will appear in the Customize User Interface dialog box and in the Menu bar. After creating the menu, we must create its submenu, using `menuman.create-submenuitem`. This submenu contains the String attributes, which is how the Menu Title is displayed.

Because the Submenu interface holds only the title, we need to get its actual submenu menu to be able to add the Macro Scripts to it. We do this using `vp_sub.get-submenu()`.

Now that we have created the menu, we can add the macros to it. We do that by creating an action item using `menuman.createactionitem` and then adding this action item to the menu using `vp_submenu.additem`. Using –1 means it will be the last item added to that menu.

Now that the menu is ready, it's time to add it to the main menu. To do so, we use `menuman.getmainmenubar` to read the main menu. Then we get the number of items already in the menu, using `main_menu.numitems()`. Using a loop, we step through each of these items using `main_menu.getitem` and we look for a title of "&Help" using `tmp_item.gettitle()`. If it's the Help menu, we store it in a variable and exit the loop.

The menu name is "&Help" because the letter H is the keyboard shortcut for that menu, and shows underlined.

Finally, we add the new menu to the main toolbar, in the same position as the Help menu is now, bumping it to the right. To do so, we use `main_menu.additem`. Any time you work with the menus, you need to update them using `menuman.updatemenubar()`.

It's a good practice to include the macros you create along with the code that places them on the menus. This makes it easier for the user to find your scripts.

Working with Quads

Quads work the same way as menus. You create a Quad menu using `var = menuman.createquadmenu`. Then you access each of the four quads using `var.getquadmenu i`, where *i* is the number of the quad you want to access.

The remaining process will be the same once you have retrieved a quad menu.

File Management

MAXScript has several commands that help us manage files, particularly keeping them filed and being able to locate them.

System Folders

Sometimes you need to know which directory max is installed in. This can be done using `getdir`.

`getdir` lists all max directories, simply specifying the folder from among these options: `#autoback`, `#drivers`, `#export`, `#expression`, `#font`, `#help`, `#image`, `#import`, `#matlib`, `#plugcfg`, `#preview`, `#scene`, `#scripts`, `#sound`, `#startupscripts`, `#ui`, and `#vpost`. `#maxroot` is used to specify the max root folder—in other words, the folder where `3dsmax.exe` is located.

If you need to know the scripts' path, you can use `scriptspath`, instead of `getdir #scripts`. Both will return the same result.

Paths

Bitmap paths and Xref paths are very important for max to work properly. You can add, get, and delete paths for both categories.

- `mappaths.add` or `xrefpaths.add` allows us to add paths to each of the search paths.

- `mappaths.count` or `xrefpaths.count` lists the number of paths in the list of search paths.

- `mappaths.get` or `xrefpaths.get` lists one of the paths. Each requires an index number.

- `mappaths.delete` or `xrefpaths.delete` removes a path from the search paths. Again, each requires an index number to identify the path.

User Interface Configuration Files

Using MAXScript you can load and save `.cui` files. These files hold the configuration of all toolbars and tabs, menu and Command Panel positions, and all display colors.

You can use `cui.loadconfig` to load any `.cui` file. All it needs is the filename to be loaded. The `cui.saveconfig()` command saves the current UI configuration, and `cui.getconfigfile()` lists the current `.cui` file.

To access UI colors, use `getuicolor` and `setuicolor`. Both require an index that will define which UI item that color relates to. Check the online Help, under User Interface Colors, for a list of all colors you can access.

External Commands

MAXScript can execute external programs and applications. You can execute DOS commands and applications.

To execute DOS commands, as well as `.bat` files or `.cmd` files, you can use `doscommand`. It requires a simple string that will be the command executed. For instance

```
doscommand "dir c:\\maps\\anim*.jpg /b >anim.ifl"
```

will create an `.ifl` file with all `anim*.jpg` files present in the specified folder.

You can also start applications and you can specify parameters to this application. To do so, you can use `shelllaunch`. It will start any application either directly or through association, and allows us to specify a command-line parameter to this application. For instance,

```
shelllaunch "d:\\movies\\anim_qt3.mov"
```

will start QuickTime or any other associated program and open this video.

Always remember to use \\ instead of a single backslash in path names.

Scene Properties

MAXScript also can access Scene Properties. This way, you can assign the properties through scripts, and create a utility that would help us manage our assets.

To access these properties, you use `fileproperties.command`, where command can be a series of commands to get, set, find, and remove properties. The File Properties dialog box (see Figure 19.11) is divided into three tabs: Summary, Contents, and Custom. You access these as `#summary`, `#contents`, and `#custom`.

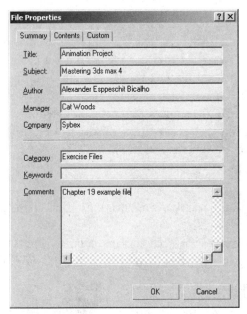

Figure 19.11 *The File Properties dialog window*

You can use `fileproperties.addproperty` to add properties to each of the sections. For instance

```
fileproperties.addproperty #summary "Title" "Animation Project"
```

will add this text to the Title field in the Summary section. The Summary section has the following fields: Title, Subject, Author, Keywords, and Comments. The Contents section is where you can edit Manager and Company, despite the fact that they are also located in the Summary page in the File Properties dialog window.

Use `max  hold` *after changing any property in the Contents section, since they are updated only when saved.*

To retrieve a property's value, you can use `fileproperties.getpropertyvalue`, but to do so, you need to know the index of the property. This is done using `fileproperties.findproperty`. If a property does not exist, the command will return 0; if the property does exist, it will return the index of that property.

For instance, you can add some properties and retrieve their values later:

```
fileproperties.addproperty #summary "Title" "Animation Project"
fileproperties.addproperty #summary "Subject" "First Shot"
fileproperties.addproperty #summary "Author" "Alexander"
t = fileproperties.findproperty #summary "Title"
v_value = fileproperties.getpropertyvalue #summary t
```

As you can see, the correct property value was retrieved and stored in v_value.

Hands-on MAXScript: File Management

Let's create a script that will manage our files, requiring the user to enter the information to be saved in the file as in Figure 19.12.

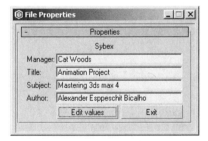

Figure 19.12 The Properties Manager script

Open `manage_properties.ms` from the CD, or start a new script and type all the commands in Listing 19.6.

LISTING 19.6: THE PROPERTIES MANAGER SCRIPT (MANAGE_PROPERTIES.MS)

```
global manage_properties_rollout, manage_properties_floater
rollout manage_properties_rollout "Properties"
(
label company "Sybex"
edittext manager fieldwidth:200 align:#right
label man "Manager:" offset:[0,-20] align:#left
```

```
edittext title  fieldwidth:200 align:#right
label tit "Title:" offset:[0,-20] align:#left
edittext subject  fieldwidth:200 align:#right
label sub "Subject:" offset:[0,-20] align:#left
edittext author   fieldwidth:200 align:#right
label aut "Author:" offset:[0,-20] align:#left
button edit "Edit values" width:98 offset:[-26,0] enabled:false
button ok "Exit" width:98 offset:[75,-26]
on manage_properties_rollout open do
   (
   fileproperties.addproperty #contents "Company" company.text
   fn read_properties section header UI =
      (
      local m = fileproperties.findproperty section header
      if m > 0 then
         (
         try
            (
            UI.text = fileproperties.getpropertyvalue section m
            UI.enabled = false
            )
         catch(UI.enabled = true)
         )
      )
   read_properties #contents "Manager" manager
   read_properties #summary "Title" title
   read_properties #summary "Subject" subject
   read_properties #summary "Author" author
   if manager.enabled == false or title.enabled == false or \
         subject.enabled == false or author.enabled == false then
      edit.enabled = true
   )
on manage_properties_rollout oktoclose do
   (
   return_value = true
   if manager.text == "" or title.text == "" or \
      subject.text == "" or author.text == "" then
      (
      messagebox "Please, all fields need to be filled."
      return_value = false
      )
```

```
        else
            return_value = true
        return_value
        )
    on edit pressed do
        (
        manager.enabled = true
        subject.enabled = true
        author.enabled = true
        title.enabled = true
        )
    on manager entered text do
        (
        fileproperties.addproperty #contents "Manager" manager.text
        max hold
        )
    on title entered text do
        (
        fileproperties.addproperty #summary "Title" title.text
        )
    on author entered text do
        (
        fileproperties.addproperty #summary "Author" author.text
        )
    on subject entered text do
        (
        fileproperties.addproperty #summary "Subject" subject.text
        )
    on ok pressed do
        (
        closerolloutfloater manage_properties_floater
        )
    on oktoclose manage_properties_rollout do
        (
        return_value = false
        if manager.text == "" or title.text == "" or \
          subject.text == "" or author.text == "" then
            messagebox "Please, all fields need to be filled."
          else return_value = true
        return_value
        )
```

```
)
fn initiate_manage_properties =
(
callbacks.removescripts id:#manage_properties
callbacks.addscript #systempostnew \
  "initiate_manage_properties()"id:#manage_properties
callbacks.addscript #systempostreset \
  "initiate_manage_properties()" id:#manage_properties
callbacks.addscript #filepostopen \
  "initiate_manage_properties()" id:#manage_properties
try(closerolloutfloater manage_properties_floater) catch()
properties_floater = newrolloutfloater "File Properties" 300 200
addrollout manage_properties_rollout properties_floater
)
initiate_manage_properties()
```

You can now save this script in the Startup folder. When any new file starts, you will be asked to enter this data. The callbacks are used to allow this to happen when the system is reset, a file is opened, or a new file is created.

Notice that we used a new event handler for the rollout. It is an oktoclose event. It allows us to specify whether or not we want to allow the user to close the dialog box—in other words, whether we want it to be modal. In our case, the user can only close the window if all fields are filled. To do this we set return_value = false, and if the user can close the dialogue, we set return_value = true. Then, the last line passes return_value as an argument to the event, which controls whether the dialog box can be closed.

We also created an Exit button, which calls closerolloutfloater. You can enhance this script, adding more fields to be filled, or automating some fields, like Author or Manager, if they are always the same people.

If you prefer not to have this script starting automatically, you can remove the callbacks, remove it from the startup folder, and create a Macro Script for it.

Summary

MAXScript can help us in many more areas than direct object manipulation. You can create scripts to do virtually anything in scene and asset management, working with files, folders, events, etc.

In the next chapter, you will learn how to create plug-in scripts to create geometry, modifiers, and render effects.

Plug-in Scripts

3ds max

Chapter 20

Plug-in scripts are scripts that behave just like any plug-in: they're seamlessly integrated into the 3ds max user interface. You can create several types of plug-in scripts: scripts that extend objects and parameters that already exist; and scripts that generate and manipulate information. Topics include:

- Creating tools

- Creating extending plug-in scripts

- Building objects using plug-in scripts

Creating Tools

Tools are scripts that are driven by mouse input, like clicking and dragging. They're essential for plug-in scripts but can also be used in Macro Scripts and other scripts.

Tools are created using the `tool` command. They require two main actions: `on mousepoint` and `on mousemove`. These actions define how the tool will behave when users click the mouse and when they drag it.

Listing 20.1 is an example of a tool. It creates a regular box and converts it to a NURBS object. Start a new script and type the code shown here, or open the `tool_nurbsbox.ms` file from the CD that accompanies this book.

LISTING 20.1: THE NURBS BOX SCRIPT (TOOL_NURBSBOX.MS)

```
tool NURBSBox
(
local st, ed1, ed2, b
on mousePoint clickNo do
    (
    if clickNo == 1 do
        (
        st = gridPoint
        in coordsys grid b = box length:0 width:0 height:0 \
            pos:gridPoint
        b.name = uniquename "NBox"
        )
    if clickNo == 3 then
        (
        convertTo b NURBSSurface
        select b
        #stop
        )
    )
on MouseMove clickNo do
    (
        if (clickNo == 2) do
            (
            ed1 = gridPoint
            d1 = abs (ed1.x - st.x)
            d2 = abs (ed1.y - st.y)
            b.length = d2*2
            b.width = d1*2
            )
```

```
        if (clickNo == 3) do
        (
            ed2 = gridPoint
            d3 = distance ed2 ed1
            b.height = d3
        )
    )
)
```

The on `mousePoint clickNo` event handlers define what the tool will do in two situations: when the mouse is first clicked (`clickNo == 1`) and when the third click happens (`clickNo == 3`).

In the first click, you create the object and assign its position. Notice that the script uses `in coordsys grid`, which creates the object in the current view/grid. Then the position is assigned using `gridPoint`. This command returns the position of the click in the active grid.

In the third click, you convert the object to NURBS, select it, and finish the tool, using #stop. The `mouseMove` event handler defines what the tool will do when the mouse is dragged. In this example, we defined two situations: when the mouse is dragged after the click, with the mouse still pressed (`clickNo == 2`); and when the mouse is dragged after the user has released the mouse button (`clickNo == 3`).

The first drag defines the box length and width. Both will be defined using the X and Y distance, also specified using `gridPoint`. The second drag defines the height of the box, using the distance between the last click and the current mouse position.

Evaluate this tool, and execute it by typing **starttool NURBSBox**. Notice that it behaves the same way as these objects are created in 3ds max.

You can also make this tool a Macro Script and assign a button to it, which will make it behave like an object being created. You will need to use these tools with plug-in scripts, in order to create the objects properly.

Creating Plug-in Scripts

There are basically three types of plug-in scripts: *extending* plug-in scripts extend an existing plug-in and adjust its parameters; *system* plug-in scripts create nodes but do not allow any editing of this creation, since they behave similarly to a system object; and *creation* plug-in scripts create new plug-ins and behave just like regular plug-ins.

In the next sections you'll see examples and applications of some of these plug-ins and learn about their differences.

Creating Extending Plug-in Scripts

The extending plug-in scripts are the easiest to create. They allow you to extend an existing plug-in, adding more parameters or simplifying the existing ones. You'll see that the extending plug-in scripts are very similar, regardless of their type. Looking at Table 20.1, you will see all the extending plug-in scripts listed; we'll only demonstrate a few of the categories, so play with the others a little, creating your own customized materials, maps, etc.

Table 20.1 Categories of Extending Plug-in Scripts

PLUG-IN	EXTENDS
Geometry	Primitives and 3D Objects (except Compound)
Shape	Shapes (except Line)
Light	Any Light object
Camera	Any Camera object
Helper	Any helper
Modifier	Any modifier
Material	Any material
Texturemap	Any texture map
Rendereffect	Any render effect
Atmospheric	Any atmospheric effect

As an example, let's create a plug-in script that will extend the box object and create a simple cube instead of a regular box. Figure 20.1 shows the Geometry tab of the Create panel after adding this plug-in.

Start a new script and type the following (this script can be found on the CD and is named `plugin_cube0.ms`):

```
plugin geometry cube
name:"Cube"
category:"Mastering 3ds max"
classID:#(0x36b2b15a, 0x60b9a9bb)
extends:Box
(
```

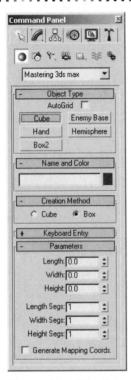

Figure 20.1 *The Cube plug-in script adds a Cube option to the Geometry tab of the Create panel.*

The `plugin` command defines the plug-in. It requires the plug-in type, which is `geometry` in this example, and a variable name (`cube`). You also need to specify the name and category of the plug-in, which will define where it will appear in the Geometry tab.

The plug-in script also requires a *classID*. The classID is a unique hexadecimal number that allows 3ds max to identify which plug-in is being used. This value is given using the `genclassid()` command, which generates a new classID for you to use in your scripts.

The classID must be unique to each plug-in and plug-in script.

The last parameter in the `plugin` command is `extends`, which defines the object that is being extended. In this example, you're extending the box object, so you used `extends:Box`.

To continue writing the script, we will define the tool. The plug-in script automatically executes the tool named Create.

In the example, continue typing:

```
tool create
(
    on mousePoint clickNo do
    (
    if clickNo == 1 do nodeTM.translation = gridPoint
    if clickNo == 2 do #stop
    )
    on MouseMove clickNo do
    (
if clickNo == 2 do
    delegate.width = sqrt(gridDist.x^2 + gridDist.y^2 + \
        gridDist.z^2)
    delegate.height = delegate.length = delegate.width
    )
    )
)
```

This tool will need the following mouse movements: the first click, mouse drag, and release. The first click will define the object's position. Within plug-in scripts, this is done using `nodeTM.translation`. You do not need to use `in coordsys grid` also.

The drag movement will define the size of the cube. That is done using the syntax `delegate.parameter`. When you need to define any parameter of the object that's being extended, use `delegate`. In our example, the width, height, and length are all equal, and they are defined by the distance between the first click and the mouse drag position. That value is specified using `griddist`. This example used a formula that calculates the distance between two points in XYZ, which is the square root of ((distance in X)^2 + (distance in Y)^2 + (distance in Z)^2).

When the mouse is released, the plug-in stops. Note that the Box rollout appears on the screen, and if you select Modify, it will continue appearing there. If you open the Track View and expand the object tracks, you will see that the box is now a subanim of the cube. This is how extending plug-ins work.

Once you add a plug-in script to a scene, it will behave just like a regular plug-in, which means that you will need to have the plug-in loaded to open the scene again. Placing the .ms file in any plug-in folder will load it as a regular plug-in.

Adding Rollouts

You can add more options and flexibility to this plug-in. A plug-in script can also present a rollout for the user to define the properties of the object. And because all the dimensions of a cube are the same, it would be nice to have a "size" option for our cube.

To add a rollout in a plug-in script, simply add it before the tool definition. If the plug-in script extends another plug-in, you need to specify whether this rollout will replace the original plug-in's user interface (UI). This is specified in the `plugin` command, using `replaceUI:true` or `false`.

Edit your script, adding `replaceUI:true` in the `plugin` command (this version of the script is named `plugin_cube1.ms` on the CD).

```
plugin geometry cube
name:"Cube"
category:"Mastering 3ds max"
classID:#(0x36b2b15a, 0x60b9a9bb)
extends:Box
replaceUI:true
```

Then, add the `rollout` clause before the tool:

```
rollout params "Parameters"
(
spinner size "Size: " range:[0,10000,0]
on size changed val do
    delegate.width = delegate.height = delegate.length = val
on params open do size.value = delegate.width
)
```

You will also need to modify the MouseMove action so that it updates the spinner value, when dragging the mouse:

```
if clickNo == 2 do
(
val = sqrt(gridDist.x^2 + gridDist.y^2 + gridDist.z^2)
delegate.width = delegate.height = delegate.length = val
params.size.value = val
)
```

Now you have the script ready. Evaluate and play with it.

Notice that now your object has a new rollout, as in Figure 20.2. When creating a new object, this rollout sometimes appears below the object's rollouts; sometimes it appears alone. In the Modify panel, only this rollout will appear, unless you have specified `replaceUI:false`, so that all rollouts will appear.

Figure 20.2 *The rollout for our Cube plug-in*

Adding Parameters in Track View

If you check the Track view, you will see that we still do not have any parameters for this object, even though it now has an interface. We need to create a parameter block.

Parameter blocks are special parameters that are saved with an object and allow direct animation of its values. Using parameter blocks will create a track in Track view for each property you want to track, making animation easier to edit and visualize. Parameter blocks are essential for creation plug-ins, since they do not extend any plug-in that already has parameters.

A parameter block can be linked to a rollout, automatically linking the variables with the UI items, making it easier to write the script, since you will not need to write any event handler code for the UI item.

To see this for yourself, add a parameter block to your cube plug-in by adding the following lines before the rollout clause:

```
parameter pblock rollout:params
(
cube_size animatable:true type:#worldunits ui:size
on cube_size set val do
    delegate.width = delegate.height = delegate.length = val
)
```

The parameter block is linked to the `params` rollout created in the previous section, because you used `rollout:params`. Then, the variable `cube_size` will be linked to the Size spinner in this rollout, because you used `ui:size`.

A parameter can have a series of properties, but the most important is its type. This defines which kind of variable the parameter is—integer, float, color, point3, Boolean, and so on (the complete list is shown in Table 20.2). In the cube example, we used World units, which will allow the user to specify this value using any configured unit in his or her system. This makes the script usable for all different measuring systems.

Table 20.2 Representing Parameter Types in the UI

UI ITEM	PARAMETER TYPE(S)
Spinner or slider	`#float`
	`#integer`
	`#time`
	`#angle`
	`#percent`
	`#colorchannel`
	`#worldunits`
Radio button	`#integer`
	`#radiobtnindex`
Check box or checkbutton	`#integer`
	`#boolean`
Colorpicker	`#color`
Pickbutton	`#node`
Mapbutton	`#texturemap`
Materialbutton	`#material`

You can also specify whether or not the parameter is animatable. If it's not animatable, it will not be displayed in the Track View.

All parameters in a parameter block can be accessed using MAXScript, and they are accessed just like any object property, using *object.property*.

Now that you have defined the parameter block, you can adjust the rest of the script to use the parameter block. Replace the code in the rollout with the following:

```
rollout params "Parameters"
(
spinner size "Size: " range:[0,10000,0]
)
```

Now edit the on MouseMove event:

```
on MouseMove clickNo do
(
if clickNo == 2 do
    size = sqrt(gridDist.x^2 + gridDist.y^2 + gridDist.z^2)
)
```

Evaluate the script now, and play with it. Notice that the Size parameter also appears in the Track View, as in Figure 20.3. This version of the script can be found on the CD as plugin_cube2.ms.

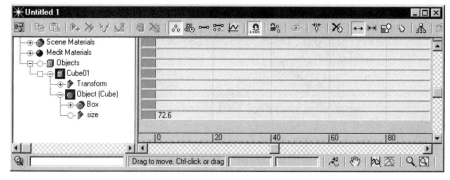

Figure 20.3 *Cube properties in Track View*

You can now animate the script like any regular object. Save this plug-in in the Plugins folder.

Let's try another example, extending a sphere to create a hemisphere object. It will have two parameters: Radius and Segments. The rollout is shown in Figure 20.4.

Figure 20.4 *The rollout displayed by the Hemisphere plug-in script*

This example will also introduce a couple of new concepts. Start a new script and type the code shown in Listing 20.2, or open the plugin_hemisphere.ms file from the CD.

LISTING 20.2: THE HEMISPHERE PLUG-IN SCRIPT (PLUGIN_HEMISPHERE.MS)

```
plugin geometry hemisphere
name:"Hemisphere"
category:"Mastering 3ds max"
classid:#(0xce445e62, 0x42606fad)
extends:Sphere
replaceui:true
(
parameters pblock rollout:params
   (
   radius animatable:true type:#worldunits ui:size
   segments animatable:true type:#integer ui:segs default:32
   on radius set val do delegate.radius = val
   on segments set val do delegate.segments = val
   )

rollout params "Parameters"
   (
   spinner size "Radius: " type:#worldunits range:[0,10000,25]
   spinner segs "Segments: " type:#integer range:[4,100,32]
   )
```

```
on create do
  (
  delegate.hemisphere = 0.5
  delegate.chop = 1
  )

tool create
  (
  on mousePoint clickNo do
    (
    if clickNo == 1 do nodeTM.translation = gridPoint
    if clickNo == 2 then #stop
    )
  on MouseMove clickNo do
    (
    if clickNo == 2 do
      radius = sqrt(gridDist.x^2+gridDist.y^2+gridDist.z^2)
    )
  )
)
```

The segments variable in the parameter block has a default value of 32. You specified a default explicitly because the default value of any parameter block is zero, which would set an incorrect parameter to our sphere.

Notice that you limited the spinner values to the actual limits of the parameters in the sphere object. You also used a new event: on create. It's called when the object is created for the first time, and it defines the object's basic configuration. In this example, it defines that the sphere is a hemisphere.

You can play with this script and add the slicing parameters to the extended version.

Extending Shapes

Extending is pretty much all that plug-in scripts can do to shapes. There's no way to create new shape objects other than the built-in shapes in 3ds max.

For instance, you can create a plug-in script that will extend the star shape and predefine some parameters. The inner radius will be 55% of the outer radius. The fillet values will be 10% of the outer radius. Start a new script and type out Listing 20.3, or open the file plugin_newstar.ms from the CD.

LISTING 20.3: THE NEW STAR PLUG-IN SCRIPT (PLUGIN_NEWSTAR.MS)

```
plugin shape Star_2
name:"New Star"
category:"Mastering 3ds max"
classID:#(0x4ca7c13d, 0x748bce49)
extends:Star
replaceui:true
(
    parameters pblock rollout:params
    (
    radius animatable:true type:#worldunits ui:size
    points animatable:true type:#integer ui:pt default:6
    on radius set val do
        (
        delegate.radius1 = val
        delegate.radius2 = val*0.55
        delegate.filletradius1 = val/10
        delegate.filletradius2 = val/10
        )
    on points set val do delegate.points = val
    )

    rollout params "Parameters"
    (
    spinner size "Radius: " range:[0,10000,0]
    spinner pt "Points: " range:[3,100,6] type:#integer
    )

    tool create
    (
        on mousePoint clickNo do
        (
        if clickNo == 1 do nodeTM.translation = gridPoint
        if clickNo == 2 then #stop
        )
        on MouseMove clickNo do
        (
        if clickNo == 2 do
            radius = sqrt(gridDist.x^2+gridDist.y^2+gridDist.z^2)
        )
    )
)
```

Notice that this script does the same as the previous scripts you have made, except that it is extending a Shape object, and it's delegating values for several parameters all at once.

You can also add regular interface items that will adjust the parameters of the object. For instance, you can create a Helix shape and define its height by selecting the distance between two objects. This cannot be done during the creation process, but it can be done in the Modify panel, as seen in Figure 20.5.

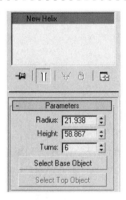

Figure 20.5 *The Modify panel's rollout for the Helix2 plug-in script*

Start a new script and type the statements in Listing 20.4, or open the file `plugin_helix2.ms` on the CD.

LISTING 20.4: THE HELIX2 PLUG-IN SCRIPT (PLUGIN_HELIX2.MS)

```
plugin shape Helix_2
name:"New Helix"
category:"Mastering 3ds max"
classID:#(0xa13154cd, 0x6c485140)
extends:Helix
replaceui:true
(

    parameters pblock rollout:params
    (
```

```
radius animatable:true type:#worldunits ui:rd
height animatable:true type:#worldunits ui:ht
turns animatable:true type:#integer ui:pt default:6
obj1 type:#node
obj2 type:#node
on radius set val do
    (
    delegate.radius1 = val
    delegate.radius2 = val
    )
on turns set val do delegate.turns = val
on height set val do delegate.height = val
)
rollout params "Parameters"
(
spinner rd "Radius: " range:[0,10000,0]
spinner ht "Height: " range:[0,10000,0]
spinner pt "Turns: " range:[1,100,6] type:#integer
pickbutton base_obj  "Select Base Object" width:140
pickbutton top_obj "Select Top Object" width:140 enabled:false
on base_obj picked obj do
    (
    obj1 = obj
    pt1 = obj.pivot
    top_obj.enabled = true
    )
on top_obj picked obj do
    (
    obj2 = obj
    height = distance obj1.pivot obj2.pivot
    )
on params open do
    (
    if obj1 != undefined do base_obj.text = obj1.name
    if obj2 != undefined do
        (
        top_obj.text = obj2.name
        top_obj.enabled = true
        )
    )
```

```
)
tool create
(
   on mousePoint clickNo do
   (
   if clickNo == 1 do nodeTM.translation = gridPoint
   if clickNo == 3 then #stop
   )
   on MouseMove clickNo do
   (
   if clickNo == 2 do
      radius = sqrt(gridDist.x^2 + gridDist.y^2 + \
         gridDist.z^2)
   if clickNo == 3
      do height = sqrt(gridDist.x^2 + gridDist.y^2 + \
         gridDist.z^2)
   )
   )
)
```

This script makes use of a new parameter type: the *node*. A node can be any object in the scene, and it allows you to access any property of the object through the variable. In this example, the nodes are the starting and ending points of the helix, and you're reading the nodes' positions and calculating the distance between them.

You prompt the user to select these points by using the two pickbuttons in the rollout. They set the obj1 and obj2 variables, when selected; they also calculate the height of the helix. We are not moving the object and we are not linking it to the others; all we are doing is defining the height using two known objects. Once the objects have been selected, their names will appear in the pickbuttons. This will happen even if the user selects the Helix2 later, because both objects were stored in the parameter blocks.

Extending Helpers

Helpers can also be extended through plug-ins. Usually, there's not much that can be done with helpers, because most of them have very few options, but you can extend a dummy object and add the missing length, width, and height options.

The next plug-in script will access the .boxsize property of a dummy and allow the user to access the length, width, and height of the dummy like any other 3ds max object, as seen in Figure 20.6.

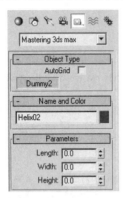

Figure 20.6 *The Helper Objects tab of the Create panel with the Dummy2 plug-in script added*

Start a new script and type the lines shown in Listing 20.5, or open the file `plugin_dummybox.ms` on the CD.

LISTING 20.5: THE DUMMY2 PLUG-IN SCRIPT (PLUGIN_DUMMYBOX.MS)

```
plugin helper dummybox
name:"Dummy2"
category:"Mastering 3ds max"
classID:#(0x648ce72d, 0x935e7b3a)
extends:Dummy
replaceui:true
(
parameters pblock rollout:params
   (
   Length animatable:true type:#worldunits ui:d_length
   Width animatable:true type:#worldunits ui:d_width
   Height animatable:true type:#worldunits ui:d_height
   on height set val do delegate.boxsize.z = val
   on length set val do delegate.boxsize.x = val
   on width  set val do delegate.boxsize.y = val
   )

rollout params "Parameters"
   (
```

```
      spinner d_length "Length: " range:[0,10000,0] type:#float
      spinner d_width  "Width:  " range:[0,10000,0] type:#float
      spinner d_height "Height: " range:[0,10000,0] type:#float
      )

  tool create
    (
    on mousePoint clickNo do
       (
       if clickNo == 1 do nodeTM.translation = gridPoint
       if clickNo == 3 do #stop
       )
    on MouseMove clickNo do
       (
       if clickNo == 2 do
          (
          length = abs(gridDist.x)*2
          width  = abs(gridDist.y)*2
          )
       if clickNo == 3 do height = sqrt(gridDist.y^2+gridDist.x^2)
       )
    )
  )
```

This script works the same way the other ones you've made. Having a resizable dummy will be very helpful for you in future projects.

Lights can also be extended, using the same process you did in the previous examples.

Extending Modifiers

Modifiers are another max element you can extend with plug-in scripts. These scripts work in the same way as our other scripts, except that modifiers do not require a tool, because no mouse action is required.

As examples, let's create two scripts. The first extends the Normalize Spline modifier, so you can use values below 1.0, since the plug-in itself doesn't allow you to do so. Another script extends the Optimize modifier, to easily set Low, Medium, or High Optimization values.

Start a new script and type out Listing 20.6, or open the CD file plugin_
normalize2.ms.

LISTING 20.6: THE NORMALIZE2 PLUG-IN SCRIPT (PLUGIN_NORMALIZE2.MS)

```
plugin modifier nspline2
name:"Normalize2"
extends:normalize_spline
replaceui:true
classID:#(0x44398c3b, 0x29422aeb)
(
parameters pblock rollout:params
   (
   Length type:#float default:20 ui:length2
   on Length set val do delegate.length = val
   )
rollout params "Parameters"
   (
   spinner length2 "Length" range:[1,10000,1] type:#float
   checkbox onoff "Enable Small Values" checked:false \
      enabled:false
   spinner mini "Mini-Length" range:[0.001,1,1] type:#float \
      scale:0.001 enabled:false
   on length2 changed val do
      (
      if length == 1.0 then
         onoff.enabled = true
        else
         onoff.enabled = false
      )
   on onoff changed state do
      (
      if state then
         (
         mini.enabled = true
         length2.enabled = false
         mini.value = 1.0
         )
        else
         (
         mini.value = 1.0
```

```
        mini.enabled = false
        length2.enabled = true
        length = length2.value
        )
    )
on mini changed val do
    (
    length = val
    )
on params open do
    (
    if length < 1.0 then
        (
        onoff.enabled = true
        onoff.checked = true
        mini.enabled = true
        mini.value = length
        length2.enabled = false
        )
      else
        (
        if length == 1.0 then
            (
            onoff.enabled = true
            length2.enabled = true
            )
        )
    )
  )
)
```

This script uses many functions in the rollout, because its operation is fairly complicated. The script allows the user to define a normal value (above 1.0), and when the value is equal to 1.0, the mini spinner will be enabled, allowing the user to specify values below 1.0, as seen in Figure 20.7. This is really needed if you have very small shapes, but dangerous if you have big ones. That's why we created a "trigger" that will enable one or the other depending on what the user needs.

The script also needs to check the length value, when it is loaded, so it can display this value correctly in the UI. This is why we used the on params open event.

Figure 20.7 *The Normalize2 modifier plug-in's rollout*

As a second example, the Optimize2 plug-in script simplifies the Optimize modifier. Start a new script and enter the code from Listing 20.7, or open the file plugin_ optimize2.ms from the CD. The result of this script is shown in Figure 20.8.

LISTING 20.7: THE OPTIMIZE2 PLUG-IN SCRIPT (PLUGIN_OPTIMIZE2.MS)

```
plugin modifier optimize2
name:"Optimize2"
extends:optimize
replaceui:true
classID:#(0x52ef94f8, 0xadb373cb)
(
parameters pblock rollout:params
   (
   power type:#integer default:1 ui:str
   on power set val do
      (
      case val of
         (
         1:   delegate.facethreshold1 = 0
         2:   delegate.facethreshold1 = 2.5
         3:   delegate.facethreshold1 = 5
         4:   delegate.facethreshold1 = 10
         )
      )
   )
)
```

```
rollout params "Parameters"
  (
  group "Optimize"
    (
    radiobuttons str "Strength:" \
        labels:#("None","Low","Medium","High")
    )
  )
)
```

Figure 20.8 *The Optimize2 modifier plug-in's rollout*

This script uses the `Strength` parameter to store the `radiobutton` index, and then, depending on the index value, passes different values to the Optimize modifier. The user has no access to these parameters unless they edit the script.

This type of plug-in script works well as a tool to standardize the animation work in a company.

Extending Materials

Materials, maps, render effects, and atmosphere plug-ins also can also be extended. Usually, you extend them to simplify the creation process and to ensure that all files in a project have the same look. This is very useful when several animators are sharing the same files.

Our first example is a plug-in script that extends the standard material and allows the user to create a simple and fast Glass material. It will display three options to the user: the glass color, index of refraction (IOR), and transparency, as seen in Figure 20.9. The remaining options are cosmetic to the material, and others are predefined by the script.

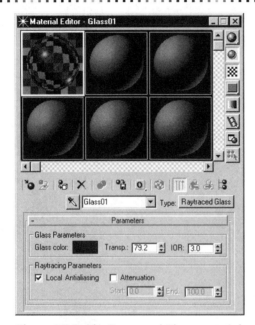

Figure 20.9 *The Raytraced Glass material in the Materials Editor*

Start a new script and enter the code from Listing 20.8, or open the file plugin_rayglass.ms from the CD.

LISTING 20.8: THE RAYTRACED GLASS PLUG-IN SCRIPT (PLUGIN_RAYGLASS.MS)

```
plugin material rayGlass
    name:"Raytraced Glass"
    classID:#(0x82b2cdc2, 0x4f77873e)
    extends:Standard replaceUI:true
(
parameters main rollout:params
 (
 Transparency type:#float default:90 ui:trans
```

```
IOR type:#float default:1.6 ui:refrac
Color type:#color default:white ui:col
on Transparency set val do
 delegate.refractionmapamount = val/2+50
on IOR set val do
 delegate.ior = val
on Color set val do
 (
 delegate.diffuse = val
 delegate.filtercolor = val/2
 delegate.ambient = val*2/5
 )
 )
rollout params "Parameters"
 (
 group "Glass Parameters"
  (
  spinner trans "Transp.: " fieldwidth:45 offset:[-90,0]
  spinner refrac "IOR: " fieldwidth:45 offset:[0,-20]
  colorpicker col "Glass color: " align:#left offset:[0,-25]
  )
 group "Raytracing Parameters"
  (
  checkbox aa "Local Antialiasing"
  checkbox atn "Attenuation" offset:[120,-20]
  Spinner st "Start:" fieldwidth:50 align:#left \
   offset:[120,0] range:[0,10000,0]
  spinner ed "End:  " fieldwidth:50 align:#left \
   offset:[210,-20] range:[0,10000,100]
  )
on aa changed state do
delegate.reflectionmap.parameters.Options__Antialiasing_Enable= \
 state
on atn changed state do
 (
 local atnx
 if state then atnx = 1 else atnx = 0
 delegate.reflectionmap.parameters.Attenuation_Mode = atnx
 delegate.refractionmap.parameters.Attenuation_Mode = atnx
 if atnx == 1 then (st.enabled = true; ed.enabled = true)
```

```
        else (st.enabled = false; ed.enabled = false)
    )
on st changed val do
    (
    delegate.reflectionmap.parameters.Attenuation_Start = val
    delegate.refractionmap.parameters.Attenuation_Start = val
    )
on ed changed val do
    (
    delegate.reflectionmap.parameters.Attenuation_End = val
    delegate.refractionmap.parameters.Attenuation_End = val
    )
on params open do
    (
    aa.state = \
    delegate.reflectionmap.parameters.Options__Antialiasing_Enable
    if delegate.reflectionmap.parameters.Attenuation_Mode == 1 then
      atn.checked = true else atn.checked = false
    if atn.checked then (st.enabled = true; ed.enabled = true)
      else (st.enabled = false; ed.enabled = false)
    )
)
on create do
    (
    delegate.reflectionmap = raytrace()
    delegate.reflectionmapamount = 15
    delegate.refractionmap = raytrace()
    delegate.shaderType = 4
    delegate.specularLevel = 78
    delegate.glossiness = 45
    delegate.Soften = 0.3
    delegate.twoSided = on
    )
)
```

Evaluate this script and select the newly created Raytraced Glass material in the Material Editor.

The script first defines all the basic parameters in the on create event. Then, the script defines a series of parameters and events that will set the object color, transparency, and IOR, and the Raytrace Map parameters, such as Local Antialiasing and Attenuation.

The values used to create the material in this script are completely predefined, not following any rule or math. 3ds max allows you to assign the original object as a sub-material of this material, so you can modify it as you wish. You can turn off the raytrace maps and even change them to other maps.

Building Objects Using Plug-in Scripts

Besides extending existing plug-ins, you can also write plug-ins that create objects from scratch. These plug-ins are divided in two categories: plug-ins that work just like system objects in 3ds max, creating other objects without allowing the user to modify them after creation; and the plug-ins that actually create data from scratch.

Only 3D geometry, render effects, modifiers, and manipulators can be created from scratch.

Creating a System-Like Plug-in

An example of a *system object* in 3ds max is the Ring Array. It creates a series of boxes and allows us to adjust and specify parameters; but after the objects are created, you can no longer manipulate those values. In MAXScript, you can write plug-in scripts that function in the same way. These plug-in scripts are a way to create a series of objects, the same way you can do with a tool, but in the form of a plug-in script. With these scripts you can also create a rollout that will adjust the creation parameters; but after the creation is ended, the objects retain no relationship with each other.

As an example, you will now create a script to draw a dummy hand—the same hand you used in Chapter 17 to animate the fingers' movement—as seen in Figure 20.10.

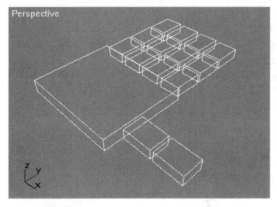

Figure 20.10 A dummy hand

Start a new script and enter the code in Listing 20.9, or open the `plugin_hand.ms` file on the CD.

LISTING 20.9: THE HAND PLUG-IN SCRIPT (PLUGIN_HAND.MS)

```
plugin geometry Hand_2
name:"Hand"
category:"Mastering 3ds max"
(
local hand,a1,a2,b1,b2,b3,c1,c2,c3,d1,d2,d3,e1,e2,e3
tool create
    (
    on mousePoint clickNo do
        (
        if clickNo == 1 do
            (
            hand = dummy pos:worldPoint name:(uniquename "Hand")
            a1 = dummy pos:worldPoint name:(hand.name + "A_01")
            a2 = dummy pos:worldPoint name:(hand.name + "A_02")
            b1 = dummy pos:worldPoint name:(hand.name + "B_01")
            b2 = dummy pos:worldPoint name:(hand.name + "B_02")
            b3 = dummy pos:worldPoint name:(hand.name + "B_03")
            c1 = dummy pos:worldPoint name:(hand.name + "C_01")
            c2 = dummy pos:worldPoint name:(hand.name + "C_02")
            c3 = dummy pos:worldPoint name:(hand.name + "C_03")
            d1 = dummy pos:worldPoint name:(hand.name + "D_01")
            d2 = dummy pos:worldPoint name:(hand.name + "D_02")
            d3 = dummy pos:worldPoint name:(hand.name + "D_03")
            e1 = dummy pos:worldPoint name:(hand.name + "E_01")
            e2 = dummy pos:worldPoint name:(hand.name + "E_02")
            e3 = dummy pos:worldPoint name:(hand.name + "E_03")
            a1.parent = b1.parent = c1.parent = d1.parent = \
                e1.parent = hand
            a2.parent = a1
            b2.parent = b1
            d2.parent = d1
            e2.parent = e1
            c2.parent = c1
            b3.parent = b2
            d3.parent = d2
```

```
            e3.parent = e2
            c3.parent = c2
            )
        if clickNo == 2 then
            (
            b1.pivot.y = b1.pos.y - b1.boxsize.y/2
            c1.pivot.y = c1.pos.y - c1.boxsize.y/2
            d1.pivot.y = d1.pos.y - d1.boxsize.y/2
            e1.pivot.y = e1.pos.y - e1.boxsize.y/2
            b2.pivot.y = b2.pos.y - b2.boxsize.y/2
            c2.pivot.y = c2.pos.y - c2.boxsize.y/2
            d2.pivot.y = d2.pos.y - d2.boxsize.y/2
            e2.pivot.y = e2.pos.y - e2.boxsize.y/2
            b3.pivot.y = b3.pos.y - b3.boxsize.y/2
            c3.pivot.y = c3.pos.y - c3.boxsize.y/2
            d3.pivot.y = d3.pos.y - d3.boxsize.y/2
            e3.pivot.y = e3.pos.y - e3.boxsize.y/2
            a1.pivot.y = a1.pos.y - a1.boxsize.y/2
            a2.pivot.y = a2.pos.y - a2.boxsize.y/2
            rotate a1 -90 Z_axis
            #stop
            )
        )
on MouseMove clickNo do
    (
    if clickNo == 2 do
        (
        hand.boxsize.x = abs(worldDist.x*2)
        hand.boxsize.y = abs(worldDist.y*2)
        hand.boxsize.z = (hand.boxsize.x + hand.boxsize.y)/15
        newsize = [hand.boxsize.x/5, hand.boxsize.y/3, \
            hand.boxsize.z*0.8]
        a1.boxsize = a2.boxsize = newsize
        b1.boxsize = b2.boxsize = b3.boxsize = newsize
        c1.boxsize = c2.boxsize = c3.boxsize = newsize
        d1.boxsize = d2.boxsize = d3.boxsize = newsize
        e1.boxsize = e2.boxsize = e3.boxsize = newsize
        b1.pos = hand.pos + [hand.boxsize.x*3/8, \
            hand.boxsize.y/2 + b1.boxsize.y*0.55,0]
```

```
c1.pos = hand.pos + [hand.boxsize.x*1/8, \
    hand.boxsize.y/2 + c1.boxsize.y*0.55,0]
d1.pos = hand.pos + [-hand.boxsize.x*1/8, \
    hand.boxsize.y/2 + d1.boxsize.y*0.55,0]
e1.pos = hand.pos + [-hand.boxsize.x*3/8, \
    hand.boxsize.y/2 + e1.boxsize.y*0.55,0]
b2.pos = b1.pos + [0, b1.boxsize.y*1.1,0]
c2.pos = c1.pos + [0, c1.boxsize.y*1.1,0]
d2.pos = d1.pos + [0, d1.boxsize.y*1.1,0]
e2.pos = e1.pos + [0, e1.boxsize.y*1.1,0]
b3.pos = b2.pos + [0, b1.boxsize.y*1.1,0]
c3.pos = c2.pos + [0, c1.boxsize.y*1.1,0]
d3.pos = d2.pos + [0, d1.boxsize.y*1.1,0]
e3.pos = e2.pos + [0, e1.boxsize.y*1.1,0]
a1.pos = hand.pos + [hand.boxsize.x/2 + \
    a1.boxsize.y*0.05, 0, 0]
a2.pos = a1.pos + [0, b1.boxsize.y*1.1, 0]
)
)
)
)
```

As you might have noticed, this script is basically a tool. It creates a series of objects and links them, when the mouse is first clicked. Then, when the mouse is dragged, the objects are resized and repositioned according to certain rules. When the user finishes dragging, the pivot point of the objects is adjusted, and the thumb is rotated.

You could not have adjusted the pivot during the dragging phase, because it would change the object's position, making us recalculate everything. In addition, when the object changes size, the pivot would have to be relocated.

In addition, notice that the script uses worldPoint instead of gridPoint. This means the user can create the hand in any viewport, but it will be aligned to the top view. This allows the script to move the pivot of the objects. More code would be needed to allow this creation in any view, because of the pivot realignment at the end of the script. You can reposition the hand at any time and manipulate its fingers with the Hand controller script from Chapter 17.

This example does not create a rollout, but if you were to add that modification, the rollout would have to manipulate the objects the same way you did here, directly addressing and adjusting their properties, and it would not allow you to manipulate the created objects once you left the Create panel.

Creating Modifiers

Using MAXScript you can write plug-ins for parametric modifiers, like the built-in 3ds max Bend, Twist, and Taper. These modifiers will change the position of vertices based on their original position, but in a parametric form, which means you will not have interactive access to the vertex position but will instead change it using a math formula.

As an example, will now write a modifier that will deform an object like a sine wave, allowing the user to define the axis, amount of deformity, and number of curves, as seen in Figure 20.11.

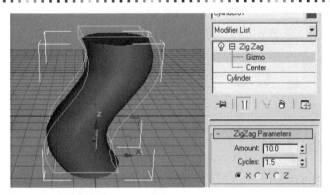

Figure 20.11 *The ZigZag modifier in action*

Start a new script and enter the code shown in Listing 20.10, or open the file named plugin_zigzag.ms from the CD.

LISTING 20.10: THE ZIGZAG MODIFIER PLUG-IN SCRIPT (PLUGIN_ZIGZAG.MS)

```
plugin simpleMod Zigzag
name:"Zig Zag"
classID:#(0xa8eba5be, 0x89ff7eab)
(
parameters main rollout:params
    (
    amount type:#worldunits ui:amtSpin default:20
    cycles type:#float ui:times default:0.5
    z_axis type:#radiobtnindex ui:zaxis default:1
    )
```

```
rollout params "ZigZag Parameters"
    (
    spinner amtSpin "Amount: " type:#float range:[-1000,1000,20]
    spinner times "Cycles: " type:#float range:[0,100,1]
    radiobuttons zaxis labels:#("X","Y","Z") coluns:3
    )
on map i p do
    (
    case z_axis of
        (
        1: p.x += amount*sin((p.z-(center.z))*pi*cycles)
        2: p.y += amount*sin((p.z-(center.z))*pi*cycles)
        3: p.z += amount*sin((sqrt(p.x^2+p.y^2)-\
                    sqrt(center.x^2+center.y^2))*pi*cycles)
        )
    p
    )
)
```

As you can see, the modifier plug-in doesn't need a tool to be created. However, it has a rollout and a parameter block like any other plug-in script.

This type of modifier plug-in works through the on map i p event. This event will be called for each vertex in the object, and will copy its position in the p variable. Then, the plug-in will modify the position and will output the new p value.

The script defines three axes, which will be called using the case expression. The position of the vertex in each axis will be modified using a sine expression. This expression has another parameter, center, which is the center position of the object. This allows you to use this value as part of the formula. In Listing 20.10, center defines where the deformation is zero, because when p.z is equal to center.z, the sine function will evaluate zero.

Notice that this modifier also has Gizmo and Center properties, which can be animated like any regular modifier.

Creating Render Effects

Render effects can also be created through MAXScript. They can access the rendered image and the rendered channels, manipulate them, and output an image at the end.

This type of script works exactly like a modifier plug-in, but the event that triggers the action is on apply bmp, where bmp is the bitmap containing the rendered image.

This way, you can manipulate the image and output another bitmap with the adjusted values.

Our next example is a script that shifts the Hue property of an image. This script will also have a nice UI, to help the user understand what is happening.

Render effect scripts that manipulate pixels, like this example, are very slow compared to regular plug-ins.

Start a new script and enter the code shown in Listing 20.11, or open the file plugin_hue.ms from the CD.

LISTING 20.11: THE CHANGE HUE PLUG-IN SCRIPT (PLUGIN_HUE.MS)

```
plugin renderEffect Hue_control
    name:"Change Hue"
    classID:#(0x31705a72, 0x4f48bbc7)
(

parameters pblock rollout:params
   (
   On_Off type:#boolean default:true animatable:true
   Hue type:#integer default:0 animatable:true ui:(h_lvl,h_slid)
   on Hue set value do
      (
      if Hue > 127 then Hue = 127
      if Hue < (-127) then Hue = (-127)
      )
   )
rollout params "Hue Settings"
   (
   local bmp1 = bitmap 255 4
   local bmp2 = bitmap 255 4

   checkbox a_only "Affect Background" checked:false
   label c_mark2 "|" pos:[160,21]
   label c_mark3 "|" pos:[160,34]
   label c_mark1 "|" pos:[160,26]
   bitmap normal_hue bitmap:bmp1 pos:[33,25]
   bitmap adjusted_hue bitmap:bmp2 pos:[33,36]
   label h_lbl "Hue" align:#left pos:[20,53]
   spinner h_lvl range:[-127,127,0] type:#integer fieldwidth:50 \
      pos:[75,52]
```

```
slider h_slid range:[-127,127,0] type:#integer
label rnd "Rendering:" align:#left
progressbar prog align:#center width:300
button reset_h "Reset" pos:[250,50]
fn make_ramp val_h =
   (
   local start_clr
   local color_ramp = #()
   start_clr = color 255 0 0
   start_hue = start_clr.hue + 127
   if (start_hue + val_h) > 255 then
     start_hue += (val_h - 255)
   else
    start_hue += val_h
   if start_hue > 255 then start_hue -= 255
   if start_hue > 255 then start_hue -= 255
   start_clr.hue = start_hue
   for i in 1 to 255 do
      (
      mid_clr = copy start_clr
      start_hue = mid_clr.hue
      if (start_hue + i) > 255 then
         start_hue += (i - 255)
        else
         start_hue += i
      if start_hue > 255 then start_hue -= 255
      if start_hue > 255 then start_hue -= 255
      mid_clr.hue = start_hue
      color_ramp[i] = mid_clr
      )
   return color_ramp
   )
fn upd_ramp =
   (
   bmp2 = bitmap 255 4
   clr = make_ramp h_level.value
   for i in 1 to 4 do setpixels bmp2 [0,i-1] clr
   adjusted_hue.bitmap = bmp2
   )
```

```
    on reset_h pressed do (h_level.value = 0; upd_ramp() )
    on h_level changed val do upd_ramp()
    on h_slid changed val do upd_ramp()
    on params open do
        (
        bmp1 = bitmap 255 4
        bmp2 = bitmap 255 4
        clr = make_ramp 0
        for i in 1 to 4 do setpixels bmp1 [0,i-1] clr
        clr = make_ramp h_level.value
        for i in 1 to 4 do setpixels bmp2 [0,i-1] clr
        adjusted_hue.bitmap = bmp2
        normal_hue.bitmap = bmp1
        )
    )
on apply bmp do
    (
    if On_Off then
        (
        for h=0 to bmp.height do
            (
            local sline = getPixels bmp [0,h] bmp.width
            for w = 1 to sline.count do
                (
                if params.a_only.checked then
                    (
                    calc = true
                    )
                  else
                    (
                    if sline[w].alpha == 0 then
                        calc = false else calc = true
                    )
                if calc then
                    (
                    slineh = sline[w].hue + Hue
                    if slineh > 255 then
                        slineh = (slineh - 255)
                        else
                          if slineh < 0 then
```

```
                            slineh = 255 + slineh
                    sline[w].hue = slineh
                    )
                )
            params.prog.value = h*100/bmp.height
            setPixels bmp [0,h] sline
            )
        params.prog.value = 0
        )
    )
)
```

Evaluate this script to add the Change Hue effect in the Rendering Effects dialog box. Notice that changing the spinner or the slider will update the bitmaps in the UI, helping us visualize the Hue change, as in Figure 20.12. These bitmaps are controlled by the functions make_ramp and upd_ramp.

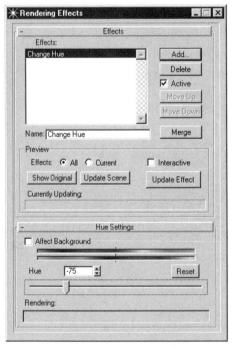

Figure 20.12 *The Change Hue render effect in action*

The script's action is in the on apply bmp section. First, it checks to see if the effect is on. Then it checks to see if the alpha channel should be calculated or not. A temporary variable is created to hold the current hue value. This value will be modified by the spinner value, which will be checked, because it cannot be bigger than 255 and not smaller than 0. At the end, the corrected value will be written to the original bmp variable.

You also used a progressbar UI item, which is a progress bar that is updated as the bitmap is processed.

As with the render() command, if you want to work with rendered channels, you need to call a specific event to create them. This event is on channelsrequired do channel_array, where channel_array is the same channel array you specify in the render() command.

This event needs to be called before the on apply bmp event, so you can use these channels in your process. Take some time now to rewrite the Render Channel script from Chapter 18 as a render effect plug-in script. It will work similarly to the File Output render effect, but you'll be able to output all channels, instead of only the three channels that are output through File Output.

Creating Manipulator Plug-ins

Manipulators are new to 3ds max 4. They allow you to interactively access an object's parameters on screen.

3ds max ships with two manipulator plug-ins: Radius and UVW Manipulator. In this example, you'll create a new manipulator that will adjust the Radius2 property of an object, which is based on the Radius manipulator script.

Let's do it step by step so you can understand the structure of this plug-in. You can find the final script on the CD in the file plugin_radius2Manip1.ms. Start a new script and enter the header of the plug-in:

```
plugin simpleManipulator radius2Manip
    name:"Radius2Manip"
    invisible:true
(
```

Next we need to specify which objects are going to be manipulated by this plug-in. to do this we use the canmanipulate event. In this case, we'll manipulate all objects that have the radius2 property, with the exception of the Torus Knot object. We do this using the following code:

```
on canManipulate target return
    (findItem (getPropNames target) #radius2) != 0 and \
    classof target != Torus_knot
```

Target, in this case refers to the object being manipulated. We use finditem to verify if radius2 is one of the properties of the object, and we verify to make sure the object's class is not Torus_knot.

The next event draws and updates the manipulator gizmo. The process is quite simple. First we delete all previous gizmos, and then we draw a new one, setting its color and size. At last, we will specify the tooltip:

```
on updateGizmos do
(
    this.clearGizmos()
    local pos = [0,0,0]
    giz = manip.makeCircle pos (target.radius2 * 1.01) 28
    this.addGizmoShape giz 0 green red
    return node.name + " radius2 = " + target.radius2 as string
)
```

In manipulator plug-ins, this refers to the manipulator plug-in itself. The manip.makeCircle command creates the circle gizmo, with a given radius and number of segments. The script uses the expression radius2 * 1.01 so that the gizmo is slightly larger than the object; otherwise, the screen redraw could make it invisible.

The next event is called when the user manipulates the gizmo in the viewport. It will read the viewport coordinates, calculate the value of the radius, and assign it to the object:

```
on mouseMove m which do
(
    local pl = manip.makePlaneFromNormal z_axis [0, 0, 0]
    local projectedPoint = [0,0,0]
    viewRay = this.getLocalViewRay m
    res = pl.intersect viewRay &projectedPoint
    if (res) then
        target.radius2 = (abs(length projectedPoint) ) / 1.01
)
)
```

In this section, manip.makeplanefromnormal defines the gizmo plane. Then, this.getlocalviewray will read the current mouse position. Pl.intersect will calculate the intersection point between the plane and the current mouse position, and will return a point relative to the gizmo origin, which is [0,0,0] in this case. If the intersection is successful, the radius2 will be set to the distance between the origin and the projected point. Because the origin is [0,0,0], this distance is the length of the projectedpoint vector. And because we multiplied the gizmo by 1.01 when you created it, we need to divide it by 1.01 to get the correct radius.

Now evaluate this script and test it with a tube, a torus, and a donut.

This plug-in would be exactly the same if we wanted to manipulate the Radius1 property. Just duplicate the script and rename all occurrences of `radius1` *to* `radius2`.

This script works well with the Tube and the Donut objects, but not very well with the Torus. This is because it's drawing the gizmo in the center of the torus object, and not in the center of the torus "ring." You can make a couple of changes in the script to fix this problem.

In the `on updategizmos` event, below `local pos = [0,0,0]` add:

```
if classof target == Torus do pos = [target.radius1,0,0]
```

This sets the gizmo center to the center of the torus "ring." Now, before the `this.addgizmoshape` statement, add the two following lines:

```
torusmatrix = (eulerangles 90 0 0) as matrix3
if classof target == Torus then giz.transform torusmatrix
```

These two lines will rotate the gizmo 90 degrees around the X axis.

Now you need to modify the `mousemove` event so it will recognize the offset and the rotation of the gizmo. After `local projectedpoint = [0,0,0]` add:

```
if classof target == Torus do
    projectedPoint = [target.radius1,0,0]
```

This matches the origin of the gizmo to the value you set on the `updategizmo` event. Now, after the `res = pl.intersect viewRay &projectedPoint` statement, add:

```
correction = 0
if classof target == torus do correction = target.radius1
```

Now substitute the `if (res)` line with the following code:

```
if (res) then
target.radius2 = (abs((length projectedPoint) - correction))/1.01
```

This code implements a `correction` variable, which by default is zero. If the object is a Torus, `correction` will be equal to `radius1`, which will then be subtracted from the distance between the origin and the point being clicked, returning the actual `radius2` value.

This final script can be found on the CD as `plugin_radius2manip2.ms`.

On the CD you can also find the `plugins_segmentsManip.ms` *file, an example that manipulates a series of segments. It uses the same concept, but it creates a different manipulator gizmo and uses a function to calculate the projection.*

Key Concept

Creating Geometry

You can also create geometry from scratch. This is done by defining vertices and faces manually, through a script. The finished script will create a parametric geometry object, with vertex and faces, just like any 3ds max object. To demonstrate, let's create a box object, with an option to have the pivot in the center instead of the base, as seen in Figure 20.13.

Figure 20.13 *The rollout for the New Box plug-in script*

Let's walk through this script step by step, so you can understand its structure. You can find the final script in the file `plugin_newbox.ms` from the CD. Start a new script and enter the header of the script, its parameter block and the rollout:

```
plugin simpleObject NewBox
name:"Box2"
classID:#(0x78f66693, 0x4c32d97b)
category:"Mastering 3ds max"
(
parameters main rollout:params
```

```
(
length type:#worldunits ui:b_length animatable:true
width  type:#worldunits ui:b_width animatable:true
height type:#worldunits ui:b_height animatable:true
center_pivot type:#boolean ui:b_pivot animatable:false
)
rollout params "Parameters"
(
spinner b_length "Length: " type:#worldunits \
    range:[-10000,10000,0] align:#right
spinner b_width  "Width: "  type:#worldunits \
    range:[-10000,10000,0] align:#right
spinner b_height "Height: " type:#worldunits \
    range:[-10000,10000,0] align:#right
checkbox b_pivot "Center Pivot"
)
```

Now that we've defined the parameter block and the rollout, we'll create the geometry. We do this by assigning the position in local X, Y, and Z coordinates, and then assigning which vertices make each face. We do not work with mapping coordinates or smoothing groups in this example. Continue writing:

```
on buildMesh do
(
if center_pivot == true then
    pvt = [0,0,-height/2] else pvt = 0
v = #()
v[1] = [-length/2,-width/2,0] + pvt
v[2] = [length/2,-width/2,0] + pvt
v[3] = [-length/2,width/2,0] + pvt
v[4] = [length/2,width/2,0] + pvt
for i in 5 to 8 do v[i] = v[i-4] + [0,0,height]
f = #()
f[1] = [1,3,4]
f[2] = [4,2,1]
f[3] = [5,6,8]
f[4] = [8,7,5]
f[5] = [1,2,6]
f[6] = [6,5,1]
f[7] = [2,4,8]
f[8] = [8,6,2]
```

```
    f[9] = [4,3,7]
    f[10] = [7,8,4]
    f[11] = [3,1,5]
    f[12] = [5,7,3]
    setMesh mesh verts:v faces:f
    )
tool create
    (
    local st
    on mousePoint click do
        case click of
            (
            1: nodeTM.translation = gridPoint
            3: #stop
            )
    on mouseMove click do
        case click of
            (
            2: (
             st = gridPoint
                length = abs(gridDist.x)*2
                width = abs(gridDist.y)*2
                )
            3: height = distance gridPoint st
            )
    )
)
```

Evaluate this script and create a box2 in any view. Then, go to the Modify tab and adjust its values. You'll see that this works just like a regular object.

The script creates a mesh by using the setmesh command. This command requires an array of vertices and an array of faces. The vertex array holds each vertex position in the local coordinate system. The face array holds a list of the vertices that make that face.

Creating More Complex Geometry

You can also create more complex geometry using a plug-in script. As an example, our next script creates an object that is similar to a cylinder with a cone on top. You will notice that this script uses many loops, to calculate the correct XYZ position of the vertex and the correct face that attaches to that vertex.

This example is a Game object that represents an enemy base in a strategy game. Let's walk through it step by step. The final script can be found in the file plugin_ enemybase.ms from the CD.

Start a new script and enter the header of the plug-in, its parameter block, the rollout and the buildmesh event:

```
plugin simpleObject Enemy_Base
name:"Enemy Base"
classID:#(0x5b4365de, 0x9244551f)
category:"Mastering 3ds max"
(
parameters main rollout:params
    (
    radius1 type:#worldunits ui:rad1 animatable:true
    radius2 type:#worldunits ui:rad2 animatable:true
    height1 type:#worldunits ui:ht1 animatable:true
    height2 type:#worldunits ui:ht2 animatable:true
    segments type:#integer ui:segs animatable:true default:12
    )
rollout params "Parameters"
    (
    spinner rad1 "Radius1: " type:#worldunits \
        range:[-10000,10000,0] align:#right
    spinner ht1 "Height1: " type:#worldunits \
        range:[-10000,10000,0] align:#right
    spinner rad2 "Radius2: " type:#worldunits \
        range:[-10000,10000,0] align:#right
    spinner ht2 "Height2: " type:#worldunits \
        range:[-10000,10000,0] align:#right
    spinner segs "Segments: " type:#integer range:[3,100,12] \
        align:#right
    )
on buildMesh do
    (
    v = #()
    v[1] = [0,0,0]
```

Now we need to create the vertices on the base of the cylinder. Their X position is radius*sin(*angle*), where the angle will be calculated depending on the number of segments.

```
for i in 1 to segments do
    (
    append v \
    [radius1*cos(i*360/segments),radius1*sin(i*360/segments),0]
    )
```

Next we create the vertices on the top of the cylinder. They're equal to the vertices on the base, except that their height is different.

```
for i in 1 to segments do
    (
    append v [radius1*cos(i*360/segments),\
        radius1*sin(i*360/segments), height1]
    )
```

Now we create the vertices on the top of the cone. They're equal to the vertices on the base, except that their radius and height are different.

```
for i in 1 to segments do
    (
    append v [radius2*cos(i*360/segments),\
        radius2*sin(i*360/segments), height1+height2]
    )
append v [0,0,height1+height2]
f = #()
```

You will start creating the faces—first, the ones on the base of the cylinder. Notice that the first vertex is constant, while the second and third vertices are variable. Then, after the loop, we must also connect the last vertex with the second one. If we didn't, the cylinder would have a seam.

```
for i in 2 to segments do
    (
    append f [1,i+1,i]
    )
append f [1,2,segments+1]
```

Now repeat the steps above for the sides and top of the object. Remember that each polygon now is made of two faces.

```
for i in 2 to segments do
    (
    append f [i,i+1,i+1+segments]
    append f [i,i+1+segments,i+segments]
    )
append f [segments+1,2,2+segments]
append f [segments+1,2+segments,1+2*segments]
for i in (2+segments) to (2*segments) do
    (
    append f [i,i+1,i+1+segments]
    append f [i,i+1+segments,i+segments]
    )
append f [2*segments+1,2+segments,2+2*segments]
append f [2*segments+1,2+2*segments,1+3*segments]
for i in 2 to segments do
    (
    append f [2+3*segments,2*segments+i,2*segments+i+1]
    )
append f [2+3*segments,3*segments+1,2*segments+2]
```

Now that every face and vertex is created, you can create the object and assign the different smoothing groups for each part of the object.

```
setMesh mesh verts:v faces:f
for i in 1 to segments do
    setfacesmoothgroup mesh i 1
for i in (segments+1) to (3*segments) do
    setfacesmoothgroup mesh i 2
for i in (3*segments+1) to (5*segments) do
    setfacesmoothgroup mesh i 1
for i in (5*segments+1) to (6*segments) do
    setfacesmoothgroup mesh i 2
)
```

Now you can write the tool that creates the object.

```
tool create
    (
    on mousePoint click do
```

```
    case click of
       (
       1: nodeTM.translation = gridPoint
       5: #stop
       )
  on mouseMove click do
    case click of
       (
       2: radius1 = sqrt(gridDist.x^2 + gridDist.y^2)
       3: height1 = sqrt(gridDist.x^2 + gridDist.y^2)
       4: height2 = sqrt(gridDist.x^2 + gridDist.y^2)
       5: radius2 = sqrt(gridDist.x^2 + gridDist.y^2)
       )
    )
 )
```

The final result of this script is displayed in Figure 20.14. This script is a good example of a plug-in script that creates geometry parametrically. It doesn't have UVW maps, however; if you want to know how to add UVW coordinates to a plug-in script, look at the online Help and at the examples supplied with 3ds max.

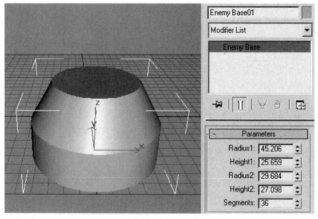

Figure 20.14 *The Enemy Base plug-in script in action*

Summary

Plug-in scripts are a complex but useful tool in 3ds max. They will sure save a huge amount of time, and help you standardize your work.

Throughout the last six chapters of the book, you've learned the concepts of MAXScript and learned ways to use it on a daily basis. However, MAXScript is much more than just what we had room for here. Exploring 3ds max is the best way to move ahead.

You can also ask questions and get support through the Web, at the Online Support Forum: `http://support.discreet.com`. There's a conference full of tips and samples only for MAXScript. You can also find information about this book and MAXScript development at `http://www.origamy.com.br`.

Part VII

Appendices

In This Part

Exporting to Web 3D with Pulse Producer and Creator

3ds max

Appendix A

Pulse technology enables 3D artists to create real-time interactive 3D content for the Web. Pulse content will play in the Pulse Player, a free plug-in that plays within Web browsers. You can also author Pulse content for QuickTime and RealPlayer.

Pulse's Producer plug-in for max allows you to export your max animations into a streamlined Web format that can be viewed on the Web in real time. Features such as morphs, character studio animations with Biped and Physique, and UVW coordinates are preserved when you export from max to Pulse's Web format. You can also bring your project files into Pulse Creator to add a variety of functionality, including complex interactivity, streaming, and texture compression.

This tutorial guides you through the process of optimizing a max animation for the Web, exporting with Pulse Producer, and adding further features in Pulse Creator to create interesting interactive 3D content for the Web.

Installing Pulse Producer and Creator

The Producer plug-in is a .dlu file that goes into your 3dsmax4\plugins directory. Creator is a stand-alone program. This tutorial uses both. The installer for both Producer and Creator is on the CD that comes with this book under the Plugins\Pulse directory. To install, double-click the PAS441.exe icon.

Optimizing Your max File for the Web

Because Pulse content resides on the Web and will be downloaded to the viewer's computer, it is important to keep file sizes low. This does not mean that quality must be sacrificed, however. Creating efficient, optimized content is the key to producing high-quality content with a small footprint. Techniques for getting the most out of max for Web output include making the polygon count as low as possible and minimizing the number and size of texture maps. A low-resolution scene has several benefits: the playback will be able to maintain a higher frame rate and the smaller file will load more quickly onto the viewer's computer.

Making Models Low-Poly

Since Pulse content is rendered in real time, keep the number of polygons as low as possible. If the file size is too large, playback performance will suffer. Content targeted toward the average viewer should not exceed 5,000 polygons in the scene. Content aimed at viewers using higher-end hardware can contain 10,000 or more polygons and still maintain an acceptable frame rate. A good target for an online character is between 1,500 and 3,000 polygons.

See the Hands-on max tutorial on optimizing models in Chapter 5. There are also good optimization tools within Creator once your model has been exported.

Unwrapping UVW Coordinates to Optimize Textures

In addition to minimizing your polygon count, keep texture map sizes to a minimum and use as few as possible. The key to making the most of every pixel of small texture maps is to use the UVW mapping features in max. The UVW coordinates in max are preserved in the exported Pulse files.

This is an alternate version of the UVW mapping method used in the Hands-on max tutorial in Chapter 7. It is quicker and simpler, but not as precise. Note the technique in the "Unwrapping the UVW Coordinates" section below for mapping symmetrical sections of a mesh to the same area of a texture map; this technique can be used with either method.

The character for this tutorial was modeled as one continuous mesh. You need to apply a single map to texture the entire model. Some areas, such as the head, would benefit from more texture resolution while others, like the pants, may be fine with less detail.

While a Multi/Sub-Object material will export to Pulse, it will be flattened, with each sub-material assigned to one piece of the exported map. This wastes vast numbers of pixels and gives you no control over assigning texture resolution where needed. Don't use Multi/Sub-Object materials for Web output.

Breaking the Model

The method used in this tutorial for assigning mapping coordinates involves separating the character into multiple pieces, assigning mapping coordinates to each piece separately, and connecting the pieces back together to be mapped as one object:

1. Open the Pulse01.max file from the maxscenes directory in the CD files for this appendix.

   To assign mapping coordinates that fit the character, you need to break the character into all the pieces that can be easily mapped by a single mapping gizmo: head, forearms, upper arms, lower legs, thighs, hands, and feet.

2. Go to the Vertex sub-object level. Select all the vertices of the head.

3. Click Detach. In the Detach dialog box, name the new object "head" and click OK.

4. Repeat steps 1 through 3 for the rest of the body parts. Start by breaking off the body into its natural cylinders, such as the upper and lower arms, thighs, and calves. Then detach the hands and feet. For extra detail, the soles of the shoes can be separated. Hands can be further articulated by detaching the thumbs and separating the palms. By assigning different object colors to the pieces, it is easy to distinguish them later when unwrapping the mapping coordinates.

Assigning Mapping Coordinates

Each object needs UVW mapping coordinates:

1. Select the head and apply a UVW Map modifier from the UV Coordinate modifier set. For the head, choose Cylindrical Mapping. A cylindrical mapping gizmo appears around the head.

2. The cylinder needs to be resized to fit the head. Go to the Gizmo sub-object level of the modifier. Adjust the size of the gizmo to fit the head by adjusting the Length, Width, and Height parameters.

3. Rotate the gizmo in the viewport to reposition the seam, denoted by a green line, to the back of the head. This seam is where the edges of the 2D texture map will converge. By placing it in the back of the head, you will ensure that the face is not distorted.

4. Repeat steps 1 through 3 for each of the body pieces. For the arms and legs, rotate the mapping gizmo so that it matches the orientation of the limbs. Position the green line so that the seam will be inconspicuous. Hands can be mapped with planar mapping. The plane must be rotated to match the orientation of the hand. The short yellow line of the planar mapping gizmo indicates the top of the texture map; the seam or green edge indicates the right side.

Unwrapping the UVW Coordinates

Once mapping coordinates have been applied to all of the objects, they are ready to be *unwrapped*. Unwrapping means assigning which vertices of the mesh correspond to which pixels of the map. You want the flat map to be distorted as little as possible while being wrapped to a 3D surface.

Let's unwrap the model:

1. Select the head and apply an Unwrap UVW modifier.

2. Click the Edit button in the modifier panel to bring up the Edit UVWs dialog box. This displays a 2D representation of the object's mapping coordinates. If you don't get this display of the object's mapping, take off the Unwrap UVW modifier and reapply the UVW Map modifier. Sometimes you may need to change the angle of the mapping gizmo or alter the placement of the seam.

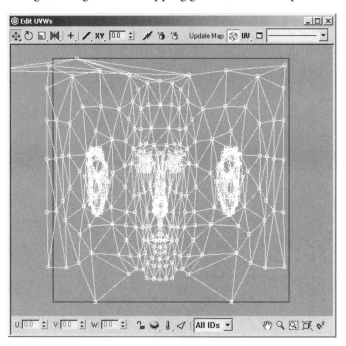

3. Close the Edit UVWs window. Right-click Editable Mesh in the stack and choose Collapse All. Click Yes to convert the object to an editable mesh. The UVW mapping coordinates you assigned are preserved with the mesh.

4. Repeat steps 1 through 3 for all the pieces.

5. Now you're ready to attach the pieces back into one mesh. Select the torso object and click Attach. Pick all the other pieces in the viewport to attach them.

6. Even though the object is a single mesh, it now has coincident vertices at each point of attachment. These need to be welded. Go to the Vertex sub-object

level. Region-select all the vertices of the object. In the Edit Geometry rollout, click Weld.

7. Select the character and apply an Unwrap UVW modifier to it. Since the UVW coordinates of the pieces are retained, the corresponding sections of the mesh will be unwrapped to separate objects in UVW space. If you click the Edit button, you will see that all these objects are currently superimposed, giving you an undecipherable display of vertices.

8. The Edit UVWs window has two sets of buttons. The set along the top of the window is used for manipulating the actual objects, while the set at the bottom of the window is used for manipulating the view. Click the Move tool at the top of the Edit UVWs window and select a vertex.

9. Click the Expand Selection button to add adjacent vertices to the selection. Continue to click the Expand Selection button until all of the vertices of that UVW object are selected.

10. Using the Zoom tool, zoom out so you have an open area. Switch back to the Move tool and drag the object to an empty area.

11. Repeat steps 8 through 10 until all the UVW pieces are separated in the Edit UVWs window.

12. Some pieces will have coincident vertices along the edges. For each edge of each object, select all the vertices along the edge. Click the Weld Selected button at the top of the Edit UVWs window to join all of the duplicates together. Repeat this step for each object.

13. One way to use map pixels efficiently is to map similar pieces with the same section of the texture map. For example, the left foot and the right foot can be mapped by the same pixels. To do this, select all the vertices of one of the objects and then click the Mirror Horizontal button. This flips the foot so that it matches the other foot. Then move one of the foot objects on top of the other and align them. Use this method for all pieces that are identical around a line of symmetry.

14. Arrange all the objects within the square representing the boundaries of the texture map. Move, rotate, and scale the various objects until they fit properly. Scaling determines the level of pixel resolution for those vertices, so make sure the head and eyeballs are scaled larger than areas that don't need as much detail.

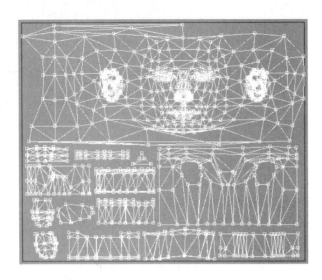

Creating a Texture Map

It can be difficult to determine which body part each object represents. To identify the pieces, you will create a reference texture map. Take a screenshot of the Edit UVWs window by pressing Alt+Print Screen. (You can also use the Texporter plug-in to export the map. Texporter is included on the CD for this book and explained in Chapter 7.) Then create your reference map in Photoshop:

1. In Photoshop, choose File → New and click OK. Press Ctrl+V to paste in the screenshot.

2. Press C to bring up the Crop tool and crop the image to the square defining the boundary of the texture map.

3. For each object, use the Lasso tool to select the area around it and fill with a different color. Make the filled area slightly larger than the boundary of the object.

4. Choose Image → Image Size and scale the image to 512×512. Flatten the image and save it as a Targa file, `colormap.tga`.

You can use maps of different aspect ratios, but maps in Pulse have to have dimension of a power of 2. Otherwise they will be scaled to the nearest power of 2 when you export. For best results, keep map dimensions to 128, 256, 512, or 1024.

5. In max, close the Edit UVWs window and open the Material Editor. Select an empty sample slot and apply the `colormap.tga` in the diffuse color map slot. Click Show Map In Viewport. Each part of the character is now a different color, making it simple to identify the pieces on the map.

6. Now that the pieces are identified, go back into Photoshop and paint a texture map over a copy of the reference map. Save it as `charactermap.tga`.

7. Back in max, replace the `colormap.tga` diffuse map with the `charactermap.tga` you just made. Just click the map button and load the new image.

Animating the Character in Max

Once you have optimized the model and the texturing for the Web, you can animate normally. Pulse Producer will export transform animation of objects or hierarchies, as well as animations using morphs, bones, and character studio Biped and Physique. FFD and parametric animations will not export. Animations using the linear, Bezier, and TCB controllers will export actual keyframes; however, Bezier and TCB keys will be converted to linear interpolation between keys. You also have the option of exporting animation using Bezier or TCB keys as samples (a keyframe is generated at a specified frequency). Biped animation exports as samples automatically. Table A.1 describes the export capabilities of Producer.

Table A.1 Exporting Capabilities of Pulse Producer

TYPE OF ANIMATION	EXPORTABILITY
Transform	Exports as keyframes or samples.
Morpher	Exports as keyframes or samples if the targets are made from moving the vertices of a copy of the original. Morphs between mesh snapshots won't export.
character studio	Exports as samples.
Linear tangents	Exports as accurate keyframes.
Bezier and TCB tangents	Exports as keyframes with linear tangents or as samples.
FFD	Doesn't export.
Parametric animation	Doesn't export.

Labeling Animation Sequences for Non-Linear Content

Pulse content is non-linear and interactive; therefore linear animations in max need to be labeled so that Pulse recognizes the sequence for export. The interface for this is adding a note track to the object in the Track view, with one key at the initial keyframe of the segment and one key at the final keyframe.

The Biped animation provided for this tutorial contains two animation sequences, one of the character picking up the box and one of him putting the box down. The box in the scene will be animated later, when the scene is imported into Pulse Creator. The hat is a separate object, and has been linked to the head bone so it animates with the rest of the body. Let's define the max sequences for export:

1. Open `Pulse05.max` from the CD files for this appendix. Select the biped, right-click it, and choose Track View Selected.

2. Open up the hierarchy of the scene, highlight the Bip01 track, and click the Add Note Track button. Add another note track for the second sequence. Each segment of animation to be exported requires a separate note track.

The note track must be on the object track of the biped or animated object, not the track containing the actual keys.

3. Click the Add Keys button. Add two keys on the first note track, one at frame 0 and one at frame 60. On the second note track, add a key at frame 60 and one at frame 100.

4. Click the Move Keys tool. Right-click the note track key at frame 0. In the Properties window that pops up, type **pickup** (the labels can't have spaces). Right-click the key in the same track at frame. Type **/pickup**. If the key is off frame 60, enter **60** in the Time field.

Producer recognizes behaviors by their syntax. The first note track key, defining the start of the animation sequence, must contain a name for the sequence, without any spaces. The second note track key, defining the end of the sequence, must contain the same name preceded by a forward slash.

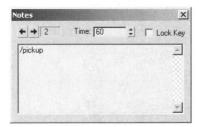

5. Label the starting key of the second note track **putdown** and the ending key **/putdown**.

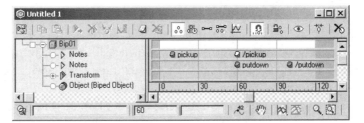

Exporting to Pulse

Now that the behaviors are defined, you are ready to export. You can export from max directly to Pulse Web files, which will automatically be embedded in an HTML page and brought up in your default browser. This also creates a Pulse Creator build (.bld) file with everything you need to open the project up in Creator to add more functionality.

Choosing Export Options

To get the best results, you can choose among various export options, some for the scene as a whole and some set per-object.

Naming the Build File

Although you can choose not to edit your `.bld` file in Creator, Producer will still create the project and all its files in the export process. Therefore, you need to assign a folder and filename for the project in order to export:

1. In the Utilities panel, click the More button. Choose Pulse. Note that the panel displays a count of the objects, polygons, and cameras in the scene.

2. Click the > button under Build File Name. Create a new folder for the project called `character1` and name your build file `character.bld` within it.

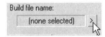

Choosing Mesh Options

The Mesh options rollout includes a variety of parameters that are set per-object. When you select an object in the scene, its name will appear in the Mesh selection set field. The rollout displays a polygon count for the object as well as whether the object has been assigned UV coordinates.

Flip Surface Normals reverses the direction of the faces on the object. Smoothing Angle specifies the maximum angle between two adjacent polygons for smooth shading. The Anti-Alias checkbox turns on anti-aliasing, although there are more anti-aliasing options if you open the file within Creator. Outline renders with a cartoon-like rendering of just outlines.

The Use Character Class option is grayed out unless you choose Manual under Class Control in the Advanced Options rollout. This is only for assigning trackball control to objects that don't have defined behaviors. It is generally better to accept the Automatic class assignments and edit them in Creator if necessary.

Light Maps

A mesh light map allows you to assign material properties to the object. Pulse computes lighting in real time by referencing a bitmap, called a *light map*, rather than using light objects. Light map calculations use a hybrid of lighting and materials calculations to render high-quality images much faster than calculating the effects of individual lights on an object's surface.

Producer ships with a selection of light maps. Light maps can also be made in any paint program, saved as a PICT, Targa, `.bmp`, or JPEG file, and copied to your `3dsmax4\Pulse\Lights` folder. To make one of your light maps the default light map, rename `default.pic` and name your map `default` (with the correct file extension).

To apply a light map to the character, select the mesh and choose BasicLB from the Mesh Lightmap pull-down menu.

Choosing Material Options

The Material options rollout sets attributes for exported texture maps. You can export texture maps as either JPEG or Targa files. Only use the JPEG format if you intend to export straight from Producer to Web files. There are better texture compression options available within Creator, if you are willing to open the project in Creator after export.

Choose Targa for this project. As you learned earlier, Pulse requires maps to have dimensions of a power of 2. You can export maps with other sizes, but they will be scaled to the nearest power of 2 in each dimension.

The Multi/Sub-Objects export option is for objects that use a Multi/Sub-Object material. Pulse consolidates these into a single map for export, and this setting allows you to choose the size of that map. It is best not to use Multi/Sub-Object materials because you will waste your texture pixels.

Choosing Behavior Options

The Behavior options rollout specifies whether to export the animation as samples or as keyframes. This is relevant when exporting animations with Bezier and TCB controllers. Refer to Table A.1 to see what types of animations can be exported. For objects with linear controllers, the keyframe option is the most efficient.

The Samples option generates keyframes at a specified frequency. For example, a value of 2 would place one keyframe for every other frame in the timeline, giving each object 15 keyframes per second. A higher Nth Frame setting will yield a smaller animation file; a lower value will provide more fidelity to the original source animation.

For this animation, choose the Samples option and leave the Nth Frame default set to 2. You will reduce keys later in Creator.

Choosing Advanced Options

The Advanced options rollout allows you to choose whether to export geometry, behaviors, sounds, and hidden objects. Although there are no hidden objects in this scene, uncheck the Hidden Objects checkbox. You generally don't want to export objects that you have hidden (morph targets, for example).

Converting and Running

Once all the options have been set, the scene is ready to be exported:

1. At the top of the Producer panel, click Convert. (Conversion takes some time.)

    This exports all the models, defined animation sequences (called *behaviors* in Pulse), and texture maps into Pulse format. All of the assets in the exported scene are also compiled into small, Web-ready files that can be viewed in the Pulse Player within a Web browser. The Export Status bar displays the progress of the current export.

2. After the conversion process is complete, Click Run. This launches a Web browser with an HTML page that contains your content.

    Note that the generated HTML page has links at the bottom for each of the defined animation sequences as well as one called Show Perf that displays the playback rate you are getting.

3. Click the Bip01:pickup link. The character stoops to pick something up. Click the Bip01:putdown link. He stoops to put something down. These commands are sent via JavaScript from the default HTML page to the Player.

You can edit the JavaScript links in the default HTML page by editing the HTML.

4. In Windows Explorer, locate the `character1` folder where you saved the project and examine the contents of the folder. Notice that Producer created folders for the various assets of the scene. The Web folder contains all of the files you need to upload to your server in order to put the content on the Internet, including the compressed Pulse Web files and the default HTML page. The other folders contain all of the source files. The current size of the `Main.pwc` file is about 450K, which is a little large for downloading over a modem. You will optimize the content within Creator to dramatically decrease the file size.

Using Pulse Creator

As you've learned already, opening your exported Pulse project in Creator allows you to access a larger palette of features for optimizing for the Web, adding more complex interactivity, and setting animations to stream, among others. Let's take the project you just exported into Creator:

1. Launch Pulse Creator. Press Ctrl+O and browse to the `character1\ character.bld` file you exported earlier or the `character1a\character.bld` file from the CD files for this appendix (in the `Pulsescenes` folder). Your file opens, showing the Build window with the filename in the window label. Expand the Main package to see the `Behavior`, `Geometry`, and `Materials` directories containing all the models, materials, and animation keys that you exported from max.

2. Double-click the word Geometry in the Build window to open up the Geometry window. This window shows the hierarchy of all the objects in the scene.

3. Click the New View button on the Geometry window toolbar. A view window opens.

There are many ways to manipulate a view in Creator. The shortcuts to remember are: press the Spacebar while dragging to pan, press Alt+Spacebar while dragging to rotate the view, and press Ctrl+Spacebar while dragging to zoom.

4. Double-click Camera in the Geometry window to open up a camera window. A camera window is a view window from the perspective of a camera. Close the unnecessary views.

5. Double-click the pickup behavior in the Behaviors directory of the Build window. This opens the Behavior Editor, where you create or edit all your animation. Notice the pickup and putdown behaviors in the left pane. Highlighting one of them displays all the keyframes of the Bip01 object. Alt-click the Bip01 object to expand its hierarchy and see all the exported keys. Every object has keys at every other frame, because the animation was exported as samples.

Optimizing the Project

The size of the main Web file for this project was about 450K. One way to reduce this is to compress the materials:

1. Expand Materials in the Build window and select the material for the character.

2. Press Ctrl+P to bring up the Properties window. In the Compress tab, choose Jpeg and drag the Quality slider to 70. This applies JPEG compression to the

character's material. Do the same thing for the BasicLB light map material, but set its Quality to 80.

3. Excessive keyframes slow download times. To reduce the number of keys, select the pickup behavior in the Build window under Behaviors and choose Behaviors ➜ Filters ➜ Remove Extra Keys. In the Remove Extra Keys window, keep the default setting (making sure All Tracks is checked) and click OK. Repeat this process for the putdown behavior.

4. Select just the Biped Footsteps track for each behavior and delete it. (Footsteps animation was not used, so you don't need any of these keys.) Click the Save button in the Build window toolbar.

5. Click Run to automatically launch a Web browser displaying your content in Pulse Player. Try the behavior links again. The animation plays just as before. However, if you look in the Web folder for the project, you will see the Main.pwc file is down to around 100K. (Note: This is saved in pulsescenes\character1b on the CD.)

3D Painting

Creator has extensive texture-mapping features, like 3D painting and decaling. The box in the scene is currently flat-shaded without textures. Let's use Creator's 3D painting tool to create a reference map for identifying sections of a texture map:

1. Click the Add Files button and load boxmap.tga from the CD files for this chapter under Materials. The boxmap material now appears in the Build window under Materials. Double-click it in the Build window to see the map divided into six sections of color.

2. Apply the boxmap material to the box by dragging it from the Build window and onto Box01 in the Geometry window.

3. To set the rendering mode, highlight Box01 in the Geometry window and choose Render ➜ Style ➜ Sphere Texture. The Sphere Texture rendering mode allows texture mapping with lighting.

4. With Box01 still selected, set the mapping mode by choosing Render ➜ Full Cubic. The full cubic mapping mode breaks up a texture map into six pieces and projects each piece along one of the six faces of a box. Now each side of the box is mapped by a different color in the map.

5. Turn off the visibility for the character in Creator by pressing Alt while clicking the visibility checkbox for the Bip01 object in the Geometry window (the visibility checkbox is the one in the column below the eye icon). Pressing the Alt key while clicking turns off visibility for the entire hierarchy.

6. Switch your view window to a front view by selecting the view and choosing Views → Orient → Front. Select the box in the Geometry window and click the Fit To Window button in the View window toolbar to center the box in the view.

7. Select Box01 in the Geometry window, and then click the Paint textures button in the main toolbar to bring up the 3D painting tool. Find the Brushes tab in the Brushes/Colors/Layers window. Draw an **F** on the box for front. After drawing, press Enter to apply the paint to the object. If you change the view or do something else before pressing Enter, you will lose your paint.

8. Click the View Presets button in the view toolbar and choose Back. Click the Fit To Window button again to center the box. Use the Paint textures tool to paint a **B** on the back face and press Enter.

9. Repeat step 8 for each view, painting an **R** on the right side, an **L** on the left, a **T** on the top, and a **U** on the underside. ("Plan" is the top view. For the underside, choose View → Object Front.) Double-click the boxmap material in the Build window to see the map edited with the letters. Click the Save button.

1 boxmap.tga

10. Open Photoshop. Open the `boxmap.tga` file in your `character1\Main\Materials` folder. Creator's painting tool is integrated with Photoshop, so that when changes are applied to an image in Photoshop and saved, Creator updates the image interactively. For this reason, it is best to keep both applications open at the same time.

11. Open up the `boxsidemap.tga` from the CD files for this appendix under `materials`. Using the Move tool, drag it into the `boxmap.tga` file opened in Photoshop. It is now on a separate layer. Make four duplicates of it by dragging the layer to the New Layer button at the bottom of the layers palette four times.

Move the layers to cover each of the sides except the top. Flatten the image (Layers palette ➜ Flatten Image), save it, and return to Creator. The material on the box reflects the changes you made in Photoshop.

12. You will map the top of the box with the decal tool in order to acquaint yourself with that tool. Highlight the box in the Geometry window. Switch to a Plan view using the View Presets and click the Fit To Window button. Click the Apply A Bitmap Decal button on the main toolbar. Browse to the `boxtopmap.tga` file from the CD files for this chapter. The map appears in the View window. Drag it to center it in the view. Holding Ctrl+Spacebar, drag upward to zoom out until the box fits the decal. Drag while holding the Spacebar if you need to pan to get the placement right. When the decal is the same size as the box in the view and in the correct position, press the Enter key to apply the decal to the box. The map is now applied to the top of the box. Click Save. (The project this far is called `character1c` in the CD files for this appendix.)

Animating with Behavior Scripts

Applying scripts within Creator gives you access to a wide range of added functionality. Many scripts ship with Creator; you can also write your own scripts. One type of script is a *behavior script*. Behavior scripts trigger a certain action as a behavior (animated sequence) is playing. In this example, the behavior script BeAttach is used to make the character pick up the box. At a specific point in time in the pickup and putdown behaviors, the script will attach or detach the box from the character's hands. (This is similar to the link controller in max.) Let's apply the script:

1. Highlight Bip01 in the Geometry window and press Ctrl+E to open its Behavior Editor. Highlight the pickup behavior and advance the timeline to 1.00 seconds by either typing in the value in the current time field at the top of the window or by manually dragging along the top of the timeline until the current time field displays 1.00.

2. Alt-click the Bip01 to expand its hierarchy and highlight the Bip01_R_Hand object. If it is difficult to see the names of all of the objects, resize the pane by dragging the vertical line separating it from the pane containing the keyframes.

3. Click the Add Script Track button in the Behavior Editor toolbar. In the Select Behavior Script window, choose BeAttachObj and click OK. Notice that a BeAttachObj script now appears as a child of the Bip01_R_Hand object.

4. Highlight the BeAttachObj script in the Behavior Editor and, making sure that the current time is 1.00 seconds, click the Set A Key On Selected Tracks button. This added key means that the behavior script will execute its action at that frame.

5. Double-click the keyframe to define the action of the behavior script in the Edit Script Key window. Click to the right of AttachName, type **Box01** into the field, and press Enter. In the AttachToName field, type in **Bip01_R_Hand**. This attaches the box to the right hand of the biped at this frame. Click OK.

6. Highlight the putdown behavior and add a BeAttachObj script to the Bip01_R_Hand. Add a key to BeAttachObj at time 1.00. In the AttachName field, type **Box01**; in the AttachToName field, type **World** to detach it from the right hand. (Behavior script actions will not be apparent in Creator; they take effect in Pulse Player.)

7 Highlight the pickup behavior so that the content will start with the character standing straight up. Save and run. Notice that when you play the pickup behavior now, the character picks up the box. When you play the putdown behavior, the character puts the box down. (The project this far is on the CD as `character1d`.) Notice that the character can be rotated. You will change this in the next section.

Adding Interactivity

You can add a great variety of interactivity to your files within Creator. Much of this is done through scripts. In this example, you will change the class of the object to one that allows user input:

1. First you will remove trackball control from the character. Highlight Bip01 in the Geometry window and press Ctrl+P to bring up its Properties window. In the Class pull-down menu at the top, the object is set to Character class. Change this to NoMouseChar to enable the character to play its behaviors without allowing trackball control.

2. Select Box01 in the Geometry window and press Ctrl+P to bring up its Properties window. Choose SmartPart from the Class pull-down menu. SmartPart allows the box to respond to mouse interaction such as clicks and rollovers. Notice that the Properties Window changed when the class of the object was changed.

There are four different interactions recognized by SmartPart: when the mouse rolls over an object (called hiliteOn), when it rolls off (called hiliteOff), and two mouse-click states that are toggled by each click of the user (called activeOn and activeOff).

The four other fields in the SmartPart properties are the same (roll on, roll off, first click, second click), except these will send a JavaScript message to the browser. If you know JavaScript, just type the code into the corresponding Event field.

3. Double-click the boxmap material in the Build window to open it in a Material window. Right-click in the window and choose Add File. Browse to the `boxmap2hi.tga` file from the CD files for this appendix under `materials`. This map is a brighter version of the box material; it was made using Curves in Photoshop.

4. Select the Box01 in the Geometry window and press Ctrl+E to open up its Behavior Editor. Create two new behaviors by clicking the New Behavior button, naming the first "boxon" and the second "boxoff."

5. Highlight the boxoff behavior and choose No in the makeButton field of the Properties window. (This means a JavaScript link will not be made in the default HTML page for this behavior).

6. With the boxoff behavior still highlighted, click the Add Texture Track button. You use a texture track to animate a change in material during a behavior.

7. Repeat steps 5 and 6 for the boxon behavior.

8. With the current time set to 0.00, highlight the boxoff behavior and texture track in the Behavior Editor. Click the Set Key For Selected Track button.

9. Select the box, press Ctrl+P, and in the Render tab of its Properties window, click one of the little arrow buttons to switch to the second material. The box turns brighter in the view window.

10. Highlight the boxon behavior and the texture track in the Behavior Editor. With the current time set to 0.00, click the Set Key For Selected Track button. Click between boxoff and boxon in the Behavior Editor; the box changes between the normal and highlighted state. Select the boxoff behavior so that it will start off in this state when the project is run.

11. Now you are ready to apply the behaviors to the SmartPart. Select Box01 in the Geometry window. Drag the boxon behavior from the Behaviors directory of the Build window to the hiliteOn field in the Properties window of the box. In the pop-up menu that appears, choose the long name. Drag the boxoff behavior to the hiliteOff field and choose the long name. The rollover interaction for the mouse is now defined.

12. Drag the pickup behavior to the activeOn field and the putdown behavior to the activeOff field. Select the long name each time.

13. Turn on the visibility of the character by Alt-clicking the visibility column of Bip01. Save and run. Notice that when the mouse moves over the box, it highlights, and when the mouse moves off, it goes back to its normal state. Also, when the box is clicked, the character picks it up, and when it is clicked again, the character puts it down. (The final project is `character1e` in the CD files for this appendix.) You can easily and quickly apply advanced interactivity to the scene this way. There are many more ways to create complex interaction using scripts in Creator.

 For more help with Pulse Producer and Creator, read the documentation that ships with the product or e-mail `devsupport@pulse3d.com`*.*

Pulse Producer and Creator project by Mark Zarich. © 2001 Pulse Entertainment, All Rights Reserved. Printed by permission.

Keyboard Shortcuts to Remember

3ds max

Appendix B

You can find out all the default keyboard shortcuts by choosing Customize → Customize User Interface and scrolling the Keyboard tab. On the same tab, you can also save a text file of the entire shortcut list (by clicking Write Keyboard Chart) and assign and save your own custom keyboard shortcuts (see Chapter 3 for details). Tables B.1 through B.5 contain the most useful keyboard shortcuts to learn for all-purpose work. This appendix also includes some other interface reminders and a reference to tables describing various sets of buttons in the interface.

Table B.1 Undo/Redo Shortcuts

FUNCTION	SHORTCUT KEY(S)
Undo object change	Ctrl+Z
Undo viewport change	Shift+Z
Redo object change	Ctrl+A
Redo viewport change	Shift+A
Hold	Alt+Ctrl+H

Table B.2 Display Shortcuts (General)

FUNCTION	SHORTCUT KEY(S)
Toggle display of command panel	3
Toggle display of main toolbar	Alt+6
Toggle display of tab panels	2
Toggle display of transform gizmo (transform tool must be selected to see the gizmo)	X
Toggle see-through display (per-object)	Alt+X
Unhide by name	5
Freeze selected	6
Unfreeze all	7

Table B.3 Viewport Display Shortcuts

FUNCTION	SHORTCUT KEY(S)
Redraw all viewports	1 (one)
Minimize/maximize viewport toggle	W
Zoom Extents All	Shift+Ctrl+Z
Zoom Extents Selected	E

Table B.3 Viewport Display Shortcuts *(continued)*

FUNCTION	SHORTCUT KEY(S)
Zoom region (in orthogonal viewports)	Ctrl+W
Zoom in	[
Zoom out	]
Zoom view	Z or roll middle mouse button
Pan view	Ctrl+P or drag with middle mouse
Arc-rotate	Alt + middle mouse drag
Toggle between Wireframe and Smooth + Highlights display	F3
Toggle display of edged faces	F4
Toggle shading of selected faces	F2
Toggle display of polygon count of selected object (vertex count when at vertex level)	Q
Toggle texture correction	Ctrl+T
Toggle display of safe frames	Shift+F
Toggle disable/enable viewport	D
Viewport Background dialog box	Alt+B
Top view	T
Front view	F
Left view	L
Perspective view	P
Bottom view	B
Back view	K
Right view	R
Axonometric User view	U
Camera view	C
Light view	Shift+4 (Spotlight = $)

Table B.4 Rendering Shortcuts

COMMAND	SHORTCUT KEY(S)
Render Scene	F10 or Shift+R
Render Last	F9 or Shift+E
Quick Render	Shift+Q
Show Last Rendered Image	Ctrl+I (letter i)

Table B.5 Miscellaneous Shortcuts

FUNCTION	SHORTCUT KEY(S)
Select By Name	H
Selection Lock toggle	Spacebar
Cycle between square, round, and fence marquee for selection	Ctrl+F
Transform Type-in dialog box	F12
Constrain to X	F5
Constrain to Y	F6
Constrain to Z	F7
Cycle through Constrain To Plane options (XY, YZ, and XZ)	F8
Snaps toggle	S
Angle snaps toggle	A
Cycle sub-object levels	Insert
Match Camera To View	Ctrl+C
Open Material Editor	M
Toggle default lighting with scene lights	Ctrl+L
Toggle Animate mode	N
Go to last frame	End
Go to first frame	Home
Toggle Play/Stop animation	/

Other Interface Tips

Other useful things to remember about the interface:

- To get back to the default perspective view angle and orientation, hide everything in the scene and Zoom Extents All (Ctrl+Shift+Z).

- To remove a button from a toolbar, Alt-drag it off the toolbar.

- Recommended custom keyboard assignments: Rotate View (for orbiting cameras quickly) and Hide Selection.

- Max 4 ships with a useful Quick Reference Card naming most of the buttons in the interface. Table B.6 lists the tables in this book that describe the use of these interface buttons.

Table B.6 Descriptions of Interface Buttons

BUTTONS	LOCATION OF TABLE
Spinner controls	Table 3.1, p.68
Create panel tabs	Table 3.2, p.69
Main toolbar	Table 3.6, p.84
Snap tools	Table 3.11, p.107
NURBS Creation toolbox	Table 6.2, p.274
Material Editor tools	Table 7.4, p.345
Time Control Area tools	Table 9.2, p.436
Track View tools	Table 9.3, p.440
F-Curve Tangent Types	Table 10.3, p.489
Virtual Frame Buffer tools	Table 13.1, p.564
RAM Player tools	Table 13.6, p.591
Video Post alignment tools	Table 14.2, p.610

Index

Note to the Reader: Throughout this index **boldfaced** page numbers indicate primary discussions of a topic. *Italicized* page numbers indicate illustrations.

A

U

V

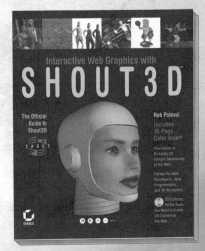

The Mastering™ 3ds max 4® CD-ROM

The CD-ROM for *Mastering™ 3ds max® 4* was designed to complement and enhance your reading experience. It contains all the .max and support files you will need to complete the exercises in the book, as well as the scripts developed in the MAXScript section of the book. Passages in the book will direct you to access files from the CD, including animations that play the final results of projects. You also get plenty of third-party bonus items to broaden your max library.

→ **Animation Files**　See sample animation clips that supplement various chapters from the book. To view animation files, go to the `AnimationFiles` folder and double-click the .mov or .avi file of your choice.

→ **Chapter Files**　If you plan to build any of the projects in the book, you can access all the files referred to in the chapters on the CD. You will find material libraries, .max files, textures to complete max scenes, and all the scripts developed in Part VI—everything you need to make your copy of *Mastering 3ds max 4* completely interactive.

→ **Software**　The CD includes more great software than we have room to describe. Topping the list is Pulse, a rich-media platform for creating interactive 3D animation on the Web. Appendix A shows how to use Pulse to export your max animations into a format that can be viewed on the Web in real time. More than twenty other great plug-ins extend or streamline max in a variety of ways. You'll find software for controlling the physics of particles, creating trails behind moving objects, modifying colors according to texture maps, simulating fluids and waves, producing translucent effects, desaturating colors based on pixel Z-depth, and even simulating dirt!

→ **MaxScripts**　A link to the `scriptspot.com` site, which hosts a collection of the latest MAXScript samples.

→ **Web Links**　The CD also provides a list of Web sites and their links to 3D industry news, forums, visual effects, animation, tools, and software. It's a great resource for 3D animators, artists, and designers.

→ **QuickTime 5**　If you don't already have QuickTime to view the animations, just go to the `QuickTime5` folder on the CD to copy it over to disk and install.

The CD is designed to run on Windows 95, 98, 2000, Windows NT Workstation 4.x. It uses the Sybex Clickme interface as an easy way for you to install the programs you want from the CD. You can also access any of the files through Windows Explorer. You may want to copy animation and project files to your hard disk to improve their performance. You will need QuickTime 5 to run the .avi files. All the .max files on the CD can be used with 3ds max 4.